EDITION 3

Effective Marketing

Creating and Keeping Customers in an e-commerce World

William G. Zikmund
OKLAHOMA STATE UNIVERSITY

Michael d'Amico
UNIVERSITY OF AKRON

SOUTH-WESTERN

™

THOMSON LEARNING

Australia · Canada · Mexico · Singapore · Spain · United Kingdom · United States

Publisher: Dave Shaut
Acquisitions Editor: Pamela M. Person
Developmental Editor: Mary H. Draper, Draper Development
Marketing Manager: Marc Callahan
Production Editor: Barbara Fuller Jacobsen
Media Technology Editor: Diane van Bakel
Media Developmental Editor: Christine Wittmer
Media Production Editor: Robin K. Browning
Manufacturing Coordinator: Sandee Milewski
Photo Manager: Cary Benbow
Photo Research: Feldman & Associates, Inc.
Internal Design: Michael H. Stratton
Cover Design: Tin Box Studio, Inc.
Cover Photographer: Stone
Production House: Lifland et al., Bookmakers
Compositor: Parkwood Composition
Printer: R. R. Donnelley & Sons Company–Roanoke Manufacturing Division

Printed in the United States of America
1 2 3 4 5   04 03 02 01

For more information contact South-Western, 5101 Madison Road, Cincinnati, Ohio 45227 or find us on the Internet at http://www.swcollege.com

For permission to use material from this text or product, contact us by
Telephone: 1-800-730-2214
Fax: 1-800-730-2215
Web: http://www.thomsonrights.com

Library of Congress Cataloging-in-Publication Data

Zikmund, William G.
    Effective marketing: creating and keeping customers in an e-commerce world/
    William G. Zikmund, Michael d'Amico.—3rd ed.
        p. cm.
    Includes index.
    ISBN 0-324-06392-X (book plus InfoTrac)
    ISBN 0-324-12569-0 (book only)
        1. Marketing. 2. Consumer behavior. 3. Export marketing. I. d'Amico, Michael. II.
Title

HF5415 .Z53 2001
658.8—dc21

                                                                                    00–051584

Creating and keeping customers in an e-commerce world.

The power of

MARK**e**TING BROWSER

Never has the science of marketing evolved more quickly than it has since the advent of the Internet. e-commerce, e-business, e-collaboration, e-strategy – all these terms and more have become integral parts of the discipline. Although the basics remain the same, e-commerce must be recognized as an integral part of marketing instruction. *Effective Marketing: Creating and Keeping Customers in an e-commerce World*, **3e** by Zikmund & d'Amico sets the bar for the next generation of marketing education by integrating e-commerce into each chapter, complete with compelling examples.

Although this edition preserves and improves upon the most popular and informative features of previous editions, it will be well worth your while to take a few minutes to look through this *Marketing* Browser to see what this innovative text has to offer. You will find a complete list of supplemental materials for both student and instructor at the end of this preface.

Integration, Illustration, Innovation

Rich media technology and streaming media programming allow users to access visuals and sound effects on the Internet. (Unfortunately, the word "technology" is often left off in discussions about rich media technology, leaving a phrase that could be misleading.) Broadcast.com is a leading aggregator and broadcaster of streaming media programming on the Web, with the network infrastructure and expertise to deliver, or "stream," hundreds of live and on-demand audio and video programs over the Internet to hundreds of thousands of users. The Broadcast.com Web site on Yahoo! Business Services offers a large selection of programming, including sports, talk and music radio, television, business events, full-length CDs, news, and full-length audiobooks. Broadcast.com broadcasts on the Internet 24 hours a day, seven days a week, and its programming includes more than 370 radio stations and networks, 30 television stations and cable networks, and game broadcasts and other programming for over 420 college and professional sports

INTEGRATED E-COMMERCE COVERAGE

Every chapter reflects the prominence and impact of e-commerce on today's New Economy. Chapter 3, *Environmental Forces in an e-commerce World: The Macro- environment*, lays the foundation for the text's extensive technological focus and introduces ways for information technology to create competitive advantage. The implications of changing technology, in particular the Internet, are integrated throughout the remaining chapters.

THE THIRD ELEMENT—PROMOTION

Marketers need to communicate with consumers. **Promotion** is the means by which marketers "talk to" existing customers and potential buyers. Promotion may convey a message about the organization, a product, or some other element of the marketing mix, such as the new low price being offered during a sale period. Simply put, promotion is marketing communication.

As an illustration of the value of promotional efforts in a marketing mix, think about Michelin tires. You probably have seen one of the television commercials featuring an adorable little baby sitting in the center of a tire. Perhaps you recall a commercial that shows several young women at a baby shower, celebrating a friend's approaching motherhood. The expectant mom is handed a large, beautifully wrapped package with a very familiar shape. She exclaims, "You guys, you didn't. You did!" when she discovers that the package contains a Michelin tire. She is even more delighted when she finds that her friends got her a whole set of tires. The commercial is quite entertaining. However, from the marketer's point of view, the most important thing for a viewer to remember is that at the end of the commercial an announcer says,

VIVID AND PROVOCATIVE EXAMPLES

Zikmund and d'Amico illustrate academic theory with compelling examples from domestic and global businesses — easily grasped examples of success and failure that bring abstract principles to life. Fresh, new e-commerce companies like Cisco Systems, Yahoo!, and Monster.com demonstrate the profound changes brought about by the Internet and information technology.

The Microenvironment—The Four Cs

The macroenvironment, the broad societal forces that affect every business and nonprofit marketer, was discussed in Chapter 3. Marketers, however, are more directly influenced by their individual microenvironments. A **microenvironment** consists of a company, its customers, and the other economic institutions that regularly influence its marketing practices.

To explain the dramatic impact of the microenvironment, it is useful to organize all microenvironmental forces into four basic categories—*company, customers, competitors,* and *collaborators.* Each of these represents a participant that performs essential business activities. We will call these the **four Cs**.[2]

INNOVATIVE, IMAGINATIVE COVERAGE OF 21ST-CENTURY MARKETING ISSUES

As always, Zikmund and d'Amico continue to refine their distinctive and popular presentation of contemporary marketing topics. Chapter 2, *Marketing Management: Strategy and Ethical Behavior*, offers competitive marketing strategies as a launching point for studying marketing mix strategies. Another core theme, relationship marketing, is introduced in Chapter 4, *The Microenvironment in an Era of Global Business*, as it discusses collaborators. The remainder of the book offers insights into managing relationships with suppliers, intermediaries and customers. And overall, a strong global perspective reminds students that marketing is, increasingly, an international discipline.

Change and Consequences

e—commerce | Changing Everything

There's a revolution under way in the music world that will eventually change the way people buy, carry, and listen to their favorite songs.[23] MP3, short for Moving Pictures Expert Group Audio Layer 3, is a way of compressing digital music so that it takes up far less space on a computer's hard disk. MP3 stores audio files on a computer in such a way that the compressed digital file is relatively small, but the song sounds near perfect.[24] MP3 technology allows songs to be "ripped" from CDs or downloaded from the Internet. Thousands of MP3 songs are distributed free over the Internet.

MP3 and other new technologies for compressing digital music are providing marketing opportunities for companies such as RealNetworks. The company calls its RealJukebox software the first complete digital music system that turns PCs into the best way to listen to music. Ten days after RealNetworks introduced RealJukebox, one million Internet users had downloaded the software, making it the most quickly accepted software product in history.[25] Within months, more than five million users had downloaded RealJukebox.

Several companies make portable MP3 players. Creative Labs' Nomad MP3 Player is magnesium-cased, is smaller than a pack of cigarettes, and weighs less than 2.5 ounces. Songs recorded in MP3 format on a Windows 95/98 PC hard disk can be easily transferred with a few mouse clicks to a Nomad connected to the computer. Its memory—half built-in, the other half on a removable postage-stamp-size flash memory card—holds about 2 hours of music. The Nomad plays for 5-plus hours on its two rechargeable AAA batteries. How good is the quality? Only golden-eared listeners would hear the difference (or care to) between the player's sound and that of a portable CD player.[26]

e-COMMERCE: CHANGING EVERYTHING!

e-commerce can force companies to change their product offerings or marketing approaches; these insights examine the technological developments that drive the process. They also serve to demonstrate the competitive advantage of quickly recognizing and adapting to market needs.

what went wrong?

Vince and Larry, the Crash-Test Dummies
Vince and Larry, the television crash-test dummies, first appeared in Department of Transportation advertising in 1984. The advertising showed Vince and Larry smashing through windshields to persuade viewers to buckle up. The message was simple: "Don't be a dummy." When the crash-test dummy campaign began, about 21 percent of the driving population wore seat belts. The percentage of Americans who use seat belts increased for years until 1996, when it reached about 68 percent. Since then, however, the percentage of people wearing seat belts has failed to rise. What went wrong?

"We've persuaded as many people as we can to wear seat belts," says Chuck Hurley, spokesman for the National Safety Council. "Now we have to look at enforcement." Some motoring organizations are concerned about stiffer laws and crackdowns. "It's a personal-liberty issue," says David Collier with the Free Roads Foundation, a Washington drivers' advocacy group. "Just like smoking or drinking. Adults have the right to do things, even if it's not necessarily good for them."

Others believed the advertising using Vince and Larry no longer worked. Murray Gaylord of the Advertising Council believed more realistic, more violent advertising was needed. The Department of Transportation agreed. It is hoping to shock drivers into buckling up with a more gruesome television campaign. Instead of using comic dummies that dust themselves off after a crash, the commercials feature live actors in simulated collisions. In one TV ad, titled "Ice Cream," a husband going to buy ice cream to satisfy his pregnant wife's late-night craving is hit head-on as he pulls out of the driveway. The ad cuts to black as viewers hear the sound of grinding metal. In another, "Cruisin'," teen-agers driving in two cars giggle and flirt until one of the cars is smashed by a speeding van. At the end of each ad, a caption asks: "Didn't see that coming? No one ever does. Buckle up."

This new advertising campaign uses a fear appeal to focus on the need for safety. It was created "to show people that you don't have to be driving dangerously to get in a wreck. It can happen to anyone, anytime."[10]

WHAT WENT RIGHT? WHAT WENT WRONG?

Zikmund and d'Amico are famous for using mini-case studies of familiar companies to illustrate chapter concepts. This popular feature focuses on the decisions made by these companies — and their consequences.

The Business of Marketing

In March of 1999, Philips and TiVo fired the first shot in a revolution that will see TV viewing habits undergo a radical change. The two collaborating companies were the first to offer a digital recording system and product category now known as a personal video recorder (PVR).

What radical change are PVRs bound to have on TV viewing? Within a few years, these "uberVCRs" will be able to record up to 100 hours of programming. Just as important, viewers will be able to skip over the ads. As a result, TV ad viewing will be cut nearly in half. So says a recent Forrester Research report that envisions an era of ubiquitous pay TV as broadcast, cable, and satellite networks scramble to replace dwindling ad dollars. Welcome to the 21st century!

What is the fuss all about? Just what is a PVR? The heart of the personal TV system is a Philips receiver: a modem-equipped set-top box that accepts

Broadcast Center, including material from Showtime, E! Entertainment Television, FLIX, HBO, Style, The Weather Channel, The Movie Channel, and ZDTV, as well as daily program recommendations, entertainment and sports-oriented editorial content, and new service updates and features.

Forrester Research's analysis of the PVR market indicates that "the two main features that drive TV sales are choice and convenience. First there was the convenience of the remote control, and then the choices offered by cable and satellite networks. The PVR puts you right in the middle of the two so you

OPENING VIGNETTES

Engaging opening vignettes capture the essence of marketing strategies and focus students on the practical application of marketing concepts. Companies students know, like Lee, Eastman Kodak, Dell, Walgreen's, Buy.com, Wal-Mart, Shell Oil, and Oscar Mayer, are some of the companies featured.

VIDEO CASES

How do real companies develop their marketing strategies and implement them? Videos developed specifically for this textbook by academic professionals focus on the challenges experienced by such innovative marketers as Ben & Jerry's, the Toronto Blue Jays, and Mercedes Black Forest Motors.

Ethics, Exercises, Insights

Ethically Right or Wrong?

The major television networks have established a "white coat" rule, which forbids medical professionals and actors portraying them from appearing in commercials. So when Chesebrough-Ponds, a unit of the Anglo-Dutch company Unilever, introduced Mentadent, a fluoride toothpaste with baking soda and peroxide, it used television commercials featuring real people who were married to dentists. The advertising objective was to educate consumers about Mentadent's unique ingredients and to communicate the dental community's acceptance of the product. The dentists' wives (and one husband) told how their spouses had recommended baking soda and peroxide for years and now recommended Mentadent. Mentadent gained a market share of approximately 5 percent in its first year.

ETHICALLY RIGHT OR WRONG?

Students are presented with ethical dilemmas at the end of each chapter and then required to take a stand — and defend it. This gives them the opportunity to experience the pull of ethical principles and apply them to specific situations.

e-exercises

http://zikmund.swcollege.com

1. Satisfying customer wants is a key aspect of the marketing concept. In order to satisfy customers, marketers must listen to what the market has to say. Some marketers use simple techniques, like suggestion boxes, to listen to the market.
   Your marketing professor wants to listen to you, the customer, so that he or she can better satisfy future customers. Send an e-mail message to your marketing professor. Include at least two things in your message: First, tell the professor what you like about this class so far. Then tell the professor what you don't like about this class so far.
2. *Reveries* is a marketing digizine that highlights what drives marketing people. Go to www.reveries.com and select a marketer whose story appears on the Web site. What motivated this person to go into marketing?
3. This chapter highlights the critical role of an organization's mission statement in the development and implementation of a marketing strategy. Use your Web browser to go to the Johnson & Johnson Company's home page at www.jnj.com. Select the link called "Our Credo" and read Credo for North America. On a sheet of paper, list five ways the credo (the organization's mission statement) differs from the mission statement of eBay (which appears on page 34) and five similarities between the mission statements of the two organizations. Bring your lists to class for discussion.
4. Go to the American Marketing Association's Web site at www.ama.org and click on Publications. Open the link for *Marketing News*, where you will find several stories from the latest issue. Read the cover story and report any examples of marketing strategy contained in the article.

Address Book (Useful Urls)

DePaul University's Institute for Business and Professional Ethics   www.depaul.edu/ethics/

E-EXERCISES AND USEFUL URLs

Rather than simply talking about the way information technologies are changing the way business is conducted around the world, each chapter invites the student to explore marketing through a series of online exercises and selected URLs.

cross-functional insights

Many theories and principles from other business disciplines can provide insights about the role of marketing in an organization. The questions in this section are designed to help you think about integrating what you have learned in other business courses with the marketing principles explained in Chapters 11 and 12.

Distribution Delivers a Standard of Living to Society The major purpose of marketing is to satisfy human needs by delivering products of various types to buyers when and where they want them and at a reasonable cost.
   How does the economic concept of scarcity relate to the distribution of a standard of living?

Channel Conflict Channel conflict refers to a situation in which channel members disagree and their relationship is antagonistic. Disagreements may relate to the channel's common purpose or the responsibility for certain activities. The behavior of one channel member may be seen as inhibiting

What would the typical small retailer's balance sheet look like?
   What should a retailer know about teamwork? What types of teams might a retailer utilize?
   What type of inventory cost system should a retailer have?

Merchant Wholesalers and Agent Wholesalers Channel members may be merchant wholesalers, which take title to the goods, or agent wholesalers, which do not take title to goods.
   Who may be a legal agent?
   How is agency authority in a channel of distribution created?
   How is an agency relationship in a channel of distribution ended?
   How does the Uniform Commercial Code apply to the relationship between manufacturers and merchant wholesalers?

Logistics Logistics describes the entire process of moving

CROSS-FUNCTIONAL INSIGHTS

It's too easy to regard marketing as an end in itself, a closed world that has little interaction with the day-to-day world. To put marketing in its proper perspective, this feature demonstrates how marketing fits into the broader landscape of business and society.

Log On and Learn
http://zikmund.swcollege.com

This online complement to the textbook is rich in educational resources.

Interactive Study Center organizes all student resources by chapter—learning objectives, e-lectures, crossword puzzles, online exercises, e-exercises, URLs, interactive quizzes.

Interactive Quizzes for each chapter include questions for student self-testing. Students get immediate feedback, including page references.

Online Exercises take students on a tour of company Web sites to explore the marketing concepts presented in each chapter. Exercises reinforce student understanding of chapter topics by having them probe into each company's marketing strategy.

e-commerce Cases feature businesses that are engaged in e-commerce activities and provide students an opportunity to explore the challenges of starting and maintaining an e-commerce business.

Appendices include Career Opportunities in Marketing, which briefly discusses a variety of marketing careers and job opportunities and portrays some of the excitement of marketing; The Business Plan and Marketing Plan; Marketing Audit, which includes a sample outline for conducting a marketing audit; Organizing the Marketing Function, which discusses ways of assigning tasks and allocating resources; and Financial and Economic Analysis for Marketers, which explains financial concepts and analytical ratios that marketing managers use in decision making.

Marketing Career Resources includes career information as well as a wealth of marketing resources, including links to marketing organizations, companies, and other related sites.

Downloadable Supplements for instructors including the instructor's manual and PowerPoint® Presentation slides.

The Power of ⓔ:
Instructor Resources

Extensive Instructor's Manual
Includes lecture outlines with abundant new e-commerce examples, chapter summaries, and answer guidelines for all end-of-chapter questions, cases, and video cases. (ISBN 0-324-06395-4)

Comprehensive Test Bank and Windows Testing Software
Over 3,000 high-quality true-false, multiple choice, and essay questions in print and Windows formats, ranked by difficulty and type to enable instructors to customize exams to meet course goals. (ISBN 0-324-06451-9)

ExamView™ Testing Software (ISBN 0-324-06394-6)

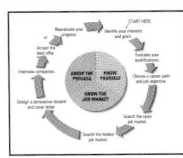

PowerPoint™ Presentation Software
Images that reinforce and illustrate major concepts from each chapter. (ISBN 0-324-06394-6)

Videos
New marketing case videos that feature the challenges faced by such innovative marketers as Burton Snowboards, La Belle Management, and the Toronto Blue Jays. (ISBN 0-324-06389-X, ISBN 0-324-06390-3, ISBN 0-324-06391-1)

Transparency Acetates
Full-color images taken from the textbook and from PowerPoint slides. (ISBN 0-324-06388-1)

Instructor's CD
All instructor resource materials, including the Test Bank, Instructor's Manual, and PowerPoint Presentation Software on a single, convenient CD. (ISBN 0-324-06394-6)

http://zikmund.swcollege.com
A rich collection of online resources for instructors and students.

The Power of ⓔ: Student Resources

Student Learning Guide
Comprehensive study guide that reinforces each chapter's major topics via chapter summaries, vocabulary-building exercises, true-false and multiple choice questions, and critical thinking activities. (ISBN 0-324-06450-0)

WizeUp Digital Edition
The WizeUp Digital Edition of *Effective Marketing* contains this complete text, powered by WizeUp software. It features powerful study tools to help you study faster and easier with a powerful search tool and digital notetaking features.

InfoTrac College Edition
With InfoTrac College Edition, students get complete, 24 hour-a-day access to full-text articles from hundreds of scholarly journals and popular periodicals such as *Newsweek, Time,* and *USA Today.* Thousands of full-length, substantive articles spanning the past four years are updated daily, indexed, and linked. And because they're online, the articles are accessible from any computer with Internet access. InfoTrac College Edition is perfect for all students, from dorm-dwellers to commuters and distance learners. (ISBN 0-324-06392-X)

WebTutor
A content rich, Web-based teaching and learning aid that reinforces and clarifies complex concepts and delivers innovative learning aids such as chapter reviews, quizzes, flashcards, Internet Exercises, and more. (on WebCT ISBN 0-324-11362-5; on Blackboard ISBN 0-324-13052-X)

Jian MarketingBuilder Express Software
Software that allows students to create their own marketing plans. (ISBN 0-538-87574-7)

New York Times Guide to Marketing
The New York Times Guide to Marketing is a collection of the best marketing-related articles from *The New York Times.* By purchasing the *Guide,* you also gain access, via password, to an online collection of the most current and relevant *New York Times* articles that are continually posted as news breaks. Also included are articles from *CyberTimes,* the online technology section of *The New York Times* on the Web. (ISBN 0-324-04182-9)

http://zikmund.swcollege.com
Access to a complete array of resources to improve success in class and in the real world.

BOOK AT A GLANCE

IN THIS EDITION

http://zikmund.swcollege.com

http://zikmund.swcollege.com

PREFACE

Over the past few years, marketing has seen the most dramatic changes ever to occur in the discipline. We live in a world in which it is difficult to imagine how we ever managed to get along without e-mail and wireless communications. Seemingly overnight, the terms *Internet, dot-com,* and *e-commerce* became part of our everyday vocabulary. Marketing has always been about adapting to change. However, the astonishing developments brought about by the Internet and improvements in information technology have changed virtually every aspect of marketing.

Consider America Online, Amazon.com, eBay, Monster.com, Real Networks, Cisco Systems, and Yahoo!. These fresh new companies are rewriting the way business is conducted. Stories about the successes and failures of e-commerce companies such as these fill the pages of the third edition of *Effective Marketing*. We believe the Internet is changing everything. It certainly has changed the revision of our book, which now integrates e-commerce considerations into all aspects of marketing strategy. The prologue is new to the book because we want to explain the impact of the Internet on marketing in what we hope is a dramatic and captivating way. Our book explains how effective marketers can gain competitive advantage through information technology and time-based competition.

Although many changes have taken place, some things about marketing remain the same. *Effective Marketing*, Third Edition, which consists of 17 chapters, is shorter than our other book, *Marketing*, Seventh Edition, but it shares many of that book's attributes. *Effective Marketing*, Third Edition, presents a lively picture of the field. It discusses academic theory, yet it is contemporary and practical. It is also very readable. In a straightforward and conversational prose style, it offers balanced coverage of marketing concepts and the practical examples that make marketing easy to understand. To enhance readers' understanding of marketing concepts and strategies, it employs current illustrations from domestic and global markets in the real world.

Effective Marketing, Third Edition, provides numerous current examples about products and companies that students can identify with. For example, Chapter 1 discusses why Buy.com resells computers and other products at or below cost. It also explains why nine innings of baseball is only one aspect of the product offered in the technologically sophisticated home of the Atlanta Braves. Chapter 2 explains how a marketing course at Northwestern University influenced the creation of Garden.com. References to Ricky Martin, Garth Brooks, Legos, PlayStation2, Palm Pilot, the NBA, and the Chicago Cubs are among the many student-oriented examples that can be found in this new edition.

Effective Marketing, Third Edition, stresses that marketing is essential to gaining a competitive advantage in a global, e-commerce marketplace. Readers will find that we have not relegated our discussion of Internet marketing to one of the last chapters in the book. However, the fact that conceptual issues about the Internet and e-commerce are not isolated in a single chapter does not mean that they are ignored. The e-commerce dimensions of the marketplace have become so pervasive that they affect virtually every aspect of marketing. These dimensions are discussed whenever an information technology perspective can help explain how marketing principles are applied in our global, e-commerce economy. We hope this structure will help students understand that 21st-century marketing managers cannot think of the e-commerce aspects of marketing as independent from the overall marketing strategy.

Effective Marketing, Third Edition, stresses the logic of marketing management so students can understand the role marketing plays in both business and not-for-profit organizations. It relates strategy and tactics to the environmental opportunities and constraints that managers must deal with daily. Effective marketing principles related to competitive strategy, total quality management, relationship marketing, and team building are emphasized throughout the book so that readers can see that there is a difference between intuitive decision making and sound marketing management.

The theories and strategies that marketing managers use to create competitive advantages have central importance in *Effective Marketing,* Third Edition. Theoretical concepts, such as those found in the study of buyer behavior, are presented so that students will understand their practical value for marketing managers. Competitive market strategies, such as those used for segmenting, targeting, and positioning, are covered early in the book. They provide a foundation for an understanding of marketing mix strategies, discussed later in the book.

Relationship marketing and collaboration with other organizations is a recurring theme in *Effective Marketing,* Third Edition. Our book stresses the fact that the marketing process does not end with the sale; it discusses how marketers establish and build relationships with customers. Many examples illustrate that both large and small businesses can apply these concepts. Our discussion of relationship marketing recognizes that the way companies like American Express and Harley-Davidson conduct business has changed dramatically in recent years. Many companies, especially those engaged in multinational marketing, are coming to rely on collaborating organizations. Chapter 4 introduces the role of collaborators, and the remainder of the book provides insights into managing relationships with suppliers, intermediaries, and customers.

DISTINCTIVE FEATURES

Effective Marketing, Third Edition, serves the needs of professors as well as those of students. Our book was written to be teachable. We made considerable effort to ensure that the pedagogy would meet the needs of modern marketing professors.

Learning Objectives   Each chapter begins with a clear statement of learning objectives so that students will know what to expect. The chapter summaries are designed around these learning objectives.

Opening Vignette   Each chapter opens with a vignette that features an actual business issue related to the topics in the chapter. Opening vignettes focus students' attention on the pragmatic aspects of the chapter. For example, Chapter 1 begins by explaining that Buy.com is a brand new company that uses the Internet to market computers. The vignette goes on to say that the company, which is losing "a couple of million dollars a month," anticipates future profits will come from the sale of advertising and ancillary services like warranties and equipment leases. And Chapter 13 opens with a discussion of how Lee Jeans used a retro image and the Buddy Lee character to connect with young consumers who, in the past, thought Lee jeans were "way off the cool meter."

e-commerce: Changing Everything   This new feature reflects the strong, new theme of the third edition and allows us to explain, in depth, how e-commerce business models are affecting marketing activity in our global economy.

What Went Right? and What Went Wrong?   These popular features illustrate successes and failures in specific marketing situations. They focus on decisions made by particular organizations and the outcomes of those decisions. For example, one What Went Right? selection tells how a pricing experiment allowed Rolling Rock to substantially increase its price and still sell more beer. Another explains how a custodian sweeping streets at Walt Disney World created a magic moment for a birthday boy whose family was late for a breakfast appointment. A What Went Wrong? box describes why having Vince and Larry, the crash-test dummies, smash through windshields to persuade consumers to wear seat belts stopped working.

Vividly Illustrated Concepts   Graphics and exhibits are designed to encourage student involvement and learning. Photos are complemented by clear, understandable captions that reinforce theories or principles explained in the text.

Global Examples   Throughout the text, numerous easy-to-understand business examples help students gain insight and perspective. Many examples reflect the changing global markets and increased competition from foreign firms faced by today's marketers. For example, in the discussion of the macromarketing environment, we point out how cultural values are not the same in different countries. One story talks about one of the latest food rages in Japan: eating fish live.

Cross-Functional Insights   We recognize that many theories and principles from other business disciplines provide additional insights into the role of marketing within an organization. The questions in the Cross-Functional Insights sections are designed to help students integrate what they have learned about management, finance, production, and other functional areas taught in business school courses with the marketing principles explained in *Effective Marketing*, Third Edition.

END-OF-CHAPTER MATERIALS

"The essence of knowledge is having it to apply it." This adage expresses our belief that students must experience a situation to truly learn. Our end-of-chapter materials have been developed with experiential learning in mind; they offer a wide range of activities to reinforce student understanding of chapter topics.

Summary   The learning objectives from the beginning of the chapter are repeated, accompanied by a brief summary of main points from the chapter.

Key Terms   To help students learn the vocabulary of marketing, key terms are listed at the end of each chapter. These terms are defined in a marginal glossary that runs through the text. In addition, a complete glossary appears at the end of the book as a reference source.

Questions for Review & Critical Thinking   These questions prompt thoughtful responses from students and require them to address practical marketing problems. Many questions are designed to stimulate the student to search for additional information about marketing. Every chapter now includes a team-building exercise to enhance students' ability to work with others.

e-exercises and Useful URLs   Because information technologies are changing the way business is conducted around the world, we have added an innovative feature to the end of each chapter in the book: a section containing Internet exercises and an address book of useful URLs. Some exercises require students to collect specific information; others are meant to hone Internet search skills. Both add interactivity to the student's education. A related feature is our Web page (http://zikmund.swcollege.com), which allows both professors and students to access voluminous instructor and student resources. The "In Case You Missed It" section of the Web page has received particularly high praise.

Ethically Right or Wrong?   Ethical issues are first introduced in Chapter 2. At the end of each subsequent chapter, students are asked to take a stand on ethical issues in the Ethically Right or Wrong? activities. These activities give students the chance to think about ethical principles and how they apply in specific business situations.

Video Cases   There are 21 end-of-chapter video cases. The exciting video segments related to the video cases spotlight marketers such as Burton Snowboards, World Gym, Second Chance Body Armor, Burke Marketing Research, and Ben & Jerry's.

ORGANIZATION OF THE BOOK

In writing a shorter book, we have not simply pared our coverage to the essentials of marketing but have organized many topics in a unique way. The material is arranged into 17 chapters that show that marketing activities are not independent but work together to achieve the organization's goals.

Chapter 1, The Nature of Marketing, places increased emphasis on the importance of creating superior customer value and using a marketing orientation to build relationships. We have incorporated a new definition of marketing, one that we believe is more understandable to students who have never been exposed to marketing. Chapter 1 introduces the marketing concept, relationship marketing, and global competition, themes that run throughout the book.

Chapter 2, Marketing Management: Strategy and Ethical Behavior, includes broad coverage of ethical principles and moral behavior, to serve as a framework and a springboard for further delineation of ethical concerns in the remaining chapters. We chose this organization because students need some background in marketing principles before they can truly understand how an organization's ethical principles influence its marketing decision making. To support an emphasis on ethics, *Effective Marketing*, Third Edition, features a section entitled Ethically Right or Wrong? at the end of each chapter. This section encourages students to think about ethical principles and how they affect decision making in specific situations.

Coverage of environmental factors has undergone major revision. Chapter 3 deals with the macroenvironment, and Chapter 4 discusses the microenvironment. Chapter 3, Environmental Forces in an e-commerce World: The Macroenvironment, lays the foundation for the text's extensive technological focus and introduces ways in which information technology can create true competitive advantage. Basic business models for making money on the Internet are introduced here.

Chapter 4, The Microenvironment in an Era of Global Business, introduces the concept of the value chain and builds a four Cs framework—Company, Customer, Competition, and Collaboration—to provide insight into managing both domestic and global relationships with suppliers, intermediaries, and customers. The chapter explains many strategic global issues within the four Cs framework. This chapter helps set the stage for a continuing discussion of the nature of competition based on quality, time, location, and price. The unique needs of global marketers—especially the need for collaborators in international marketing activity—are introduced in this chapter.

Chapter 5, Information Technology and Marketing Research, explains why information is essential to effective decision making. The revised chapter updates information on using the Internet to collect secondary data and expands the discussion about conducting Internet surveys.

Chapter 6, Consumer Behavior, provides a model and an overview of consumer behavior. It concentrates on both the psychological dimensions of the decision-making process and the sociological and cultural factors influencing the consumer.

Chapter 7, Business Markets and Organizational Buying, has been substantially revised to reflect how the advent of e-commerce and global business has remarkably changed organizational buying. The growing importance of the Internet in business-to-business marketing is explained in engaging examples such as the one about Cisco Systems, Inc.

Chapter 8, Market Segmentation, Targeting, and Positioning Strategies, applies the behavioral theories discussed in other chapters to the concepts of market segmentation. The chapter shows how both large multinational firms and small domestic marketers can use market segmentation, targeting, and positioning strategies. For instance, one example explains why the crossover marketing strategy of country artists, such as Shania Twain and Faith Hill, to appeal to a more mainstream pop or rock audience has not been adopted by the Dixie Chicks. The chapter includes a discussion of data-based marketing, mass customization, and flexible manufacturing. The opportunities for one-to-one marketing are explored.

Chapter 9, Basic Concepts about Goods, Services, and Ideas, discusses the elements of products and explains branding and packaging strategies. It has been revised to explain how our e-commerce world has shaped product strategy. For example, because Fogdog.com and many other Web site URLs serve as brand names or company names, the name before the "dot-com" should be selected with as much care as any other brand name. Another example deals with the fact that registering an address on the Internet does not establish the owner's right to receive trademark protection. The chapter includes discussion of the special concerns of the marketers of services who create products that consumers can neither touch nor closely examine before purchase. One e-commerce feature compares establishing an online service relationship with beginning a dating relationship.

Chapter 10, Strategies for New Products and the Product Life Cycle, opens with a discussion of Philips and TiVo, the first companies to offer a digital recording system and a product category now known as a personal video recorder. This innovative new product is expected to create a revolution that will see TV viewing habits undergo a radical change. The chapter addresses the nature of new products and the characteristics associated with new product successes. It goes on to depict the new product development process and to address the fact that most new products fail. The discussion of various strategies used over the course of product life cycles and the ethical issues associated with the marketing of products provides students with a practical understanding of how these issues can be addressed in both domestic and foreign markets.

The major purpose of marketing is to satisfy human needs by delivering products of various types to buyers when and where they want them and at a reasonable cost. Chapter 11, The Nature of the Supply Chain and Distribution, sets the stage for the discussion of the place element of the marketing mix. The chapter incorporates a new section about electronic marketplaces on the Internet. The text discusses how these emerging intermediaries are dramatically reshaping distribution strategies. This new edition of *Effective Marketing* reflects the growing importance of logistical systems and supply chain management in the success of the firm.

Chapter 12, Retailing, Direct Marketing, and Wholesaling, has greatly expanded coverage of direct marketing, especially of e-tailing. The chapter explains how interactivity is a fundamental and vital aspect of an Internet retail strategy. Shopbots and other technological innovations in retailing are discussed. The retailing strategies of Amazon.com, Priceline.com, Buy.com, Garden.com and many other e-tailers are discussed.

Chapter 13, Integrated Marketing Communications, focuses on the need for all elements of the promotional mix to work together. The chapter opens with an example about Lee Jeans' new marketing approach. Special attention is paid to communication theory and strategies for promotional campaigns. The chapter concludes with a discussion of the ethics of persuasion.

Chapter 14, Advertising and Public Relations in an e-commerce World, has been updated to reflect the reclassification in media caused by recent technological changes. The categories of personal and mass media no longer accurately describe the tools of marketing. We separate interactive (non-human) technologies such as the Internet from media that involve interaction with a person. Examples about Internet advertising companies such as AllAdvantage, which pays its members for visiting Web sites and watching ads, illustrate the overlap between personal and mass media. Among the new topics included is the custom delivery of personalized marketing messages via the Internet.

Chapter 15, Personal Selling, Sales Management, and Sales Promotion, explains the changing role of the salesperson in today's digital world. The chapter includes extensive coverage of sales force automation. It explains how companies like salesforce.com and other Internet innovations have made personal selling more efficient and effective. It also highlights the growing importance of sales promotions in marketing strategies.

Chapter 16, Introduction to Pricing Concepts, and Chapter 17, Pricing Strategies and Tactics, address the function of price in the allocation of goods within economies and the practical role price plays in the marketing mix. Much of the material deals with pricing objectives and discusses how pricing strategy is developed to satisfy these objectives. The book retains a very pragmatic approach to this key element of the marketing mix.

There are five appendices on our Web site at http://zikmund.swcollege.com. Appendix A, Career Opportunities in Marketing, provides information to help students learn how to identify career options using the Internet. (In addition to the appendix itself, students will find links to two related Web sites: Wired Resumé and Career Center.) Appendix B, The Business Plan and Marketing Plan, is new. Related materials can be found at http://www.bplans.com. Appendix C, Marketing Audit, has a sample outline for conducting a marketing audit. Appendix D, Organizing the Marketing Function, discusses ways of assigning tasks, grouping tasks into organizational units, and allocating resources to those units. Appendix E, Financial and Economic Analysis for Marketers, explains financial concepts and many analytical ratios that marketing managers use in their decision making. Because these are Internet appendices, professors can introduce this material at any point in the academic term.

EXTENSIVE INSTRUCTOR RESOURCES

A professor's job is demanding. Thus, we expect professors to demand a lot from the publisher and the authors of *Effective Marketing,* Third Edition. Both the textbook and the accompanying instructor's materials have been developed to help instructors excel when performing their vital teaching function.

Instructor's Manual (ISBN: 0-324-063954)   The *Instructor's Manual,* developed by the authors and Faye W. Gilbert, University of Mississippi, and updated by Thomas J. Quirk, Webster University, has been designed to serve as a rich source of materials for enhancing and organizing lectures. The *Instructor's Manual* is also available on CD-ROM for those who want to edit or expand the content of each chapter. Each chapter contains the following information:

Chapter Scan, with new e-commerce Enhancements

Learning Objectives, with a Brief Chapter Summary

Key Terms

Answer guidelines for each chapter's Questions for Review & Critical Thinking and e-exercises

Discussion guidelines for Ethically Right or Wrong? features

Discussion guidelines for Take a Stand questions

Discussion guidelines for critical thinking and video cases

Test Bank (0-324-064519)   The *Test Bank for Effective Marketing,* Third Edition, has been significantly revised by Thomas Ainscough at the College of William and Mary. Each question has been carefully written to support key chapter topics. Particular attention has been paid to developing a variety of test questions that properly evaluate student learning, measure retention, and probe for deeper understanding of topics. With over 3,000 questions, this high-quality *Test Bank* includes multiple-choice, true/false, short answer, and essay questions. Each question is coded for difficulty level and includes a textbook page reference. To further facilitate use, the questions have been categorized according to Bloom's taxonomy for cognitive complexity: recall, comprehension, calculation, and application.

Complete Video Package (0-324-06389X, 0-324-063911, and 0-324-063903)
Written and designed by a team of academics to enrich and support chapter concepts, the video cases present real marketing issues faced by a variety of service and manufacturing organizations. The video cases challenge students to study the busi-

ness issues and develop solutions to business problems. The Instructor's Video Guide, included in the *Instructor's Manual,* outlines the key teaching objectives of each video case and offers suggested answers to the critical thinking questions.

ExamView Testing Software (0-324-063946)   All items from the printed *Test Bank* are available on the Instructor's CD-ROM with ExamView Testing Software, an automated testing program that allows instructors to create exams by selecting provided questions, modifying questions, and adding questions. The software is available in Windows and MS-DOS versions and is provided free to instructors at educational institutions that adopt the text. Instructors can also have tests created and printed by calling Thomson Learning (South-Western) at 1-800-423-0563 between 8:30 a.m. and 6 p.m. EST.

PowerPoint Presentation Software (0-324-063946)   Prepared by Eric J. Karson of St. Joseph's University, these slides of key chapter concepts enhance lecture organization and reduce preparation time. Images can easily be edited, added, or deleted. All you need is Windows to run the PowerPoint viewer, and an LCD panel for classroom display. The PowerPoint slides can also be downloaded from the Instructor Resources portion of http://zikmund.swcollege.com.

***Effective Marketing,* Third Edition Web Site**   For a closer look at the technological focus of *Effective Marketing,* Third Edition, visit the online complement to the text at http://zikmund.swcollege.com. There you will find the following features:

Downloadable Instructor Resources

Student Online Learning Center

Online quizzes

Internet exercises and related URLs

"In Case You Missed It" (interesting marketing examples and useful tidbits from Michael d'Amico, updated monthly during the academic year to add spice to your lectures)

Marketing Trivia

Marketing career information, Wired Resumé, and Career Center

Internet Appendixes

e-marketing cases

Transparency Acetates (0-324-063881)   Over 200 full-color images are available as transparency acetates. The set includes images from the textbook and from the PowerPoint slides.

Instructor's Resource CD-ROM (0-324-063946)   All of the instructor's resource materials are available on a convenient CD, including the *Test Bank, Instructor's Manual,* and PowerPoint Presentation Software.

STUDENT RESOURCES

***Student Learning Guide* (0-324-064500)**   The *Student Learning Guide* for *Effective Marketing,* Third Edition, was written by Thomas J. Quirk of Webster University. For each chapter, this comprehensive guide includes a chapter summary, vocabulary-building matching exercises, vocabulary-building fill-in-the-blank exercises, true/false questions, multiple-choice questions, and experiential activities.

WebTutor on WebCT (0-324-113625)   This content-rich, Web-based teaching and learning aid reinforces and clarifies complex concepts. For each chapter, WebTutor includes a summary of key topics, a variety of quizzes to determine where a student needs additional study, flashcards, quizzes, additional Web links, threaded discussion, and more. WebTutor also provides rich communication tools for use by both instructors and students, including a course calendar and chat and e-mail functions.

WizeUp Digital Edition   The WizeUp Digital Edition of *Effective Marketing* contains the complete textbook, powered by WizeUp software. It features powerful study tools to help you study faster and easier. With the digital version, you can instantly find exactly what you need with powerful search tools, add notes anywhere in the textbook, search, sort, and print your notes to make a custom study guide, and much more.

InfoTrac College Edition (0-324-06392X)   With InfoTrac College Edition, students get complete, 24 hour-a-day access to full-text articles from hundreds of scholarly journals and popular periodicals such as *Newsweek, Time,* and *USA TODAY.* InfoTrac College Edition is perfect for all students, from dorm-dwellers to commuters and distance learners.

JIAN *MarketingBuilder Express* (0-538-875747)   The JIAN *MarketingBuilder Express* was written by Erika Matulich of Texas Christian University. The book and software provide hands-on assistance to students who are assigned to write a marketing plan. *MarketingBuilder Express* covers topics such as selecting a client, presenting information, creating a marketing plan outline, preparing a situation analysis, writing strategies, and evaluating performance.

***The New York Times Guide to Marketing* (0-324-041829)**   *The New York Times Guide to Marketing* is a collection of the best marketing-related articles from *The New York Times.*

OUR REVIEWERS ARE APPRECIATED

Special thanks go to the following insightful and creative professors who developed the supplements: Faye W. Gilbert, who developed valuable materials for the *Instructor's Manual* along with Thomas J. Quirk; Thomas Ainscough, who carefully revised and improved the *Test Bank;* Geoff Lantos of Stonehill College, who helped prepare the instructor's materials for the Ethically Right or Wrong? activities; Eric J. Karson of St. Joseph's University, who creatively designed the PowerPoint presentation slides; and Thomas J. Quirk, who significantly enhanced the third edition of the *Student Learning Guide.*

Dennis Bristow, St. Cloud State University; Nita Paden, Northern Arizona University; and Donald Olsen, University of Phoenix, reviewed various drafts of the manuscript to evaluate scholarly accuracy, writing style, and pedagogy. The many changes in this edition are based on their suggestions. We gratefully acknowledge their contributions in helping us point *Effective Marketing* toward the 21st century.

Our thanks also go to the following individuals for their earlier contributions.

Thomas L. Ainscough
University of Massachusetts-Dartmouth

Patricia Baconrind
Fort Hays State University

Todd Baker
Salt Lake City Community College

Joe Ballenger
Stephen F. Austin State University

John Beisel
Pittsburgh State University

Phil Berger
Weber State College

Michael Bolin
Abilene Christian University

Wendy Bryce
Western Washington University

William Carner
University of Texas-Austin

Barbara Dyer
Ohio University

Linda Gerber
University of Texas-Austin

Jack Gifford
Miami University

Vicki Griffis
University of South Florida

Pola Gupta
University of Northern Iowa

Frederick Hebein
California State University-San Bernardino

Craig Hollingshead
Marshall University

Richard Houser
Southern Methodist University

Tim Johnson
University of Tennessee-Knoxville

Craig A. Kelley
University of Texas-Austin

William Kilbourne
Milwaukee Area Technical College

Terry Kroeten
Concordia College

Ron E. LaFreniere
Shoreline Community College

Rajshek Lai Javalgi
Cleveland State University

Robert Lambert
Belmont College

Timothy Longfellow
Illinois State University

Lawrence J. Marks
Kent State University

Michael Mayo
Kent State University

Lee Meadow
Northern Illinois University

Leonard Miller
College of Eastern Utah

Rusty Mitchell
Inver Hills Community College

Susan A. Peterson
Scottsdale Community College

John Porter
West Virginia University

Murphy Sewall
University of Connecticut

Frederick Stephenson
University of Georgia

Kenneth Thompson
University of North Texas

Sue Umashankar
University of Arizona

Charles Vitaska
Metropolitan State College of Denver

Timothy W. Wright
Lakeland Community College

ACKNOWLEDGMENTS

The first two editions of *Effective Marketing* were well received by professors and, more importantly, by students of marketing. We appreciate the compliments and praise we have received from our fellow professors at universities and colleges around the country.

The third edition of *Effective Marketing* was the result of the hard work of many people at South-Western College Publishing. Our sponsoring editor, Pamela Person, was both very involved and very supportive. It is an understatement to say that we greatly appreciate Pamela's help. Her fresh perspective and understanding of the needs of both instructors and students have enhanced this project. We applaud her efforts. For deftly managing the onerous details of this project and for ensuring that the supplements meet our high standards, we thank our developmental editor, Mary Draper. Her sincere efforts and always optimistic personality encouraged us on many occasions.

Production editor Barb Fuller Jacobsen was always available and acted as a necessary sounding board about production issues. We appreciate the rapport we shared with her. Moreover, her meticulous attention to detail and her concern for the quality of our book made a big difference. Her expertise in bookmaking will be apparent to all who peruse this book. We are in her debt.

The efforts of copy editor Quica Ostrander, designer Mike Stratton, photo manager Cary Benbow, and production coordinator Sally Lifland resulted in a book that is lucid in exposition and a paragon of the state of the art in publishing. They did a great job. Their creative talent and special skills provide evidence that marketing is both an art and a science. Robin Browning and Christine Wittmer deserve special appreciation for creating a cool Web site and for providing indispensable help with the video and other multimedia materials.

We owe many long-term debts as well to our parents, professors, families, and friends. George Zikmund, who spent his entire life in sales and sales management, was responsible for leaving to his son an indelible sense of the practical side of marketing. Philip Cateora, as an assistant professor of Principles of Marketing at the University of Colorado, inspired a directionless young man to major in marketing. Phil Campagna later served as a wise marketing mentor at Remington Arms Company. Learning to understand marketing — and to be both book smart and street smart — takes many years, and these long-term debts are impossible to repay. We hope this book will pass on our parents', teachers', and mentors' insights to others.

William G. Zikmund
Michael F. d'Amico

AUTHORS

William G. Zikmund

A native of the Chicago area, William G. Zikmund now lives in Tulsa, Oklahoma. He is a professor of marketing at Oklahoma State University. He received his bachelor's degree in marketing from the University of Colorado, a master's degree from Southern Illinois University, and a Ph.D. in business administration from the University of Colorado. Zikmund worked in marketing research for Conway Millikin Company and Remington Arms Company before beginning his academic career. In addition, he has extensive consulting experience with many business and not-for-profit organizations.

During his academic career, Zikmund has published dozens of articles and papers in diverse scholarly journals. In addition to *Effective Marketing,* Zikmund has written *Marketing, Exploring Marketing Research, Essentials of Marketing Research, Business Research Methods,* and a work of fiction, *A Corporate Bestiary.*

A member of many professional organizations, Zikmund has served on the editorial review boards of the *Journal of Marketing Education, Marketing Education Review,* the *Journal of the Academy of Marketing Science,* and the *Journal of Business Research.* He is an active teacher who strives to be creative and innovative in the classroom.

Michael d'Amico

Michael d'Amico was born and bred in Hoboken, New Jersey. He now lives in Akron, Ohio and is a professor of marketing at the University of Akron. D'Amico graduated from the Georgetown University School of Foreign Service, received his master's degree from Rutgers University, and earned his Ph.D. in business administration at Texas Tech University. Before attending Rutgers, he worked in sales and marketing positions in Washington, D.C. and New York City, and he now serves frequently as a consultant to not-for-profit, political, and commercial organizations and as a board member for such organizations as Goodwill Industries.

D'Amico has published over one hundred proceedings, journal, and business press articles and has co-edited several proceedings and texts. Currently co-editor of the *Marketing Management Journal,* he is also a past president of the Marketing Management Association and past national vice-president of Pi Sigma Epsilon, the national marketing fraternity. D'Amico has won a number of teaching awards and was selected by the Professional Fraternities Association as its 1997–1998 Outstanding Collegiate Chapter Advisor for his work with Pi Sigma Epsilon. He is a currently past national president of Mu Kappa Tau, the Marketing Honorary Society.

To Tobin and Noah Zikmund
Kathy and Alyse d'Amico

THE INTERNET IS TRANSFORMING SOCIETY. TIME IS COLLAPSING. DISTANCE IS NO LONGER AN OBSTACLE. CROSSING OCEANS TAKES ONLY A MOUSE CLICK. PEOPLE ARE CONNECTED 24 HOURS A DAY, 7 DAYS A WEEK. "INSTANTANEOUS" HAS A NEW MEANING. SOME SAY THE INTERNET IS CHANGING EVERYTHING. EVERYTHING, ESPECIALLY COMMERCE.

e commerce
The power of e

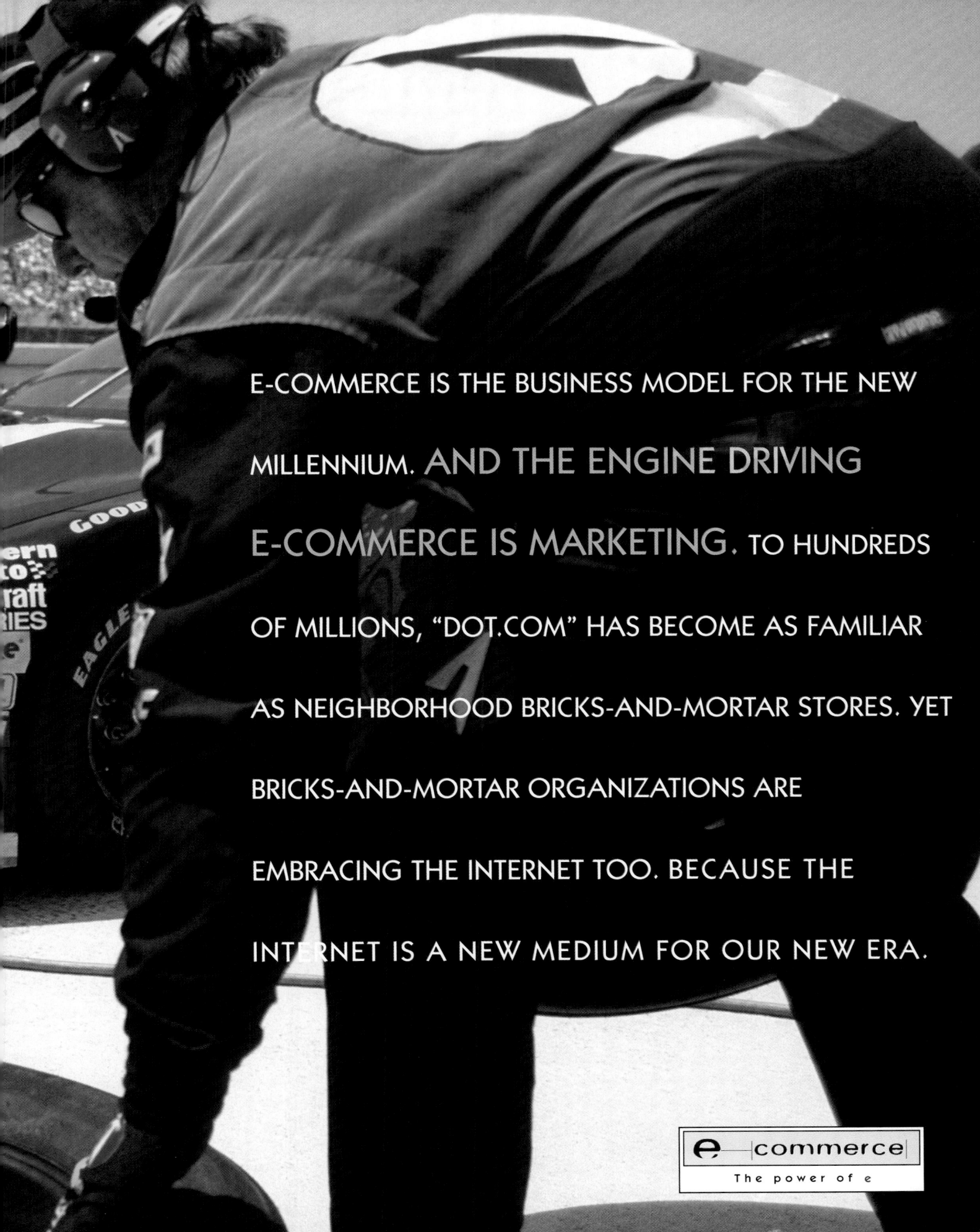

E-COMMERCE IS THE BUSINESS MODEL FOR THE NEW MILLENNIUM. AND THE ENGINE DRIVING E-COMMERCE IS MARKETING. TO HUNDREDS OF MILLIONS, "DOT.COM" HAS BECOME AS FAMILIAR AS NEIGHBORHOOD BRICKS-AND-MORTAR STORES. YET BRICKS-AND-MORTAR ORGANIZATIONS ARE EMBRACING THE INTERNET TOO. BECAUSE THE INTERNET IS A NEW MEDIUM FOR OUR NEW ERA.

e-commerce
The power of e

THE INTERNET IS A COMMUNICATION MEDIUM.

COMMUNICATION PROVIDES THE FOUNDATION FOR ALL

MARKETING ACTIVITY. THE INTERNET IS A DISTRIBUTION

MEDIUM. DISTRIBUTION—BRIDGING THE PHYSICAL SEPARATION

BETWEEN BUYERS AND SELLERS—IS WHERE MARKETING'S

ROOTS LIE. THE INTERNET IS A TRANSACTION

MEDIUM. EXCHANGE IS THE ESSENCE OF MARKETING.

MARKETING'S SUM AND SUBSTANCE INVOLVES MAKING

TRANSACTIONS AND BUILDING RELATIONSHIPS WITH

CUSTOMERS—CREATING AND KEEPING CUSTOMERS.

e-commerce

The power of e

THE INTERNET ALLOWS A ONE-ON-ONE CONNECTION BETWEEN MARKETERS AND CUSTOMERS. IT OFFERS A WEB OF OPPORTUNITIES. THE INTERNET IS TRANSFORMING HOW MARKETERS CONDUCT BUSINESS. MARKETING IS BEING REDEFINED. EFFECTIVE MARKETING, 3RD EDITION HIGHLIGHTS MARKETING IN A BORDERLESS, E-COMMERCE WORLD. BECAUSE THE INTERNET IS TRANSFORMING SOCIETY—CHANGING EVERYTHING.

The Nature of Marketing

chapter 1

Sitting atop a bluff overlooking the Pacific, Scott Blum's house is a modernist fantasy that sticks out from the drab, conservative homes around it. Most of the other houses in Ritz Cove, a plush, gated community just south of Laguna Beach, Calif., are typical, albeit large, examples of Orange County architecture. A mishmash of Mediterranean styles—Ionic columns, red-tiled roofs, walled courtyards, wrought-iron hardware—the houses are painted in muted whites, pinks, or browns.

Not Scott's house. His 6,800-square-foot home is a set of interconnected geometric shapes built from poured concrete, green glass, and stainless steel, a sleek design that somehow suits its natural surroundings. "Some people tried to stop me from building it," says Blum, 35. "They even threatened to sue me." But they picked the wrong guy to intimidate. Scott Blum has made a living out of getting what he wants. And he really wanted oceanfront property in Ritz Cove. Back in 1984, Blum (rhymes with "plum") was a 19-year-old parking-lot attendant at the adjacent Ritz-Carlton Hotel. "I told the other attendants that someday I was going to own a house in that development," says Scott. In 1998, after four years of legal wrangling, he and his wife, Audrey, moved in.

Today, Blum may have enough money to buy the whole development, and the hotel, if he so chooses. Buy.com, the e-commerce company he founded only a few years ago, has potential stock market valuation of over a billion dollars. Scott, who is chairman of the company, owns 65% of the stock.

The marketing plan for Buy.com, headquartered in Aliso Viejo, Calif., is as bold—or reckless—as the design of Scott's house. The company resells computers and other products at or below cost, and is now losing "a couple of million dollars a month." But that's the plan: Like other e-commerce companies, including FreePC.com and online auction house OnSale, Buy.com aims to build a large base of loyal customers who will return again and again to its Web site to buy products. The goods themselves are an inducement to bring visitors to the Web site. The anticipated profits will come from the sale of advertising and ancillary services like warranties and equipment leases.

It's too early to say whether this type of marketing plan will work, but Buy.com is furthest along in implementing the strategy. The company's slogan, "the lowest prices on earth," is attracting customers. Buy.com launched its Web site in November 1997. At first it sold only computers, but now it offers software, books, videos, and electronic games, with CDs and other products soon to come. In its first full year of operations, Buy.com had about $125 million in revenues. Its current growth rate indicates that Buy.com is off to one of the fastest starts of any U.S. company.

It's not enough for Blum. He's purchased the rights to more than 4,000 Web addresses covering all kinds of products that he might sell, including Buymusic.com, Buystuff.com, Buytoys.com, and even Buycars.com. "My goal is to reach $10 billion in revenue with 1% gross margins on product sales," he says. And he'd like to get there by 2003.[1]

The Internet has created a thriving e-commerce industry. It has changed the way people buy products and the way organizations conduct business. Who shops online? Who prefers personalized service in shopping malls? Why do people visit certain Web sites and not others? What makes them return again and again to places like Yahoo! and Buy.com? How important is the price of a product? What do marketers do that motivates consumers to place Internet orders with credit cards? Does privacy matter? Is being socially responsible an important concern for a marketing organization? Are all e-commerce businesses the same? The answers to questions like these lie in the field of marketing, the subject of this book.

Marketing Affects Our Daily Lives

Perhaps you have thought of some answers to the questions we asked in the introduction. After all, you probably have surfed the Internet. Certainly you have visited shopping centers, examined retail displays, compared prices, dealt with salespeople, and evaluated and purchased a wide range of products. If you think about it, as customers, we all play a part in the marketing system, so we all know something about marketing. We all recognize brand names like Nike and Energizer and their corporate and product symbols such as the Nike "Swoosh" and the Energizer Bunny. Television advertising has been both an irritant and a source of pleasure to us all.

Some aspects of marketing are, of course, more widely known than others. The brand names shown in Exhibit 1-1 are probably quite familiar to you. The brand names in Exhibit 1-2 probably are not—they identify corporations most consumers seldom encounter directly. These companies supply goods and services that are used to produce other goods and services, thus performing important marketing activities behind the scenes. Although most of us deal regularly with retailers and sales clerks, we encounter wholesalers, industrial sales representatives, and advertising agents less frequently. Indeed, there are many aspects of marketing that many people have never considered systematically. To fully understand marketing, you must first know what it is and what it includes.

This chapter begins by explaining the nature of marketing and the essential marketing activities that make up the marketing mix. Next, the chapter explores how managers adapt the marketing mix in response to changes in uncontrollable forces in the environment. The chapter then looks at the marketing concept and the importance of an organization's establishing a cross-functional commitment to a consumer orientation, long-term success, and the building of relationships. Finally, the chapter explores the important role marketing plays in society and its role in your professional career.

e x h i b i 1-1

You Already Know Something About Marketing

Some Important Marketing Companies You May Not Have Encountered Directly

Marketing—What Is It?

As you will see, there are several ways to consider the subject of marketing, so there are a number of ways to define the term itself. Because for most people marketing has a business connotation, it is best to begin by discussing marketing from a business perspective. Marketing, as the term implies, is focused on the marketplace. (In fact, for shoppers of past generations, the word *marketing* meant going to a store or market to buy groceries.) A businessperson who is asked the question "What is marketing?" might answer that marketing is selling, or advertising, or retailing. But notice that these are marketing activities, not definitions of marketing as a whole.

At the broadest level, the function of marketing activities is to bring buyers and sellers together. At the beach, the thirsty sunbather seeks the Coke stand owner. The owner is, in turn, interested in selling soft drinks to satisfy the customer's thirst. The owner's marketing activities, such as locating the stand at the beach and advertising the price on a sign, help bring buyer and seller together. The owner's goal is to consummate a sale to satisfy a customer. This, of course, is a simple example. A more sophisticated situation requires more complex marketing activities.

Suppose you were the vice-president of marketing for Sara Lee Bakery, the maker of frozen cheesecakes and other frozen desserts. Production—which is an important business activity, but not a marketing activity—would not be directly under your control. Instead, your marketing activities might be identified as conceiving and developing products, determining prices, advertising, selling, distributing products to consumers, and servicing customers after sales have been made. And even this extensive list is not complete.

> At the broadest level, the function of marketing activities is to bring buyers and sellers together.

A full understanding of marketing requires recognition of the fact that product development activities and product modifications are planned in response to the public's changing needs and wants. A major marketing activity, then, is paying continuous attention to customers' needs—identifying and interpreting those needs before undertaking other activities, including production. Although most marketing activities are intended to direct the flow of goods and services from producer to consumer, the marketing process begins with customer analysis even before the product is produced.

Again consider Sara Lee. The company experienced declining sales of its frozen cheesecakes during 1997 and 1998. When the company investigated its problem, marketers uncovered a major shift in Americans' eating behavior, connected to consumers' limited free time. For instance, an increasing number of Americans are eating their meals away from home.[2] A whole new culture of "dashboard dining" has developed as the car has become a regular place where people eat. In addition, when families dine at home, they often seek the convenience of ready-made or hassle-free entrees available from restaurants, supermarkets, or packaged food marketers. The company also learned that consumers were more likely to have dessert in front of the TV at 9 p.m. than to take time to eat cheesecake after dinner. Discussions with families created a better understanding of their changing needs and resulted in a new product: Sara Lee Cheesecake Bites. The product consists of individual cheesecake servings, which can be eaten straight from the freezer.[3] When marketers understand consumer needs, they find it easier to bring buyers and sellers together.

Not-for-Profit Organizations Are Marketers Too!

"Perform a death-defying act—eat less saturated fat." The American Heart Association makes this appeal in an advertisement, yet the American Heart Association

From a broad perspective, marketing includes the activities of not-for-profit organizations, such as tourist councils. Ireland markets the island country's natural beauty and historic castles. The advertisement for Ireland shown here also promotes the opportunity to enjoy good food and to stay in world-class hotels, bed and breakfast lodges, and traditional Irish cottages.

The city of Lawrence, Kansas, offers brochures and free information about the region. Promoted in this advertisement are the Jayhawks of yesteryear, who helped keep Kansas a free state, and the University of Kansas's basketball team that shares their name.

does not seek to make a profit, nor does it charge a price for most services. Is the American Heart Association engaging in marketing? Are your university, church, and local police department marketers? If we take a broadened perspective of marketing, the answer is unquestionably "Yes."

If the concept of marketing is broadened to include not-for-profit organizations, then the primary characteristic of marketing is that it involves an **exchange process** in which two or more parties exchange, or trade, something of value. An economic transfer of goods or services in exchange for money is the most frequently analyzed marketing transaction. However, exchanges also occur in a politician's campaign, a zoo's fund-raising drive, or an antismoking group's program. When a donation is made to a political campaign, to a zoo, or to an antismoking effort, something is given and something is received—even though what is received may be intangible, such as a feeling of goodwill or a sense of satisfaction. In each situation, there has been a transaction, either between an individual and a group or between two individuals. The common characteristic in these situations is the set of activities necessary to bring about exchange relationships. Additional examples of exchanges include offering to vote or volunteer for a candidate who pledges to work hard for his or her constituents, donating blood to help the sick and injured, and spending time working for a United Way campaign—the reward for all of which is a sense of satisfaction. Because all these activities involve an exchange, they may be viewed from a marketing perspective.

Exchange process
The interchange of something of value by two or more parties.

A Definition of Marketing

The Buy.com and Sara Lee examples illustrate what marketing is like in well-managed businesses. The American Heart Association example illustrates that not-for-profit organizations engage in marketing. Thinking about these examples should help you understand that the three organizations share a common marketing goal—to facilitate the exchange or transfer of a product, regardless of whether the product is a good, service, or idea, so that both the marketer and the customer profit in some way. This principle of exchange comprises the key aspect of the definition of marketing.

Marketing is the process of influencing voluntary exchange transactions in which one party to the transaction can be envisioned in some fashion as a customer of the other, the marketer. The marketing process involves communication and requires a mechanism or system to carry out the exchange of the marketer's product for something of value.[4] Our definition emphasizes five fundamental aspects of marketing:

- two or more parties
- something that is given up by each
- something that is received by each
- some level of communication between the parties
- some mechanism or system to perform the exchange

Marketing
The process that seeks to influence voluntary exchange transactions between a customer and a marketer. The marketing process involves communication and requires a mechanism or system to carry out the exchange of the marketer's product for something of value.

Every exchange requires two or more parties: One party conceives and develops a product to market, and another party acquires the product and provides something in return. In business, companies give up their product, which may be a good, service, or an idea, for a price. Both participants in the exchange, acting on the basis of their perceived self-interest, expect to gain something; revenues satisfy the marketer's objectives, and products satisfy the consumer's needs. Effective marketing involves using the resources of an entire organization to create exchanges between the marketer and the customer so that both parties are satisfied.[5]

The basic function of bringing marketers (suppliers) together with consumers (buyers) cannot be accomplished without communication. Communication is the means to exchange information. Communication between a prospective buyer and a seller can be face to face or can occur through a variety of media. Effective marketers carefully select both message and media when they communicate the value of what they offer to potential customers.

A mechanism or system to perform the exchange may be as basic as a physical exchange of possessions between two people. Or it may be a complicated series of distribution activities involving the transfer of ownership and possession to get shoes made in Italy to shoe stores in Los Angeles. Effective marketers develop efficient systems to carry out exchanges.

Keeping Customers and Building Relationships

So far, our discussion of marketing has focused on the idea of creating exchanges. To put it another way, we have talked about getting customers; but keeping customers is equally important. Marketers want customers for life. Effective marketers work to build long-term relationships with their customers. The term **relationship marketing** (or relationship management) communicates the idea that a major goal of marketing is to build long-term relationships between a company and the parties who contribute to the company's success.

Once an exchange is made, effective marketing stresses managing relationships that will bring about additional exchanges. Effective marketers view making a sale not as the end of a process but as the start of the organization's relationship with a customer. Satisfied customers who want to purchase the same product in the future will return to a company that has treated them well in the past. If they need a related item, satisfied customers know the first place to look. The key aspects of our definition of marketing are illustrated in Exhibit 1-3.

Relationship marketing
Marketing activities aimed at building long-term relationships with the people (especially customers) and organizations that contribute to a company's success.

> Effective marketers view making a sale not as the end of a process but as the start of the organization's relationship with a customer.

e x h i b i **1-3** The Definition of Marketing: Three Examples

| | EXCHANGE | | |
ORGANIZATION	WHAT THE ORGANIZATION GIVES UP	WHAT THE CONSUMER GIVES UP	CUSTOMER SATISFACTION/ RELATIONSHIP BUILDING
Sara Lee	Offers individual servings of cheesecake that are hassle-free and can be eaten straight from the freezer	Spends money	Enjoyment of ready-made, tasty desserts Convenience has value for today's family Quality food from an established company
American Heart Association	Dispenses useful public service information, provides health care, and conducts medical research Expresses gratitude for donations	Donates money or volunteer time that helps the American Heart Association provide services	Sense of doing good Knowledge that time or money is well spent to benefit others Knowledge that "someone might do the same for me or one of my loved ones" in a time of need
Atlanta Braves' Turner Field	Offers nine innings of baseball, interactive entertainment, food and beverages, and television broadcasts of games, all of which have value for the fan	Pays for tickets, interactive games, food, beverages, souvenirs, etc., providing revenue for the Braves	Enjoyment of game and ballpark visit Sense of involvement with team Sense of loyalty

In summary, marketers strive to initiate exchanges and build relationships. More simply, you can think of marketing as an activity aimed at getting and keeping customers. It is the marketer's job to use the resources of the entire organization to create, interpret, and maintain the relationship between the company and the customer.

What Is a Market?

The root word in the term *marketing* is *market*.[6] A **market** is a group of potential customers for a particular product who are willing and able to spend money or exchange other resources to obtain the product. The term can be somewhat confusing, because it has been used to designate buildings or places (the Fulton Fish Market, the European Market), institutions (the stock market), and stores (the supermarket), as well as many other things. But each usage—even the name of a building in which trading is carried out—suggests people or groups with purchasing power who are willing to exchange their resources for something else. It will become clear as you read this book that the nature of the market is a primary concern of marketing decision makers.

The Marketing Mix

Planning and executing the conception, pricing, promotion, and distribution of ideas, goods, and services are essential marketing activities.[7] These interrelated and interdependent activities are performed to encourage exchange and build relationships. The term **marketing mix** describes the result of management's creative efforts to combine these activities.[8] Faced with a wide choice of product features, messages, prices, distribution methods, and other marketing variables, the marketing manager must select and combine ingredients to create a marketing mix that will achieve organizational objectives.

The marketing mix may have many facets, but its elements can be placed in four basic categories: product, place (distribution), promotion, and price. These are commonly referred to as the **four Ps of marketing**, or—because they can be influenced by managers—as the controllable variables of marketing.[9] Because virtually every possible marketing activity can be placed in one of these categories, the four Ps constitute a framework that can be used to develop plans for marketing efforts. Each of the 4Ps is introduced in this section.

THE FIRST ELEMENT—PRODUCT

The term **product** refers to what the business or nonprofit organization offers to its prospective customers or clients. The offering may be a tangible good, such as a car; a service, such as an airline trip; or an intangible idea, such as the importance of parents' reading to their children.

Because customers often expect more from an organization than a simple, tangible product, the task of marketing management is to provide a complete offering—a "total product"—that includes not only the basic good or service but also the "extras" that go with it. The core product of a city bus line may be rides or transportation, for example, but its total product offering should include courteous service, buses that run on time, and assistance in finding appropriate bus routes.

Consider an Atlanta Braves baseball game at Turner Field as a product. The stadium design reflects the charm and nostalgia of baseball's past. A Braves Museum and Hall of Fame, housing more than two hundred artifacts, enhances the traditional atmosphere of the stadium. However, state-of-the-art Turner Field is also a baseball theme park where "20th century tradition meets 21st century technology." There are interactive games to test fans' hitting and pitching skills, as well as knowledge of baseball trivia; electronic kiosks with touch screens and data banks filled with scouting reports on 300 past and present Braves, along with the Braves' Internet home page; a dozen 27-inch television monitors mounted above

Market
A group of potential customers who may want a particular product and who have the resources, the willingness, and the ability to purchase it.

Marketing mix
The specific combination of interrelated and interdependent marketing activities in which an organization engages to meet its objectives.

Four Ps of marketing
The basic elements of the marketing mix: product, place (distribution), price, and promotion; also called the controllable variables of marketing, because they can be controlled and manipulated by the marketer.

Product
A good, service, or idea that offers a bundle of tangible and intangible attributes to satisfy consumers.

A product is what is offered to customers. A concert by Ricky Martin is not a tangible good, but it is a product nonetheless. Developing a product, even a concert, requires making certain that it has the characteristics and features the customer wants. Every product, whether it is a good, a service, or an idea, requires marketing. Some organizations are effective marketers that create value for their customers, and others are not.

http://www.rickymartin.com

the Braves' Clubhouse Store, broadcasting all the other major league games in progress, and a video ticker-tape screen underneath, spitting out up-to-the-minute scores and stats.[10] The product idea behind Turner Field is that, for many fans, it is not enough to just provide nine innings of baseball. The Atlanta Braves are no longer just a baseball team—they are in the business of offering assorted entertainment products that provide fun, amusement, and diversion for fans. Effective marketers like those in the Atlanta Braves organization realize what a product is.

The product the customer receives in the exchange process is the result of a number of product strategy decisions. Developing and planning a product involves making sure that it has the characteristics and features customers want. Selecting a brand name, designing a package, developing appropriate warranties and service plans, and other product decisions are also part of developing the "right" product. Product strategies are addressed in Chapters 9 and 10.

As you will see, product strategies must take into consideration the other three elements of the marketing mix. Price, distribution, and promotion enhance the attractiveness of the product offering.

what went wrong?

McDonald's McDonald's in the United Kingdom chose a tartan design for new "host" and "hostess" uniforms in all of its 764 U.K. restaurants. By most accounts, the ties, scarves, and waistcoats in the tartan fabric were considered to be attractive. However, soon after the uniforms began to appear in the restaurants, it became clear that McDonald's had breached British etiquette. What went wrong?

Different Scottish tartans historically belong to individual clans, or families, whose members in days gone by were typically fiercely competitive with each other, sometimes to the point of bloodshed. Where McDonald's tripped up was in choosing the tartan belonging to Clan Lindsay, rivals of the Donalds. An enraged Godfrey Lord Macdonald, chief of Clan Donald (who allegedly commands the allegiance of every Donald, Macdonald, and McDonald worldwide), complained of a "complete lack of understanding of the name." He says there are nineteen Macdonald tartans the company could have chosen from.[11]

Place, or **distribution**, activities involve bridging the physical separation between buyers and sellers to assure that products are available at the right place. Determining how goods get to the customer, how quickly, and in what condition are decisions that are made to place products where and when buyers want them. Transportation, storage, materials handling, and the like are physical distribution activities. Selecting wholesalers and retailers or choosing to be an e-commerce company operating exclusively on the Internet are decisions about the structure and extent of distribution. We will have a great deal to say about distribution via the Internet in later chapters. However, before we do, we will explain the traditional distribution activities.

The examples so far have shown that every organization engages in marketing. Not every organization, however, has the resources or ability to manage all the activities that make up the distribution process. Thus, organizations may concentrate on activities in which they have a unique advantage and rely on wholesalers, retailers, and various other specialists to make the distribution process more efficient. For example, the Pepsi-Cola Corporation, which specializes in the production and promotion of soft drinks, finds it efficient to utilize independent bottlers and retailers to distribute its products to the ultimate consumer.

A **channel of distribution** is the complete sequence of marketing organizations involved in bringing a product from the producer to the consumer. Its purpose is to make possible transfer of ownership and/or possession of the product. Exhibit 1-4 illustrates a basic channel of distribution consisting of the manufacturer, the wholesaler, the retailer, and the ultimate consumer. Each of these four engages in a transaction that involves movement of the physical good and/or a transfer of ownership (title) of that product. As you look at Exhibit 1-4, consider the following definitions:

A **manufacturer** is an organization that recognizes a consumer need and produces a product from raw materials, component parts, or labor to satisfy that need.

A **wholesaler** is an organization that serves as an intermediary between manufacturer and retailer to facilitate the transfer of products or the exchange of title to those products, or an organization that sells products to manufacturers or institutions that resell the products (sometimes in another form). Exhibit 1-4 shows the type of wholesaler that sells to retailers. Wholesalers neither produce nor consume the finished product.

A **retailer** is an organization that sells products it has obtained from a manufacturer or wholesaler to the ultimate consumer. Retailers neither produce nor consume the product.

The **ultimate consumer** is the individual who buys or uses the product for personal consumption.

The actual distribution path that a product or title takes may be simpler or much more complex than the one illustrated in Exhibit 1-4. For example, a computer manufacturer such as Gateway or Dell may provide information about its products on the Internet, allow customers to place orders on the Internet, and then ship directly to a buyer. Various distribution systems are explained in Chapters 11 and 12.

Excluded from the channel of distribution are numerous specialists that perform specific facilitating activities for manufacturers, wholesalers, or retailers—for example, the airline or the railway that transports a product from Boston to Philadelphia or the advertising agency on Madison Avenue that creates the advertising message and selects the appropriate media. These specialists, or *collaborators,* are hired because they can perform a certain marketing activity in a basic marketing channel more efficiently or more effectively than a producer can. However, they are not among the organizations included in our definition of channel of distribution.[12]

Place (distribution)
The element of the marketing mix that encompasses all aspects of getting products to the consumer in the right location at the right time.

Channel of distribution
The sequence of marketing organizations involved in bringing a product from the producer to the consumer.

Manufacturer
An organization that recognizes a consumer need and produces a product from raw materials, component parts, or labor to satisfy that need.

Wholesaler
An organization that serves as an intermediary between manufacturer and retailer to facilitate the transfer of products or the exchange of title to those products, or an organization that sells to manufacturers or institutions that resell the product (perhaps in another form). Wholesalers neither produce nor consume the finished product.

Retailer
An organization that sells products it has obtained from a manufacturer or wholesaler to the ultimate consumer. Retailers neither produce nor consume the product.

Ultimate consumer
An individual who buys or uses a product for personal consumption.

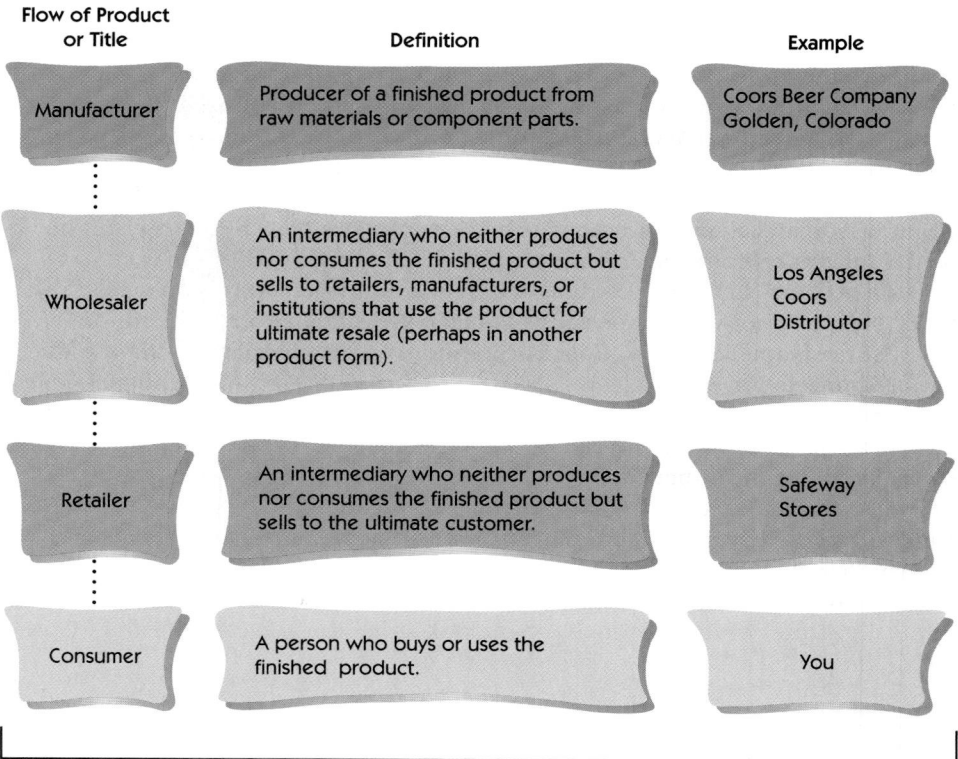

Who Is Involved in a Basic Channel of Distribution?

Flow of Product or Title	Definition	Example
Manufacturer	Producer of a finished product from raw materials or component parts.	Coors Beer Company Golden, Colorado
Wholesaler	An intermediary who neither produces nor consumes the finished product but sells to retailers, manufacturers, or institutions that use the product for ultimate resale (perhaps in another product form).	Los Angeles Coors Distributor
Retailer	An intermediary who neither produces nor consumes the finished product but sells to the ultimate customer.	Safeway Stores
Consumer	A person who buys or uses the finished product.	You

It is important to realize that distribution mixes vary widely even among companies selling directly competitive products. For example, Avon and Amway use sales representatives selling directly to consumers as their primary source of distribution; Gillette and Colgate-Palmolive, selling similar goods, deal with many wholesalers and retailers in their distribution systems. Further, a single organization may use different methods of distribution in different parts of the world.

THE THIRD ELEMENT—PROMOTION

Promotion
The element of the marketing mix that includes all forms of marketing communication.

Marketers need to communicate with consumers. **Promotion** is the means by which marketers "talk to" existing customers and potential buyers. Promotion may convey a message about the organization, a product, or some other element of the marketing mix, such as the new low price being offered during a sale period. Simply put, promotion is marketing communication.

As an illustration of the value of promotional efforts in a marketing mix, think about Michelin tires. You probably have seen one of the television commercials featuring an adorable little baby sitting in the center of a tire. Perhaps you recall a commercial that shows several young women at a baby shower, celebrating a friend's approaching motherhood. The expectant mom is handed a large, beautifully wrapped package with a very familiar shape. She exclaims, "You guys, you didn't. You did!" when she discovers that the package contains a Michelin tire. She is even more delighted when she finds that her friends got her a whole set of tires. The commercial is quite entertaining. However, from the marketer's point of view, the most important thing for a viewer to remember is that at the end of the commercial an announcer says, "Michelin—because so much is riding on your tires." Michelin's promotion accomplishes its task: It communicates the message that Michelin provides high-quality, safe tires and peace of mind for parents.

Advertising, personal selling, publicity, and sales promotion are all forms of promotion. Each offers unique benefits, but all are forms of communication that inform, remind, or persuade. For example, advertising with Tony the Tiger saying "They're GR-R-Reat!" reminds us of our experiences with Kellogg's Frosted Flakes. Or, when an IBM sales representative delivers a personal message during a sales presentation, this personal selling effort may be designed to explain how IBM's experience on the Internet and its computer servers help pro-

The day we found a monster in our mailroom

This happened in Tokyo. A Japanese mother returned a kid's parka to us. And somebody in Shipping discovered a toy in the pocket — a goofy, 4-inch monster.

Well, figuring some little kid would miss it, he sent it back.

The next thing you know, we received a postcard from a very grateful mother.

Seems that goofy monster was her kid's *favorite* toy.

Mind you, we get cards and letters all the time at Lands' End® – thanking us for the little *unexpected* things we do.

A lady in Germany wrote that she ordered a necktie for her son – who usually doesn't wear ties – asking us to send him instructions on how to tie it.

Instead, one of our people tied one to show him how. And sent it in a gift box, for extra measure.

And then, there's the English chap who sent back one of our Original Attaches – well worn –

asking us to repair a broken zipper.

We sent him a brand new Attache. He wrote back that not only was he delighted by the replacement – he even likes the new color better.

Wherever Lands' End customers are, we try to do right by them, just as we do here at home.

Only here, we've been doing it for thirty years and more.

© 1999 Lands' End, Inc.

Guaranteed. Period.

LANDS' END

For our free catalog, call: 1-800-296-8124
or mail to: 1 Lands' End Lane, Dodgeville, WI 53595.

Name _____
Address _____
City _____ State _____ Zip _____
Phone ( ) _____ Day/Night (whole one)
Fax: 1-800-332-0103 www.landsend.com/catalogs/228

vide business solutions. The essence of all promotion is communication aimed at informing, reminding, or persuading potential buyers.

Different firms emphasize different forms of promotional communication, depending on their marketing objectives. Some firms advertise heavily, for example, whereas others advertise hardly at all. A firm's particular combination of integrated communication tools is its promotional mix. The topic of promotion and integrated marketing communications is addressed in greater detail in Chapters 13–15.

THE FOURTH ELEMENT—PRICE

The money—or something else of value—given in exchange for something is its **price**. In other words, price is what is exchanged for a product. The customer typically buys a product with cash or credit, but the price may be a good or service that is traded. In not-for-profit situations, price may be expressed in terms of volunteered time or effort, votes, or donations.

Marketers must determine the best price for their products. To do so, they must ascertain a product's value, or what it is worth to consumers. Once the value of a product is established, the marketer knows what price to charge. However, because consumers' evaluations of a product's worth change over time, prices are subject to rapid change.

According to economists, prices are always "on trial." Pricing strategies and decisions require establishing appropriate prices and carefully monitoring the competitive marketplace. Price is discussed in Chapters 16 and 17.

Price
The amount of money or other consideration—that is, something of value—given in exchange for a product.

THE ART OF BLENDING THE ELEMENTS

A manager selecting a marketing mix may be likened to a chef preparing a meal. Each realizes that there is no one best way to mix ingredients. Different combinations may be used, and the result will still be satisfactory. In marketing, as in cooking, there is no standard formula for a successful combination of ingredients. Marketing mixes vary from company to company and from situation to situation.

MARKETING MIX ELEMENT	COMPANY OR ORGANIZATION	EXAMPLE
PRODUCT		
Product development	Procter & Gamble	Swiffer (electrostatic dust mop)
	First USA	Wingspan Bank.com (online banking)
Product modification	Palm Computing	Palm Pilot III C offers 256 colors on hand-held computer screen
	Charles Schwab	Schwab's broker service can now be accessed via the Internet
	Mattel	Barbie doll has a redesigned midsection that eliminates the seam and enables the doll to twist and bend at the waist without joints showing.
Branding	3M Company	Scotch brand cellophane tape
	World Wrestling Federation	XFL (professional football league)
Trademark	Michelin	Tire Man
Warranty	Sears	"If any Craftsman hand tool ever fails to give complete satisfaction, Sears will replace it free."
PLACE (DISTRIBUTION)		
Channel of distribution	Hoover Vacuum	Ships directly to Wal-Mart
	U.S. Postal Service	Sells stamps by mail order, in vending machines, on-line, and at post offices
Physical distribution	South-Western College Publishing	Uses FedEx to transport rush orders
PROMOTION		
Advertising	Yahoo!	"Do you Yahoo?"
	The Advertising Council	"Remember, only you can prevent forest fires."
Personal selling	Girl Scouts	Door-to-door cookie sales
	Hitachi	Sales representatives sell fiber-optic communication systems to business organizations
Sales promotion	Metropolitan Life Insurance	Gives away "Let's Go Mets" T-shirts at New York Mets baseball games
	The American Red Cross	Emphasizes the importance of donating blood by giving Nabisco Lifesaver candies and a T-shirt with the "life saver" theme
Publicity	Garth Brooks (singer)	Gives free concert in Central Park
	Susan G. Komen Breast Cancer Foundation	Race for the Cure 5K runs
PRICE		
Price strategy	Absolut Country of Sweden Vodka	Expensive
	eBay	Auction pricing on the Internet

Exhibit 1-5 provides examples of many marketing mix elements. The vast majority of marketers agree that the blending of these elements is a creative activity. For example, though both firms are successful at selling motorcycles, the marketing mix strategies of Honda and Harley-Davidson differ greatly. Far greater differences can be seen in marketing mixes for different products, such as Penn tennis balls and Steinway pianos. The field of marketing encompasses such differing approaches because the design, implementation, and revision of a marketing mix is a creative activity.

Some experts claim that marketing is—or could be—a science. Certain aspects of marketing, such as the gathering and analyzing of information by marketing researchers, are indeed scientific in nature. The fact remains, however, that there are no pat solutions in marketing. Even frequently encountered problems have unique aspects requiring creative solutions. This absence of certainty may annoy those who are accustomed to solving math or accounting problems and arriving at one "right" answer. But marketing is different. Its relationship to the ever-changing environment requires that it be dynamic, constantly altering its approaches to suit the marketplace. Each product's marketing mix must be critically analyzed and altered as the environment changes and new problems develop.

The Marketing Environment— Coping with the Uncontrollable

All organizations operate within environments. That is, all organizations, whether for profit or not for profit, are surrounded by, and must contend with, external forces. Except in rare instances, managers cannot govern these external environmental forces; therefore, the forces are called **uncontrollable variables**. Uncontrollable variables affect both consumers' behavior and organizations' development of effective marketing mixes, as shown in Exhibit 1-6.

Uncontrollable variable
A force or influence external to the organization and beyond its control.

Inflation provides an example of an external environmental force. Organizations' reactions to high inflation rates are easy to spot in their pricing policies. Consumers' reactions to economic conditions such as shortages of materials and high land prices are similarly predictable: They are likely to build fewer homes. Such a decline will in turn reduce the demand for bulldozers, concrete mixers, nails, and even work clothes.

The influence of some environmental forces—for example, changes in social values and lifestyles—may be more subtle. Consider that most people in your grandparents' day—and certainly your great-grandparents' day—thought it a vice for children to eat between meals.[13] Today, most parents allow children to eat a series of small meals and snacks throughout the day. Parents today differ from those of past generations in their beliefs about whether a 5 p.m. cookie can "spoil" their children's dinner. Many view snacks not just as a form of sustenance but as a means to buy peace. Mothers tuck lollipops in their purses to appease restless children in church. They prepare goody bags for car trips of more than 30 minutes.

e x h i b i 1·6

Consumer Behavior and the Marketing Mix Are Shaped by Environmental Forces

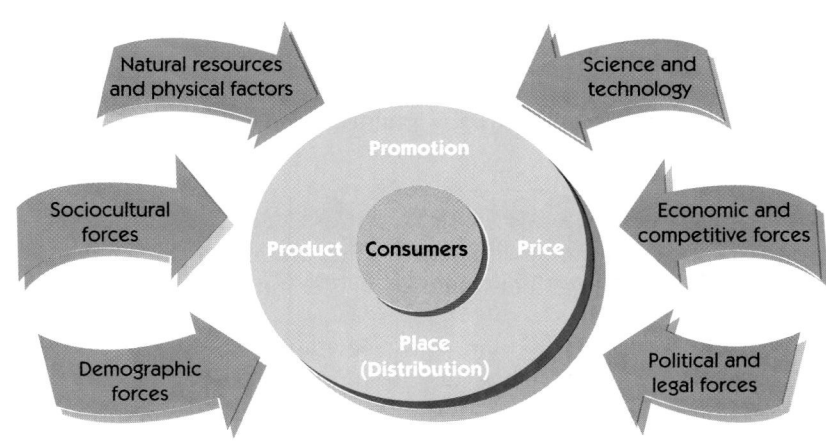

Marketing managers must be able to recognize and analyze subtle uncontrollable variables of this kind so that they can plan marketing mixes compatible with the environment. For example, marketers have responded to the snacking trend with convenient, disposable, single-serving packages containing sweet and colorful snacks that appeal to children. To appeal to parents, they communicate health claims that stress the real fruit juice or added nutrients in candy and cereals.

Reacting and adapting to competition, economic forces, social trends, government regulations, and the many other environmental influences surrounding an organization is a major part of a marketing manager's job. On one hand, the manager may try to change or influence the environment in some way. Although environmental forces are, for the most part, beyond the control of any individual organization, a group of organizations may be able to influence some aspect of its environment through political lobbying or some other such activity. On the other hand, the marketing mix is controlled by the organization. The marketing manager can adjust the marketing mix to reflect changes in the environment. The proper timing of a marketing decision is often the factor that determines success. Determining the correct time to enter and exit a market, for example, may rest on an analysis of the external environment.

> Reacting and adapting to the many environmental influences surrounding an organization is a major part of a marketing manager's job.

Environmental factors affect all organizations, even the largest and wealthiest companies. Because of their important influence on marketing decisions, environmental forces are discussed in depth in Chapters 3 and 4.

Modern Marketers Use the Marketing Concept

An organization's level of marketing sophistication is often reflected in its goals and in the general principles underlying the way it conducts its activities. Marketing sophistication can be judged in terms of whether an organization is oriented toward production, sales, or marketing. These orientations also describe the prevailing philosophies of certain historical eras.[14] Exhibit 1-7 illustrates the differences among the orientations.

PRODUCTION ORIENTATION—"AS LONG AS IT'S BLACK"

Production orientation
Organizational philosophy that emphasizes physical production and technology rather than sales or marketing.

Marketing managers with a **production orientation** and philosophy focus their efforts on physical production and stress developments in technology. Henry Ford's famous description of the Model T—"You can have any color you want as long as it's black"—sums up the prevailing attitude of the production orientation.

Organizations with a production orientation typically do best in a seller's market, in which demand exceeds supply. Manufacturers simply produce a high-quality product and expect to sell it easily. Before the turn of the century, production-oriented organizations were more common than they are today. Today, few organizations in the United States can survive for long if they maintain a philosophy that gives little thought to marketing.

SALES ORIENTATION—FOCUS ON TRANSACTIONS

Sales orientation
Organizational philosophy that emphasizes selling existing products, whether or not they meet consumer needs, often through aggressive sales techniques and advertising.

The philosophy of an organization with a **sales orientation** is to change consumers' minds to fit the product. This philosophy is epitomized by the slogan "Push! Push! Sell! Sell!"

Organizations with a sales orientation stress aggressive promotional campaigns to "push" their existing products. These organizations concentrate on selling what they make rather than on learning what will best satisfy consumers and then marketing those products. Sales-oriented organizations focus their efforts on the **transaction**, which is the completion of a single exchange agreement or, more

Transaction
A single completed exchange agreement; a one-time sale.

	FOCUS	MEANS	GOAL	ILLUSTRATIVE COMMENTS
PRODUCT ORIENTATION	Manufacturing	Making high-quality products	Produce as much product as possible	"You can have any color you want as long as it's black." "Make the best product you can and people will buy it." "I know people want my kind of product."
SALES ORIENTATION	Selling existing products	Aggressive sales and advertising efforts	Maximize sales volume	"You don't like black? I'll throw in a set of glassware!" "Sell this inventory no matter what it takes." "Who cares what they want? Sell what we've got."
MARKET ORIENTATION	Fulfilling actual and potential customer needs and wants	Consumer orientation, profit orientation, and integrated marketing	Make profits by ensuring customer satisfaction	"Find out what consumers want before you make the product." "Maybe people don't want 'the best' product. Find out what they do want." "I'm going to find out what the people want."

simply put, an immediate sale. This focus on transactions (sometimes called *transaction marketing*) encourages organizations to emphasize short-run increases in sales of existing products rather than long-run profits. Short-term sales maximization is a paramount goal of these organizations.

The sales orientation is perhaps most common during economic periods when supply exceeds demand, such as the Great Depression (1929–1933). Companies that maintain a sales orientation while competitors move on to a market-oriented philosophy may find themselves in difficulty.

MARKET ORIENTATION—ESTABLISHING AND MAINTAINING RELATIONSHIPS

Companies that have superior skill in understanding and satisfying customers are said to have a market orientation or to be market-driven.[15] Organizations with a **market orientation** embrace the idea of an organization-wide focus on learning customers' needs so that they can offer **superior customer value**—that is, so that they can satisfy customer needs better than their competitors do. These organizations realize that they must view themselves not as producing goods and services but as developing long-term relationships with customers—as doing the things that will make people want to continue to do business with them rather than with their competitors.[16]

THE MARKETING CONCEPT—THE FOUNDATION OF A MARKET ORIENTATION

Being market-oriented means adopting the philosophy known as the marketing concept. The **marketing concept**, which is central to all effective marketing thinking, planning, and action, relates marketing to the organization's overall purpose—to survive and prosper by satisfying a clientele—and calls on management and employees to do three things.

1. To be *consumer-oriented* in all matters, from product development to honoring warranties and service contracts
2. To stress *long-run success* rather than short-term profits or sales volume
3. To adopt a *cross-functional perspective* to achieve a consumer orientation and long-run profitability

Companies that subscribe to this philosophy have a market orientation.

Market orientation
Organizational philosophy that emphasizes developing exceptional skill in understanding and satisfying customers so that the organization can offer superior customer value.

Superior customer value
The consumer's attribution of greater worth or better ability to fulfill a need to a certain product compared to its competitors.

Marketing concept
Organizational philosophy that stresses consumer orientation, long-range profitability, and the integration of marketing and other organizational functions. The marketing concept, which focuses on satisfying consumers' wants and needs, is the foundation of a market orientation.

In market-oriented organizations, products are designed to solve customer problems. Marketing managers for Wearever recognized that bakers want to avoid burned cookies at all costs. When they created insulated cookie sheets to solve this consumer problem, sales soared.

http://www.wearever.com

Consumer orientation
An organization's understanding that the organization must create goods and services with the consumer's needs in mind.

Consumer Orientation

Consumer orientation is the first aspect of the marketing concept. The consumer, or customer, should be seen as "the fulcrum, the pivot point about which the business moves in operating for the balanced interests of all concerned."[17] Organizations that have accepted the marketing concept try to create goods and services with the customer's needs in mind. Effective marketers recognize that they must offer products that consumers perceive to have greater value than those offered by competitors.

It follows that a marketing manager's initial goal must be to determine what the customer wants. It is better to find out what the customer wants and offer that product than to make a product and then try to sell it to somebody. A company that subscribes to the marketing concept, then, must figure out what customers need—sometimes before they figure it out themselves. In many instances, the technological innovations of visionaries are the roads to customer need satisfaction. However, most effective marketers must gather and analyze information to understand factors, such as competitive alternatives, that influence consumer needs.

According to most marketing thinkers, consumer orientation—the satisfaction of customer wants—is the justification for an organization's existence. Consider the following examples:

- While visiting one McDonald's outlet, the chairman of the board of McDonald's restaurants encountered a sign ordering customers to "MOVE TO THE NEXT POSITION." He made sure that such signs were removed from all McDonald's outlets, stating, "It's up to us to move to the customer."

- Procter & Gamble developed Dryel to allow consumers to care for their "Dry Clean Only" clothes right at home. Consumers use the Dryel home dry-cleaning kits instead of going to the dry cleaners. The Dryel kit won't damage fine fabrics by getting them wet. The Dryel fabric care system helps protect clothes from shrinking, stretching, or fading caused by dryer heat. This new product fills a consumer need for quick, easy, and affordable dry cleaning without problems.

Many organizations that have adopted the marketing concept realize that the organization must see itself not as producing goods and services but as "buying customers, as doing the things that will make people want to do business with it."[18] Progressive companies wisely spend a great deal of time and effort learning about consumers. Unfortunately, not all firms have adopted a consumer orientation as their philosophy—but it is rare for such firms to survive in the long run.

Long-Term Success

Even though the marketing concept stresses a consumer orientation, an organization need not meet every fleeting whim of every customer. Implicit in the marketing concept are two assumptions: that the organization has competition and that it wishes to continue to exist. Therefore, the marketing concept accents long-term profits, not simply current profitability.

what went right?

Walt Disney World The Senior Vice-President of Resort Operations at Walt Disney World believes in magic customer moments. He describes his philosophy about empowering employees to be consumer-oriented below:

One of the most important things that we train staff members to do is service recovery. That's when you walk into a situation and you can tell that something has gone wrong—and you do whatever it takes to fix the problem. That's also an opportunity for what we call a "magic moment."

We once had a family that wanted to celebrate a child's birthday at a "character breakfast"—a buffet in which Disney characters mingle with guests, sign autographs, and pose for photographs. But this family was late and didn't make the seating. The next show was scheduled for lunch, which was also booked.

Members of the family were sitting on a bench outside the restaurant, waiting for an opening, when one of our employees walked by and saw that these people were not happy campers.

The employee found out what the problem was and said, "Let me see what I can do." He was able to get them into the lunch show, seat them right up front, and make sure that the birthday boy's favorite character sang "Happy Birthday" to him and that all of the characters danced around the family's table. That was a magic moment—a quick recovery from what could have been a very disappointing birthday.

The best part? The employee who did that recovery was a custodian—a guy just walking by with a broom, sweeping up cigarette butts. But all of our employees, from janitors and dishwashers to hotel managers, know they have the ability—and the responsibility—to improve the experience of any guest.[19]

Consumers would prefer that the price of a new Mercedes-Benz be under $15,000. But because the manufacturing and marketing costs associated with such a car far exceed that figure, DaimlerChrysler manufacturer of the Mercedes, and its distributors would soon be out of business if they attempted to satisfy that particular consumer desire. Not only consumer wants but also costs and profits must be taken into consideration in determining a competitive market offering.

The marketing concept's focus on long-term success (profitability) leads to the idea that organizations should not seek sales volume for the sake of volume alone. Sales volume can be profitless, and a firm can actually increase its sales volume while decreasing its profits—for example, when big discounts attract more customers but result in less income. It may be possible to "buy volume" by advertising heavily, cutting prices to levels below cost, or using other methods. Few marketing analysts see this as a profitable strategy, however. As most aggressive price cutters ultimately find out, the profit requirements of an operation regulate marketing activities over all but the shortest time periods.

It's been said that "Marketing is an attitude, not a department." This phrase expresses the perspective of market-oriented organizations, which expect other business functions, such as operations, to perform certain marketing activities. In market-oriented hotels, for example, door people, reservations clerks, housekeeping staff, and other service personnel strongly influence guests' satisfaction with the hotel. An aspect of their jobs is to understand the important role their services play in the hotel's marketing activities.

The marketing concept's focus on long-term success recognizes that building relationships with customers can both increase customer responsiveness and decrease the cost of dealing with loyal customers. Keeping customers coming back is a great way to ensure organizational success.

Marketing Is a Cross-Functional Activity

Marketing personnel do not work in a vacuum, isolated from other company activities. The actions of people in such areas as production, credit, and research and development may affect an organization's marketing efforts. Similarly, the work of marketers affects these other departments. Managers must integrate and coordinate marketing functions with other corporate functions so that they are all directed toward achieving the same objectives.

Problems are almost certain to develop unless an integrated, company-wide marketing effort is maintained. Difficulties may arise when a focus on consumer needs is viewed as the responsibility solely of the enterprise's marketing department. Other functional areas may have goals that conflict with customer satisfaction or long-term profitability. For instance, the engineering department will want long lead times for product design, with simplicity and economy as major design goals. Marketing, however, will want short lead times and more complex designs, including optional features and custom components. Similarly, the finance department may want fixed budgets, strict spending justifications, and short-term prices that always cover costs, whereas the marketing department may seek flexible budgets, looser spending rationales, and short-term prices that may be less than costs but that allow markets to be developed quickly.

> Marketing personnel do not work in a vacuum, isolated from other company activities.

In the last decade, progressive organizations recognized that to achieve consumer-oriented goals, such as new product development, marketing had to be carried out as a cross-functional activity, not a distinct and separate business function. To say that marketing is a **cross-functional activity** is to say that people with many different job titles and functions within the organization (and even outside the organization) have an impact on the goals set by marketing executives. In today's business organization, traditional functional distinctions have become blurred. This book takes a cross-functional perspective on marketing. Much more will be said about the cross-functional nature of marketing in future chapters.

Cross-functional activity
An activity carried out by individuals from various departments within an organization and from outside the organization, all of whom have a common purpose.

This advertisement for DuPont proclaims: "Recycled carpet is now in full bloom." The advertising communicates that DuPont is socially responsive and markets products that are compatible with nature. Antron by DuPont is a nylon fiber, made from recycled nylon, that can be used for carpets, cushioning, soundproofing materials, and other environmentally friendly products. The company's management believes its environmentally conscious marketing efforts are an important part of its success.

http://www.dupont.com/dcf/antron

recycled carpet is now **in full bloom.**

We planted the seeds in 1991 with the DuPont Carpet Reclamation™ Program. So far, we've collected over 35 million pounds of used commercial carpet, turning it into auto parts, sod reinforcements, cushioning, soundproofing materials and industrial flooring. And now, we're able to make a new Antron® nylon fiber with recycled nylon, for carpets with the perfect balance of style, performance and sustainability. Call 1-800-4DUPONT or visit www.dupont.com/antron to learn more. Antron®. There is no equal.

Antron
Only by DuPont

Marketing and Society

Marketing must be examined not only in terms of its role in individual organizations but also in terms of the important role it plays in society. Before we explain, a note on terminology is in order. When referring to mar-

what went wrong?

Building a Better Mousetrap   Many organizations fail to understand that producing a "quality product" is not, in itself, enough to ensure success in the marketplace. Numerous products fail because marketing efforts are off target or inadequate. Examples of some products that failed to meet company success standards are listed below.

Crystal Pepsi (clear cola drink)

Coca-Cola Company's OK Cola

Minute Maid Vitamin soft drinks

McDonald's Arch Deluxe

Apple's Newton (personal digital assistant)

Fruit of the Loom laundry detergent

Levi's Tailored Classics (sports coats and slacks)

Happy Face (facial washing cream)

Small Miracle Shampoo

Vaseline Intensive Care Shampoo

Pink Panther Flakes (cereal)

Kream Krunch (cereal)

Breakfast Mates (milk-cereal combination pack)

Finger Frostings (candied frosting in cups to be eaten with fingers)

Thirsty Dog (flavored bottled water for pets)

Clear Miller Beer

Clipper (Miller's dark, low-calorie beer)

HELP (canned liquid fruit beverage concentrate)

Great Loaf (bread mix for meatloaf)

Learning what went wrong and why products failed contributes to future successes. Throughout the remainder of this book, we will look at examples of marketing failures as well as marketing successes.

---

keting as the aggregate of marketing activities within an economy or as the marketing system within a society, some prefer to use the term **macromarketing**. Thus, marketing may be split in the same way economics is split into microeconomics and macroeconomics. Our preference is simply to use the term *marketing*, making its meaning clear by the context in which it is discussed. Marketing's role in society can be illustrated by the description of marketing (or macromarketing) as "the delivery of a standard of living to society." It may seem a bit grandiose to describe marketing in this way, but some reflection will bear out the truth of that statement.

When you think of the aggregate of all organizations' marketing activities (especially if you include transportation and distribution activities), you can see that the efficiency of the system for moving goods from producers to consumers may substantially affect a society's well-being. Consider undeveloped countries. Transportation, storage, and other facets of distribution are vital undertakings; but in many undeveloped nations, marketing intermediaries such as wholesalers are inefficient or even nonexistent. In at least some cases, less developed countries may be poor because their marketing systems are too primitive or inefficient to deliver an improved quality of life. To reach a higher level of economic well-being, such a country must improve its macromarketing.

The recognition that marketing activity plays an important role in society has led a number of marketing thinkers to refine the marketing concept philosophy. The marketing concept stresses satisfying consumer needs at a profit. The **societal marketing concept**, which can be in perfect harmony with the marketing concept, requires that marketers consider the collective needs of society as well as individual consumers' desires and the organization's need for profits.[20]

An example of a company that emphasizes the societal marketing concept is Patagonia. It produces useful and durable products with an eye to minimizing waste and damage to the environment.[21] Patagonia was the first company to market outdoor clothing made from modern synthetic fleece. Stylish and functional pullovers

Macromarketing
The aggregate of marketing activities in an economy or the marketing system of a society, rather than the marketing activities of one firm (micromarketing).

Societal marketing concept
Organizational philosophy that stresses the importance of considering the collective needs of society as well as individual consumers' desires and organizational profits.

are fashioned out of fiber from recycled plastic bottles. The company uses only hemp and organic cotton, grown without pesticides or fertilizers, to make its shirts. Children's shirts are made of scraps left over when fabric is cut out for larger garments. Patagonia allocates 1 percent of its sales to environmental causes. These actions reflect a marketing philosophy that recognizes that every customer, as a member of society, has a long-term stake in conserving the earth's resources as well as a short-term need for outdoor wear. Patagonia, then, has adopted a societal marketing philosophy that integrates the fulfillment of consumers' short-term preferences with what is best for consumers and society in the long run.

What consumers want and what benefits society often are in harmony. That appears to be the case with Patagonia. Consumers, society, and the organization may all benefit from the business's societal concerns. Sometimes, however, there can be conflicts between consumers' expressed preferences and an organization's interpretation of what is good for society. Many McDonald's customers, especially teenagers, loved McDonald's french fries when they were cooked in beef tallow. However, McDonald's believed that the fat content of some of its menu items, like french fries, was too high. It stopped frying french fries in beef tallow because it felt a responsibility to offer as healthy a menu as possible. Marketers adhering to the societal marketing concept believe that the organization must reconcile any differences between customers' expressed preferences for goods and services and the organization's interpretation of what is good for society.

Why Study Marketing?

Why study marketing? One practical reason is that marketing offers many career opportunities, including opportunities in advertising, sales, product management, retail store management, and other fields. Appendix A on the Zikmund/d'Amico Web site (http://zikmund.swcollege.com) provides additional information to help you learn what career options are available and what preparation is required for employment in these fields.

You may not be planning a career in marketing. This does not mean that the study of marketing holds nothing for you. You may end up working for a business organization in some capacity, in which case you will work with employees who are actively engaged in marketing activity. The study of marketing principles can help you become a more productive, valuable co-worker. In addition, many of the skills and tools of marketing can be applied in other functional areas of business.

If you are planning to own your own business, marketing is the name of the game, and you must understand it to be successful. After you finish this course, you will know why this is so.

We have already mentioned that marketing is used by organizations and people outside the business world. Indeed, when you look for a job, you will be engaged in marketing yourself. The marketing principles and skills you learn in this course will help you achieve the goals you have set for your career. Marketing skills can also help you become a more knowledgeable consumer, as you will better understand the marketing practices that influence your purchases.

There is yet another reason for studying marketing. Learning how people in a society view marketing and how it functions in an increasingly global environment is part of being an educated person. Marketing is a pervasive aspect of our culture that has a dramatic impact on world affairs. It is a fascinating subject, and we hope you will enjoy studying it.

Summary

The function of marketing is to bring buyers and sellers together, and the primary emphasis of marketing is an exchange process requiring that two or more parties trade things of value.

1) Define marketing and discuss marketing in its broadened sense.

Marketing is the process that seeks to influence voluntary exchange transactions in which one party to the transaction can be envisioned as a customer of the other, the marketer. The marketing process involves communication and requires a mechanism or system to carry out the exchange of the marketer's product for something of value. Effective marketing consists of a consumer-oriented mix of business activities planned and implemented by a marketer to facilitate an exchange so that both parties profit in some way. Consumers may exchange money, votes, blood, or something else to obtain the marketer's offering.

2) Identify the elements of the marketing mix.

The marketing mix consists of four major elements: product, place (distribution), promotion, and price. These are basic to any organization and are adjusted and combined by the marketing manager to achieve the organization's goals. Thus, marketers plan and execute the conception, pricing, promotion, and distribution of ideas, goods, and services to create exchanges that will satisfy individual and organizational objectives.

3) Understand that marketers must contend with external environmental forces.

The marketing environment consists of uncontrollable forces that influence consumer behavior and represent both opportunities for and constraints on an organization. The marketing manager's task is to adjust an organization's marketing mix to cope with the external environment. This involves anticipating environmental changes that will affect the organization. Correct environmental assessment makes marketing decisions more successful.

4) Explain the marketing concept.

The marketing concept is a philosophy of business and a set of objectives enabling organizations to offer superior customer value. According to this concept, market-oriented organizations can succeed by focusing on consumers' wants and needs, long-term rather than short-term success, and an integrated marketing effort. Market-oriented organizations embrace the idea that they can satisfy customer needs better than their competitors. Production orientation and sales orientation are less effective alternative philosophies.

5) Recognize the contribution of marketing to a country's economy and way of life.

Marketing delivers a standard of living to society. The aggregate of all organizations' marketing activities, especially their transportation and distribution activities, affects a society's economic well-being. The efficiency of the system for moving goods from producers to consumers is an important factor determining a country's quality of life.

6) Define the societal marketing concept.

The societal marketing concept, which can be in perfect harmony with the marketing concept, stresses the need for marketers to consider the collective needs of society as well as individual consumer desires and the organization's need for profits. It recognizes that every consumer, as a member of society, has both long-term and short-term needs.

7) Explain the importance of studying marketing.

This book will help you learn what career options are available in marketing. It explains how the study of marketing principles can help people with non-marketing careers become more productive, valuable workers. In addition, many of the skills and tools of marketing are essential for those who plan to own their own business. Marketing skills can also help individuals become more knowledgeable consumers. Marketing is a pervasive aspect of our culture. Learning how people in a society view marketing and how it functions in an increasingly global environment is part of being an educated person.

Key Terms

channel of distribution (p. 11)
consumer orientation (p. 18)
cross-functional activity (p. 20)
exchange process (p. 7)
four Ps of marketing (p. 9)
macromarketing (p. 21)
manufacturer (p. 11)
market (p. 9)
market orientation (p. 17)

marketing (p. 7)
marketing concept (p. 17)
marketing mix (p. 9)
place (distribution) (p. 11)
price (p. 13)
product (p. 9)
production orientation (p. 16)
promotion (p. 12)
relationship marketing (p. 8)

retailer (p. 11)
sales orientation (p. 16)
societal marketing concept (p. 21)
superior customer value (p. 17)
transaction (p. 16)
ultimate consumer (p. 11)
uncontrollable variable (p. 15)
wholesaler (p. 11)

Questions for Review & Critical Thinking

1. Think about what you did this morning. In what ways did marketing affect your activities?

2. Define marketing in your own words.

3. If marketing activities involve exchange, what isn't a marketing activity?

4. Do lawyers, accountants, doctors, and dentists need marketing?
5. Why is relationship marketing important?
6. Identify some goods, services, or ideas that are marketed by not-for-profit organizations.
7. What are the elements of the marketing mix?
8. Describe the marketing mixes used by these organizations:
   a. McDonald's
   b. Your local zoo
   c. A group attempting to reduce air pollution
   d. The Xerox Corporation
9. The marketing concept is profit oriented. What kinds of profit does it stress? How does this orientation apply to nonprofit organizations?
10. Identify an organization in your college town that, in your opinion, has not yet adopted the marketing concept. What evidence can you offer?
11. How might a firm such as Pillsbury conduct its business if it were (a) a production-oriented company, (b) a sales-oriented company, or (c) a market-oriented company?

12. Given the existence of the marketing concept, why do so many products fail? Why are consumer groups still displeased with many products and companies?
13. How can an organization's management prove that it has adopted the marketing concept?
14. A zoo designer says she begins work by asking "In what sort of landscape would I want to observe this animal?" Discuss this approach to design in terms of the marketing concept.
15. Can a small business embrace the marketing concept philosophy as discussed in this chapter?
16. What role does marketing play in society?
17. What is the societal marketing concept?
18. Form small groups as directed by your instructor. Select an international company such as Nike, a local bank, or another familiar company, and identify the key aspects of the company's marketing mix. Discuss as a class the decisions each group makes.

http://zikmund.swcollege.com

The Internet is a communication, distribution, and exchange medium that is having a dramatic impact on marketing. We discuss the Internet and e-commerce in all remaining chapters of this textbook. Because of the importance of the Internet to marketing, all of the remaining chapters contain an Internet exercise feature called e-exercises. The exercises in this feature will give you the chance to enhance your understanding of marketing by using the Internet.

Another aspect of the e-exercises is the Address Book (useful URLs)—a directory of interesting and educational Web addresses. The first of these appears below.

Address Book (Useful URLs)

American Marketing Association	http://www.ama.org
South-Western College Publishing	http://www.swcollege.com

Ethically Right or Wrong?

Ethical issues are discussed in Chapter 2. A feature entitled Ethically Right or Wrong? ends each of the remaining chapters. This feature gives you the chance to take a stand on ethical issues and think about your ethical principles and how they would apply in specific situations.

VIDEO CASE 1-1
Burton Snowboards (A):
The Company That Jake Built

On the outskirts of Burlington, Vermont, sits an office with an old chairlift spanning the parking lot and a skate ramp out back. Next to the entrance, an I-beam is planted diagonally into the ground with one word stenciled on it: Burton. The current incarnation of over 20 years of innovation and commitment to the sport, this building and company have roots that run deep into the history of snowboarding.

In the mid-1960s Jake Burton was one of thousands of kids to get hooked on Sherman Poppen's Snurfers. It might have only been a toy, but it was still surfing on snow. Shocked that not much had progressed ten years later, he bid the Manhattan business world farewell to become a snowboard "shaper." The year was 1977. He moved up to Londonderry, Vermont, and started making and riding his first boards. The world's first snowboard factory was born.

The early years were an experiment in grassroots business. In the second year, Burton Snowboards moved into a farmhouse in Manchester—the facility that would go on to produce such classics as Burton's Backhill and Performer snowboards. Working in the living room, dining room, basement, and barn, a crew of four or five people produced, sold, and repaired all the early Burton models. The toll-free customer service line rang in the bedroom, at all hours. If orders for boards were low, Jake would load up his Volvo wagon and visit up to ten shops a day offering his latest designs.

In the first few years, snowboarding was an underground sport struggling on sledding hills and snow-covered golf courses. To move it to the next level, Jake lobbied hard for local ski areas to open their lifts to snowboarders. In the early '80s, he succeeded in convincing Stratton to give it a shot. Others followed—Jay Peak, Stowe, Sugarbush, Killington. The opening of eastern resorts led to growth for the sport—and became a major factor in Burton's product innovation. Edgeless wooden boards that were fine in powder no longer cut it on the ice of a Vermont ski area. To this day, eastern conditions drive innovation at Burton—if it doesn't work in Vermont, it doesn't get made.

Since 1992, Burton Snowboards has been leading the industry from its factory in Burlington, Vermont. The same motivation that took Jake from the garage in Londonderry to the barn in Manchester guided Burton from Manchester to Burlington: the commitment to making the world's best snowboarding equipment and to growing the sport.

Within the ever-expanding walls of Burton's modern facilities in Burlington beats the same heart that beat years ago in a garage in Londonderry, Vermont. Two things matter more than all else: riders and riding. They always have. The drive to innovate and develop next-generation products is relentless. Then again, if it dumps, the innovation might have to wait until noon.[22]

Burton markets snowboards and snowboarding equipment and nothing else. Its products include snowboards, bindings, boots, gloves, hats, and snowboarding clothing.

QUESTIONS

1. Who are the likely customers of a company such as Burton? What do they get in exchange for the price they pay for a snowboard or snowboard equipment? In other words, in your opinion, what is the product being marketed by Burton? What customer needs does this product satisfy?

2. Explain the 4Ps of the marketing mix using Burton as an example.

3. How might a company such as Burton implement the marketing concept?

4. Burton markets snowboards and snowboarding equipment and nothing else. Would it be a good idea to expand its business?

Lawn Care of Wisconsin

It's hard to imagine anything worse befalling a business that promises customers lush, green grass than what happened to Terry Kurth's Lawn Care of Wisconsin, Inc., a few years ago. To Kurth's horror, grass of customers who had signed up for a top-of-the-line lawn-care program was mysteriously turning brown.

Kurth had begun the business, which operates Barefoot Grass Lawn Service franchises in Madison and Little Chute, Wis., nine years earlier, and it grew healthily, thanks to a reputation for quality lawn maintenance. When customers began calling to report brown areas, and competitors got wind of an epidemic of "burned" Barefoot Grass lawns, its reputation and health were in grave danger.

Sleuthing solved the brown grass mystery. The company keeps extensive records—date, employee name, products applied, etc.—on each property worked on. The affected lawns had a common denominator: All had been treated with a granular fertilizer that contained a fungicide. Kurth, who has an agronomy degree, asked a University of Wisconsin plant pathologist to inspect some of the lawns, and he said they looked like they had been damaged by atrazine.

Atrazine? It is designed to eliminate grass in cornfields, corn being one of the few plants it doesn't affect. Kurth called the fertilizer supplier, asking that someone fly in to meet with him. A representative of the supplier arrived the next day; he reported his company had already performed lab tests and had found random atrazine contamination. The supplier stopped making atrazine at the plant where the fertilizer came from, but what of the problem at hand?

The supplier agreed to pay for damage repair, but it was up to Kurth and his managers to do the repairing. They gave affected customers an information sheet—most of them before their grass started turning brown. Then, calling in outside landscaping firms to help get the job done faster, they applied activated charcoal to affected lawns. There were 325 in all, and the process was messy, staining clothing and equipment. However, the atrazine was neutralized, and lawns were renovated. Sometimes reseeding was adequate; sometimes an entire lawn was removed and replaced with sod.

"Though our customers were overwhelmingly impressed," Kurth says, "we felt they deserved an additional thank-you for their understanding." Each received a gift box containing an assortment of meats that could be grilled while they were out on their lawns, reminding them of how Barefoot Grass Lawn Service had taken care of them.[23]

QUESTIONS
1. What is the product being marketed by Lawn Care of Wisconsin? What customer needs does this product satisfy?
2. Which of the philosophies/orientations toward marketing discussed in the text has Lawn Care of Wisconsin embraced?
3. Why did the company provide its customers with a gift assortment of meats?

Marketing Management: Strategy and Ethical Behavior

chapter 2

LEARNING OBJECTIVES

After you have studied this chapter, you will be able to . . .

1) Differentiate between marketing strategy and marketing tactics.

2) Discuss the role of marketing planning at the corporate level, at the strategic business unit level, and at the operational level of management.

3) Understand the concept of the organizational mission.

4) Understand the nature of a competitive advantage.

5) Understand the importance of total quality management strategies in product differentiation.

6) Discuss demarketing.

7) Explain the market/product matrix.

8) Identify the stages in the strategic marketing process.

9) Describe marketing objectives and marketing plans.

10) Discuss the concept of positioning.

11) Understand the nature of marketing ethics and socially responsible behavior.

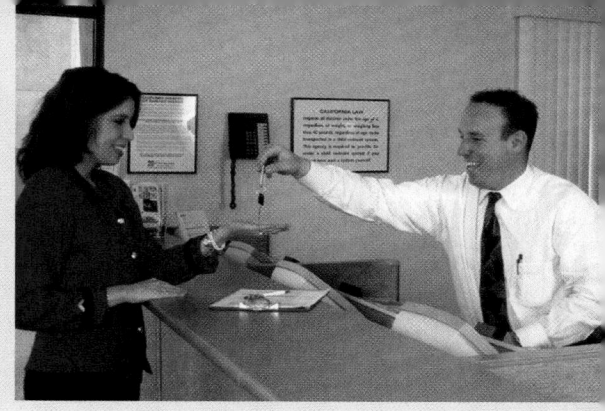

What if you were asked to name the biggest rent-a-car company. And what if you were told that the answer is not Hertz or Avis, but Enterprise Rent-a-Car. Would you say you've barely heard of them? It's okay; most frequent fliers have never come near an Enterprise office. And that's just fine with

Enterprise. While Hertz, Avis, and lots of little companies were cutting one another's throats to win a point or two of the "suits and shorts" market from business and vacation travelers at airports, Enterprise invaded the hinterlands with a completely different strategy—one that relies heavily on doughnuts, ex–college frat house jocks, and your problems with your family car.

In the 44 years since it was founded in St. Louis, Enterprise has blown past everybody in the industry. It now owns more cars (310,000) and operates in more locations (2,800) than Hertz.

Enterprise's approach is astoundingly simple: It aims to provide a spare family car if your car has been hit, or has broken down, or is in for routine maintenance. Typically, you pay 30 percent less for an Enterprise car than for one from an airport. And your insurance or warranty usually picks up part of the tab. The paperwork is minimal and the rental process is quick.

Wow! How simple! So why haven't Hertz and Avis made road kill out of Enterprise? And how come Hertz's CEO concedes he "missed a big opportunity" by letting Enterprise run away with this business? Because the replacement business is harder than it looks, and because years ago Enterprise developed a bunch of quirky but simple hiring and promotion practices that have produced a culture perfectly suited to its part of the industry.

Instead of massing 10,000 cars at a few dozen airports, Enterprise sets up inexpensive rental offices just about everywhere. As soon as one branch grows to about 150 cars, the company opens another a few miles away. Once a new office opens, employees fan out to develop chummy relationships with the service managers of every good-size auto dealership

and body shop in the area. When your car is being towed, you're in no mood to figure out which local rent-a-car company to use. Enterprise knows that the recommendations of the garage service managers will carry enormous weight, so it has turned courting them into an art form. On most Wednesdays all across the country, Enterprise employees bring pizza and doughnuts to workers at the garages.

Enterprise is also betting that when you're stuck, you won't be in the mood to quibble about prices. Yes, it has cars for $16 a day—the amount many insurance policies pay for replacement rentals. But those are often tiny Geo Metros; about 90 percent of people pay more for a bigger car. Enterprise buys cars from a wide variety of American, Japanese, and European automakers. To reduce costs, it keeps its cars on the road up to 6 months longer than Hertz and Avis do.

Enterprise doesn't just wait for your car to break down to capture you as a customer. A huge chunk of its recent growth has come as auto dealers increasingly offer customers a free or cheap replacement while their cars are in the shop for routine maintenance. Enterprise has agreements with many dealers to provide a replacement for every car brought in for service. At major accounts, the company sets up an office on the premises, staffs it for several hours a day, and keeps cars parked outside so customers don't have to travel back to the Enterprise office to fill out paperwork.

Unusual hiring and promotion practices drive much of the company's hustle and rapid growth. Virtually every Enterprise employee is a college graduate; in a unionized, labor-intensive industry that seeks to keep wages low, that's unusual enough. But there's more. Hang around Enterprise people long enough, and you'll notice that despite their informal exteriors, most seem to have the competitive, aggressive air of the ex-athlete. It's no accident. Brainy introverts need not apply, says the company's chief operating officer. "We hire from the half of the college class that makes the upper half possible," he adds wryly. "We want athletes, fraternity types—especially fraternity presidents and social directors. People people."

The social directors make good salespeople, able to chat up service managers and calm down someone who has just been in a car wreck.[1]

Enterprise built itself around a marketing strategy that differentiated the company from its competitors. As this example illustrates, developing a marketing strategy is crucial to an organization's success. Marketing strategy is the subject of this chapter.

The chapter begins by discussing the activities of marketing managers and defining marketing strategy. Next, it discusses planning at various levels in the organization, giving special attention to the organizational mission and to planning for marketing at the strategic business unit level. It then addresses each stage in the strategic marketing process. A discussion of execution and control follows the material on marketing planning. Finally, the chapter introduces the topic of ethics and social responsibility in marketing, an important and pervasive topic that will be discussed further throughout the text.

Marketing Management

Organizations, whether charities, universities, or giant global businesses like the Microsoft Corporation, must have managers. Managers develop rules, principles, and ways of thinking and acting that allow the organization to attain its goals and objectives.

Corporate managers, or top managers, are the executives responsible for the entire organization. Top managers, with titles such as chief executive officer (CEO) and executive vice president, recognize that at the corporate level, marketing is a business philosophy rather than a series of activities. An important part of their job is to ensure that all business functions work together to achieve marketing success. Managers at the middle levels of the organization are responsible for the management of marketing efforts for goods and services in the organization's business units.

Marketing
management
The process of planning, executing, and controlling marketing activities to attain marketing goals and objectives effectively and efficiently.

Marketing management is the process of planning, executing, and controlling marketing activities to attain marketing goals and objectives effectively and efficiently. Of course, the time, effort, and resources associated with Johnson & Johnson's introduction of a new flavor of dental floss differ from the time, effort, and resources associated with Microsoft's development of computer software that understands normal spoken language, a project that Microsoft has been working on for years. Yet in both cases, success depends on planning, execution, and control. These are the basic functions of management at every level.

Managers in today's dynamic and rapidly changing business world confront extraordinary challenges that were rarely encountered a decade ago. Today's marketing manager must be flexible and versatile to deal with changes that come more quickly and are more dramatic, complex, and unpredictable than ever before.[2] Because marketing managers must deal with change, the marketing

> Today's marketing manager must be flexible and versatile to deal with changes that come more quickly and are more dramatic, complex, and unpredictable than ever before.

what went wrong?

Northwest Airlines A veteran pilot walked off the plane at Las Vegas airport because he did not like the in-flight meal. He told the crew of the Boeing 757 he was leaving to find something else to eat. Unable to turn up anything he liked in the departure lounge, the pilot took a cab to buy food outside the airport. For 90 minutes, he left a loaded plane standing at an airport gate and 150 frustrated passengers waiting to fly to Detroit.

Effective marketers realize that properly executing an appropriate strategy—that is, doing things right—can make the difference between success and failure. Northwest Airlines terminated the pilot who felt he could not get a "decent meal" at the airport.[3]

management process is a continuous one: Planning, execution, and control are ongoing and repetitive activities. A major aspect of dealing with change is the development of appropriate strategies.

What Is a Marketing Strategy?

Marketers, like admirals and generals, must develop strategies to help them attain the objectives they seek. The military planner's endeavors can end more disastrously than those of business people, but the loss of the means to make a living, the closing of a factory, and the "defeat" of a product in the marketplace are serious matters indeed to the workers, investors, and executives involved. Many executives have noticed similarities between military strategy and marketing strategy. Therefore, a number of military terms—*strategy, tactics, campaigns, maneuvers,* and so on—have been adopted by business people, just as they have been by football coaches, to relate their organizational activities to those of competitors. Because of its widespread usage, the term *strategy* has been defined in many different ways.[4] For our purposes, a specific definition is appropriate: A **marketing strategy** consists of a plan identifying what basic goals and objectives will be pursued and how they will be achieved in the time available. A strategy entails commitment to certain courses of action and allocation of the resources necessary to achieve the identified goals.

Members of the armed forces describe strategy as what generals do and tactics as what lower officers, such as captains and lieutenants, do. This description rightly suggests that tactics are less comprehensive in scope than strategies. **Tactics** are specific actions intended to implement strategy. Therefore, tactics are most closely associated with the execution of plans.

The basic strategy at McDonald's, for example, is to have clean, family-type restaurants that offer friendly service, high-quality food, and good value. Offering Happy Meals for children at reasonable prices is a tactic used to implement this strategy. It encourages consumers to bring their families to McDonald's because high-quality children's meals are a good value there. Providing pamphlets explaining that your fork is the only thing that is not nutritious in a McSalad Shaker is another specific action that helps convey the idea that McDonald's offers an assortment of high-quality food for the entire family. McDonald's uses many tactics like these to implement its "quality, service, cleanliness, and value" strategy.

Planning—Designing a Framework for the Future

Recall that the basic functions of management are planning, execution, and control. In this part of the chapter, we focus on planning.

Marketing strategy
A plan identifying what marketing goals and objectives will be pursued and how they will be achieved in the time available.

Tactics
Specific actions intended to implement strategies.

Parmalat is the world's largest producer of milk. In developing countries like Brazil and China, its strategy is to convince mothers that children need dairy products on a regular basis. The advertisements shown here depict children dressed as animals, with the caption "Because We Are Mammals." Choosing whether to portray children as pandas, lambs, and other animals is a tactical decision.

http://www.parmalat.com.br

Planning
The process of envisioning the future, establishing goals and objectives, and designing organizational and marketing strategies and tactics to be implemented in the future in order to achieve the goals.

Planning is the process of envisioning the future, establishing goals and objectives, and designing organizational and marketing strategies and tactics to be implemented in the future in order to achieve these goals. The planning process consists of analyzing perceived opportunities and selecting courses of action that will help achieve the organization's objectives most efficiently. Marketing managers plan what future activities will be implemented, when they will be performed, and who will be responsible for them.

The purpose of planning is to go beyond analysis of the present and to attempt to predict the future and devise a means to adjust to an ever-changing environ-

e x h i b i 2-1

Three Levels of Administration

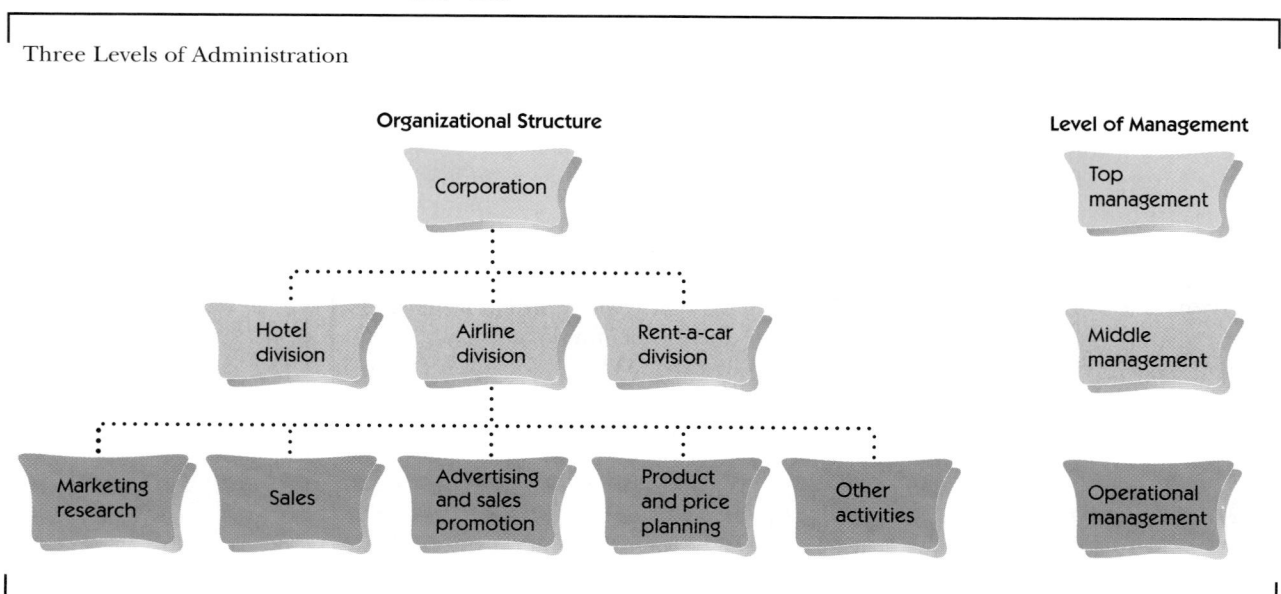

ment before problems develop. Planning helps an organization shape its own destiny by anticipating changes in the marketplace rather than merely reacting to those changes. For example, an organization that anticipates changes in the public's and legislators' attitudes toward the need for recyclable packaging may plan to convert to "environmentally friendly" packaging before laws require it to do so. Planning allows a manager to follow the maxim "Act! Don't react." In short, planning involves deciding in advance.

Planning goes on at various organizational levels. For simplicity's sake, we will say that planning occurs at three levels of the organization: top management, middle management, and operational, or first-line, management. These levels are shown in Exhibit 2-1.

Strategic planning is long-term planning by top management that specifies an organization's primary goals and objectives. Top management focuses on determining long-term strategies for the entire organization. As we move down the levels in Exhibit 2-2, the focus of planning narrows. At the middle management level, planning strategy and tactics for business units (such as divisions) and specific products becomes a more important job dimension. Middle-level marketing managers are responsible for planning the marketing mix strategy, allocating resources, and coordinating the activities of operational managers. At the level of operational management, **operational planning,** which concerns day-to-day functional activities, becomes dominant. Thus, whereas a vice president of marketing (a top-level manager) spends most of his or her time planning new products and strategy modifications for entire product lines, a sales manager (an operational manager) concentrates on supervising and motivating the sales force. Exhibit 2-2 shows how the focus of planning and basic strategic and tactical questions vary at the three major levels of the organization.

Strategic planning
Long-term planning dealing with an organization's primary goals and objectives, carried out primarily by top management; also called *corporate strategic planning.*

Operational planning
Planning that focuses on day-to-day functional activities, such as supervision of the sales force.

exhibi 2-2

A Manager's Level in the Organization Dictates the Focus of Planning

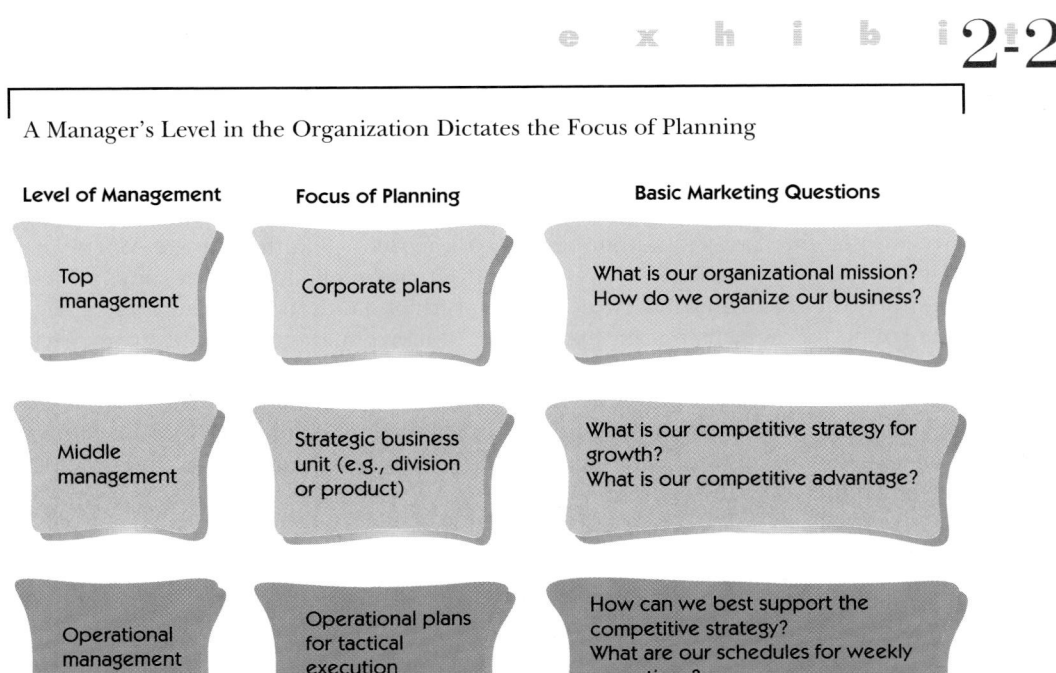

Level of Management	Focus of Planning	Basic Marketing Questions
Top management	Corporate plans	What is our organizational mission? How do we organize our business?
Middle management	Strategic business unit (e.g., division or product)	What is our competitive strategy for growth? What is our competitive advantage?
Operational management	Operational plans for tactical execution	How can we best support the competitive strategy? What are our schedules for weekly operations?

This DuPont advertisement reads "To Do List for the Planet. Number 6. Develop medicines that fight HIV. (Did that)." It goes on to say "Pressing ahead on next generation medicines. Would love to see the day no one has this disease." This ad provides a clear-cut statement of the company's mission, which involves discovering and developing the miracles of science.

http://www.dupont.com

Top Management Makes Corporate Strategic Plans

As previously stated, top management plans strategies for the organization as a whole. Answers to questions such as "What business are we in?" and "How do we organize our business?" help top executives determine comprehensive strategies for long-term growth. This section describes how the decisions top managers make about the organizational mission provide a framework for establishing the organization's strategic business units.

DEFINING THE ORGANIZATIONAL MISSION

Organizational mission statement
A statement of company purpose. It explains why the organization exists and what it hopes to accomplish.

Developing an organizational or corporate mission is a strategic decision that influences all other marketing strategies. An **organizational mission statement** is a broad statement of company purpose. It explains why the organization exists and what it hopes to accomplish. It provides direction for the entire organization. For example, when the Ford Motor Company was founded in 1903, Henry Ford had a clear understanding that cars should not be only for the rich—that the average American family needed economical transportation in the form of a low-priced car. Ford also had the insight to know that he could use product standardization and assembly-line technology to accomplish this mission. Modern marketers should strive to have an equally clear sense of each aspect of the business domain in which they operate.

eBay is the world's largest personal online trading community. eBay created a new market: efficient one-to-one trading in an auction format on the Web. The mission statement of eBay provides a particularly clear understanding of the principles on which the company operates:

> We help people trade practically anything on earth. eBay was founded with the belief that people are honest and trustworthy. We believe that each of our customers, whether a buyer or a seller, is an individual who deserves to be treated with respect. We will continue to enhance the on-line trading experiences of all our constituents—collectors, hobbyists, small dealers, unique item seekers, bargain hunters, opportunistic sellers, and browsers. The growth of the eBay community comes from meeting and exceeding the expectations of these special people.[5]

Product success, industry leadership, and even an organization's survival depend on satisfying the consumer. In defining the broad nature of its business, a company must take a consumer-oriented perspective. It must avoid short-sighted, narrow-minded thinking that will lead it to define its purpose from a product/production orientation rather than a consumer orientation. Thus, Motorola defines itself as being in the wireless communication business, not just as a maker of cellular phones or pagers. Companies, like Disney, that make movies should see themselves as being in the entertainment business ("using our imagination to bring happiness to millions") rather than the movie business. A firm's failure to define its purpose from a broad consumer orientation is referred to as **marketing myopia**.[6]

Many organizational mission statements include ethical credos. Marketing ethics is discussed later in this chapter.

STRATEGIC BUSINESS UNITS HAVE A MARKET FOCUS

The organizational mission and other strategic corporate goals, once established, provide a framework for determining what organizational structure and business models are most appropriate to the organization's marketing efforts. The organizational structure of a company that markets only a single product or service will be relatively simple. However, many organizations—for example, General Electric—operate a diverse set of businesses. General Electric's businesses range from the marketing of light bulbs to the marketing of aircraft engines. For the medium-sized and large organizations that engage in diverse businesses, establishing strategic business units is another aspect of corporate-level planning.

A **strategic business unit (SBU)** is a distinct unit of the overall parent organization, such as a company, division, department, or product line, with a specific market focus and a manager who has the authority and responsibility for managing all unit functions. For example, a bank may have a real estate division, a commercial division, and a trust division, as well as a retail division that offers traditional banking services for the general public. The logic that underlies the concept of the strategic business unit is best illustrated with an example. Consider these statements: Procter & Gamble does not compete against Kimberly-Clark, and Dow Chemical does not compete against Union Carbide. Competition isn't carried on at the corporate level but at the individual business-unit level. Thus, Procter & Gamble's Pampers compete against Luvs disposable diapers, a Kimberly-Clark product. Dow might compete with Union Carbide for certain types of chemical customers but not others. Acknowledgment of this simple reality has led top managers to identify separate manageable units or autonomous profit centers within their organizations so that performance can be monitored at the level of individual business activities rather than at the overall corporate level only.

The idea is that each SBU operates as a "company within a company." The SBU is organized around a business model and cluster of offerings that share some common element, such as being aimed at a particular target market or being produced with certain technology. The **business model** refers to the fundamental strategy underlying the way a business unit operates. For example, Dell Computer's business model has two basic components: direct-order buying and a build-to-order process. People can buy a PC directly from Dell by phone, by fax, or over the Internet, but not in stores. Dell's Web site lets a customer pick a PC and see how the price changes when various component parts are added or subtracted. Dell doesn't build a PC until one is ordered. Then, workers in its plants assemble the PC according to the buyer's specifications, and the PC is delivered to the customer. Dell's business model does not require the company to inventory assembled PCs.[7]

Organizations that have several different business models typically have more than one SBU. For example, Kay-Bee toys is one of the growing number of retailers that operate business in retail stores as one SBU and Internet operations as another SBU.

Marketing myopia
The failure of a company to define its organizational purpose from a broad consumer orientation.

Strategic business unit (SBU)
A distinct unit—such as a company, division, department, or product line—of an overall parent organization, with a specific marketing focus and a manager who has the authority and responsibility for managing all unit functions.

Business model
The fundamental strategy underlying the way a business unit operates.

Corporate Strategy Filters Down to Other Levels

An SBU has control over its own business model and marketing strategy. Its sales revenues may be distinguished from those of other SBUs in the organization. It can thus be evaluated individually and its performance measured against that of specific external competitors. This evaluation provides the basis for allocating resources.

Corporate-level strategies outline broad principles that are expected to filter down through the organization. Exhibit 2-3 depicts how corporate strategies influence marketing strategies at the business-unit level and at the operational level. Although corporate-level planning strongly influences the marketing planning activities within strategic business units, SBU managers tend to be closer to their customers, and their customer knowledge shapes their planning.

Marketing Strategies at the SBU Level

Corporate-level strategies that define the organization's purpose provide a framework for marketing strategies within the business units. The responsibility for planning the SBU marketing strategy for a division or for individual products is assigned to middle managers. From a corporation perspective, the managers in charge of SBUs are at a level below the organization's top managers. However, within the SBU they are key executives. These marketing managers focus on three key aspects of SBU strategies: (1) establishing a competitive advantage, (2) implementing a total quality management strategy, and (3) planning business-unit growth strategies.

BUSINESS-UNIT STRATEGIES FOR COMPETITIVE ADVANTAGE

Competitive advantage
Superiority to or favorable difference from competitors along some dimension important to the market.

One of the most common business-unit goals is to establish and maintain a **competitive advantage**—to be superior to or favorably different from competitors in a way that is important to the market. Illustrations of two basic marketing strategies (there are many others) should help you understand what a business-unit strategy is and how it can allow a company to establish a competitive advantage.

A **price leadership strategy,** or low-cost/low-price strategy, emphasizes producing a standardized product at a very low per-unit cost and underpricing all competitors.[8] For example, Southwest Airlines offers rock-bottom prices. Unlike most other domestic airlines, Southwest does not offer long-distance flights. It links city pairs with frequent flights, almost like a shuttle airline. It does not offer preflight seat selection, hot meals, or baggage transfer to other airlines. It rewards customers who purchase paperless tickets via the Internet. Its low-cost/low-price strategy has been successful because Southwest passes the savings from its efficient, no-frills service on to consumers. Low-cost/low-price strategies often capitalize on cheaper resources in foreign countries, producing a product comparable in quality to those of competitors and marketing it at a rock-bottom price.

Your devices eat a lot of batteries. Don't let them eat your money, too.

MAXIMUM POWER. FOR LESS.

A **differentiation strategy** emphasizes offering a product that is unique in the industry, provides a distinct advantage, or is otherwise set apart from competitors' brands in some way other than by price. The product's styling, a distinctive product feature, likeable advertising, faster delivery, or some other aspect of the marketing mix is designed to produce the perception that the product is unique. The heart of a differentiation strategy is to create, for the consumer, value that is different from or better than what competitors offer. Consider, for example, 3M's strategy to enter the scouring pad business. Steel wool soap pads had been on the market for almost 80 years when 3M introduced Scotch-Brite Never Rust Soap Pads, made from 100 percent recycled plastic beverage bottles, with biodegradable and phosphorus-free soap. Scotch-Brite's tremendous success was a result of 3M's differentiation strategy to market soap pads that look and feel like competing brands but do not rust or splinter.

Price leadership strategy
A strategy whereby a marketer emphasizes underpricing all competitors.

Differentiation strategy
A strategy whereby a marketer offers a product that is unique in the industry, provides a distinct advantage, or is otherwise set apart from competitors' brands in some way other than price.

TOTAL QUALITY MANAGEMENT TO ACHIEVE DIFFERENTIATION

In working to differentiate their products, many organizations implement total quality management strategies. These strategies make market-driven quality a top priority.

Today, effective marketing organizations have implemented total quality management programs. These programs are not the exclusive domain of marketing managers, because production quality control and other business activities are integral aspects of their implementation. However, they are in tune with the marketing concept, since the definition of quality comes from the consumer.

The philosophy underlying the implementation of a total quality management strategy is epitomized in this statement by a Burger King executive: "The customer is the vital key to our success. We are now looking at our business through the customers' eyes and measuring our performance against their expectations, not ours."[9] A company that employs a total quality management strategy must evaluate

Cross-functional team
A team made up of individuals from various organizational departments who share a common purpose.

Demarketing
A strategy (or strategies) intentionally designed to discourage all or some consumers from buying a product.

quality and value through the eyes of the customer. Every aspect of the business must focus on quality and continuous improvement. For example, management may institute a performance appraisal system to evaluate employees in terms of the service they provide to customers. Further, the organization may establish cross-functional teams that strive for continuous improvement.

Cross-functional teams are composed of individuals from various organizational departments, such as engineering, production, finance, and marketing, who share a common purpose. Current management thinking suggests that cross-functional teams help organizations focus on core business processes, such as customer service or new product development. Working in teams reduces the tendency of employees to focus single-mindedly on an isolated functional activity. The use of cross-functional teams to improve product quality and increase customer value is a major trend in business today.

In some situations, total quality managers determine that a marketing strategy must be aimed at reducing consumption or discouraging buying. **Demarketing** is the name of a strategy (or group of strategies) intentionally designed to discourage all or some customers from buying or consuming a product either temporarily or permanently. Suppose, for example, that a manufacturing firm finds that it has a temporary shortage of finished goods because of a scarcity of raw materials. To reduce customer demand, the firm might use demarketing strategies, such as reducing advertising, increasing prices, instituting a rationing system, or some other, more original activity.

Is demarketing different from the first-come, first-served, take-it-or-leave-it attitude a marketer of goods in short supply might take? Yes. Demarketing stresses a key aspect of marketing, consumer satisfaction. Demarketing attempts to change consumers' attitudes so that they will understand the temporary situation and be satisfied with less. It emphasizes maintaining high quality and trying to keep customers over the long run rather than antagonizing them with a take-it-or-leave-it attitude. This is why demarketing fits into an overall total quality management strategy.

Businesses often encounter situations that warrant demarketing strategies. McDonald's offering of one of ten different Teenie Beanie Baby figures with the purchase of a Happy Meal sold nearly 100 million Happy Meals in only 10 days. But the Beanie Baby promotion was flawed by a great underestimation of demand. The program was supposed to last 35 days, but many retail outlets quickly

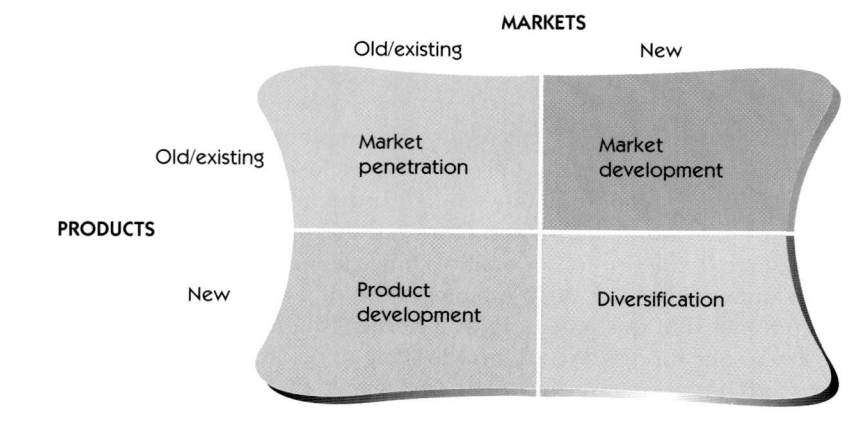

e x h i b i **2·4**

The Market/Product Matrix

MARKETS

	Old/existing	New
Old/existing	Market penetration	Market development
New	Product development	Diversification

PRODUCTS

sold every Beanie Baby in stock. In Chicago (at the time home of the NBA world-champion Bulls), newspaper advertisements proclaimed "Harder to get than Bulls tickets" and indicated that McDonald's was sorry if the shortage caused any inconvenience. The demarketing effort's purpose was to maintain customers' trust in their relationship with McDonald's.

When the marketers of new products underestimate demand, advertisements often stress that the shortages will be temporary, with messages such as "We're sorry if you can't find our new [name of brand]. But we're sure you'll find it worth the wait."

In some situations, excess demand or overcrowding is unalterable, and demarketing is a long-term strategy. In Washington, D.C., the Metro subway system engages in selective demarketing by raising rates during morning and evening rush hours. The fare increase discourages tourists, shoppers, and others who could use the subway in non-rush hours from traveling during peak periods.

PLANNING BUSINESS-UNIT GROWTH STRATEGIES

Managers responsible for strategic business units manage existing products and plan new products. They seek opportunities for business growth in new or existing markets. The **market/product matrix**, which broadly categorizes alternative SBU opportunities in terms of basic strategies for growth, serves as a planning tool. Exhibit 2-4 shows how the matrix cross-classifies market opportunities and product opportunities.

Market-Related Strategies for Existing Products

An organization seeking to expand sales of existing products has two major strategy paths available to it. One is **market penetration**. This strategy seeks to augment sales of an established product by increasing use of the product by existing customers in existing markets. Arm & Hammer has, with considerable success, convinced existing customers to purchase more baking soda by showing them new and creative ways to use the product. One suggestion, offered in advertisements and on packages, is to put an open box of baking soda in the refrigerator to reduce food odors. For consumers who feel uncomfortable throwing out a box of baking soda once it has been in the refrigerator for a time, the company suggests that the product be poured down the kitchen drain to freshen the drain. This strategy gave baking soda two new uses and gave buyers a way to dispose of the product in a manner that performed yet another odor-killing task. A similar technique is used by cereal companies, which frequently demonstrate how a cereal such as Cheerios or Rice Krispies can be used to make cookies, snack foods, and other non-breakfast items. Consumers are encouraged to try, for example, "cooking with Kellogg's."

A somewhat different strategy is **market development**, whereby the organization attempts to

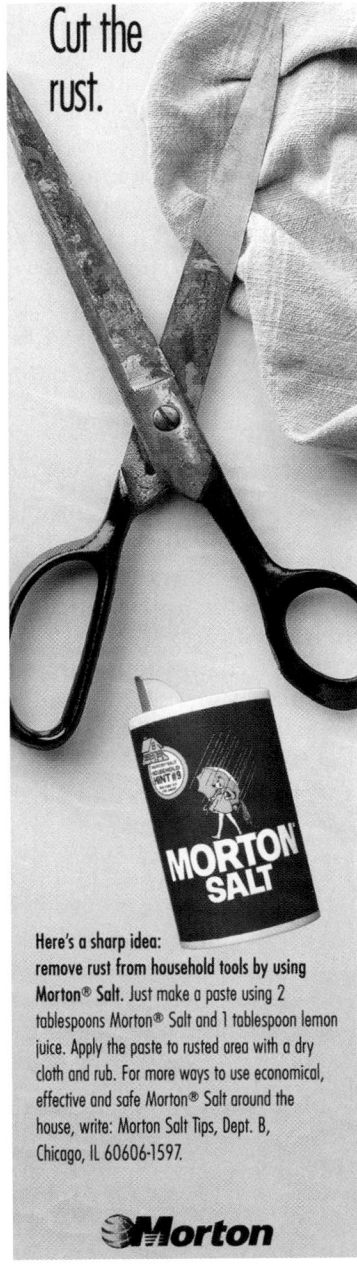

Cut the rust.

Here's a sharp idea: remove rust from household tools by using Morton® Salt. Just make a paste using 2 tablespoons Morton® Salt and 1 tablespoon lemon juice. Apply the paste to rusted area with a dry cloth and rub. For more ways to use economical, effective and safe Morton® Salt around the house, write: Morton Salt Tips, Dept. B, Chicago, IL 60606-1597.

Morton

Market/product matrix
A matrix that includes the four possible combinations of old and new products and old and new markets. The purpose of the matrix is to broadly categorize alternative opportunities in terms of basic strategies for growth.

Market penetration
A strategy that seeks to increase sales of an established product by generating increased use of the product in existing markets.

Market development
A strategy by which an organization attempts to draw new customers to an existing product, most commonly by introducing the product in a new

Increased product usage may be an objective for a market penetration strategy. Morton Salt uses a market penetration strategy to encourage existing users to increase usage of its product.

draw new customers to an existing product. The most common market development strategy is to enter a new geographical area. The recent changes in Eastern Europe present a market development opportunity for many multinational organizations. The markets that are now growing in the Czech Republic, Slovakia, Lithuania, and other countries previously without market economies expand the sales potential of existing products.

The desire to expand the demand for an existing product need not come from the belief that an existing market is shrinking. It might derive from the fact that an organization has the capacity to produce more product or believes that in some other way its assets are not being utilized to the fullest.

Market-Related Strategies for New Products   Nothing is more important to a company's long-term survival and growth than the successful introduction of new products. Consider, for example, that Lego, along with the Massachusetts Institute of Technology, spent more than 10 years developing a new robot-building toy called Mindstormers. Mindstormers sets, which contain Lego blocks, sensors, and software, allow users to build robots that walk and pick up objects in response to commands issued through a personal computer. Lego is in the process of developing other new products using the latest innovations in electronics technology. At Rubbermaid, one-third of the company's annual sales volume comes from products that are less than 5 years old. Every year, the company introduces more than 400 new products to the market.[10] Both Lego and Rubbermaid understand the critical importance of **product development**, which is the process of marketing innovative products or "new and improved" products in existing markets.

> Nothing is more important to a company's long-term survival and growth than the successful introduction of new products.

Marketing new products to a new set of customers is called **diversification**. When Sega Corporation felt a need to diversify outside its video-game operations, it created two high-tech, virtual-reality theme parks in Japan. Its expansion into North America with simulator rides that are part video game and part 3D movie is a major diversification effort for Sega.

A company that diversifies expands into an entirely new business. Often the company's marketing research staff and its engineering research and development staff are instrumental in identifying market opportunities and product ideas for diversification.

An alternative approach to developing new products internally is to acquire new products by merging with another company or purchasing products from other companies. Upon finding that busy Americans were substituting bagels, muffins, and pastries for a bowl of breakfast cereal, Kellogg, the cereal maker, followed this strategy when it purchased Lender's, a bagel maker.

The Strategic Marketing Process

Marketing managers engage in many diverse activities, ranging from creating new strategies to evaluating whether existing strategies are effective and efficient. The term **strategic marketing process** refers to the entire sequence of managerial and operational activities required to create and sustain effective and efficient marketing strategies. There are six major stages in the strategic marketing process:

1. Identifying and evaluating opportunities
2. Analyzing market segments and selecting target markets
3. Planning a market position and developing a marketing mix strategy
4. Preparing a formal marketing plan
5. Executing the plan
6. Controlling efforts and evaluating the results

Product development
A strategy of marketing innovative or "new and improved" products to existing markets.

Diversification
A strategy of marketing new products to a new market.

Strategic marketing process
The entire sequence of managerial and operational activities required to create and sustain effective and efficient marketing strategies.

The Six Stages of the Strategic Marketing Process

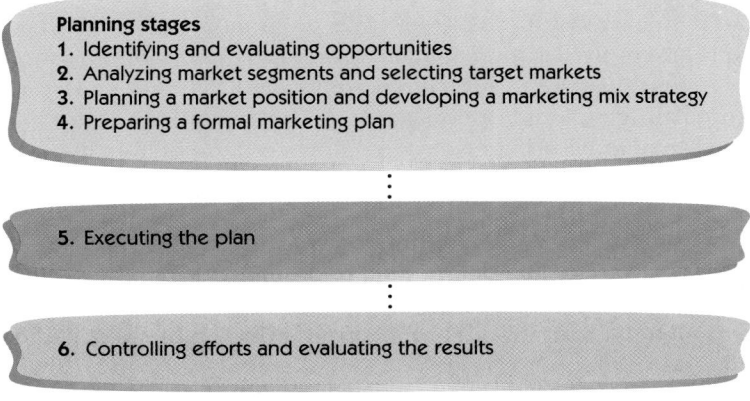

Planning stages
1. Identifying and evaluating opportunities
2. Analyzing market segments and selecting target markets
3. Planning a market position and developing a marketing mix strategy
4. Preparing a formal marketing plan

5. Executing the plan

6. Controlling efforts and evaluating the results

As Exhibit 2-5 shows, the first four stages involve planning activities to develop a marketing strategy that will satisfy customers' needs and meet the goals and objectives of the organization. The latter two stages involve execution and control to make the plan work.

The various activities involved in developing a marketing strategy may be carried out by a number of people over varying time periods, and the actual sequence of decisions may differ among organizations. Nevertheless, each stage is crucial to effective strategy development.

STAGE 1: IDENTIFYING AND EVALUATING OPPORTUNITIES

The powerful and ever-changing impact of environmental factors presents opportunities and threats to every organization. Opportunities occur when environmental conditions favor an organization's attaining or improving a competitive advantage. Threats occur when environmental conditions signal potential problems that may jeopardize an organization's competitive position. The marketer must be able to "read" the environment and any changes in it accurately and to translate the analysis of trends into marketing opportunities.

An environmental change may be interpreted as a threat or an opportunity, depending on the nature of an organization's or a strategic business unit's competitive position. Declining at-home per-capita coffee consumption is clearly an unfavorable trend and an environmental threat to coffee marketers. The marketers of soft drinks, however, will see this trend as an opportunity to sell more of their products by convincing consumers to drink cola in the morning. Effective managers analyze threatening situations and foresee problems that may result. Then they adapt their strategies in the hope of turning threats into opportunities. For example, after Stamps.com and E-stamps got approval from the U.S. Postal Service to market stamps on the Internet, Pitney Bowes, the leader in mechanical postage metering machines, had to adapt and develop digital postage software of its own.

Situation analysis is the diagnostic process of interpreting environmental conditions and changes in light of an organization's ability to capitalize on potential opportunities and ward off problems. Situation analysis requires both environmental scanning and environmental monitoring so that the organization can

Situation analysis
The interpretation of environmental attributes and changes in light of an organization's ability to capitalize on potential opportunities.

Environmental scanning
Information gathering designed to detect changes that may be in their initial stages of development.

Environmental monitoring
Tracking certain phenomena to detect the emergence of meaningful trends.

SWOT
Acronym for internal strengths and weaknesses and external opportunities and threats. In analyzing marketing opportunities, the decision maker evaluates all these factors.

Strategic gap
The difference between where an organization wants to be and where it is.

understand change. **Environmental scanning** is information gathering designed to detect indications of changes that may be beginning to develop. For example, by scanning the environment, Vanity Software Publishing determined that increased attention was being paid to repetitive stress injuries suffered by office workers who were spending long periods of time at their computers. In response, the company developed ErgoBreak for Office. ErgoBreak is a software package designed to interrupt, at regular intervals, whatever other program a worker is using. Periodically one of five cartoon characters appears on a worker's computer screen and leads a short exercise to stretch out a body part that may have gone numb from manipulating a mouse or doing some other repetitive action.[11]

Environmental monitoring involves tracking certain phenomena, such as sales data and population statistics, to observe whether any meaningful trends are emerging. For example, data indicate that Americans' breakfast eating habits are changing. The number of eggs consumed in the morning has declined dramatically in the last 20 years. People now focus on quick and easy meals. In particular, environmental monitoring shows that, as part of the trend toward simpler and more convenient breakfast food, bagel consumption has increased 150 percent in the last decade.[12]

Scanning and monitoring provide information that allows marketers to interpret environmental conditions and to determine the timing and significance of any changes. When these processes accomplish their purpose, situation analysis serves as both a warning system that alerts managers to environmental threats and an appraisal system that makes managers aware of the benefits associated with certain opportunities.

SWOT Analysis Situation analysis also requires an inward look at the organization. An organization should evaluate its internal strengths and weaknesses in relation to the external environment. You may find the acronym **SWOT**—which stands for internal *strengths* and *weaknesses* and external *opportunities* and *threats*—helpful in remembering that the purpose of situation analysis is to evaluate both the external environment and the internal environment.

Exhibit 2-6 illustrates how situation analysis involves both identifying environmental threats and opportunities and evaluating organizational strengths and weaknesses. Marketing managers consider environmental trends in light of organizational goals to determine the organization's desired position—where it wants to be. Such an analysis allows the organization to assess its present situation. Chances are good that the desired position differs somewhat from the actual position. The difference between the two can be called the **strategic gap**. Planning is

e x h i b i **2-6**

Situation Analysis Helps Match Opportunities to the Organization

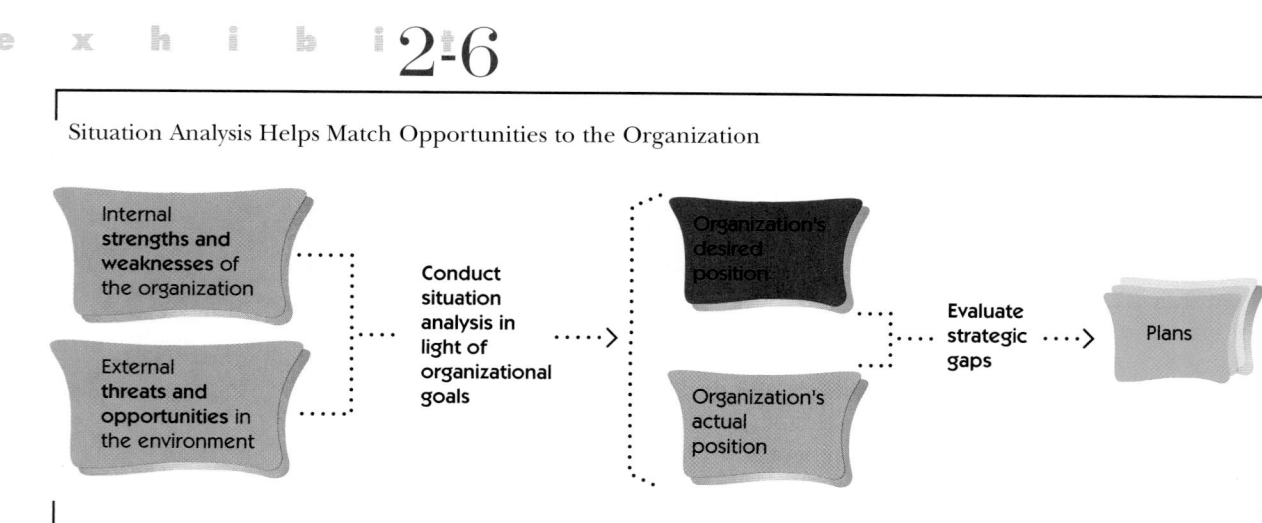

aimed at closing the gap so that the organization can move from a situation it doesn't want to one that it does want.

STAGE 2: ANALYZING MARKET SEGMENTS AND SELECTING TARGET MARKETS

As stated in Chapter 1, a market is a group of individuals or organizations that are potential customers for the product being offered. There are many types of markets. The most fundamental way of distinguishing among them is on the basis of the buyer's use of the good or service being purchased. When the buyer is an individual consumer who will use the product to satisfy personal or household needs, the good or service is a consumer product sold in the **consumer market**. When the buyer is an organization that will use the product to help operate its business (as when a furniture manufacturer purchases wood) or will resell the product (as when an office equipment wholesaler purchases a fax machine), the good or service is an organizational, or business, product sold in the **organizational market**, or **business market**.

A **market segment** is a portion of a larger market. Thus, African Americans constitute a segment of the total U.S. market. African Americans between the ages of 30 and 40 are a smaller, more narrowly defined segment. Female African Americans between the ages of 30 and 40 who use electric rather than gas stoves are a still smaller market segment. Market segments can be defined in terms of any number of variables from race or gender to air travel behavior. **Market segmentation** is the dividing of a heterogeneous mass market into a number of segments. The segments considered by analysts to be good potential customers for an organization's product are likely to become the organization's **target markets**—that is, the specific groups toward which the organization aims its marketing plan. Identifying and choosing targets, rather than trying to reach everybody, allows a marketer to tailor marketing mixes to a group's specific needs. As the old adage states, "You can't be all things to all people." A firm selects a target market because it believes it will have a competitive advantage in that particular segment.

Market segmentation is such an important topic that it will be treated more fully in Chapter 8. Suffice it to say here that identifying and evaluating marketing opportunities (the first stage in the six-stage strategic marketing process) must be followed by a decision about where marketing efforts will be directed—that is, by market segmentation and targeting—before the next step, planning a market position and developing a marketing mix, can be undertaken.

STAGE 3: PLANNING A MARKET POSITION AND DEVELOPING A MARKETING MIX

Planning a market position and constructing a marketing mix is the third step in the development of a marketing strategy. After selecting a target market, marketing managers position the brand in that market and then develop a marketing mix to accomplish the positioning objective. **Positioning** relates to the way consumers think about all the competitors in a market. A **market position**, or **competitive position**, represents how consumers perceive a brand relative to its competition. Each brand appealing to a given market segment has a position in relation to competitors in the buyer's mind. DiGiorno Rising Crust Pizza positions itself as comparable to pizzeria pizza rather than to other cook-at-home frozen pizzas. The company positions the pizza as being different from conventional frozen pizzas by emphasizing the pizza's rising crust, which gives it a "fresh-baked taste." Grasshoppers by Keds are positioned as inexpensive shoes for practical consumers—"If you feel the need to spend more on shoes, you could always buy two pairs." The object of positioning is to determine what distinct position is appropriate for the product. Positioning will be discussed more fully in Chapter 8. At this point, however, you should recognize that an organization's strategy for positioning its product relative to the competition will shape its marketing mix.

Consumer market
The market consisting of buyers who use a product to satisfy personal or household needs.

Organizational market, or business market
The market consisting of buyers who use a product to help operate a business or for resale.

Market segment
A portion of a larger market, identified according to some shared characteristic or characteristics.

Market segmentation
Dividing a heterogeneous market into segments that share certain characteristics.

Target market
A specific market segment toward which an organization aims its marketing plan.

Positioning
Planning the market position the company wishes to occupy. Positioning strategy is the basis for marketing mix decisions.

Market position, or competitive position
The way consumers perceive a product relative to its competition.

College students comprise an important market segment to the marketers of credit card services. The Visa credit card positions itself as the most widely accepted credit card. The marketing objective is to communicate the message that Visa can be used in many unexpected places, even at colleges for payment of tuition.

Accepted at more schools than you were.

It's *everywhere* you *want to be.*

Marketing plan
A written statement of the marketing objectives and strategies to be followed and the specific courses of action to be taken when (or if) certain events occur.

Marketing objective
A statement of the level of performance that an organization, SBU, or operating unit intends to achieve. Objectives define results in measurable terms.

As mentioned in Chapter 1, developing a marketing mix requires planning the four Ps: product, price, promotion, and place (distribution). Much of the remainder of this book, especially Chapters 9 through 17, discusses what marketing mix elements are appropriate under varying circumstances. The blend of ingredients, as well as the relative importance of each element in the mix, may differ for different types of products and different positioning strategies.

STAGE 4: PREPARING A FORMAL MARKETING PLAN

The preparation of the formal marketing plan is the final planning stage of the strategic marketing process. A formal **marketing plan** is a written statement of the marketing objectives and strategies to be followed and the specific courses of action to be taken when (or if) certain future events occur. It outlines the marketing mix, explains who is responsible for managing the specific activities in the plan, and provides a timetable indicating when those activities must be performed. Certain aspects of the plan may ultimately be scrapped or modified because of changes in society or in other portions of the market environment. Establishing action-oriented objectives is a key element of the marketing plan. A **marketing objective** is a statement about the level of performance the organization, SBU, or operating unit intends to achieve. Objectives are more focused than goals because they define results in measurable terms. For example, "to increase our dollar-volume share of the Japanese market from 9 percent to 15 percent by December 31 of this year" describes the nature and amount of change (a 6 percent increase), the performance criterion (market share as measured by percentage of dollar volume), and the target date for achieving the objective.

Marketing plans may be categorized by their duration: long-term (5 or more years), medium-term (2 to 5 years), or short-term (1 year or less). Long-term marketing plans usually outline basic strategies for the strategic business unit's growth. Most organizations prepare an annual marketing plan because marketing activities must be coordinated with annual financial plans and other budgetary plans that follow the fiscal year. (See Appendix B on our Web site, http://zikmundswcollege.com, for a more extensive discussion of business plans and marketing plans. See http://www.bplans.com for numerous business and marketing plans.)

STAGE 5: EXECUTING THE MARKETING PLAN

Once marketing plans have been developed and approved, they must be executed, or carried out. In fact, the words *executive* and *execute* both come from the Latin word meaning to "follow out" or "carry out." Making a sales presentation, inspecting proofs of advertising copy, setting prices and discounts, and choosing transportation methods are all aspects of executing a marketing plan.

Execution, or implementation, of a plan requires organizing and coordinating people, resources, and activities. Staffing, directing, developing, and leading subordinates are major activities used to implement plans. Clearly, the best marketing plans can fail if they are not properly executed. Speakers at sales meetings are fond of describing the salesperson who read every book on planning for success, spent every waking hour developing approaches to customers and getting all aspects of his sales career in perfect order, but who never sold a thing and was fired. Why? He never got out of the house to sell anything! Planning is extremely important, but it means little without execution.

An important aspect of the middle-level marketing manager's job is to supervise the execution of the marketing plan. Translating the plan into action is a task delegated to operational managers and their staffs. Operational managers, such as a district sales manager or a manager of the jewelry department in a Nordstrom department store, plan activities that will support the business-level marketing strategy. They make specific plans that clearly set out the marketing tactics to be executed. For example, if the organization's marketing plan sets a 25 percent increase in sales volume as an objective, the regional sales manager may plan to employ two additional sales representatives during the next month. Then the manager may implement the necessary marketing activities, such as hiring and training the new employees and directing their selling efforts, so that the objectives can be met. Mistakes may be made in the completion of any task. These mistakes—some minor, some perhaps unavoidable, but all damaging to some degree—are errors of execution. For example:

- Instructions on the front of Lite Way brand salad dressing packages read, "Just mix with water and cider vinegar." On the reverse side of the package, the instructions read, "Mix with low-fat milk and cider vinegar."
- A television commercial for a Cadillac Catera showed the car illegally crossing a double yellow line to pass.[13]
- The Iowa Department of Transportation inaccurately printed 1,700,000 maps identifying the Fort Dodge Correctional Facility (the state prison) as the Fort Dodge Recreational Facility.

We do not mean to be negative. Most marketing plans are properly executed. We do, however, want to emphasize that "the best-laid plans of mice and men" may go astray. Proper execution should never be taken for granted.

Execution
The carrying out of plans; also called *implementation*.

The Association of American Publishers has as an objective encouraging reading, especially among 18- to 34-year-olds. The advertisement shown here portrays avid reader Whoopi Goldberg reading *Peter Pan,* one of her favorite books. The slogan, "Get Caught Reading," is a tactic in the campaign.

http://www.publishers.org

Get caught reading.

Whoopi Goldberg reading PETER PAN.

Lisa Sharples, her husband Cliff, and their good friend Jamie O'Neill had all taken professor Louis W. Stern's marketing channels course at Northwestern University. They had learned to distinguish the supply chain—how a product physically moves from the supplier's point of origin to end user—from the channel of distribution system in which ownership of a product changes hands from the producer to the buyer. After they graduated, all held the conviction that the Internet represented a potent new channel. At the time, few people had grasped its potential. "We said, 'This is a medium that can provide a whole new set of services to the consumer,'" recalls O'Neill. "It was not just a way to distribute information more widely."

In 1995, all up and quit their jobs at Trilogy Software Inc., in Austin, Texas, where the three had worked for only 10 weeks. On the morning after, the new partners gathered around a whiteboard in the Sharpleses' garage and began brainstorming a design for the perfect Internet business. For months they lived off O'Neill's Visa card and peanut-butter-and-jelly sandwiches. On Friday nights they would treat themselves to dinner at a local restaurant, the Iguana Grill, where margaritas salved the week's wounds. The founders' memories of that first summer are elemental. "It was hot, and we had no money," says Lisa.

They had the strategy. Now all they needed was the right business.

The three founders were looking for a fragmented market that they could consolidate before drawing the attention of another consolidator or category killer. "The idea was to find an industry where no one company had channel power," says Lisa. They had to be able to source quality products and get them to customers quickly and reliably. They had to build a brand name. To guarantee repeat business they had to build a community, which meant producing an unending flow of content for their Web site. Customers would flock to the site like coffee drinkers drawn to the familiar environs of the neighborhood Starbucks.

They had to hit a grand slam by creating the category and building the brand at the same time. And they had to do it quickly and with limited funds before a larger competitor took note and threw ten times as much money into the niche.

While the founders searched for an appropriately fragmented industry, they also knew it could not be a commodity business. "We did not want to end up in a price war," recalls Lisa. The surest way to protect margins was to provide an abundance of useful information, which, they hoped, would build trust and a sense of community and create a willingness on the part of buyers to pay a premium. Finally, they needed a business with strong repeat-purchasing patterns. "We needed to be able to remarket to the consumer," says Lisa.

Throughout the long, hot summer, the names of various industries went up on the whiteboard, only to be erased once the partners started asking questions. One model they studied was that of Peapod, the Internet grocer, but they decided not to follow it, because food is a commodity business. They also looked at apparel but reasoned, "How much information do people really need when they buy a sweater?" according to Lisa.

One day, Lisa, who was interested in crafts, volunteered, "What about beads on-line?"

"No," came the reply.

Then, free-associating, she asked, "What about seeds online?"

"No."

"Wait a minute," she said. None of the three was an avid gardener, but Lisa had relatives who gardened. The idea felt right to her. She announced she was taking off for the University of Texas business-school library, where she embarked on three days of research on the gardening industry. She returned with enough information to combat the skepticism of the other two partners. Gardening, she reported, was at least a $40-billion-a-year business. It was highly fragmented; no player accounted for more than 1 percent of the market. There were few national brands—for good reason:

STAGE 6: CONTROLLING EFFORTS AND EVALUATING THE RESULTS

Control

The process by which managers ensure that planned activities are completely and properly executed.

The purpose of managerial **control** is to ensure that planned activities are executed completely and properly. The first aspect of control is to establish acceptable performance standards. Control also requires investigation and evaluation. Investigation involves "checking up" to determine whether the activities necessary to the execution of the marketing plan are in fact being performed. Actual performance must then be assessed to determine whether organizational objectives have been met. Performance may be evaluated, for example, in terms of the number of sales calls made or new accounts developed. Sales and financial figures may also be judged to appraise individual or organizational successes.

Control activities provide feedback to alert managers, indicating whether to continue with plans and activities or to change them and take corrective action. Marketing executives may discover, by means of a control activity, that actions that were part of the marketing plan are not being carried out "in the field." When this happens, either the marketing plan must be corrected to reflect environmental realities or the persons responsible for carrying out the plan must be more strongly motivated to achieve organizational goals.

you can't warehouse live plants. Gardening is a regional, if not local, phenomenon, tied to climate and soils. And yet gardeners are affluent and willing to pay widely varying prices for the same item, based on their perception of quality and the amount of expert advice being delivered.

Research with family and friends revealed there was no one-stop shop for gardeners and no single reliable body of advice or information. Moreover, as Cliff puts it, "The supply chain was broken." Baby boomers had commandeered the hobby with a vengeance, but the industry had failed to change with the times. Most suppliers still operated as if gardening meant seeds arriving sometime in the spring and tomatoes being canned for winter. Yet gardening had become the new extreme sport for a graying generation. It was now about ordering ornamental fruit trees by mail and having them arrive, without fail, on Tuesday, because you were leaving on Wednesday on a three-day business trip.

Cliff refers to that cohort of high-octane, competitive gardeners as "the Pottery Barn generation"—people who are short on time, yet hungry for knowledge about how to do things in an artful way. "The interest is now about fashion, collection, and decoration," he says. "It's about designing your exterior space the way you would think about your interior space."

Developing a proprietary company network designed to tie together the numerous gardening suppliers and the company that would be named Garden.com was perhaps the key concept in the 80-page business plan that the founders dropped on the desk of venture capitalist John Thornton, general partner at Austin Ventures, in the late summer of 1995. What the plan articulated was this: Gardening was a highly fragmented industry. No distributor had ever sought to tie suppliers together nationwide—as had been done in so many other industries—because the industry mind-set resisted it. Besides, the technology to do so had theretofore not existed. But O'Neill reasoned that with the Internet established, the technology hurdle had been cleared. So if a traditional industrial company could distribute drill bits and drywall sourced from a national supplier base, then why not asters and azaleas? After all, 10 percent of all plants sold were already purchased by mail order.

Garden.com's strategy was simple but very ambitious: Find the best suppliers in each gardening category and sign them to exclusives. All of a supplier's on-line sales would go through Garden.com. In return, the company would not sign up any direct competitors of that supplier. The company and its suppliers would be tied together by a proprietary "extranet" integrated with the muscle of Federal Express.

O'Neill says the idea was to make it seem to the consumer as though everything came out of a warehouse in Texas, when, in fact, it was being drop-shipped from multiple locations around the country. "The power is in the idea of tying all these niche growers together into a virtual store," says O'Neill. "I got the Zen of that business model—and the customer reaction is awesome. A really well executed one-stop shop is an extremely powerful tool from the customer's standpoint."

And from the suppliers' as well, O'Neill adds. "Instead of going in and saying, 'You know, Mr. Grower, we demand x percent gross margin,' we said, 'We'll spend all this money on marketing, on service calls, on finding new customers for you. Now, look at how much we save you by taking all this cost out, and we'll base gross margin on that. You can have an exclusive. In exchange, we are going to do a lot of work that needs to get done to make for a happy customer. We want a fair margin, but you will not spend a penny until we sell the first product.'"

Garden.com's kinder, gentler approach was a carrot to its suppliers. The company also had, and still has, an offer-you-can't-refuse mind-set. Garden.com has a mutual exclusivity with its suppliers. Of course, this also means that if a gardening supplier doesn't talk to Garden.com, the company will go to the supplier's competitor.[14]

A **marketing audit** is a comprehensive review and appraisal of the total marketing operation. It requires a systematic and impartial review of an organization's recent and current operations and its marketing environment. The audit examines the company's strengths and weaknesses in light of the problems and opportunities it faces. Because the marketing audit evaluates the effectiveness of marketing activities, it is often best performed by outside consultants or other unbiased personnel. The topic of managerial control, including a more extensive discussion of the marketing audit, is explored in Appendix C on our Web site.

Marketing audit
A comprehensive review and appraisal of the total marketing operation, often performed by outside consultants or other unbiased personnel.

INTERRELATIONSHIPS AMONG PLANNING, EXECUTION, AND CONTROL

Planning, execution, and control are closely interrelated. A consideration of the marketing environment leads to the formulation of marketing plans. These in turn must be executed. The execution of the plans must then be controlled through investigation and evaluation. The results or findings generated during the control phase provide a basis for judging both the marketing plans and their execution and serve as new inputs for further planning and execution. Thus, a series of logical steps is maintained, as shown in Exhibit 2-7.

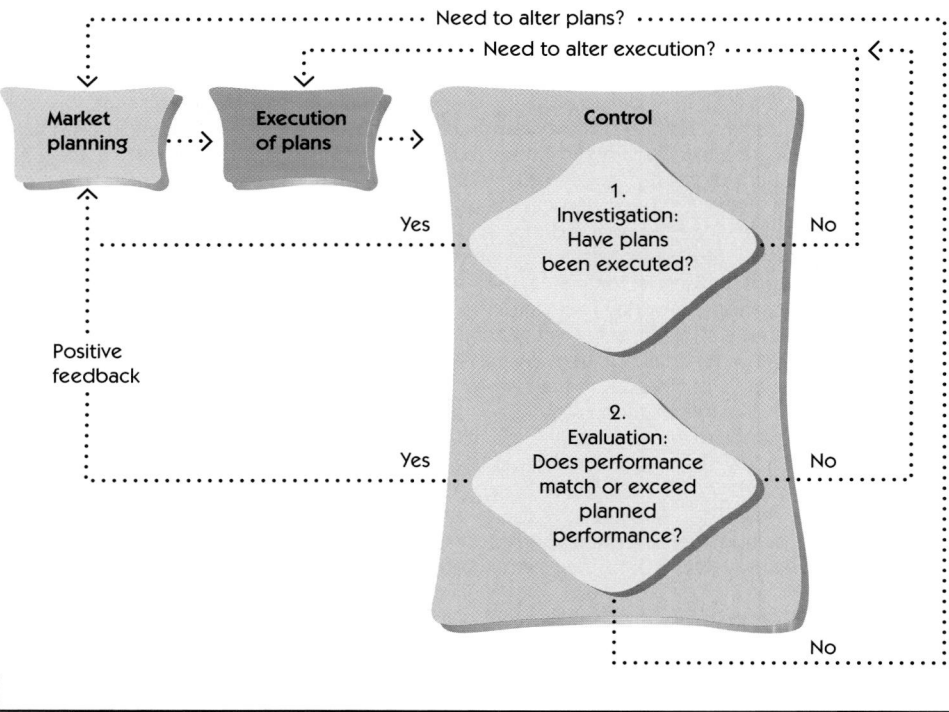

Planning, Execution, and Control Are Interrelated

Planning, execution, and control of marketing strategy and tactics are also interrelated because each has ethical dimensions. Understanding the nature of marketing ethics is essential for anyone who plans to be a manager. The remainder of this chapter addresses this issue.

Managerial Ethics and Socially Responsible Behavior

In recent years, many highly publicized stories about organizations—and individuals in organizations—that did not act according to high ethical standards have appeared on television and in newspapers and magazines. For example, there was a barrage of criticism about the Exxon Valdez oil spill and the company's efforts to reduce the damage to the Alaskan environment. And marketers of batteries received so much criticism about the mercury, cadmium, and other toxic metals in batteries that Energizer virtually eliminated mercury from its Green Power batteries, while other battery marketers began to package toxic batteries in such a way that they could be returned to the manufacturer for recycling.

> In order to be socially responsible, an organization must acknowledge a responsibility broader than its legal responsibility.

Society clearly expects marketers to obey the law, but in order to be socially responsible, an organization must acknowledge a responsibility broader than its legal responsibility. **Social responsibility** refers to the ethical principle that a person or an organization must become accountable for how its acts might affect the interests of others.[15] Every marketing manager makes decisions that have ethical implications.

Social responsibility
The ethical principle that a person or an organization must become accountable for how its acts might affect the interests of others.

what went wrong?

The Lorax? Has the Lorax, Dr. Seuss's curmudgeonly woodlands character "who speaks for the trees," sold out to logging interests? That's what the Heritage Forest Campaign charged in a letter sent to Dr. Seuss Enterprises, the organization that licenses use of Dr. Seuss characters.

Seuss's cartoon creature is being used on the Web to solicit schoolchildren's money for American Forests, a national conservation group based in Washington, D.C. For $2.95, children can become "Lorax Helpers" and have a tree planted in their names in the Dr. Seuss Lorax Forest, part of a project to replace South Carolina trees destroyed by hurricane Hugo (go to http://www.randomhouse.com/seussville and then click on "Games"). The Heritage Forest Campaign, another Washington-based environmental group, says the American Forests board includes representatives from logging companies that favor clear-cutting of forests—a practice Heritage officials say would have irked Dr. Seuss (Theodore Geisel), who died in 1991.

Champion International Corp., a major logging concern that uses the controversial technique, is represented on American Forests' board, and R. Neil Sampson, a senior fellow at the group, urged that clear-cutting remain "a management option" in congressional testimony in 1994.

In the 1971 children's book, the Lorax confronted loggers about forest destruction: "Sir! You are crazy with greed."

Ken Rait, director of the Heritage Forest Campaign, wrote to Susan O'Sullivan, vice president of marketing and licensing at Dr. Seuss Enterprises, worried that trees planted in the American Forests project might ultimately be cut by its corporate supporters. "Will you free the Lorax, so that he can once again speak for the trees?" Rait wrote. O'Sullivan defends the licensing decision as a sound one. "American Forests is a wonderful organization," she says. "It has wonderful projects and one we're very proud of." American Forests spokesman Craig Nobel says the group "supports limits on the size of clear-cuts, and the purpose of [its reforestation effort] is not future timber product."

American Forests is the country's oldest nonprofit citizen conservation group. But the Heritage Forest Campaign thinks the organization isn't "green" enough for an icon like the Lorax to hook up with. In the famous Seuss story, however, it is business interests—represented by the "Once-ler"—that are swayed by the Lorax and ultimately pass out seedlings and propagate his creed: "The word of the Lorax seems perfectly clear. Unless someone like you cares a whole awful lot, nothing is going to get better. It's not."[16]

THE NATURE OF ETHICS

Ethics involves values about right and wrong conduct. **Marketing ethics** are the principles that guide an organization's conduct and the values it expects to express in certain situations.[17] In the marketing context, **moral behavior** is individual or organizational activity that exhibits ethical values.

Ethical principles reflect the cultural values and norms of a society. **Norms** suggest what ought to be done under given circumstances. They indicate approval or disapproval, what is good or bad. Many norms in Western society are based on the Judeo-Christian ethic. Being truthful is good. Being fair—doing unto others as you would have them do unto you—meets with approval. Other norms have a utilitarian base.[18] Norms may arise from a concern about the consequences of one's actions: "You ought to obey product safety laws, or you may go to jail." Norms may also arise from expectations about how society should function: "It is good that a company's shareholders receive its profits, because profits are the shareholders' reward for investment and risk taking."

Some ethical principles of personal conduct dictated by broad norms have direct counterparts in marketing actions. Being truthful, a societal norm, and avoiding deceptive, untruthful advertising are closely linked. Where such clear-cut links

Marketing ethics
The principles that guide an organization's conduct and the values it expects to express in certain situations.

Moral behavior
Individual or organizational marketing activity that embodies the ethical values to which the individual or organization subscribes.

Norm
A social principle identifying what action is right or wrong in a given situation.

exist, the expected moral behavior is relatively clear. Some actions, such as murdering a competitor, are so noticeably contrary to societal norms that they would be morally indefensible in all circumstances. Although morally acceptable behavior may be clear-cut in many circumstances, in others, determining what is ethical is a complicated matter open to debate.

RESOLVING ETHICAL DILEMMAS

Ethical dilemma

A predicament in which a marketer must resolve whether an action that benefits the organization, the individual decision maker, or both may be considered unethical.

An **ethical dilemma**, for a marketer, is a predicament in which the marketer must resolve whether an action that benefits the organization, the individual decision maker, or both may be considered unethical.[19] An ethical dilemma may arise when two principles or values are in conflict. It may be that a corporation president values both high profits and—like most people in society in general—a pollution-free environment. When one of these values or preferences in any way inhibits the achievement of the other, the business person is faced with an ethical dilemma. Problems also arise when others do not share the principles or values that guide a marketer's actions. Consider these questions: Is it wrong to pay a bribe in a foreign country where bribery is a standard business practice? Should the Brooklyn Museum avoid showing an art exhibit if its anti-religious overtones offend certain museum-goers but not others? How a marketer answers these questions involves resolving ethical dilemmas.

In many situations, individuals agree on principles or values but have no fixed measure by which to judge actions. An engineer can calculate exactly how strong a steel girder is and a chemist can usually offer the right formulation of chemicals necessary to perform a task, but the business executive often cannot be so precise. Even in instances when specific laws would seem to guide action, the laws and their application may be subject to debate. Although marketers and other business people often pride themselves on their rational problem-solving abilities, the lack of permanent, objective ethical standards for all situations continues to trouble the person seeking the ethical course of action in business.

Thus, there rarely is an absolute consensus on what constitutes ethical behavior. Different people, and even a single person, can evaluate a question from several different perspectives. For example, the belief that smoking is injurious to health has led to regulations that restrict smoking in airplanes and other public places and ban cigarette commercials from radio and television. Yet to some, this is a controversial matter. Of course, good health is important, but what about a restaurant's desire to give cigar smokers freedom of choice?

In general, when marketing decision makers encounter ethical dilemmas, they consider the impact of the organization's actions and operate in a way that balances the organization's short-term profit needs with society's long-term needs. For example, a cookie marketer, such as Keebler, knows that people buy cookies because they taste good. It also knows certain inexpensive cooking oils that enhance taste are not as low in saturated fat as other, more expensive ingredients. The company may conduct extensive research to find a way to reformulate the cookies by changing to more healthful ingredients while maintaining the cookies' good taste. More specifically, marketers must ask what is ethical in a particular situation. They must establish the facts of the situation and determine if their plans are compatible with the organization's ethical values. They must determine at what point certain marketing practices become ethically questionable. Is it ethical for a sales representative to pay for a purchasing agent's lunch? To give the purchasing agent a gift on his or her birthday? To arrange for an all-expenses-paid vacation for the agent if the sales representative's company gets a big contract?[20]

To help marketers act in a socially responsible manner, President John F. Kennedy outlined the consumer's basic rights: the right to be informed, the right to safety, the right to choose, and the right to be heard. Since Kennedy's pronouncement, others have argued that consumers have other rights, such as the right to privacy and the right to a clean and healthy environment. Arguments have been made that children have special rights because they have not developed mature reasoning powers.

Members of the American Marketing Association (AMA) are committed to ethical professional conduct. They have joined together in subscribing to this Code of Ethics embracing the following topics:

Responsibilities of the Marketer

Marketers must accept responsibility for the consequences of their activities and make every effort to ensure that their decisions, recommendations, and actions function to identify, serve, and satisfy all relevant publics: consumers, organizations and society. Marketers' professional conduct must be guided by:

1. The basic rule of professional ethics: not knowingly to do harm;
2. The adherence to all applicable laws and regulations;
3. The accurate representation of their education, training and experience; and
4. The active support, practice and promotion of this Code of Ethics.

Honesty and Fairness

Marketers shall uphold and advance the integrity, honor, and dignity of the marketing profession by:

1. Being honest in serving consumers, clients, employees, suppliers, distributors and the public;
2. Not knowingly participating in conflict of interest without prior notice to all parties involved; and
3. Establishing equitable fee schedules including the payment or receipt of usual, customary and/or legal compensation for marketing exchanges.

Rights and Duties of Parties

Participants in the marketing exchange process should be able to expect that:

1. Products and services offered are safe and fit for their intended uses;
2. Communications about offered products and services are not deceptive;
3. All parties intend to discharge their obligations, financial and otherwise, in good faith; and
4. Appropriate internal methods exist for equitable adjustment and/or redress of grievances concerning purchases.

It is understood that the above would include, *but is not limited to,* the following responsibilities of the marketer:

In the area of product development and management:

• Disclosure of all substantial risks associated with product or service usage
• Identification of any product component substitution that might materially change the product or impact on the buyer's purchase decision
• Identification of extra-cost added features

In the area of promotions:

• Avoidance of false and misleading advertising
• Rejection of high pressure manipulations, or misleading sales tactics
• Avoidance of sales promotions that use deception or manipulation

In the area of distribution:

• Not manipulating the availability of a product for purpose of exploitation
• Not using coercion in the marketing channel
• Not exerting undue influence over the resellers' choice to handle a product

In the area of pricing:

• Not engaging in price fixing
• Not practicing predatory pricing

• Disclosing the full price associated with any purchase

In the area of marketing research:

• Prohibiting selling or fund raising under the guise of conducting research
• Maintaining research integrity by avoiding misrepresentation and omission of pertinent research data
• Treating outside clients and suppliers fairly

Organizational Relationships

Marketers should be aware of how their behavior may influence or impact on the behavior of others in organizational relationships. They should not encourage or apply coercion to obtain unethical behavior in their relationships with others, such as employees, suppliers or customers.

1. Apply confidentiality and anonymity in professional relationships with regard to privileged information.
2. Meet their obligations and responsibilities in contracts and mutual agreements in a timely manner.
3. Avoid taking the work of others, in whole or in part, and representing this work as their own or directly benefiting from it without compensation or consent of the originator or owner.
4. Avoid manipulation to take advantage of situations to maximize personal welfare in a way that unfairly deprives or damages the organization or others.

Any AMA member found to be in violation of any provision of this Code of Ethics may have his or her Association membership suspended or revoked.

Rights like these are embodied in organizations' and associations' codes of conduct. A **code of conduct** establishes a company's or a professional organization's guidelines with regard to its ethical principles and what behavior it considers proper. The American Marketing Association's Code of Ethics appears in Exhibit 2-8.

Code of conduct
A statement establishing a company's or a professional organization's guidelines with regard to ethical principles and acceptable behavior.

Following a code of conduct helps resolve some ethical dilemmas but not others. Many ethical dilemmas involve issues that are not black and white, and individuals often have to resolve such dilemmas by using their own judgment, based on their own ethical values. The checklist that follows offers some good general advice about considering ethical dilemmas.[21]

1. Recognize and clarify the dilemma.
2. Get all possible facts.
3. List the options—all of them.
4. Test each option by asking "Is it legal? Is it right? Is it beneficial?"
5. Make your decision.
6. Double-check your decision by asking "How would I feel if my family found out about this? How would I feel if my decision were printed in the local newspaper?" Do you still feel you made the correct decision?
7. Take the action if warranted.

ETHICAL DIMENSIONS OF MARKETING STRATEGY

It should be clear by now that ethical values influence many aspects of marketing strategy.[22]

Throughout this book, you will see that laws and ethical considerations can affect every aspect of an organization's marketing mix, which, in turn, can influence the level of its profits. Similarly, ethical considerations can play a part in the development and implementation of that mix. Exhibit 2-9 presents some ethical questions that may be raised concerning the four major elements of the marketing mix. In considering them, remember that ethical issues are philosophical in nature and that not everyone may agree on solutions to ethical dilemmas.[23] However, there has been an undeniable trend toward broadening the social responsibility of marketing organizations beyond their traditional role as economic forces.

e x h i b t 2-9 Selected Ethical Questions Related to the Marketing Mix

PRODUCT	PROMOTION	PRICE	DISTRIBUTION
• Who must accept responsibility for an injury caused by a product that was used improperly? • Is the package a source of unnecessary environmental pollution?	• Can advertising persuade consumers to purchase products that they don't really want? • What effect does advertising have on children?	• Should pricing laws protect consumers or protect small business? • Do the poor really pay more?	• Should modern shopping malls be built in low-income areas? • If a retailer wishes to carry only one of a manufacturer's products, should the manufacturer be able to force the retailer to carry all of its products?

Summary

This chapter discusses marketing strategy and tactics and explains how marketing managers must plan, execute, and control the organization's marketing activities.

1) Differentiate between marketing strategy and marketing tactics.

A strategy is a long-range plan to determine what basic goals and objectives will be pursued and how they will be achieved in the time available. A strategy entails a commitment to certain courses of action and allocation of the resources necessary to achieve the identified goals. Tactics are specific actions intended to implement strategy.

2) Discuss the role of marketing planning at the corporate level, at the strategic business unit level, and at the operational level of management.

Top management engages in strategic planning to determine long-term goals for the entire organization. Managers at the strategic business unit level plan strategies for the business unit and for individual products. Operational managers are concerned with planning and executing the day-to-day activities of the organization.

3) Understand the concept of the organizational mission.

An organizational mission is a statement of a company's purpose. It explains why an organization exists and what it hopes to accomplish.

4) Understand the nature of a competitive advantage.

A business or product that is superior to or favorably different from its competitors in a way that is important to the market has a competitive advantage. It may offer the same quality at lower cost or some unique feature, for example.

5) Understand the importance of total quality management strategies in product differentiation.

Adopting a total quality management strategy is one of the most common ways marketers differentiate their products. They do this by adjusting marketing strategy to assure that their products offer customers better quality and thus greater satisfaction than competitors' products.

6) Discuss demarketing.

In general, marketers engage in demarketing when a product is in short supply. It is a marketing strategy intended to diminish demand while maintaining consumer satisfaction during the shortage period.

7) Explain the market/product matrix.

The market/product matrix broadly categorizes the opportunities of a strategic business unit in terms of strategies for growth. The four strategies are market penetration, market development, product development, and product diversification.

8) Identify the stages in the strategic marketing process.

The strategic marketing process includes the following six stages:

1. Identifying and evaluating opportunities
2. Analyzing market segments and selecting target markets
3. Planning a market position and developing a marketing mix
4. Preparing a formal marketing plan
5. Executing the plan
6. Controlling efforts and evaluating results

9) Describe marketing objectives and marketing plans.

Marketing objectives are statements about the level of performance the organization, strategic business unit, or operating unit intends to achieve. Marketing plans are written statements of the marketing objectives and strategies to be followed and the specific courses of action to be taken when (or if) certain events occur.

10) Discuss the concept of positioning.

Each product occupies a position in the consumer's mind relative to competing products. A key marketing objective is to determine what position the company wishes a given product to occupy. Positioning is accomplished through the development and implementation of a marketing mix.

11) Understand the nature of marketing ethics and socially responsible behavior.

Social responsibility refers to the ethical principle that people or organizations must be accountable for how their acts might affect the interests of others. Ethics involves values about right and wrong conduct. Marketing ethics are the principles that guide an organization's conduct and the values it expects to express in certain situations. Moral behavior on the part of marketers is activity that exhibits ethical values. Ethical principles reflect the cultural values and norms of a society. Marketing decisions often have ethical dimensions and may involve ethical dilemmas.

Key Terms

business model (p. 35)
code of conduct (p. 51)
competitive advantage (p. 36)
consumer market (p. 43)
control (p. 46)
cross-functional team (p. 38)
demarketing (p. 38)
differentiation strategy (p. 37)
diversification (p. 40)
environmental monitoring (p. 42)
environmental scanning (p. 42)
ethical dilemma (p. 50)
execution (p. 45)

market development (p. 39)
market penetration (p. 39)
market position, or competitive position (p. 43)
market/product matrix (p. 39)
market segment (p. 43)
market segmentation (p. 43)
marketing audit (p. 47)
marketing ethics (p. 49)
marketing management (p. 30)
marketing myopia (p. 35)
marketing objective (p. 44)
marketing plan (p. 44)

marketing strategy (p. 31)
moral behavior (p. 49)
norm (p. 49)
operational planning (p. 33)
organizational market, or business market (p. 43)
organizational mission statement (p. 34)
planning (p. 32)
positioning (p. 43)
price leadership strategy (p. 37)
product development (p. 40)
situation analysis (p. 41)

Questions for Review & Critical Thinking

1. What are the three major tasks of marketing management?
2. Distinguish between a strategy and a tactic.
3. Based on some of Pepsi's print and television ads, what do you think the company's marketing strategy is?
4. Why are marketing planning activities important?
5. Describe your interpretation of the organizational missions of several corporations or not-for-profit organizations (perhaps Toshiba, Digital Equipment Corporation, Walt Disney Productions, Eastman Kodak, and Ford Motor Company).
6. Several corporate slogans are listed below. Discuss how each reflects a corporate mission.
   a. FedEx: "When it absolutely, positively has to be there overnight."
   b. Panasonic: "Just slightly ahead of our time."
   c. Lexus: "The relentless pursuit of perfection."
   d. The Equitable Financial Companies: "We have great plans for you."
   e. Raytheon: "Where quality starts with fundamentals."
   f. Disney: "Using our imagination to bring happiness to millions."
   g. Merck: "To preserve and improve life."
7. What is a strategic business unit? What are the basic growth strategies for SBUs?
8. What is the role of total quality management in marketing strategy?
9. What is competitive advantage? Suppose you were the marketing manager for Saturn automobiles. What marketing strategies would you develop to compete with imports?
10. Is it possible for two competing companies to have the same goal but to use different marketing strategies to reach the goal?
11. Describe the stages in the strategic marketing process.
12. What is positioning? How is Dr Pepper positioned relative to Coke and Pepsi?
13. Choose a retail store or a manufacturing company in your local area. Study the company and identify its marketing plan. In your opinion, is the plan a sound one? Is it being executed well or poorly? Give evidence to support your answers.
14. Identify some typical execution errors.
15. What are marketing ethics?
16. What are some examples of socially responsible behavior and socially irresponsible behavior?
17. How do codes of conduct help marketers make strategic decisions?
18. Discuss how marketing managers might work in teams with managers of other functional areas, such as production, in planning a marketing strategy.

---

e-exercises | http://zikmund.swcollege.com

1. Satisfying customer wants is a key aspect of the marketing concept. In order to satisfy customers, marketers must listen to what the market has to say. Some marketers use simple techniques, like suggestion boxes, to listen to the market.

   Your marketing professor wants to listen to you, the customer, so that he or she can better satisfy future customers. Send an e-mail message to your marketing professor. Include at least two things in your message: First, tell the professor what you like about this class so far. Then tell the professor what you don't like about this class so far.
2. *Reveries* is a marketing digizine that highlights what drives marketing people. Go to http://www.reveries.com and select a marketer whose story appears on the Web site. What motivated this person to go into marketing?
3. This chapter highlights the critical role of an organization's mission statement in the development and implementation of a marketing strategy. Use your Web browser to go to the Johnson & Johnson Company's home page at http://www.jnj.com. Select the link called "Our Credo" and read Credo for North America. On a sheet of paper, list five ways the credo (the organization's mission statement) differs from the mission statement of eBay (which appears on page 34) and five similarities between the mission statements of the two organizations. Bring your lists to class for discussion.

4. Go to the American Marketing Association's Web site at http://www.ama.org and click on Publications. Open the link for *Marketing News*, where you will find several stories from the latest issue. Read the cover story and report any examples of marketing strategy contained in the article.

Address Book (Useful URLs)

DePaul University's Institute for Business   http://www.depaul.edu/ethics/
   and Professional Ethics

Better World 'Zine   http://www.betterworld.com

Ethically Right or Wrong?

The major television networks have established a "white coat" rule, which forbids medical professionals and actors portraying them from appearing in commercials. So when Chesebrough-Ponds, a unit of the Anglo-Dutch company Unilever, introduced Mentadent, a fluoride toothpaste with baking soda and peroxide, it used television commercials featuring real people who were married to dentists. The advertising objective was to educate consumers about Mentadent's unique ingredients and to communicate the dental community's acceptance of the product. The dentists' wives (and one husband) told how their spouses had recommended baking soda and peroxide for years and now recommended Mentadent. Mentadent gained a market share of approximately 5 percent in its first year.

QUESTIONS

1. Why do you think the networks have established the "white coat" rule?
2. By using dentists' spouses, did Chesebrough-Ponds sidestep the networks' codes of ethics?

TAKE A STAND

1. Many critics say that Wendy's should stop wrapping its products in packages that just end up littering the neighborhood. Do you agree?
2. Do you think that tobacco companies should be put out of business because their products cause cancer and other health problems and annoy many people who do not smoke?
3. Government could do more to control television programs considered by some to be offensive (such as those on the *Playboy* TV network) and recordings judged by some to be obscene (like those of Snoop Doggy Dogg). Take a stand.
4. It's been said that people learn ethical principles at home. Can a business teach ethical behavior?
5. A North Dakota aquaculture researcher is raising a freshwater variety of red claw lobsters in the hope of creating a market for the product. The red claw lobster is not as large as the saltwater Maine lobster—in fact, it is actually a large Australian crayfish. If the North Dakota lobsters weigh at least 6 ounces, the law allows them to be marketed as lobsters. Would it be ethical to market these as lobsters without mentioning that they were not real lobsters?

VIDEO CASE 2-1

Second Chance Body Armor

Second Chance manufactures and markets modern, wearable, concealable body armor for law enforcement officers around the world. The general public typically refers to the company's products as "bulletproof" vests. A more detailed description of Second Chance's products can be viewed at http://www.secondchance.com.

Second Chance's mission statement appears below.[24]

THE SECOND CHANCE BODY ARMOR MISSION STATEMENT

Second Chance is the inventor and world's most successful manufacturer of modern, wearable, concealable body armor. Our "bulletproof" vests save more lives every year than any other manufacturer. For over twenty-five years . . . through five generations of technology, . . . Second Chance vests have been distinguished by their superb design, superior wearability, guaranteed fit, high value, and flawless field performance.

But concealable body armor is not all we excel in. Our unsurpassed tactical/special-purpose armor jackets, extraordinary new anti-puncture Corrections vests, and rough stock Rodeo protective vests are also important examples of how we deliver on our personal protection mission.

Safety has always been our number one priority! Second Chance views its unequalled lifesaving history as both a challenge and a responsibility. The challenge is to continuously improve our products and services, so that more lives can be saved. As the industry leader, our responsibility is to always merit all our customers' trust . . . to set the best examples for others.

To achieve our personal protection mission we have established these Operating Principles:

1. Constant focus on meeting and/or exceeding each individual customer's needs.
2. World leadership in product designs, high value and competitive prices.
3. Unimpeachable market conduct and integrity; truthful, ethical product representation.
4. Unsurpassed, continuously improving quality, in all facets of our operation.
5. Minimum organizational structure; maximum participatory management.
6. Equal opportunity and respect for human differences.
7. Individual empowerment; positive, stimulating work environment.
8. Strong supplier partnerships that optimize product wearability and performance.
9. Fair and reasonable profits that support jobs, R&D growth, and diversification.
10. Corporate citizenship, officer safety education, and appropriate public sector relations.

QUESTIONS

1. Evaluate the Second Chance mission statement. Does it give the reader a clear idea about the company's philosophy?
2. How important are marketing growth strategies for a small- to medium-sized company like Second Chance?

Ben & Jerry's (A)

Ben & Jerry's Homemade, Inc., the Vermont-based manufacturer of ice cream, frozen yogurt, and sorbet, was founded in 1978 in a renovated gas station in Burlington, Vermont, by childhood friends Ben Cohen and Jerry Greenfield, with a $12,000 investment ($4,000 of which was borrowed). They soon became popular for their innovative flavors, made from fresh Vermont milk and cream. The company currently distributes ice cream, low fat ice cream, frozen yogurt, sorbet, and novelty products nationwide as well as in selected foreign countries in supermarkets, grocery stores, convenience stores, franchised Ben & Jerry's scoop shops, restaurants, and other venues.

Ben & Jerry's gives away 7.5 percent of its pre-tax earnings in three ways: through the Ben & Jerry's Foundation, through employee Community Action Teams at five Vermont sites, and through corporate grants made by the Director of Social Mission Development. The company supports projects that are models for social change—projects that exhibit creative problem solving and hopefulness. The Foundation is managed by a nine-member employee board and considers proposals relating to children and families, disadvantaged groups, and the environment.

In 1988 Ben & Jerry's Homemade, Inc. created a document called the *Statement of Mission.*

STATEMENT OF MISSION

Ben & Jerry's is dedicated to the creation and demonstration of a new corporate concept of linked prosperity. Our mission consists of three interrelated parts. Underlying the mission is the determination to seek new and creative ways of addressing all three parts, while holding a deep respect for individuals inside and outside the company, and for the communities of which they are a part.

Product To make, distribute and sell the finest quality all natural ice cream and related products in a wide variety of innovative flavors made from Vermont dairy products.

Economic To operate the Company on a sound financial basis of profitable growth, increasing value for our shareholders, and creating career opportunities and financial rewards for our employees.

Social To operate the Company in a way that actively recognizes the central role that business plays in the structure of society by initiating innovative ways to improve the quality of life of a broad community—local, national, and international.[25]

QUESTION

1. Ben & Jerry's mission links product, economic, and social issues. Is this a practical business strategy?

Environmental Forces in an e-commerce World: The Macroenvironment

L E A R N I N G   O B J E C T I V E S

After you have studied this chapter, you will be able to . . .

1) Describe the domestic and foreign environments in which marketers operate and their effects on organizations.

2) Understand that the physical environment influences marketing activity.

3) Understand that social values and beliefs are important cultural forces.

4) Explain how demographic trends, such as changes that have occurred in the American family, influence marketers.

5) Understand that technology, especially digital technology and the Internet, are having a significant impact on marketing and society.

6) Explain the various ways in which economic conditions influence marketers.

7) Appreciate how the three levels of U.S. law and the laws of other nations can influence marketing activity.

The idea behind Black Rock Golf Corporation's Killer Bee driver was ludicrously simple. Its main selling point wasn't sophisticated aerodynamics or new composite materials; it was merely that the club was longer.

Although most drivers are 43 to 45 inches long, the clubs introduced in 1995 by start-up Black Rock measured either 46 or 48 inches. That extra length translated into extra distance off the tee, claimed the company's cofounders, Hugh "Rocky" Thompson and Jack Rule, both professional golfers who have played on the Senior PGA Tour. "They thought they had found the Holy Grail," recalls Christopher Cooper, Black Rock's former chief operating officer.

Mindful that rivals might easily copy the Killer Bee—after all, no patent protected the extra length—Thompson and Rule rushed their product to market. They didn't do what golf-equipment manufacturers typically do before mass-producing a new club: They didn't ask the sport's governing authority, the U.S. Golf Association (USGA), to certify that their design conformed to its standards. Bypassing the USGA would turn out to be a fatal mistake.

It was Thompson, known as a "short hitter" on the PGA Tour, who had discovered that a longer club could extend his drives and who had recognized its commercial potential. He and Rule raised $1.2 million in seed capital from private investors and revved up production of the Killer Bee. Rather than competing in stores against established rivals like Callaway and Cobra, Black Rock appealed directly to customers in cable-TV infomercials on the Golf Channel. Wearing an outlandish yellow-and-black-striped outfit, Thompson brandished the Killer Bee and urged viewers to order it for $200 by telephoning an 800 number.

Many did. In 1995 sales swelled to almost $5 million. Flush with overnight success, by 1997 the company was producing a full line of clubs, including a $350 titanium-headed version of the Killer Bee, and, Cooper says, was "looking forward to a big year."

But that was not to be. In February 1997 the USGA notified Black Rock that the face markings on the Killer Bee and two of the company's other metal woods violated the measurement requirements of the association's rule 4-1e. By not seeking the USGA approval early on, Black Rock ran a big risk. "When you are spending so much time and money to develop a club, you want to have a letter of conformance on file from the USGA," says Don Anderson, president and CEO of GolfGear International, a golf-club manufacturer based in Huntington Beach, Calif.

Because many golfers will buy only clubs sanctioned by the USGA, the ruling stalled sales. Although the USGA reversed its decision two months later, by then Black Rock had returned 10,000 clubs to its manufacturer in Taiwan for refurbishing, at a total cost of $500,000. Hobbled during the prime selling months of March and April, the company never regained its balance. In 1997 its revenues plummeted 22 percent from the previous year's, and it lost $2.7 million. On July 17, 1998, Black Rock filed for Chapter 7 bankruptcy.[1]

The Killer Bee driver and the entire Black Rock Golf Corporation failed because the company incorrectly interpreted environmental forces influencing its business. This chapter discusses marketing's environment. Because the growth of the Internet is such a dramatic force shaping marketing practices, special attention is given to new Internet technologies and e-commerce business models. The chapter begins with a brief introduction to international aspects of the environment. Then it describes the various components of the macroenvironment: the physical environment, sociocultural forces, demographic forces, science and technology, economic forces, and politics and laws.

A World Perspective for the 21st Century

You may drive a Toyota, a Mazda, or a Mercedes. You may fill your tank at a Shell service station with gasoline refined from crude oil from Nigeria or Venezuela. You may sign the charge slip with a Bic pen. Each of these products comes from a foreign company and is made available in the United States as a result of international marketing. Today, we live in a global village. It is difficult to think of many business matters that do not influence or are not themselves influenced by events or activities in other areas of the world. Jet-age transportation, satellite television networks, computer modems, e-mail, and other electronic technologies are reshaping and restructuring the patterns of business. The world is getting smaller, and the external environment is taking on a more global character.

Some organizations that market products only in their home countries are influenced solely by environmental forces operating in the **domestic environment.** However, in today's global economy, most corporations must anticipate and respond to opportunities and threats in **foreign environments** as well. (See Exhibit 3-1.) It may be easier to envision how a large multinational corporation like Xerox or Honda is influenced by forces from both the domestic and foreign environments than to understand how uncontrollable foreign forces affect the marketing activities of, say, a small local electronics retailer. Yet both large and small organizations—indeed, the entire economy—can be influenced by forces thousands of miles away from their home countries.[2] And tomorrow's marketing managers will face even more global competition than managers of the late 20th century.

The Macroenvironment

Whether it is the domestic environment, a foreign environment, or the world environment that is under consideration, the environment can be divided into two categories: the macroenvironment and the microenvironment. The broad societal forces that influence every business and nonprofit marketer comprise the **macroenvironment.** Every company, however, is more directly influenced by a

Domestic environment
The environment in an organization's home country.

Foreign environment
The environment outside an organization's home country.

Macroenvironment
Broad societal forces that shape the activities of every business and nonprofit marketer. The physical environment, sociocultural forces, demographic factors, economic factors, scientific and technical knowledge, and political and legal factors are components of the macroenvironment.

e x h i b i **3-1**

Forces in Both the Domestic and the Foreign Environments Influence the Marketing Mix

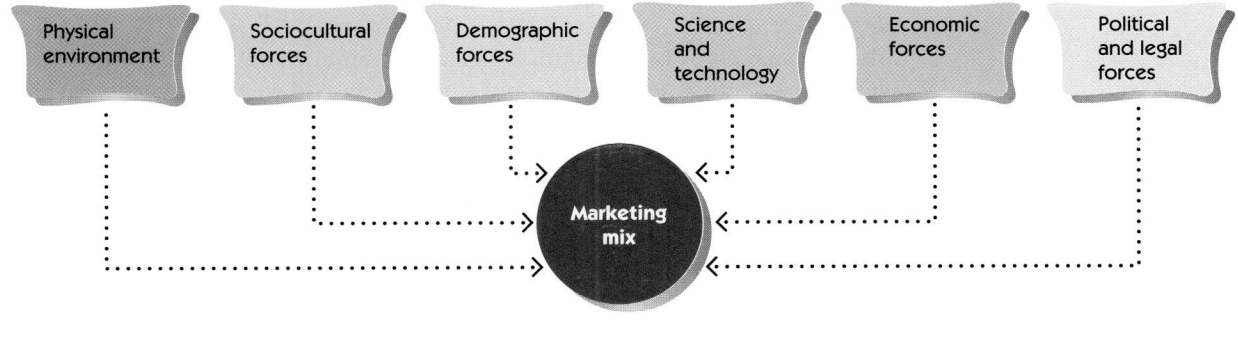

Macroenvironment Influences on the Marketing Mix

microenvironment consisting of its customers and the economic institutions that shape its marketing practices.

The discussion in this chapter describes the macroenvironment. Chapter 4 deals with the more direct domestic and global influences that comprise the microenvironment. The macroenvironment consists of the physical environment, sociocultural forces, demographic forces, scientific and technical knowledge, economic forces, and political and legal forces. (See Exhibit 3-2.)

Microenvironment
Environmental forces, such as customers, that directly and regularly influence a marketer's activity.

The Physical Environment

The **physical environment** consists of natural resources, such as minerals and animal populations, and other aspects of the natural world, such as changes in ecological systems. The availability of natural resources may have a direct and far-reaching impact on marketing activities in a geographic region. Areas rich in petroleum, for example, may concentrate on the production and marketing of fuel oil, kerosene, benzene, naphtha, paraffin, and other products derived from this natural resource.

Marketing is influenced by many other aspects of the natural environment as well. Climate is one example. It is not difficult to understand why umbrella sales are greater in rainy Seattle than in desert-like Tucson or why more winter clothing is sold in Minneapolis than in Miami.

Climate also greatly influences the timing of marketing activities. In India, more than 65 percent of all soft drinks are sold during the blazing hot months of June through September, for instance. Marketers adapt their strategies to such environmental differences. Kmart, for example, identifies every item stocked in its stores by climate. It knows that climate influences not only what is purchased but when. Grass seed, insect sprays, snow shovels, and many other goods must be in the right stores at the correct time of year.

Finally, consideration of the physical environment of marketing must include an awareness of activities or substances harmful to the earth's ecology. Smog, acid rain, and pollution of the ocean are among the many issues in this category. Such issues are highly interrelated with aspects of the sociocultural environment.

Ford's Focus automobile offers an example of an inventive ecological marketing strategy. The Ford factory in Saarlouis, Germany shreds denim jeans, then packs the treated fabric under the hood of every Focus as sound-deadening material. Marketing ecologically safe products and making efforts, as Ford does, to help preserve or revitalize the physical environment is often called **green marketing.**

Physical environment
Natural resources and other aspects of the natural world that influence marketing activities.

Green marketing
Marketing ecologically safe products and promoting activities beneficial to the physical environment.

Sociocultural Forces

Every society has a culture that guides everyday life. In the environment of marketing, the word **culture** refers not to classical music, art, and literature but to social institutions, values, beliefs, and behaviors. Culture includes everything people learn as members of a society, but does not include the basic drives with which people are born.

Culture is shaped by humankind. It is learned rather than innate. For example, people are born with a need to eat—but what, when, and where they eat, and whether they season their food with ketchup or curdled goat's milk, is learned from a particular culture. Similarly, the fact that many U.S. women are free from traditional restraints, whereas few Saudi women are, is a cultural phenomenon. Material artifacts and the symbolic meanings associated with them also vary by culture.

VALUES AND BELIEFS

A **social value** embodies the goals a society views as important and expresses a culture's shared ideas of preferred ways of acting. Social values reflect abstract ideas about what is good, right, and desirable (and bad, wrong, and undesirable). For example, we learn from those around us that it is wrong to lie or steal. The following social values reflect the beliefs of most people in the United States:

Freedom. The freedom of the individual to act as he or she pleases is a fundamental aspect of U.S. culture.

Achievement and success. The achievement of wealth and prestige through honest efforts is highly valued. Such achievement leads to a higher standard of living and improves the quality of life.

Work ethic. The importance of working on a regular basis is strongly emphasized. Those who are idle are considered lazy.

Equality. Most Americans profess a high regard for human equality, especially equal opportunity, and generally relate to one another as equals.

Patriotism/nationalism. Americans take pride in living in the "best country in the world." They are proud of their country's democratic heritage and its achievements.

Individual responsibility and self-fulfillment. Americans are oriented toward developing themselves as individuals. They value being responsible for their achievements. The U.S. Army's slogan "Be all that you can be" captures the essence of the desirability of personal growth.[3]

A **belief** is a conviction concerning the existence or the characteristics of physical and social phenomena. A person may believe, for example, that a high-fat diet causes cancer or that chocolate causes acne. Whether a belief is correct is not particularly important in terms of a person's actions. Even totally foolish beliefs may affect how people behave and what they buy.

It is the marketer's job to "read" the social environment and reflect the surrounding culture's values and beliefs in a marketing strategy. For example, a marketer might consider indications that American women's values about the importance of careers may be changing. Research has shown that many women believe that the stress caused by their multiple roles—wife, mother, career woman, nurse, chauffeur—is too intense. Social values are changing to play down work and to focus on family and on emotional enhancement of personal life. (An associated trend toward casual living and relaxed dress codes has caused the sales of sheer pantyhose to decline.) In the 21st century, American women will continue to work, but they will be more interested in leisure and in spending more time with family. Such changing

> It is the marketer's job to "read" the social environment and reflect the surrounding culture's values and beliefs in a marketing strategy.

Culture
The institutions, values, beliefs, and behaviors of a society; everything people learn, as opposed to the basic drives with which people are born.

Social value
A value that embodies the goals a society views as important and expresses a culture's shared ideas of preferred ways of acting.

Belief
A conviction concerning the existence or the characteristics of physical and social phenomena.

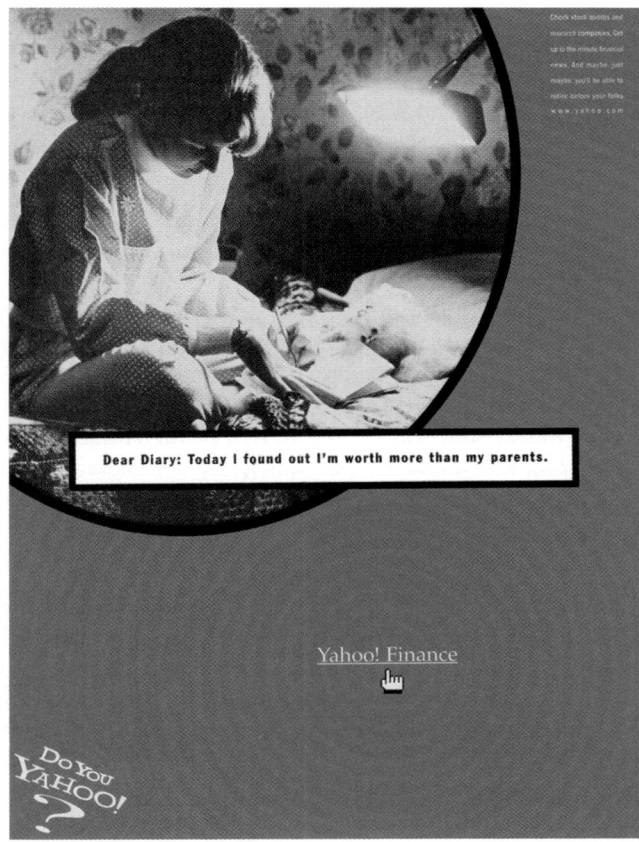

Dear Diary: Today I found out I'm worth more than my parents.

Yahoo! Finance

DO YOU YAHOO!?

social values could result in more spending on products that offer fantasy, romance, humor, and fun.

Values and beliefs vary from culture to culture. Understanding why people in foreign countries behave and react as they do is discussed in Chapter 4. In fact, because social values have such a pervasive impact on marketing, they are discussed in almost every chapter in this book.

Demographics

The terms *demography* and *demographics* come from the Greek word *demos,* meaning "people" (as does the word *democracy*). **Demography** may be defined as the study of the size, composition (for example, by age or racial group), and distribution of the human population in relation to social factors such as geographic boundaries. The size, composition, and distribution of the population in any geographic market will clearly influence marketing. Because demographic factors are of great concern to marketing managers, we discuss some basic demographic information and trends in this section. A wealth of demographic statistics for the United States can be found in the *Statistical Abstract of the United States* (http://www.census.gov/prod/www/statistical-abstract-us/html) or in other sources on the Internet.[4]

Demography
The study of the size, composition, and distribution of the human population in relation to social factors such as geographic boundaries.

THE U.S. POPULATION

The population of the United States is constantly changing. If marketers are to satisfy the wants and needs of that population, they must be aware of the changes that are occurring and the directions in which these changes are moving the population.

The U.S. Bureau of the Census estimated that there were 274 million people living in the United States when the 21st century began on January 1, 2000. It has been predicted that the population will reach 300 million in the year 2011. (Go to http://www.census.gov/population/www/projections/natproj.html for a wealth of data about population projections.) The U.S. birth rate is 14.6 per thousand, and the death rate is 8.6 per thousand. The birth rate is expected to continue to decline. About 51.2 percent of the population is female, and about 48.8 percent is male.[5]

Migration Migration has always been an overwhelmingly important demographic factor in the United States. Much attention has been paid to the effect of Cuban and Haitian migrations into southern Florida and the general migration into the Sunbelt states. However, migration into and around the country has been going on for hundreds of years.

The center of population is represented by the intersection of two lines, one dividing the population equally into a northern and a southern half and the other, into an eastern and a western half. The 1790 U.S. census showed the center of population to be 23 miles east of Baltimore, Maryland. In 1790 the population center was actually under the waters of the Atlantic Ocean, because virtually the entire population of the country was concentrated along the East coast and the coastline is curved. The 1990 census moved the population center to Crawford County, Missouri, near Cherryville. Each census since 1790 has moved the point farther south and west.

Urbanization The United States—and, in fact, the entire world—has become increasingly urbanized since the nineteenth century. In the United States, the expansion of some metropolitan areas has brought neighboring cities and their suburbs so close together that they have, for all practical purposes, merged. Two examples of this phenomenon are the string of communities stretching from north of Los Angeles to Tijuana, Mexico, and the Northeast Corridor, which extends from Boston to Washington, D.C.

In fact, the 1990 census showed that more than half of the people in the United States live in the 39 metropolitan areas (that is, central cities and suburbs) with populations of more than 1 million. Approximately 80 percent live in the nation's metropolitan areas—up from 56 percent in 1950.

Growth in U.S. metropolitan areas has not meant growth in the central cities. Crowded conditions, high crime rates, and other discomforts associated with city life, coupled with the great numbers of private cars owned by Americans, have encouraged the much-discussed "flight to the suburbs" of people seeking to enjoy a blend of country and city living. It is growth in suburban areas that has caused the populations of metropolitan areas to remain stable and even to rise. Indeed, the most dramatic growth of the past decade was in the suburbs.[6] Many of these suburbs, such as Palo Alto, California, have become so large that they are in essence cities in themselves. Many citizens of these "second cities" work near their homes and do not commute into the older metropolitan areas to work or shop.

Baltimore, Maryland is part of the urban area known as the Northeast Corridor, which extends from Boston to Washington, D.C. As this area has become increasingly urbanized, the suburbs of cities such as Annapolis, Maryland, have become "second cities" with high population densities.

State Populations: Percent Change, 1990–1998, and Other Demographic Facts[7]

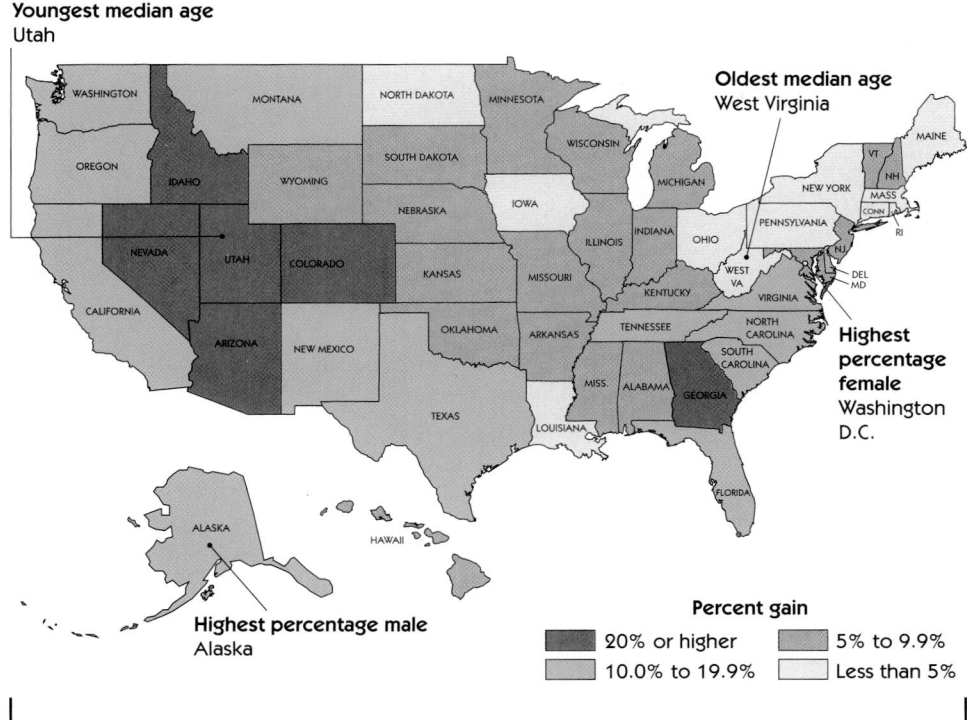

Growth in the Sunbelt   Exhibit 3-3 shows state population change between the years 1990 and 1998. The states of the southern and western United States, sometimes called the Sunbelt, grew most rapidly during the past two decades. Between the 1980 and 1990 censuses, almost all (87 percent) of the net gain in the U.S. population was in the South and West. Between 1990 and 1995, more than 4 million people immigrated to the United States from other countries, and more than half of these people (54 percent) went to California, Texas, and Florida.

California, the most populous state, held the rank of fifth-fastest-growing state in 1990, but dropped to eighteenth during the 1990–1998 period, when it grew by just 9.7 percent. This growth occurred despite California's heavy out-migration—that is, despite the fact that many Californians moved to other states. In fact, California lost more from out-migration than it gained from migration of people from other states into California.[8] Texas grew by 16.3 percent, and New York grew by only 1 percent. Nevada, Idaho, Utah, and Colorado showed the highest percentage rates of population growth. (However, the rate of population growth can be somewhat misleading; these states have always been, and continue to be, small in terms of population in spite of high growth rates.)

It is important to remember that long-term trends reflect the past and not necessarily the future. For example, as suggested earlier, it appears that the vast migration of people from other states to California is over.

Age and Generations   When the very first U.S. census was taken in 1790, the median age of the population was only 16 years. Today, the median age is 35.2 years. That means that half the population is older and half younger than 35.2.

GENERATION	YEAR BORN	AGE IN 2000	U.S. POPULATION	PERCENTAGE OF U.S. POPULATION
Seniors				
GI Generation	Pre–1930	71+	25.3	9.1%
Depression	1930–1939	61–70	17.8	6.5
War Babies	1940–1945	55–60	15.6	5.7
Baby Boomers	1946–1964	36–54	77.4	28.2
Generation X	1965–1976	24–35	44.9	16.4
Generation Y	1977–1994	6–23	70.7	25.8
Millennials	1995+	0–5	22.9	8.3

A consumer's age category—or, as demographers say, age cohort—has a major impact on his or her spending behavior. Teenagers spend a great deal of money on movies, soft drinks, and fast foods, for example. Many senior citizens spend a lot on travel and prescription drugs. Understanding the age distribution of the population helps marketers anticipate future trends. Exhibit 3-4 shows the distribution of U.S. generations by age for 2000.

The U.S. population has been growing older in recent decades, and this trend is expected to continue. The trend has occurred for two reasons. One is a lowering of the death rate, and the other is aging of the "baby boomers." The lowering of the death rate means that more people are living longer today. The average life expectancy in the United States has increased to 76 years, and people over 65 years of age constitute one of the fastest-growing segments of the population. Many of these senior citizens do not fit the stereotype of an oldster sitting in a rocking chair waiting for a Social Security check. They are healthy and active, with sufficient finances to enjoy sports, entertainment, international travel, and other things they may have denied themselves while raising families. Some estimates indicate that nearly half of all savings account interest is earned by people over 65. This fact has particular significance to bank marketers but should be considered by all other marketers as well. The "graying of America" has been as potent an influence on U.S. marketing as was the baby boom of years past.

The *baby boom* is the name for the tremendous increase in births that occurred in the United States between 1946 and 1965, in the 20 years following World War II. Four out of every ten adults are baby boomers. The impact of the baby boom age cohort on U.S. society has been far-reaching, and as these consumers age, they should continue to exert a major influence on marketing strategies for many goods and services. By 2000, all baby boomers were over 35 years old, and many were in their mid-50s. These are the peak earning and spending years. This entry of baby boomers into middle age is having a major impact on marketers of investment plans for retirement, health care services, and products such as Centrum Silver vitamins.

Seniors and baby boomers have received a great deal of attention, but other age cohorts should not be overlooked. The generation of Americans born between 1965 and 1976, who grew up with television as a central influence in their lives, is often called *Generation X*. Generation X is smaller than the baby boom generation. Nevertheless, the 45 million young adults born between 1965 and 1976 make up the second-largest group of adults in U.S. history. This self-reliant, entrepreneurial, and socially tolerant generation overtakes baby boomers as a primary market for most product categories in 2001.

Another group of consumers came into being between 1977 and 1994, when adult baby boomers who had postponed starting families began having children, creating an "echo" of the baby boom, or a baby "boomlet."[10] Because the oldest members of this group are just in their early 20s, demographers have not settled on a universally accepted name. We will use the term *Generation Y,* but they are also known as Echo Boomers. The more than 70 million in this generation, who are growing up very accustomed to computers and the Internet, are going to have a major impact on American marketing. The *Millennium Generation* is the name for young children.

The effects of the Generation Y baby boomlet can be illustrated by focusing on education. After years of decline, America's elementary school enrollment began rising in 1985 and continues to do so today. By the fall of 1999, there were 53.2 million children enrolled in public and private school.[11] Think of the implications for the marketers of scissors, construction paper, and school glue! College enrollments in the 1999/2000 academic year set a record, at almost 15 million. The growth in the pre-teen and teenage groups has tremendous implications for the marketing of entertainment media, music, consumer electronics, fashion items, and many other products. Generation Y represents a sizable pool of people who will, in 10 or 15 years, be forming households and having and raising children. They will then constitute prime markets for homes, furniture, appliances, and other durable products.

Profile of the "Average American Consumer" What is the "average American consumer" like? Because of the many variables involved, there is no true average American. But it is interesting to try to paint a picture of one. First, there are more women than men in the United States, so the average American is female. And as we mentioned earlier, the median age of Americans is 35.2. The median number of years of schooling in the United States is 12.7. Thus, the "average American" is a woman about 35 years old with a high school education and perhaps a year of college.

The Changing American Household What is the typical U.S. household like? Father, mother, and two children? Wrong! Fewer than 10 percent of all households include husband, wife, and exactly two children. Married couples with any number of children account for only one-fourth of all households. Single-parent households and households composed of unmarried individuals have proliferated in the past 20 years. In 1998, there were almost 100 million U.S. households—up from 81 million in 1980. The number of people in the average household declined from 3.14 in 1970 to 2.76 persons in 1980 and 2.63 persons in 1990.

Single-Person and Single-Parent Households Single-person households—that is, people living alone—account for one of every four households, yet they constitute only 9 percent of the population. The fact that there are single-person households demonstrates that, although many people think a household is the same as a family, it need not be. A household is a dwelling unit occupied by a group of related people, a single person, or several unrelated people who share living quarters. Today, according to the Census Bureau, nonfamily households account for approximately 30 percent of all households.

There are several reasons for the increase in single-person households. More people than ever before have never been married, and young singles are remaining single longer. A high percentage of marriages end in divorce. The longer life expectancy of women means that widows constitute a sizable population segment; the number of households maintained by women with no husband present doubled between 1980 and 1990 (from 5.5 million to 10.7 million). An aging mother (or father) may live alone or may live in a retirement community that provides meal services and other assistance.

There are also single-parent households, which account for 27.3 percent of all households. Many of these are headed by women who are divorced or who have never married. (Approximately 28 percent of all U.S. births are to unmarried women.) But the number of single-parent households headed by men is growing

Many marketers are increasingly focusing their attention on Generation Y, the group defined as those born after 1977. Generation Y has grown up during prosperous times, experiencing a life of economic security and rapidly changing technology. They are a breed of computer-savvy youngsters who are unafraid of taking risks.

2.5 times as fast as the number headed by women. Buying behavior in a single-parent household may be different from that in the two-parent household. For example, a teenager may play the shopper role and have the primary responsibility for preparing meals.

Working Women   The advent of the modern career-oriented woman is, in itself, a major change in the American family. With increasing career orientation have come changes in the age at which women have children and in the numbers of women who choose not to have children at all.

The number of people in the work force has grown rapidly in the past decade and will continue to do so. The labor force grew from 128 million workers in 1993 to at least 137 million in 1998. By 2000, women represented 47 percent of the labor force. In more than 60 percent of married-couple households, both the husband and wife work, up from about 40 percent in 1960. Forecasters predicted that in 2000, fewer than 20 percent of all households would be "traditional" husband-wife households with only one partner employed outside the home.

Obvious changes in the marketplace reflect these developments: Many stores are open late at least one or two nights per week. Many retailers offer catalogs or Web sites that permit working people to shop at their convenience. Easily prepared microwave dinners are commonplace. Take-out food, whether from a restaurant or from the prepared-foods section of a supermarket, has gained great popularity.

Family and Household Income   The U.S. Bureau of the Census defines a family as a group of two or more persons related by birth, marriage, or adoption and residing together. The annual median family income in the United States was $47,469 in 1998, up from $29,943 in 1990 and from $21,023 in 1980.[12]

In 1998, 20 percent of U.S. households had incomes above $75,000, and 20 percent had incomes below $16,200. The top 5 percent had incomes above $132,000. More than two-thirds of all households earning more than $100,000 were headed by college graduates. The average annual income of college graduates was about double that of high school graduates who did not graduate from college.

In 1998, the wealthiest 20 percent of households earned almost 50 percent of all household income.[13]

The upper-income group has expanded, in part because of an increase in the number of affluent two-income married couples. Working wives contribute about 40 percent of family income. This affluent group has considerable discretionary income, and it has an impact on the market for luxury goods.

According to the IRS, about 40,000 Americans have $10 million or more in assets. Of these wealthy people, 27,000 had a net worth between $10 and $20 million and 13,000 were worth over $20 million. Many luxury products are targeted for this demographic group.

A Multicultural Population   The United States has a multicultural population—that is, a population made up of many different ethnic and racial groups. One out of every five U.S. residents is African American, Hispanic, Asian, Native American Indian, Eskimo, or a member of another minority group.[14] Census Bureau statistics show that in 1998, African Americans (Blacks) represented almost 13 percent of the U.S. population, Hispanic Americans about 11 percent, and Asian Americans about 4 percent. These three minorities account for approximately 34 million, 30 million, and 10 million people, respectively. (See Exhibit 3-5.) Native Americans account for less than 1 percent of the population.

The trend is clearly toward increased diversity. In the 1960s, nine out of ten Americans were white. Today, about three out of four Americans are non-Hispanic whites. Only a small percentage of immigrants are of European origin. Immigrants, along with Hispanic Americans and African Americans, tend to have more children than the non-Hispanic white population. If these immigration and birth-rate trends continue, the United States will continue to become increasingly diverse.

The Census Bureau has revealed some trends in the United States' multicultural population. Two trends are perhaps the most significant for the entire country:

- The number of Asians and Pacific Islanders living in the United States doubled between 1980 and 1990, increased by 35 percent between 1990 and 1998, and will double again by the year 2020.
- The number of Hispanic Americans is increasing. Many demographers have predicted that Hispanic Americans will replace African Americans (and other blacks) as the largest U.S. minority group before the year 2020.

The trend toward diversity and a multicultural society has had its greatest impact on certain regions of the country. For example, most of the growth in the Asian American population has been in California, and most of the growth in the Hispanic population has been in Florida, Texas, and California. In certain cities in these states, such as San Diego, non-Hispanic whites account for less than 50 percent of the population.

America's Growing Diversity[15]

e   x   h   i   b   i **3-5**

GROUP	PERCENT GROWTH 1990–1998	POPULATION IN MILLIONS, 1998	PERCENT OF TOTAL U.S. POPULATION
Blacks	13%	34.4	12.7%
Hispanics	9	30.3	11.0
Asian and Pacific Islanders	35	10.5	4.0

WORLD POPULATION

The world population exceeds 6 billion people. (See Exhibit 3-6.) Because markets consist of people willing and able to exchange something of value for goods and services, this total is of great marketing significance. However, the exponential growth of population, particularly in less developed countries, puts a heavy burden on marketing. The distribution of food, for instance, is a marketing problem whose solution may prove crucial to the survival of this planet. The world population is expected to grow by at least 140 million per year during the first decade of the 21st century. That's about 16,000 new people per hour. The United Nations estimates the world population will reach 8.9 billion in 2050.[16] However, marketers must also recognize that in certain regions of the world, such as western Europe, population is declining. Italians, for example, are marrying later, having babies later, and having fewer children.

> Vigorous international trade cannot be effectively implemented and maintained unless marketers concern themselves deeply with what is going on in "the rest of the world."

Although the bulk of this section has dealt with the demography of the U.S. market, it is important to remember that the future of both developed and developing economies is well served by vigorous international trade. Such trade cannot be effectively implemented and maintained unless marketers concern themselves deeply with what is going on in "the rest of the world." Three areas of the world—North America, Europe, and the Pacific Rim countries surrounding Japan—are economically important areas where global competition can be intense. They will receive special attention in our discussions throughout this book.

e x h i b i 3-6

World Population Growth

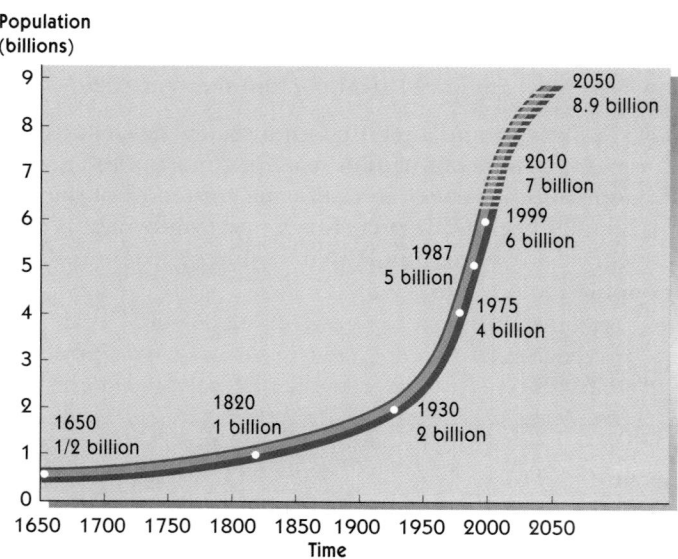

Science and Technology

Although the two terms are sometimes used interchangeably, **science** is the accumulation of knowledge about human beings and the environment, and **technology** is the application of such knowledge for practical purposes. Thus, the discovery that certain diseases can be prevented by immunization is a scientific discovery, but how and when immunization is administered is a technological issue.

Like other changes in the macroenvironment, scientific and technological advances can revolutionize an industry or destroy one. Examples of organizations that suffered because they did not adapt to changing technology are easy to find. Western Union's telegrams, which were sent by an electromechanical device, were made obsolete by telephones, computers, and fax machines. More recently, Atari and several other marketers of video games fell victim to competitors, such as Sony Playstation and Nintendo, that were more technologically advanced, with higher-performance microprocessors.

DIGITAL TECHNOLOGY AND THE INTERNET: CHANGING EVERYTHING

Historians and anthropologists have pointed out that technological innovations can change more than the way business is done in an industry. Indeed, major technological innovations can change entire cultures. For example, the mechanical clock made regular working hours possible.[17] The invention of the steam engine and railroads and the mass production of automobiles changed the way people thought about distance—the words *near* and *far* took on new meaning.[18] Television changed the way people think about news and entertainment.[19]

"Today's computer technology can be characterized by the phrase *digital convergence.* Almost all industries, professions, and trades are being pulled closer together by a common technological bond: the digitizing of the work product into the ones and zeros of computer language."[20] Digital technology, especially the Internet, is having such a profound impact on marketing and society that it deserves special attention.[21]

THE INTERNET

The **Internet** is a worldwide network of computers that gives users access to information and documents from distant sources. People using the Internet may be viewing information stored on a host computer halfway around the world. The **World Wide Web (WWW)** refers to a system of Internet servers, computers supporting a retrieval system that organizes information into Hypertext documents called Web pages. (Hypertext is a computer language that allows the linking and sharing of information in different formats. HTTP [HyperText Transfer Protocol] is the most commonly used method for transferring and displaying information formatted in either HTML [HyperText Markup Language] or XML [Extensible Markup Language] on the Internet.)

In our prologue, we said that the Internet is transforming society. Time is collapsing. Distance is no longer an obstacle. "Instantaneous" has a new meaning. Our intent was to impress on the reader that the Internet is the most important communication medium to come along since television. The Internet, as a new medium for our new era, is a macroenvironmental force that is having a profound impact.

We are among those who believe that the Internet is changing everything—especially commerce. We firmly believe that e-commerce is the business model for the new millennium and that marketing's role has been changed forever by the Internet. This does not mean that the familiar neighborhood brick-and-mortar stores and all traditional marketing institutions like shopping centers will disappear, but it does mean that they will adapt and change as new forms of Internet marketing become more prevalent.

> The Internet is changing everything—especially commerce.

Science
The accumulation of knowledge about humans and the environment.

Technology
The application of science for practical purposes.

Internet
A worldwide network of private, corporate, and government computers that gives users access to information and documents from distant sources.

World Wide Web (WWW)
A portion of the Internet; a system of Internet servers—computers that support specially formatted documents.

The scientific discovery that prolonged exposure to the sun can cause skin cancer certainly affected suntan lotion marketers. Similarly, the knowledge that aspirin may help reduce the risk of heart attack has led to changes in the advertising messages for this product.

PORTALS

As you probably know, over the past few years, most major corporations, government agencies, universities, newspapers, TV networks, and libraries have set up e-mail systems and Web sites. The introductory page, or opening screen, of a Web site is called the *home page*. The home page provides basic information about the purpose of the Web site, along with a "menu" of selections, or links, that lead to other screens with more specific information. Thus, each page can have connections, or hyperlinks, to other pages, which may be on the organization's own computer or on any computer connected to the Internet.

The Internet can be thought of as the world's largest public library. This means that the Internet user can be faced with a retrieval and filtering burden—it takes time to search various Web sites and determine if the information you want is there. To solve this problem, many companies such as Yahoo!, Excite, AltaVista, and NBCi have established themselves as portals to the Internet. A **portal** is a Web site that offers a broad array of resources and services, such as news services, search engines, e-mail, discussion forums, and online shopping. The first portals were online service providers (for example, America Online), but now most service providers with search engines have transformed themselves into Web portals. Many marketers view the portal business as a media business that can attract and retain a larger audience. Advertising, which pays the bills and thus allows a company access to an audience, is prevalent on portals (and many other Web sites). In Internet jargon, attracting *eyeballs* (visitors who view the Web site) and maintaining *stickiness* (having people spend a substantial amount of time at the site) are important goals for developers of portals and other marketers who understand the Internet's role as an advertising medium. During one week in May 2000, Yahoo! had 24,050,718 visitors to its Web site, who spent an average of 27 minutes and 35 seconds at the site. In contrast, eBay had 4,464,678 visitors to its site, but the average time spent on the site was 51 minutes and 14 seconds.[22]

Portal
A Web site that offers a broad array of resources and services, such as news services, search engines, e-mail, discussion forums, and online shopping.

PERSONALIZED CONTENT ON WEB SITES

Today's information technology allows marketers to deliver personalized content to a computer user's desktop. Computer software known as "smart agents" or "intelligent agents" can find information without the user's participation and then store text, images, and links on the user's computer for later viewing. These smart information delivery systems (known by a variety of technical names, including *push phase technology*) are capable of learning an Internet user's preferences and automatically searching out information at selected Web sites and then distributing this information. Smart information delivery allows a portal Web site to become a one-on-one medium for each individual user. MyYahoo, MyExcite, and MyAltaVista are portal services that personalize Web pages. Users can get stock quotes on their investment portfolios, news about favorite sports teams, local weather, and other personalized information. Users can customize the sections of the service they want delivered. Many Web sites, such as Amazon.com, include technology that allows personalized online shopping.

TRACKING WEB ACTIVITY

Personalized information delivery systems may use surveys of customer preferences, or they may use "cookies." **Cookies,** or "magic cookies," are small computer files that a content provider can download onto the computer of someone who visits the provider's Web site. Cookies allow the Web site computer to record a user's visit, then track other Web sites that person visits, and store this info in a file

e—commerce | Changing Everything

There's a revolution under way in the music world that will eventually change the way people buy, carry, and listen to their favorite songs.[23] MP3, short for Moving Pictures Expert Group Audio Layer 3, is a way of compressing digital music so that it takes up far less space on a computer's hard disk. MP3 stores audio files on a computer in such a way that the compressed digital file is relatively small, but the song sounds near perfect.[24] MP3 technology allows songs to be "ripped" from CDs or downloaded from the Internet. Thousands of MP3 songs are distributed free over the Internet.

MP3 and other new technologies for compressing digital music are providing marketing opportunities for companies such as RealNetworks. The company calls its RealJukebox software the first complete digital music system that turns PCs into the best way to listen to music. Ten days after RealNetworks introduced RealJukebox, one million Internet users had downloaded the software, making it the most quickly accepted software product in history.[25] Within months, more than five million users had downloaded RealJukebox.

Several companies make portable MP3 players. Creative Labs' Nomad MP3 Player is magnesium-cased, is smaller than a pack of cigarettes, and weighs less than 2.5 ounces. Songs recorded in MP3 format on a Windows 95/98 PC hard disk can be easily transferred with a few mouse clicks to a Nomad connected to the computer. Its memory—half built-in, the other half on a removable postage-stamp-size flash memory card—holds about 2 hours of music. The more sophisticated Nomad Jukebox portable music player has its own hard drive, which allows it to store the music equivalent to the contents of 150 CDs. How good is the quality? Only golden-eared listeners would hear the difference (or care to) between the player's sound and that of a portable CD player.[26]

that uses an identification code embedded in the cookie in place of the person's name (which in most cases the company that owns the Web site never knows). For example, if you look up a weather report at a Time Warner Pathfinder Web site such as http://www.fortune.com by keying in a zip code, the Web site computer notes where you live (or maybe where you wish you lived!). The computer then notes what else you look up—perhaps stock quotes (though Time Warner does not make note of specific stocks). If you visit the Tech Guide, the cookie will record your interest in technology. Then, the next time you visit this Web site, computer software might serve up an ad for a modem or an online brokerage firm or a restaurant in Mountain View, California, depending on what the computer's managed to learn.[27]

Cookies
Small computer files (downloaded onto the computer of someone who visits a provider's Web site) that track and record a user's visit.

RICH MEDIA AND STREAMING CONTENT

Rich media technology and streaming media programming allow users to access visuals and sound effects on the Internet. (Unfortunately, the word "technology" is often left off in discussions about rich media technology, leaving a phrase that could be misleading.) Yahoo!'s Broadcast.com is a leading aggregator and broadcaster of streaming media programming on the Web, with the network infrastructure and expertise to deliver, or "stream," hundreds of live and on-demand audio and video programs over the Internet to hundreds of thousands of users. The Broadcast.com Web site on Yahoo! Business Services offers a large selection of programming, including sports, talk and music radio, television, business events, full-length CDs, news, and full-length audiobooks. Broadcast.com broadcasts on the Internet 24 hours a day, seven days a week, and its programming includes more than 370 radio stations and networks, 30 television stations and cable networks, and game broadcasts and other programming for over 420 college and professional sports teams.[28]

Currently, streaming media programming is in its infancy. As the technology improves, there will be more and more streaming media content available to

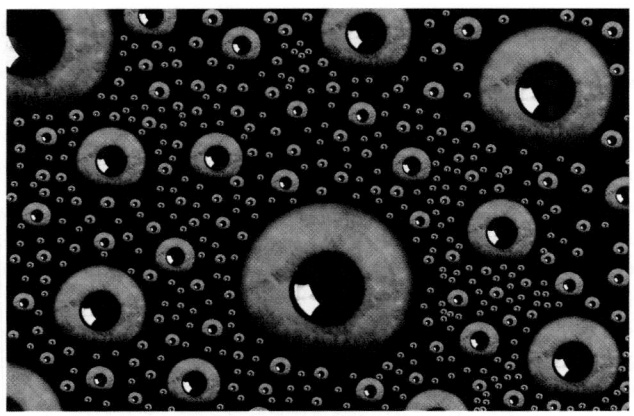

Providing access to an audience is one Internet business model. In Internet jargon, "counting eyeballs" refers to estimating the size of an audience. "Stickiness" refers to a Web site's ability to keep visitors at the Web site.

Internet users on demand. As you can see, the Internet is a new medium for our new era.

BASIC BUSINESS MODELS: HOW TO MAKE MONEY ON THE INTERNET

Several examples of Internet marketing have already been presented. Many additional examples and discussions of e-commerce will appear throughout this textbook. At this point, we will just briefly mention four basic Internet business models.[29]

Selling goods or services on line. Garden.com, discussed in Chapter 2, is an example of this type of business model. eBay's auctions and automatic downloads of software are other examples of this type of business model.

Providing access to an audience. America Online provides advertisers access to more than 25 million people.

Selling subscriptions to a Web site. A number of premium Web sites require subscription payments. For example, The *Wall Street Journal*'s interactive edition and TheStreet.com provide premium investment information that only subscribers can access.

Selling admissions. Some Internet events are like pay-per-view television events. As streaming media technology improves, this business model is likely to become more prevalent.

Many marketing activities, such as service delivery, automatic generation of newsletters, and customized advertising, require multidimensional business models with more complex Internet implications. We will cover these at the appropriate places in the textbook.

"We do all our business over the Internet."

As our discussion of the Internet illustrates, scientific and technological forces have a pervasive influence on the marketing of most goods and services. Because changes related to science and technology can have a major impact, organizations of all types must monitor these changes and adjust their marketing mixes to meet them.

Economic and Competitive Forces

Economic and competitive forces strongly influence marketing activity at all levels. In this section, we discuss macromarketing concerns—economic systems and general economic conditions. In Chapter 4, when we discuss the microenvironment, we will consider how competitive forces influence an individual firm's activities.

ECONOMIC SYSTEMS

A society's **economic system** determines how it will allocate its scarce resources. Traditionally, capitalism, socialism, and communism have been considered the world's major economic systems. In general, the western world's economies can be classified as modified capitalist systems. Under such systems, competition, both foreign and domestic, influences the interaction of supply and demand. Competition is often discussed in this context in terms of competitive market structures.

The competitive structure of a market is defined by the number of competing firms in some segment of an economy and the proportion of the market held by each competitor. Market structure influences pricing strategies and creates barriers to competitors wishing to enter a market. The four basic types of competitive market structure are *pure competition, monopolistic competition, oligopoly,* and *monopoly.*

Pure competition exists when there are no barriers to competition. The market consists of many small, competing firms and many buyers. This means that there is a steady supply of the product and a steady demand for it. Therefore, the price cannot be controlled by either the buyers or the sellers. The product itself is homogeneous—that is, one seller's offering is identical to all the others' offerings. The markets for basic food commodities, such as rice and mushrooms, approximate pure competition.

The principal characteristic of **monopolistic competition** is product differentiation—a large number of sellers offering similar products differentiated by only minor differences in, for example, product design, style, or technology. Firms engaged in monopolistic competition have enough influence on the marketplace to exert some control over their own prices. The fast-food industry provides a good example of monopolistic competition.

Oligopoly, the third type of market structure, exists where a small number of sellers dominate the market. Oligopoly is exemplified by the commercial aircraft industry, which is controlled by two large firms: Boeing and Airbus Industries. Getting established in an oligopoly like the commercial aircraft industry often requires a huge capital investment, which presents a barrier to new firms wishing to enter the industry. The distinguishing characteristic of an oligopoly, however, is not the size of the companies involved, as measured by assets or sales volume, but their control over the marketplace, as measured by market share. Each of the companies in an oligopoly has a strong influence on product offering, price, and market structure within the industry. The companies do not, however, generally compete on price.

Finally, markets with only one seller, such as a local telephone company or electric utility, are called monopolies. A **monopoly** exists in a market in which there are no suitable substitute products. Antitrust legislation strictly controls monopolies in the United States.

ECONOMIC CONDITIONS

Economic conditions around the world are obviously of interest to marketers. The most significant long-term trend in the U.S. economy has been the transition to a service economy. There has been a continuing shift of workers away from

Economic system
The system whereby a society allocates its scarce resources.

Pure competition
A market structure characterized by free entry, a homogeneous product, and many sellers and buyers, none of whom can control price.

Monopolistic competition
A market structure characterized by a large number of sellers offering slightly differentiated products and exerting some control over their own prices.

Oligopoly
A market structure characterized by a small number of sellers who control the market.

Monopoly
A market structure characterized by a single seller in a market in which there are no suitable substitute products.

manufacturing and into services, where almost 80 percent of U.S. jobs are to be found. This shift has greatly affected economic conditions as well as marketing activity.[30] The marketing of services is an important topic which is discussed throughout this book.

THE BUSINESS CYCLE

Business cycle

Recurrent fluctuations in general economic activity. The four phases of the business cycle are prosperity, recession, depression, and recovery.

The **business cycle** reflects recurrent fluctuations in general economic activity. The various booms and busts in the health of an economy influence unemployment, inflation, and consumer spending and saving patterns, which, in turn, influence marketing activity. The business cycle has four phases:

- Prosperity—the phase in which the economy is operating at or near full employment and both consumer spending and business output are high
- Recession—the downward phase, in which consumer spending, business output, and employment are decreasing
- Depression—the low phase, in which unemployment is highest, consumer spending is low, and business output has declined drastically
- Recovery—the upward phase, when employment, consumer spending, and business output are rising

Because marketing activity, such as the successful introduction of new products, is strongly influenced by the business cycle, marketing managers watch the economic environment closely. Unfortunately, the business cycle is not always easy to forecast. The phases of the cycle need not be equal in intensity or duration, and the contractions and expansions of the economy do not always follow a predictable pattern. Furthermore, not all economies of the world are in the same stage of the business cycle. So a single global forecast may not accurately predict activity in certain countries.

what went right?

Motorola   The fact that the average Chinese citizen does not own a telephone has worked to one company's advantage in an unexpected way. With so few telephones to be beckoned to, who could have guessed that the Chinese would go bonkers over that familiar summoning device—the pager? The passion spread so quickly in China during the nineties that Motorola was astonished. The answer to this mystery: Resourceful Chinese use the pager not as an accessory to the phone, but as a sort of primitive substitute for it. The conventional phone system has a penetration rate of some three to four lines for every 100 Chinese, meaning that even if you find a phone, the other party might not be in a position to receive your call. Only the well-heeled business person can surmount this annoyance with a costly cellular phone.

So native genius stepped into the breach. Chinese paging subscribers spontaneously devised a method of carrying code books, allowing them to interpret numeric messages flashed on their pagers: 75416, for example, might mean sell gravel at 6,500 yuan a ton or bring home a cabbage for dinner. Today's pagers have alphanumeric displays that read out short bursts of Chinese characters, eliminating the need for number codes. They also come in stylish packages, priced so a moderately successful worker can afford one: from about $120 for a basic model to $220 for one with a Chinese character readout. . . . There are some 14 million paging subscribers in China, probably half or more of them Motorola customers.[31]

Marketing strategies in a period of prosperity differ substantially from strategies in a period of depression. For example, products with "frills" and "extras" sell better during periods of prosperity than in periods when the economy is stagnant or declining. During periods of depression or recession, when consumers have less spending power, lower prices become more prominent considerations in spending decisions.

Politics and Laws

The **political environment**—the practices and policies of governments—and the **legal environment**—laws and regulations and their interpretation—affect marketing activity in several ways. First, they can limit the actions marketers are allowed to take—for example, by barring certain goods from leaving a country, as when Congress passed the Export Administration Act, which prohibited the export of strategic high-technology products to nations such as Iran and Libya. Second, they may require marketers to take certain actions. For instance, cookies called "chocolate chip cookies" are required to contain chips made of real chocolate, and the surgeon general's warning must appear on all cigarette packages. Last, policies and laws may absolutely prohibit certain actions by marketers—for example, the sale of products such as narcotic drugs and nuclear weapons—except under the strictest of controls. Political processes in other countries may have a dramatic impact on international marketers. For example, the dissolution of the former Soviet Union was an historic political action that totally changed the business climate and opened new markets in newly independent states such as Russia, Lithuania, and Ukraine. When the British ended their 156-year colonial control of Hong Kong in 1997, Hong Kong embarked on an uncertain new era under the sovereignty of Communist China. It remains to be seen how this major political change will affect marketers who do business in Hong Kong in the 21st century.

Developments in Rwanda illustrate how uncertain political situations are and how swiftly they can change. The movie *Gorillas in the Mist* inspired thousands of international tourists to travel to Rwanda to pay $170 per hour to observe mountain gorillas in the Varunga volcanoes. However, soon after the 1994 civil war in Rwanda began, virtually all international tourism stopped—and Rwanda lost the huge revenues that tourism had provided. Of course, not all political and legal influences involve dramatic changes like those in Rwanda. Laws, in particular, tend to have a stable, long-term influence on marketing strategy. For example, almost all countries with commercial airlines have long-standing bans on foreign ownership of these businesses.

Political environment
The practices and policies of governments.

Legal environment
Laws and regulations and their interpretation.

THREE LEVELS OF U.S. LAW

Legislation intended to maintain a competitive business environment, to protect consumers from dangerous products or unethical practices, and to preserve the natural environment can be found at the federal, state, and local levels. Because each of these levels has various departments, subdepartments, regulatory boards, and political subdivisions, such as counties and townships, it is possible that a single marketing organization could confront some 82,688 sets of laws and regulations.[32] When

Chinese parents are limited by government regulations to one child. As a result, Chinese parents—along with grandparents, great-grandparents, aunts, and uncles—are spoiling their children by showering them with everything from candy to toys to computer games. These only children, called Little Emperors, may not have brothers or sisters, but they benefit from the "six-pocket syndrome"—as many as six adults may be indulging the whims of each child.

In 1999 the California Prune Board sought a name change. It believes "dried plums" has a more positive connotation than "prunes." The labeling change required approval by the Food and Drug Administration.

Disney explored the possibility of building a theme park in Virginia to celebrate America's heritage, the company learned that its plans would be reviewed by more than 30 state, local, and federal agencies and it would have to obtain at least 72 permits.[33]

The Federal Level At the federal level of government, the U.S. Department of Justice, the Food and Drug Administration, the Federal Trade Commission, and many other agencies enforce a multitude of laws affecting business. The degree of specialization of some laws and agencies is suggested by the examples in Exhibit 3-7.

Much federal control involves **antitrust legislation,** which prohibits restraint of trade, monopolies, price fixing, price discrimination, deceptive practices, misrepresentations in the labeling of products, and other behavior that tends to lessen competition. The Sherman Antitrust Act (1890), the Clayton Act (1914), and the Federal Trade Commission Act (1914) are the major antitrust laws.

One major federal agency—the **Federal Trade Commission (FTC),** established in 1914—affects virtually all marketers on a regular basis. The FTC was given broad powers of investigation and jurisdiction over "unfair methods of competition." Initially, the FTC was to draft a fixed list of "unfair practices." It soon became clear that no list could be developed to cover all situations. Thus, though the FTC publishes guidelines and uses past decisions as precedents for solving current problems, each situation investigated by the FTC is judged individually. Marketing managers, therefore, face considerable uncertainty in trying to develop programs that can withstand FTC scrutiny. Examples of political and legal constraints on

Antitrust legislation
Federal laws meant to prohibit behavior that tends to lessen competition in U.S. markets. The major antitrust laws are the Sherman Antitrust Act (1890), the Clayton Act (1914), and the Federal Trade Commission Act (1914).

Federal Trade Commission (FTC)
Federal agency established in 1914 by the Federal Trade Commission Act to investigate and put an end to unfair methods of competition.

e x h i b i **3-7** Sample of Specialized Federal Legislation Affecting Business

LEGISLATION	MAJOR PROVISIONS
Federal Hazardous Substances Act (1960)	Requires warning labels on hazardous household chemicals
Kefauver-Harris Drug Amendment (1962)	Requires that manufacturers conduct tests to prove drug effectiveness and safety
Child Protection and Toy Safety Act (1969)	Prevents marketing of products so dangerous that adequate safety warnings cannot be given
Consumer Credit Protection Act (1968)	Requires that lenders fully disclose true interest rates and all other charges to credit customers for loans and installment purchases
Public Health Smoking Act (1970)	Prohibits cigarette advertising on TV and radio and revises the health hazard warning on cigarette packages
Poison Prevention Labeling Act (1970)	Requires safety packaging for products that may be harmful to children
Child Protection Act (1990)	Regulates the number of minutes of advertising on children's television
Telecommunications Act (1996)	Deregulation allows local and long-distance phone companies and other telecommunications companies to compete with each other

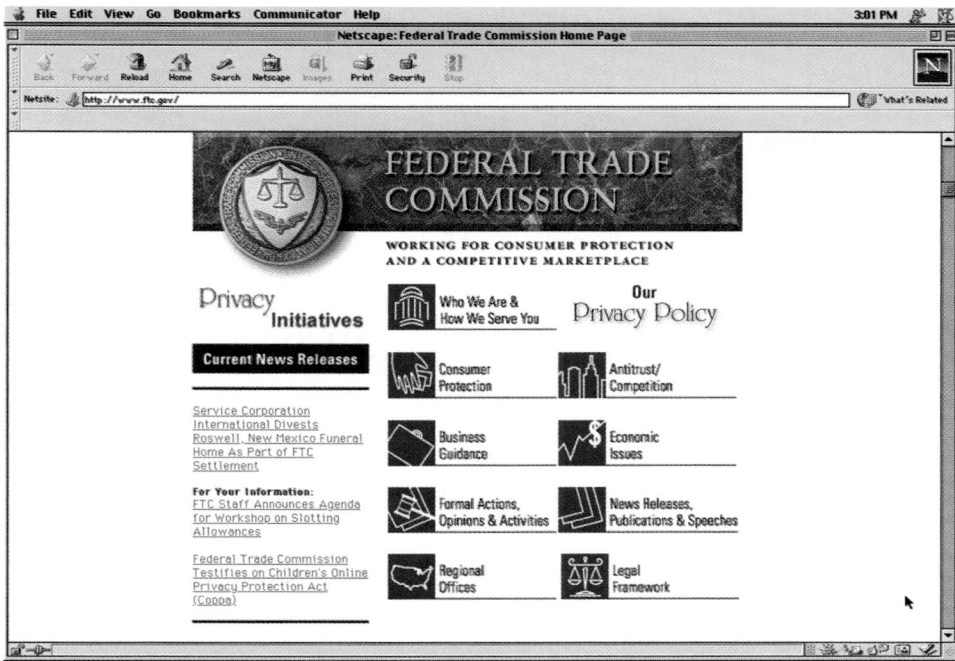

The Federal Trade Commission (FTC) enforces a variety of federal antitrust and consumer protection laws. It works to ensure that unfair or deceptive acts or practices do not occur.

http://www.ftc.gov

marketing are easy to find. For example, the Food and Drug Administration has ordered cosmetic companies, such as Avon, Revlon, and Estee Lauder, to stop claiming that their so-called anti-aging skin creams can "reverse aging or make basic underlying changes in the skin." According to the FDA, wording such as "rejuvenate, repair or renew skin" and "retard or counteract aging" could subject anti-aging creams to the same regulations as drugs, because it suggests that "a function or structure of the body will be affected by the product."[34]

It would be impossible to discuss all U.S. legislation dealing with marketing in this introductory treatment of the subject. Exhibit 3-8 summarizes selected federal legislation that affects most marketers. Additional milestone legislation affecting major portions of the marketing mix is discussed throughout the book.

The State Level   Most states have created laws and agencies that parallel those at the federal level. Most states have departments of agriculture, commerce, labor, and so on, and state-level consumer protection laws dealing with foods, manufactured goods, lending, real estate, banking, and insurance are commonplace.

All states have laws that can affect organizations' marketing mixes. Today, Jet Skis, Wave Runners, and other personal watercraft propelled by powerful jets of water can travel at speeds up to 60 miles per hour. With personal watercraft-related injuries and fatalities on the rise, states are beginning to regulate their use. The state of Oregon has imposed new water-bike speed limits as strict as 5 mph in certain circumstances. And other states are drafting laws controlling reckless riders. State laws are a powerful environmental force influencing marketing and consumer behavior.

The Local Level   Cities, townships, villages, and counties are all empowered to pass laws and ordinances and to create regulatory agencies. In most areas, health department inspectors check restaurants and motels, weights and measures inspectors check to ensure that scales are honest, and city and county prosecutors investigate misleading and unfair business practices. Local zoning laws affect where businesses such as meat processors, wholesalers, and retailers may be

ACT	PURPOSE
Sherman Antitrust Act (1890)	Prohibits combinations, contracts, or conspiracies to restrain trade or monopolize
Clayton Act (1914)	Prohibits price discrimination, exclusive dealer arrangements, and interlocking directorates that lessen competition
Federal Trade Commission Act (1914)	Created the FTC and gave it investigatory powers
Robinson-Patman Act (1936)	Expanded Clayton Act to prohibit sellers from offering different deals to different customers
Wheeler-Lea Act (1938)	Expanded powers of FTC to prevent injuries to competition before they occur
Celler-Kefauver Act (1950)	Expanded Clayton Act to prohibit acquisition of physical assets as well as capital stock in another corporation when the effect is to injure competition
Magnuson-Moss Act (1975)	Grants the FTC the power to determine rules concerning warranties and provides the means for class action suits and other forms of redress
Consumer Goods Pricing Act (1975)	Repealed "fair-trade" laws and prohibited price maintenance agreements among producers and resellers
Fair Debt Collection Act (1980)	Requires creditors to act responsibly in debt collection (e.g., bans false statements) and makes harassment of debtors illegal
FTC Improvement Act (1980)	Provides Congress with the power to veto the FTC industrywide Trade Regulation Rules (TRR) and limits the power of the FTC
Federal Antitampering Act (1983)	Prohibits tampering with a product and threats to tamper with a product
Americans with Disabilities Act (1990)	Prohibits discrimination against consumers with disabilities (e.g., stores and hotels must be accessible to shoppers or guests who use wheelchairs)
Nutritional Labeling and Education Act (1990)	Requires that certain nutritional facts be printed on food product labels
North American Free Trade Agreement (1993)	Allows for free trade between U.S., Mexico, and Canada without tariffs and trade restrictions
Millennium Digital Commerce Bill (1999)	Ensures that contracts will not be denied the legal effect that they otherwise would have under state law solely because they are in electronic form or because they were signed electronically
Electronic Signatures Law (2000)	An act to regulate interstate commerce by electronic means by permitting and encouraging the continued expansion of electronic commerce through the operation of free-market forces and other purposes

located. Local government units may tax some products but not others, require that certain stores be closed on Sunday, or, as in New York City, legislate that all bars must be closed for at least 1 hour a day and all customers removed from the premises. A common local control on marketing is the issuing of vendors' licenses. In most cases, the licenses are not sold to make money for local governments, although this can be a factor, especially in the case of liquor licenses. The major reason for licensing is so that licenses can be denied to organizations that violate laws or local customs.

Marketing is not only constrained by the legal environment; it can be helped by it as well. For example, retailers use laws to help protect themselves against shoplifting.

INTERNATIONAL LAWS

Companies operating their businesses in global markets must pay attention to international laws and the laws of foreign lands. Laws and legal systems that govern the marketing of products in foreign countries vary tremendously. For example, in Brazil, advertisers found guilty of harming or misleading consumers may be fined up to $500,000 or given a prison sentence of up to 5 years. This is a harsh punishment by U.S. standards. The rules of competition, trademark rights, price controls, product quality laws, and a number of other legal issues in individual countries may be of immense importance to a global marketer, such as Coca-Cola.

Furthermore, not only individual countries, but also multinational bodies, have legal systems to deal with international commerce. **Multinational marketing groups** are groups of countries aligned to form a unified market with minimal trade and tariff barriers among participating member countries. An example is the European Union. The European Parliament and the Court of Justice deal with legal issues for the European Union.

Time is an overarching environmental factor, as each environmental factor changes over time. Some, like technology, are highly sensitive to change. Others, like culture, change more slowly.

Multinational marketing group
A group of countries aligned to form a unified market with minimal trade and tariff barriers among participating member countries.

Summary

All organizations are influenced by the environments in which they operate.

1) Describe the domestic and foreign environments in which marketers operate and their effects on organizations.

Marketing managers must adjust an organization's marketing mix to cope with the domestic environment and often foreign environments as well. In both cases, the marketing environment consists of uncontrollable forces that provide opportunities and constraints. The environment can be divided into two categories: the macroenvironment and the microenvironment. The macroenvironment includes the physical environment, sociocultural forces, demographic forces, science and technology, economic forces, and politics and laws. The microenvironment consists of forces directly influencing the marketer, such as customers. Correct environmental assessment makes marketing decisions more successful.

2) Understand that the physical environment influences marketing activity.

The physical environment consists of natural resources, such as minerals and animal populations, and other aspects of the natural world, such as changes in ecological systems. Climate or the availability of natural resources may have a direct and far-reaching impact on marketing activities in a geographic region.

3) Understand that social values and beliefs are important cultural forces.

A social value embodies the goals a society views as important and expresses a culture's shared ideas of preferred ways of acting. A belief is a conviction concerning something's existence or characteristics. It is the marketer's job to "read" the social environment and reflect the surrounding culture's values and beliefs in a marketing strategy.

4) Explain how demographic trends, such as changes that have occurred in the American family, influence marketers.

Important demographic trends include the aging of the population, a general trend toward having fewer children, an increase in the number of households, and greater cultural diversity. These and other demographic factors not only affect the demand for goods and services but also lead to variations in pricing, distribution, and promotion.

5) Understand that technology, especially digital technology and the Internet, are having a significant impact on marketing and society.

Scientific and technological advances can revolutionize an industry or destroy one. The Internet is reshaping the way business is conducted around the world. The advent of portals as media businesses and the development of streaming media technology have been of particular significance. The basic models for doing business over the Internet are selling goods or services online, providing access to an audience, selling subscriptions to a Web site, and selling admissions.

6) Explain the various ways in which economic conditions influence marketers.

The competitive structure of a market is defined by the number of competing firms in some segment of an economy and the proportion of the market held by each competitor. Pure competition, monopolistic competition, oligopoly, and monopoly are the four basic market structures, and they have different influences on pricing strategies and barriers to competition. The business cycle—prosperity, recession, depression, and recovery—reflects recurrent fluctuations in general economic activity. The various booms and busts in the economy influence unemployment, inflation, and consumer spending and savings patterns, which, in turn, influence marketing activity.

7) Appreciate how the three levels of U.S. law and the laws of other nations can influence marketing activity.

Federal laws control many business activities, such as pricing and advertising by manufacturers, wholesalers, and retailers. The FTC, in particular, affects almost all marketers. State laws also deal with many areas of business, including foods, manufactured goods, lending, real estate, banking, and insurance. Local laws affect zoning and licensing, among other things. Laws that govern the marketing of products in foreign countries and in multinational marketing groups vary tremendously and will affect any organization that engages in international marketing.

Key Terms

antitrust legislation (p. 78)
belief (p. 62)
business cycle (p. 76)
cookies (p. 73)
culture (p. 62)
demography (p. 63)
domestic environment (p. 60)
economic system (p. 75)
Federal Trade Commission (FTC)
   (p. 78)

foreign environment (p. 60)
green marketing (p. 61)
Internet (p. 71)
legal environment (p. 77)
macroenvironment (p. 60)
microenvironment (p. 61)
monopolistic competition (p. 75)
monopoly (p. 75)
multinational marketing group
   (p. 81)

oligopoly (p. 75)
physical environment (p. 61)
political environment (p. 77)
portal (p. 72)
pure competition (p. 75)
science (p. 71)
social value (p. 62)
technology (p. 71)
World Wide Web (WWW) (p. 71)

Questions for Review & Critical Thinking

1. What domestic and foreign environmental factors might have the greatest influence on each of the following firms?
   a. General Motors
   b. McDonald's
   c. Starbucks (coffee)
   d. Humana Hospitals
2. What impact would the development of efficient solar energy have on each of the following industries?
   a. The housing industry
   b. The automobile industry
   c. Another industry of interest to you
3. Evaluate Americans' continuing concern for physical fitness from the point of view of each of the following:
   a. A manufacturer of packaged foods
   b. A leasing agent for an office building
   c. A maker of athletic shoes and clothing

4. World population is rising much more quickly than the U.S. population. What opportunities does this present to U.S. marketers? What constraints?
5. What is a household? What do you predict will be the nature of households in the year 2010?
6. Ethnic or racial groups are often served by small companies, such as makers of specialty foods. Why might a large firm such as Procter & Gamble, Toyota, or Miller Brewing Company avoid marketing to such groups?
7. What businesses would be influenced if a fire destroyed a telephone switching station and it took two weeks to get local service working?
8. What U.S. states seem to be bellwether states— that is, states that exhibit macroenvironmental trends before the rest of the country does?
9. Are economic forces the most important environmental influences on marketing activities?

10. The text mentioned that, over the course of history, the development of new technologies, such as the steam engine and the automobile, has profoundly changed the marketplace. What technologies are the driving forces changing today's marketplace?

11. What laws are unique to your state?

12. How much can marketers control political and legal influences on the marketing mix?

13. Form small groups as directed by your instructor. As a group, come to a consensus on the five environmental factors that will most strongly influence an industry designated by your instructor. Discuss as a class the groups' conclusions and how each group came to a consensus.

 **e—exercises** | http://zikmund.swcollege.com

1. Go to http://www.census.gov and look at the Population Clock to find the Census Bureau's estimate of the U.S. population on today's date.
2. The ClickZ Network is a good place to keep track of environmental changes in e-commerce. Go to http://www.clickz.com and write a short report on trends affecting marketing activity.
3. The Australian National University maintains a Web page that keeps track of leading demographic information facilities worldwide. Go to http://coombs.anu.edu.au/ResFacilities/DemographyPage.html to find a list of more than 150 interesting Web pages.
4. Most tables from the Census Bureau's 1999 *Statistical Abstract* are on the Internet at http://www.census.gov/prod/www/statistical-abstract-us.html. (Publications listed are in the portable document format [PDF]. In order to view these files, you will need the Adobe Acrobat Reader, which is available for free from the Adobe Web site.) Go to the Census Bureau's site and get some statistics to profile your home state.

Address Book (Useful URLs)

American Demographics Magazine	http://www.marketingtools.com/publications/AD/index.htm
The Living Internet	http://www.livinginternet.com
The Information Economy	http://www.sims.berkeley.edu/resources/infoecon/
Popular Science Magazine	http://www.popsci.com
AmosWeb	http://www.amosweb.com
FindLaw	http://www.findlaw.com

Ethically Right or Wrong?

Once upon a time, Disney wanted to build a new theme park that explored American history. The company planned to locate the park in northern Virginia, 35 miles from Washington, D.C., and near many Civil War battlefields and other historical sites that are now part of the National Park System. Most Virginians supported the Disney plan—including the governor, who envisioned the creation of 19,000 jobs. However, critics argued that history should not be presented in an amusement park setting and that Disney's "competitive" effort would result in fewer visits to real historical sites. In addition to asserting that Disney would trivialize U.S. history, critics argued that the park would cause air pollution and traffic gridlock. Although some residents of the area welcomed the prospect of a theme park, others believed it would disrupt the community's tranquil lifestyle. After several years of planning, Disney abandoned the project.

QUESTIONS

1. In abandoning its plans, did Disney make a socially responsible decision, or was it unfairly forced to abandon its plans because of macroenvironmental factors?
2. In your judgment, should the park be built at a different location in Virginia or in Maryland?

TAKE A STAND

1. Should products with high sodium levels, such as fast-food hamburgers and breakfast sausage, be advertised on children's television?
2. Should English be made the national language of the United States? Should all products have labels in English only?
3. Tokyo-based Ito-Yokado owns a 70 percent share of the 7-Eleven convenience store chain. Should this fact be stated on a decal posted in store windows?
4. Dr. Dre and Snoop Doggy Dogg, gangsta rappers, have been accused of making rap recordings that promote black-on-black crime, advocate violence, and use derogatory, profane, and misogynist lyrics. Is gangsta rap a product that should be marketed? Marketed aggressively on daytime radio?
5. A lawsuit was filed by men who were denied employment by the Hooters restaurant chain, known for its scantily clad female bartenders and servers. Should the restaurant chain be required to hire men as bartenders and servers?

VIDEO CASE 3-1
Comedian Mark Lundholm

Today, Mark Lundholm is a comedian. In the past he was an alcoholic, drug addict, street person, tax evader, check forger, and prison inmate. His comedy career began after he became clean and sober in an Oakland, California rehabilitation program.

A drug rehabilitation program needed someone to add some humor to treatment programs in prisons and rehabilitation centers. Mark felt his life story about recovery was filled with materials for an on-stage routine. He took the job. Over the years Mark has paid his dues. In addition to his treatment center routines that focus around AA's 12-step program, he performs in comedy clubs for "normies"—normal people—and on college campuses.

QUESTIONS
1. What environmental forces influence a comedy product—that is, the act's content and presentation?
2. Does a comedian need to have a marketing strategy?
3. How might individual target audiences—alcoholics and addicts, "normies," and college students—have different entertainment needs?

The Microenvironment in an Era of Global Business

4

chapter

LEARNING OBJECTIVES

After you have studied this chapter, you will be able to . . .

1) Understand that the four Cs of marketing portray the microenvironment.

2) Recognize how marketing creates economic utility for customers.

3) Identify the various types of competitors and understand how marketers anticipate and react to competitors' strategies.

4) Describe the value chain and explain why it must be managed.

5) Understand the importance of global competition in today's economy.

6) Understand that the four Cs are shaped by global forces.

7) Explain the importance of understanding global cultures.

8) Understand the different levels of management involvement and ownership in international marketing.

When Wal-Mart opened its first store in Argentina four years ago, it found itself cast in the unaccustomed role of David—against a Goliath of a competitor in Carrefour, the French general merchandise chain. And finding a slingshot has been anything but easy. Carrefour's position in Argentina is formidable. Argentine shoppers have long felt at home in its stores, much as they historically have taken to other things French, from the lines of their dress fashions to their late dining habits. Argentine painters, architects, and psychologists have all taken cues from France. Even the tango was only fully accepted by polite Argentine society after it became a hit in post–World War I Paris.

Carrefour has been so readily accepted in Argentina since it arrived in 1982 that it is now the country's largest retailer. Still, Wal-Mart executives felt that if Carrefour's fleur-de-lis logo could catch on in the Francophile Argentina of the 1980s, the yellow Wal-Mart smiley face could do the same when the cultural winds here seemed to be blowing America's way. Globalization, and with it American cultural influences, swept through the country in the early 1990s, and by 1995 Argentines were beginning to dress more casually, drink more beer and less wine, and even acquire a taste for jazz and the blues. And English was replacing French as the primary foreign language taught in schools.

So with typical Yankee can-do confidence—some would call it arrogance—Wal-Mart entered the Argentine market with a team of American managers and the same basic store model that worked from Des Moines to Dallas.

The meat counters featured American cuts like T-bone steaks, not the rib strips and tail rumps that Argentines prefer. Cosmetics counters were filled with bright-colored rouge and lipstick, though Argentine women tend to like a softer, more natural look. And jewelry displays gave prominent placement to emeralds, sapphires, and diamonds, while most women prefer wearing gold and silver. The first few stores even had hardware departments full of tools and appliances wired for 110-volt electric power; the standard throughout Argentina is 220.

But the miscalculations went beyond the merchandise mix, and all the way to the widths of store aisles and the carpeting on the floor. Only by trial and error did Wal-Mart learn that far more Argentine customers than Americans were in the habit of stopping at a store each day. The much greater traffic meant more sales of small items, but also aisles that always seemed overcrowded and floors that always seemed dirty and wore out rapidly. In entering Argentina, Carrefour had kept its Frenchness fairly subtle. At Wal-Mart, however, it soon became clear that the Americanness was too obvious, and counterproductive. Analysts in Argentina and on Wall Street say the company racked up huge losses in its first few years in Argentina. Carrefour better understood from the beginning the local idiosyncrasies and managed its strategy around local conditions.[1]

Chapter 3 discussed the macroenvironment, the collection of broad societal forces that affect every business and nonprofit marketer. However, a marketer like Wal-Mart is more directly influenced by microenvironmental forces, such as competition from Carrefour. This chapter begins by defining the four Cs of the microenvironment. It then explains global forces, such as cultural differences in shopping behavior, in the context of an organization's microenvironment.

The Microenvironment—The Four Cs

The macroenvironment, the broad societal forces that affect every business and nonprofit marketer, was discussed in Chapter 3. Marketers, however, are more directly influenced by their individual microenvironments. A **microenvironment** consists of a company, its customers, and the other economic institutions that regularly influence its marketing practices.

To explain the dramatic impact of the microenvironment, it is useful to organize all microenvironmental forces into four basic categories—*company, customers, competitors,* and *collaborators.* Each of these represents a participant that performs essential business activities. We will call these the **four Cs.**[2]

Exhibit 4-1 illustrates how macroenvironmental forces shape a company's microenvironment, which in turn affects the marketing mix decisions the company makes.

COMPANY

The first of the four Cs is the **company,** the business or organization itself. Marketing, although very important, is only one functional activity of an organization. Every marketer must work with people in the organization who perform nonmarketing tasks. For example, in a large manufacturing company, manufacturing, engineering, purchasing, accounting, finance, and personnel are all part of the internal company environment. These functional activities, the level of technology, and the people who perform them have an impact on marketing. Marketers, for example, work within the framework of the corporate mission set by top managers who are responsible for the company's operations. Companies like 3M, Sony, and Disney have several divisions and market many different goods

Microenvironment
A company, its customers, and the other economic institutions that influence its marketing practices.

Four Cs
The microenvironmental participants that perform essential business activities: company, customers, competitors, and collaborators.

Company
A business or organization that offers products and services to consumers.

e x h i b i **4-1**

The Macroenvironment and the Microenvironment:
Forces That Shape the Marketing Mix

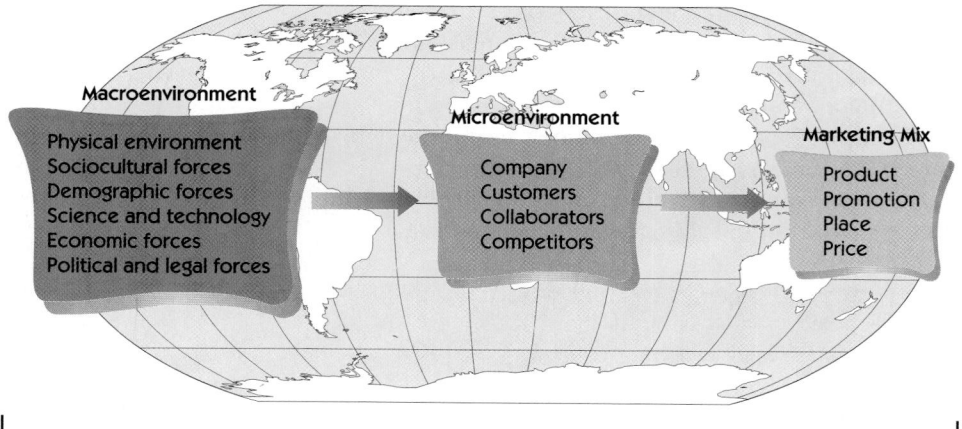

and services. The way one product is marketed often affects the marketing of other company products.

Owners and managers in today's companies must strive to be flexible to keep up with dynamically changing business environments. In doing so, they often take an entrepreneurial approach to running the business. An **entrepreneur** is someone willing to undertake a venture to create something new. In the traditional view, an entrepreneur is a single individual who sees an opportunity and is willing to work long and hard to turn an idea into a business. Entrepreneurs are typically creative, optimistic, and hard-working individuals who risk their own money to start small companies to make something happen.[3] The story of the entrepreneurial development of the personal computer is well known. Starting out in a garage, two risk-taking individuals with a vision built the first personal computers and then developed Apple Computer into a multinational corporation. Entrepreneurs who assume all the risks associated with their innovative ideas have always been in the forefront of new product development.

The top managers of many large organizations try to instill an entrepreneurial spirit in their employees. To avoid confusion with the traditional definition of entrepreneur, we define an **intrapreneurial organization** as a large organization that encourages individuals to take risks and gives them the autonomy to develop new products as they see fit.

Managers of intrapreneurial companies try to create company cultures that encourage employees to be proactive. That is, these companies favor organizational structures that allow employees to initiate marketing action swiftly rather than forcing them to follow rigid bureaucratic procedures before taking action. As the chief executive officer of Sara Lee—global marketer of Hanes, Playtex, Coach leatherwear, and Sara Lee brands—says, "Decentralized management is our point of difference. Why do you think big businesses are imploding all over America? They cannot match the creativity that can come out of individual, highly motivated small businesses. We operate about 100 discrete profit centers, each with a chief officer and a management team."[4]

CUSTOMERS

Customers are the lifeblood of every company. A company that does not satisfy its customers' needs will not stay in business over the long run. It is difficult to think of a more direct influence on marketing than the gaining or losing of customers.

Historically, consumer needs have been discussed in terms of economic utility. **Economic utility** is the ability of a good or service marketed by an organization to satisfy some aspect of a consumer's wants or needs. There are four specific types of economic utility: form utility, place utility, time utility, and possession utility.

In converting raw materials into finished goods, an organization's production department alters the materials' form. It creates **form utility.** However, transforming leather and thread into a purse does not create form utility unless the new shape formed by the materials satisfies a consumer need. Marketing helps production create form utility by interpreting consumers' needs for products of various configurations and formulations.

Bridging the physical separation between buyers and sellers is where marketing's roots lie. Products available at the right place—that is, where buyers want them—have **place utility.** A bottle of Pepsi-Cola at a bottling plant far from a consumer's hometown has considerably less place utility than does a Pepsi in a consumer's refrigerator.

Making products or services available when consumers need them creates **time utility.** A bank may close at 6:00 p.m., but by maintaining a 24-hour automatic teller machine, it produces additional time utility for its customers.

The fourth type of utility is created at the conclusion of a sale, when the transfer of ownership occurs. House owners enjoy greater freedom to alter their homes, such as the right to paint walls bright orange, than do house renters; they

Entrepreneur
A risk-taking individual who sees an opportunity and is willing to undertake a venture to create a new product or service.

Intrapreneurial organization
An organization that encourages individuals to take risks and gives them the autonomy to develop new products as they see fit.

Customer
One who buys a company's goods or services.

Economic utility
The ability of a good or service marketed by an organization to satisfy a consumer's wants or needs. Economic utility includes form utility, place utility, time utility, and possession utility.

Form utility
Economic utility created by conversion of raw materials into finished goods that meet consumer needs.

Place utility
Economic utility created by making goods available where consumers want them.

Time utility
Economic utility created by making goods available when consumers want them.

When the U.S. Postal Service issued its Classic Movie Monsters series of stamps, it did so in October. This coincided with the Halloween holiday, which added time utility to the product offering.

Possession utility
Economic utility created by transfer of physical possession and ownership of the product to the consumer.

Competitor
One of two or more rival companies engaged in the same business.

Product category
A subset of a product class containing products of a certain type.

Product class
A broad group of products that differ somewhat but perform similar functions or provide similar benefits.

Brand
A name or some other identifying feature that distinguishes one marketer's product. Much competition is among brands.

Price competition
Competition based on price. It is especially important in the marketing of products that are not distinctive, such as raw materials. Price competition is associated with possession utility.

have **possession utility.** Possession utility satisfies the consumer's need to own the product and to have control over its use or consumption.

These economic utilities serve as the underlying bases of competition, discussed in the following section.

COMPETITORS

Days Inn and Holiday Inn are competitors. So are two plumbing companies in your neighborhood. **Competitors** are rival companies engaged in the same business. Your competitors are interested in selling their products and services to your company's customers and potential customers. One of the fundamental marketing tasks is identifying and understanding the competition. The marketer does this by analyzing product classes, product categories, and brands.

Product categories are subsets of a **product class.** For example, household cleaners, taken together, constitute a product class, but the subdivisions of liquids, powders, and sprays are product categories. Similarly, beer is a product class. There are a number of product categories within that class, including regular beer, light beer, dark beer, and imported beer.

To complete their view of competition, marketing managers must consider the matter of brand. **Brands** identify and distinguish one marketer's product from those of its competitors. You are familiar with hundreds of brands of products. For example, the light beer category includes brands such as Miller Lite, Coors Light, Bud Light, and many others.

All three groupings—product class, product category, and brand—must be considered in answering the question "Who is the competition?" A liquid cleaner like Top Job can be used to clean floors. So can a powdered cleaner like Spic and Span. Liquid Lysol can do anything that spray Lysol can do, except provide the convenience of the spray can itself.

In a sense, any cleaner, beer, or hotel can compete against any other member of its product class. However, brands of products compete primarily within product categories. A marketer must of course be aware of the entire class of goods or services being marketed, but it is the product category that contains the major competitors, because the category reflects a specific consumer's wants, needs, and desires.

The Four Types of Competition   There are four general types of competition: price, quality, time, and location. These types of competition are related to the utilities described earlier.

To obtain possession utility, consumers must pay a price. That is, they must exchange something of value, called a price, for the good or service they desire. Economists have spent a great deal of time investigating **price competition.** In general, a price that is lower than competitors' prices will attract customers. However, note that economic price theory is based on the *ceteris paribus* assumption. That is, all things other than price are assumed to remain the same.

Form utility increases as product quality improves. Many businesses choose to compete on the basis of product quality rather than on the basis of price. **Quality-**

based competition is more complex than price competition because consumers define quality in many different ways. Durability and reliability are traditionally associated with quality. So are design, color, style, and many other attributes that determine the physical nature of products. Prompt, polite, and friendly service is also associated with consumers' perception of quality. If all other things, including price, are equal, the higher the perceived quality, the more likely consumers are to buy a product.

Time-based competition is directly associated with time utility. To put it simply, buyers prefer to take possession of their goods exactly when they need them, which is often as soon as possible. Time-based competition is very important in many industries, especially those in which customers view competing products as virtually identical. Moreover, time is becoming more important as a competitive weapon in a world of ever-faster global communications. A marketing manager in today's competitive environment "has to think like a fighter pilot. When things move so fast, you can't always make the right decision—so you have to learn to adjust to correct more quickly."[5] State Farm Insurance's claims representatives once used ballpoint pens, paper, and stacks of huge manuals in their offices to estimate damage from fires and other disasters. Today, they use laptop computers to review building data and calculate and print estimates right at the site of the damage. Using modern information technology has reduced processing time for claims from weeks to hours.

> Time is becoming more important as a competitive weapon in a world of ever-faster global communications.

Location-based competition is the effort to provide more place utility than competitors do. Location is extremely important for retail businesses. The 7-Eleven conveniently located at a high-traffic intersection will sell more milk and soft drinks than a grocery store located on a little-traveled road. A small store inside a shopping mall has many drop-in customers who came to the mall to shop at the large department stores.

Today, the Internet allows marketers, even small businesses, to connect instantly with customers all over the globe. In traditional business situations, bridging the physical separation between buyers and sellers meant having a better geographical location, but today barriers caused by distance are easier to overcome than they once were.

Competitive Advantage

In Chapter 2 we mentioned that a company strives to obtain an edge, or competitive advantage, over industry competitors. To establish and maintain a competitive advantage means to be superior to or different from competitors in some way. More specifically, it means to be superior in terms of price, quality, time, or location. A company may achieve superiority by operating a more efficient factory, by selling its products at a lower price, by designing better-quality products, by being the first on the market

Quality-based competition Competition based on quality. Quality-based competition is associated with form utility.

Time-based competition Competition based on providing time utility by delivering a product when the consumer wants it.

Location-based competition Competition based on providing place utility by delivering a product where the consumer wants it.

e-commerce | Changing Everything

Imagine a world in which time seems to vanish and space seems completely malleable. Where the gap between need or desire and fulfillment collapses to zero. Where distance equals a microsecond in lapsed connection time. A virtual world created at your command. Imagine a world in which everything you do, from work to education, is clothed as an entertainment-like experience, veiled by technology so subtle and transparent that you have no idea it is there at all. Habits, attitudes, opinions, preferences, expectations, demands, perceptions, and needs all adapt unwittingly to an environment in which immediacy rules.

All of this may sound like material for a science fiction thriller. But it is very nearly the world we are living in today. Technology is transforming our existence in profound ways, and the pace of change is speeding up, not slowing down. Almost all technology today is focused on compressing to zero the amount of time it takes to acquire and use information, to learn, to make decisions, to initiate action, to deploy resources, to innovate. When action and response are simultaneous, we are in *real time*.

Real time is ... our sense of ultra-compressed time and foreshortened horizons. ... The change in our consciousness of time is the creation of ubiquitous programmable technology producing results at the click of a mouse or the touch of a button or key. Real time occurs when time and distance vanish, when action and response are simultaneous.[6]

America Online, the leading online services company, has a multiyear strategic alliance with the National Basketball Association (NBA) and the Women's National Basketball Association (WNBA). The collaboration calls on AOL to feature and promote NBA and WNBA content and offer NBA and WNBA merchandise for sale across AOL's family of Web sites. In exchange, AOL receives on-air promotion during NBA games on the TNT and TBS networks, as well as WNBA game telecasts, and will benefit from significant advertising in other NBA programming.

Collaborator
A person or company that works with a marketing company. Collaborators help the company run its business but are not actually part of the company.

Supplier
An organization that provides raw materials, component parts, equipment, services, or other resources to a marketing organization; also called a *vendor*.

Value chain
Chain of activities by which a company brings in materials, creates a good or service, markets it, and provides service after a sale is made. Each step creates more value for the consumer.

with an innovation, or by satisfying customers in other ways. In other words, market-oriented organizations can use many alternative strategies to outperform competitors in terms of price, quality, time, or location.

COLLABORATORS

For an organization, buying materials and supplies, hiring an advertising agency, or getting a loan from a bank requires that one company work with another company. These companies are collaborators. A **collaborator** is a person or a company that works with your company. Collaborators help a company run its business but they are not part of the company. They are often specialists who provide particular services or supply raw materials, component parts, or production equipment.

Collaborators that provide materials, equipment, and the like are called **suppliers.** Hyatt Hotel Corporation believes that establishing long-term relationships with a supplier benefits both companies. Whether it's sheets and linens, emergency fire exit signs, or cheesecakes, Hyatt buyers circle the globe looking for the highest-quality products. After Hyatt settles on a supplier, the company works hard at maintaining that relationship.

The terms *alliances, networks,* and *informal partnerships,* as well as others, have been used to describe the kinds of relationships just mentioned. However, the term *collaborators* works well because it implies that two companies are engaged in an ongoing relationship. In today's business climate, companies must be flexible and able to change quickly. Working with collaborators helps companies enhance their flexibility, especially in global marketing activities and e-commerce activities. For example, America Online and computer maker Gateway have a collaborative agreement for e-commerce: America Online gains a prominent position on Gateway's desktop computer screens, while Gateway benefits from promotion of its computers across the Internet through America Online's service.

The number of collaborative relationships has grown significantly in recent years, and organizational collaborations are expected to be increasingly important during the 21st century. Contemporary organizations no longer perform all business activities internally. Managers recognize that collaborators may have special competencies that allow them to excel at certain tasks. Managers in today's companies believe that there is value in making joint commitments and sharing resources.

Some companies' marketing strategies are highly dependent on collaborations. In fact, business thinkers have created a name for organizations that use collaboration extensively: *virtual corporations.* The word *virtual* is derived from terminology used in the early days of the computer industry. The term *virtual memory* described a way of making a computer act as if it had more storage capacity than it really possessed.[7] Thus, the so-called virtual corporation, which appears to be a single enterprise with vast capabilities, is the result of numerous collaborations with companies whose resources are called on only when they are needed.

The Value Chain

Operating a business involves a system of activities and relationships with collaborators. Each part of the system—each link in the chain—adds value to the product customers ultimately buy. Exhibit 4-2 shows what is known as a **value chain.**[8] The exhibit illustrates the relationships between a company and its customers and some

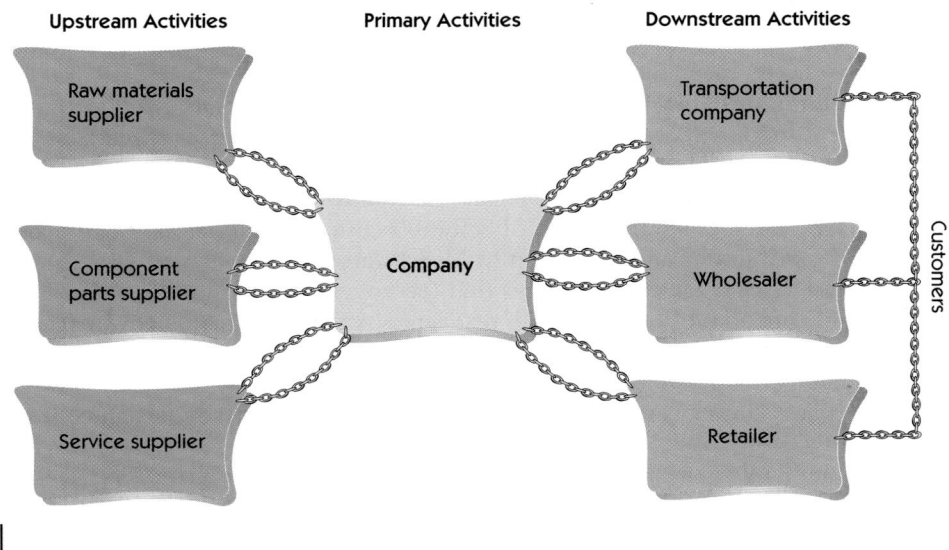

A Simple Value Chain

of its collaborators by dividing activities into primary, upstream, and downstream activities. Notice that before the company engages in its primary operations, such as production, accounting, and pricing, it engages in *upstream activities*, such as purchasing equipment and materials from suppliers. *Downstream activities*, performed after the product has been produced, require dealing with other collaborators, such as transportation companies and retailers. These upstream and downstream activities are called *supportive activities*. They provide the support necessary for carrying out primary activities or for concluding the sale of goods or services to the final buyer. Value chains may be more complex than the one illustrated here. However, at this point in the book we wish to make the point that collaborators in the value chain create new value together.[9] These companies link themselves together to achieve a common purpose. Each company values the skills that its partners bring to the collaboration. By linking their companies' capabilities, the collaborators can increase the value that the ultimate customer obtains.

Core Competencies

Before establishing the role of each collaborator in the value chain, marketers should ascertain the company's core competencies. A **core competency** is a proficiency in a critical functional activity—such as technical know-how or a particular business specialization—that helps provide a company's unique competitive advantage. The company may be able to do something that its competitors cannot do at all or that they find difficult to do even poorly.[10] Simply put, core competencies are what the organization does best.

A company enhances its effectiveness by concentrating its resources on a set of core competencies that will allow it to achieve competitive superiority and provide unique or differentiated value for customers. For example, Nike manufactures only key

A company enhances its effectiveness by concentrating its resources on a set of core competencies that will allow it to achieve competitive superiority and provide unique or differentiated value for customers.

Core competency
Expertise in a critical functional area or aspect of a particular business that helps provide a company's unique competitive advantage; what a company does best.

technical components of its Nike Air system. All of its shoe production is performed by Asian collaborators. Research and development for product design and marketing are Nike's core competencies, not production.

Outsourcing
Buying or hiring from
outside suppliers.

An understanding of core competencies helps managers determine what value-creating activities can be outsourced. **Outsourcing** means having certain activities performed by collaborators—outside sources. Outsourced activities, such as the production of major parts or subassemblies by suppliers or the operation of an Internet Web site, may be integral to a company's operations. Consider the collaboration behind MySchwab.com, a Web site that provides free financial information, current stock market news, and other investment tools personalized for individual investors. The Charles Schwab Company, a stock brokerage firm, collaborates with Excite, a Web portal, because customization technology is one of Excite's competencies—but not one of Schwab's core competencies. Excite benefits from the promotion of Excite.com by MySchwab.com.

The major reason for outsourcing is that few companies possess adequate resources and capabilities to perform all primary activities, upstream activities, and downstream activities themselves. In today's era of intense global competition, it would be almost impossible for any organization to have all the necessary competencies to excel at every activity in its value chain. Companies that recognize this fact carefully plan their collaborations with other companies so that they can combine complementary strengths to increase customer value.

Companies often have problems when they stray too far from their core competencies. Burger King, for example, expanded its menu with Snickers ice cream bars, chef salads, and Breakfast Buddy and bagel sandwiches. It offered a special dinner service, which included fried shrimp brought to customers' tables by staff. After several years of broadening its offerings, the company realized it had veered

MySchwab.com is a Web site that offers free financial information, current stock market news, and other investment tools and resources. The Charles Schwab Company collaborates with Excite because Excite.com customization technology creates added value. Companies link themselves together to achieve a common purpose; each company values the skills that its partner brings to the collaboration.

http://www.myschwab.com

too far from its core competencies. Burger King retrenched. It decided to concentrate on the business it knew best—the burger, fries, and drink business. The company now stresses flame broiling, taste, and value.

Relationship Management

Effective executives stress managing the relationships that make the value chain productive. These managers work to build long-term relationships with suppliers, resellers, and ultimately customers who buy their products for consumption. The term **relationship management** refers to a major goal of business: building long-term relationships with the parties that contribute to a company's success.

Companies strive to initiate collaborations and build loyalties. It is the manager's job to create, interpret, and maintain the relationships between the company and its collaborators.

The Impact of Global Forces on the Four Cs

"On a political map, the boundaries between countries are as clear as ever. But on a competitive map, a map showing the real flows of financial and industrial activity, those boundaries have largely disappeared."[11] The world has become a global economy in which corporations market their products in many areas outside their home countries. In consumer electronics, for instance, Japanese marketers like Sony and Panasonic have high market shares in the United States and compete effectively throughout the world. Not only marketing but also manufacturing has taken on an international character for some organizations. Honda lawn mowers, for example, are manufactured in Swepsonville, North Carolina. Is this an American product or a Japanese product?

An organization that sells its products beyond the boundaries of its home nation engages in international marketing. **International marketing** involves a marketing strategy that views the world market rather than a domestic market as the forum for marketing operations.

In thinking about marketing in the global economy, it is important to remember two key economic terms. **Imports** are foreign products purchased domestically. **Exports** are domestically produced products sold in foreign markets. Today, U.S. exports amount to almost a trillion dollars. In 1998 imports were approximately $1,110 billion.[12] The goods accounting for much of this trade were crude oil and refined petroleum products, automobiles, industrial raw materials, and capital goods.

Many U.S. companies are thoroughly involved in multinational marketing. Gillette, Coca-Cola, and Johnson & Johnson earn well over 50 percent of their profits overseas. The U.S. government encourages U.S. companies to expand their international marketing efforts, and the United States is a major exporting country in terms of absolute dollar volume.

The United States has passed through a transition period from a domestic orientation to a global orientation. At one time, an American marketer could be content to ignore world trade and compete with other domestic marketers for business in the growing U.S. economy. Today, however, with multinational organizations employing global marketing strategies, a domestic marketer must be aware of foreign competitors' influences not only in international markets but also in its own domestic market. Competition is global, and the future of marketing is global. Companies must therefore analyze microenvironments in various parts of the world.[13] For that reason, it is useful to consider the impact of global forces on the four Cs. We begin by looking at the global consumer.

CUSTOMERS—THE ERA OF THE GLOBAL CONSUMER

International marketers, like marketers in their home countries, focus on satisfying customer needs. Understanding why people in foreign countries behave and react as they do requires knowing how their values and beliefs affect the success

Relationship management
The building and maintaining of long-term relationships with the parties that contribute to an organization's success; the sales function of managing relationships with customers and ensuring that they receive appropriate services.

International marketing
Marketing across international boundaries; also called *multinational marketing*.

Import
A foreign product purchased domestically.

Export
A domestically produced product sold in a foreign market.

of marketing efforts.[14] As mentioned in Chapter 3, values and beliefs vary from culture to culture. What seems like a normal idea, or even a great idea, to marketers in one country may be seen as unacceptable or even laughable by citizens of other lands. Consider these examples about food preferences:

- When Campbell's offered its familiar (to Americans) red and white–labeled cans of soup in Brazil, it found cultural values there too strong for this product to overcome. Brazilian housewives apparently felt guilty using the prepared soups that Americans take for granted. They believed that they would not be fulfilling their roles as homemakers if they served their families a soup they could not call their own. Faced with this difficulty, Campbell's withdrew the product. However, the company discovered that Brazilian women felt comfortable using a dehydrated "soup starter" to which they could add their own special ingredients and flair. To market soup in Japan, on the other hand, the marketer must realize that soup is regarded there as a breakfast drink rather than a dish served for lunch or dinner.

- Some 80 percent of Indians are Hindu, adherents of a religion that prohibits the eating of beef and considers cows to be a sacred symbol. Instead of the Big Mac, the Indian menu features the Maharaja Mac—"two all-mutton patties, special sauce, lettuce, cheese, pickles, onions on a sesame-seed bun." For the strictest Hindus, who eat no meat at all, there are rice-based patties flavored with peas, carrots, red pepper, beans, coriander, and other spices. McDonald's, which has restaurants in more than 100 countries, adapts its menu to local tastes around the world.[15]

- The latest trend in Japanese restaurants is to eat fish live. Trendy establishments serve flounder that flaps around on the plate. Shrimp are featured in a dish called "dance," and are expected to do just that. Shrimp and flounder are by no means the only entrees expected to move around a lot. Other attractions include firefly squid, sea bream, and young yellowtail. Waiters bring the fish in wiggling, their eyes and mouths moving, then quickly slice open the midsection and gut it, so the fish is ready to eat. Like sushi or sashimi, the slices are dipped in soy sauce and horseradish. Lobster is served belly up, with an incision made along the length of the tail so diners can get at the meat. Small squid and eels are eaten whole.[16]

Industrial buyers and government workers may also behave differently in different cultures. In some countries, business dealings are carried on so slowly that U.S. business people are frustrated by what they perceive as delays. Yet this customary slowness may be seen by their hosts as contributing to a friendly atmosphere. Government officials in some countries openly demand "gifts" or "tips," without which nothing gets done. Of course, this practice is illegal in the United States because it conflicts with American social values.

English is spoken in many countries, but sometimes the language in English-speaking countries is not quite the same. A pickup truck is called a *bakkie* in South Africa, a *ute* in Australia, and a *utility vehicle* in New Zealand. What Americans call a bar is a *pub* in Great Britain, a *hotel* in Australia, and a *boozer* in New Zealand. And if you are in Canada, a *hoser* is just another *bubba*.

LANGUAGE

Language is an important part of culture, and the international marketer must be aware of

what went wrong?

Gestures Speak Louder Than Words "I knew I'd committed a monumental goof. But I just couldn't imagine how." A young computer salesman from New Jersey is remembering his first overseas sales pitch. The scene was his company's offices in Rio, and it had gone like a Sunday preacher's favorite sermon. As he looked around the table, he knew he had clinched the sale. Triumphantly, he raised his hand to his Latin customers and flashed the classic American okay sign—thumb and forefinger forming a circle, other fingers pointing up.

The sunny Brazilian atmosphere suddenly felt like a deep freeze. Stony silence. Icy stares. Plus embarrassed smirks from his colleagues.

Calling for a break, they took him outside the conference room and explained. Our hero had just treated everyone to a gesture with roughly the same meaning there as the notorious third-finger sign conveys so vividly here. Apologies saved the sale, but he still turns as pink as a Brazilian sunset when retelling the tale.

It is only natural when you find yourself at sea in the local language to use gestures to bail yourself out. . . . Gestures pack the power to punctuate, to dramatize, to speak a more colorful language than mere words. Yet, like the computer sales representative, you may discover that those innocent winks and well-meaning nods are anything but universal.[17]

its subtleties. For example, although the French words *tu* and *vous* both mean "you," the former is used to address a social equal or an inferior and the latter to signify formality and social respect. In Japan, "yes" may mean "yes, I understand what you said," not necessarily "yes, I agree." Numerous marketing mistakes have resulted from misinterpretations of language by unwary translators. The Chevrolet brand name Nova translates into Spanish as "no go." Tomato paste becomes "tomato glue" in Arabic. Translated into Spanish, Herculon carpet is "the carpeting with the big derriere." The straightforward slogan "Come alive with Pepsi!" has been translated as "Come out of the grave with Pepsi!" and "Pepsi brings your ancestors back from the grave." Gestures, too, can be misinterpreted, as illustrated in the What Went Wrong? feature.

CULTURAL SYMBOLS

Another aspect of culture is cultural symbols. A *cultural symbol* stands for something else and expresses a particular meaning shared by members of a society. Symbols may be verbal or nonverbal. The color white may represent purity, for example. A bull may represent strength. Such symbols may act as powerful unconscious forces, silently working to shape consumer attitudes and behavior. The use of cultural symbols can thus be of great importance in a marketing effort.

As with language, failure to fully understand cultural symbols can produce unpredictable results. According to myth, the site of the Aztec city of Tenochtitlan, now Mexico City, was revealed to its founders by an eagle bearing a snake in its talons. This image, now the official seal of Mexico, appears on the country's flag. To commemorate Mexico's Flag Day, two local McDonald's restaurants managed by U.S. citizens papered their serving trays with placemats embossed with a representation of the national emblem. Mexican government agents were infuriated when they discovered their beloved eagle splattered with ketchup. Authorities swooped down and confiscated the disrespectful placemats.[18]

ETHNOCENTRISM

More often than not, as in the McDonald's placemats example, failure to understand the market leads to unpleasant results. One reason that many managers fail to fully understand foreign cultures and marketing is that people tend to be ethnocentric. **Ethnocentrism** is the tendency to consider one's own culture and way of life as the natural and normal ones. We may mistakenly expect others to share these feelings. This unconscious use of our own cultural values as a reference point has been called the *self-reference criterion*. People doing business in a foreign country may be using the self-reference criterion, or being ethnocentric, when they think their domestic strategy or reputation is better than that of any competitor in that country. But exporting one's own biases into foreign markets results in mistakes—such as when U.S. companies attempted to sell large U.S.-built cars with steering wheels on the left side for use in overcrowded Japanese streets, where cars are driven on the left side of the road.

Many Americans expect foreign business people to conduct business the same way people do in the United States. However, often this is not the case. For example, assuming that it is appropriate to send a woman sales representative to Saudi Arabia, Yemen, or some other country in the Middle East shows a lack of understanding of cultural values. The women's movement has not had much impact in many Middle Eastern countries. Marketers must avoid such cultural nearsightedness by consciously recognizing its potentially biasing impact.

Although consumers will no doubt continue to differ from country to country, they are developing some similar tastes and preferences as the business world becomes more global. Global marketers should recognize both similarities and differences among customers in different areas of the world and incorporate this knowledge into their marketing strategies.

This advertisement for Telstra says "For newcomers, Asia can be a confusing place. Customs, rituals and ways of doing business completely different to what you're used to. That's why you should talk to Australia's Telstra." It communicates the message that a company that is not familiar with the customs of Asia should talk to the Australian telecommunications company that knows its way around.

http://www.telstra.com.au

MULTINATIONAL ECONOMIC COMMUNITIES

Marketers often view global customers from a regional perspective, reflecting a trend toward economic integration and the formation of multinational economic communities. A **multinational economic community** is a collaboration among countries to increase international trade by reducing trade restrictions. The formation of economic communities not only makes it easier for member nations to trade with each other but also makes it easier for outsiders to trade with member nations.

Perhaps the best-known economic community is the European Union, also known as the European Community or the Common Market. As shown in Exhibit 4-3, it consists of Portugal, France, Ireland, the United Kingdom, Spain, Denmark, Germany, the Netherlands, Belgium, Luxembourg, Italy, Greece, Austria, Finland, and Sweden. Although Europeans had been working on a "borderless" economy for more than 30 years, 1992 finally marked the elimination of national trade barriers, differences in tax laws, conflicting product standards, and other restrictions that had kept the member nations from being a single market. Trade within this union is very similar to trade among U.S. states—borders are of minimal significance, and there are no customs controls. In 1999 the Euro became the common currency in the European Union.

Multinational economic community
A collaboration among countries to increase international trade by reducing trade restrictions. Typically, a group of countries forms a unified market within which there are minimal trade and tariff barriers; the European Union is an example.

e x h i b i **4-3**

Map of European Union

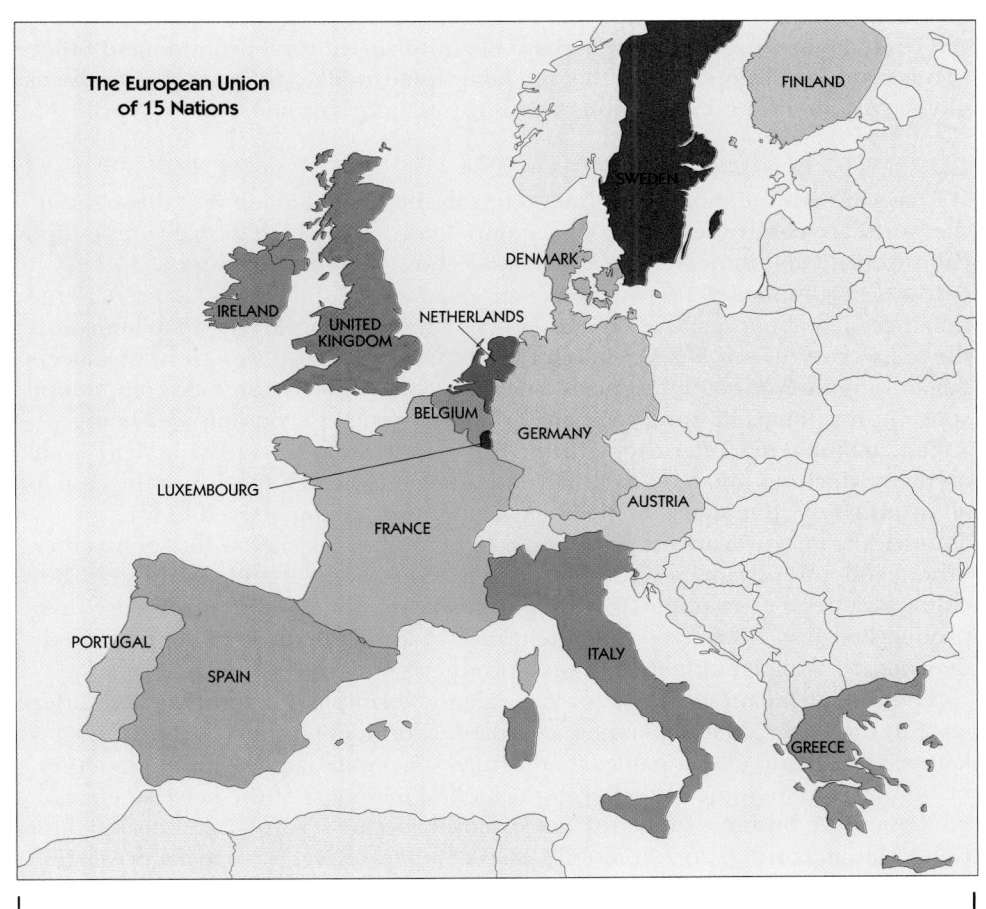

The European Union offers a single market with more than 325 million consumers—an enormous marketing opportunity. It has been estimated that, since 1992, the European Union has been the largest single market in the world. Today, spending within the European Union exceeds $50 trillion. Each year, U.S. companies sell more than $500 billion of goods and services in the European Union. Furthermore, this group of economic partners may soon encompass most of the continent. Iceland, Norway, and Switzerland approved a pact that over time will integrate these countries with the European Union. Three former Eastern bloc countries—the Czech Republic, Hungary, and Poland—are seeking associate status with the European Union.

In North America, the stage has been set for the development of a single trading market of more than 360 million people. NAFTA, the North American Free Trade Agreement, was passed by the United States Congress in 1993. NAFTA reduced trade barriers, allowed for increased foreign investment, promoted cross-border manufacturing, and, in general, helped increase free trade among Mexico, Canada, and the United States. NAFTA allows companies in Canada and the United States to take advantage of low-cost labor in Mexico. Mexico benefits from the infusion of capital and technology. All three countries are believed to be more competitive with other nations. NAFTA has already had a major impact on production location, imports, exports, and unemployment in selected industries.

Tariff
A tax imposed by a government on an imported product. A tariff is often intended to raise the price of imported goods and thereby give a price advantage to domestic goods.

Tariffs are taxes imposed by a nation on selected imported goods brought into that nation to make those goods more costly in the marketplace. When NAFTA went into effect, the United States canceled tariffs on 60 percent of Mexican goods that had been subjected to taxes. Other tariffs are being phased out over a 15-year period. Mexican consumers increasingly are buying U.S. products whose production requires technology that Mexico does not yet possess. Consumers in the United States increasingly purchase Mexican agricultural products and other goods produced by operations that are labor-intensive. We will continue to discuss global customers and their unique needs throughout this book.

COMPETITORS IN A WORLDWIDE ARENA

We have already mentioned that marketers in the United States and throughout the world are confronted with global competition. Intensified global competition can stimulate and improve domestic competition in an industry. For example, consumers complained for years that American automobile manufacturers were unconcerned about quality and inattentive to market needs. When Japanese and European cars gained a large share of the U.S. auto market, American producers began to remedy these deficiencies. Such improvements in domestic competition spur improvements in living standards as well as general economic well-being.

International marketers hope they can compete on a "level playing field"—an arena in which no one has an "unfair" advantage. However, this is not the case for all products or all markets. Sometimes competitors headquartered in foreign countries enjoy government subsidies or benefit from legislation that grants them other economic advantages in their home markets. Sometimes laws are shaped by cultural values. For example, foreign marketers are not allowed to advertise their products on Iran's two state-owned television channels because of the perceived detrimental Western influence of such products.[19]

The role of Japanese *keiretsu* provides a good example of a fundamental difference in the ways U.S. and Japanese companies conduct business in Japan. A keiretsu is a group of companies that form a "corporate family." Bound together by mutual shareholdings or other financial ties, members of the keiretsu engage in cooperative business strategies. For example, because Toyota's keiretsu includes Koito Manufacturing, an automobile parts company, Koito has special privileges when supplying parts to Toyota. Outside companies find it difficult to compete with members of Toyota's keiretsu in marketing products to Toyota.

what went wrong?

American Sanctions Against France The United States and Canada imposed 100 percent tariffs on some European products in July 1999 in retaliation for the European Union's refusal to import North American beef raised with growth-enhancing hormones.

The French products affected by the special taxes are foie gras, truffles, Dijon mustard, and Roquefort cheese. Tariffs on the blue-veined Roquefort cheese, especially popular on salads and in salad dressings, could hurt France the most because it exports about 28 metric tons a year to the United States.

Because of these sanctions against France, McDonald's and Coca-Cola were singled out for unofficial reprisals. Some cafés in the Roquefort region near the southern city of Toulouse banned Coke or added surcharges to increase its price several times. McDonald's, which has some 400 restaurants in France, became the target of protests. At the outset, farmers held usually good-humored picnics outside McDonald's restaurants, offering local produce rather than Big Macs. At a protest in Cahors, a cow wearing a banner proclaiming "I was not raised on hormones" ambled alongside a farmer.

However, in August of 1999, the demonstrations in towns in southern France were less amiable. French farmers dumped tons of manure on several McDonald's restaurants in protest against the U.S. sanction. One restaurant was occupied, another was badly damaged. Graffiti painted on the walls in Arles, near the Mediterranean coast, declared the superiority of locally made Roquefort cheese over U.S. burgers. "Roquefort first, McDo go home," it read.

French farm leaders said, "McDonald's is just a symbol for us, it could have been Coke." They are angry about the sanctions and the growing U.S. domination of food and agricultural markets. McDonald's accused the farmers of dragging it into a conflict for which it is not responsible.[20]

As mentioned earlier, governments often protect certain domestic industries by imposing tariffs on imports, to restrict the activity of foreign companies. Tariffs can have a dramatic impact on foreign competitors. Because the imported products are more expensive (as a result of the tariff), domestic production may be encouraged or consumption of the imported products may be discouraged. For example, at one time the United States imposed a high tariff (50 percent) on imported motorcycles with engines larger than 700cc. Harley-Davidson, the only American-owned motorcycle manufacturer, made no motorcycles with engines smaller than 1000cc and did not care about small-engine motorcycles. As a consequence of the tariff on imported large-engine motorcycles, Harley-Davidson dominated the U.S. market for such machines. Clearly, the existence of high restrictive tariffs in a country can discourage competitors from another nation from marketing in that country.

Import quotas, or government-imposed limits on a type of imported good, are another restrictive factor. Countries trying to promote domestic production or encourage consumption of domestic goods may impose quotas on certain imported products. Some quotas set absolute limits, and goods can be imported only until the set level is reached. After that, no further imports are allowed. Other quotas are linked with tariffs so that an extremely high tariff is levied on goods imported beyond the quota limit. There are are two extreme forms of restriction. An **embargo** is a government prohibition against trade, often focused on a particular product. A **boycott** is the refusal of some group or a government to buy a certain product. Either tactic may completely shut down trade with a particular country.

Governments may impose a variety of other restrictive controls to discourage foreign companies from doing business in their markets. Sometimes countries

Import quota
A limit set by a government on how much of a certain type of product can be imported into a country.

Embargo
A government prohibition against trade, especially trade in a particular product.

Boycott
The refusal of some group to buy certain products. A government may enforce a boycott of the products of some other country.

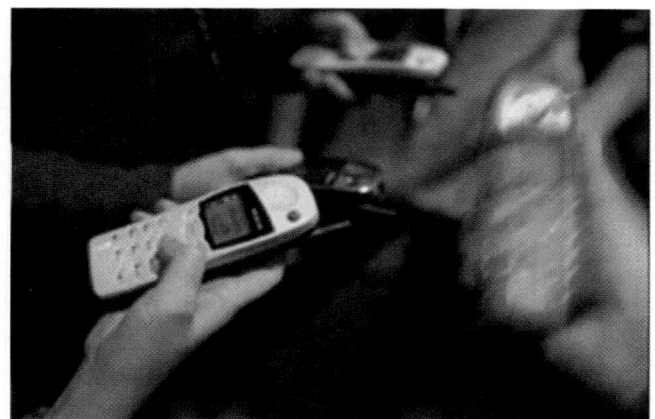

Nokia is a Finnish company that has become a global leader in wireless telecommunications and mobile telephony. Nokia's newest phones incorporate Internet access. As the world's leading mobile phone supplier, Nokia must deal with tariffs, import quotas, and government regulations around the world.

http://www.nokia.com

require that all trade with other nations be approved by some form of central ministry. This allows a government to impose various types of controls over goods brought into the country. Still other nations set up restrictive criteria to eliminate the importing of certain products. A local government may, for instance, establish buying criteria for food products that effectively prevent food products from being shipped in from certain countries.

Even when there is a level playing field without government restrictions, an exporter may face disadvantages relative to domestic competitors. Procter & Gamble's Pampers, for example, could not beat stiff competition in the Australian and New Zealand markets. Pampers were imported, rather than manufactured locally, and high transportation costs and currency fluctuations meant they had to be priced higher than the competing products.[21]

THE COMPANY AS AN INTERNATIONAL MARKETER

Not all U.S.-based companies choose to market their products outside the United States. A bagel bakery may limit its marketing to New York City, for instance. The bakery's resources or market demand may justify this strategy. Large corporations, of course, are more likely to find it advantageous to spend considerable time and effort marketing beyond their national boundaries. But not even all large corporations engage in international marketing. Southwest Airlines, for example, chooses to market its services only within the United States.

The company that does opt to expand into international marketing must consider the same fundamental marketing concepts that apply in domestic marketing. That is, uncontrollable environmental factors must be analyzed, and target markets must be determined. Competitive market positions must be considered, and marketing mix strategies must be planned and executed to appeal to these target markets.

Political stability, tariffs, and exchange rates are some of the factors that a company must take into account when it is making the decision to market in another country. The factors that affect a company's decision to enter a certain market are discussed in Chapter 8.

Direct investment in manufacturing facilities and marketing operations reflects a long-term, high-level commitment to international marketing.

If a company decides to do business in a certain market, it must make decisions about what degree of ownership and management involvement it will pursue. Market potential, the organization's experience in international marketing, the organization's willingness to subject itself to risks, and host country policies often influence these decisions. A multinational marketer may choose to be involved at different levels in different countries. The basic types of in-

STRATEGY	LOCATION OF PRODUCTION FACILITY	FOREIGN COMPANY'S PRIMARY INVOLVEMENT	OWNER OF FOREIGN OPERATION	CAPITAL OUTLAY REQUIRED BY DOMESTIC COMPANY
INVESTMENT WITHOUT COLLABORATORS				
Direct foreign investment	In foreign country	Provides native work force, sales force, and/or intermediaries	Domestic company	High
Direct exporting	In domestic country	None	None	Low
INVESTMENT WITH COLLABORATORS				
Indirect exporting	In domestic country	Acts as intermediary to ensure distribution and sales in foreign country	Company acting as intermediary is foreign owned	Low
JOINT VENTURES				
Licensing/international franchising	In foreign country	Has right to manufacture and service the product and use product name; conducts local marketing efforts	Foreign owned, according to contract	Low
Contract manufacturing	In foreign country	Manufactures product according to specifications	Production facility is foreign owned	Low
Joint ownership venture	In foreign country	Participates as partner	Facilities are owned jointly by domestic and foreign companies, in proportions determined by contract	Moderate to high

volvement in international markets are direct investment, exporting, and joint venturing. We examine direct investment and direct exporting next. With indirect exporting and joint venturing, we move into the area of collaborations, discussed in the next section. Exhibit 4-4 outlines these strategies.

If foreign market demand is great, a company may invest directly in manufacturing and marketing operations in a host foreign country. This strategy is called **direct foreign investment,** or full ownership. Coca-Cola owns bottling plants in Guangzhow (Canton) and other cities in China, for example. Several Japanese automobile manufacturers have built automobile plants in the United States. This approach enables the automakers to minimize the shipping expenses and political pressures associated with selling foreign-made cars in the U.S. market. In other instances, an organization may invest directly in plant operations in developing countries to take advantage of low-cost labor. Whatever the reason, direct investment in manufacturing facilities and marketing operations reflects a long-term, high-level commitment to international marketing.

Many risks are associated with a long-term direct investment strategy. For example, Turkey's disastrous 1999 earthquake seriously affected multinational companies operating in that nation. The possibility that China might invade Taiwan is another type of risk. In some countries, a change in governments may lead to nationalization of foreign companies' assets—that is, a transfer of the assets to the

Direct foreign investment
Investment in production and marketing operations located in a foreign country.

Exporting
Selling domestically produced products in foreign markets.

Direct exporting
Exporting in which a company deals directly with a foreign buyer without the assistance of a collaborator.

Indirect exporting
Exporting in which a company uses the assistance of a collaborator to deal with a foreign buyer.

Export management company
A company that specializes in buying from sellers in one country and marketing the products in other countries. Such companies typically take title to the products.

Joint venture
An arrangement between a domestic company and a foreign company to set up production and marketing facilities in a foreign market.

Licensing
An agreement by which a company (the licensor) permits a foreign company (the licensee) to set up a business in the foreign market using the licensor's manufacturing processes, patents, trademarks, trade secrets, and so on, in exchange for payment of a fee or royalty.

new government. If the risk of nationalization of a multinational's operations is high, direct investment becomes less attractive.

In contrast to direct investment, **exporting** is a relatively low-level commitment to international marketing. Exporters, manufacturing or harvesting in their home countries, sell some or all of their products in foreign markets. Such distribution may be accomplished either directly, through the company's sales force, or indirectly, through intermediaries. (Thus, exporting may or may not involve collaborators.) There is no investment in overseas plant or equipment in either case.

A firm may use **direct exporting** when it wants greater control over the foreign sales of its product. Direct exporting can take several forms. Some companies use their own traveling salespeople, who make occasional visits to overseas markets to try to sell the product there. To be successful, these salespeople must cultivate the right prospects and understand what is required to conduct business in another culture. Other companies establish a domestic-based export department or division. The scope of this unit is determined in part by the degree of commitment the company has to international marketing. Many companies market their products via the World Wide Web to buyers in other countries. When it receives an Internet order, the company ships the product directly to the customer.

In many cases, marketers using direct exporting still maintain a domestic perspective. Organizations with domestic outlooks do not always meet with success in the exporting arena. Therefore, some marketers choose to establish overseas sales offices, branches, or distributors to maintain a continuing presence in the host country or overseas market. Such an organization can develop a better understanding of the differences in foreign markets than can salespeople who make only occasional visits.

COMPANIES WORK THROUGH GLOBAL COLLABORATIONS

Global collaborations have increased as a result of the globalization of the marketplace. Using export management companies, engaging in joint ventures, and outsourcing to companies operating outside the United States have allowed U.S. companies to marshal more resources for international marketing.

Indirect exporting is one approach that involves the use of collaborators. With **indirect exporting,** a domestic company does not deal directly with overseas customers. Instead, it sells a portion of its inventory to some intermediary that conducts business in the company's home country; the intermediary then distributes the product in foreign markets. The major strength of the intermediary is its access to and relationship with foreign customers. Some companies that export indirectly do not do so routinely; rather, they view the international marketplace simply as a place to get rid of surplus inventory or unwanted products. Others use indirect exporting continuously and systematically. Whatever the degree of indirect exporting, the company uses its domestic sales force to sell its products to the intermediaries.

Companies often develop collaborative relationships with **export management companies,** intermediaries that specialize in buying from sellers in one country and marketing the products in other countries. Export management companies, which assume ownership of the goods, reduce the risk of multinational marketing for companies that lack a great deal of exporting experience. Like other wholesalers, export management companies perform many distribution functions for sellers. However, in most cases, their primary functions are selling and taking responsibility for foreign credit. Other intermediaries that represent companies in overseas selling activities include various types of *export agents,* who do not take title to the goods.

In a **joint venture,** domestic and host companies join to set up production and marketing facilities in an overseas market. Unlike exporting, joint venturing involves some agreement for production of the product on foreign soil.

There are several forms of joint venturing. (Refer to Exhibit 4-4.) One simple method is **licensing,** in which a domestic company (the licensor) that wishes to

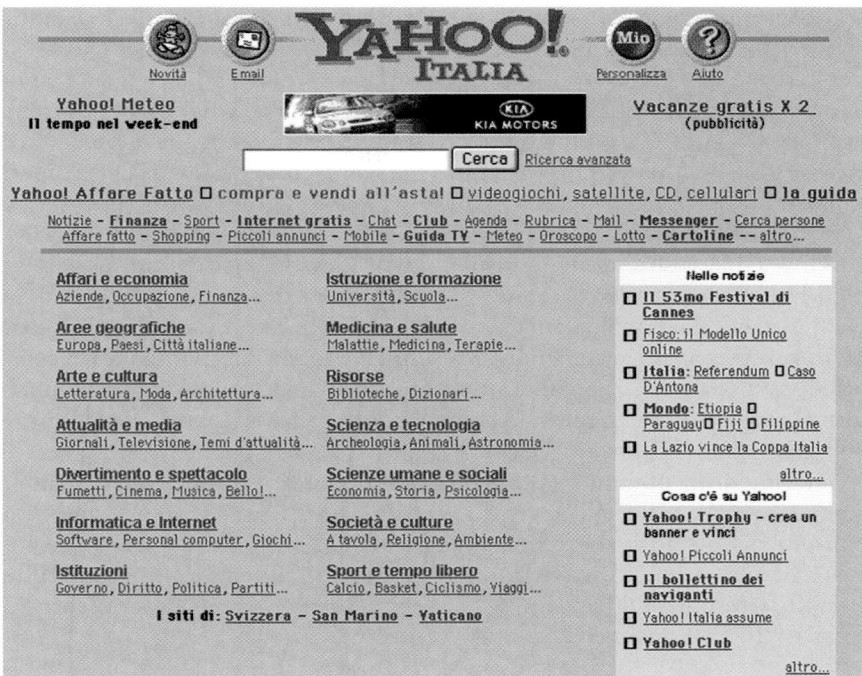

Yahoo!'s portal operations are worldwide. It has direct investments or joint ventures in Australia, New Zealand, China, Japan, Korea, Singapore, Taiwan, Brazil, Canada, Denmark, France, Germany, Ireland, Norway, Spain, Sweden, the United Kingdom, and Italy. Each country's Yahoo!, such as this one from Italy, reflects the language and interests of the area.

http://it.yahoo.com

do business in a particular overseas market enters into a licensing agreement with an overseas company (the licensee). The agreement permits the licensee to use the licensor's manufacturing processes, patents, trademarks, trade secrets, and so on, in exchange for payment of a fee or royalty. Licensing provides a means to conduct business in a country whose laws discourage foreign ownership. One disadvantage of licensing is loss of managerial control. The foreign company makes key decisions without input from the licensor. On the positive side, a licensee may have a greater understanding of the local culture, experience with the local distribution system, and the marketing skill required to succeed in the foreign market.

International franchising is a form of licensing in which a company establishes overseas franchises in much the same way it establishes franchises in its own country. Because many franchisors desire consistency, franchising agreements are most common in markets where conditions are similar to those in the domestic market. A potential disadvantage of international franchising is the possibility that this type of operation will foster future competitors. Sometimes, after gaining enough training and experience, franchisees start their own rival companies.

Some companies believe that the risks of licensing are too great and prefer to maintain greater marketing control. These companies use **contract manufacturing.** In such an agreement, a company agrees to permit an overseas manufacturer to produce its product. The domestic company supplies the product specifications and the brand name, and the foreign company produces the product under that label for the domestic company. Overseas sales of the product are typically handled and controlled by the domestic company. In Mexico and Spain, for instance, Sears may establish its own stores; but rather than filling these stores with imported products, it often uses local manufacturers to produce Sears-label products to specifications. In many foreign markets, contract manufacturing also offers the opportunity to use labor that is less expensive, thus yielding lower product prices or greater savings to the company.

A final form of joint venturing is the **joint ownership venture.** Under this arrangement, the domestic and foreign partners invest capital and share ownership

International franchising
A form of licensing in which a company establishes foreign franchises. Franchising involves a contractual agreement between a franchisor (often a manufacturer or wholesaler) and a franchisee (typically an independent retailer) by which the franchisee distributes the franchisor's product.

Contract manufacturing
An agreement by which a domestic company allows a foreign producer to manufacture its product according to its specifications. Typically, the domestic company then handles foreign sales of the product.

Joint ownership venture
A joint venture in which domestic and foreign partners invest capital and share ownership and control.

and control of the partnership in some agreed-on proportion. Ownership is not always equal. Whirlpool is typical of customer-driven companies striving to be competitive in this age of global competition. It works with collaborators to gain competitive advantage through joint ownership ventures around the world. Whirlpool jointly manufactures and markets products under 12 major brand names in about 140 countries. With its collaborators, Whirlpool claims the No. 1 market share in Latin America, while in Europe it holds the No. 3 slot.[22]

A common reason for entering into a joint ownership venture is that some countries that restrict foreign ownership of investments require such an arrangement. Mexico bars total foreign ownership of Mexican advertising agencies, for example. International agencies such as J. Walter Thompson, Inc. must therefore be involved in joint ownership ventures if they wish to operate in Mexico. In some other countries, the government requires that the local company maintain a majority interest in the venture, keeping foreign control in the company under 50 percent.

Sharing of technology is often a reason for a joint venture. American wireless giant Motorola and Sega Enterprises Ltd. of Japan, one of the leading video game console makers, have formed a strategic alliance to jointly develop a technology that will allow users to access and run games and other forms of entertainment software through cellular phones, pagers, and other wireless devices, such as personal digital assistants (PDAs).

what went right?

Pokémon The Pokémon (PO-kay-mon) trading-card game is currently one of the hottest crazes in America. The WB network's Pokémon show is the highest-rated Saturday morning children's series on either broadcast or cable television. Pokémon began with a video game in Japan in 1995. Pokémon, or "pocket monsters," refers to both the game and the fantasy characters who populate it. These mini-monsters range from smiling, rounded blobs to fire-breathing dragons and faceless objects, and sport such odd names as Wartortle, Kakuna, Pikachu, Charizard, and Blastoise.[23]

Pokémon's licensing agreements with many American companies, including the WB network, sometimes allow the marketer to modify the product for the American market. The English-language version of the Japanese *Pokémon* TV series requires considerable reworking before it airs on American television net-

works.[24] When 4Kids Productions receives an episode in Japanese, the first thing the company does is a literal translation. The script is then rewritten until the flow of the story works and the humor is more appropriate for the American market. The music is all replaced, because the music in the Japanese version is very sparse and Western audiences are used to cartoon series with music all the way through. 4Kids also does some minor editing for things that might be offensive to a U.S. audience. It's usually not a big problem, but sometimes the human characters slap or smack one another, and the company figures out a way to tone it down. Finally, the company digitally removes the Japanese characters on street signs, storefronts, business cards, etc. If possible, the characters are replaced with graphic symbols, but occasionally the company has to go with an English word.

Another reason for joint ownership ventures is financial. A U.S. company may wish to set up European operations but may find it expensive. A joint ownership venture with a European firm may be the solution. A key to the success of a joint ownership venture, as with any type of partnership, is finding and keeping the right mix of companies. Foreign and U.S. firms do not always have the same views. Europeans tend to be engineering-oriented, for instance. The term *marketing* may simply mean "sales" to them. In contrast, American companies often put marketing first. Management becomes difficult when the partners disagree on fundamental components of the business. Whatever the level of collaboration, finding the right partner reduces differences and is vital to success.

Summary

1) Understand that the four Cs of marketing portray the microenvironment.

The microenvironment consists of the company, its customers, and other economic institutions that shape its marketing practices. Thus, the effect of the microenvironment is regular and direct. It is useful to organize all microenvironmental forces into four basic categories: company, customers, competitors, and collaborators. These are called the four Cs. Each C represents a participant that performs essential business activities. The company is the business or organization itself. Customers are the lifeblood of every company; a company that does not satisfy customers' needs will not stay in business in the long run. Competitors are rival companies engaged in the same business. Collaborators are persons or companies that work with a marketing company.

2) Recognize how marketing creates economic utility for customers.

Marketing includes designing, distributing, and storing products; scheduling their sale; and informing buyers about them. It thus helps to create form utility and creates place, time, and possession utility. Together, these constitute economic utility. By creating economic utility, marketing delivers a standard of living to society.

3) Identify the various types of competitors and understand how marketers anticipate and react to competitors' strategies.

Competitors are rival companies interested in selling their products and services to the same group of customers and potential customers. Companies compete on the basis of price, quality, time, and/or location. In general, a price that is lower than competitors' prices will attract customers. Many businesses choose to compete on the basis of quality rather than on the basis of price. Quality-based competition is more complex than price competition because consumers define quality in many different ways. Time-based competition focuses on the fact that buyers prefer to take possession of their goods exactly when they need them, which is often as soon as possible. Location-based competition is based on providing more place utility than competitors do. To establish and maintain a competitive advantage means to be superior to or different from competitors in terms of price, quality, time, or location. This superiority may be accomplished by operating a more efficient factory, by selling at a lower price, by designing better-quality products, or by satisfying customers in other ways.

4) Describe the value chain and explain why it must be managed.

The value chain is the system of collaborative activities and relationships involved in operating a business. Each link in the chain adds value to the product customers ultimately buy. By managing these collaborations, companies free up their resources so that they can concentrate on what they do best. Having every organization in the value chain focus on its particular core competencies results in less expensive, better-quality products.

5) Understand the importance of global competition in today's economy.

The United States—as well as the rest of the world—has passed through a transition period from a domestic orientation to a global orientation. Today, with multinational organizations employing global marketing strategies, a domestic marketer must be aware of foreign competitors' influence not only in international markets but also in its own domestic market. Markets have been internationalized, competition is global, and the future of marketing is global.

6) Understand that the four Cs are shaped by global forces.
Because competition is global, companies must analyze microenvironments in various parts of the world. The four Cs often vary by country and culture. International companies often focus on satisfy-

ing customer needs by working with collaborators to gain a competitive advantage.

7) Explain the importance of understanding global cultures.

Understanding why people in foreign countries behave and react as they do requires knowing how their values and beliefs affect the success of marketing efforts. Language and cultural symbols vary from culture to culture. Ethnocentrism is the tendency to consider one's own culture and way of life as the natural and normal ones.

8) Understand the different levels of management involvement and ownership in international marketing.

Direct investment and direct exporting are basic types of involvement in international markets that do not require foreign collaborators. Indirect exporting and joint ventures require working with collaborators. Joint venturing takes one of four forms: licensing, franchising, contract manufacturing, or joint ownership.

Key Terms

boycott (p. 101)
brand (p. 90)
collaborator (p. 92)
company (p. 88)
competitor (p. 90)
contract manufacturing (p. 105)
core competency (p. 93)
customer (p. 89)
direct exporting (p. 104)
direct foreign investment (p. 103)
economic utility (p. 89)
embargo (p. 101)
entrepreneur (p. 89)
ethnocentrism (p. 98)
export (p. 95)
export management company (p. 104)

exporting (p. 104)
form utility (p. 89)
four Cs (p. 88)
import (p. 95)
import quota (p. 101)
indirect exporting (p. 104)
international franchising (p. 105)
international marketing (p. 95)
intrapreneurial organization (p. 89)
joint ownership venture (p. 105)
joint venture (p. 104)
licensing (p. 104)
location-based competition (p. 91)
microenvironment (p. 88)
multinational economic community (p. 99)
outsourcing (p. 94)

place utility (p. 89)
possession utility (p. 90)
price competition (p. 90)
product category (p. 90)
product class (p. 90)
quality-based competition (p. 91)
relationship management (p. 95)
supplier (p. 92)
tariff (p. 100)
time utility (p. 89)
time-based competition (p. 91)
value chain (p. 92)

Questions for Review & Critical Thinking

1. State what each of the four Cs stands for, and give an example of each.
2. Who are a professional soccer team's competitors?
3. What are the core competencies of the following organizations?
   a. Levi Strauss
   b. Southwest Airlines
   c. Chicago Bulls
   d. AT&T
   e. Sony
4. Identify the participants in a value chain that brings automobiles to the ultimate consumer.
5. Identify the competitive advantages of the following products:
   a. Lennox air conditioners
   b. Barnes and Noble bookstores
   c. DeBeers diamonds
   d. Visa credit cards
   e. eTrade stockbroker

6. List ten foreign products sold in the United States. How many have you purchased?
7. Why is global collaboration growing in importance?
8. Explain how global competition affects a small business in your college town.
9. What factors affect a company's ability to compete in international markets?
10. Compare and contrast direct foreign investments and joint ownership ventures.
11. Suppose you are the marketing manager of a company that outsources key components of the product it manufactures. What are the job titles of the people in the supplier companies with which you work? Should your company maintain total control of the supplier companies, or should you try to think of the suppliers as your collaborators in a joint effort?

1. Go to the Yahoo! search engine (http://www.yahoo.com) and enter "European Union" as a search phrase. What type of information is available?
2. Use the Internet to learn what you can about Indonesia. Visit the CIA *World Factbook* at http://www.odci.gov/cia/publications/factbook/index.html. Then navigate to "Indonesia." What type of information is available?
3. Babel Fish is an online language translator. Go to http://babelfish.altavista.com/translate.dyn and you'll be able to translate from English to French, German, Italian, Spanish, or Portuguese. Enter "creating and keeping customers" and translate it into one of these languages.

Address Book (Useful URLs)

3D Atlas Online	http://www.3datlas.com
Michigan State University Center for International Business Education and Research	http://ciber.bus.msu.edu/
Advertising Age International	http://www.AdAgeInternational.com

Ethically Right or Wrong?

The United States has had a series of confrontations with China over trade. A number of politicians believe that the federal government should impose tariffs on Chinese exports to the United States unless Beijing cracks down immediately on pirating of American music, movies, and computer software.

It is estimated that Chinese factories churn out 70 million compact discs and other illegally copied products every year. The cost to American industry is about $1 billion in lost sales. American businesses are especially concerned about Chinese exports of these illegal products to other countries in Asia.

The U.S. government could impose a 100 percent tariff on all goods exported from China to the United States. These sanctions could harm a variety of Chinese industries, including some state-run factories closely linked to government leaders and their families. They could also cost American consumers if, because of the sanctions, prices go up on Chinese-made items ranging from consumer electronics to toys and clothing.

QUESTIONS

1. How might China's culture influence its values about intellectual property rights and pirating American music, movies, and software?
2. If China continues to pirate, should sanctions be imposed?
3. Should standards of business ethics be the same throughout the world?

TAKE A STAND

1. Often, when a company enters into a collaborative relationship with a single supplier, other suppliers are locked out of doing business with that company for several years. Is this practice consistent with the free enterprise system?
2. Is it ethical for a company to engage in international trade and work with collaborators in the People's Republic of China, a communist country that has been accused of human rights violations?

VIDEO CASE 4-1
Etec (A)

Etec was founded by an inventor and a former police officer. The company markets AutoCite, which is short for Automatic Citation Issuance System. Using this handheld computer and printing device, a police officer can write and record traffic violations much more efficiently. Today, AutoCite is used by police departments in more than 350 cities, municipalities, and college campuses. However, Etec sold only three units in its first two years of operation.

AutoCite is durable and works in all types of weather. A police officer who gives multiple tickets in a given location does not have to reprogram location information into the AutoCite. This allows the officer to produce more tickets in a given time period.

Etec believes that the product would prove equally beneficial to law enforcement agencies in Australia, New Zealand, Canada, Mexico, and many other countries around the world.

QUESTIONS
1. What political, economic, and cultural forces are most likely to influence Etec's global strategy?
2. Which of the international marketing strategies listed in Exhibit 4-4 would you choose for Etec?

cross-functional insights

Many theories and principles from other business disciplines can provide insights about the role of marketing in an organization. The questions in this section are designed to help you think about integrating what you have learned about management, finance, production, and other business functions with the marketing principles explained in Chapters 1 through 4.

Marketing Concept/Market-Driven Organizations The marketing concept stresses consumer orientation, long-run profitability, and integrating marketing functions with other corporate functions. Companies that have superior skill in understanding and satisfying customers are said to be market-driven.

What are the key revenue and expense items that influence an organization's long-run profitability?

Are entrepreneurs consumer-oriented? What characteristics of entrepreneurs would help them become successful marketers?

What traits should a person have to be a leader in a market-driven organization?

Does management contingency theory apply to marketing leadership positions?

Customer Satisfaction Market-oriented organizations embrace an organization-wide focus to learn their customers' needs so they can offer superior customer value—that is, so they can satisfy customer needs better than their competitors. Marketers should strive to increase customer satisfaction.

How important is a company's corporate culture in such efforts? What type of corporate culture would contribute most to the achievement of the goal of satisfying customers?

What type of performance appraisal system could be used to evaluate employees in terms of customer satisfaction?

Organizational Mission Top managers decide on the organizational, or corporate, mission. This strategic decision influences all other marketing strategies. An organizational mission is a statement of company purpose. It explains why the organization exists and what it hopes to accomplish. It provides direction for the entire organization. When we discussed corporate mission statements, we looked at the mission from a marketing perspective.

What aspects of a mission statement would be important to a manager of human resources? A manager of engineering? A financial manager?

Total Quality Management A company that employs a total quality management strategy must evaluate quality through the eyes of the customer. Every aspect of the business must focus on quality. For example, management may institute a performance appraisal system to evaluate employees in terms of the service they provide to customers. Further, all participants must strive for continuous improvement.

Total quality management requires the cooperation of marketing, production, and many other functional areas of the business. How should this coordination be managed?

How important is knowledge of statistical analysis and statistical process control in analyzing a total quality management system?

What type of performance appraisal system could be used to evaluate employees in terms of the quality of goods and services produced?

Do companies need to solicit the opinions of as many employees as possible to be successful in a total quality effort?

Differentiation Strategy A differentiation strategy emphasizes offering a product that is unique in the industry, pro-

vides a distinct advantage, or is otherwise set apart from competitors' brands in some way other than price.

How do the laws of supply and demand apply to a marketer of branded goods or services that seeks to differentiate them from those of competitors? Would economists and marketers give the same answer to this question?

SWOT Situation analysis is the diagnostic activity of interpreting environmental conditions and changes in light of the organization's ability to capitalize on potential opportunities and to ward off problems. SWOT stands for external Strengths and Weaknesses and internal Opportunities and Threats.

How would a company's financial analysts look at internal opportunities and threats?

How would a top executive's concerns about internal opportunities and threats differ from those of a marketer, if at all?

What is opportunity cost, and how does it relate to the strategic marketing process and SWOT analysis?

Competitive Advantage One of the most important goals of a business unit is to establish and maintain a competitive advantage—to be superior to or favorably different from competitors in a way that is important to the market.

Marketers think that increasing customer satisfaction through product development is the key to competitive advantage. In what other ways might a top executive have the organization strive for competitive advantage?

Discuss marketing strategies aimed at gaining competitive advantage in the context of antitrust laws such as the Sherman Antitrust Act and the Federal Trade Commission Act.

Diversification Marketing new products to a new set of customers is called diversification.

What economic factors might bar a company from entering a market?

What organizational changes are necessary when a company diversifies?

Control To marketers, the purpose of managerial control is to ensure that planned activities are completely and properly executed.

What role does accounting play in the marketing control process?

Do organizational conflicts arise between marketers and accountants because of different perspectives on control activities?

Four Cs Working with collaborators is becoming increasingly important.

What organizational adjustments must be made when a company decides to collaborate with another company?

Core Competencies A core competency is expertise in a critical functional area or aspect of a particular business that helps provide a company's unique competitive advantage.

At what level in the organization are core competencies determined? By what process?

International Marketing International marketing involves the adoption of a marketing strategy that views the world market rather than a domestic market as the basis for marketing operations.

What adjustments must a company make in its organizational structure when it becomes an international organization?

Information Technology and
Marketing Research

5

chapter

L E A R N I N G   O B J E C T I V E S

After you have studied this chapter, you will be able to . . .

1) Explain why information is essential to effective marketing decision making.

2) Explain the importance of worldwide information systems.

3) Describe a decision support system.

4) Explain the contribution of marketing research to effective decision making.

5) Describe the stages in the marketing research process.

6) Explain how exploratory research relates to specific marketing management problems.

7) Understand why secondary data are valuable sources of information.

8) Understand the uses of surveys, observation, and experiments.

9) Demonstrate your knowledge of the purposes of sales forecasting.

10) Evaluate the advantages and disadvantages of the various forecasting methods.

Since the late 1970s, Shell Oil's prestige as a premier company had gradually slipped away. Employees were feeling low, and so were shareholders. How could the company regain its status in the industry?
Shell needed to figure out what made a corporation first-rate in the minds of consumers. So in 1995, Shell conducted a series of focus groups and one-on-one interviews among various segments of the population, including minorities, youths, residents of neighborhoods near Shell plants, legislators, academics, even employees and retirees of Shell. Top companies, people told researchers, delivered more than just a good product or service. They were an integral part of their communities. And while Shell Oil, which traces its roots back to 1912, was a household name, most people knew very little about the company. Of course, consumers expected Shell to excel in its core business—oil. But they had higher expectations than that.

In response to this information from the market, Shell developed several videos that communicated the company's central values. Another round of qualitative research evaluated the various messages and, ultimately, helped shape the strategy for a promotional campaign. Shell's expertise in the oil industry was a factor to consumers, but so was its promise to be socially responsible. Shell needed to underscore that promise.

A survey was conducted to determine what messages clicked with the target audience. Would it be something about Shell's innovative chemists or the company's environmental efforts? Social issues, things that related directly to people's lives, resonated strongest. Shell might be proud of its scientists, but consumers knew Shell as an oil company first. The campaign had to start with the familiar—and introduce Shell's technological know-how later.

Shell's advertising agency developed 12 campaigns with social themes. Research was conducted on each campaign to see which commercials delivered and which backfired. At each stage in the testing process, the advertising agency tweaked the creative strategy. The "Count on Shell" campaign, featuring a mix of safety messages, was the last one tested. It turned out to be the best of the bunch. People liked that the ads addressed the quality of their lives. The advertisements put a face on Shell, providing consumers with meaningful information they could use, like what to do if a tire blows out on the highway. Ironically, in its quest to revitalize its image, Shell had come full circle. Its successful "Come to Shell for Answers" campaign of the late 1970s and early '80s had been based on the same concept. Shell management worried that "Count on Shell," so close in concept to its predecessor, would seem like old news. But researchers stood firm: The idea behind the campaign—that Shell could help consumers in their lives—was critical to the company's identity. The researchers won.

Since the launch of this promotional campaign, recall of Shell advertising has jumped to 32 percent from 20 percent among "opinion influencers," adults who've addressed a public meeting or participated in other civic activities recently. Traffic to http://www.countonshell.com has risen more than 18,000 percent, and a million copies of Shell's free safety brochures have been distributed.[1]

Although many factors contributed to Shell Oil's resurgence, marketing research was a major factor. Clearly, Shell understands how important systematic research is to modern marketing managers. This chapter focuses on how marketing managers use marketing information, especially marketing research, to influence decisions about marketing activities. The chapter begins with a discussion of the role information plays in the marketing decision-making process and goes on to discuss worldwide information systems, decision support systems, and data-based marketing. The stages in the marketing research process are then described in detail. The chapter ends with an explanation of the importance of accurate sales forecasting.

Information: The Basis of Effective Marketing

Marketing managers spend much of their time making decisions. An integral aspect of decision making is the analysis and evaluation of information about the organization's customers, environment, and marketing activities. To be effective, the marketer needs to gather enough information to understand past events, to identify what is occurring now, and to predict what might occur in the future. Good, timely marketing information is an extremely valuable management tool because it reduces uncertainty and the risks associated with decision making. Marketing information can lead the marketing manager to develop new products, to improve existing products, and to make changes in price, promotion, and distribution strategies and tactics. Information can also help define problems or identify opportunities. Once a marketing problem or opportunity is identified, further pertinent information can be systematically gathered to help the marketing manager deal objectively with the situation.

When you're not informed, it shows.

It happens to the best of us. Discovering you lack a critical piece of business information can leave you crying on the inside. Presenting Hoover's Online. Our incisive editorial coverage runs the gamut of business — from travel to money, from company profiles to career development — so you'll never look foolish. **Know thy stuff.** www.hoovers.com

HOOVER'S ONLINE

Worldwide information system
An organized collection of telecommunications equipment, computer hardware and software, data, and personnel designed to capture, store, update, manipulate, analyze, and immediately display information about worldwide business activity.

Worldwide Information Systems in the 21st Century

The well-being of business organizations that hope to prosper in the 21st century depends on information about the world economy and global competition. Contemporary marketers require timely and accurate information from around the globe to maintain competitive advantages. In today's world, managers find that much information is available instantaneously. This fact has changed the nature of marketing decision making.

As a result of increased global competition and technological advances, worldwide information systems have been developed. A **worldwide information system** is an organized collection of telecommunications equipment, computer hardware and software, data, and personnel. Such a system is designed to capture, store, update, manipulate, analyze, and immediately display information about worldwide business activity.[2] Worldwide information systems are made possible by satellite communication, high-speed microcomputers, electronic data interchanges, fiber optics, CD-ROM data storage, fax machines, the Internet, and other technological advances involving interactive media. For example, when executives at Motorola must make pricing decisions about cellular phones for their European markets, they can get information about international currency and exchange rates immediately, without leaving their desks. A salesperson who needs information about a corporation's executives can access a full report on the corporation from a remote location using a personal communication device and the Internet. A marketing manager who requires a bibliography on a particular subject can generate hundreds of abstracts and articles with a few simple keystrokes.

Consider these examples of the dramatic influence of worldwide information systems on the way two organizations do business.

- Every evening, Wal-Mart transmits millions of characters of data about the day's sales to its apparel suppliers. Wrangler, a supplier of blue jeans, shares some of the data and a model that interprets the data. It also shares software applications that allow the company to replenish stocks in Wal-Mart stores. This decision support system determines when to send specific quantities of specific sizes and colors of jeans to specific stores from specific warehouses. The result is a learning loop that lowers inventory costs and leads to fewer stockouts.

- At any moment, on any day, United Parcel Service (UPS) can track the status of its shipments around the world. UPS drivers use hand-held electronic clipboards, called delivery information acquisition devices (DIAD), to record data about each pickup or delivery. The data are then entered into the company's main computer for record keeping and analysis. Then, using a satellite telecommunications system, UPS can track any shipment for its customers.

Facing a public increasingly critical of logging in national forests, the U.S. Forest Service uses information systems and a technique called "seen-area analysis" to plan national forests.[3] The information systems help foresters tuck clear-cuts behind ridges, shield them from view with "beauty strips"—veneers of trees maintained to hide bare patches—and identify areas where they can use "partial cut" techniques to subtly thin the forest without ruining the view.

The age of global information has begun, and worldwide information systems have already changed the nature of business. Yet, as amazing as today's technology is, it will seem primitive as the 21st century advances.

Data and Information

Before we go on, we must define the difference between information and data. **Data** are simply facts—recorded measures of certain phenomena—whereas **information** is a body of facts in a format suitable for use in decision making. The proper collection of data is the cornerstone of any information system. The data collected should be pertinent, timely, and accurate. There are two types of data: primary data and secondary data. **Primary data** are data gathered and assembled specifically for the project at hand. For example, a company that designs an original questionnaire and conducts a survey to learn about its customers' characteristics is collecting primary data. **Secondary data** are data previously collected and assembled for some purpose other than the project at hand. Secondary data come from both internal sources, such as accounting records, and sources external to the organization, such as the U.S. Bureau of the Census. Generating information may require collecting secondary data, primary data, or both.

Data
Facts and recorded measures of phenomena.

Information
Data in a format useful to decision makers.

Primary data
Data gathered and assembled specifically for the project at hand.

Secondary data
Data previously collected and assembled for some purpose other than the one at hand.

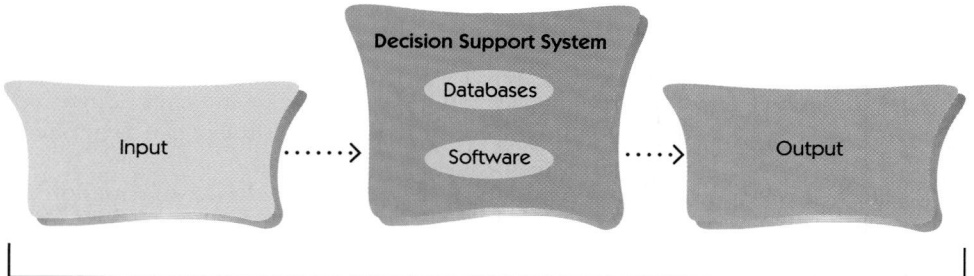

The Decision Support System

Decision Support Systems

To store data and to transform data into accessible information, companies use computer systems called **decision support systems.**[4] Such systems serve specific business units within a company. A large organization may have several decision support systems linked into its worldwide information system.

The purpose of a decision support system is to allow decision makers to answer questions through direct interaction with databases. As Exhibit 5-1 shows, the system consists of databases and software.

A **database** is a collection of data, arranged in a logical manner and organized in a form that can be stored and processed by a computer. For example, customer names, addresses, zip codes, and previous purchases may be contained in a company's internal database. Internal records collected by accounting and other company reports provide product data about sales, shipments, costs, and so on. A typical product manager may ask for weekly (or daily) computer-generated reports on sales by geographical area, inventory reports, back-order reports, and other information that managers use to improve performance.

Many commercial organizations, such as Information Resources, ABI/Inform, and Dow Jones News/Retrieval, assemble and market computerized databases. These companies make retail sales figures, economics statistics, industry news, journal articles, and other data accessible instantaneously via the Internet.

The **software** portion of a decision support system consists of various types of programs that tell computers, printers, and other hardware what to do. Advances in spreadsheet and statistical software have revolutionized the analysis of marketing data. A decision support system's software allows managers to combine and restructure databases, assess relationships, estimate variables, and otherwise analyze the relevant databases.

Most of today's software is so user-friendly that it is easy for nonexperts to maintain direct control over a computer's tasks and outcomes. A manager sitting at a computer workstation can instantaneously retrieve data files and

Decision support system
A computer system that stores data and transforms them into accessible information. It includes databases and software.

Database
A collection of data, arranged in a logical manner and organized in a form that can be stored and processed by a computer.

Software
Various types of programs that tell computers, printers, and other hardware what to do.

Pizza Hut maintains a database on what types of pizza people have previously ordered.

http://www.pizzahut.com

can request special creative analyses, in which information is refined, modified, or generated in a tailor-made format. At Kmart, a computerized point-of-sale checkout system and a satellite communications system linked to a marketing decision support system allow managers at headquarters to retrieve and analyze up-to-the-minute sales data on all merchandise for the company's 2,400 stores.

Intranets

If a company's decision support system is a private data network that uses Internet standards and technology, it is called an **intranet**.[5] The information on a company's intranet (data, graphics, even video and voice) is available only inside the organization. Thus, a key difference between the Internet and an intranet is that "firewalls," or security software programs, are installed to limit access to only those employees authorized to enter the system.[6]

Using Internet features, such as electronic mail, Web pages, and browsers, a company builds its own intranet, which is a communications and data resource at that specific company.[7] Company information is accessed using the same point-and-click technology people are accustomed to using to access the Internet. Managers and employees use links to get complete, up-to-date information. An intranet lets authorized personnel—some of whom may previously have been isolated on departmental local area networks—look at product drawings, employee newsletters, sales reports, and other kinds of company information. In short, setting up an intranet adds the functionality of the World Wide Web to an organization's existing worldwide information system.

Many organizations give external collaborators, such as suppliers or customers, access to portions of their intranets. These **extranets** allow all parties to obtain key information whenever it is needed. They may reduce service costs, and they help build and maintain strong relationships between the parties.

Intranet
A company's private decision support system that uses Internet standards and technology.

Extranet
The portions of an organization's intranet that are shared by external collaborators, such as suppliers or customers.

Data-Based Marketing

Many organizations create databases containing huge amounts of data about individual customers and potential customers. Marketers use this information to generate computerized mailing lists and individualized promotional messages. The practice of using databases of customers' names, addresses, phone numbers, past purchases, responses to previous offers, and demographic characteristics in making marketing decisions is referred to as **data-based marketing**. Databases may be compiled by the organization and/or purchased from organizations that specialize in mailing lists or other forms of databases. *Relational database software* is an important part of data-based marketing because it allows marketers to relate records in one database, such as sale representatives' customer orders, to records in another database, such as products ready to ship.[8]

> Data-based marketing has implications for many aspects of marketing strategy, especially market segmentation and relationship marketing.

Data-based marketing
The practice of using databases of customers' names, addresses, phone numbers, past purchases, responses to previous offers, and demographic characteristics in making marketing decisions.

In recent years, organizations have begun using the Internet to compile databases. For example, the first time Internet users visit certain Web sites, they must fill out a registration request before they get access to the site. The marketer can collect address information and ask visitors about such matters as their interests and demographic background. Then, through use of relational database software, this information can be combined with other databases.

Data-based marketing has implications for many aspects of marketing strategy, especially market segmentation and relationship marketing. This topic will be discussed throughout the book.

Marketing research

The systematic and objective process of generating information for use in marketing decision making.

What Is Marketing Research?

Any discussion of the importance of information to the marketer must include a discussion of marketing research. Marketing research allows managers to make decisions based on objective data, gathered systematically, rather than on intuition.

What is the distinction between marketing research and other forms of marketing information? Even without a formal research program, a manager will have some information about what is going on in the world. Simply by reading the newspaper or watching TV, he or she may discover that a competitor has announced a new product, that the inflation rate is stabilizing, or that a new highway will be built and a shopping mall erected north of town. All of these things may affect the marketer's business, and this information is certainly handy to have, but is it the result of marketing research?

The answer to this question is no. **Marketing research** is the systematic and objective process of generating information for use in making marketing decisions. This process includes defining the problem and identifying what information is required to solve the problem, designing a method for collecting information, managing and implementing the collection of data, analyzing the results, and communicating the findings and their implications.[9]

This definition suggests that marketing research is a special effort rather than a haphazard attempt at gathering information. Thus, glancing at a news magazine on an airplane or overhearing a rumor is not conducting marketing research. Even if a rumor or a fact casually overheard becomes the foundation of a marketing strategy, that strategy is not a product of marketing research because it was not based on information that was systematically and objectively gathered and recorded. The term *marketing research* suggests a specific, serious effort to generate new information. The term *research* suggests a patient, objective, and accurate search.

Although marketing managers may perform the research task themselves, they often seek the help of specialists known as marketing researchers. The researchers' role requires detachment from the question under study. If researchers cannot remain impartial, they may try to prove something rather than to generate objective data. If bias of any type enters into the investigative process, the value of the findings must be questioned. Yet this sort of thing can happen relatively easily. For example, a developer who owned a large parcel of land on which she wanted to build a high-price, high-prestige shopping center conducted a survey of customers' buying habits to demonstrate to prospective mall occupants that there was an attractive market for such a center. By conducting the survey only in elite neighborhoods, she generated "proof" that area residents wanted a high-prestige shopping center.

Misleading "research" of this kind must be avoided. Unfortunately, business people with no knowledge of proper marketing research methods may inadvertently conduct poorly designed, biased studies or may be sold such work by marketing research firms. All business people should understand marketing research well enough to avoid these mistakes.

The Stages in the Research Process

Marketing is not an exact science like physics, but that does not mean that marketers and marketing researchers should not try to approach their jobs in a scientific manner. Marketing research is a systematic inquiry into the characteristics of the marketplace, just as astronomy is a systematic investigation of the stars and planets. Both use step-by-step approaches to gain knowledge.

The steps in the research process are highly interrelated, and one step leads to the next. Moreover, the stages in the research process often overlap. Disappointments encountered at one stage may necessitate returning to previous stages or even starting over. Thus, it is something of an oversimplification to present marketing research as a neatly ordered sequence of activities. Still, marketing research often follows a generalized pattern of seven stages. These stages are (1) defining the problem, (2) planning the research design, (3) selecting a sample, (4) collecting data, (5) analyzing data, (6) drawing conclusions and preparing a report, and (7) following up.

Again, these stages overlap and affect one another. For example, the research objectives outlined as part of the problem definition stage will have an impact on sample selection and data collection. In some cases, the "later" stages may be completed before the "early" ones. A decision to sample people of low educational levels (stage 3) will affect the wording of the questions posed to these people (stage 2). The research process, in fact, often becomes cyclical and ongoing, with the conclusions of one study generating new ideas and suggesting problems requiring further investigation. Within each stage of the research process, the researcher faces a number of alternative methods, or paths, from which to choose. In this regard, the research process can be compared to a journey.[10] On any map, some paths are more clearly charted than others. Some roads are direct; others are roundabout. Some paths are free; others require the traveler to pay a toll. The point to remember is that there is no "right" or "best" path. The road taken depends on where the traveler wants to go and the amounts of time, money, ability, and other resources available for the trip.

Although there is no "right" path, the researcher must choose an appropriate one—that is, one that addresses the problem at hand. In some situations, where time is short, the quickest path is best. In other circumstances, where money, time, and personnel are plentiful, the chosen path may be long and demanding.

Exploring the various paths marketing researchers encounter is the main purpose of this section, which describes the seven stages of the research process. Exhibit 5-2 illustrates some choices researchers face at each stage.

STAGE 1: DEFINING THE PROBLEM

The idea that **problem definition** is central to the marketing research process is so obvious that its importance is easily overlooked. Albert Einstein noted that "the formulation of a problem is often more essential than its solution."[11] This is valuable advice for marketing managers and researchers who, in their haste to find the right answer, may fail to ask the right question. Too often, data are collected before the nature of the problem has been carefully established. Except in

Problem definition
The crucial first stage in the marketing research process—determining the problem to be solved and the objectives of the research.

The Marketing Research Process

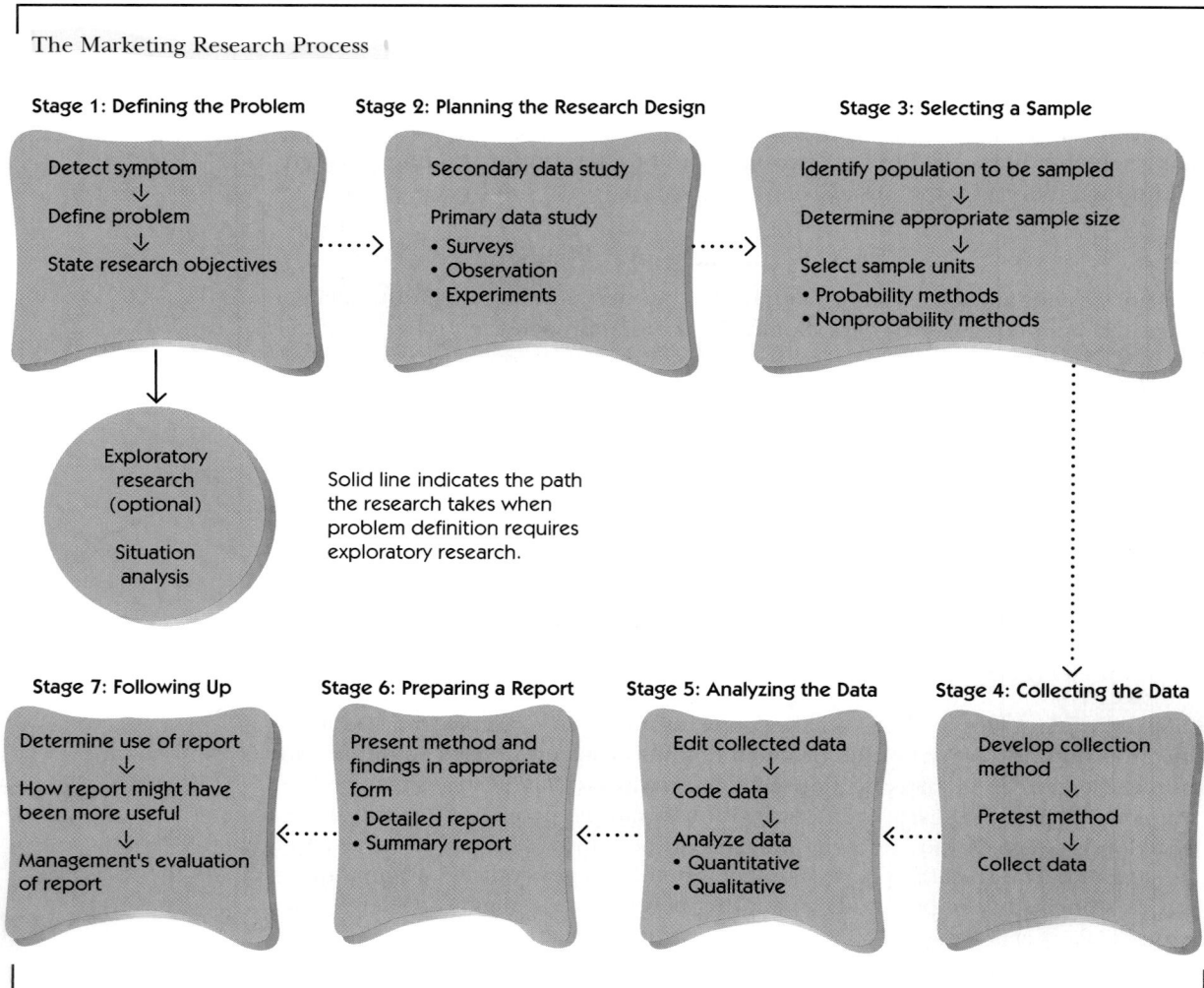

Stage 1: Defining the Problem

Detect symptom
↓
Define problem
↓
State research objectives

Stage 2: Planning the Research Design

Secondary data study

Primary data study
• Surveys
• Observation
• Experiments

Stage 3: Selecting a Sample

Identify population to be sampled
↓
Determine appropriate sample size
↓
Select sample units
• Probability methods
• Nonprobability methods

Exploratory research (optional)

Situation analysis

Solid line indicates the path the research takes when problem definition requires exploratory research.

Stage 7: Following Up

Determine use of report
↓
How report might have been more useful
↓
Management's evaluation of report

Stage 6: Preparing a Report

Present method and findings in appropriate form
• Detailed report
• Summary report

Stage 5: Analyzing the Data

Edit collected data
↓
Code data
↓
Analyze data
• Quantitative
• Qualitative

Stage 4: Collecting the Data

Develop collection method
↓
Pretest method
↓
Collect data

cases of coincidence or good luck, such data will not help resolve the marketer's difficulties. Researchers are well advised to remember the adage "a problem well defined is a problem half solved."

Problems Can Be Opportunities   On many occasions, the research process is focused not on a problem but on an opportunity. For example, a toy maker who has developed a fabulous new item might face the "problem" of determining what age groups will most likely want the toy or which advertising media are the best to use. In this happy circumstance, the problem definition stage of the research might well be called the "opportunity definition" stage. The point is that the problems addressed by marketing research are frequently "good" problems and not disasters.

> The problems addressed by marketing research are frequently "good" problems and not disasters.

Don't Confuse Symptoms with the Real Problem   There is a difference between a problem and the symptoms of that problem. Pain, for example, is the symptom of a problem. The cause of the pain, perhaps a broken leg, is the problem. In marketing, falling sales are a symptom that some aspect of the marketing mix is not working properly. Sales may be falling because price competition has intensified or because buyer preferences have changed. Defining the general nature of the problem provides a direction for the research.

Consider the case of Ha-Psu-Shu-Tse brand fried Indian bread mix. The owner of the company thought that his product, one of the few Native American food products sold in the United States, was selling poorly because it was not advertised heavily. This feeling led him to hire a management consulting group to research new advertising themes. The consultants suggested, instead, that the product's brand name, Ha-Psu-Shu-Tse (the Pawnee word for "red corn"), might be the main problem. They proposed that consumer attitudes toward the name and product be the starting point of research. In effect, the consultants were reluctant to choose advertising, one component of the marketing mix, as the area of concern without checking for more basic causes of the product's difficulties. The researchers did not confuse symptoms with the real problem.

As Exhibit 5-3 shows, defining the problem begins with the detection of symptoms. If managers are uncertain about the exact nature of the problem, they may spend time analyzing and learning about the situation. For example, they may discuss the situation with others, such as sales representatives, who are close to the customers. They may conduct exploratory research to shed more light on the situation and reveal more details about the problem. Exploratory research is optional and is not used in all research projects.

Finally, as Exhibit 5-3 shows, the problem is defined, and a series of research objectives related to the problem are stated. No decisions about the remaining stages of the marketing research process should be made until managers and researchers clearly understand the objectives of the research about to be undertaken.

Exploratory Research   As noted earlier, **exploratory research** is sometimes needed to clarify the nature of a marketing problem. Management may know, from noting a symptom such as declining sales, that some kind of problem is "out there" and may undertake exploratory research to try to identify the problem. Or, management may know what the problem is but not how big or how far-reaching it is. Here too, managers may need research to help them analyze the situation.

Exploratory research
Research to clarify the nature of a marketing problem.

e   x   h   i   b   i 5-3

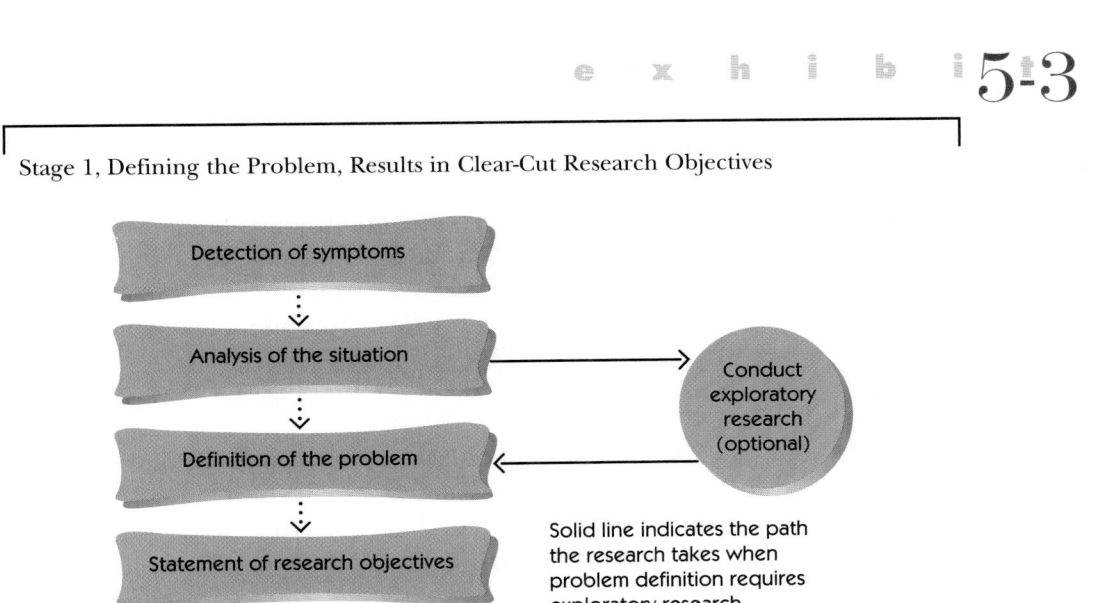

Stage 1, Defining the Problem, Results in Clear-Cut Research Objectives

Detection of symptoms

Analysis of the situation

Definition of the problem

Statement of research objectives

Conduct exploratory research (optional)

Solid line indicates the path the research takes when problem definition requires exploratory research.

Focus group interviews are a popular form of exploratory research. Groups of 6 to 10 people give their comments and reactions to new product ideas or explain why they buy certain products.

Focus group interview
A loosely structured interview in which a group of 6 to 10 people discusses a product or focuses on some aspect of buying behavior.

Providing conclusions is not the purpose of exploratory research. Its purpose is simply to investigate and explore. Usually, exploratory research is undertaken with the expectation that other types of research will follow and that the subsequent research will be directed at finding possible solutions.

In any research situation, it is generally best to check available secondary data before beginning extensive data collection. Some work at a library, on the Internet, or with an internal database may save time and money. However, there isn't any set formula that outlines exactly how to analyze a situation.

Sometimes checking secondary sources may not be the appropriate first step. Instead, a short series of interviews with a few customers may be in order. For example, suppose a fast-food restaurant is considering adding a low-fat menu or a line of tacos to its standard menu of hamburgers. Marketing managers might begin their research by conducting some unstructured interviews with customers. Customers might surprise management with negative comments on the proposed additions. Exploratory research in this case could serve to identify problem areas or point to a need for additional information.

Although there are many techniques for exploratory research, our discussion will highlight one popular method—the focus group interview—to illustrate the nature of exploratory techniques.

Focus group interviews are loosely structured interviews with groups of 6 to 10 people who "focus" on a product or some aspect of buying behavior. During a group session, individuals are asked to comment on and react to new product ideas or explain why they buy (or do not buy) certain products. Researchers later analyze those comments for useful ideas, such as that a product is "too high-priced" or "looks like it would break easily." Focus group research is extremely flexible and may be used for many purposes—for example, to learn what problems consumers have with products. During one of Rubbermaid Inc.'s focus groups on housewares, a woman accused the industry of sexism.[12] "Why do companies continue to treat brooms and mops like they were 'women's tools'?" she complained. "They're poorly designed and second-class to hammers and saws, which are balanced and molded to fit men's hands. Brooms and mops make housework more miserable, not easier." At the time, Rubbermaid did not make cleaning products, but the woman's remarks eventually convinced the company that an opportunity awaited. After five years of research and development, Rubbermaid introduced a line of about 50 cleaning products and brushes designed to make cleaning easier, with handles that fit comfortably in consumers' hands and bristles angled to reach tight spaces.

What Is a "Good" Research Objective? Marketers contemplating a research project must decide exactly what they are looking for. For example, a local Big Brothers and Sisters organization might have the following research objectives:

• To determine males' awareness of the Big Brothers and Sisters organization
• To determine males' awareness of the organization's need for volunteers
• To determine males' willingness to volunteer as big brothers
• To determine a demographic profile of those most likely to volunteer

A formal statement of the problem(s) and the research objective(s) must be the culmination of Stage 1 of the research process. These provide the framework for the study.

STAGE 2: PLANNING THE RESEARCH DESIGN

After researchers have clearly identified the research problem and formulated a hypothesis, the next step is to develop a formal research design. The **research design** is a master plan that identifies the specific techniques and procedures that will be used to collect and analyze data about a problem. The research design must be carefully compared to the objectives developed in Stage 1 to assure that the sources of data, the data collected, the scheduling and costs involved, and so on are consistent with the researchers' main goals.

"First, they do an online search."

Research design
A master plan that specifically identifies what techniques and procedures will be used to collect and analyze data about a problem.

At the outset, the researchers should determine if the data they need have already been generated by others or if primary research is required. In other words, as Exhibit 5-2 suggests, researchers planning a research design must first choose between using secondary data and using primary data.

Research Designs Using Secondary Data As we have mentioned, data already in the researcher's decision support system or in the library may provide an adequate basis for a formal research effort. For example, a marketer of mobile homes might know that sales of this product rise as building permits for traditional homes decline. Using government figures showing the numbers of building permits issued and trends in home building, the mobile home seller can develop a quantitative model to predict market behavior. In this case, the research design involves the analysis of secondary data only.

Meaningful secondary data may come from internal sources, such as company databases, or external sources, such as government agencies, trade associations, and companies that specialize in supplying specific types of data. Exhibit 5-4 shows some examples of the types of secondary data that are available.

The primary advantages of secondary data are that (1) they almost always are less expensive to collect than primary data and (2) they can be obtained rapidly. Secondary sources must be used with care, however, as they have certain disadvantages:

- Secondary data are "old" and possibly outdated.
- Some data are collected only periodically. For example, the population census is taken only once a decade. Comparatively up-to-date estimates are often available in such cases, however.
- Data may not have been collected in the form preferred. Sales figures may be available for a county but not for a particular town within that county, for example.
- Users of secondary data may not be able to assess the data's accuracy. For example, previous researchers may have "bent" the data to "prove" some point or theory.

In general, a basic disadvantage of secondary data is that they were not collected specifically to meet the researcher's needs. The manager's task is to determine if the secondary data are pertinent and accurate.

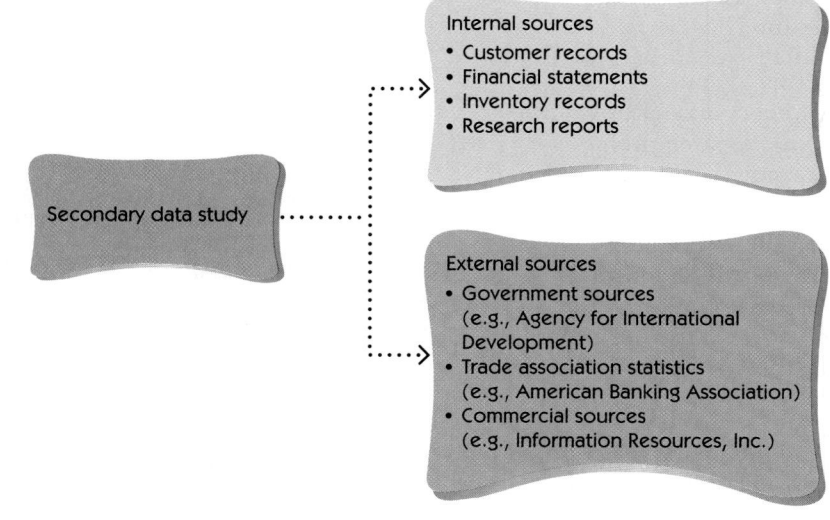

Secondary Data Sources

Secondary data study

Internal sources
- Customer records
- Financial statements
- Inventory records
- Research reports

External sources
- Government sources
  (e.g., Agency for International
  Development)
- Trade association statistics
  (e.g., American Banking Association)
- Commercial sources
  (e.g., Information Resources, Inc.)

The Internet as a Source of Secondary Data As described in Chapter 3, the Internet is a worldwide network of computers that gives users access to information and documents from distant sources. Many managers see the Internet as the world's largest public library, because both noncommercial and commercial organizations post secondary data there. A wealth of data from reliable sources is available. For example, the United States Library of Congress (http://www.loc.gov) provides the full text of all versions of House and Senate legislation and the full text of the *Congressional Record.*

The Internet is very user-friendly; information can be viewed using a mouse and menu-based software system called a Web browser. Netscape and Microsoft Explorer are two popular Web browsers that allow the user to enter a uniform resource locator, or URL. For example, the user might type in the URL for the U.S. Small Business Administration, which is http://www.sbaonline.sba.gov. The URL

Seemingly overnight, secondary data have become digital. For those who are "wired," the Internet is currently the research medium of choice. Every marketing researcher working in the 21st century needs to understand how to access and use the Internet.

opens the SBA's Web site, where there are many statistics about small business organizations in the U.S. economy.

A search engine is a computerized directory that allows users to search the Internet for information indexed in a particular way. Most portals, such as Yahoo!, Hotbot, Excite, AltaVista, and Snap, contain comprehensive and accurate Internet search engines. All a researcher has to do is type the search term in plain English or click on key words and phrases.

Anyone can access most Web sites without previous approval. However, many commercial sites require that the user have a valid account and password to access a site. For example, the Wall Street Journal Interactive is a valuable resource; however, only subscribers who pay a fee can read it via the Internet.

e-commerce Changing Everything

Privacy on the Internet is a controversial issue. A number of groups question whether it is an invasion of privacy to use Web site questionnaires, registration forms, and other means of collecting personal information from visitors to a site. Many marketers argue that their organizations don't need to know who the user is because the individual's name is not important for their purposes. However, they do want to know certain information (such as demographic characteristics or product usage habits) associated with an anonymous profile. A Web advertiser could reach a targeted audience without having access to identifying information. Of course, unethical companies may ignore this restriction.

In July of 1998, America Online established a new privacy policy. AOL will not read customers' email, collect any information about Web site visits, or give key data to other organizations without authorization. AOL will seek parents' written approval to get data from children at sites targeting kids. Research shows that people are more willing to disclose sensitive information if they know a Web site's privacy policy. For this reason, many high-traffic Web sites such as Yahoo! and Lycos have privacy statements, which visitors can easily access. Organizations such as the Electronic Frontier Foundation and the Online Privacy Alliance are involved in developing privacy guidelines.[13]

Research Designs Using Primary Data   Researchers who find that no appropriate secondary data are available can choose from three basic techniques for collecting primary data: surveys, observation, and experiments.

Surveys Primary data are commonly generated by survey research. Survey results on one topic or another are reported almost daily by the news media. Most adult Americans have been stopped by interviewers at shopping centers or voting places or have received mailings or phone calls from survey takers. In general, a **survey** is any research effort in which data are gathered systematically from a sample of people by means of a questionnaire. Researchers using surveys may collect data by means of telephone interviews, mailed questionnaires, personal interviews (either door-to-door or in shopping malls or some other public place), or some other communication method such as fax or the Internet.

Survey research has several advantages. For one thing, surveys involve direct communication. How better to provide buyers with what they want than to first ask them what they want? For example, U.S. automobile makers operate style research clinics to appraise consumer reactions to car designs. First, mock-ups of proposed designs are constructed; then consumers, or respondents, are recruited through short telephone interviews. These respondents are brought in to a showroom and shown a car mock-up along with competing autos from around the world. As the "buyers" look over the cars, professional interviewers ask for their reactions to virtually every detail. The survey results are then given to designers in Detroit.

When surveys are properly planned and executed, they are quick, efficient, and accurate means of gathering data. Survey research can involve problems, however. Careless researchers may design or conduct surveys improperly and thus produce incorrect and worthless results—that is, results marked by **systematic bias**. The survey questions might be poorly worded, respondents might be reluctant to provide truthful answers, the sample may not be representative, or mistakes might be made entering data into the computer.

Exhibit 5-5 summarizes the advantages and disadvantages of the most popular types of surveys. You can see from this exhibit that choosing one method over another involves trade-offs. For instance, a low-cost mail survey takes more time and is less versatile than a higher-cost personal interview at the consumer's doorstep.

Survey
Any research effort in which data are gathered systematically from a sample of people by means of a questionnaire. Surveys are conducted through face-to-face interviews, telephone interviews, and mailed questionnaires.

Systematic bias
A research shortcoming caused by flaws in the design or execution of a research study.

	PERSONAL INTERVIEW		MAIL-IN QUESTIONNAIRE	TELEPHONE INTERVIEW	INTERNET SURVEY
	DOOR-TO-DOOR	SHOPPING MALL			
Speed of data collection	Moderate to fast	Fast	Researcher has no control over return of questionnaire	Very fast	Instantaneous
Respondent cooperation	Good	Moderate	Moderate—poorly designed questionnaire will have low response rate	Good	Varies depending on Web site
Flexibility of questioning	Very flexible	Very flexible	Highly standardized format is very inflexible	Moderately flexible	Extremely flexible
Questionnaire length	Long	Moderate to long	Varies depending on purpose	Moderate	Modest
Possibility for respondent misunderstanding	Low	Low	Highest—no interviewer to clarify questions	Moderate	High
Influence of interviewer on answers	High	High	None	Moderate	None
Cost	Highest	Moderate to high	Lowest	Low to moderate	Low

How does the researcher choose the appropriate survey technique? The marketing problem itself generally suggests which technique is most appropriate. An advertiser whose message appears in a broadcast seen by many viewers, like the Super Bowl or the World Series, might contact viewers in their homes via telephone to gather reactions to its commercials. A manufacturer of industrial equipment might choose a mail survey because the executives it wishes to question are hard to reach by phone. A political party might prefer to employ a door-to-door personal survey so that voters can formulate and voice their opinions on current issues. In these examples, the cost, time, and perhaps accuracy involved vary. It is the researcher's job to weigh the advantages and disadvantages of each method and find the most appropriate way to collect the needed data.[14]

Wording survey questions appropriately is a skill that must be learned. The questionnaire writer's goals are to avoid complexity and use simple, accurate, conversational language that does not confuse or bias the respondent. The wording of questions should be simple and unambiguous so that the questions are readily understandable to all respondents.

Consider, for example, the following question:

Should The Limited continue its excellent gift-wrapping program?
☐ Yes
☐ No

The gift-wrapping program may not be excellent at all. By answering "yes," a respondent is implying that things are just fine as they are. But by answering "no," she implies that The Limited should discontinue the gift wrapping. Questions should be worded so that the respondent is not put in this sort of bind.[15]

Many respondents are susceptible to leading questions, such as "You do agree that U.S. automobiles are a better value than Japanese automobiles, don't you?" Leading questions should be avoided.

Sometimes rating scales are used to measure consumers' attitudes. Two of the most common attitude scales are the Likert scale and the semantic differential. A Likert scale asks respondents to indicate the degree of agreement with a statement, as in the following example:

Timberland boots are expensive.

Strongly agree   Agree   Undecided   Disagree   Strongly disagree

A semantic differential identifies a company, store, brand, or the like and asks the respondent to place a check mark on a bipolar rating scale, as in the following example:

Timberland boots

Expensive __:__:__:__:__:__:__ Inexpensive

Observation   If the purpose of a research effort is to note actions that are mechanically or visually recordable, observation techniques can form the basis of that effort. **Observation research** involves the systematic recording of behavior, objects, or events as they are witnessed. Companies that sell space on outdoor billboards are interested in traffic patterns—specifically, the numbers of cars and people passing the billboard installations each day. Mass transit organizations may want to know how many people ride each bus and where most of them get on or off. In both cases, the information could be recorded either by human observers or by mechanized counters.

Observation can be more complicated than these simple nose-counting examples might suggest. For example, Fisher-Price's Play Laboratory is a well-stocked day-care center where toy designers and marketing researchers sit behind a one-way mirror to observe children who are trying out new toys. They observe how long children play with various toys and evaluate whether prototype toys catch children's interest.

"Mystery shoppers" can be used to check on salespeople's courtesy or product knowledge. Researchers disguised as customers, store employees, or product demonstrators might subtly observe consumer reactions to prices, products, package designs, or display cases, leaving the consumers unaware that their behavior was being observed.

The greatest strength of observation is that it permits the recording of what actually occurs in a particular situation. Its biggest weakness is that the observer cannot be sure *why* the observed behavior occurred. Still, in some cases, it is enough to know *that* something happened.

Experiments   Experiments have long been used by scientists attempting to discover cause-and-effect relationships. Almost every day, you can read news stories about experimental groups of white mice that were exposed to some substance and then developed more cancers than mice in groups not so exposed. The assumption, of course, is that the substance involved increased the chance of developing cancer. A properly run **experiment** allows an investigator to change one variable, such as price, and then observe the effects of the

Observation research
The systematic recording of behavior, objects, or events as they are witnessed.

Experiment
A research method in which the researcher changes one variable and observes the effects of that change on another variable.

Observation research has revealed that shoppers who spend more time in a store will purchase more. It also shows that when a woman is in a store with a man she will spend less time than when she is alone or shopping with another woman or a child. A houseware retailer observed the following average times: woman shopping with female companions: 8 minutes, 15 seconds; woman with children: 7 minutes, 19 seconds; woman alone: 5 minutes, 2 seconds; and woman with a man: 4 minutes, 41 seconds.[16] The reasons for the differences in shopping times were revealed only in later analyses.

change on another variable, such as sales. Ideally, the experimenter holds all factors steady except the one being manipulated, thus showing that changes are caused by the factor being studied.

Marketing researchers use experimental techniques both in the marketplace ("in the field") and in controlled, or laboratory, situations. For example, McDonald's conducted experiments in the marketplace to determine if it should add a single-slice McPizza to its menu. The company sold the product in *test markets*—cities where a test product is sold just as it would be if it were marketed nationwide. Test markets provide a trial run to determine consumers' reactions and actual sales volume. For McDonald's, sales of the pizza slices were disappointing, and the company discontinued its plans to market pizza to adults. The company is currently test marketing pizza in children's Happy Meals.

what went right?

Rolling Rock   For many years Rolling Rock beer was a regional brand in western Pennsylvania. Its signature package was a long-neck green bottle with a white painted label featuring icons such as a horse head, a steeplechase fence, and the number "33," which concludes a legend about the beer being brought to you "from the glass-lined tanks of Old Latrobe." Rolling Rock beer, now marketed by Labatt USA, expanded nationally during the 1980s by focusing on core consumers who purchased specialty beers for on-premise consumption and were willing to pay prices higher than those for national brands such as Budweiser.

As years went by, packaging options expanded to include bottles with mystique-less paper labels for take-home consumption, often packaged in twelve-packs. In the mid-1990s, in response to a competitive explosion from microbrews, Rolling Rock added Rock Bock, amber Rock Ice, and a number of other items to its product line. They failed. Sales stagnated. In New York and other crucial markets, price reductions to the level of Budweiser and Miller became inhibiting aspects of its marketing program. Marketing executives held the view that the longneck painted bottle was the heart of the brand. However, earlier efforts to develop cheaper imitations of the painted-label look had not achieved success.

Rolling Rock executives decided to conduct a massive marketing research project. Researchers recruited consumers at shopping malls to engage in a shopping experiment in a mock store. In the "store," beer drinkers found shelves stocked with beer—not just specialty beer but beer at every price range from sub-premium up. Consumers, given money to spend (in the form of chips), were exposed to "old-bundle" packages (the old graphics and the paper-label stubbies) and "new-bundle" packages (two new graphics approaches, including the one ultimately selected, and painted-label longnecks), at a variety of price points. They were asked to allocate money for their next ten purchases. Some were even invited to take the "new-bundle" packages home with them for follow-up research.

As the executives had hoped, the research results did not leave any room for interpretation: Not only did the new packages meet with consumers' strong approval, but consumers consistently indicated that they would be willing to pay more for the brand in those packages. In fact, they not only were *willing* to pay more, but *expected* to pay more, particularly those already loyal to Rolling Rock. In three regions—the Northeast, Southeast, and West—purchase intent among users increased dramatically both at prices 20 cents higher per six-pack and at prices 40 cents higher. The increase in purchase intent was milder in the Midwest, but there Rock already commanded a solid premium over Bud and other premium beers. The sole exception to that trend was in the brand's core markets in Pennsylvania and Ohio, where Rock has never entirely escaped its shot-and-a-beer origins—and even there, purchase intent declined by only 2 percent at each of the higher prices.[17]

In contrast, advertisers often use laboratory settings to test advertising copy. One group of subjects is shown a television program that includes one version of an advertisement. A second group views the same program with a different version. Researchers compare the groups' responses. Research like this is conducted in a controlled setting, rather than a natural setting, to increase researchers' control of environmental variables. Such an experiment is known as a **laboratory experiment**.

Selecting the Research Design   After considering research alternatives, a marketing researcher must pick one. Because there are many ways to tackle a problem, there is no one "best" research design. Certain techniques are simply more appropriate than others.

For example, what technique should the Chicago Museum of Science and Industry use to determine which of its exhibits is the most popular? A survey? (Could you really expect visitors to remember and rate all the museum's exhibits?) Experimentation? (Would you close off the exhibits one at a time and count the complaints associated with each closing?) Secondary data? (That might tell you what exhibits are most popular at other museums.) The Chicago Museum's researcher actually suggested the simple and inexpensive observation technique of keeping track of how frequently the floor tiles had to be replaced in front of each exhibit—indicating which exhibit drew the heaviest traffic. Of course, had the museum been in a hurry for information, another method would have been more appropriate, but the floor tile approach gave museum operators a good measurement over time at a low cost. (By the way, the chick-hatching exhibit was the most popular.)

STAGE 3: SELECTING A SAMPLE

Once a researcher has determined which research design to use, the next step is to select a sample of people, organizations, or whatever is of interest. The methods for selecting the sample are important for the accuracy of the study.

Though sampling is a highly developed statistical science, we all apply its basic concepts in daily life. For example, the first taste (or sample) of a bowl of soup may indicate that the soup needs salt, is too salty, or is "just right." **Sampling**, then, is any procedure in which a small part of the whole is used as the basis for conclusions regarding the whole.

A **sample** is simply a portion, or subset, of a larger **population**. It makes sense that a sample can provide a good representation of the whole. A well-chosen sample of lawyers in California should be representative of all California lawyers. Such a sample can be surveyed, and conclusions can be drawn about California lawyers, making surveying all of them unnecessary. A survey of all the members of a group is called a **census**. For a small group—say, a group comprising the presidents of all colleges and universities in Nebraska—sampling is not needed. All the presidents can easily be identified and contacted.

Sampling essentially requires answering these three questions:

1. *Who is to be sampled?* Specifying the **target population**, or the total group of interest, is the first aspect of sampling. The manager must make sure the population to be sampled accurately reflects the population of interest. Suppose a department store manager who wants to analyze the store's image in the community at large uses current credit-card records to develop a survey mailing list. Who will be surveyed? Only current credit-card customers, not noncredit customers, and certainly not noncustomers, though these groups may be important parts of "the community at large."

    Lists of customers, telephone directories, membership lists, and lists of automobile registrations are a few of the many population lists from which a sample may be taken. Selecting a list from which to draw a sample is a crucial aspect of sampling. If the list is inaccurate, the sample may not be representative of the larger population of interest.

Laboratory experiment
An experiment in a highly controlled environment.

Sampling
Any procedure in which a small part of the whole is used as the basis for conclusions regarding the whole.

Sample
A portion or subset of a larger population.

Population
In marketing research, any complete group of people or entities sharing some common set of characteristics; the group from which a sample is taken.

Census
A survey of all the members of a group (an entire population).

Target population
The population of interest in a marketing research study; the population from which samples are to be drawn.

2. *How big should the sample be?* The traditional tongue-in-cheek response to this question—"big enough"—suggests the true answer. The sample must be big enough to properly portray the characteristics of the target population. In general, bigger samples are better than smaller samples. Nevertheless, if appropriate sampling techniques are used, a small proportion of the total population will give a reliable measure of the whole. For instance, the Nielsen TV ratings survey, which appears to be highly accurate, involves only a few thousand of the 103 million U.S. households. The keys here are that most families' TV viewing habits are similar and that the "Nielsen families" are selected with meticulous care to assure the representativeness of the sample.

3. *How should the sample be selected?* The way sampling units are selected is a major determinant of the accuracy of marketing research. There are two major sampling methods: probability sampling and nonprobability sampling.

When the sampling procedures are such that the laws of probability influence the selection of the sample, the result is a **probability sample**. A *simple random sample* consists of individual names drawn according to chance selection procedures from a complete list of all people in a population. All these people have the same chance of being selected. The procedure is called *simple* because there is only one stage in the sampling process.

When sample units are selected on the basis of convenience or personal judgment (for example, if Portland is selected as a sample city because it appears to be typical), the result is a **nonprobability sample.** In one type of nonprobability sample, a *convenience sample*, data are collected from the people who are most conveniently available. A professor or graduate student who administers a questionnaire to a class is using a convenience sample. It is easy and economical to collect sample data this way; but unfortunately, this type of sampling often produces unrepresentative samples. Another nonprobability sample, the *quota sample*, is often utilized by interviewers who intercept consumers at shopping malls. With this type of sampling, people are chosen because they appear to the interviewers to be of the appropriate age, sex, race, or the like.

Probability sample
A sample selected by statistical means in such a way that all members of the sampled population had a known, nonzero chance of being selected.

Nonprobability sample
A sample chosen on the basis of convenience or personal judgment.

STAGE 4: COLLECTING DATA

Once the problem has been defined, the research techniques chosen, and the sample to be analyzed selected, the researcher must actually collect the needed data. Whatever collection method is chosen, it is the researcher's task to minimize errors in the process—and errors are easy to make.

Generally, before the desired data are collected, the collection method is pretested. A proposed questionnaire or interview script might be tried out on a small sample of respondents in an effort to assure that the instructions and questions are clear and comprehensible. The researcher may discover that the survey instrument is too long, causing respondents to lose interest, or too short, yielding inadequate information. The **pretesting** provides the researcher with a limited amount of data that will give an idea of what can be expected from the upcoming full-scale study. In some cases, these data will show that the study is not answering the researcher's questions. The study may then have to be redesigned. After pretesting shows the data collection method and questionnaire to be sound, the data can be collected.

Pretesting
Conducting limited trials of a questionnaire or some other aspect of a study to determine its suitability for the planned research project.

STAGE 5: ANALYZING THE DATA

Once a researcher has completed what is called the *fieldwork* by gathering the data needed to solve the research problem, those data must be manipulated, or processed. The purpose is to place the data in a form that will answer the marketing manager's questions.

Processing requires entering the data into a computer. Data processing ordinarily begins with a job called **editing**, in which surveys or other data collection instruments are checked for omissions, incomplete or otherwise unusable responses, illegibility, and obvious inconsistencies. As a result of the editing process, certain collection instruments may be discarded. In research reports, it is common to encounter phrases like this: "One thousand people were interviewed, yielding 856 usable responses." The process may also uncover correctable errors, such as the recording of a usable response on the wrong line of a questionnaire.

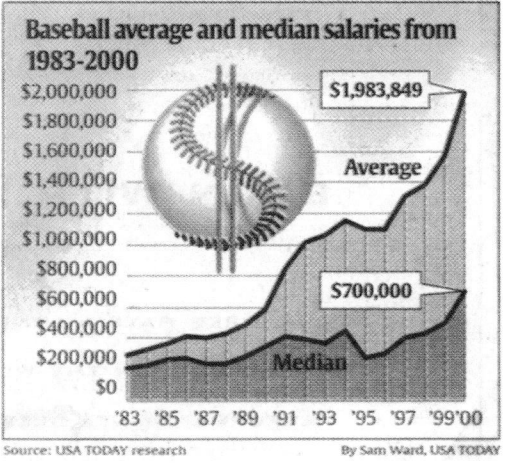

Baseball average and median salaries from 1983-2000

$1,983,849

Average

$700,000

Median

'83 '85 '87 '89 '91 '93 '95 '97 '99'00

Source: USA TODAY research   By Sam Ward, USA TODAY

In the data-analysis stage, researchers calculate averages and look for trends to decide what the information means to marketing managers.

Once the data collection forms have been edited, the data undergo **coding**. That is, meaningful categories are established so that responses can be grouped into classifications usable for computer analysis. For example, for a survey focusing on response differences between men and women, a gender code, such as 1 = male and 2 = female, might be used.

After editing and coding, the researcher is ready to undertake the process of analysis. **Data analysis** may involve statistical analysis, qualitative analysis, or both. The type of analysis used should depend on management's information requirements, the research hypothesis, the design of the research itself, and the nature of the data collected.

A review of the many statistical tools that can be used in marketing research is beyond the scope of this book. They range from simple comparisons of numbers and percentages ("100 people, or 25 percent of the sample, agreed") to complex mathematical computations requiring a computer. Statistical tools such as the t-test of two means, the chi-square test, and correlation analysis are commonly used to analyze data. It may be surprising, in light of the availability of these and many other techniques, that a great number of studies use statistics no more sophisticated than averages and percentages.

Editing
Checking completed questionnaires or other data collection forms for omissions, incomplete or otherwise unusable responses, illegibility, and obvious inconsistencies.

Coding
Establishing meaningful categories for responses collected by means of surveys or other data collection forms so that the responses can be grouped into usable classifications.

Data analysis
Statistical and/or qualitative consideration of data gathered by research.

STAGE 6: DRAWING CONCLUSIONS AND PREPARING A REPORT

Remember that the purpose of marketing research is to aid managers in making effective marketing decisions. The researcher's role is to answer the question "What does this mean to marketing managers?" Therefore, the end result of the research process must be a report that usefully communicates research findings to management. Typically, management is not interested in how the findings were arrived at. Except in special cases, management is likely to want only a summary of the findings. Presenting these clearly, using graphs, charts, and other forms of artwork, is a creative challenge to the researcher and any others involved in the preparation of the final report. If the researcher does not communicate the findings so that marketing managers can understand them, the research process has been, in effect, a total waste.

STAGE 7: FOLLOWING UP

After the researcher submits a report to management, he or she should follow up to determine if and how management responded to the report. The researcher should ask how the report could have been improved and made more useful. This is not to say that researchers should expect that managers will always agree with a report's conclusions or pursue its suggested courses of action. Deciding such things is, after all, the role of managers, not of researchers. Marketing management, for its part, should let researchers know how reports could be improved or how future reports might be made more useful.

Marketing Research Is a Global Activity

Marketing research, like all business activity, has become increasingly global. Many companies have far-reaching international marketing research operations. Upjohn, for example, conducts marketing research in 160 different countries.

Companies conducting business in foreign lands must understand the nature of customers in these markets. Although the nations of the European Union now share a single market, research shows that consumers in the EU do not share identical tastes for many consumer products. Marketing researchers have learned that there is no such thing as a typical European consumer—the nations of the European Union are divided by language, religion, climate, and centuries of tradition. Scantel Research, a British firm that advises companies on consumer color preferences, found inexplicable differences in the way Europeans take their medicine. The French pop purple pills; the English and Dutch prefer white ones. Consumers in all three countries dislike bright red capsules, which are big sellers in the United States.[18] This example illustrates that companies doing business in Europe must learn whether and how to adapt to local customs and buying habits.

Decisions about international strategies and tactics should be based on sound market information. But in many foreign nations, U.S. marketing researchers encounter circumstances far different from those to which they are accustomed. To begin with, there is rarely much secondary data available. American researchers are lucky; there are volumes of data about the people and markets in the United States. But in some countries, no census has ever been taken. People in some developing nations seem to take the view that anyone wanting to pry into another person's life must have less than honorable motives. Often, too, lack of data and unfamiliar social patterns make it difficult for a researcher to use all the tools available. It may be impossible to develop carefully planned samples. Telephone directories may not include the entire population and may be woefully out of date. Street maps are unavailable in many cities in South America, Central America, and Asia. In fact, in some large metropolitan areas of the Near East and Asia, streets are unnamed and the houses on them are unnumbered.

In spite of these hardships, marketing research does take place around the globe. ACNielsen, the television ratings company, is the world's largest marketing research company. More than 60 percent of its business comes from outside the United States. Although the nature of marketing research varies around the globe, the need for marketing research and accurate information is universal.

Sales Forecasting: Research about the Future

Marketing managers need information about the future to make decisions today. They need to ask "What will be the size of the market next year?" "How large a share of the market will we have in 5 years?" "What changes in the market can we anticipate?" Sales forecasting involves applying research techniques to answering questions like these.

Sales forecasting is the process of predicting sales totals over some specific future period of time. An accurate sales forecast is one of the most useful pieces of information a marketing manager can have, because the forecast influences so

> An accurate sales forecast is one of the most useful pieces of information a marketing manager can have, because the forecast influences so many plans and activities.

Sales forecasting
The process of estimating sales volume for a product, an organizational unit, or an entire organization over a specific future time period.

many plans and activities. A good forecast helps in the planning and control of production, distribution, and promotion activity. Forecasting may suggest that price structures need to be adjusted or that inventory holdings should be changed, for example. Because operational planning greatly depends on the sales forecast, ensuring the accuracy of the forecast is important. Mistakes in forecasting can lead to serious errors in other areas of the organization's management. For example, an overestimate of sales can lead to an overstocking of raw materials; an underestimate can mean losing sales because of material shortages.

The sales forecast provides information for the control function by establishing an evaluation standard. Management uses it to gauge the organization's marketing successes and failures. Without a standard, there is no way to measure the success or failure of any endeavor.

BREAK-DOWN AND BUILD-UP FORECASTING

Sales forecasts are focused on company sales, but they may also make use of forecasts of general economic conditions, industry sales, and market size. A bank, for example, may use the Wharton forecast of the U.S. economy to develop its own forecast for the banking industry. Based on that forecast, bank management will try to estimate the demand for loans at its various branch locations. This approach—that is, starting with something big, like the U.S. gross domestic product, and working down to an industry forecast, and then a company forecast, and even a product forecast—is called the **break-down method** of forecasting.

The **build-up method** starts with the individual purchaser and then aggregates estimates of sales potential into progressively larger groups. For example, a tool manufacturer might estimate that 10 percent of all electrical contractors in Georgia will buy a drill during a specified period, 15 percent of all carpenters in Georgia will buy a drill, and so on. Adding subtotals for each state leads to a build-up forecast.

THE THREE LEVELS OF FORECASTING

There are three levels of forecasting reflected in the forecast of market potential, the forecast of sales potential, and the sales forecast.

- **Market potential** refers to the upper limit of industry demand, or the expected sales volume for all brands of a particular product type during a given period. Market potential is usually defined for a given geographical area or market segment under certain assumed business conditions. It reflects the market's ability to absorb a type of product.
- **Sales potential** is an estimate of an individual company's maximum share of the market, or the company's maximum sales volume for a particular product during a given period. Sales potential reflects what demand would be if the company undertook the maximum sales-generating activities possible in a given period under certain business conditions.
- The **sales forecast**, or expected actual sales volume, is usually lower than sales potential because the organization is constrained by resources or because management emphasizes the highest profits rather than the largest sales volume.

CONDITIONAL FORECASTING—"WHAT IF?"

Forecasters often assume the upcoming time period will be like the past. However, marketing is carried on in a dynamic environment. An effective forecaster recognizes that a forecast will be accurate only if the assumptions behind it are accurate. Therefore, organizations often create three versions of each forecast: one based on optimistic assumptions, one based on pessimistic assumptions, and one based on conditions thought to be "most likely." The most likely forecast is not always halfway between the other two. In bad times, "most likely" might be awfully close to disaster. The advantage of this threefold forecasting approach is that the forecaster clearly distinguishes between what is predicted and what is possible.

Break-down method
A sales forecasting method that starts with large-scale estimates (for example, an estimate of GDP) and works down to industrywide, company, and product estimates. See also *build-up method*.

Build-up method
A sales forecasting method that starts with small-scale estimates (for example, product estimates) and works up to larger-scale ones. See also *break-down method*.

Market potential
The upper limit of industry demand. That is, the expected sales volume for all brands of a particular product during a given period.

Sales potential
The maximum share of the market an individual organization can expect during a given period.

Sales forecast
The actual sales volume an organization expects during a given period.

FORECASTING BY TIME PERIODS

A good forecast specifies the time frame during which the forecasted goal is to be met. Managers frequently use expressions like "short term," "long term," and "intermediate term" to describe these time periods. Such expressions can mean almost anything, depending on the marketing problem under discussion. For novelty items such as snap bracelets, the difference between the short and the long term may be very short, indeed. Such products may have a life of only a month and then disappear from the market. Established products like Honda motorcycles and Lawn Boy lawn mowers may survive for years or even decades.

Though situations vary, there is general agreement that a short-term forecast covers a period of a year or less and that long-term forecasts cover periods of 5 to 10 years. The intermediate term is anywhere in between.

Generally, forecasting time frames do not go beyond 10 years. For some products, such as automobile tires, it should be safe to assume that a market will exist 10, 20, or even 50 years into the future. But it is not safe to assume that any product will be around "forever." Some forecasters do make such long-range forecasts. The problem is that the longer the time period, the greater the uncertainty and risk involved. The level of uncertainty increases immensely for each year of the forecast.

As time frames become longer, what starts as a forecast can become a fantasy. The history of business is littered with stories of managers who encountered disastrous failure because they assumed that an existing market situation would remain unchanged indefinitely. Marketing's dynamic environment does not offer the safety long-term planners would like to have. Thus, many forecasters revise sales forecasts quarterly, monthly, or weekly, as the situation warrants.

FORECASTING OPTIONS

There is no best way to forecast sales. This does not mean that the marketing manager faces total chaos and confusion. It does mean that there are many different methods, ranging from simple to complex, for forecasting. Some methods that have been used to forecast sales are executive opinion, analysis of sales force composites, surveys of customer expectations, projection of trends, and analysis of market factors.

Surveys of Executive Opinion Top-level executives with years of experience in an industry are generally well informed. Surveying executives to obtain estimates of market potential, sales potential, or the direction of demand may be a convenient and inexpensive way to forecast. It is not a scientific technique, however, because executives may be biased, either consciously or unconsciously, and thus overly pessimistic or overly optimistic. Used in isolation, executive opinion has many pitfalls. But the opinions of seasoned industry executives may be a useful supplement to one or more of the other forecasting methods.

Surveying customers' expectations is a method of forecasting sales of established products.

Analysis of Sales Force Composite Asking sales representatives to project their own sales for the upcoming period and then combining all these projections is the sales force composite method of forecasting. The logic underlying this technique is that the sales representative is the person most familiar with the local market area, especially the activity of competitors, and therefore is in the best position to predict local behavior. However, this method may yield subjective predictions and forecasts based on a perspective that is too limited.

Surveys of Customer Expectations Surveying customer expectations simply involves asking customers if they intend to purchase a service or how many units of a product they intend to buy. This method is best for established products. For a new product concept, customers' expectations may not indicate their actual behavior.

Projection of Trends Identifying trends and extrapolating past performance into the future is a relatively uncomplicated quantitative forecasting technique. Time series data are identified and even plotted on a graph, and the historical pattern is projected onto the upcoming period. Thus, if sales have increased by 10 percent every year for the last 5 years, the trend suggests that next year's sales should also increase by 10 percent. An advantage of projecting past sales trends is that the company's accounting records can provide the needed data. This common method of forecasting can work well in mature markets that do not experience dynamic changes, since the underlying assumption is that the future will be somewhat like the past. However, if environmental change is radical or if new competitors are entering the market, blindly projecting trends may not be useful and may even be detrimental.

Analysis of Market Factors The market factor method of forecasting is used when there is an association between sales and another variable, called a **market factor**. For example, population is a general market factor that will help determine whether sales potential for Coca-Cola is higher in Albany, New York, or Salt Lake City, Utah. Similarly, new housing starts may predict lumber sales. When a number of factors are combined into an *index*, the result is referred to as a multiple **market factor index**, or market index. Correlation methods and regression methods are mathematical techniques that may be used to identify the degree of association between sales and a market factor.

Market factor
A variable, associated with sales, that is analyzed in forecasting sales.

Market factor index
An index derived by combining a number of variables that are associated with sales.

Summary

Effective marketing management relies on accurate, pertinent, and timely information, supplied in appropriate form by a well-designed decision support system.

1) Explain why information is essential to effective marketing decision making.

The marketing manager needs timely, systematically gathered information about the organization's customers, environment, and marketing activities. Without it, the marketing manager has no accurate basis on which to make decisions. Information reduces uncertainty and helps to define problems and identify opportunities.

2) Explain the importance of worldwide information systems.

A worldwide information system is an organized collection of telecommunications equipment, computer hardware and software, data, and personnel. The system is designed to capture, store, update, manipulate, analyze, and immediately display information about worldwide business activity. The well-being of business organizations that hope to prosper in the 21st century depends on such information. The Internet is among the various communication media that are changing the way organizations obtain information from around the globe.

3) Describe a decision support system.

A decision support system includes (1) databases that provide logically organized data and (2) a set of software systems for managing data. Decision support systems allow organizations to engage in data-based marketing and data mining.

4) Explain the contribution of marketing research to effective decision making.

Marketing research is intended to provide objective information about marketing phenomena to reduce uncertainty and lead to more rational and effective decisions.

5) Describe the stages in the marketing research process.

Marketing research studies generally follow seven major steps: (1) defining the problem, (2) planning the research design, (3) selecting a sample, (4) collecting data, (5) analyzing data, (6) drawing conclusions and preparing a report, and (7) following up.

6) Explain how exploratory research relates to specific marketing management problems.

Exploratory research clarifies the nature of problems that are not clearly understood so that further research can be conducted.

7) Understand why secondary data are valuable sources of information.

Secondary data have already been collected and assembled. They may be obtained quickly and inexpensively.

8) Understand the uses of surveys, observation, and experiments.

Primary data are collected through surveys, observation, and experiments. Surveys are used to gather information about large groups of people by mail, Internet, telephone, personal interview, or other communication medium. Observation is used to record actual behavior. Experiments are tightly controlled research designs that manipulate an experimental variable and measure its effect under controlled conditions.

9) Demonstrate your knowledge of the purposes of sales forecasting.

Sales forecasting is the prediction of an organization's anticipated sales over a specific time period. The forecast is used to plan such activities as production scheduling, distribution, and promotion and to measure the success of these activities. Good forecasting improves planning and control.

10) Evaluate the advantages and disadvantages of the various forecasting methods.

Surveys of executive opinion, sales force composites, and surveys of customers are forecasting methods based on the opinions of experienced individuals or consumers. Personal biases or lack of knowledge may, however, affect the results. Trend analysis is appropriate in some situations but assumes that the future will be like the past. Market factor analysis and published indices are useful when sales are affected by certain external variables.

Key Terms

break-down method (p. 133)
build-up method (p. 133)
census (p. 129)
coding (p. 131)
data (p. 115)
data analysis (p. 131)
database (p. 116)
data-based marketing (p. 117)
decision support system (p. 116)
editing (p. 131)
experiment (p. 127)
exploratory research (p. 121)
extranet (p. 117)
focus group interview (p. 122)

information (p. 115)
intranet (p. 117)
laboratory experiment (p. 129)
market factor (p. 135)
market factor index (p. 135)
market potential (p. 133)
marketing research (p. 118)
nonprobability sample (p. 130)
observation research (p. 127)
population (p. 129)
pretesting (p. 130)
primary data (p. 115)
probability sample (p. 130)
problem definition (p. 119)

research design (p. 123)
sales forecast (p. 133)
sales forecasting (p. 132)
sales potential (p. 133)
sample (p. 129)
sampling (p. 129)
secondary data (p. 115)
software (p. 116)
survey (p. 125)
systematic bias (p. 125)
target population (p. 129)
worldwide information system (p. 114)

Questions for Review & Critical Thinking

1. What role does marketing research play in the development of marketing strategies and the implementation of the marketing concept?
2. Some marketing managers seem unable to manage information as well as they perform their other duties. Why might that be?
3. Define or describe, in your own words, each of the following:
   a. Worldwide information system
   b. The Internet
   c. Database
   d. Decision support system
   e. Data-based marketing
   f. Marketing research
4. What does marketing research do for the manager? What doesn't it do?
5. What is exploratory research? Give an example of its proper application.
6. What are the stages in a formal research project? Which is the most important?

7. Why might a marketing manager choose to investigate secondary data rather than primary data?
8. What are the strengths and weaknesses of the following marketing research methods?
   a. Mail surveys
   b. Telephone surveys
   c. Observation studies
   d. Experiments
   e. Internet surveys
9. What are the primary considerations in the selection of a sample?
10. Give some examples of population lists from which samples may be drawn.
11. What is the difference between a forecast of market potential, a forecast of sales potential, and a sales forecast?
12. What market factors might help predict market potential for the following products?

a. Forklift trucks
b. Chain saws
c. Soft drinks
d. Playground equipment
13. What forecasting method would be best for each of the following products?
   a. Cigars
   b. The Palm Pilot hand-held computer
   c. Tickets to baseball games at your university
14. What do the executive opinion survey and the sales force composite methods have in common?
 15. Form small groups as directed by your instructor. Select a local retailer or a campus organization. Define a marketing problem or a marketing opportunity facing that organization, and design a questionnaire that will yield information to help the organization solve the problem or take advantage of the opportunity.

 **e—|exercises|** http://zikmund.swcollege.com

1. The Spider's Apprentice is a Web site that provides many useful tips about using search engines. Go to http://www.monash.com/spidap.html to learn the ins and outs of search engines.
2. Marketers scan the environment for changes in social values and beliefs. Go to the Harris Organization's home page at http://www.harrisinteractive.com. Select the News option. Read the results of a recent survey. What are the implications for marketers of the societal attitudes the survey reports? Make a list of five businesses that would be affected by the results of the survey you accessed.

Address Book (Useful URLs)

New York Public Library	http://www.nypl.org
Penn Library Business Reference Desk	http://www.library.upenn.edu/resources/reference/business/ref-business.html
NPD Group Inc.	http://www.npd.com
Ipsos-ASI: The Advertising Research Company	http://www.asiresearch.com
Advertising Research Foundation	http://www.arfsite.org

Ethically Right or Wrong?

Survey researchers hired by television networks often interview voters in presidential elections as they leave polling places. These "exit polls" are often concluded as much as an hour before the voting ends so that a news director can have the results ready in time to project the winner as soon as the local polls close. Many residents on the west coast believe that when national television news networks make early projections about presidential races before polls close on the west coast, local voting behavior, especially turnout, is affected. The networks argue that they should not withhold the polling results once they are known.

QUESTION
1. Is broadcasting early election projections an ethical practice?

TAKE A STAND
1. Should an individual's answers to a survey be confidential?
2. Is it ethical to telephone someone at 9:30 p.m. and ask him or her to participate in a survey?
3. Representatives of a private cemetery begin their telephone sales solicitations for cemetery plots by saying they are conducting a survey. Is this ethical?

|cases|

VIDEO CASE 5-1
Burke Inc.

Burke Inc. provides a number of management consulting services to clients around the world. Burke has four business units: Burke Marketing Research, Burke Customer Satisfaction Associates, Burke Strategic Consulting Group, and the Training and Development Center.

Burke Marketing Research provides full-service custom marketing research, analysis, and consulting for consumer and business-to-business product and service companies to help them understand marketplace dynamics worldwide. Services include product testing, brand equity research, pricing research, market segmentation, image and positioning studies, and a wide range of other marketing research services. Burke has been providing marketing research services to Blue Chip companies since 1931. Burke has tremendous depth of experience in all forms of research designs, including telephone, Internet, mail, and mall intercept.

Burke Marketing Research procedures are typical of most suppliers of custom research studies. A client may come to Burke indicating it has a marketing "problem." Burke will spend some time investigating the problem and then submit a research proposal to the client. If the client approves the proposal, Burke conducts the fieldwork and prepares a research report.

QUESTIONS
1. Outline the steps in the marketing research process.
2. How might a company like Burke help a client in each step of the marketing research process?

Toronto Blue Jays (A): Data-Based Marketing

The Toronto Blue Jays major league baseball team began playing in the American League East on April 7, 1977. The Blue Jays defeated the Chicago White Sox that day, but at the end of its first season the team finished last in the division. The Blue Jays were the American East League Champions in 1985, 1989, 1991, 1992, and 1993, and both the American League and World Series Champions in 1992 and 1993.

Today, the Blue Jays play in a covered stadium called the Sky Dome. The Blue Jays' management is very concerned about building, maintaining, and enhancing relationships with fans.

The Blue Jays have always kept records of corporate and season ticket holders' addresses. However, contemporary database software and decision-support systems now allow the company to generate computerized mailing lists and individualized promotional messages.[19]

QUESTIONS

1. What is the difference between data and information?
2. What type of data might the Blue Jays collect and record from the organizations and individual fans who purchase tickets for games at the Sky Dome?
3. Provide some examples of ways that the Blue Jays could use the database to increase sales or improve customer satisfaction.

Consumer Behavior

LEARNING OBJECTIVES

After you have studied this chapter, you will be able to . . .

1) Understand the basic model of consumer behavior.

2) Describe the consumer decision-making process and understand factors, such as consumer involvement, that influence it.

3) Appreciate the importance of perceived risk, choice criteria, purchase satisfaction, and cognitive dissonance.

4) Recognize the influence of individual factors, such as motives, perception, learning, attitude, and personality, on consumer behavior.

5) Explain the nature of culture and subculture in terms of social values, norms, and roles.

6) Characterize social class in the United States.

7) Explain the influence of reference groups on individual buyers.

8) Examine the roles in the joint decision-making process.

When Lisa Spence and Tege Millikin of Longview, Texas, first started making scrapbooks in 1996, they merely wanted to preserve memories of their young children. Since then, the two friends have spent thousands of dollars on supplies for their hobby, including dozens of scissors with special blades, acid-free paper so photos won't yellow, and die-cut shapes and stickers to decorate the pages. But they won't specify exactly how much they've spent. "We don't want our husbands to know," confides Mrs. Spence during a recent scrapbook convention in Arlington, Texas, that attracted about 1,000 participants.

Forget quilting. The craft industry's hottest trend is the scrapbook, the fancier the better. The Hobby Industry Association estimates that sales of scrapbooks and supplies now exceed $200 million, up from virtually nothing in 1995.

What lifted scrapbooks out of the scrap heap, and why now? Hobbyists say it's a homespun backlash against technology (and something to do when a spouse is on-line), a balm for workaholic guilt and a simple yearning for family tradition. "Families are really disjointed today," says Susan Brandt, assistant executive director of the Hobby Industry Association. Scrapbooks, she adds, harken back to a time "when things were simpler and people were together." Demographics are another factor: "Boomers having babies didn't hurt," she says.

Assembling memory books has become a social outlet for women in their 20s, 30s and 40s. Some devote entire rooms in their homes to the hobby, and host "cropping parties," where neighbors gather to compile pages for their books.

But these aren't your grandmother's scrapbooks. Today's keepsakes are organized by themes, and feature photographs cut with special scissors ($10), pages decorated with mock fabric borders ($10), labels written with fade-resistant pens (about $3), color-coordinated background paper (one pack: $5) and metallic stickers ($5).

Preservation has become another gold mine. Photos in old scrapbooks faded because they were mounted on highly acidic paper and under plastic sheets. Today's scrapbookers demand special buffered paper that costs several dollars per page.

Scrapbook enthusiasts are so gadget-happy that old products are being refashioned to cash in on demand. With a deft bit of labeling, Leeco Industries, an Olive Branch, Mississippi, manufacturer of office filing systems, has transformed its standard-issue filing box into the "Cropper Hopper," a caddy for scrapbook tools and supplies.

MJDesigns Inc., a Texas-based chain of 57 craft stores, now devotes 100 feet of shelf space in each store to scrapbooks. And it has plans for expansion because its scrapbook departments are jammed with scrapbook customers who spend an average of $60 to $80 per visit.[1]

Creative Memories, a company in St. Cloud, Minnesota, uses a Tupperware-like "party plan" format to promote scrapbooking. Its sales force visits customers in their homes to sell scrapbook products and hosts parties where the scrapbook products can be demonstrated. It's a far cry from the old-fashioned home party. But some of the same business fundamentals apply. There's a captive audience, low marketing costs, and an aura of social pressure that can be lucrative for purveyors. A 1990 University of Chicago study showed that while there's no requirement to buy, 97 percent of party attendees do, in part because they feel an obligation to their host.[2]

Spending extravagantly on scrapbooks and accessories and preserving photos in memory books as a social outlet are examples of consumer behaviors that influence the marketing mix. They also show how fascinating, yet baffling, consumer behavior can be.

This chapter begins our explanation of why people buy. The chapter opens by developing a model that gives an overview of consumer behavior. It then explains the consumer decision-making process and the psychological factors that influence this process. Finally, it describes sociocultural factors in consumer behavior.

What Is Consumer Behavior?

Effective marketing must begin with careful evaluation of the problems faced by potential customers. This evaluation is essential because, according to the marketing concept, marketing efforts must focus on consumers' needs and provide answers to buyers' problems. A key to understanding consumers' needs and problems lies in the study of consumer behavior. A knowledge of consumer behavior gives the marketing manager information he or she can use to increase the chance of success in the marketplace.

Consumer behavior consists of the activities people engage in when selecting, purchasing, and using products so as to satisfy needs and desires. Such activities involve mental and emotional processes, in addition to physical actions.[3] Consumer behavior includes both the behavior of ultimate consumers and the business behavior of organizational purchasers. However, many marketers prefer to use the term *buyer behavior* when discussing organizational purchasers.

A Simple Start—Some Behavioral Fundamentals

Our discussion of consumer behavior starts with a basic building block: Human behavior of any kind (B) is a function (f) of the interaction between the person (P) and the environment (E)—that is, $B = f(P, E)$. Simple though it is, this formula says it all.[4] Human behavior results when a person interacts with the environment. Whether behaviors are simple or complex, they flow from the person's interaction with environmental variables.

Consumer behavior
The activities people engage in when selecting, purchasing, and using products so as to satisfy needs and desires.

e x h i b i 6-1

A Consumer Behavior Model of the Decision-Making Process: How It Works and What Influences It

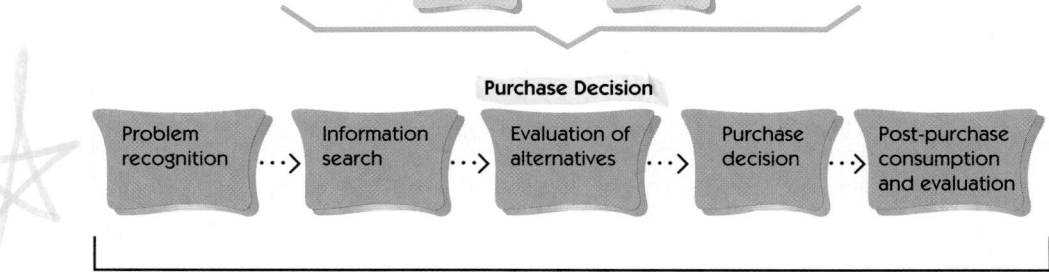

Exhibit 6-1 expands the basic formula for behavior, $B = f(P, E)$, into a more elaborate model of consumer decision making.[5] The model presents a decision-making process influenced by numerous interdependent forces rather than any single factor. Activities of marketers, such as advertising on television, are environmental forces, as are social forces such as culture and family. The characteristics of the individual, such as the person's attitudes and personality, may also influence the decision-making process at a particular moment.

The Decision-Making Process

Marketers who study consumer behavior are ultimately interested in one central question: How are consumer choices made? One important determinant is the situation in which a decision is made. With regard to situation, there are three categories of consumer decision-making behavior: routinized response behavior, limited problem solving, and extensive problem solving.

Routinized response behavior is the least complex type of decision making. Here, the consumer has considerable experience in dealing with the situation at hand and thus needs no additional information to make a choice. To a cola drinker, deciding on a particular brand is a routine matter accomplished in a matter of seconds. The purchase of a new house by a consumer or a fleet of trucks by an organization, however, usually requires **extensive problem solving.** The process may take months to complete, with a series of separate decisions made at different points. **Limited problem solving** is an intermediate level of decision making in which the consumer has some previous purchasing experience but is unfamiliar with stores, brands, or price options.

The "snap judgment" and the more extensive processes are more closely related than they may seem. The routine decision to purchase a particular brand of

Routinized response behavior
The least complex type of decision making, in which the consumer bases choices on his or her own past behavior and needs no other information.

Extensive problem solving
In-depth search for and evaluation of alternative solutions to a problem.

Limited problem solving
An intermediate level of decision making between routinized response behavior and extensive problem solving, in which the consumer has some purchasing experience but is unfamiliar with stores, brands, or price options.

The decision-making process is often shaped by the level of consumer involvement. This advertisement says, "Own one and you'll understand." It humorously points out that owners of Infiniti vehicles are highly involved with their cars.   http://www.infinitimotors.com

INFINITI.   OWN ONE AND YOU'LL UNDERSTAND.

Consumer involvement

The extent to which an individual is interested in and attaches importance to a product and is willing to expend energy in making a decision about purchasing the product.

cola is likely to have been preceded by a series of trials and errors in which the consumer tested different brands of cola before becoming able to make a routine choice. Both the routine choice and the more extensive problem-solving procedures may involve the same series of steps completed at different speeds.

Related to these problem-solving situations is the consumer's involvement in the purchase. The level of **consumer involvement** has to do with the importance an individual attaches to a product and the energy he or she directs toward making a decision. High involvement occurs when the decision to be made relates to a product that is of high interest and personally relevant to the individual. The buying situation (buying a birthday gift, for example) and the product's price may also be factors contributing to high involvement. A person who is highly involved with a product will exert more energy in decision making than a person whose involvement is low. Involvement may include both thoughts and feelings, so high involvement can mean thinking more strongly, feeling more strongly, or both.[6] A new mother is likely to be highly involved in the selection of a pediatrician but far less involved in the purchase of safety pins.

Exhibit 6-2 illustrates the decision-making steps in a high-involvement situation, in which there is extensive problem solving. It also shows a low-involvement situation, which usually requires only a limited information search and no evaluation.

Let us look more closely at these steps, focusing primarily on situations in which extensive problem solving takes place. Remember, however, that (1) different consumers pass through these steps at different speeds and (2) the five-step process is not necessarily completed once it has begun. Many buyers take a long time to reach the purchase stage, if only because of a shortage of money. Others do not reach the purchase stage at all because they evaluate alternatives and determine that no available alternatives are satisfactory.

e x h i b i **6-2**

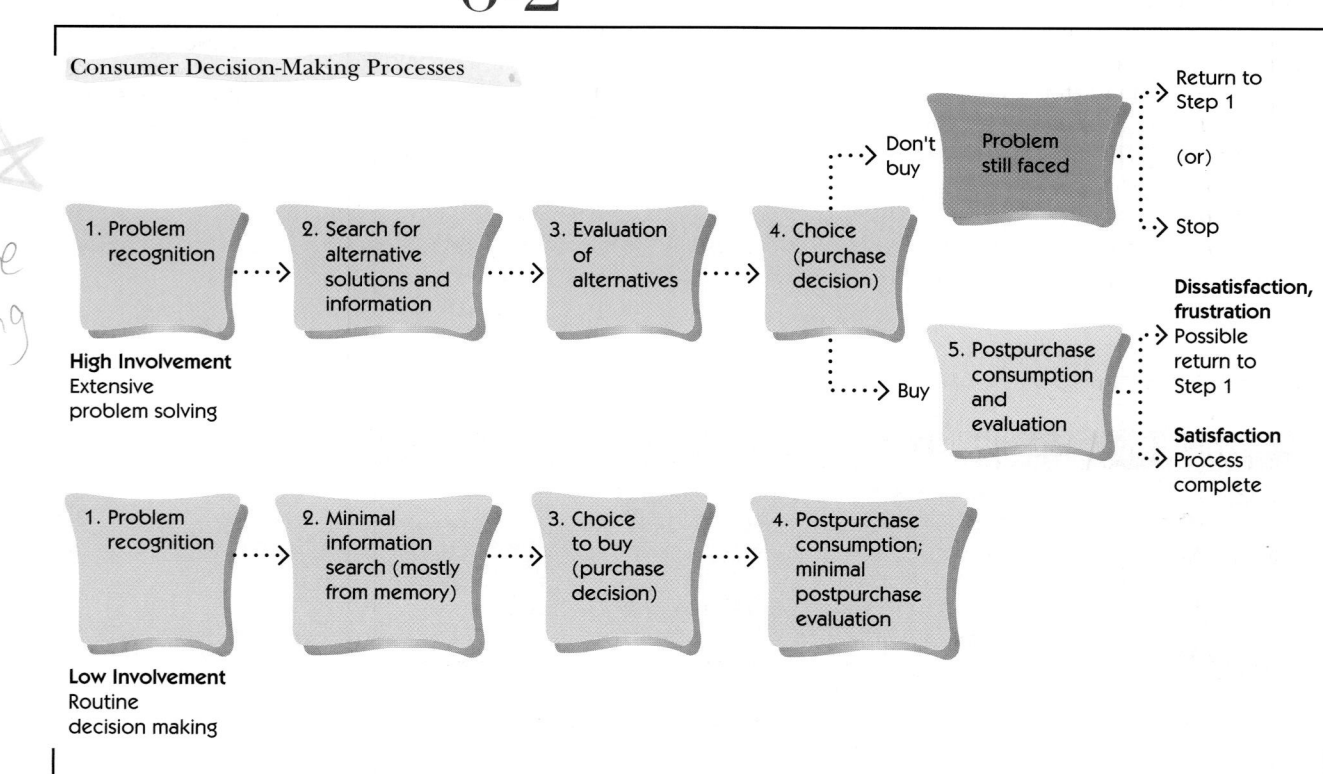

Consumer Decision-Making Processes

STEP 1: PROBLEM RECOGNITION

When a tire blows out on your car as you are driving on an interstate highway, problem recognition is instantaneous. Alternatively, problem recognition can be a more complex, long-term process. A person whose car occasionally "dies" and isn't very shiny or attractive anymore may start to recognize a problem in the making. Perhaps when the new automobile models become available, she becomes aware that her needs are not completely satisfied. **Problem recognition** is the awareness that there is a discrepancy between an actual and a desired condition. The person who has become aware that a new car is in order may take a bit of time getting one. However, a smoker who realizes that he is lighting the last cigarette in the pack is likely to make a purchase decision very rapidly, passing through steps 2 and 3 of the decision-making process so quickly as to appear to have skipped them. For all practical purposes, he has skipped these stages, because he already has the necessary information stored in his memory. Marketers know that routinized buyer behavior is difficult to alter. A buyer who devotes some time and consideration to decision making opens up more opportunities for effective marketers to appeal to him and to offer a product that may satisfy his need. Of course, marketers of the most popular brands of cigarettes, gum, and candy are happy that their regular customers have developed a routinized approach to solving problems.

STEP 2: SEARCH FOR ALTERNATIVE SOLUTIONS AND INFORMATION

Even the habitual buyer of Snickers candy bars is very likely to consider, however briefly, some other choices before selecting Snickers as usual. However, the search for alternatives and information about those alternatives is most easily observed among highly involved buyers who are purchasing a product for the first time or making a purchase that could have major financial, social, or other consequences.[7]

That buyers in such positions behave as they do is explained by the theory of **perceived risk**—the consumer's perception that there is a chance the product may not do what it is expected to do. These consumers perceive that their actions may produce unpleasant consequences that cannot be anticipated with anything approaching certainty.

Consumers encounter several types of risk when they purchase expensive clothing, for example: Is the clothing too expensive? Will it be durable? What will my friends say? Will I look good? Exhibit 6-3 identifies several types of risk that may concern potential buyers.

Buyers seek to reduce feelings of uncertainty by acquiring information. They may read advertisements. They may take family members or friends shopping with them. They may want the salesperson or some expert to tell them that the

Problem recognition
The awareness that there is a discrepancy between an actual and a desired condition.

Perceived risk
Consumers' uncertainty about the consequences of their purchase decisions; the consumer's perception that a product may not do what it is expected to do.

Types of Risk That Concern Potential Buyers e x h i b i 6-3

TYPE OF RISK	TYPICAL CONCERN
Performance risk	The brand may not perform its function well; it may not work; it may break down.
Financial risk	The buyer may lose money, pay too much, or miss buying something else.
Physical risk	The product may be harmful to the user's health; it may cause injury.
Social risk	Friends, relatives, or significant others may not approve of the purchase.
Time-loss risk	Maintenance time or time required to return the product to the place of purchase may be excessive.

Consumers shopping on the Internet often have high levels of perceived risk. One of the most widespread consumer complaints about buying products over the Internet is the lack of immediate, personalized help with what are often simple questions. LivePerson.com offers a service to solve this problem. LivePerson.com is a company that provides e-businesses with a support staff who can answer questions over the Internet. LivePerson allows Web site visitors to engage in a real-time text conversation with a customer service representative, using the same mechanism they use to browse the Web. Because consumers often ask similar questions, many of the answers are pre-formatted. That way, customer service representatives can click on an icon and send what appear to be personalized answers to frequently encountered questions. The customer experiences active, live customer service. By adding the ability for live customer service agents to interact with Web users, LivePerson.com enables companies to upgrade their customer service to a more humanized level. Internet shoppers reduce feelings of uncertainty by acquiring information. [8]

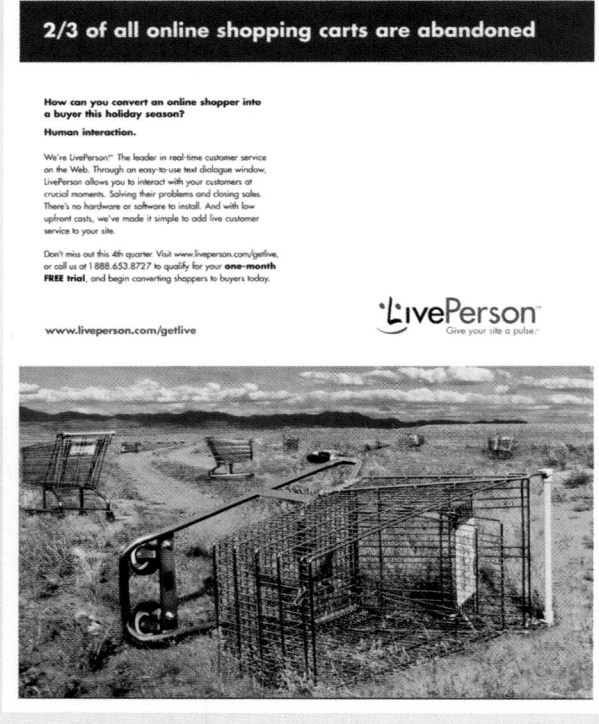

product is well made and a very popular item. In other words, consumers engage in an **information search** to acquire information that will reduce uncertainty and provide the basis for evaluation of alternatives. The information search may be internal or external.

Internal search is the mental activity of retrieving information from memory. After an individual has recognized a problem, the first step in solving it is to scan memory for pertinent information. Information stored in memory may have come from prior purchase behavior, advertising, conversations with friends, or other experiences. When the buying situation facing the consumer differs from past situations, however, an internal search may not provide enough information.

External search—the gathering of information from sources other than memory—may require time, effort, and money. External search is most likely to occur in high-involvement situations; it tends to be quite limited in low-involvement situations. Consumers gather external information from experience (such as shopping), personal sources (such as friends), public media (such as newspaper articles and the Internet), and marketer-dominated sources (such as magazine advertisements).

Marketers provide numerous sources of information to satisfy the consumer's need to reduce risk. Guarantees, a liberal return policy, store displays or advertisements showing that a product actually delivers what is promised,

Information search

An internal or external search for information carried out by a consumer to reduce uncertainty and provide a basis for evaluating alternatives.

and a pledge that "We service what we sell" may reduce the consumer's concern about perceived risk. These efforts are not "tricks." To reduce uncertainty, most consumers prefer to deal with companies that give such assurances.

In low-involvement situations, in which the customer conducts almost no external search (and even internal search is minimal), it is extremely important for the company's brand name to be prominent in

Buyers seek to reduce feelings of uncertainty by acquiring information.

the customer's memory. Thus, assuming consumers spend little time making decisions about soft drink choices, an effective marketing strategy is to make the name Coca-Cola, for example, prominent in consumers' minds. Often, in such situations, the objective of advertising is to create awareness and familiarity through repetition. Messages should remain simple, because the consumer is not highly involved. However, in high-involvement situations, consumers may be more receptive to more complex messages, and the advertising may emphasize information about comparative features of competing brands, stressing the unique benefits of the advertiser's brand.

STEP 3: EVALUATION OF ALTERNATIVES

Evaluation of alternatives begins when an information search has clarified or identified a number of potential solutions to the consumer's problem. Often the alternative solutions are directly competing products. An alternative to a Vermont skiing vacation may be a skiing vacation in Aspen or St. Moritz, for example. Other times, however, the alternative to a skiing vacation in Vermont is a new station wagon. The outcome of the evaluation process is usually the ranking of alternatives, the selection of a preferred alternative, or the decision that there is no acceptable alternative and that the search should continue.

In analyzing possible purchases, the prospective buyer considers the appropriate choice criteria. **Choice criteria** are the critical attributes the consumer uses to evaluate alternatives. For an automobile tire, product features such as expected average mileage, warranty, brand name, and price might be typical choice criteria. Which choice criteria are used depends on the consumer and the situation. For example, some people who need automobile tires may buy them at the neighborhood service station even if prices there are higher than at other places. They may feel that the time saved is worth the extra dollars spent. They may know the local station owner and want to give him some business. They may be trying to keep on the station owner's good side just in case they ever need emergency help. Or they may want to deal with a local seller so that they can complain if something goes wrong.

Many buyers appear not to want to evaluate too many factors when choosing among alternatives. The average person looking for a new car does not want (or cannot understand) the kinds of facts and figures mechanical engineers could provide. The typical car buyer wants very simple facts: The car looks good; the car dealer is a good guy. The buyer does not want an analysis of the car's aerodynamics or an art expert's opinion of its looks. In fact, Honda's "We make it simple" promotions were based on the finding that many consumers are confused about optional accessories and mechanical details. Offering only cars with "standard options" simplifies the choice criteria and the buying situation.

STEP 4: CHOICE—PURCHASE DECISIONS AND THE ACT OF BUYING

Sooner or later the prospective buyer must make a purchase decision or choose not to buy any of the alternatives available. Assuming the decision maker has decided which brand to purchase and where it will be purchased, the mechanics of the purchase must be worked out. The actual purchase behavior may be simple,

Turn it on **Pioneer**

Now getting 15 different artists on one CD doesn't require a natural disaster.

The decision to purchase a compact disc recorder is a high-involvement decision for most first-time buyers. And before consumption can follow the purchase, the consumer must connect the recorder to a CD player/changer and learn how to record music. Pioneer uses a KISS— "Keep It Simple, Stupid"—philosophy and a one-touch record button system to avoid frustrating consumers. The Pioneer compact disc recorder automatically fine tunes the laser for the best sound quality. When the recording is done the disc can be played on any CD player.

http://www.pioneerusa.com

Choice criteria
The critical attributes a consumer uses to evaluate product alternatives.

One aspect of the act of buying is determining how to pay for the purchases. Today, this may involve a decision to use an electronic wallet such as PocketCard.

http://www.pocketcard.com

Purchase satisfaction
The feeling on the part of the consumer that the decision to buy was appropriate because the product met expectations.

Cognitive dissonance
The tension that results from holding two conflicting ideas or beliefs at the same time; in terms of consumer behavior, the negative feelings that a consumer may experience after making a commitment to purchase.

especially if the buyer has either a credit card or a checkbook with a sufficient balance. However, the decision to buy can bring with it a few other related decisions. For example, should the tire buyer get new valve stems too? How about a lifetime wheel-balancing agreement with the seller?

STEP 5: POSTPURCHASE CONSUMPTION AND EVALUATION

Consumption naturally follows the purchase. If the decision maker is also the user, the matter of **purchase satisfaction** (or dissatisfaction) remains. In some cases, satisfaction is immediate, as when the buyer chews the just-bought gum or feels pleased that the decision-making process is over. Frequently, after making a purchase, we think to ourselves or tell others, "Well, I bought a great set of tires today." Patting ourselves on the back in this way is an attempt to assure satisfaction. We are telling ourselves that we are pleased with the purchase because our expectations have been confirmed. In this case, marketing has achieved its goal of consumer satisfaction.[9]

However, the opposite can occur—a consumer can feel uneasy about a purchase. Will the tires be good on snow? Will someone be surprised that I bought this brand instead of that one? Second thoughts can create an uneasy feeling, a sensation that the decision-making process may have yielded the wrong decision. These feelings of uncertainty can be analyzed in terms of the theory of cognitive dissonance. In the context of consumer behavior, **cognitive dissonance** is a psychologically uncomfortable postpurchase feeling. More specifically, it refers to the negative feelings, or "buyer's remorse," that can follow a commitment to purchase. Cognitive dissonance results from the fact that people do not like to hold two or more conflicting beliefs or ideas at the same time. Suppose the car owner has bought the tires and has left the shop; there's no turning back now. She wonders, "Should I have bought Michelin tires instead, even though the price was a bit higher?" Dissonance theory describes

> When marketers understand that any choice can create cognitive dissonance, they can seek to support their customers' choices.

such feelings as a sense of psychic tension, which the individual will seek to relieve. Each alternative has some advantages and some disadvantages. Buyers reduce cognitive dissonance by focusing on the advantages of the purchase—by carrying out postpurchase evaluation in a way that supports the choice made. Buyers may seek reinforcement from friends or from the seller. They may mentally downgrade the unselected alternatives and play up the advantages of the selected brand to convince themselves that they made the right choice. Effective marketers don't want dissatisfied customers. When marketers understand that any choice can create cognitive dissonance, they can seek to support their customers' choices. Promising good service, telling the buyer to come right back if there's any trouble and "we'll fix it up," and giving a toll-free hot line number are good business. Fulfilling customer expectations, which leads to satisfaction, is the purpose of many marketing activities.[10]

what went right?

Sauder Woodworking Sauder Woodworking became a leader in the red-hot ready-to-assemble furniture business by recognizing what customers want and by understanding that marketing does not end when the sale is made. It promotes its ready-to-assemble furniture not as a cheap alternative to factory-ready furniture but as good furniture that just happens to come in a box. The company is highly skilled at anticipating changing lifestyle and retail trends, but it also recognizes that it must offer furniture that consumers perceive to have greater value than products offered by competitors. Attention to the small details is an important part of Sauder's marketing effort. For instance, Sauder's products—from computer workstations to entertainment centers to stand-alone wardrobes—are famous for their easy-to-follow assembly instructions. The company believes the instructions are as much a part of the product as the wood that goes into it. All instructions are tested in sixth-grade classrooms to ensure that after the purchase has been made customers will be able to assemble a product. Sauder knows that fulfilling customers expectations leads to postpurchase satisfaction.[11]

Individual Factors That Shape the Decision-Making Process

Taking a decision-making perspective reveals a great deal about consumers' problem-solving behavior. But consumer behavior is complex, and there is much more to learn. Now that we have presented an overview of decision-making processes, we can explore the psychological variables that activate and influence them.

MOTIVATION

Marketers wish to know the underlying causes of buying behavior. They wish to know how consumer behavior gets started, is directed toward certain products, and is stopped. Psychologists explain such behavior in terms of motivation.

Motivation and Needs Defined **Motivation** is an activated state within a consumer that causes the consumer to initiate goal-directed behavior. When a person is motivated, he or she is in a state of arousal that serves to energize behavior and direct it toward a goal. A **need** reflects the lack of something that would benefit the person—a gap between the consumer's actual and desired state. The larger the gap between the consumer's actual and desired state, the more motivated the consumer is to solve the problem. Notice that this definition is consistent with our description of the problem-recognition step of the decision-making process. Problem recognition is, in effect, the creation of a consumer need state. Needs are always within people, but they may not be strong enough to cause the people to act. When, by whatever means, a need is activated, it becomes a **motive**. Thus, jogging may stimulate the basic human need to quench thirst, which is always present. The motive to find and drink a beverage to satisfy a thirst is an aroused need. An **incentive** (in this case, water or Gatorade) can be any object, person, or situation that an individual believes will satisfy a particular motive.

What is it that arouses motives? What gets people going? In general, it is either an internal force or an external stimulus. For example, when a person is hungry, internal biological mechanisms (grumbling stomach, empty feeling) arouse behaviors aimed at satisfying that hunger. The hungry person satisfies the motive of alleviating hunger by following the steps in Exhibit 6-4, a simple model of motivated behavior. The unfulfilled motive pushes the person toward

Motivation
An activated state that causes a person to initiate goal-directed behavior.

Need
The gap between an actual and a desired state.

Motive
An aroused need that energizes behavior and directs it toward a goal.

Incentive
Something believed capable of satisfying a particular motive.

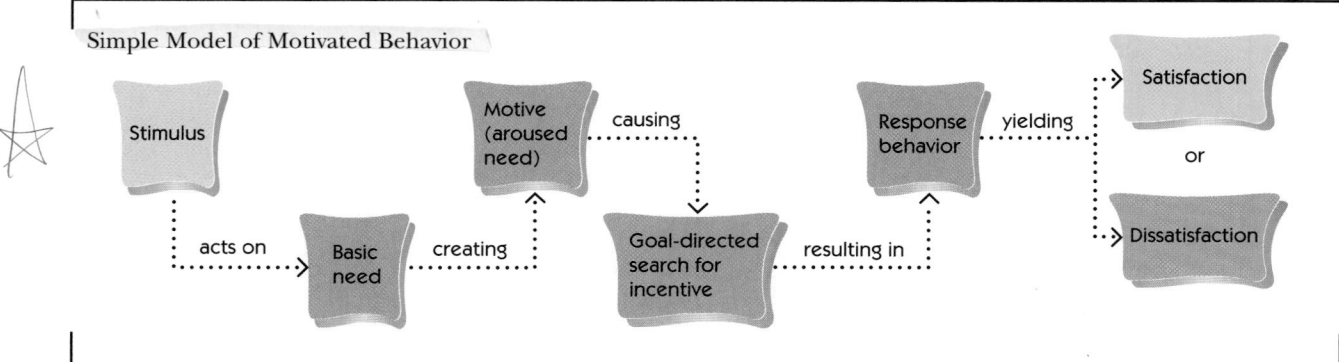

Simple Model of Motivated Behavior

Stimulus — acts on → Basic need — creating → Motive (aroused need) — causing → Goal-directed search for incentive — resulting in → Response behavior — yielding → Satisfaction or Dissatisfaction

an incentive that will satisfy the motive. The hungry person may respond by reaching for a candy bar on the desk, strolling to the refrigerator, or going out to a store or restaurant.

Physiological need
A need based on biological functioning, like the needs for food, water, and air.

Social and psychological need
A need stemming from a person's interactions with the social environment.

Classifying Needs and Motives   Many psychologists have attempted to classify needs and motives. There is little agreement among these classifications. In fact, the only area of commonality is the general agreement that people have two basic groups of needs. The first group is made up of **physiological needs**, or needs stemming from biological and genetic mechanisms. The second group consists of **social and psychological needs**, or needs resulting from a person's interaction with the social environment. For example, many Americans have a high need for achievement. An example of marketers who deal with both sorts of needs is food marketers. Humans need food to live (a physiological need), but the social environment creates other needs. For example, some people patronize elegant restaurants to show that they are more successful than the Joneses next door (a social need).

This advertisement for Allstate's insurance service appeals to homeowners' safety needs. In a basement filled with paint cans and other flammable liquids, it shows a match snaking toward invisible fumes from a gas pilot. It provides a toll-free number where consumers can obtain information on home fire safety.

http://www.allstate.com

A flash fire. It happens when invisible fumes creep along your floor and make contact with a gas pilot light. So please make sure flammable liquids are tightly sealed and stored far away from gas appliances. For more information on home fire safety, see an Allstate Agent or call 1-888-ALLSFTY. **Being in good hands is the only place to be.** **Allstate** You're in good hands.

Maslow's Hierarchy of Needs   Abraham Maslow, a psychologist, believed that even though each individual is unique, all humans have certain needs in common. Maslow identified these needs and ordered them from the most basic to the highest-level need. His needs hierarchy provides the basis for many theories of motivation. The five classes identified by Maslow, which are shown in Exhibit 6-5, are as follows:[12]

1. Physiological needs (food, water, air, sex, control of body temperature)
2. Safety needs (security and protection from threats)
3. Love and social needs (affection and feelings of belonging)

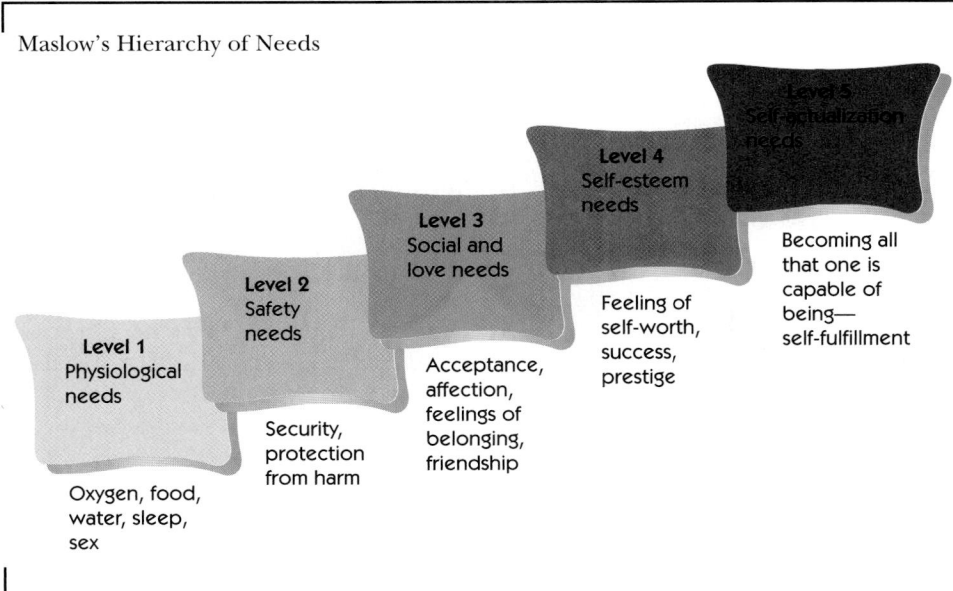

Maslow's Hierarchy of Needs

Level 5
Self-actualization needs

Level 4
Self-esteem needs

Level 3
Social and love needs

Level 2
Safety needs

Level 1
Physiological needs

Oxygen, food, water, sleep, sex

Security, protection from harm

Acceptance, affection, feelings of belonging, friendship

Feeling of self-worth, success, prestige

Becoming all that one is capable of being— self-fulfillment

4. Self-esteem needs (feelings of self-worth, achievement, respect of others, prestige)
5. Self-actualization needs (self-fulfillment, becoming what one is capable of becoming)

Maslow believed that individuals try to fill the most basic needs first. He suggested that a largely satisfied need is no longer a motivator of behavior. (It is not necessary for the need to be totally satisfied.) People move on to try to satisfy higher-level needs as lower-level needs are met. It follows from this that, for example, the need for food does not motivate people who are regularly well-fed in the same way it motivates people who regularly go hungry. In countries where hunger and even starvation are major problems, food is marketed almost entirely through simple distribution. No inducement other than availability is required. But U.S. marketers of food know that they must appeal to higher-level needs. Thus, Rice-a-Roni is "the San Francisco treat" and Weight Watchers Chocolate Dessert Sensations offer "Total indulgence. Zero guilt." Dining as San Franciscans do or indulging oneself is not essential to maintaining life, but it may be appealing to consumers seeking affection or self-esteem.

Finally, consumers may seek to meet lower-level and higher-level needs at the same time. The person who is installing a home burglar or fire alarm system to satisfy a need for safety may also be seeking social acceptance and self-esteem by exercising, eating healthy foods, and dressing well to gain the respect of others.

Motivation and Emotion   **Emotions** are states involving subjectively experienced feelings of attraction or repulsion. There is a complex interrelationship between motivation and emotion. Romantic love, joy, fear, and anger are some of the emotions that may be associated with a motivated state.

Have you ever gone shopping because you were bored or made an impulsive purchase because you needed a little variety in your life? Most people answer "yes" to this question. The experiential perspective on consumer behavior suggests that consumers shop or buy certain products to have fun, to enjoy the process of shopping, and to achieve increased levels of arousal. These are motivations influenced by emotion.

In the past, marketers classified motives based on the role emotions played in the motivation. Therefore, motives were incorrectly grouped in two distinct categories:

Emotion
A state involving subjectively experienced feelings of attraction or repulsion.

what went wrong?

Vince and Larry, the Crash-Test Dummies
Vince and Larry, the television crash-test dummies, first appeared in Department of Transportation advertising in 1984. The advertising showed Vince and Larry smashing through windshields to persuade viewers to buckle up. The message was simple: "Don't be a dummy." When the crash-test dummy campaign began, about 21 percent of the driving population wore seat belts. The percentage of Americans who use seat belts increased for years until 1996, when it reached about 68 percent. Since then, however, the percentage of people wearing seat belts has failed to rise. What went wrong?

"We've persuaded as many people as we can to wear seat belts," says Chuck Hurley, spokesman for the National Safety Council. "Now we have to look at enforcement." Some motoring organizations are concerned about stiffer laws and crackdowns. "It's a personal-liberty issue," says David Collier with the Free Roads Foundation, a Washington drivers' advocacy group. "Just like smoking or drinking. Adults have the right to do things, even if it's not necessarily good for them."

Others believed the advertising using Vince and Larry no longer worked. Murray Gaylord of the Advertising Council believed more realistic, more violent advertising was needed. The Department of Transportation agreed. It is hoping to shock drivers into buckling up with a more gruesome television campaign. Instead of using comic dummies that dust themselves off after a crash, the commercials feature live actors in simulated collisions. In one TV ad, titled "Ice Cream," a husband going to buy ice cream to satisfy his pregnant wife's late-night craving is hit head-on as he pulls out of the driveway. The ad cuts to black as viewers hear the sound of grinding metal. In another, "Cruisin'," teen-agers driving in two cars giggle and flirt until one of the cars is smashed by a speeding van. At the end of each ad, a caption asks: "Didn't see that coming? No one ever does. Buckle up."

This new advertising campaign uses a fear appeal to focus on the need for safety. It was created "to show people that you don't have to be driving dangerously to get in a wreck. It can happen to anyone, anytime."[13]

"emotional" versus "rational." Distinctions of this sort, though not entirely accurate, are still in use. They persist because they serve to remind marketers that consumers, and even organizational buyers, are not strictly rational.

PERCEPTION

Although the idea of "reality" may at first seem straightforward, individuals differ in how they perceive reality. For example, no two people perceive a product, store, or advertisement in exactly the same way. Perception takes place through the senses. To perceive is to see, hear, taste, feel, or smell some object, person, or event and to assign meaning to it in the process.

Products offered by marketers provide many examples of how perceptions differ. A three-year-old car may appear to be just a used automobile to some, but a teenager may be thrilled to have it as a first car. The teenager's parents may see the car in a different light. The used-car dealer may view it in still another. Their images of the automobile—their perceptions—are very different.

Perception
The process of interpreting sensations and giving meaning to stimuli.

Perception, then, is the process of interpreting sensations and giving meaning to stimuli. This process occurs because people constantly strive to make sense of the world and, when faced with new sensations or data, seek patterns or concepts that relate new bits of information to each other and to past experience. Perception is the interpretation of reality, and each of us views reality from a different perspective.

What Is Selective Perception?   Individuals receive information, or stimuli, by hearing, seeing, touching, tasting, and smelling. How they organize and interpret these stimuli in the decision-making process—that is, how they gain information from them—depends on their involvement in the decision-making process, their abilities to experience sensations, the context in which they encounter the stimuli, their intelligence and thought processes, and even their moods. These factors combine to create a mental phenomenon known as **selective perception**—that is, the tendency of each individual to screen out certain stimuli and to color or interpret other stimuli with meanings drawn from personal background.

The cover of *Travel and Leisure Golf* magazine in Exhibit 6-6 shows one way in which people add meaning to and interpret stimuli. The cover's title includes the words "Travel" and "Leisure" plus the letter G, the model's head, and the letters l and f. Yet most people read "Golf" because of the human tendency to mentally "fill things in" or "finish things off." This aspect of perception is called **closure**. Many advertisements make use of this process by not showing the product at all, showing only part of it, or showing only its shadow. The viewer supposedly becomes more involved with the advertisement through the process of closure. A person who does not experience closure will be annoyed by the advertisement, so the closure idea is used only when the product is very well known and the advertiser is sure that the viewer can complete the picture.

Selective perception may involve selective exposure, selective attention, or selective interpretation. Selective exposure exists because individuals seek out certain stimuli and avoid other stimuli. For example, many subscribers to satellite TV systems choose to block out the reception of certain nonfamily channels. Thus, one way consumers avoid stimuli is simply to avoid exposure to them. This is **selective exposure**. So is spending all weekend watching the premium sports channels they purchased.

Selective perception
The screening out of certain stimuli and the interpretation of selected other stimuli according to personal experience, attitudes, or the like.

Closure
An element of perception whereby an observer mentally completes an incomplete stimulus.

Selective exposure
A perceptual screening device whereby individuals selectively determine whether they will be exposed to certain stimuli.

e x h i b i **6-6**

A Design That Capitalizes on Closure

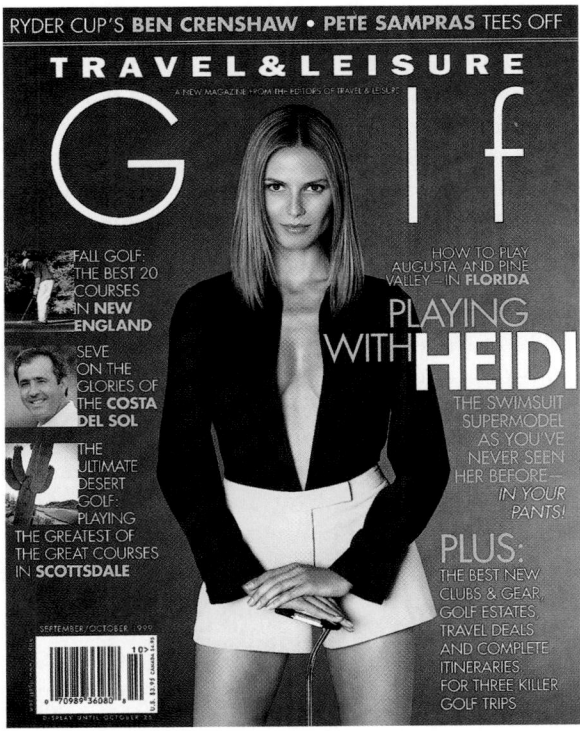

Selective attention
A perceptual screening device whereby a person does not attend to a particular stimulus.

Selective interpretation
A perceptual screening device whereby a person forms a distorted interpretation of a stimulus whose message is incompatible with his or her values or attitudes.

Stimulus factor
A characteristic of a stimulus—for example, the size, colors, or novelty of a print advertisement—that affects perception.

Individual factor
A characteristic of a person that affects how the person perceives a stimulus.

Brand image
The complex of symbols and meanings associated with a brand.

Even if individuals are exposed to information, they may not want to receive certain messages, so they screen these stimuli out of their experience. They pay no attention—at least, no conscious attention—to the stimuli. This is **selective attention**. For example, a person who has just purchased a new PlayStation 2 video game system does not want to hear an advertisement announcing that Sega's prices have just been cut in half, so the person may not pay attention to such advertisements.

Finally, even a person who pays attention may distort a newly encountered message that is incompatible with his or her established values or attitudes. This is **selective interpretation**. The owner of a Ford pickup truck is likely to distort information detailing why Dodge Rams are better trucks than Fords, for example. Looking carefully at perception teaches the truth of the adage "It's not what you (the marketer) say, it's what they (consumers) hear."

There is not much the marketer can do to overcome selective exposure other than to carefully plan the placement of advertisements so that they reach target customers. Selective attention may be overcome with attention-getting messages. The size of an advertisement, the colors used, sounds, and many other **stimulus factors** have been shown to have considerable effect on the amount of attention a viewer will give an advertisement. Attention is also influenced by the *context* of the stimulus factors, such as the novelty of a picture or setting.

More subtly, an advertisement may gain increased attention by featuring aspects that speak to the viewer's needs, background, or hopes, because perception is also influenced by **individual factors**. Generally a full-page color advertisement will attract more attention than a quarter-page advertisement in black and white. However, a black-and-white advertisement offering the hope of "a better appearance" to balding men is likely to attract a lot of attention among its target group, balding men, because they are highly involved. Similarly, advertisements promising help in losing weight will be noticed by people who need this help, even if the advertisements don't grab the attention of other people. Many rules of advertising (use color, don't be wordy) can be broken when the target consumers are willing to devote attention to an ad that means something to them. This illustrates a basic fact about the perception of advertising: Consumers pay attention to advertisements when the products featured interest them.

Perception and Brand Image Marketing   Product distinctions often exist in the minds of consumers and not in the products themselves. The symbolic meaning associated with brand distinctions, developed as a result of selective perception, is known as **brand image**. A brand image is a complex of symbols and meanings associated with a brand. Over the years, for example, General Mills has established a strong image for its Betty Crocker brand. The image is one of dependability and honesty—valuable images for a food product. There never was a real Betty Crocker, but the General Mills products are good and reliable, just like Betty's image. Research has shown that brand image can be the key factor in a buying decision.

It has been shown in formal research that with a number of products—among them cola and beer—consumers cannot distinguish between brands once the labels have been removed.[14] That perception of reality is extremely important in brand image marketing is demonstrated in various "taste test" ads on television. Diet 7Up, for example, humorously portrays a blindfolded man nervously awaiting a firing squad. After taking a "taste test" in which he, of course, cannot read the label, the blindfolded man indicates he prefers Diet 7Up to Diet Coke.

Subliminal Perception   Can advertisers send messages of which people are not consciously aware? In the 1950s, there was considerable controversy about the possibility of this so-called subliminal advertising. In an alleged movie theater "experiment," the phrases "Eat popcorn" and "Drink Coca-Cola" were supposedly flashed on the screen so rapidly that people were unaware of

Symbolism is not subliminal, nor are embedded messages "hidden" in pictures.

YOU'VE GOT TO SEE IT IN **EPSON**

WITH ORDINARY PRINTERS, YOU SEE THE STRIPES ON THE ZEBRA.

WITH OUR PRINTER, YOU SEE THE WOMAN ON THE ZEBRA.

Take a quick look at this advertisement before reading on. Did you see only a herd of zebras? Take a second look. The advertisement says, "With our printer you can see the woman on the zebra." Do you now see a woman riding one of the zebras? Perception is the process of interpreting sensations and giving meaning to stimuli. Effective marketers recognize the importance of perception in consumer behavior.

http://www.epson.com

Our 1440 dpi reveals her every detail. And when the company that made the amazing camouflage gear she's wearing needed a sales report – and needed it fast – the printer they selected was an EPSON Stylus® Color 900. Aside from the incredible resolution you see, it also creates sharp text at up to 12 ppm and color up to twice as fast as other competitors at comparable dpi. Which is the kind of performance that always sets it ahead of the herd.

INTRODUCING THE EPSON STYLUS COLOR 900 BUSINESS PRINTER WITH 1440 DPI.

Only EPSON® color ink jet printers have the exclusive PerfectPicture® Imaging System for: 1440 x 720 dpi • A 3-picoliter dot – the smallest in the industry, for sharpest detail • Fast print speeds – up to 12ppm black/10ppm color • Ethernet/LocalTalk options • PC/Mac/USB compatibility. For more information, call 1-800-GO-EPSON or visit www.epson.com.

Epson Stylus Color 900. Ultrafast business printer. $449

These advertisements show how stimulus factors can be used to attract attention. In the Dodge ad, the red four-leaf clover in a field of green three-leaf clover communicates the message that Dodge is different. In the Tropicana ad, color sets the products apart from the brown and white background photo.

http://www.4adodge.com

http://www.tropicana.com

Dodge Different.

them. Sales in the movie theater were reported to have increased 58 percent for popcorn and 18 percent for Coca-Cola. Psychologists, alarmed at this result, seriously studied the "experiment" and concluded that it had lacked scientific rigor. Subsequent investigations of *subliminal perception* (perception of stimuli at a subconscious level) suggested that advertisers trying to achieve "perception without awareness" would face technical problems so great that the public need not be apprehensive about the possibility. Subliminal stimuli are simply too weak to be effective. For example, only very short messages can be communicated subliminally, and the influence of selective perception tends to be stronger than the weak stimulus factors.[15]

It is interesting to note that the public frequently misuses the word *subliminal.* Symbolism is not subliminal, nor are embedded messages "hidden" in pictures. Neither symbolism nor embedded messages are perceived at a subconscious level—that is, without the individual's knowing of their existence.

LEARNING

If you were asked to identify a brand of light bulbs, what brand would you name? Would you say General Electric? If so, you'd be agreeing with 86 percent of consumers asked this question. Furthermore, 55 percent of consumers said they would pick GE the next time they bought a light bulb. Most consumers have learned to be loyal to GE brand light bulbs. How does such learning take place?

How Learning Occurs   Learning occurs as a result of experience or of mental activity associated with experience. Thus, the expression "older and wiser" is not far from the mark, because older people have had the opportunity to learn from many experiences. Experiences related to product usage, shopping, and exposure to advertisements and other aspects of marketing add to consumers' banks of knowledge and influence their habits.

Learning is defined as any change in behavior or cognition resulting from experience or interpretation of experience. Suppose a package or display—say, for a crayon whose marks can be cleaned away with soap and water—attracts the attention of a shopper, and the shopper gives the product a try. If the crayon works to the customer's satisfaction, she learns through experience that the new product is acceptable. If it does not, she learns that instead. This knowledge becomes information in the consumer's memory. **Memory** is the information-processing function that allows people to store and retrieve information.

A type of learning called *social learning* can occur through observation of the consequences of others' behavior. For example, a younger child observes an older sibling's punishment and learns to avoid that punishment by avoiding the situation that brought it about. Similarly, buyers often purchase products recommended by other people who have used these products. Much television advertising is based on the

Learning
Any change in behavior or cognition that results from experience or an interpretation of experience.

Memory
The information-processing function involving the storage and retrieval of information.

idea that social learning occurs when people watch others on television. Viewers observe the satisfaction that others, such as Michael Jordan, apparently derive from a product, and they learn by interpreting these experiences.

Many theories attempt to explain exactly how learning occurs. All of the widely accepted theories acknowledge the great importance of experience. One important viewpoint focuses on **operant conditioning**, a form of learning believed to occur when a response, such as a purchase, is followed by a reinforcement, or reward. Exhibit 6-7 illustrates the consumer learning process according to this theory. Here, some aspect of the product (or something or someone associated with the product) provides the stimulus, and the purchase is the consumer's response to the stimulus. If the product proves to be satisfactory, the consumer receives a reward—a **reinforcement**. In fact, the consumer makes the purchase with the hope that satisfaction will follow. When it does, the effect is to strengthen (reinforce) the stimulus-response relationship. Learning takes place as this phenomenon occurs over and over.

NOTHING ELSE
IS A PEPSI

This Pepsi advertisement appeared in the souvenir program of a minor league baseball team. Can you see a batter, a ball, and a fielder? Is this a subliminal advertisement? No, it isn't, because you can see the ball players. Subliminal perception is perception of stimuli at a subconscious level. The Pepsi advertisement is an effective advertisement targeted at a baseball-oriented audience.

http://www.pepsi.com

Operant conditioning
The process by which reinforcement of a behavior results in repetition of that behavior.

Reinforcement
Reward. Reinforcement strengthens a stimulus-response relationship.

e x h i b i **6-7**

Effects of Reinforcement on Consumer Behavior: First Trial and Repeat Purchase

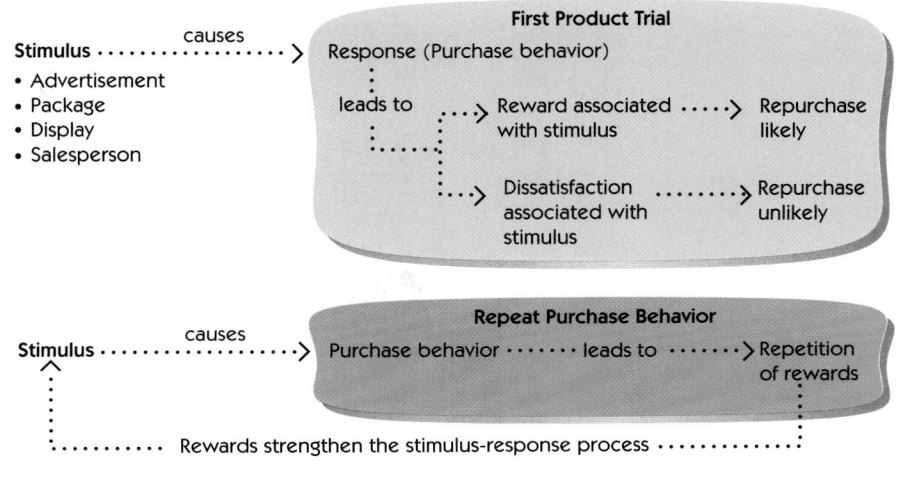

First Product Trial

Stimulus ·········· causes ·········> Response (Purchase behavior)
- Advertisement
- Package
- Display
- Salesperson

leads to ····> Reward associated ·····> Repurchase
with stimulus   likely

····> Dissatisfaction ········> Repurchase
associated with   unlikely
stimulus

Repeat Purchase Behavior

Stimulus ·········· causes ·········> Purchase behavior ······· leads to ·······> Repetition
of rewards

········· Rewards strengthen the stimulus-response process ···········

Some theories of learning stress the importance of repetition in the development of habits. For example, the more you are exposed to a television message such as Smucker's claim that "With a name like Smucker's, it has to be good," the more likely it is that you will learn the content of the sales message. Similarly, repeatedly rewarding a behavior strengthens the stimulus-response relationship. More simply, repeated satisfaction creates buying habits and loyal customers.

Learning Theories and Marketing   Most learning theories are compatible with marketing activities and marketing's key philosophy, the marketing concept. The theories assert that positive rewards or experiences lead to repeated behaviors. The marketing concept stresses consumer satisfaction, which leads to repeat purchases and long-term profitability for the organization.

ATTITUDES

Attitude
An individual's general affective, cognitive, and behavioral responses to a given object, issue, or person.

An **attitude** comprises an individual's general affective, cognitive, and behavioral responses to a given object, issue, or person.[16] People learn attitudes. In terms of marketing, they learn to respond in a consistently favorable or unfavorable manner to products, stores, advertising, and people. Notice that because attitudes are learned, it is possible to change them. This is a goal of much promotional activity.

The ABC Model: A Three-Part Theory of Attitudes   The ABC model is the traditional way to view attitudes. In this view, an attitude has three parts. The A component is the *affective*, or emotional, component. It reflects a person's feelings toward an object. Is the brand good or bad? Is it desirable? Likable? The B component is the *behavioral* component, which reflects intended and actual behaviors toward the object. This component is a predisposition to action. The C component is the *cognitive* component. It involves all the consumer's beliefs, knowledge, and thoughts about the object—the consumer's perception of the product's attributes or characteristics. Is it durable? Expensive? Suitable as a gift for Aunt Mary? The ABC model is graphically portrayed at the top of Exhibit 6-8.

e x h i b i 6-8

Two Views of the Nature of Attitudes

The Traditional ABC View: Three Components

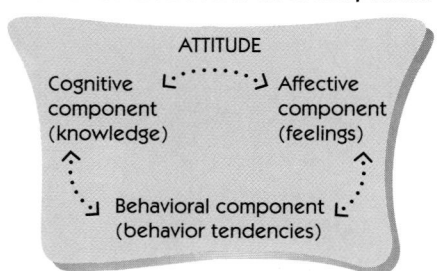

A Modern View: An Emphasis on Affect

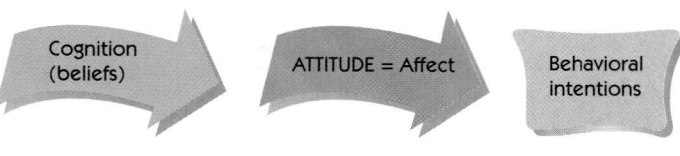

Modern Attitude Theory Stresses Affect   In recent years, attitude theory has changed. The current practice is to define attitude as affect. Attitude is thus seen as a consumer's feelings about products or brands. The shift in view does not discount the importance of cognitive or behavioral components but simply does not define them as components of attitude. Indeed, as Exhibit 6-8 shows, in this view attitudes are based on cognitive beliefs. Behavioral intentions are in turn influenced by both cognitions and attitude (affect).[17]

How Do Attitudes Influence Buying Behavior?   Let's examine a consumer's attitude toward the Kodak Advantix camera. The consumer may hold several cognitive beliefs about the product. One of her beliefs might be that it takes clear pictures. Another might be that its features make it easy to switch back and forth from a regular shot to a wide-angle shot. She may have certain feelings about the camera as well—for example, she may feel that Kodak is a good brand or that the Kodak is desirable because it is the "official camera" of the Olympics. In the current view, these feelings, and her cognitive beliefs, make up her attitude—which may create a predisposition to buy the product.

Note that the consumer's attitude serves as a general indicator of her possible behavior toward the attitudinal object. That is, the consumer will *consider* buying the product—she will not necessarily buy it. A favorable attitude toward a particular brand may not result in purchase of that brand. After all, consumers have attitudes toward competing brands as well. Furthermore, attitudes are not the sole determinant of behavior. Situational, financial, and motivational forces, as well as attitudes, influence behavior. Because attitudes are situational, their effects are controlled by circumstances. Most Americans have very favorable attitudes toward Rolls Royce and Mercedes automobiles, yet not many own one of these cars. Many people admire—that is, have attitudes that favor—mansions surrounded by well-tended formal gardens. Few people live in such places, however. Attitudes may also be affected by other attitudes. People who don't like winter weather will probably not like skiing or snowmobiling and aren't likely to plan to live out their days in Minnesota.

Thus, it is difficult to predict a specific behavior from an attitude toward a single object. Nevertheless, in many situations, there is consistency between attitudes and behavior. For example, you may think that the personnel in a certain department store are friendly. You may also think that the store is clean and the prices are reasonable. These beliefs may lead you to have a positive attitude toward the store. In turn, your purchasing behavior may be consistent with your attitude. Much managerial strategy is based on the assumption that, all other things being equal, a positive attitude toward a store or brand will predispose the consumer to shop at the store or use the brand.

PERSONALITY AND SELF-CONCEPT

We have been discussing several individual differences in consumer behavior. Where do such differences come from? Many individual differences in human behavior are related to personality and self-concept.

What Is Personality?   Like many psychological terms, the word *personality* is used in nontechnical ways in everyday conversation. When Bill says "Mike gets along well with others because he has a pleasing personality," the word is not being used technically. In consumer behavior theory, **personality** is the fundamental disposition of an individual and the distinctive patterns of thought, emotion, and behavior that characterize that individual's response to the situations of his or her life. Personality especially refers to the most dominant characteristics, or traits, of a person, such as introversion or extroversion. Many personality traits have been identified—for example, dominance, gregariousness, self-confidence, masculinity, prestige-consciousness, conservativeness, and independence. It is reasonable to expect such traits to affect behavior. Introverts and extroverts might be expected to purchase different types of automobiles, for example.

Personality
The fundamental disposition of an individual; the distinctive patterns of thought, emotion, and behavior that characterize an individual's response to life situations.

Self-concept is an individual's perception and appraisal of himself or herself. According to self-concept theory, consumers shop at stores and purchase goods and services that reflect and enhance their self-concepts.

Self-concept
An individual's perception and appraisal of himself or herself.

Self-Concept: How People See Themselves

The term **self-concept** refers to an individual's perception and appraisal of himself or herself. Of course, the appraisal of others plays a part in the formation of self-concept. Ultimately, though, the self-concept is the person's own picture of who he or she is (the "real" self) and who he or she would like to be or is in the process of becoming (the "ideal" self). According to self-concept theory, consumers shop at stores and purchase goods and services that reflect and enhance their self-concepts.

Personality Theory Evaluated

The hypothesized relationship of personality (including self-concept) to buying and other aspects of consumer behavior has been studied extensively. The results of such studies indicate that personality theory has only limited power to explain why one brand is chosen over another and that marketing managers can make only scant use of theories of personality in formulating their marketing strategies. That is, investigating personality in isolation from other factors, such as demographic characteristics, is not an effective method of predicting specific consumer behavior. Nevertheless, the intuitive appeal of a relationship between personality and consumer behavior leads some marketing practitioners to base strategy on notions associated with personality theory.

Problems with the practical application of personality research led to the development of psychographic profiles of consumers, discussed in Chapter 8. The focus of personality theory in psychology is on the person as a person, whereas consumer behavior theory focuses on the person as a consumer, emphasizing traits related closely to day-to-day consumer activities. This seems to be a more appropriate way for marketing managers to implement ideas about individual differences in consumers.

Interpersonal Influences on the Decision-Making Process

We have examined many individual factors that influence the decision-making process. But as Exhibit 6-1 showed, environmental influences also exert an effect. In this section, we focus on sociocultural aspects of the environment. The lives of consumers are subject to countless sociocultural forces, including those created by the culture, the subculture, and various groups. Sociologists refer to these forces as *interpersonal influences.*

SOCIAL VALUES, NORMS, AND ROLES

People hold certain social values, follow certain norms, and fill certain roles. As you will see, values, norms, and roles have various sources, from the overall culture to much smaller social groups.

Social Values Chapter 3 defined social values as the goals that a society views as important. As such, they reflect the moral order of a society and give meaning to social life. For example, winning is a value considered important by the sports-oriented U.S. society.

Norms Norms are rules of conduct to be followed in particular circumstances. Behavior appropriate to one situation may be inappropriate to another; thus, norms are "situation specific." In the United States, one general social norm is that pedestrians avoid touching each other. Jostling and crowding together are to be avoided in most circumstances, and persons who do not follow this norm are rewarded with angry stares or comments. At a parade, however, crowding and pushing are more acceptable. The norm changes with the situation.

Norms, like values, strongly affect people's lifestyles and day-to-day behavior patterns, including consumer behavior. The increasingly commonplace norm of not smoking in certain public places influences the planning of owners or managers of restaurants, airports, and shopping malls. Another example of a norm is the custom of buying a diamond engagement ring. Many couples would not even consider a ruby or an emerald engagement ring.

Norms vary from culture to culture. The Japanese who visit the Tokyo Disneyland are far more restrained than the Americans who visit Disneyland in this country. For example, passengers on the rides in Japan do not raise their hands in the air and scream as do their American counterparts. It is not the accepted norm.

Roles　Any social institution, from the smallest group to the largest organization, creates and defines roles for its members. These, like norms, are customary ways of doing things. **Roles** define appropriate behavior patterns in reference to other roles. Thus, the role of son or daughter includes expected behavior patterns that differ from but correspond with the behavior patterns expected of someone in a parental role. The role of a wage earner and that of a student also imply different behaviors. Students tend to dress in jeans and T-shirts because this is consistent with their status as students. However, during a job interview, students of business administration may dress more formally and carry attaché cases to act out their potential roles as business people.

Roles obviously carry over into purchasing situations. There are consumer roles and seller roles. The shopper expects to have certain rights and expects the store employee to fulfill certain obligations.[18] Furthermore, an employee in an expensive fur salon is expected to behave differently from a check-out clerk at Kmart.

Role
A cluster of behavior patterns considered appropriate for a particular person in a particular social setting, situation, or position.

CULTURE

Many values, norms, and roles come from a person's overall culture. The term *culture*, though frequently used, is difficult to define clearly because it covers so much about the way a society operates. Recall that a culture consists of values, beliefs, and customary behaviors learned and shared by the members of a particular society. Essential to the concept of culture is the notion that culture is learned rather than innate. Thus, that children are born is natural, but how the mating process is conducted and how the children that result from it are treated are cultural.

It is important for marketers to understand the many aspects of culture. Culture obviously varies from place to place around the globe and affects the success of marketing worldwide.

SUBCULTURES: CULTURES WITHIN CULTURES

Within any society there is a dominant culture. However, there are also cultural differences. Language differences are an example. Some countries (Canada and Belgium, for example) have two or more official languages (Switzerland has four). In China, five major and many minor languages are spoken. In the United States, several

In our diverse society, there are many subcultures based on race, language, religion, and geography. Preferences for foods and music and forms of socializing can be strongly influenced by values, norms, and roles prescribed by the subculture.

Subculture
A group within a dominant culture that is distinct from the culture. Members of a subculture typically display some values or norms that differ from those of the overall culture.

language groups can be identified. Nowadays, almost 20 percent of the U.S. population speaks Spanish.

A **subculture** is a group within a dominant culture that is distinct because it differs from the dominant culture in one or more important ways—in language, demographic variables such as ethnic or racial background, or geographical region, for example. The subculture will also differ from the overall culture in some values, norms, and beliefs.

Within the U.S. culture, there are many subcultures. Subcultures made up of particular racial or ethnic groups, such as the African American, Hispanic, and Jewish subcultures, are easiest to identify, but the marketer must recognize the many other subcultural differences. These may be as simple as regional differences in food preferences.[19] In the northeastern states, people often eat lamb chops, for example, but in west Texas, beef is the staple and lamb chops are hard to find. Subcultural differences provide marketers with challenges and with potentially rich segmentation possibilities.

SOCIAL CLASSES

Social class
A group of people with similar levels of prestige, power, and wealth whose thinking and behavior reflect a set of related beliefs, attitudes, and values.

Within every culture there are social classes. A **social class** is a group of people with similar levels of prestige, power, and wealth whose thinking and behavior reflect a set of shared beliefs, attitudes, and values. Exhibit 6-9, which summarizes one view of U.S. social classes, shows six discrete groups. Class structure is actually more like an escalator, however, because it runs from bottom to top without any major plateaus.

Social class explains many differences in behavior patterns and lifestyles. Social class may have a major impact on shopping patterns or products purchased. An advertisement for Lucchese boots, which are exquisitely tooled and made from the finest leathers, states that the boots are "available only at finer stores." This simple phrase may stop some readers from further consideration of these boots. Why? One of the classic studies in consumer behavior explains that the lower-status woman believes that if she goes into a high-status department store, the

e x h i b i t 6-9 The American Class System in the 20th Century—an Estimate[20]

CLASS (PERCENTAGE OF POPULATION)	ANNUAL INCOME	PROPERTY	OCCUPATIONS	EDUCATION
Upper class (less than 3%)	Very high	Old wealth, great new wealth	Investors, heirs, capitalists, corporate executives, highly placed civil and military leaders	Liberal arts education at elite schools
Upper-middle class (12%)	High	Property accumulated through savings	Upper managers, professionals, successful small business owners	College, often with graduate training
Middle class (32%)	Average	Some savings	Small business owners, lower managers, farmers, semiprofessionals, nonretail sales operatives, and clerical workers	Some college, high school
Working class (38%)	Modest	Some savings	Skilled labor, unskilled labor, retail sales operatives	High school
Upper-lower class (10%)	Low	No savings	Working poor, sometimes unemployed	Grade school, some high school
Lower-lower class (less than 10%)	Poverty	No savings	Welfare recipients	Grade school or illiterate

clerks will snub or insult her in various subtle ways, making it clear that she does not "belong." Members of different social classes know which stores and products are for people of their class.

The impact of social class on consumer behavior is often indirect. For example, most people live in neighborhoods made up of people from their own class. If the purchases these people make are directly affected by small membership groups within their neighborhoods, they are indirectly touched by the influence of social class.

Among the upper middle class, the *nouveaux riches* (the "newly rich") are most likely to purchase furs or yachts, because these products signify achievement. The expensive car, the big house, private college for the kids, a summer home, a boat, and frequent vacations are all symbolic expressions of success. This kind of buying behavior was well described by the turn-of-the-century American economist Thorstein Veblen, who coined the term **conspicuous consumption**. Veblen, in criticizing people who buy products simply to be seen consuming them or to display them, hit on a fact of human nature. Consumption of certain items is a means to express one's social class status. Although you may snicker along with Veblen at this behavior, the desire to show off may be real and quite important to a person who aspires to or has achieved membership in a higher social class, and thus a marketer should not ignore it.

REFERENCE GROUPS

Each individual belongs to many groups. From a marketing perspective, the most important are reference groups. A **reference group** is a group that influences an individual because that individual is a member of the group or aspires to be a member of it. The reference group is used as a point of comparison for self-evaluation.

A **membership group** is a group an individual is actually part of. Examples include clubs, the freshman class, and UCLA alumni. Such groups strongly influence members' behavior—including consumer behavior—by exerting pressure to conform, or peer pressure. The individual is free to join or withdraw from a *voluntary* membership group, such as a group of college peers or a political party. Sometimes, however, the individual has little or no choice about group membership. For example, people approaching middle age may not like that fact, but they nevertheless make changes in their lives as a result of the influence of their middle-aged peers.

A second major type of reference group is the **aspirational group**. Individuals may try to behave or look like the people whose group they hope to join. Thus, a little brother may try to act like a big brother and his buddies, or a little sister may try to act like a big sister's teenage friends. Similarly, the young business manager may choose to "dress for success." This usually means dressing like the women or men the manager hopes to join one day in the organization's higher ranks.

Reference Groups Influence Some Products More Than Others   The use of some products is highly subject to group influence. Examples include clothing, cars, and beer consumed publicly. The use of other products is subject to almost no group pressure. These products are so mundane or so lacking in visibility that no one uses them to express self-concept. The risks of using the "wrong" brand in private are small. One rarely hears comments about someone's eating Libby's canned peaches instead of Del Monte's. Note that some product categories can be subject to reference group influences regardless of

Conspicuous consumption
Consumption for the sake of enhancing social prestige.

Reference group
A group that influences an individual because that individual is a member of the group or aspires to be a member.

Owners of Harley-Davidson motorcycles strongly identify with the membership group of Harley owners. They often fancy Harley riders as cowboys, desperadoes, or knights in shining armor. Marketers at Harley-Davidson exert considerable effort to make Harley owners feel special and part of the Harley-Davidson tradition. The company endorses a club (the Harley Owners Group, or HOG), a newsletter *(Hog Tales)*, and many special events. For example, ZZ Top has played at HOG-members-only shows sponsored by Harley-Davidson.

http://www.hog.com

Membership group
A group to which an individual belongs. If the individual has chosen to belong to the group, it is a voluntary membership group.

Aspirational group
A group to which an individual would like to belong.

the brand name or design: "Why don't you break down and get an air conditioner, Harry?" "You mean you use instant coffee? No, thank you!" Reference groups, then, may influence the type of product consumed, the brand purchased, or both.

Opinion Leaders   Groups frequently include individuals known as opinion leaders. **Opinion leaders** might be friends who are looked up to because of their intelligence, athletic abilities, appearance, or special abilities, such as skill in cooking, mechanics, or languages.[21] In any group, the role of opinion leader with respect to buying behavior moves from member to member, depending on the product involved. If someone is planning to buy a car, that person may seek the opinion or guidance of a friend or family member who is thought to know about cars. The same person might seek a different "expert" when he or she is buying stereo equipment or good wine or investment plans.

In certain situations, the most powerful determinant of buying behavior is the attitude of those people the individual respects. Thus, word-of-mouth recommendations may be important buying influences. One reason that marketers try to satisfy their customers is their hope that the customers will recommend the product or organization to members of their social groups. The best thing a homeowner can hear when hiring a house painter, for example, is that the painter did a good job on a neighbor's or friend's house.

THE FAMILY

The United States Census Bureau defines a **family** as a group of two or more persons related by birth, marriage, or adoption and residing together. An individual's family is an important reference group. Family members interact face-to-face and respond to each other's total personalities rather than on the basis of particular roles. It is not surprising that the values people hold, their self-concepts, and the products they buy are influenced by their families. That influence may continue to be strong throughout a person's life. The family is the group primarily responsible for the **socialization process**—that is, the passing down of social values, norms, and roles. Socialization includes the learning of buying behavior. Children observe how their parents evaluate and select products in stores. They see how the exchange process takes place at the cash register and quickly learn that money or a credit card changes hands there. That is how children learn the buying role. When children receive money as a gift or allowance and are permitted to spend it, they act out the buying role, thus learning an activity they will perform throughout their lives.

SITUATIONAL FACTORS

In addition to interpersonal influences, another environmental influence on the decision-making process is the situation. Consider the gasoline-buying consumer who is late for an appointment and notices the tank is nearly empty. The situational pressure may increase the importance of convenient location in the choice of gas station and decrease the importance of other attributes. It would be impossible to list all the situational influences on buying behavior. However, it is important to appreciate that a consumer may purchase one brand in one situation and another in a different situation.

Joint Decision Making

Some consumer choices are made not by individuals but by groups of two or more people. This is referred to as **joint decision making** (or household decision making). Family members may, for example, choose a car or a house together. Or spouses or partners may sit down together to talk over insurance purchases, furniture purchases, or retirement plans. Despite this image of togetherness, most purchase decisions are dominated by one group member. In the case of the family group, the parents dominate rather than the grade-school children. Older chil-

Opinion leader
A group member who, because of some quality or characteristic, is likely to lead other group members in particular matters.

Family
A group of two or more persons related by birth, marriage, or adoption and residing together.

Socialization process
The process by which a society transmits its values, norms, and roles to its members.

Joint decision making
Decision making shared by all or some members of a group. Often, one decision maker dominates the process.

dren may have greater influence—as when the teenage son, who "knows all about cars," advises his parents on the selection of a new auto. Typically, different group members take the dominant role in group decision making for different purchases. Even though changing sex roles are influencing traditional roles in family decision making, in most households the husband frequently dominates decisions relating to purchases of insurance, while decisions regarding clothing for the children, food, and household furnishings are most often dominated by the wife. This pattern reflects society's norms and traditional role expectations. Decisions made by husband and wife together are common when entertainment, housing, and vacation choices are being made. It should be noted that changes taking place in our society are making the process of identifying the major decision influencer more difficult.

To simplify the discussion, we have not mentioned the distinctions among consumers' roles during the buying effort. However, there are several roles to be played in any buying decision. These roles are (1) the buyer, who, narrowly defined, is the person who goes to a store and actually purchases a product; (2) the user, who, narrowly viewed, is the person who actually consumes or uses the product; and (3) the decision maker, who decides which product or brand to buy. Think about it for a while. Each role could be played by a different person, or all could be played by the same person, or the roles could be played by any combination of people.

The purchase of baby food is the classic example of a situation in which different people play different roles. The baby eats the food but is denied any comment on it. The buyer could be an older child sent to the store by Mom. Mom is the decision maker who, based on her own experience, the influence of advertisements, or her mother's suggestions, has determined which brand of baby food to buy. The purchase of gum or a haircut, however, may involve only one person performing all three roles.

In more complex buying decisions, such as the purchase of a new home or a family automobile, a family member may also play the role of influencer or gatekeeper. The **influencer** expresses an opinion about the product or service to persuade the decision maker ("Dad, we need to sell the station wagon and buy a car that won't embarrass me"). The **gatekeeper** controls the flow of information ("I won't tell Bob about the house on Rockwood Drive because I liked the one on Hazel Boulevard better").

The focus of marketing changes with the role structure of the buying decision. When only one person is involved, marketing can be more concentrated than when several people in different roles are involved. In the baby food example, whom should the marketer attempt to reach? The decision maker—the person with the real say in the matter—should be the target. Thus, baby food advertisements appear in publications read by mothers as well as on TV and radio programs that reach mothers. These advertisements stress the concerns of mothers, such as nutrition. These are matters that neither the baby nor the older sibling sent to the store really cares about.

Influencer
A group member who attempts to persuade the decision maker.

Gatekeeper
A group member who controls the flow of information to the decision maker.

Summary

Understanding consumer behavior helps the marketer bring about satisfying exchanges in the marketplace. Consumer behavior is affected by a variety of individual and interpersonal (sociocultural) factors, which influence the decision-making process. Marketers must take these factors into account.

1) Understand the basic model of consumer behavior.
Consumer behavior results from the interaction of person and environment, $B = f(P, E)$. Consumer behavior theorists have expanded and explained this basic model with many theories.

2) Describe the consumer decision-making process and understand factors, such as consumer involvement, that influence it.
The decision-making process varies depending on how routine the consumer perceives the situation to be. For decisions involving extensive problem solving, consumers follow a multistep process:

(1) recognizing the problem, (2) searching for alternative solutions, (3) evaluating those alternatives, (4) deciding whether to buy, and (5) if a purchase is made, evaluating the product purchased. Many internal and environmental factors affect this process, including consumer involvement as well as situational influences such as physical settings, social circumstances, and economic conditions.

3) Appreciate the importance of perceived risk, choice criteria, purchase satisfaction, and cognitive dissonance.

Perceived risk is the consumer's uncertainty about whether a product will do what it is intended to do. Choice criteria are those critical attributes the consumer uses to evaluate a product alternative. Purchase satisfaction on the consumer's part means that marketing has achieved its goal. However, the consumer may instead experience cognitive dissonance—a sense of tension and uncertainty—after deciding to make a purchase. Marketers must address all these issues if satisfactory exchanges are to take place.

4) Recognize the influence of individual factors, such as motives, perception, learning, attitude, and personality, on consumer behavior.

Motivation theory attempts to explain the causes of goal-directed behavior in terms of needs, motives, incentives, and drives. Needs can be classified in many ways. Maslow's needs hierarchy ranks human needs from the most basic (physiological) to the highest (self-actualization). As the lower needs are satisfied, the higher needs become more important. Perception is the process of interpreting sensations and stimuli. Each person's perceptions differ at least slightly from everyone else's. Selective perception is the process of screening out or interpreting stimuli—including marketing stimuli. Learning is important to marketing because consumers learn to favor certain products and brands and to dislike others.

Consumers also learn to have certain attitudes. Personality reflects the individual's consistent ways of responding to his or her environment.

5) Explain the nature of culture and subculture in terms of social values, norms, and roles.

Marketers look at culture as the values, beliefs, and customary behaviors that the members of a society learn and share. Insofar as consumers in a society share a culture, they think and act in similar ways. A subculture is a group within a dominant culture that has values and distinctive characteristics not shared with the larger culture. Cultures and subcultures prescribe certain values, norms, and roles for the members.

6) Characterize social class in the United States.

A social class is a group of people with similar levels of prestige, power, and wealth. According to one view, U.S. society may be roughly divided into six social classes determined by wealth, education, occupation, and other measures of prestige. People in different social classes differ in lifestyle, purchase preferences, and shopping and consumption patterns.

7) Explain the influence of reference groups on individual buyers.

Groups strongly influence individuals' behavior. Reference groups, including membership and aspirational groups, provide points of comparison by which an individual evaluates himself or herself. These groups have many direct and indirect influences on purchasing behaviors.

8) Examine the roles in the joint decision-making process.

Roles in the joint decision-making process include buyer, user, and decision maker, as well as influencer and gatekeeper for more complex decisions. In general, the decision maker should be the focus of marketing efforts.

Key Terms

Questions for Review & Critical Thinking

1. Use the consumer decision-making model shown in Exhibit 6-2 to explain how an individual might arrive at each of the following decisions:
   a. To buy a pack of Doublemint chewing gum
   b. Not to buy a BMW convertible
   c. To buy a new house
   d. Not to take a group of three children to the Ice Capades

2. Using examples from your own experience, explain how the following have affected your purchasing behavior:
   a. Extensive problem solving
   b. Perceived risk
   c. Choice criteria
   d. Cognitive dissonance

3. What might a marketer do to reduce cognitive dissonance in the following situations?
   a. A consumer purchases an automobile.
   b. A wholesaler agrees to carry an industrial product line.
   c. A parent purchases an expensive video game for her children.
   d. A man purchases a magazine subscription and wants to be billed later.

4. Tell how the last major purchase you made involved a perceived risk and information search behavior.

5. Name the five levels in Maslow's needs hierarchy. Which group of needs is the most powerful?

6. What is selective perception? How does it influence behavior?

7. Use learning theory to explain why consumers repurchase the same products repeatedly.

8. How do unfavorable consumer attitudes lead to behaviors that are undesirable?

9. What kinds of purchases might be particularly influenced by a buyer's personality and self-image? Name some products and explain your choices.

10. Distinguish between norms and values.

11. How might the marketers at McDonald's be influenced by cultural forces in U.S. marketing? In international marketing?

12. How likely is it that the following people would purchase a ticket to the ballet, to a professional baseball game, and to Disneyland?
   a. A 34-year-old steelworker who graduated from high school
   b. A 44-year-old college professor
   c. A 21-year-old executive secretary
   d. A 21-year-old counter helper at Burger King

13. Is a reference group likely to influence the purchase of the following products or brands?
   a. Laundry detergent
   b. Shampoo
   c. Polo sports shirt
   d. Wristwatch
   e. Athletic club membership
   f. Milk

14. How much joint decision making by a husband and wife would you expect for the following purchases?
   a. Life insurance
   b. Steam iron
   c. Private school education
   d. Box of candy

15. Form small groups as directed by your instructor. Outline the consumer decision-making process for choosing a college or university. Discuss as a class each group's outline of the process.

 **exercises** | http://zikmund.swcollege.com

1. Go to SRI Consulting's Business Intelligence Center home page at http://www.future.sri.com.
2. Select the Values and Lifestyles (VALS) Program link and read some of the background information on the VALS system. Select iVALS—Internet VALS—to complete a VALS survey online. When you have completed your questionnaire, select the Submit button to submit your completed questionnaire. Wait for the analysis (your answers will be analyzed in less than a minute). What is your primary VALS type? What is your secondary VALS type?

Address Book (Useful URLs)

Association for Consumer Research	http://www.acrweb.org/
Society for Consumer Psychology	http://www.cob.ohio-state.edu/scp/
Yankelovich Partners MONITOR	http://www.yankelovich.com/monitor/index.htm

Ethically Right or Wrong?

Theodore Levitt and Sterling Hayden have both written about human consumption needs. These two views appear below.[22]

Theodore Levitt

The "purpose" of the product is not what the engineer explicitly says it is, but what the consumer implicitly demands that it shall be. Thus the consumer consumes not things, but expected benefits—not cosmetics, but the satisfactions of the allurements they promise; not quarter-inch drills, but quarter-inch holes. . . .

The significance of these distinctions is anything but trivial. Nobody knows this better, for example, than the creators of automobile ads. It is not the generic virtues that they tout, but more likely the car's capacity to enhance its user's status and [sexuality]. . . .

Whether we are aware of it or not, we in effect expect and demand that advertising create these symbols for us to show us what life might be, to bring the possibilities that we cannot see before our eyes and screen out the stark reality in which we must live.

Sterling Hayden

What does a man need—really need? A few pounds of food each day, heat, and shelter, six feet to lie down in—and some form of working activity that will yield a sense of accomplishment. That's all—in a material sense. And we know it. But we are brainwashed by our economic system until we end up in a tomb beneath a pyramid of time payments, mortgages, preposterous gadgetry, playthings that divert our attention from the sheer idiocy of the charade.

QUESTIONS

1. What might each author say about the other's viewpoint?
2. Does advertising create needs?
3. Which of these two views is ethically correct?

TAKE A STAND

1. After a winter storm, your car is covered with ice. There is an old spray can of de-icer in the basement. You read the ingredients and discover it contains chlorofluorocarbons. Do you use the spray?
2. You purchase a new copy of Microsoft Office at a computer store. Several weeks later a friend says he would like to have a copy of Microsoft Office and asks you to make a copy for him. Do you make the copy?
3. Is using embedded stimuli in advertisements immoral?
4. Mark McGwire's historic 62nd home-run ball was recovered by a computer analyst who worked part-time as a groundskeeper for the St. Louis Cardinals. He gave the ball to McGwire instead of selling it for the estimated million dollars it was worth to a collector. Was this the right thing to do?

VIDEO CASE 6-1

Vermont Teddy Bear (A)

In November of 1902, President Theodore Roosevelt was on a hunting trip in Mississippi while trying to settle a boundary dispute between Mississippi and Louisiana. Being an accomplished outdoorsman, he liked to bag big game.

However, his hunt was going poorly that day, and he couldn't seem to find anything worthy of discharging his rifle. His staff, trying to accommodate him, captured a Louisiana black bear cub for the President to shoot, but he could not. The thought of shooting a bear that was tied to a tree did not seem sporting, so he spared the life of the black bear cub and set it free.

A famous political cartoonist for the *Washington Star*, Mr. Clifford Berryman, drew a cartoon titled, "Drawing the Line in Mississippi," which used the story of the President refusing to shoot the bear as a metaphor for how he dealt with the boundary dispute.

The cartoon became famous throughout Washington and was reprinted nationally, sparking the imagination of toy manufacturer Morris Michtom of Brooklyn, N.Y. He asked for and received President Roosevelt's permission to use his name for the hand-sewn bears that he and his wife made, and the "Teddy Bear" was born.

Today, the Vermont Teddy Bear Company is the largest maker of handcrafted, American-made teddy bears. The company markets an extensive line of bears for kids (Red Riding Hood Bear and Pajama Bear); bears based on sports (Soccer Bear and Cheerleader Bear); bears based on occupation (Teacher Bear and Doctor Bear); and bears based on other themes. The Vermont Teddy Bear Company specializes in the Bear-Gram Gift, which includes

- A hand-crafted, fully jointed teddy bear that's guaranteed for life. The Classic Teddy Bears are made in Vermont, and no two are alike.
- A choice of over 100 different outfits and accessories to personalize the teddy bear for every interest or special occasion
- A delicious candy treat
- A personal message inside a gift card
- A fun, colorful gift box that even has an airhole to ensure the teddy bear gets lots of fresh air on his or her journey

The Bear-Gram Gifts are shipped directly to customers or gift recipients for birthdays, anniversaries, and other special occasions.[23]

QUESTIONS

1. What place do teddy bears have in the American culture?
2. Is the purchase of a teddy bear as a gift a high- or low-involvement buying decision?
3. Outline the decision-making process for the purchase of a Vermont Teddy Bear as a birthday present.

Business Markets and Organizational Buying

chapter | 7

LEARNING OBJECTIVES

After you have studied this chapter, you will be able to . . .

1) Identify and characterize the types of organizations that make up the business, or organizational, market.

2) Know the steps involved in an organizational buying decision.

3) Characterize the three basic organizational buying situations: the straight rebuy, the modified rebuy, and the new task purchase.

4) Understand how the Internet is changing the way business-to-business marketing occurs.

5) Explain why the buying center concept is important in business-to-business marketing.

6) Appreciate the needs of organizational buyers and explain how marketers can react to those needs.

7) Describe NAICS and analyze its usefulness to marketers.

TimeDance is one of those Internet head-slappers. You know. The why-didn't-I-think-of-that kind of slap. The Redwood City, Calif., startup company has tackled one of the most annoying business tasks: setting up a meeting. TimeDance has made sure that you never encounter that nightmare scenario in the

IBM television commercial—the one where everyone shows up in a room and then wonders who called the meeting. And it does so with an elegant and deceptively simple Web solution.

To arrange a meeting between far-flung people, you first register at http://www.timedance.com. Then you create an event by entering date, time, and location. You enter the names and e-mail addresses of the people you'd like to have show up and click a button to send out the request. (Now they know who's calling the meeting.) You can suggest several time slots to your potential guests. Send the information with just a click, and your invitees receive a form (HTML or plain text) on which they can choose the most convenient time and say whether they'll attend.

TimeDance collects the responses and then sends you e-mail asking you to check the status of your meeting. Logging on to the TimeDance Web site, you'll find each attendee listed with a check mark if he or she has accepted, an "x" if you were turned down, or a question mark if TimeDance is still waiting for an answer. If you've given invitees a choice of times, a clever bar graph shows the preferred slots and who can attend when—a useful feature to ensure that you get the key people.

Several neat tricks make your task even easier. Don't want to type all those names and addresses? Just upload the list of names and e-mail addresses from Outlook, Act, or Organizer. TimeDance will also connect your invitees to a Web site called MapBlast if they need directions to the meeting. If you're trying to get a group of people together to discuss something that needs to be attended to quickly, TimeDance is a welcome innovation that will help you get around phone tag and endless negotiations.[1]

TimeDance markets to businesses and nonprofit organizations, not to ultimate consumers. Just as a consumer products marketer needs to know its customers' buying behaviors, TimeDance knows it is important to understand the needs of its organizational customers and the nature of buyer-seller relationships in business markets. This chapter investigates how organizational buying behavior differs from the buying behavior of ultimate consumers.

The chapter begins by defining business-to-business marketing and organizational buying behavior. Then it explains the different types of organizational buying decisions and the role of the buying center. Finally, it discusses the nature of industrial demand and the characteristics of business markets.

Organizational Buying Behavior

A business marketing transaction takes place whenever a good or service is sold for any use other than personal consumption. In other words, any sale to an industrial user, wholesaler, retailer, or organization other than the ultimate consumer is made in the business market. Such sales involve **business-to-business marketing,** or **B2B marketing.**

All products other than consumer products are organizational products. They are sold in the business market and are used to help operate an organization's

business. The term *organizational* is broader than the terms *business* or *industrial,* but both of the latter terms remain in common use. In fact, the term *business market,* which, narrowly defined, would only refer to manufacturers, service marketers, wholesalers, and retailers, is broadly used by most marketing writers to include organizational buyers such as governments, churches, and other nonprofit entities.

Faced with indecision as to whether a product is a consumer product or an organizational product, ask these two questions:

1. Who bought it?
2. Why did they buy it?

Notice that it is not necessary to ask the question "What did they buy?" For example, airline travel may be a consumer or an organizational product, depending on who bought it and why it was purchased. The fact that the purchase is an airline ticket is not relevant to its classification in this regard.

What, then, do organizations buy? Manufacturers require raw materials, equipment, component parts, supplies, and services. Producers of nonmanufactured goods require many of these same products. Wholesalers and retailers purchase products for resale, as well as equipment such as trucks, shelving, and computers. Hospitals, zoos, and other nonprofit organizations use many goods and services to facilitate the performance of their business functions, as do federal, state, and local governments. In fact, the federal government is the largest single buyer of organizational products. In participating in business-to-business exchanges, all these organizations display **organizational buying behavior.** Exhibit 7-1 illustrates some of these behaviors.

Business-to-business marketing
Also known as *B2B marketing;* marketing aimed at bringing about an exchange in which a product or service is sold for any use other than personal consumption. The buyer may be a manufacturer, a reseller, a government body, a nonprofit institution, or any organization other than an ultimate consumer. The transaction occurs so that an organization may conduct its business.

You might confuse Tyco International with a toy company that has a similar name. However, Tyco International is a business-to-business marketer, not a consumer products marketer. It markets products that control the flow of liquids and gases, undersea fiber optic cable, disposable healthcare products, and other products sold in the business market.

http://www.tyco.com

Organizational buying behavior
The decision-making activities of organizational buyers that lead to purchases of products.

SEGMENT OF ORGANIZATIONAL MARKET	TYPICAL BUYING SITUATION
Agriculture	A farmer purchases a tractor from a farm equipment dealer.
Mining, forestry, fishing	Reading and Bates purchases offshore drilling equipment from the manufacturer.
Construction	A home construction company hires a CPA firm.
Manufacturers of consumer goods	The Smucker's Co. supplies fruit filling for Kellogg's Pop Tarts.
Manufacturers of industrial goods	Boeing purchases steel as a raw material from United States Steel.
Wholesalers and retailers (resale market)	Bloomingdale's purchases towels from a wholesaler.
Health care	Little Company of Mary Hospital purchases blood transfusion equipment.
Information	Cox Cable makes a decision as to whether to offer WGN as part of its programming.
Service industries	Southwest Airlines purchases peanuts for its airline passengers.
Nonprofit organizations	The San Diego Zoo hires an advertising agency to produce TV commercials.
Government	The federal government asks for competitive bids on solar panels for a space telescope.

Buying is a necessary activity for all business and not-for-profit organizations. In organizational buying situations, the process for purchasing goods and services, such as semiconductors and accounting services, may be complex. Purchasing agents and other organizational members determine the need for goods and services, engage in information-seeking activities, evaluate alternative purchasing actions, and negotiate the necessary arrangements with suppliers.

Placing an order with a supplier is generally not a simple act. Organizational buying takes place over time, involves communications among several organizational members, and entails financial relationships with suppliers.

Characteristics of the Business Market

The agricultural, financial, and manufacturing industries are quite different from one another, yet they share some basic characteristics that are typical of the business market. First, particular business markets often contain relatively few customers. Often these customers are geographically concentrated. Even though some American automakers have moved production facilities to the Sun Belt, for example, their headquarters remain mostly in their traditional center, Detroit.

A second characteristic of business markets is that the demand for goods and services is *derived*. A reduction in consumer demand for housing has a tremendous and obvious impact on the building supply products industry. Similarly, downturns in the economy may cause people to cut back on their use of airlines, which in turn reduces the need for airplane fuel and the parts and tools used in airplane maintenance. Ultimately, even the demand for such mundane items as the brooms used to sweep out airline hangars will decline as airline usage declines. All of these examples demonstrate a basic truth: All organizational demand depends ultimately on consumer demand. It is **derived demand**—that is, derived from consumer demand.

The effects of derived demand on marketing efforts are important to business-to-business marketers, and not just because those effects are potentially devastating.

Derived demand
Demand for a product that depends on demand for another product.

Lycra®, by DuPont, is an ingredient that makes stretch pants stretch. The demand for Lycra is derived from the demand for clothing marketed by Liz Claiborne and other companies that use Lycra to add comfort, fit, and freedom of movement to clothing.

http://www.lycra.com

Derived demand presents certain opportunities. Under some circumstances, the business-to-business marketer can stimulate the demand for the consumer product on which demand for the organizational product depends. For example, advertisements suggesting that milk is better in unbreakable plastic jugs may be sponsored by the producers of plastic jugs or the manufacturers of machines that make plastic jugs. Recognizing a trend of declining per capita beef consumption, the Beef Industry Council targeted advertisements to consumers in an attempt to reverse the trend. Pork producers and lamb producers have done much the same thing, even though all these organizations represent farmers and ranchers who are several steps removed from the consumer in the channels of distribution.

A third characteristic of business markets is that organizational buyers prefer to buy directly from the manufacturer or producer. This preference may come from the desire to buy in large quantities or to avoid intermediaries in an effort to obtain a better price. It may also be a function of the technical complexity of many of the products these buyers use and the fact that many such products are made to order. (Consider how the U.S. government purchases weapon systems, for example.) For all of these reasons, the desire to deal directly with producers is understandable.

A fourth characteristic of business markets is that organizational purchasers have comparative expertise in buying. They buy, almost always, in a scientific way, basing decisions on close analyses of the product being offered and careful comparisons with competing products. Moreover, terms of sale, service, guarantees, and other such factors are likely to be carefully weighed. If a product is a highly technical one, the buyer may assign properly trained engineers or scientists to participate in the purchase decision. For a major purchase decision, a committee will likely be formed to evaluate certain factors such as the business-to-business marketer's product, technical abilities, and position relative to competitors. Strategic alliances may be formed to work out technological problems. For example, Fujitsu's engineers shared technologies and worked closely with product developers at Sun Microsystems to jointly develop a new microchip for Sun's workstations.

The focus of much business-to-business marketing has shifted from the single transaction to the overall buyer-seller relationship—a focus known as *relationship marketing.*

A fifth characteristic of business markets is the importance of repeated market transactions. The focus of much business-to-business marketing has shifted from the single transaction to the overall buyer-seller relationship—a focus known as *relationship marketing.* By establishing strong working relationships, suppliers and customers can work together to improve distribution processes and other joint activities. In fact, many business-to-business marketers form **strategic alliances,** or informal partnerships, with their customers. For example, GE buys a couple hundred thousand computers from Dell. Their strategic alliance includes the GE@dell.com Web site, which

Strategic alliance
An informal partnership or collaboration between a marketer and an organizational buyer.

has special pricing for GE. Only GE employees can access this site. Because GE has guidelines and rules about the types of computers different types of employees can order, GE@dell.com's system is designed so that engineers can order one kind of machine, scientists can order another kind of computer, and so on. Dell's Web site system is linked to GE's, allowing a frictionless, paperless flow of information for those who are purchasing computers. The Internet is a very efficient medium for conducting repeat business. Because the Internet is having such a dramatic impact on business-to-business marketing, we devote a separate section to this topic later in the chapter.

We have already discussed the sixth characteristic of business markets, but it is worth repeating. Business-to-business marketing has

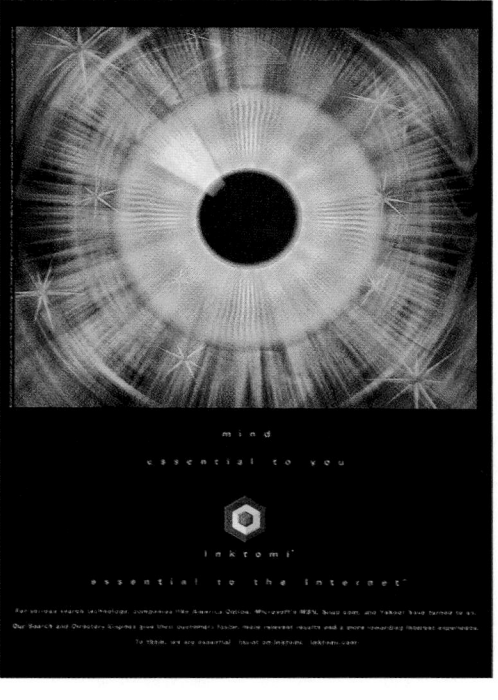

Inktomi is a B2B marketer in the new e-commerce economy. By storing, or "caching," the most frequently requested Internet material on network servers nearest to the people who request it, Inktomi aims to make Web traffic flow faster for organizational buyers such as America Online. Inktomi also markets search engine and directory software used by portals such as Yahoo! and Lycos's HotBot. B2B marketers often form strategic alliances with organizational buyers who have comparative technical expertise and prefer to buy direct.

http://www.inktomi.com

become a global activity. Global competition can be intense, and taking a world perspective is essential. In many instances, a business-to-business marketer's main competition does not come from its home country. Indeed, it may have no domestic competitors. Taking a global perspective is important to marketers selling in consumer markets, of course, but in business markets it is so crucial that it may determine the survival of the marketer's business. Managers in business-to-business marketing organizations often find that their decisions about international strategy are the most vital decisions they make.

The characteristics of organizational customers mentioned here and summarized in Exhibit 7-2 do not relate to every organizational buyer. Furthermore, they

e x h i b i t **7-2**

Major Characteristics of the Business Market

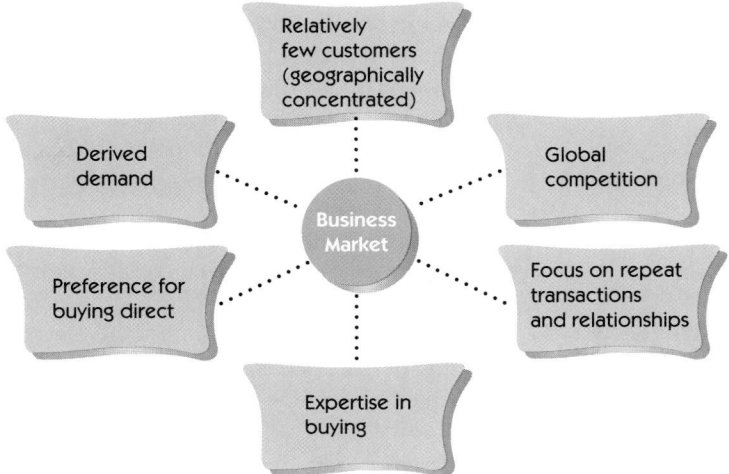

by no means constitute an exhaustive list of such factors. But they do give some indications of how marketers deal with these special buyers. The fact that there are often relatively few buyers, who may be geographically concentrated and who prefer to deal directly with suppliers, encourages—indeed, often mandates—the extensive use of personal selling. The technical nature of many of the products and the expertise of the persons engaged in making purchase decisions demand a well-trained sales force with an extensive knowledge of the products they sell. Representing a maker of nuclear power plants is quite different from selling Legos or Hot Wheels Playsets to Christmas-shopping grandparents. The various characteristics of business markets often combine to permit a marketer to identify almost all potential customers. This capability can make personal selling, which is usually expensive, a cost-efficient marketing tool.

Three Kinds of Buying

The buyer of organizational goods and services, whether chemicals, machinery, or maintenance services, may go through a decision-making process similar to, but more complex than, the consumer decision-making process discussed in Chapter 6. As shown in Exhibit 7-3, organizational buying behavior may be viewed as a multistage decision-making process. However, the amount of time and effort devoted to each of the stages, or **buy phases**, depends on a number of factors such as the nature of the product, the costs involved, and the experience of the organization in buying the needed goods or services. Consider these three situations:[2]

- An organization regularly buys goods and services from the same suppliers. Careful attention may have been given to selection of the suppliers at some earlier time, but the organization is well satisfied with them and with the products they offer. The organization buys from these suppliers virtually automatically. This is the **straight rebuy** situation. Everything from pencils to legal advice to equipment may be bought this way if the buyer is satisfied with the supplier's past performance.

Buy phase
One of the stages of the multistage process by which organizations make purchase decisions.

Straight rebuy
A type of organizational buying characterized by automatic and regular purchases of familiar products from regular suppliers.

e x h i b i **7-3** Buy Phases: Steps in Organizational Decision Making

STEP	DESCRIPTION
1. Identification of a Need	• Anticipation of pending need or recognition of a problem • Determination of how to solve the problem • Determination of the characteristics of the needed good or service • Establishment of buying responsibility and authority
2. Establishment of Objectives	• Description of precise product specifications • Identification of quantities needed and deadlines to be met • Estimation of associated service needs
3. Identification of Suppliers and Evaluation of Alternatives	• Search for and qualification of potential sources • Request for proposals from possible suppliers • Evaluation of proposals
4. Selection of Suppliers and Negotiations	• Selection of qualified suppliers • Negotiation of terms • Signing of contract
5. Establishment of Relationship	• Selection of an order routine • Provision of feedback and evaluation • Maintenance of regular communication

- An organization is discontent with current suppliers or suspects that "shopping around" may be in its best interest. It knows what products are needed and who the likely suppliers are. This is the **modified rebuy** situation. Here, too, any type of good or service may be involved.
- An organization is facing a new problem or need and is not certain what products or what suppliers will fill the need. If the purchase is expected to be a very expensive one, the sense of concern and uncertainty is heightened. This is **new task buying**.

In each situation, the length of the decision-making process and the amount of time devoted to each buying phase may vary, depending on what is being purchased.

Understanding the types of buying situations and behavior found in organizations is extremely important for organizational marketers, just as understanding consumer behavior patterns is important for marketers of consumer products. Each buying situation suggests a different marketing mix—an adjustment of the four major elements to fit particular circumstances.

A marketing manager whose customer is facing a new task buying situation, for example, should understand that the target customer is uncertain what steps should be taken to satisfy his or her organization's needs. Such a buyer probably will require a good deal of information about the supplier, its products, and its abilities to deliver and service the products. This suggests a marketing mix that stresses promotion, especially communication of information that will help the customer evaluate alternatives and understand why the company doing the marketing is the one to choose.

A buyer in a modified rebuy mode might require information of another type. This buyer knows something of what is needed and who likely suppliers are. In such a case, communications built around very specific problem areas might be appropriate. If the target buyer is searching for new suppliers, the marketer must find out why. Have deliveries been late? Have there been product failures? Are prices perceived as too high? The marketer must be aware of such problems and show the target buyer why dealing with this supplier can solve them.

In the case of the straight rebuy, the marketer—who is in the strong position of being the supplier benefiting from the rebuy situation—wants to make sure that the target customer does not become discontent and continues to make regular purchases. Maintaining the relationship is the key marketing objective.

The Internet and e-commerce

The Internet is dramatically changing business-to-business marketing and the way organizational buying occurs. Buying over the Internet has been called *electronic commerce*. Consider General Electric, a major corporation that markets power systems, aircraft engines, plastics, medical systems, and hundreds of other products in the business market. GE does more than a billion dollars' worth of business on its Trading Process Network Web site. A salesperson no longer needs to make a call to companies engaged in straight rebuys. Buyers just go to the company's Web site, find information about goods and services, select the products they need, and e-mail their orders. Many business-to-business marketers have found that providing extra customer value on the Internet both increases sales and reduces the cost of making a sales transaction.

An Internet Web site provides a number of advantages to organizational buyers. They appreciate having product and pricing information readily available through a company's Web site. Technical documents and marketing information no longer need to be mailed or faxed to organizational buyers, because they can be sent to customers and collaborators in the value chain over the marketing company's intranet, which is connected to the Web site. Sophisticated Web sites

Modified rebuy
An organizational buying situation in which a buyer is not completely satisfied with current suppliers or products and is shopping around rather than rebuying automatically.

New task buying
An organizational buying situation in which a buyer is seeking to fill a need never before addressed. Uncertainty and lack of information about products and suppliers characterize this situation.

(such as Cisco System's, discussed in the What Went Right? feature) allow customers to select a particular product configuration and learn its exact cost.

Customer service representatives may not have to spend as much time on the telephone answering questions about the status of orders in progress. Many Internet sites, such as the Federal Express site, use a tracking number system that permits customers to learn the status of a shipment. Customers also like the idea of being able to get product configuration information and price quotes at their own pace, rather than using e-mail or voice mail to contact a sales representative or customer service worker and then waiting for the company representative to get back to them later on.[3] Simply by eliminating some telephone tag (leaving messages back and forth repeatedly before finally contacting each other), the Internet can save great amounts of time. FAQ (Frequently Asked Questions) lists on Web sites also provide added value to prospective customers.

In competitive bidding situations, the Internet can increase the number of bidders and include suppliers from around the world. General Electric has cut the length of the bidding process in its lighting division from 21 days to 10. Because requesting bids is so easy, purchasing managers contact more suppliers. The result of this increased competition has been the lowering of the cost of goods by 5–20 percent. Advanced software lets GE purchasing managers specify whom they want their request for bids to go to and describe the type of information, such as technical drawings, bidders should provide. The software then manages the bids as they come back, eliminating unacceptable bids and handling further rounds, finally notifying the bidders of the outcome.[4]

The Cross-Functional Buying Center

As mentioned earlier, many people may be involved in an organizational buying decision. How do marketers manage to consider all these persons, their motives, and their special needs? It is a complicated and difficult task. However, the concept of the buying center helps marketing managers to visualize the buying process and to organize their thinking as they develop the marketing mix. The **buying center** in any organization is an informal, cross-departmental decision unit whose primary objective is to acquire, distribute, and process relevant purchasing-related information. In somewhat simpler terms, the buying center includes all the people and groups that have roles in the decision-making processes of purchasing. Because all these people and groups take part, they are seen as having common goals and as sharing in the risks associated with the ultimate decision. Membership in the buying center and the size of the center vary from organization to organization and from case to case. In smaller organizations, almost everyone may have some input; in larger organizations, a more restricted group may be identifiable. The buying center may range in size from a few people to perhaps 20.

Buying center
An informal, cross-departmental decision unit, the primary objective of which is to acquire, distribute, and process relevant purchasing-related information.

what went right?

Cisco Systems Cisco Systems Inc., the leading supplier of networking hardware including routers, local- and wide-area-network switches, and dial-up access servers, has been selling its products through its Web site since 1996. Through its far-reaching Cisco Connection Online (CCO), in 1998 Cisco took 41 percent of its orders online, averaging $10 million a day in e-commerce. In 1999, Internet sales were even more impressive. The Web site accounted for 73 percent of the company's orders and $22.8 million a day. Cisco is selling billions of dollars' worth of networking products annually, making it by far the biggest e-commerce marketer in the world.

Cisco is in the networking business, so it's hardly surprising that a company whose products help connect . . . businesses on the Internet would be selling its wares online. But the company is setting the pace . . . in the way it's employing some fancy new technology to support the cyber-selling process. . . . The company initially used its Web address (http://www.cisco.com) to offer customers product information as well as service. But in March 1996, Cisco Marketplace went online, offering customers the ability to configure their own products without having to depend on a salesperson. . . . Cisco Marketplace includes an Internetworking Product Center containing information on 12,800 parts. . . . Customers who have been granted access to do business with the company online can use the e-store 24 hours a day from anywhere in the world.

The secret to the company's e-commerce success is the system's built-in intelligence that filters out erroneous orders before they can even get into the process. This is done through a sophisticated sales-configuration software package. By shifting much of its business to the Web, Cisco is easing the burden on its order-entry staff, who typically had to correct or re-work 10 to 15 percent of all orders that came in by fax. With the configurator built into the Cisco Marketplace Web site, 100 percent of the orders the company receives over the Web site are correct the first time. The placement of a correct order . . . reduces the lead time Cisco needs to deliver the product by 2 to 3 days.

. . . The accuracy of orders is ensured because the system guides the customer through a series of questions to design the product's capabilities. Instead of being turned away, customers who pick combinations that won't work are guided to make alternative choices based on which aspects of the product have greater priority for their needs.

. . . Cisco's Web site has made it better able to meet its customers' demands because its salespeople are not just order takers. The sales force can build relationships with customers and focus on more important issues as a result of not having to handle the transaction carried out on the Internet.

Cisco is enjoying the fruits of being one of the early adopters of Web-based selling technology. Its business-to-business marketing strategy has created a massive advantage for Cisco.[5]

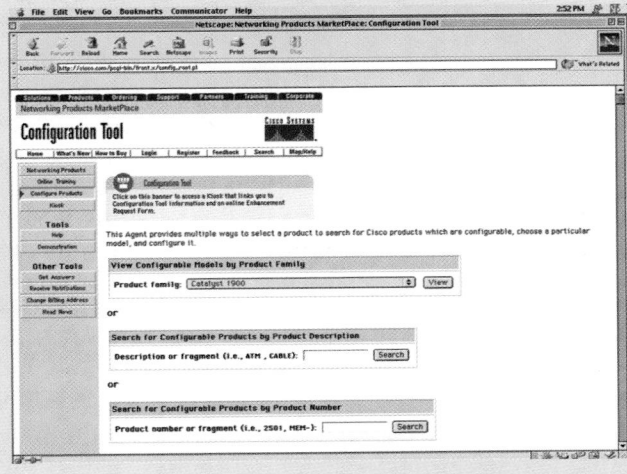

When thinking in terms of a buying center, keep in mind that the center is not identified on any organization chart. A committee officially created to decide on a purchase is likely to be but one part of the buying center. Other members have unofficial but important roles to play. Indeed, membership in the buying center may actually change as the decision-making process progresses. As the purchasing task moves from step to step, individuals with expertise in certain areas are likely to step out of the process as others are added. Again, membership in a buying center is informal, so no announcements are likely to be made of who has been dropped and who has been added.

> The cross-functional buying center is not identified on any organizational chart.

Buying centers, then, include a wide variety of individuals who work in different functional areas of the organization. In other words, buying centers are cross-functional. One example comes from a study of the buying of air compressors for manufacturing plants. The following individuals and groups were all found to be involved in some part of the purchasing decision: president, vice president of engineering, vice president of manufacturing, plant facilities manager, maintenance supervisor, chief electrician, and purchasing department personnel. Each member of a buying center has an official place in the organizational structure as well as an unofficial one in the buying center. Official organizational roles may influence roles in the buying center. For example, the formal organization of a hospital might include a purchasing department that screens all marketers of hospital equipment, even though the physicians, surgeons, and hospital executives actually have more influence over the decision-making process. Furthermore, in general, roles vary with the complexity of the product under consideration. As complexity increases, engineers and technicians may have a greater say in purchasing decisions. If the product is not complex or if a regular purchasing pattern has been developed and agreed on, a purchasing agent or some other formally identified buyer is likely to have buying responsibility.

ROLES IN ORGANIZATIONAL BUYING

In a sense, in spite of its apparent complexity, buying behavior in buying centers is like buying behavior in households, discussed in Chapter 6. There, different members of the household play certain roles in the purchase decision. We can identify five similar roles in organizational buying behavior: users, buyers, gatekeepers, deciders, and influencers.

Users are employees or managers who will actually use what is purchased. Although a retail sales clerk may be the user of a computerized cash register, he or she may have little influence on the decision to buy the product.

The **buyer** has the formal authority to purchase the product and is often responsible for choosing a supplier and negotiating the terms of the purchase. A purchasing agent may fill the role of buyer. Alternatively, a purchasing agent may gather information, such as product specifications and prices, after which engineers or others within

User
The buying-center role played by the organizational member who will actually use the product.

Buyer
The buying-center role played by the organizational member with the formal authority to purchase the product.

In many physicians' offices and other small businesses, the roles of user (the person who actually uses the product), decider (the person who actually makes the decision), and buyer (the person with the formal authority to make the decision) are played by the same person.

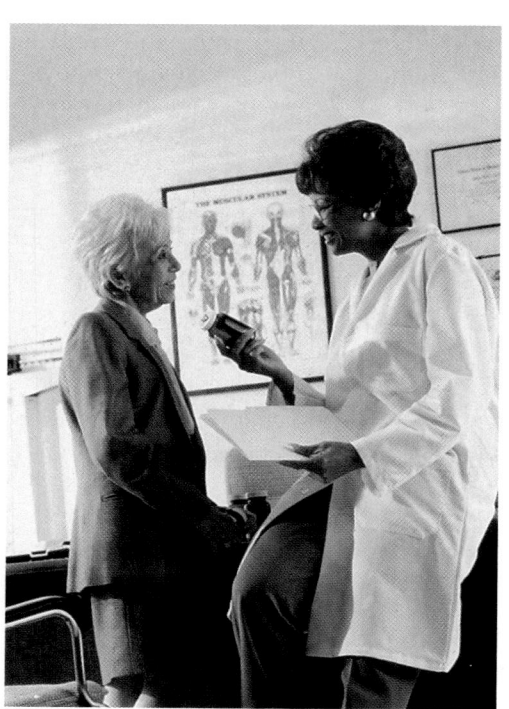

the organization make the buying decision. Collecting and passing on—or withholding—information is known as the **gatekeeper** function. In some cases, the "gate" may be opened or closed by someone who has very little to do with the process otherwise. For example, suppose a secretary requests new word processing software. The office manager who supervises the secretary may act as gatekeeper by simply passing along (or failing to pass along) the request to higher management. Perhaps, though, the office manager has the ultimate responsibility to decide whether the secretary will get the new software. In that case, the office manager is also the **decider**—the person who makes the actual purchase decision. In any case, marketers must direct much of their effort toward gatekeepers because they control the flow of information related to the purchase.

The **influencer** affects the purchase decision by supplying advice or information. In a software purchase, a consultant may supply technical information and may thus act as an influencer. (Note that an outsider can play a role in the buying center.) A secretary in another department may act as an influencer by relating past experiences with a particular product. Influence can also take the form of information about what course of action those in high positions in the organization prefer; whoever provides such information is an influencer.

Remember that a person in a particular position may play several roles and that a particular role may be played by persons in several types of positions. Note also that the importance of a particular role varies from decision to decision. You can see that a buying center is often loosely constructed and somewhat difficult to identify clearly. Nevertheless, because of its potent influence, the marketer should devote time and effort to investigating the effects of the buying center on the marketing situation at hand.

Why Do Organizations Buy?

Is organizational buying behavior based on rational buying criteria, or do emotional motives come into play? Reasonable observers must acknowledge that good sales skills and effective advertisements often appeal to an organizational buyer's emotional need to buy "the best" or to take pride in the products purchased. However, one compelling argument explains why emotional buying motives are not likely to be the most important ones: No organizational buyer would put his or her job and reputation on the line by purchasing a product simply because a friendly salesperson satisfied some emotional need of that buyer. By entertaining a prospect, a sales representative may satisfy certain of that prospect's needs for affiliation, but if the sales goes through, it's because the product meets all the rational criteria used by the purchaser to judge the product. That is, the emotional reasons are almost always supplemental buying criteria.

There are many rational reasons for buying. The importance of each factor varies from situation to situation, and some factors may not come into play in a given purchase decision. This discussion focuses on a few of the most influential purchasing criteria.

PRODUCT QUALITY

Product quality can be an extremely important purchasing criterion. Organizations make certain purchases without carefully analyzing the products they are buying simply because the costs and risks involved in making a bad choice are not very great. Paper clips and thumbtacks are all pretty much alike, for example, and are often bought without close scrutiny. However, most goods and services bought by organizations are not like that, and organizational buyers are usually careful. In fact, many products are made according to the buyer's own specifications, indicating that the buyer closely considers exactly what quality is required in a product purchased for a given task. In many industries, such as aerospace and defense, the reliability of the component part is the most important criterion.

Gatekeeper
The buying-center role played by the organizational member who controls the flow of information related to the purchase.

Decider
The buying-center role played by the organizational member who makes the actual purchasing decision.

Influencer
The buying-center role played by organizational members (or outsiders) who affect the purchase decision by supplying advice or information.

Many organizations have adopted total quality management (TQM) programs that directly affect the organizational buying decision. A manufacturer that promises its customers defect-free products will not tolerate parts suppliers that do not adopt TQM programs of their own. Thus, not only must product quality conform to customer requirements; it may have to exceed the expectations of organizational buyers. High quality, as the customer defines it, is a major reason for buying.

ISO, the International Organization for Standardization, publishes international quality-control standards which are rapidly taking hold in Europe and elsewhere around the globe. ISO 9000 is a standard of quality management, represented by a certificate awarded by one of many independent auditors, attesting that a company's factory, laboratory, or office has met quality management requirements determined by the International Organization for Standardization. The ISO 9000 standards do not tell a manufacturer how to design a more efficient earth mover or build a more reliable industrial robot. But they provide a framework for showing customers how a company tests products, trains employees, keeps records, and fixes defects. Think of ISO 9000 not as another variant of total quality management but as a set of generally accepted accounting principles for documenting quality procedures. With an estimated 30,000 or more certificates issued worldwide, the standard is rapidly becoming an internationally recognized system, comprehensible to buyers and sellers. In addition, the International Organization for Standardization has published ISO 14000, which is a guide for environmental standards that relate to product design.[6]

RELATED SERVICES

Service is an important variable in organizational purchasing. Before a sale is completed, the marketer may have to demonstrate the ability to provide rapid delivery, repair service, or technical support. After the sale, the supplier had better be able to deliver the promised services, because "downtime" costs money and may be a great source of frustration for the buyer of, for example, an office photocopier, a computer, or an assembly-line conveyor system.

In business-to-business marketing, relationship marketing often means effectively being part of a collaborator's organization. Red Star Specialty Products, a Universal Foods company, is a global leader in the manufacture of flavor enhancers, yeasts, and natural and synthetic colors for foods, beverages, and other products. It offers food-processing companies, beverage companies, and other customers applications support, technical seminars, prototype products, and a technically trained staff of field representatives. Maintaining and enhancing relationships with its customers by providing extra services is a vital aspect of Universal Foods' B2B marketing efforts.

PRICES

Price can be the single most important determining factor in many organizational buying decisions. There is an old adage that says "Farmers are price takers, not price makers." It suggests that farmers (who are organizational marketers) face keen competition in a marketplace where the products sold are more or less the same. Not all organizational marketers are quite so much at the mercy of market forces as farmers, but many organizational goods and services face strong competition from products that are close substitutes. In such situations, price is likely to be the key to completing a sale. To heighten the effects of competition on price, organizational buyers often gather competitive bids from suppliers.

Organizational buyers can be expected to analyze price carefully, examining not just the list price but also any discounts, terms of sale, and credit opportunities that accompany a purchase agreement. Further, some buyers make a distinction between first cost (initial price) and operating cost (price over a specific time period). Such cost analysis, as well as their thorough knowledge of the product, allows organizational buyers to make detailed comparisons of value, increasing the importance of price as a buying criterion.

RELIABLE DELIVERY AND INVENTORY MANAGEMENT

For many organizations, the assurance of reliable delivery of purchases is essential. A related concern, inventory management, may also be an important buying criterion. These issues are often addressed through the development of strategic alliances with collaborators.

BENEFICIAL ORGANIZATIONAL COLLABORATION

As business becomes more global and as information technology advances, organizational buyers are increasingly concerned with collaborative efforts and with building strategic alliances with other organizations. For example, strategic alliances related to inventory management may take the form of single-sourcing.

Single-sourcing occurs when an organization buys from a single vendor. Usually, in such situations, the organizational marketer works closely with the buyer to ensure that inventory items are delivered just as the buyer's inventory is being depleted. The seller may, for example, ship tires to an auto manufacturer so that they arrive exactly when needed in the production process and in the quantity needed. The degree of cooperation may be so great that buyer and seller share information technologies and a common database reflecting the customer's current inventory. Such single-sourcing is likely to involve electronic data interchanges between companies.

In Chapter 4, we argued that a company enhances its effectiveness by concentrating its resources on a set of core competencies. Many organizations buy from collaborators who have competencies in tasks the organization chooses not to perform itself. Hence, the potential for continuity in a relationship with the same seller because of common goals, mutual trust, and compatible business processes is an important reason for buying. This is particularly true for wholesalers and retailers who are members of a channel of distribution. Business-to-business distribution and supply-chain management strategy are discussed in Chapters 11 and 12.

THE BOTTOM LINE

The relative importance of each of the major organizational buying criteria—product quality, service, price, and delivery—may vary with the buyer, the situation, or the product. For example, research showed that customers of Copperweld Robotics, a producer of industrial robots, wanted answers to three questions, in the following order: (1) Will the product do the job? (2) What service is available? (3) What is the price? Copperweld knows that, for buyers of industrial robots, service is a top priority. If one component of the robot doesn't work, the customer's whole production line shuts down. Providing service after a sale is Copperweld's number-one way of creating and maintaining customer relationships.

In general, in any organizational buying decision, the buying criteria interact. Each contributes to the final

Single-sourcing
Purchasing a product on a regular basis from a single vendor.

BreezeNET is a new wireless networking system. Educational organizations buy from BreezeNet because its software helps them save money and improve their operations. In the business market, improving the "bottom line" is an important buying criterion.

http://www.breezecom.com

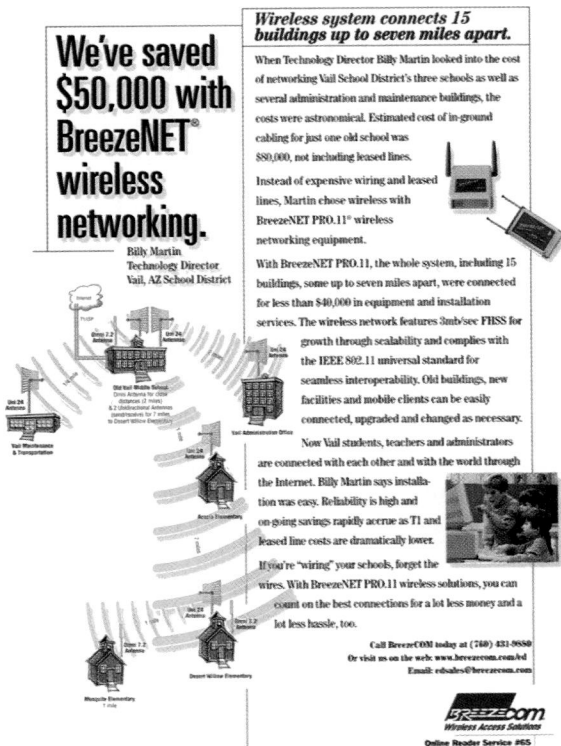

We've saved $50,000 with BreezeNET® wireless networking.

Billy Martin
Technology Director
Vail, AZ School District

Wireless system connects 15 buildings up to seven miles apart.

When Technology Director Billy Martin looked into the cost of networking Vail School District's three schools as well as several administration and maintenance buildings, the costs were astronomical. Estimated cost of in-ground cabling for just one old school was $80,000, not including leased lines.

Instead of expensive wiring and leased lines, Martin chose wireless with BreezeNET PRO.11® wireless networking equipment.

With BreezeNET PRO.11, the whole system, including 15 buildings, some up to seven miles apart, were connected for less than $40,000 in equipment and installation services. The wireless network features 3mb/sec FHSS for growth through scalability and complies with the IEEE 802.11 universal standard for seamless interoperability. Old buildings, new facilities and mobile clients can be easily connected, upgraded and changed as necessary.

Now Vail students, teachers and administrators are connected with each other and with the world through the Internet. Billy Martin says installation was easy. Reliability is high and on-going savings rapidly accrue as T1 and leased line costs are dramatically lower.

If you're "wiring" your schools, forget the wires. With BreezeNET PRO.11 wireless solutions, you can count on the best connections for a lot less money and a lot less hassle, too.

Call BreezeCOM today at (760) 431-9880 Or visit us on the web: www.breezecom.com/ed Email: edsales@breezecom.com

BREEZECOM
Wireless Access Solutions
Online Reader Service #65

VeriSign calls itself a "trust services" company. The firm is the largest distributor of digital certificates used for identification purposes on computer networks. The company's digital IDs protect access to information over intranets, extranets, and the Internet. This allows for safer communication and e-commerce activities where security and access control are needed.

For example, health care service providers need a way to verify the identity of their online subscribers, especially when highly personal, critical, and confidential drug prescription information is at stake. PCS Health Systems, one of the nation's largest pharmacy benefit managers and a wholly owned subsidiary of Rite Aid Corporation, is using VeriSign's Go Secure! services to secure pcsRx.com. Secured by VeriSign's trust services, this new Web site—http://www.pcsRx.com—provides a wide range of personalized health information and online prescription management services for more than 50 million PCS cardholders.

Over 150,000 Web sites have purchased the company's digital certificates, and nearly 4 million individuals have been issued certificates for use in online surfing and buying. Microsoft has anointed VeriSign's system its "preferred provider" of digital IDs for use in the company's Web browser, Internet Explorer. Netscape's Navigator browser also supports the use of VeriSign's digital certificates. All Fortune 500 companies with a Web presence and all of the top 40 electronic commerce Web sites use VeriSign digital certificate services.

VeriSign's success is in no small part due to derived demand resulting from Internet growth. However, its success is also related to the market the company serves. It only makes sense that the e-commerce security market would rally behind one technology and make that the "standard" security system. It's almost a winner-take-all situation, and VeriSign has had the lead for some time now.[7]

decision, and each affects the importance of the others. Yet they often boil down to one overriding factor: the need to operate an organization. General Motors' truck and coach division emphasizes features like corrosion resistance and low fuel consumption in its advertising. The strategy is based on the belief that GM customers buy trucks not because they like them, but because they need them to earn a profit.

NAICS: Classifying Business Markets

A wide variety of profit and not-for-profit institutions make up the business market. Knowing how many of each kind of organization are in operation, where they are located, their size, and so on can help marketers conduct research and plan marketing strategies. Fortunately, a great deal of information is available on business markets. Although much of this information is gathered by private companies, governmental agencies are also important sources.

North American Industry Classification System (NAICS)
A numerical coding scheme developed by the governments of the partners in the North American Free Trade Agreement and used to classify a broad range of organizations in terms of the type of economic activity in which they are engaged.

Standard Industrial Classification (SIC) system
A numerical coding system developed by the U.S. government and (until the advent of NAICS) widely employed by organizational marketers to classify organizations in terms of the economic activities in which they are engaged.

One tool for researching the organizational marketplace is the **North American Industry Classification System (NAICS)**. NAICS, a numerical coding scheme developed by the governments of the partners in the North American Free Trade Agreement, is used to classify a broad range of organizations in terms of the type of economic activity in which they are engaged.

As of 1997, the North American Industry Classification System replaced United States', Canada's, and Mexico's separate classification systems with one uniform system for classifying industries.[8] In the United States, NAICS replaced the **Standard Industrial Classification (SIC) system**, in use since the 1930s. The North American Industry Classification System allows marketers to better compare economic and financial statistics and ensures that such statistics keep pace with the changing global economy.

In a marked change from the old SIC system, NAICS reflects the enormous changes recently in technology and in the growth and diversification of services. New NAICS industry sectors include the following:

1. The Information Sector, which covers industries that create, distribute, or provide access to information, including satellite, cellular, and pager communications; online services; software and database publishing; motion picture, video, and sound recording; and radio, television, and cable broadcasting.
2. The Health Care and Social Assistance Sector, which organizes those industries by intensity of care and recognizes new industries, such as HMO medical centers, outpatient mental health care, and elderly continuing care.
3. The Professional, Scientific, and Technical Services Sector, which recognizes industries that rely primarily on human capital, including legal, architectural, engineering, interior design, and advertising services.

SECTOR	TWO-DIGIT CODE
Agriculture, Forestry, Fishing, and Hunting	11
Mining	21
Utilities	22
Construction	23
Manufacturing	31–33
Wholesale Trade	42
Retail Trade	44–45
Transportation and Warehousing	48–49
Information	51
Financial and Insurance	52
Real Estate and Rental Leasing	53
Professional, Scientific, and Technical Services	54
Management of Companies and Enterprises	55
Administrative and Support, Waste Management, and Remediation Services	56
Educational Services	61
Health Care and Social Assistance	62
Arts, Entertainment, and Recreation	71
Accommodation and Foodservices	72
Other Services (except Public Administration)	81
Public Administration	92

The major divisions used in the system are shown in Exhibit 7-4. The two-digit codes in the exhibit can be extended to three digits, four digits, or more to identify finer and finer gradations of differences within any particular area. Consider Information. The two-digit code is 51. Publishing Industries (511), Motion Picture and Video Industries (512), and Broadcasting and Telecommunications (513) are examples of groups with three-digit codes within the Information sector. The four-digit code within the Broadcasting and Telecommunications group for Telecommunications is 5133, and the five-digit code for Wireless Telecommunications Carriers (except Satellite) is 51332.

The new North American Industry Classification System (like the old Standard Industrial Classification system it replaced) is important to marketers because it is a guide to vast amounts of information published by the federal government. The *Census of Retail Trade,* the *Census of Manufacturing, County Business Patterns,* and many other useful government publications are based on this system. Furthermore, because government agencies use the system so heavily in generating government statistics, most private companies that generate marketing research data also use it.

Summary

The behavior of organizational buyers often differs significantly from that of ultimate consumers. Marketing managers must understand the special characteristics of this market.

1) Identify and characterize the types of organizations that make up the business, or organizational, market.

The business, or organizational, market is composed of businesses, nonprofit groups, charitable and religious organizations, governmental units, and other

nonconsumers. Business markets often contain a relatively small number of geographically concentrated customers who prefer to buy directly from the manufacturer or producer or service provider. Organizational purchasers buy, almost always, in a scientific way, basing decisions on their expertise. Business-to-business marketing has become a global activity, typically involving repeated market transactions and strategic alliances. Consumer buying decisions affect many organizations because demand for products in the organizational marketplace is derived demand. That is, organizational demand ultimately depends on consumer demand, even when organizational purchasing decisions are far removed from consumers.

2) Know the steps involved in an organizational buying decision.

Organizational buying takes place over time, involves communications among several organizational members, and requires financial relationships between an organization and its suppliers. An organizational buying decision is the result of a multistage process that includes (1) anticipating or recognizing a problem, (2) determining the characteristics and quantity of the product needed, (3) describing product specifications and critical service needs, (4) searching for and qualifying potential sources, (5) acquiring and analyzing proposals, (6) evaluating proposals and selecting suppliers, (7) selecting an order routine, and (8) using feedback to evaluate performance.

3) Characterize the three basic organizational buying situations: the straight rebuy, the modified rebuy, and the new task purchase.

The straight rebuy requires no review of products or suppliers; materials are reordered automatically when the need arises. The modified rebuy occurs when buyers are discontent with current products or supplier performance and investigate alternative sources. The new task purchase involves evaluating product specifications and reviewing possible vendors in a purchase situation new to the organization.

4) Understand how the Internet is changing the way business-to-business marketing occurs.

The Internet has dramatically changed business-to-business marketing and the way organizational buying occurs. In buying over the Internet, or electronic commerce, organizational buyers go to a supplier's Web site, find information about goods and services, select the products they need, and e-mail their orders. Many business-to-business marketers have found that providing extra customer value on the Internet both increases sales and reduces the cost of making a sales transaction.

5) Explain why the buying center concept is important in business-to-business marketing.

The buying center is an informal network of people who have various roles in the purchasing decision process. The people and their roles vary over time. Roles include users, buyers, gatekeepers, deciders, and influencers. Marketers must identify members of the buying center and evaluate their importance at various stages of the process in order to target marketing efforts most effectively.

6) Appreciate the needs of organizational buyers and explain how marketers can react to those needs.

Needs of organizational buyers include high-quality products, related services, low price, and reliable delivery (perhaps including enhanced inventory management). The relative importance of these factors may vary with the buyer, the situation, or the product. The marketer must first determine what these needs are and then react to them through appropriate adjustments in the marketing mix.

7) Describe NAICS and analyze its usefulness to marketers.

NAICS, a coding method used to classify many organizations, can be used to identify products, individual manufacturers, purchasers of various products, and other useful facts. Governments, trade associations, and other sources use these codes to categorize information. Marketers who understand the system have access to vast amounts of published data and can use the codes to determine market potentials and gain other insights into the structure of markets.

Key Terms

business-to-business marketing (p. 172)
buy phase (p. 176)
buyer (p. 180)
buying center (p. 178)
decider (p. 181)
derived demand (p. 173)
gatekeeper (p. 181)

influencer (p. 181)
modified rebuy (p. 177)
new task buying (p. 177)
North American Industry Classification System (NAICS) (p. 184)
organizational buying behavior (p. 172)

single-sourcing (p. 183)
Standard Industrial Classification (SIC) system (p. 184)
straight rebuy (p. 176)
strategic alliance (p. 174)
user (p. 180)

Questions for Review & Critical Thinking

1. In what ways does business-to-business marketing differ from consumer marketing?
2. Compare and contrast the consumer's decision-making process and the organization's decision-making process.
3. For the organization purchasing each of the following products, indicate whether the buying task will be a straight rebuy, a modified rebuy, or new task buying. Briefly explain your answers.
   a. Lawn maintenance for the Mercedes-Benz regional headquarters building in suburban New Jersey
   b. Roller bearings to be component parts for Snapper lawn mowers
   c. An industrial robot to perform a function currently done manually
   d. Personal computers for top-level managers
4. What difficulties for sellers are suggested by the buying center concept?
5. What variables might be used to estimate demand for the following products?
   a. Paper clips
   b. Staplers
   c. Lubricants for industrial-quality drill presses
   d. Forklift trucks
6. Define derived demand, and give an example of its effect on the sale of packaging materials.
7. Is a business-to-business marketer more likely to stress personal selling or advertising in promoting a product? Why?
8. Form small groups as directed by your instructor. Pick a local business organization and identify at least four job titles held by managers and employees. Discuss who might influence the company's buying decisions for straight rebuys, modified rebuys, and new task buying.

 **exercises** http://zikmund.swcollege.com

You will find the entire North American Industry Classification System at http://www.census.gov/epcd/www/naics.html. Explore the information given for one or more of the industries listed in Exhibit 7-4. Identify three products that have codes of at least four digits.

Address Book (Useful URLs)

International Organization for Standardization	http://www.iso.ch/
Dun & Bradstreet	http://www.dnb.com
Manufacturing Extension Partnership	http://www.mep.nist.gov/

Ethically Right or Wrong?

A purchasing agent likes to work with Company A, though its prices are rarely the lowest. The purchasing agent solicits competitive bids from Company A and from Companies B and C, which are known for very high quality products but also extremely high prices. Companies D and E, whose products meet the organization's quality specifications and whose prices are generally the lowest in the industry, are not invited to submit bids. Company A, whose product meets minimum quality specifications, wins the contract.

QUESTION

1. Is this ethical?

1. A purchasing agent attends a lewd party, sponsored by a company that wants to do business with the agent's company. Should the purchasing agent have attended?
2. A company gives preferential treatment to minority-owned raw materials suppliers. Is this a good policy?

|case|

VIDEO CASE 7-1
Weather Or Not, Inc.

Sara Croke was known for her accuracy as a TV weather forecaster, she says, but that didn't cut any ice when a contract with a Kansas City station ran out and she set up shop as a private forecaster under the name Weather Or Not, Inc. Potential clients kept saying no.

Construction companies and other outdoor businesses insisted they could get what weather information they needed from TV or radio, even though she frequently heard lamentations like: "They said it was going to rain yesterday, so I sent my guys home. Then the sun came out, and now the general contractor's all over me for losing a day."

It wasn't until she went to a small business development center that the cloud over Croke's sales efforts began to lift. The center helped her find her initial market—those already spending money on forecasts.

Walked through her first government bid, Croke got a 6-month contract with KCI Airport. It paid $230 a month which, she says, "I supplemented with unemployment checks."

A business writer, sent her way by the center, wrote about accurate rainout forecasts Croke had given the groundskeeper at Royals Stadium (the writer didn't know the forecasts were free), and that led to her first construction-firm contract. Unlike similar firms Croke had approached, this one already had a private forecaster but was dissatisfied.

Next Croke added marketing training to the meteorological training she already had. A sales consultant provided a play-by-play of how to make cold calls, design proposals and marketing packets, and—most important—close sales.

"The No. 1 factor became relating bad weather to bad profits," Croke says. "Instead of 'I know all about weather,' it became 'I know you guys got caught last week with that surprise rain. Weather Or Not's clients had several hours' warning before the rain started. They prepared and didn't lose a dime.'"

Also, Croke would point out weather broadcasts gave information for an area up to 100 miles wide, while she would find out each morning where clients' projects would be, pinpoint information, and call clients if weather changes were likely. Construction supervisors or tournament-running golf pros had other things to do besides sit and watch the weather all day, she would note. Now they could have "someone baby-sitting the weather for them."

Today Weather Or Not, which started out in 1986 in Croke's one-bedroom apartment, is in two sites in Westwood, Kansas. It is staffed by an office manager; four forecasters, including a chief meteorologist; and Croke, who pulls a 4–9 A.M. forecasting shift and then concentrates on sales.

Clients have increased along with personnel. They include company CEOs who, for example, change travel plans when warned that ice will glaze over a corporate jet's destination. Thanks in part to satellite technology, Weather Or Not can retrieve the time and place of lightning strikes anywhere in the U.S.—a one-phone-call time-saver of value to insurance companies and lawyers. The same technology makes it possible to warn people running a golf tournament hundreds of miles away that lightning is approaching their area.

Croke sees much growth ahead in these areas, and in mail-order sale of radios that sound an alarm at any hour when severe weather threatens. Dollars that a business spends with her firm in a year can be made back, she says, in minutes.[9]

QUESTIONS
1. What is the broad industry classification for a company like Weather Or Not?
2. Identify the type of organizational buying situation faced by most of Weather Or Not's customers.

Market Segmentation, Targeting, and Positioning Strategies

chapter 8

LEARNING OBJECTIVES

After you have studied this chapter, you will be able to . . .

1) Define the term *market*.

2) Explain the concept of market segmentation.

3) Relate the identification of meaningful target markets to the development of effective marketing mixes.

4) Distinguish among undifferentiated, concentrated, differentiated, and custom marketing strategies.

5) Demonstrate the effect of the 80/20 rule and the majority fallacy on marketing strategy.

6) List the market segmentation variables most commonly used by marketing managers and explain how marketers identify which ones are appropriate.

7) Explain the purpose of a positioning strategy.

In their second album outing, the Dixie Chicks remained firmly rooted in country. But their marketing didn't. Spurning the strategy of successful country artists such as Shania Twain and Faith Hill, the Dixie Chicks have opted not to become crossover artists—meaning they won't water down their country sound to appeal to a more mainstream pop or rock audience, considered a safer marketing tack by many.

In so doing, the group is becoming a case study in how music companies are acceding to the wishes of new artists, forgoing short-term sales gains and, instead, managing their music assets for the long term.

Rather than changing the music, marketing executives at Sony Music Nashville are building a "crossover strategy" that utilizes different media, touring, and promotion to broaden the market appeal of the Dixie Chicks.

The Dixie Chicks were profiled in a new spinoff of VH1's "Behind the Music" show that did a series on current artists. The series focuses on musical acts of the '60s, '70s, and '80s and rarely profiles country artists.

To promote the release of their second album, *Fly*, the group was booked to appear during the Lilith Fair tour, which customarily features a broad range of mostly rock and pop female artists and doesn't normally include country acts. The Lilith tour exposed them to people who don't listen to country radio. The group also brings its music to the masses by producing a syndicated half-hour radio concert with the AMFM Inc. radio networks and launched a new single, "Ready to Run," with the release of the Richard Gere/Julia Roberts movie "Runaway Bride." Both "Ready to Run" and a remake of "You Can't Hurry Love" are on the movie's soundtrack CD.

The Chicks are searching for more ties with consumer-product marketers, as a follow-up on the group's appearance in an advertising campaign for Candies shoes. This effort allowed the Dixie Chicks to get exposure in *Elle* and *Harper's Bazaar* and other magazines they wouldn't normally be in.

Advertising for their album *Me* appeared on WB's "Dawson's Creek" and NBC's "Friends." The Dixie Chicks also advertised on cable's Lifetime Television and VH1, which played their first video even after the group rejected the network's request for a remixed version leaving out the banjos and fiddles.

Ever since the release of *Wide Open Spaces*, a double-platinum CD that sold 6 million copies, there has been tremendous temptation to go mainstream. Big sales and interest in the Chicks also whetted the appetite of many non-country music stations to play their music.

But some stations requested that the music be "remixed," said Sony Music executives, to create a mainstream rock/pop music feel without the country-tinged instruments. The Chicks believe that this would alter their sound and the personality of their music. The strategy is to allow the Dixie Chicks to keep their "country" soul and musical integrity while targeting a broader market.[1]

Understanding the nature of various market segments is an important aspect of marketing strategy. This chapter considers in greater depth the definitions of the terms *market* and *market segmentation*. It discusses how marketers, such as the Dixie Chicks and Sony Music Nashville, determine which target marketing strategy will best serve their objectives. Then it examines the many variables used to segment consumer and organizational markets. Finally, it considers how marketers develop positioning strategies.

What Is Market Segmentation?

We have already defined what a market is but let us look again at that definition. A *market* is a group of actual or potential customers for a particular product. More precisely, a market is a group of individuals or organizations that may want the good or service being offered for sale and that meet these three additional criteria:

1. They have the ability or purchasing power to buy the product being offered.
2. They have the willingness to spend money or exchange other resources to obtain the product.
3. They have the authority to make such expenditures.

Economics textbooks often give the impression that all consumers are alike. Economists frequently draw no distinctions among different types of buyers, as long as they have a willingness and an ability to buy. Young and old buyers, men and women, people who drink 12 beers a day and those who drink one beer on New Year's Eve are all lumped together. Experience tells marketers, however, that in many cases buyers differ from one another even though they may be buying the same products. Marketers try to identify groups and subgroups within total markets—that is, they try to segment markets.

Recall that market segmentation consists of dividing a heterogeneous market into a number of smaller, more homogeneous submarkets. Almost any variable—age, sex, product usage, lifestyle, expected benefit—may be used as a segmenting variable, but the logic behind the strategy is always the same.

- Not all buyers are alike.
- Subgroups of people with similar behavior, values, and/or backgrounds may be identified.
- The subgroups will be smaller and more homogeneous than the market as a whole.
- It should be easier to satisfy smaller groups of similar customers than a large group of dissimilar customers.

Usually, marketers are able to cluster similar customers into specific market segments with different, and sometimes unique, demands. For example, the computer software market can be divided into two segments: the domestic market and the foreign market. The domestic market can be segmented further into business users and home users. And the home user segment can be further subdivided into sophisticated personal computer users, people who hate personal computers but have one so their children can use

Quaker State 4x4 is a motor oil targeted toward the segment of the market composed of owners of sports utility vehicles, light trucks, and minivans. Historically, motor oil marketers expected drivers to understand the grades of motor oils. However, the distinction between, for example, 10W40 oil and 5W30 oil was not meaningful to most consumers. Quaker State 4x4's segmentation strategy provides a meaningful difference to a distinguishable—and sizable—segment of the market.

http://www.quakerstate.com

it for schoolwork, people who use computers only for e-mail, and so on. The number of market segments within the total market depends largely on the strategist's ingenuity and creativity in identifying those segments.

Needless to say, a single company is unlikely to pursue all possible market segments. In fact, the idea behind market segmentation is for an organization to choose one or a few meaningful segments and concentrate its efforts on satisfying those selected parts of the market. Focusing its efforts on these targeted market segments—that is, *targeting*—enables the organization to allocate its marketing resources effectively. Concentrating efforts on a given market segment should result in a more precise marketing program satisfying specific market needs.

As mentioned in Chapter 2, the market segment, or group of buyers, toward which an organization decides to direct its marketing plan is called the *target market.* The target market for Shower Shaver, for example, is that subgroup of women who shave their legs in the shower.

Because it is possible to segment markets in so many ways, target marketing opportunities abound. For example, there are "left-hander" shops specializing in products for left-handed people, tobacco shops catering to wealthy pipe smokers, and dress shops that target women who wear certain clothing sizes. In addition, numerous products bear the names or symbols of sports teams, such as the San Francisco 49ers or the Chicago Bulls, and are marketed to team fans. Some companies even sell items to people who hate particular teams—a once-popular sports-related item was the "I Hate the Yankees Hanky." As you can see, the process of segmentation provides hints on how to market to the targeted segments identified.

Selection of a target market (or markets—in some cases, more than one may be selected for a product) is a three-step process, as shown in Exhibit 8-1. First, the total market, consisting of many different customers, is studied and broken down (or *disaggregated*) into its component parts—that is, individual customers, families, organizations, or other units. The customers are then regrouped by the marketing strategist into market segments on the basis of one or several characteristics that segment members have in common. Then the strategist must target segments to which the organization will appeal. When that is done, the strategist has answered the question "What are our target markets?"

CHOOSING MEANINGFUL MARKET SEGMENTS

Target marketing rests on the assumption that differences among buyers are related to meaningful differences in market behavior. The identification of market

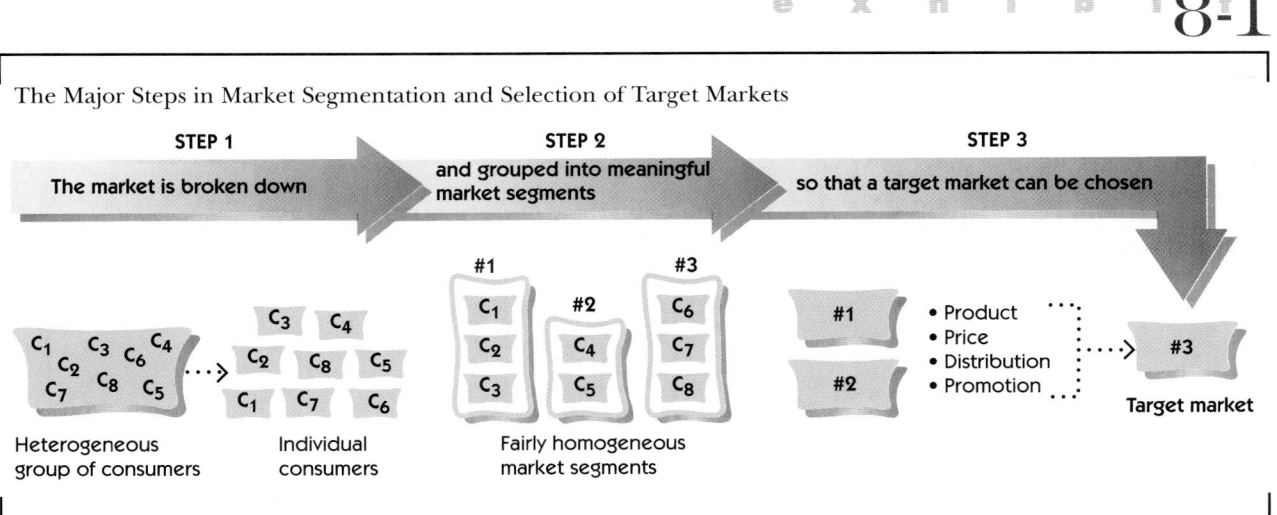

The Major Steps in Market Segmentation and Selection of Target Markets

STEP 1 — The market is broken down

STEP 2 — and grouped into meaningful market segments

STEP 3 — so that a target market can be chosen

Heterogeneous group of consumers

Individual consumers

Fairly homogeneous market segments

• Product
• Price
• Distribution
• Promotion

Target market

Although they both have identical ingredients, pop and soda are completely different things depending on what part of the country you're in. Effective marketers seek to find characteristics that meaningfully segment markets.

IT'S HARD TO SELL
"POP"
TO PEOPLE WHO DRINK
"SODA."

Every savvy marketer knows that, although they both have identical ingredients, pop and soda are completely different things depending on what part of the country you're in. On local television stations, you can speak to customers in the language they identify with. Local television lets you to concentrate your message in the areas where you sell the most product. For a better way to connect your brand to local communities, call the Television Bureau of Advertising toll free at 1-877-488-2529 or see our site at www.tvb.org. **LOCAL TV** A better connection

segments that are not meaningful has little value. The following five criteria make a segment meaningful:

1. The market segment has one or more characteristics that distinguish it from the overall market. These characteristics should be stable over time.
2. The market segment has a market potential of significant size—that is, large enough to be profitable.
3. The market segment is accessible through distribution efforts or reachable through promotional efforts.
4. The market segment is responsive. The market segment has a unique market need, and the likelihood is high that the segment will respond favorably to a marketing mix tailored to this need.
5. The segment's market potential should be measurable. Ease of measurement facilitates effective target marketing by helping to identify and quantify group purchasing power and to indicate the differences among market segments. Although ease of measurement is desirable, it is not mandatory.

Exhibit 8-2 outlines these criteria. Whether a company achieves its general goal of profitability can depend on how well marketers use the criteria to identify target markets. Selecting a group that is not easily distinguishable or accessible, or appealing to a segment that is too small to generate adequate sales volume, or selecting a group that the company is unable to attract is not effective market segmentation.

Consider an example. Cuban citizens form a possible market segment. This is a large group. But even assuming it has unique market demands, this segment is

e x h i b i 8-2

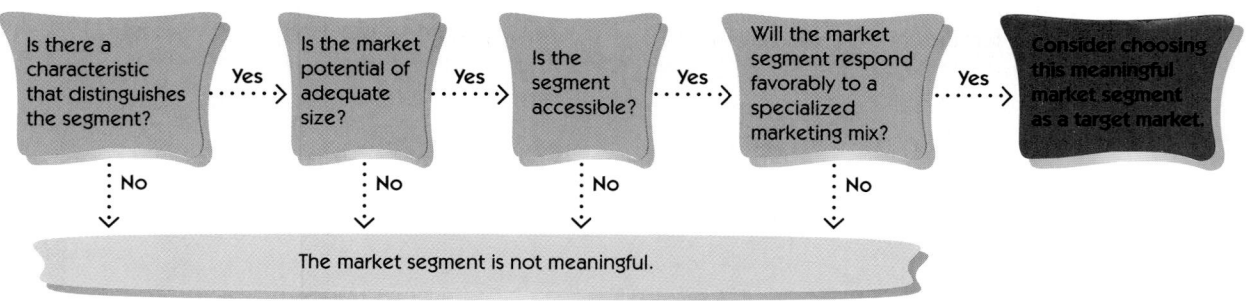

Determining Whether a Market Segment Is Meaningful

Is there a characteristic that distinguishes the segment? → Yes → Is the market potential of adequate size? → Yes → Is the segment accessible? → Yes → Will the market segment respond favorably to a specialized marketing mix? → Yes → Consider choosing this meaningful market segment as a target market.

No ↓ No ↓ No ↓ No ↓

The market segment is not meaningful.

not meaningful. The U.S. government has placed an embargo on exports to Cuba, and these restrictions have completely shut down trade with the island. Thus, the market segment consisting of Cubans living in Cuba does not meet the criterion of accessibility.

One product that successfully appealed to a meaningful market segment was the First Alert Traveling Smoke and Fire Detector. The product was designed for the sizable

number of frequent travelers who worry about hotel fires. Marketers can reach frequent travelers through specific promotional efforts (for example, advertising in in-flight magazines). Offering a high-quality portable smoke alarm at a fair price by mail is a marketing mix that may appeal to the specialized needs of this market segment. Thus, First Alert met the criterion of meaningfulness.

THE MARKET SEGMENT CROSS-CLASSIFICATION MATRIX

Effective marketers segment the markets they address and then select attractive target markets.[2] Some do this almost unintentionally, even without realizing it—as did the owner of a small grocery store located in the Seattle area. The store serves only a small portion of the Seattle market, perhaps an area of a few blocks. In a sense, by choosing the store's location, the store's owner has "segmented" and "targeted" the market geographically. However, proper market segmentation and target marketing generally involve serious consideration of a total market, the variables that can be used to identify meaningful segments in that market, and the creation of marketing mixes aimed at satisfying the needs of chosen target segments.

One way marketers can identify target markets is to use a **cross-classification matrix**, a grid that helps isolate variables of interest in the market. Exhibit 8-3 shows the cross-classifications the owners of a new tennis shop in New York City might use to segment the retail market for tennis equipment. First, the total group of people interested in tennis is cross-classified using a geographic variable and the variable of sex. Then the chosen segment is cross-classified with income and level of tennis skill. It appears from Exhibit 8-3 that our tennis shop's selected target market is the group of females interested in tennis who shop in Manhattan, are intermediate or advanced players, and have annual incomes over $100,000. The variables used to segment the tennis market can be portrayed on a single, three-dimensional figure, as in Exhibit 8-4 (page 197). However, if more than three variables are employed, graphical portrayal becomes increasingly difficult.

Cross-classification matrix
A grid that helps isolate variables of interest in the market. For example, a geographic variable might be cross-classified with some other variable of interest, such as income.

MATCHING THE MIX TO THE TARGET MARKET

Having determined that its target segment will be women with incomes over $100,000 who are intermediate and advanced tennis players, the tennis shop owners must develop a marketing mix aimed at satisfying that group of consumers. This process can be very difficult, even risky. Yet the segmentation effort itself simplifies some of the choices to be made.

Cross-Classification Used by a New York City Tennis Shop to Identify Market Segments

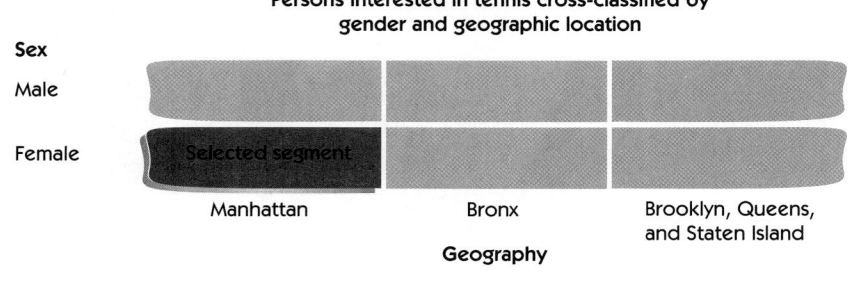

Persons interested in tennis cross-classified by gender and geographic location

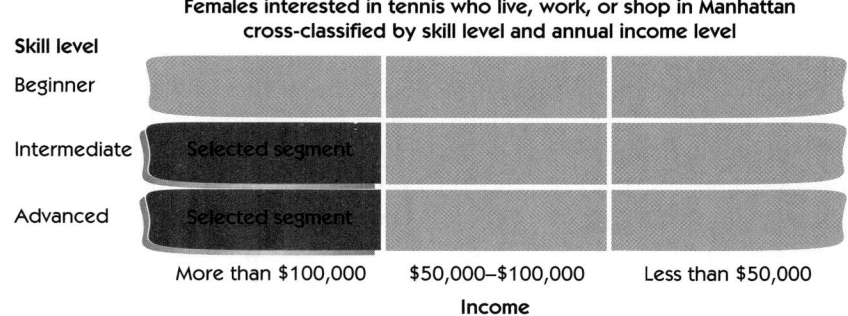

Females interested in tennis who live, work, or shop in Manhattan cross-classified by skill level and annual income level

1. What brands should be stocked? Those that appeal to female players who are not beginners. Names such as Prince, K-Swiss, and Ellese appeal to this segment.
2. Should credit cards be accepted? Probably so, because the shop is dealing with women who have high incomes and, therefore, good credit.
3. What newspapers should be used to advertise the store? The best choice is most likely *The New York Times*, which appeals to upscale readers, rather than the *Daily News* or *New York Post*, which appeal to downscale readers.

This example shows how market segmentation and target marketing can help not only in identifying whom to target but also in suggesting how to make the appeal.

Four Strategies for Target Marketing

The idea of zeroing in on a given market segment suggests analogies with rifles and shotguns. The shotgun approach spreads marketing efforts widely, while the rifle approach allows for greater precision by focusing on one target market. We can develop the logic of this analogy by examining four target marketing strategies based on the uniqueness of consumer segments and organizational objectives.

UNDIFFERENTIATED MARKETING: WHEN EVERYONE IS A CUSTOMER

Sometimes, when a marketing manager asks, "What is our market?" the answer turns out to be "Almost everyone who has any use for our type of product." When marketers determine that there is little diversity among market segments, they may engage in mass marketing. A firm selling hacksaw blades, brass or silver polish, or garbage cans to consumers may find it more efficient not to distinguish among market segments. This absence of segmentation, which is illustrated in Exhibit 8-5, is called **undifferentiated marketing**.

Undifferentiated marketing
A marketing effort not targeted at a specific market segment but designed to appeal to a broad range of customers. The approach is appropriate in a market that lacks diversity of interest.

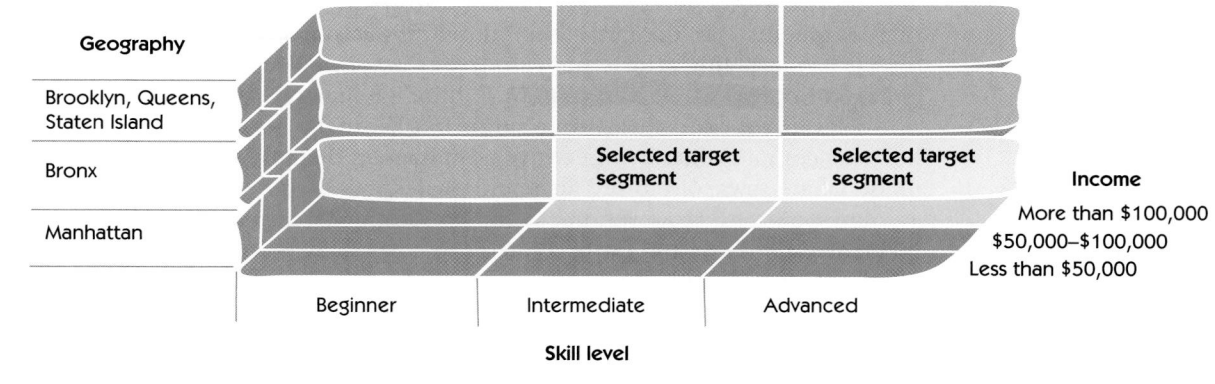

A Three-Dimensional Portrayal of the Cross-Classification Matrices Shown in Exhibit 8-3

In some situations, undifferentiated marketing may result in savings in production and marketing costs, which can be passed on to consumers in the form of lower prices. After all, it should be cheaper to make and sell only one car model in one color, as Henry Ford did with the Model T, than to produce and sell tens of models in many colors and with various options, as General Motors does today. However, the attempt to appeal to everyone may make an organization extremely vulnerable to competition.

Even producers of common, unexciting products like salt have found this out. No-Salt, Lite Salt, sea salt, popcorn salt, flavored salts, noniodized salt, and other such products chip away at the customer base of a marketer of common table salt. Similarly, all facial tissues may be pretty much alike, but a product marketed in a package illustrated with Winnie-the-Pooh characters may appeal to buyers with small children. Although "everyone" buys salt and tissues, buyers' secondary desires (for example, to please a child with a Winnie-the-Pooh package) may provide the basis for segmentation. The undifferentiated brand cannot offer such specialized benefits.

Undifferentiated marketing can succeed. A small grocery store in a small, isolated town seeks all the people in that town as its customers. The store operator can construct one well-prepared marketing mix to please all, or at least most, customers.

The Undifferentiated Marketing Approach

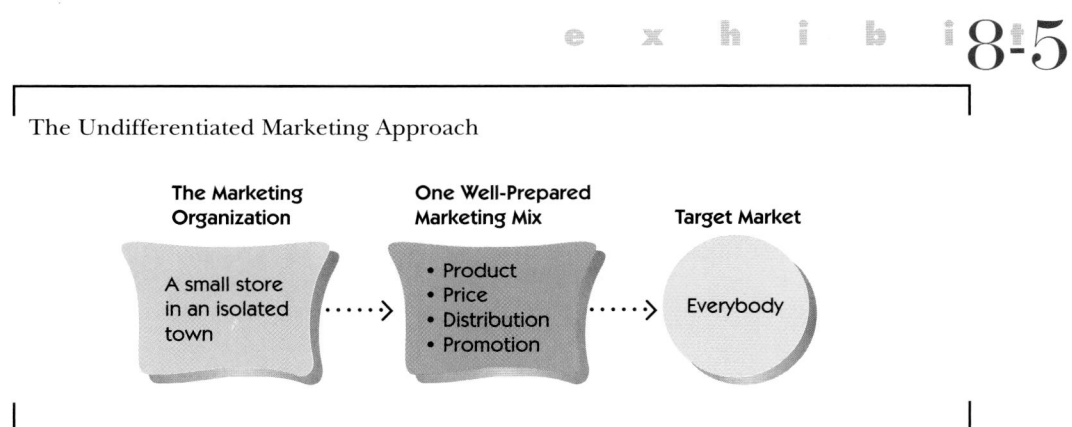

Suppose a chain saw manufacturer identifies three major market segments: the casual or occasional user (such as the suburban homeowner), the farm segment, and the professional lumberjack segment. Each of these user groups has special needs; each uses chain saws in different ways; each reads different magazines and watches different television programs. If the chain saw marketer selects just one of these segments (say, the farm user), develops an appropriate marketing mix, and directs its marketing efforts and resources toward that segment exclusively, it is engaged in **concentrated marketing**. Exhibit 8-6 illustrates this strategy.

A firm might concentrate on a single market niche because management believes its company has a competitive advantage in dealing with the selected segment. Chain saws sold to the farm and professional segments are generally gasoline-powered. However, the casual-user segment, with less demanding performance standards and far fewer acres to cover, may be content with less powerful electric saws. Thus, a manufacturer of gasoline-powered lawn mowers may decide to produce gas-powered chain saws, while a maker of electric tools might find that its existing production facilities are compatible with the production of electric chain saws. Each can select market segments that provide a match between company goals and abilities and customer needs. Concentrated marketing strategies can be employed by both firms.

Examples of firms that concentrate their marketing efforts are easy to find. There are jewelers and clothing manufacturers that produce goods with price tags that seem ridiculous to most people. Such products are sold to a small but wealthy market segment. Radio stations use concentrated marketing when they target their programming to a market segment that prefers a particular type of music. That is why you don't often hear rock, classical, and country music on the same station.

Can a business-to-business marketer practice concentrated marketing? The answer is yes. An example: Leo Burnett is one of the ten largest advertising agencies in the United States, yet it has fewer than fifty clients. Burnett focuses its efforts on servicing a small number of affluent clients with huge advertising budgets.

Concentrated marketing
Development of a marketing mix and direction of marketing efforts and resources to appeal to a single market segment.

e x h i b i t **8-6**

The Concentrated Marketing Approach

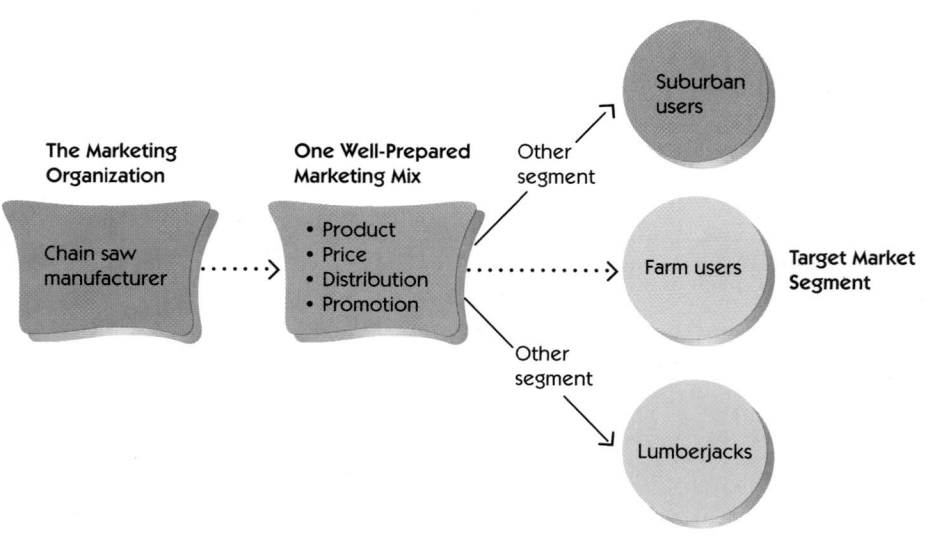

Specializing seems to work, for in this volatile business, more than half of Burnett's clients have been with the agency for more than 10 years.

Concentrated marketing is not without its risks. If an organization specializes its efforts, it lacks diversity and has the problem of "putting all its eggs in one basket." If the market segment is too narrow or if growth in the market segment slows, major financial problems arise.

Both Toysmart.com and Red Rockets ceased their Internet toy store operations in 2000. The market segment of Internet toy shoppers was too small to support eToys, Toys "Я" Us.com, faoschwarz.com, as well as these newcomer competitors.

An organization that is extremely successful in targeting a single segment may have great difficulty targeting other segments later. Cadillac spent years concentrating on older, well-to-do consumers who wanted big cars. When it tried to reach younger, upwardly mobile consumers with smaller cars, the company was too well entrenched in one market segment to diversify into others.

The 80/20 Principle   Concentrating on one market segment is often more attractive when the marketer knows that a small percentage of all users of a product accounts for a great portion of that product's sales. The **80/20 principle** is the name given to this phenomenon whereby 20 percent of the customers buy 80 percent of the product sold. This 20 percent (which may really be 25 percent or some similar percentage) may be called "heavy users" or "major customers." For example, marketers of beer know from marketing research that blue-collar workers are the "heavy users" in the beer market. The 80/20 principle operates in both consumer and organizational markets.

> Clearly, it may be better for a marketer to go after a small, seemingly less attractive market segment than to pursue the same customers that everyone else is after.

The Majority Fallacy   Concentrating on the largest segment or the segment of heaviest users may not be the best course of action. Some organizations mistakenly aim at such a segment just because it is so obviously attractive. These organizations have fallen hook, line, and sinker for the majority fallacy. The **majority fallacy** is the name given to the blind pursuit of the largest, or most easily identified, or most accessible market segment. Why is it a fallacy? Simply because the segment they are pursuing is the one that everybody knows is the biggest or "best" segment, it probably attracts the most intense competition and may actually prove less profitable to firms competing for its attention. Although Procter and Gamble's Prell and Pert shampoos are aimed at broader markets than its dandruff-fighting Head and Shoulders, Head and Shoulders—a more specialized product—sells more than the other two brands combined, because many other marketers aim their products at the users of regular shampoo.

Clearly, the majority fallacy points out that it may be better for a marketer to go after a small, seemingly less attractive market segment than to pursue the same customers that everyone else is after. Thus, although most brewers market to the heavy user, some brewers succeed by offering smaller bottles of beer to people who don't drink much beer or very expensive beer to beer drinkers celebrating a special occasion. Many microbreweries target the gourmet beer drinker segment rather than the blue-collar segment.

80/20 principle
In marketing, a principle describing the fact that usually a relatively small percentage of customers accounts for a disproportionately large share of the sales of a product.

Majority fallacy
The blind pursuit of the largest, or most easily identified, or most accessible market segment. The error lies in ignoring the fact that other marketers will be pursuing this same segment.

Business travelers represent about 40 percent of United Airlines passengers, but account for more than 70 percent of its revenues.[3] Those business travelers who fly most often, known as "road warriors," represent only 65 percent of all business travelers but 37 percent of United's revenues. Although the percentages are not exactly 80 and 20, this is a good example of the 80/20 principle.

http://www.united.com

Foofoo is a play on the word *frou-frou.* Foofoo.com targeted upwardly mobile young professionals looking for luxury goods and services. The company hoped its upscale target market would expand the meaning of the slang word to encompass all sorts of indulgences, including travel and fine cuisine. Unfortunately, Foofoo targeted too narrow a market segment with upscale shoppers. The company failed in 2000. The Web site featured information supplied mostly through partnerships with magazines like *Men's Health, Food and Wine,* and *Elle,* and it sold goods from retailers like J. Crew and Cigars International.

Differentiated marketing

A marketing effort in which a marketer selects more than one target market and then develops a separate marketing mix for each; also called *multiple market segmentation.*

DIFFERENTIATED MARKETING: DIFFERENT BUYERS, DIFFERENT STRATEGIES

Of course, it is possible for an organization to target its efforts toward more than one market segment. Once the various segments in a total market have been identified, specific marketing mixes can be developed to appeal to all or some of the submarkets. When an organization chooses more than one target market segment and prepares a marketing mix for each one, it is practicing **differentiated marketing,** or **multiple market segmentation**. For example, Marriott Corporation markets its hotel/motel service in many different price ranges. Residence Inns, Marriott Courtyards, Fairfield Inns, Marriott Hotels, and Marriott Resort Hotels appeal to different buyers attempting to satisfy different needs. Marriott thus practices differentiated marketing.

Using a differentiated marketing strategy exploits the differences between market segments by tailoring a specific marketing mix to each segment. For instance, the chain saw manufacturer that decided to concentrate on only one of three market segments could have, given appropriate resources, attempted to appeal to each segment of the chain saw market. This would have meant a greater investment of money and effort, because each segment would have required its own specially tailored product, price, distribution, and promotion.

Of course, some markets are much more diverse than the chain saw illustration suggests. A good example of an industry facing a wide diversity of customers is the hair-coloring industry. Some customers want to change hair color, some want to cover traces of gray, and some want to highlight or brighten hair. Within these large customer groups, additional segments can be found. Exhibit 8-7 illustrates how Clairol segments the hair-coloring market. In this case, identifying the segments is not particularly difficult. The real work and expense come in creating the marketing mixes that satisfy all the segments.

The Differentiated Marketing Approach

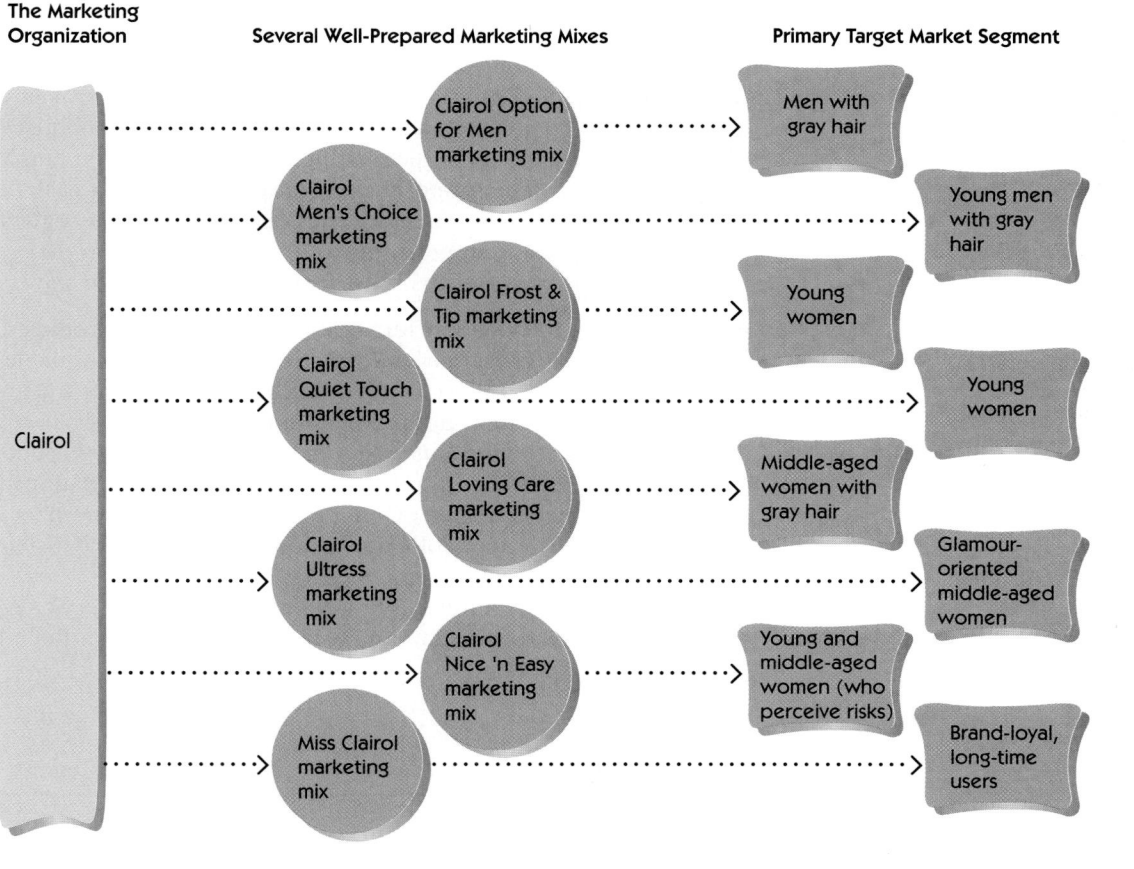

Differentiated marketing is applicable to many situations, and in many cases, it is easy to implement. For example, a popular way for a manufacturer to attract a differentiated market—and one that requires relatively little effort—is by producing different-sized packages of the same product.

Although differentiated marketing is appropriate in many situations, it must be used with care. As this approach becomes more elaborate, costs increase. This fact must be taken into account as the marketing manager considers the value of focusing on different segments' needs. Competitive conditions, corporate objectives, available resources, and alternative marketing opportunities for other product lines all influence the decision to utilize a differentiated market segmentation strategy.

CUSTOM MARKETING: TO EACH HIS OR HER OWN

Sometimes the market facing a given marketing manager is so diverse, and its members so different from one another, that no meaningful groups of customers can be identified. When this kind of diversity exists, a special kind of marketing effort is necessary. This situation requires **custom marketing**, the attempt to satisfy each customer's unique set of needs. In this case, the marketer must develop a marketing mix suitable to each customer.

Custom marketing
A marketing effort in which a marketer seeks to satisfy each customer's unique set of needs. In effect, each customer is an individual market segment.

A manufacturer of industrial robots faces such a prospect. Industrial robots are usually custom-designed to fit the buyer's special manufacturing problems. Each buyer demands a unique product, with special size and strength characteristics, depending on the job to be done. Each will probably require delivery and installation at a given location, thus somewhat altering the marketer's distribution system. In addition, individual customers may have difficult technical questions, requiring salespeople with broad technical knowledge. The salesperson, who is the key element in promotional efforts, may be required to alter the company's pricing structure to fit the custom-designed product's cost. In all, for our robot maker, each prospect may be considered a market segment, as illustrated in Exhibit 8-8.

Marketers of services, such as architects, tailors, and lawyers, often employ custom marketing strategies. The nature of these services requires that each customer be treated in a unique way. Effective marketers of custom services recognize this need for unique treatment as an opportunity to promote the notion that each customer gets exactly what he or she wants. Customers can have it their way.

Going One-on-One Using Information Technology   Chapter 5 introduced the topic of data-based marketing. The new information technologies available today allow a data-based marketer to track customers individually and then customize its marketing efforts. This form of customized marketing is sometimes called *one-on-one marketing*, but we prefer the term *data-based marketing*. (Later in this book we will show how data-based marketing is intertwined with customer relationship marketing and direct marketing strategies.) Going one-on-one with customers is made possible by digital information technologies: customer databases and systems that support mass customization.

With today's information technology, the role of personalized service can be greatly expanded if a company maintains a customer database. Wyndham Hotels,

e x h i b i **8-8**

The Custom Marketing Approach

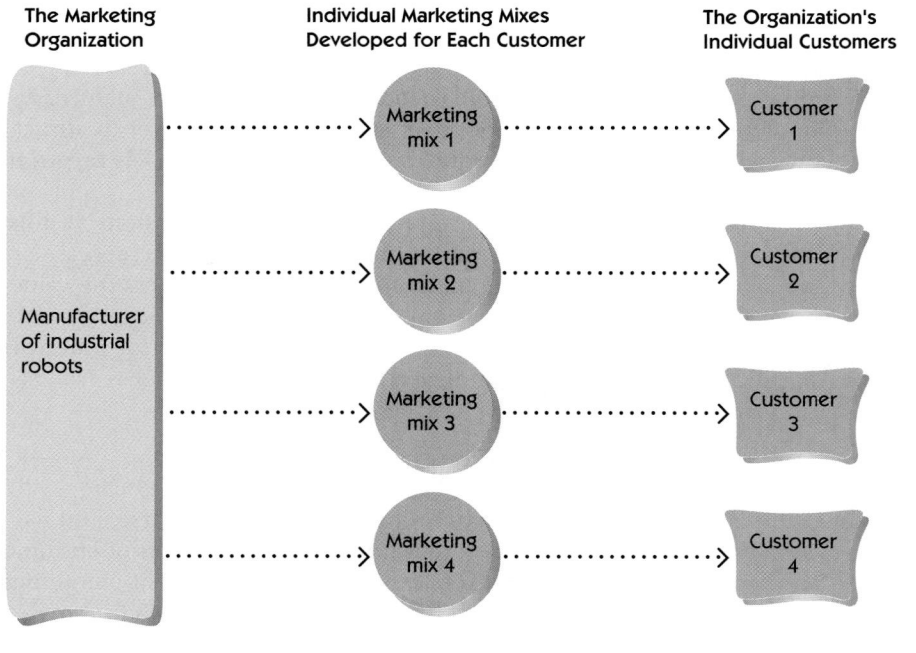

The Marketing Organization	Individual Marketing Mixes Developed for Each Customer	The Organization's Individual Customers
Manufacturer of industrial robots	Marketing mix 1	Customer 1
	Marketing mix 2	Customer 2
	Marketing mix 3	Customer 3
	Marketing mix 4	Customer 4

for instance, maintains a detailed database on its frequent guests. Doormen greet arriving guests by name, and reservation agents know without asking whether a guest prefers a nonsmoking room or one on an upper rather than a lower floor. Rooms are stocked with favorite snacks and magazines that fit the guests' interests.[4] The hotel chain's relationship marketing goal is to have a circle of friends, with the customer at the center.

> Going one-on-one with customers is made possible by digital information technologies: customer databases and systems that support mass customization.

Many marketers use information in customer databases to create computer-generated mailing lists, individualized promotional messages, and personalized Web pages. In other words, computer technology has made it possible for a marketer to learn more about customers' habits and preferences and then adopt a custom marketing strategy with individualized promotional messages or personalized product offerings. Data-based marketing helps the company form relationships with customers.

Exhibit 8-9 summarizes the characteristics of the four basic market segmentation strategies.

Mass Customization   In addition to making data-based marketing possible, new technologies are changing the face of traditional custom marketing in many ways. A mass production process results in low-cost, standard goods and services. Mass customization calls for flexibility and quick responsiveness to give customers exactly what they want. **Mass customization** is a strategy that mobilizes the combined power of mass production technologies and computers to make varied, customized products for small market segments. In fact, in many situations, such as in personalized greeting card kiosks, products are customized for one or a very few customers. Today, for example, a person who wishes to purchase a Dell Computer can visit Dell's Web site (http://www.dell.com), select a basic model, and see how the price changes when choosing alternative configurations from a menu of features and accessory items. A wide variety of "personalized" computers is possible because mass customization is used rather than traditional mass production.

Mass customization
A strategy that combines mass production with computers to produce customized products for small market segments.

Typical Characteristics of the Basic Market Segmentation Strategies

e x h i b i 8-9

STRATEGY	MARKET SEGMENT	MARKET CHARACTERISTICS	COMPANY OBJECTIVES	MAJOR DISADVANTAGES	EXAMPLE
Undifferentiated Marketing	Everyone	Little diversity	Production savings	Competitors may identify segments	Chicago Museum of Science and Industry
Concentrated Marketing	One select segment	Targeted segment has special needs	Gain competitive advantage by specialization; use one well-prepared marketing mix to meet segments with special segment needs	Lack of diversity; market segment may be too narrow; intense competition for majority segment	Rolls Royce
Differentiated Marketing	Multiple segments	Wide diversity of customers	Exploit differences among market segments; maximize market share	Extensive resources required	Starbucks Coffee
Custom Marketing	Complete segmentation	Each customer is unique	Satisfy each customer's unique needs	High marketing costs	Hitachi industrial robots

what went right?

Lexus Lexus would like consumers to feel that ownership of an exclusive car entitles them to membership in an exclusive club: The Lexus Club. Lexus believes that people who have already purchased a Lexus are an important target market. Lexus keeps in steady contact with current owners and prospective buyers through data-based marketing. For example, before ads for its new GS 300 model appeared, all Lexus owners received a letter alerting them to "the new Lexus," the same positioning line used later in traditional media ads. The letter even included an offer for a free videotape on the new car.

Lexus also mailed the letters and videotapes to key prospects, primarily owners of competing models such as the Infiniti J30, the BMW 535i, and the Mercedes-Benz 300E.

At the same time, Lexus has built a dossier on its buyers. The division has logged every new Lexus owner into a database totaling more than 3,000,000 names. The company uses the database to analyze the characteristics of the existing Lexus owners, in hopes of extending those characteristics to a broader market.

Lexus faces a problem common to all luxury car marketers: The buyer group is small.

Only about 9 percent of all cars sold are luxury vehicles, with near-luxury cars representing an additional 3.8 percent, according to *Automotive News*.

This makes advertising in the mass media, such as network TV or general magazines, inherently wasteful. So in addition to direct mailings to its customers, Lexus engages in the promotion of special events and sports sponsorships.

But because Lexus owners report higher satisfaction than owners of any other company's cars, they are the best promoters of the brand through a proven tool: word of mouth. That's why Lexus strives to keep its customer base excited about what the automaker is doing.

Lexus marketing executives see data-based marketing and special promotions as a means to build relationships. The company's relationship marketing can keep a customer in the fold while identifying common denominators among customers. Because Lexus sees its owner base as a significant source of word-of-mouth endorsements, it attempts to keep this target market excited about the Lexus brand.[5]

Flexible manufacturing system
A group of machines integrated through a central computer and able to produce a variety of similar but not identical products.

Marketers can offer mass customization to very small and specialized market segments because of technological advances in manufacturing that allow for the coordination of relatively autonomous process or task modules. **Flexible manufacturing systems** are replacing mass production with mass customization because more flexible, computerized production technologies are making it possible to make products both in large volume and in great variety. These manufacturing systems also allow changes in design or style to be made rapidly. For example, Panasonic consumer electronics products are replaced with modified models approximately every 90 days. At Dell, the company doesn't build a PC until one is ordered.

The ability to produce reasonably priced, made-to-order items is perhaps the greatest benefit of mass customization. Levi Strauss has known for some time that many women—those who fall right in the middle of the size ranges—are not satisfied with standard-sized blue jeans. Using mass customization and flexible manufacturing, Levi's developed a Personal Pair Program to solve this problem. At selected Original Levi's Stores, a trained sales associate will take a woman's measurements, enter the measurements into a computer, and send the information via modem to a Levi's factory in Tennessee. In approximately 3 weeks, the customer can either pick up her Personal Pair jeans or, for a small extra fee, have them sent directly to her. The ability to mass-customize products often allows marketers to charge a price higher than that of mass-produced items, but lower than that of hand-made items. Further, retailers reduce inventory and do not have to mark down unsold items.

Identifying Market Differences

Marketing is a creative activity, and many marketing success stories are the results of the creative identification of market segments with unsatisfied needs. The essence of market segmentation strategy is looking for differences within total markets on which to base the development of successful marketing mixes. Marketers ask, "What variables are associated with meaningful differences?" Unfortunately, there is no simple, irrefutable answer to this question, because the bases for differentiating market segments are virtually unlimited. For example, Mercedes-Benz automobiles are sold to the prestige auto segment. No More Tangles creme rinse and shampoo are aimed at mothers who recognize their children's need for "tangle-free hair without tears" (and who have a personal need to get through bath time without a lot of crying and fussing). Purina Puppy Chow is for puppy owners, Dog Chow is for owners of grown dogs, and Purina Fit and Trim is for owners of overweight dogs.

Two factors make the task of dealing with the almost limitless bases for market segmentation easier to handle. One is that the variables can be categorized into major groups, making them somewhat simpler to use and to remember. Exhibit 8-10 shows various ways of segmenting consumer markets. The other simplifying factor is that, although the possible segmenting variables are numerous, a far smaller number of variables are, in fact, the ones most commonly used. We look next at variables commonly used in segmenting consumer markets. Then we discuss segmentation in organizational markets.

Geographic Segmentation   Simple geography can be an important basis for market segmentation. The demand for suntan lotion is far greater in Florida, for example, than in Saskatchewan. In some cases, a geographic variable might indicate

e x h i b i 8-10

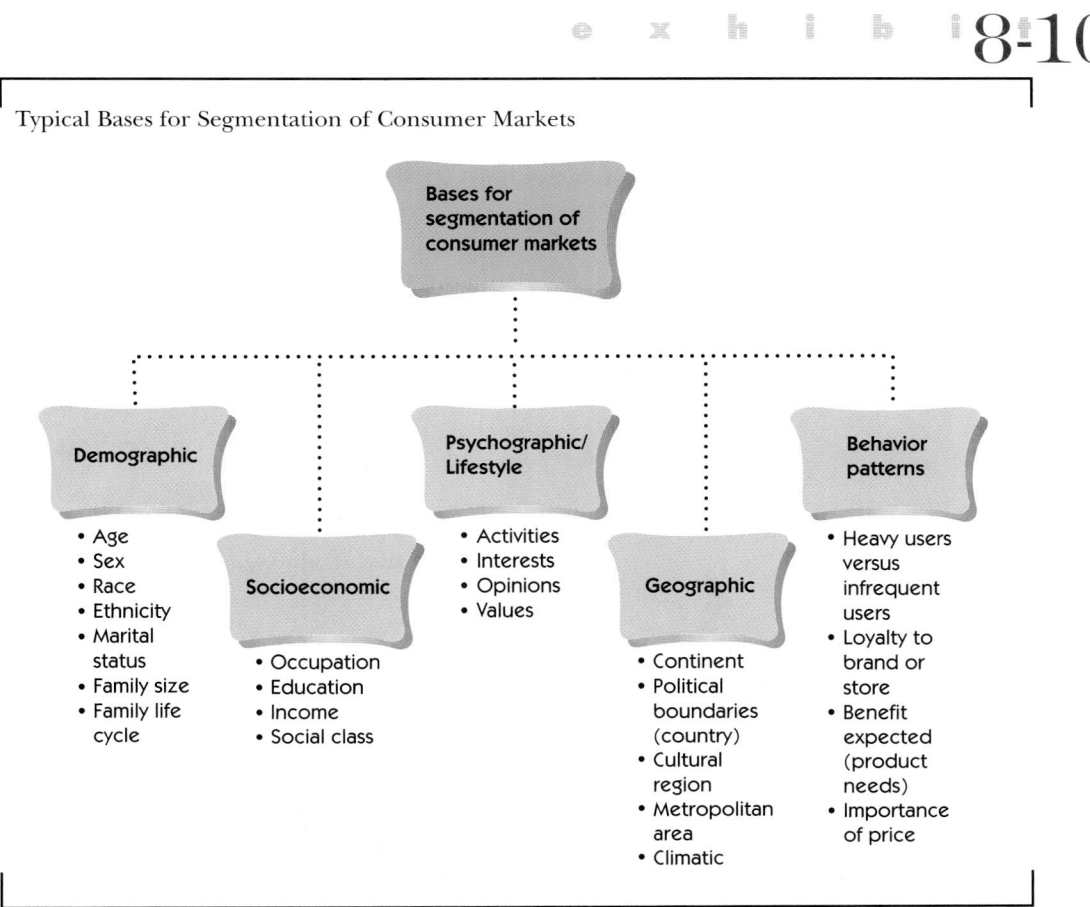

Typical Bases for Segmentation of Consumer Markets

to a marketer that there is absolutely no demand for a certain product in a certain area, such as for snow shovels in Puerto Rico.

Geographic market segmentation often begins with the broad distinction between domestic and foreign markets. Organizations that market their products outside their own countries are engaged in international, or multinational, marketing. International marketers recognize that people in different nations may have different needs. In Argentina, for example, most Coca-Cola is consumed with food, but in many Asian countries it is rarely served with meals. Not all U.S.-based firms choose to market their products outside the United States. An organization's resources or market demand may not justify this strategy. However, many firms find it advantageous to spend considerable time and effort marketing beyond their national boundaries.

Geographic segmentation also includes distinctions based on continents, cultural regions, and climate. Another basis for geographic segmentation is political boundaries, such as state and city lines. However, populations are not always adequately described by such political boundaries. Marketers are most concerned with the population map—where the people are—rather than with such matters as the "line" that separates Billings Heights, Montana, from Billings, Montana. Everyday expressions—"Greater New York," "the Dallas–Fort Worth Metro-Plex," and "the Bay Area"—indicate that there is no distinct political boundary line for certain market segments.

Demographic Segmentation   Demographic characteristics, such as sex, age, marital status, family size, and ethnicity, are segmentation variables that are easily understood. Their relationship to different product needs has been well established. Measurement of demographic characteristics and of their relationships to purchasing behavior is not difficult. Further, information about the demographic composition of markets is widely available from a variety of sources. For these reasons, demographic characteristics are among the most commonly used segmentation variables.

Chapter 3 discussed several demographic trends. This section illustrates how a few demographic variables have been used as bases for segmentation.

Age   Infants and toddlers, young children, teenagers, adults, and senior citizens are typical age-based market segments. Classifying consumers into age groups like these is useful when people of different ages have different purchasing behaviors.

Many marketers, including Snowball.com, target their efforts toward the 77 million Americans born since 1977. What the popular press has labeled Generation Y, Snowball.com calls the i generation. Generations generally get their "names" from the major events that occur during their formative years. Which do you think will be used 20 years from now—Generation Y (because it followed Gen X) or the Internet generation?

http://www.snowball.com

what went right?

Delia's Catalog The morning after the Delia's catalog arrives, the halls of Paxton High School in Jacksonville, Fla., are buzzing. That's when all the girls bring in their copies from home and compare notes. '"Everyone loves Delia's," says Emily Garfinkle, 15. "It's the big excitement."

If you've never heard of Delia's, chances are you don't know a girl between 12 and 17. The five-year-old direct mailer has become one of the hottest names in Gen Y retailing by selling downtown fashion to girls everywhere. Already, the New York cataloger, which racked up sales of $98 million over the past three quarters, has a database of 4 million names, and its fastest growth may still lie ahead: Gen Y's teen population won't peak for five or six years.

Tight Focus. A lot of thriving Gen Y companies fell into the market by accident. Not Delia's. Founders Stephen Kahn, a 33-year-old ex-Wall Streeter, and Christopher Edgar, his ex-roommate at Yale University, realized that few retailers had taken the trouble to learn this market. So they carefully honed the Delia's concept: cutting-edge styles and mail-order distribution with a Gen Y twist.

Delia's trendy apparel is definitely not designed with mom and dad in mind. "I think the clothes are too revealing,'" says Emily's mother, Judy. "I tell her I'll buy her anything she wants at the Gap." But Emily dismisses the Gap as "too preppy," preferring Delia's long, straight skirts and tops with bra-exposing spaghetti straps. Delia's order form even includes tips on how to order pants so they conform to the parentally despised fashion of drooping well below the hips, with hems dragging. In keeping with Gen Y preferences, the catalog illustrates these fashions with models who look like regular teen-agers, not superglam androgynes.

Delia's youthful image isn't just a facade. Most of the company's 1,500 employees are well under 30. And its phone reps—mostly high school and college students—do more than take orders: They offer tips and fashion advice. "Delia's speaks the language of its consumers," says Wendy Liebmann, president of consultant WSL Marketing.

Instead of mass-market advertising, Delia's gets the word out in the ways Gen Y prefers: with local campaigns such as catalog drops in schools and with hot Web sites. In 1997, the company bought http://www.gURL.com, a popular fashion, chat, and game site for girls. It also launched its own Web site, with news and entertainment stories, catalog-request forms, e-mail, and online shopping. That effort helped buy some buzz for Delia's stock, which has gyrated between $4 and $32 a share over the past year. In December, buoyed by news of an on-line shopping venture, the stock shot up more than 50%, to a recent 15.

So far, the company has sold mostly clothing, but it has recently branched out into home furnishings, such as bean bag chairs and throw rugs. "Girls like to do their rooms," says Kahn, who defines his business by its customers rather than by a product category. He foresees a day when Delia's will get these girls their first credit card, first car loan, and first mortgage. "We'll follow them and broaden our offerings," says Kahn.

Next up: boys. The company recently bought TSI Soccer Corp., a sportswear catalog, and launched Droog, a catalog for boys. "We are going to own this generation," Kahn says. Or at least a sizable portion of its members' wallets.[6]

Changing age distributions may dramatically affect a company targeting an age-based market. The heaviest consumption of soft drinks, for example, occurs among teenagers. An increase of four million 13- to 24-year-olds would represent an annual consumption gain of three billion cans of soft drink.

Many marketers target their efforts toward Generation Y, the 77 million Americans born since 1977. Generation Yers are growing up during the most prosperous domestic economy ever. In many cities, teens have an abundance of job offers, from lifeguarding to baby-sitting to burger flipping. Parents are flourishing, too, and sharing the wealth with their kids. Consequently, teens are flush. And they are spending on technology and fashion. Cell phones, beepers, personal computers, and the Internet are all part of their daily lives. So are shopping and socializing in malls. The average teen visits shopping venues 54 times a year, compared with 39 times for the typical shopper. Because Generation Yers are a video generation, marketers who target this segment are often high-tech. For example, Hot Topic, a 138-store chain that sells clothing emblazoned with images of rock bands and pro wrestling stars, has about 20 video monitors in its offices continuously tuned to MTV to catch the slightest fashion nuance.[7]

At the beginning of this century, only one person in 25 was over 65. Today, one person in 5 is over 65. With the growth in the number of older consumers, more firms will be targeting this market segment with products—such as appliances with large letters and big control knobs—that reflect the needs of older people.

Family Life Cycle   A marketer of trash compactors, refrigerators, or credit cards might concentrate efforts on households or families rather than on individual consumers. To such marketers, knowing the composition of households is important.

When the word *family* is mentioned, most people think first of parents and their children. However, families are diverse, in part because they change over time. The **family life cycle,** a series of traditional stages through which most families pass, helps describe how diverse families may be. Exhibit 8-11 shows that people marry, raise children, and live together after the children go out on their own. Individuals may pass through these stages at different rates of speed, and the process may be preceded by cohabitation or disrupted by divorce or death of a spouse. It is difficult to say exactly what a "normal" family is.

Family life cycle
A series of stages through which most families pass.

e x h i b i 8-11

A Modernized Family Life Cycle[8]

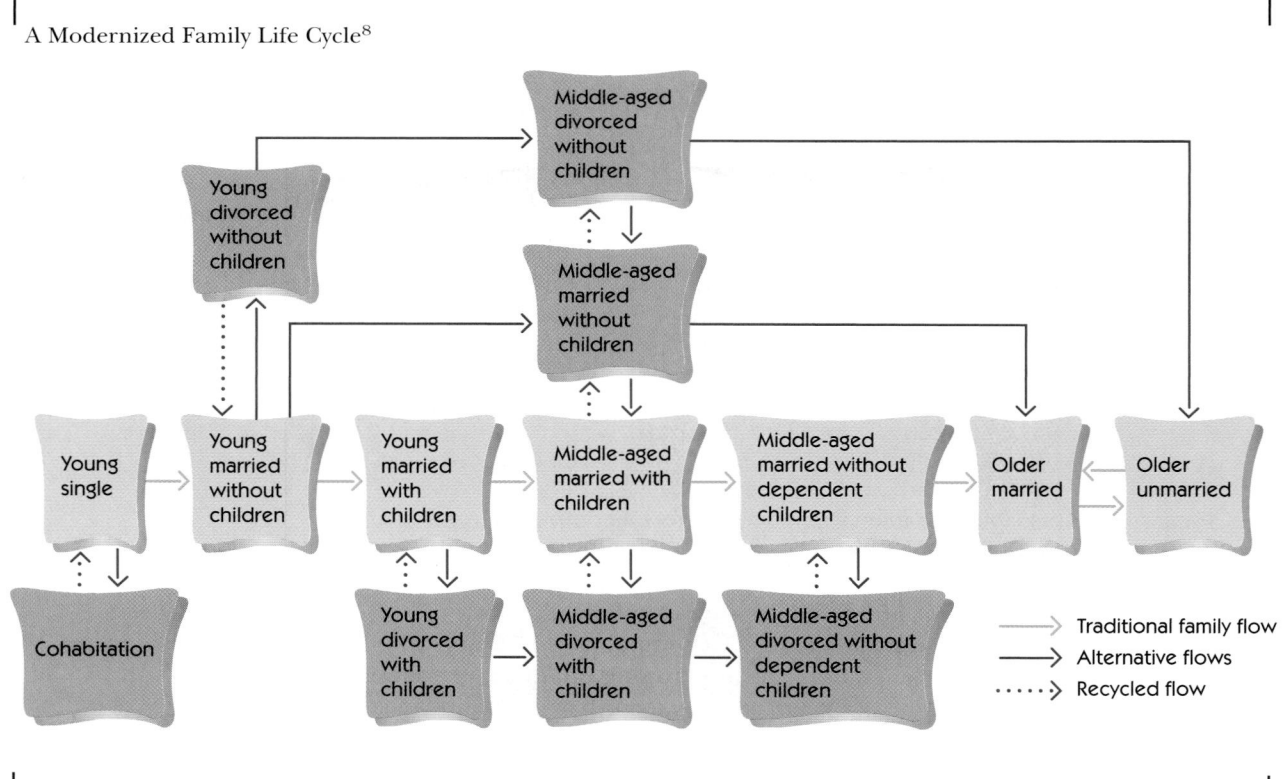

Many service marketers use the family life cycle to segment markets. This advertisement communicates the message that when a family with young children visits Universal Studios, they will be rewarded with 100% pure enjoyment.

http://www.universal studios.com

Family responsibilities and the presence of children may have a much stronger influence on spending behavior than age, income, or other demographic variables. Therefore marketing managers may use the family life cycle as a basis for segmentation for entertainment, household furniture, appliances, and many other product categories. Consider several people in their twenties: one may be single, one may be married without children, and one may be married with two children ages 1 and 3. In regard to spending behavior, these consumers are likely to have little in common. Exhibit 8-12 lists some products more likely to be used during certain life-cycle stages than during others.

Consumption Patterns of Families in
Several Life-Cycle Stages[9]

e x h i b i 8-12

STAGE	CONSUMPTION PATTERNS
Young single	Outdoor sporting goods, sports cars, fashion clothing, entertainment, and recreation services
Young married without children	Recreation and relaxation products, home furnishings, travel, home appliances
	High purchase rate of durables
Young married with children	Baby food, clothing, and furniture; starter housing; insurance; washers and dryers; medical services and supplies for children; toys for children
Young single parent	Money-saving products, frozen foods, rental housing, child care, time-saving appliances, and foods
Middle-aged married with children at home	Children's lessons (piano, dance, etc.); large food purchases (respond to bulk-buying deals); dental care; higher-priced furniture, autos, and housing; fast food restaurant meals
Middle-aged married without children at home	Luxury products, travel, restaurants, condominiums, recreation
	Make gifts and contributions; have high discretionary incomes and solid financial position
Older (married or single)	Health care, home security, specialized housing, specialized food products, recreation geared to the retired

The market for Olestra fat substitute products in foods has been analyzed using psychographic segmentation. Research found that "determined dieters" and "heavy snackers" were most predisposed to embrace Olestra. Groups labeled "naturalists" and "taste purists" were least likely to be attracted to Olestra products.[10]

http://www.olean.com

SOCIOECONOMIC BASES OF SEGMENTATION

Socioeconomic variables are special demographic characteristics that reflect an individual's social position or economic standing in society. A professor may have a low economic position but a respectable social standing. A surgeon usually rates high in both areas. An unskilled laborer may rate low in both. Socioeconomic factors such as occupation and income are often combined with other demographic variables to describe consumers (for example, white, male, professional, aged 35 to 40, making $75,000 or more).

Social class is one socioeconomic variable that can be used to distinguish groups of customers. Although Americans, perhaps disliking the term *class*, tend to speak of rich and poor people rather than high- and low-class people, class distinctions do exist. There is a considerable difference between a married couple with high-school educations making a combined annual income of $50,000 as toll collectors on the New Jersey Turnpike and a married couple who are both graduates of the Harvard Medical School earning a combined income of $400,000 a year practicing in Beverly Hills, California. And the difference is not just the money they make. The doctors may have attended prep schools and prestigious private colleges, inherited wealth, and come from families that have known the good life for generations. They may listen to classical music, dine frequently at posh restaurants, and travel out of the country for their vacations. The other couple probably does not. Consider this as a final comparison: If each couple were suddenly to earn an extra $20,000, how would each be likely to spend it? Would they spend it differently?

LIFESTYLE AND PSYCHOGRAPHIC SEGMENTATION

Lifestyle
An individual's activities, interests, opinions, and values as they affect his or her mode of living.

Psychographics
Quantitative measures of lifestyle.

A **lifestyle** is a pattern in an individual's pursuit of life goals—in how the person spends his or her time and money. An individual's activities, interests, opinions, and values represent the person's lifestyle. You probably know someone who has a "workaholic" lifestyle or an "outdoor" lifestyle, for example. Quantitative measures of lifestyles are known as **psychographics.** Such measures represent an attempt to "get inside the customer's head" and find out what people actually think.

Psychographic market segmentation provides a richer portrait of consumer groups than simple demographic information can yield. Psychographic measurement does not replace demographic measures but enhances them. For example, one father of young children may continue the activities that occupied him before the children arrived—perhaps golf, tennis, and partying. Another father in the same stage of the family life cycle may drop his sports and social activities to devote more time to the children. The two demographically similar men differ in terms of lifestyle, or psychographic variables.

Lifestyles and psychographics are often used to segment markets. *Outdoor Life, Flying, Travel and Leisure,* and many other magazines define their target markets by lifestyle, for example. By reaching certain lifestyle segments, the magazines provide advertising media for other marketers who wish to appeal to those segments. Psychographic variables are more difficult to deal with than demographic and socioeconomic variables. Library research can tell the marketer approximately how many male Hispanic Americans there are in California, for instance, but there are no statistics on the number of care-free people or good family men. Therefore, marketers typically use psychographic variables in combination with other variables. For example, marketers might decide that one segment of Porsche buyers consists of "self-indulgent thrill-seekers," rather than "conservative traditionalists." They might then define a "self-indulgent" consumer demographically as a single male, 25 to 45, college-educated, earning $100,000 or more a year. The psychographic variable is thereby tied in with more concrete demographic and economic descriptions.[12]

SEGMENTATION BY BEHAVIOR PATTERNS

Individual consumers exhibit different behavior patterns and consumption habits worthy of marketers' attention. Some consumers purchase apparel only at specialty men's or women's shops, for example, while others buy their clothing at department stores, in discount shops, or from catalogs. These shopping habits are behavior patterns that may be used as bases for segmentation. Buyers can vary their consumption from heavy use to nonuse. Therefore, in many cases, consumption patterns provide a good basis for market segmentation. Both the New York Mets and the New York Metropolitan Opera offer season tickets to heavy users of their products. Similarly, airlines such as Delta and American make product (service) usage and brand loyalty the basis for their frequent flyer programs. Flyers who take regular trips have different product needs than do occasional flyers. Banks are aware that many of their customers are long-term clients who loyally deal with only one institution—thus, banks invent slogans like "a full-service bank" and "the only bank you'll ever need." Light users or nonusers of the same bank's services require a different marketing mix, perhaps one stressing convenient locations or free merchandise for new depositors. Banks and many other marketers of services target some existing customers by using a technique known as cross-selling. **Cross-selling** refers to marketing activities designed to sell new, "extra" services to customers who already buy an existing service. Thus, a bank may make it easy for a customer with a home mortgage loan to obtain a low-cost safety deposit box and a checking account with a credit line.

Another differentiating aspect of consumer behavior involves

Cross-selling
Marketing activities used to sell new services to customers of an existing service.

The marketers of Zippo lighters conducted a survey and discovered that 30 percent of the company's customers were collectors. After learning that a large market segment had different reasons for purchasing a Zippo, the company started working more closely with retailers, built a database, established a "collectible of the year" promotion, and increased the lighter line to include more than 500 different models.

http://www.zippo.usa.com

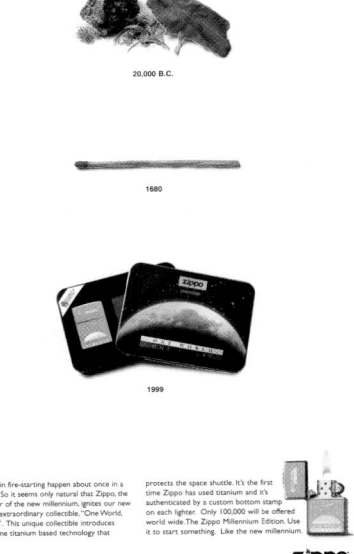

20,000 B.C.

1680

1999

Revolutions in fire-starting happen about once in a millennium. So it seems only natural that Zippo, the official lighter of the new millennium, ignites our new era with an extraordinary collectible, "One World, One Future": This unique collectible introduces TVD, the same titanium based technology that protects the space shuttle. It's the first time Zippo has used titanium and it's authenticated by a custom bottom stamp on each lighter. Only 100,000 will be offered world wide. The Zippo Millennium Edition. Use it to start something. Like the new millennium.

zippo
Use it to start something.

Check out www.zippo-usa.com for a chance to win the Zippo Millennium Limited Edition lighter.
Zippo. It works or we fix it free.™ Proudly made in USA.

consumers' product knowledge, beliefs about products and brands, and reasons for purchase. The sophisticated, knowledgeable buyer of stereo equipment is, for marketing purposes, almost totally different from the novice buyer. The veteran buyer knows what to look for, what questions to ask, where to buy, where to get service, and even what the price should be. The novice knows almost nothing of these things and so looks to salespeople for guidance. The novice seeks a store with a good reputation and trustworthy salespeople. The veteran buyer trusts his or her own knowledge and judgment. Furthermore, the major benefits sought by consumers are likely to vary considerably. Seeking to identify groups of customers by the benefits they seek is called **benefit segmentation.** Even when two or more buyers are purchasing exactly the same product, the expected benefits may vary. Just as the commercial says, some people buy Miller Lite because it tastes great, others because it's less filling.

Consumption patterns may also differ with circumstances. The purchase occasion may prove to be the underlying force creating consumption patterns and thus may be useful in distinguishing among buyer groups. A holiday drinking glass decorated with a Christmas tree or Santa Claus is obviously geared to buyers planning seasonal entertaining rather than to people looking for everyday glassware. Lava soap and similar hand cleaners are to be used when a person's hands are especially dirty, messy, or greasy.

Benefit segmentation
A type of market segmentation by which consumers are grouped according to the specific benefits they seek from a product.

what went wrong?

Porsche After having sold a record 30,000 automobiles in the United States in 1986, Porsche sold only 4,000 or so in 1993. Price was partly responsible. During the 1980s, the price of a Porsche 911 Carrera coupe was less than the average U.S. household's annual income. In 1993, the price was about 25 percent higher because of the strength of the Deutschemark and a luxury tax passed by Congress. However, after conducting marketing research to learn what market segments were prime customers, Porsche Cars North America found out increased price wasn't the only thing that had gone wrong.

The research showed that the demographics of Porsche owners were utterly predictable. The typical owner is a 40-something male college graduate earning over $200,000 per year. The psychographics, however, were of more interest. Porsche owners fell into the rather unusual—and not necessarily flattering—lifestyle categories shown below.

Porsche's vice president of sales and marketing found the results astonishing. He said, "We were selling to people whose profiles were diametrically opposed. You wouldn't want to tell an elitist how good he looks in the car or how fast he could go."

As a result of its new insights about its target markets, Porsche has cut its prices, launched a new advertising campaign, and introduced a redesign of its classic rear-engine car, the 911.[13]

TYPE	PERCENT OF ALL OWNERS	DESCRIPTION
Top Guns	27	Driven, ambitious types. Power and control matter. They expect to be noticed.
Elitists	24	Old-money blue bloods. A car is just a car, no matter how expensive. It is not an extension of personality.
Proud Patrons	23	Ownership is an end in itself. The car is a trophy earned for hard work, and who cares if anyone sees them in it?
Bon Vivants	17	Worldly jet setters and thrill seekers. The car heightens the excitement in their already passionate lives.
Fantasists	9	Walter Mitty types. The car is an escape. Not only are they uninterested in impressing others with it, they also feel a little guilty about owning one.

Direct marketers, especially those who sell through catalogs sent by mail, often use zip codes as a basis for market segmentation. The phrase "birds of a feather flock together" is quite appropriate here. People and households in the same zip code area often have similar demographic and socioeconomic characteristics. **Geodemographic segmentation** refers to the combination of demographic variables with a geographic variable, such as zip code, to characterize clusters of like individuals. Claritas Corporation's PRIZM system has analyzed each of the 36,000 zip codes in the United States and classified them into 40 market segments. Each segment has a colorful name such as Shotguns and Pickups (large rural families with modest means) or Gray Power (active retirement communities).

Geodemographic segmentation
A type of market segmentation by which consumers are grouped according to demographic and lifestyle variables, such as income and age, as identified by a geographic variable, such as zip code.

Segmenting Business Markets

To a great extent, business markets may be segmented by use of variables similar to the ones just discussed. The difference, of course, is that, instead of using characteristics and behavior of the individual consumer, the segmenter uses characteristics and behavior of the organization. For example, when marketers of electrical resistors decided to investigate their market on the basis of benefit segmentation, a study of the benefits sought from electrical resistors uncovered two major benefit segments. Military engineers purchasing for the government and engineers purchasing for consumer electronic companies both sought performance stability and reliability. But military buyers were concerned with failure rate and promptness in review of specifications, while low price was the major benefit sought by the consumer products engineers.

Exhibit 8-13 shows that business markets may be segmented on the basis of geography, organizational characteristics, purchase behavior and usage patterns, and organizational predispositions.

e x h i b i **8-13**

Selected Bases for Segmentation of Business Markets

Bases for segmentation of organizational markets

Geography	Organizational characteristics	Purchase behavior and usage patterns	Organizational predisposition or policy
• Political boundaries (cities, states, etc.) • Domestic/international boundaries	• Industry type • Organizational size • Technology used	• Order size (heavy vs. light usage) • Centralized vs. decentralized purchasing • Type of rebuy (e.g., straight rebuy vs. new task)	• Product knowledge • Benefits sought • Organizational problems • Multiple vs. single supplier policy

Finding the "Best" Segmentation Variable

As has already been suggested, the "best" segmentation variable is the one that leads the marketer to the identification of a meaningful target market segment. Some experts have argued that the benefits customers seek from products are the basis for all market segments. This may be so. After all, that idea supports the view that consumer orientation is the foundation of the marketing concept.

But geographical differences and buyers' characteristics contribute to differences in the benefits consumers are seeking. Thus, many segmentation variables may be found to be working together, complementing one another. The heavy user of Coors Light, for example, is somewhere between the ages of 21 and 34, is in the middle or upper income group, lives in an urban or suburban area, belongs to a health club, buys rock music, travels by plane, gives parties and cookouts, rents videos, and is a heavy viewer of television sports.[14] Because variables often complement each other, it is in the marketer's interest to target the best bundle of segmenting variables—two to five or more—so that the most advantageous match of market and marketing mix can be achieved. The marketer's goal is to segment the market in a way that helps the organization select market opportunities compatible with its ability to provide the right marketing mix.

Positioning: The Basic Focus for the Marketing Mix

After a target market has been selected, marketing managers choose the position they hope the brand will occupy in that market. Recall that *market position*, or competitive position, represents the way consumers perceive a brand relative to its competition. The thrust of a typical positioning strategy is to identify a product's or brand's competitive advantage and to stress relevant product characteristics or consumer benefits that differentiate the product or brand from those of competitors.

For example, Pepperidge Farm's Goldfish was for years positioned as a premium snack product. However, consumer research indicated that the product had the highest appeal in households with children under 12, who liked the way they tasted. And their mothers liked Goldfish because they were baked, not fried. As a result, the Goldfish brand was positioned less as a premium product and more as a fun, kid-oriented snack that moms and kids could agree on. ("It's one snack that it's OK to get hooked on.") Of course, as mentioned in the discussion of market segmentation, a brand cannot be all things to all people. Thus, positioning a brand—perhaps even altering product formulations to emphasize certain product attributes—may cause long-term problems. Further, a competitor may enter the market and position its product directly against the established product. This is known as **head-to-head competition** (or "me, too" competition). The objective here is to occupy the same position as a competitor, rather than to position away from competitors. For example, Burger King introduced its Big King burger to compete head-to-head with the Big Mac.

Head-to-head competition
Positioning a product to occupy the same market position as a competitor.

The retro-styled PT Cruiser is part minivan, part truck, part car, and part hot rod. It is shorter than a Neon subcompact but has as much interior room as the average minivan. Chrysler PT Cruiser is a vehicle that blends many characteristics to create an all-new product category: the flexible activity vehicle.

http://www.chrysler.com

Positioning decisions are easier when marketing research has clearly identified how consumers in different market segments perceive various competing offerings. Often, marketers draw positioning maps, sometimes based on sophisticated computer models, to illustrate how consumers see each com-

Positioning Maps for Tea

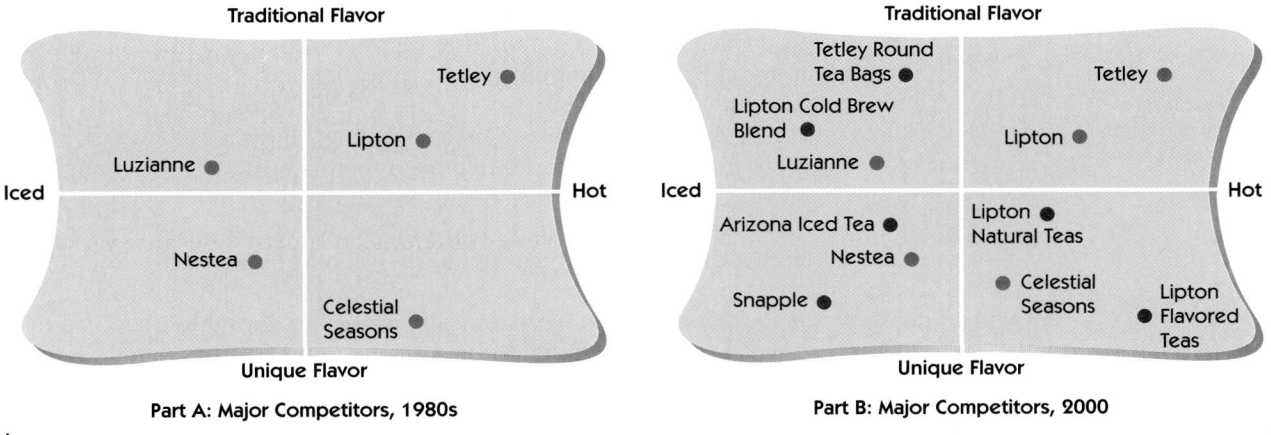

Traditional Flavor

Iced — Hot

Unique Flavor

Part A: Major Competitors, 1980s

Tetley ●
Lipton ●
Luzianne ●
Nestea ●
Celestial Seasons ●

Traditional Flavor

Iced — Hot

Unique Flavor

Part B: Major Competitors, 2000

Tetley Round Tea Bags ●
Lipton Cold Brew Blend ●
Luzianne ●
Tetley ●
Lipton ●
Lipton ● Natural Teas
Arizona Iced Tea ●
Nestea ●
Snapple ●
● Celestial Seasons
Lipton ● Flavored Teas

petitor's product. Exhibit 8-14 shows positioning maps for tea based on two product characteristics: flavor (traditional versus unique) and serving temperature (iced versus hot). A map such as this reflects benefit segmentation.

The map in Part A illustrates that when Luzianne entered the tea market, it was positioned as being exclusively for iced tea, and it was alone in this position. Lipton and Tetley were perceived to be quite similar to each other (served hot and offering a traditional flavor). Positioning maps can help pinpoint opportunities and problems. Part B reflects how competitors, after recognizing Luzianne's success, offered brands that were more clearly differentiated in consumers' minds from the traditional hot teas.

Positioning maps may indicate a void in the market. In other words, if a map shows no brands in a particular quadrant or area, there may be room for a new product. Sometimes research is conducted to determine what characteristics an "ideal brand" would have. If there is no competing product in the "product space" that the ideal brand would occupy on the map, a market opportunity may exist.

In the tea example, positioning was based on certain product characteristics. Consumers view competing offerings from many other perspectives as well. For example, consumers may evaluate a brand or product relative to offerings in another product class—low-saturated-fat olive oil relative to high-saturated-fat butter, for example—or according to purchase situation or usage occasion—an ordinary table wine versus a wine for a

This Rain Clean Clorox Bleach advertisement declares that no bargain bleach has a fragrance like it. Rain Clean Clorox Bleach positions itself as unbeatable compared to bargain bleach.

http://www.clorox.com

celebration. A marketer planning positioning strategy must take these perspectives into account.

When marketing managers are confident that they understand how consumers see their brand's position in relation to the competition, they must decide if they wish to maintain that position or reposition the brand. Ethan Allen introduced a new Country Colors collection, a reasonably priced natural-color furniture line, and advertised it on "Friends" because it wanted to reposition itself as a furniture maker with something for everyone rather than a company that makes expensive furniture for older consumers.[15] **Repositioning** may require rethinking the benefits offered to consumers through the marketing mix. Cascade brand dishwasher detergent, which for years was positioned as a powder with a pure rinse formula, was repositioned as a new "no pre-wash" tablet. The improved and premium-priced detergent was also given a new name, Cascade-Complete, to play up the "no need to rinse" aspect of the product. Note also that a brand may establish different positions for different market segments. For example, Cheerios positions its cereal as having muscle-building power for kids and cholesterol-lowering properties for middle-aged adults.

The target market strategy and the positioning strategy provide the framework for the development of the marketing mix. Thus, target marketing, positioning, and the marketing mix are highly interdependent. More will be said about each of these topics in future chapters.

Repositioning
Changing the market position of a product.

Summary

Market segmentation is one of marketing's most powerful tools. Whatever variables they use, effective marketers try to identify meaningful target segments so that they can develop customer-satisfying marketing mixes.

1) Define the term market.

A market is composed of individuals or organizations with the ability, willingness, and authority to exchange their purchasing power for the product offered.

2) Explain the concept of market segmentation.

In order to identify homogeneous segments (subgroups) of heterogeneous markets, marketing managers research an entire market, separate it into its parts, and regroup the parts into market segments according to one or more characteristics, such as geography, buying patterns, demography, and psychographic variables.

3) Relate the identification of meaningful target markets to the development of effective marketing mixes.

Marketing mixes are effective only if they satisfy the needs of meaningful target markets. A meaningful target market has a significant (and, ideally, measurable) market potential, is distinguishable from the overall market, is responsive, and is accessible through distribution or promotional efforts.

4) Distinguish among undifferentiated, concentrated, differentiated, and custom marketing strategies.

An undifferentiated marketing strategy is used if no meaningful segment can be identified. If one meaningful segment is the target of an organization's marketing mix, the concentrated marketing strategy is used. If several market segments are targeted, the differentiated marketing strategy is employed. When markets are so distinctive that each customer requires a special marketing mix, the custom marketing strategy is appropriate. Data-based marketing and mass customization are changing the nature of traditional custom marketing.

5) Demonstrate the effect of the 80/20 rule and the majority fallacy on marketing strategy.

According to the 80/20 principle, the majority of a product's sales are accounted for by a small percentage of the buyers. These users constitute an attractive target market; however, competitors often target this market as well. Failure to take the strength of the competition into account is the majority fallacy. One purpose of market segmentation is to identify segments that may have gone undetected by competitors.

6) List the market segmentation variables most commonly used by marketing managers and explain how marketers identify which ones are appropriate.

In consumer markets, segmentation variables include demographic, socioeconomic, psychographic, and geographic factors, as well as behavior and consumption patterns and consumer predispositions. In business markets, geographical areas, organizational characteristics, purchase behavior and usage patterns, and organizational predispositions and policies are used as segmentation variables. The appropriateness of any one variable or combination of variables varies considerably from case to case. The marketing manager must determine which variables will isolate a meaningful target market.

7) Explain the purpose of a positioning strategy.
Each brand appealing to a given market segment has a position in the consumer's mind. The pur-pose of a positioning strategy is to identify a product's or brand's competitive advantage and to stress relevant product characteristics or consumer bene-fits that differentiate the product or brand from those of competitors.

Key Terms

benefit segmentation (p. 212)
concentrated marketing (p. 198)
cross-classification matrix (p. 195)
cross-selling (p. 211)
custom marketing (p. 201)
differentiated marketing (multiple market segmentation) (p. 200)

80/20 principle (p. 199)
family life cycle (p. 208)
flexible manufacturing system (p. 204)
geodemographic segmentation (p. 213)
head-to-head competition (p. 214)

lifestyle (p. 210)
majority fallacy (p. 199)
mass customization (p. 203)
psychographics (p. 210)
repositioning (p. 216)
undifferentiated marketing (p. 196)

Questions for Review & Critical Thinking

1. Why do organizations practice market segmentation?
2. Think of some creative ways the following organizations might segment the market.
   a. A rental car company
   b. A zoo
   c. A personal computer manufacturer
   d. A science magazine
3. What are some unusual ways markets have been segmented?
4. Identify and evaluate the target market for the following products.
   a. *The Wall Street Journal*
   b. The Chicago Cubs
   c. Timberland boots
   d. Perrier bottled water
   e. *Wired* magazine
5. What questions should a marketer ask to determine if a market segment is meaningful?
6. Think of examples of companies that use undifferentiated marketing, concentrated marketing, differentiated marketing, and custom marketing. Why is the strategy appropriate in each instance?

7. Should firms always aim at the largest market segment?
8. What is the relationship between data-based marketing and mass customization?
9. How might Levi's segment the men's clothing market? How might Anheuser-Busch segment the market for beer?
10. What variable do you think is best for segmenting a market?
11. What variables might a business-to-business marketer use to segment a market?
12. What is positioning? Provide some examples.
13. Identify the positioning strategy for the following brands.
    a. 7-Up
    b. American Airlines
    c. AT&T long-distance service
    d. Gateway computers
14. Form small groups of four or five students. Assume you have been hired by a rental car company as consultants. Research and identify a market segmentation strategy and a positioning strategy for the company.

e—exercises

1. Abbott Wool's Market Segment Resource Locator provides numerous links to information and Web sites related to market segmentation. Go to http://www.awool.com and answer the following questions.
   a. What type of information can be obtained about the African-American market, the Asian-American market, and the Hispanic-American market?
   b. Select the teen segment. What type of information can be obtained about this market segment?
2. Go to the Census Bureau's home page at http://www.census.gov. What three states are forecasted to increase the most in population between 1995 and 2020? What is the expected growth of the Asian-American market? The Hispanic market?

Address Book (Useful URLs)

Statistics Canada	http://www.statcan.ca/start.html
Pampers Parenting Institute	http://www.totalbabycare.com
iGolf	http://www.igolf.com
Big Yellow: NYNEX Interactive Yellow Pages	http://www.niyp.com
Claritas: Developers of the PRIZM System	http://www.claritas.com

Ethically Right or Wrong?

After careful research, the Uptown cigarette was targeted to a group that had a higher-than-average number of heavy smokers. Research showed that the target market liked the product, its name, and its attractive black and gold package. However, there were intense protests when the product was introduced to the public, because Uptown was the first cigarette targeted to African Americans. According to some critics, this minority group, which has a higher percentage of smoking-related illnesses than other groups, was a target market chosen on the basis of racism.

QUESTION

1. Is segmentation based on race ethical?

TAKE A STAND

1. Is the marketing of sugar-coated cereals on Saturday morning television programs good for society?
2. There are many people who watch TV evangelists and consider themselves "born again." Is it ethical for a consumer products marketer to sell products to consumers on the basis of religion?
3. Dakota cigarettes were designed to be marketed to active working-class women. Is this ethical?

VIDEO CASE 8-1

LaBelle Management

In 1948, Norman LaBelle decided he would have more fun running a restaurant than selling used cars, and the result was the opening of the Pixie Restaurant, in Mount Pleasant, Michigan. Complete with car-hop waitresses and great inexpensive food (Coney Dogs and Bitty Burgers), the Pixie quickly became a popular place with both the local population and the fast-growing enrollment at Central Michigan University. 1972 saw the creation of The Sweet Onion, whose original menu was built on a limited selection of soups, sandwiches, and dinners. Another, perhaps more consequential, event of 1972 was when McDonald's entered the Mount Pleasant market. The franchise operation became a strong competitor for LaBelle. It did not take long for LaBelle management to realize that if it wanted to stay competitive, it had to factor the restaurant chain franchise concept into its marketing strategy. Two years later, a Big Boy Restaurant was added to the LaBelle restaurant line in Mount Pleasant, followed by three more locations. Next came Ponderosa Steakhouses, with three locations. In 1980, LaBelle opened a second location of The Sweet Onion in Midland.

In the 1980s and 1990s, LaBelle added 17 more Ponderosas. It further expanded with Bennigan's Irish Pub and Italian Oven restaurants (pasta and pizza from wood-burning ovens). Today, LaBelle owns and operates 30 hotel and restaurant locations in Indiana and Michigan. At one time it expanded into the southern market. Unfortunately, it did not learn to adapt to regional tastes before it had to close these restaurants.

In Mount Pleasant, LaBelle operates all six of its restaurant concepts: the Pixie (now with a retro, nostalgic theme), The Sweet Onion, Italian Oven, Big Boy, Bennigan's, and Ponderosa Steakhouse. Although LaBelle management realizes that the restaurants compete with each other, it also believes that each serves a separate market segment.[16]

QUESTIONS

1. What criteria might LaBelle use to determine restaurant market segments in the Mount Pleasant market?
2. How might marketing strategy, targeting certain market segments, change with each of LaBelle's six restaurants?

CRITICAL THINKING CASE 8-2
VALS™ 2

The Values and Lifestyles System (VALS) is a popular psychographic classification scheme. The VALS 2 typology, developed by SRI International, segments U.S. adults based on psychological attributes that drive consumer buying behavior. VALS 2 classifies consumers based on their answers to 35 attitudinal statements and 4 demographic questions.

Using the VALS national database of products, media, and services, manufacturers and advertisers identify the consumer groups who are most naturally attracted to their products and services. This enables them to select an appropriate consumer target. Marketers design their advertising messages for the target using words and images intended to appeal to the target. They then put the advertising in media that the target actually uses. (VALS tracks the television, magazine, and radio preferences of each of the eight consumer groups annually.)

Consumer data by VALS type is provided by linkages with Simmons' annual *Survey of the American Household*, SRI's retail financial services survey, MacroMonitor, and other databases.

Marketers also apply VALS™ to direct marketing using GeoVALS to identify zip codes and groups that contain large concentrations of their target consumers. Other products include iVALS, which measures and represents consumer preferences in online environments, and Japan VALS™, which segments Japanese consumers based on their psychographic profiles.

VALS is built on two key concepts: self-orientation and resources. Self-orientation determines what in particular about the self or the world is the meaningful core that governs a person's activities in life. According to VALS, consumers are motivated by principle, status, or action. Principle-oriented consumers are guided in their choices by abstract, idealized criteria rather than by feelings, events, or desire for approval and opinions of others. Status-oriented consumers look for products and services that demonstrate their success to their peers. Action-oriented consumers are guided by a desire for social or physical activity, variety, and risk taking.

Resources include the full range of psychological, physical, demographic, and material means and capacities consumers have to draw on. Resources encompass education, income, self-confidence, health, eagerness to buy, and energy level. Resources run on a continuum from minimal to abundant.

Based on these dimensions, VALS 2 defines eight segments of adult consumers, as illustrated in the accompanying art and table. Actualizers and Strugglers represent the upper and lower ends of the resource dimension. The other six groups—Fulfilleds, Believers, Achievers, Strivers, Experiencers, and Makers—represent combinations of self-orientation and resource availability.

VALS™ 2 Segmentation System[17]

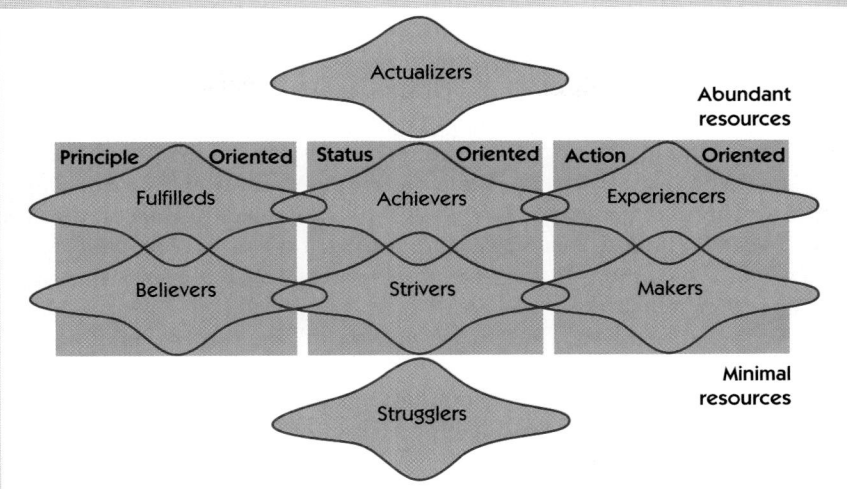

Characteristics of VALS™ 2 Market Segments[18]

CONSUMER TYPE	PERCENT OF POPULATION	MEDIAN AGE	DISTINCTIVE PURCHASE BEHAVIORS
Actualizers	10	42	Possessions reflect a cultivated taste for finer things in life
Fulfilleds	10	55	Desire product functionality, value, and durability
Believers	17	58	Favor American products and established brands
Achievers	14	39	Prefer products that demonstrate success to peers
Strivers	14	36	Emulate those with impressive possessions
Experiencers	13	24	Avid consumers of clothing, fast food, music, movies, and videos
Makers	11	35	Unimpressed by material possessions (except those with a practical purpose)
Strugglers	10	67	Modest resources limit purchases to urgent needs

For example, both Achievers and Strivers are status-oriented consumers, but Achievers have more resources. Achievers are successful career and work-oriented people who value structure, predictability, and stability over risk, intimacy, and self-discovery. They are deeply committed to their work and families, and their social lives are structured around family, church, and business. As consumers, they favor established products and services that demonstrate their success to their peers. Strivers seek motivation, self-definition, and approval from the world around them. They are striving to find a secure place in life. Unsure of themselves and with limited economic, social, and psychological resources, they are deeply concerned about the opinions and approval of others. They may try to emulate people who own more impressive possessions, but what they wish to obtain is often beyond their reach.[19]

QUESTIONS

1. Evaluate VALS 2 as the basis for a market segmentation strategy.
2. What types of products are most likely to benefit from segmentation based on VALS 2?

cross-functional insights

Many theories and principles from other business disciplines can provide insights about the role of marketing in an organization. The questions in this section are designed to help you think about integrating what you have learned in other business courses with the marketing principles explained in Chapters 5 through 8.

Decision Support Systems for Marketing Decision support systems serve specific business units in a company. A decision support system is a computer system designed to store data and transform the data into accessible information. Its purpose is to allow decision makers to answer questions through direct interaction with databases.

What database software might be used by marketing research managers?

What spreadsheet software might be used by marketing research managers?

What statistical software might be used by marketing research managers?

In what ways must a marketer's decision support system be coordinated with the organization's information system?

Research Is Systematic and Objective Marketing research allows managers to make decisions based on objective, systematically gathered data rather than intuition.

How can a knowledge of statistical hypothesis testing help a marketing researcher?

What steps might a marketing researcher take in testing a statistical hypothesis about a mean?

Simple Random Sampling A sample is simply a portion, or subset, of a larger population. It makes sense that a sample can provide a good representation of the whole. A simple random sample consists of individuals' names drawn according to chance selection procedures from a complete list of all people in a population.

Discuss the types of statistical errors associated with simple random sampling.

How much control does a statistician have over the probability that an error will occur?

How likely is the occurrence of random sampling error?

A mail questionnaire includes a question that can be answered either *excellent, good, fair,* or *poor.* If simple random sampling is utilized, what statistical test will determine if the observed distribution is different from the expected uniform distribution?

Sales Forecasting Sales forecasting is the process of predicting sales totals over some specific future period. An accurate sales forecast is one of the most useful pieces of information a marketing manager can have because the forecast influences so many plans and activities. Identifying trends and extrapolating past performance into the future is a relatively uncomplicated quantitative forecasting technique. Time series data are identified and even plotted on a graph, and the historical pattern is projected for the upcoming period. The market factor method of forecasting may be used when there is an association between sales and another variable, or factor.

How could correlation analysis be used to identify market factors?

How could regression analysis be used to forecast sales?

How might the moving averages method be used in the projection of sales trends?

Consumer Behavior Consumer behavior consists of the activities people engage in when selecting, purchasing, and using products so as to satisfy needs and desires. Such activities involve mental and emotional processes in addition to physical actions.

Explain economists' theories about consumer behavior and how they differ from marketers' theories.

The concept caveat emptor ("let the buyer beware") was introduced in the 16th century. What is the history of this concept in the 20th century? Is it an important aspect of consumer behavior?

Buying Center The buying center in any organization is an informal, cross-departmental decision unit whose primary objective is the acquisition, dissemination, and processing of relevant purchasing-related information.

What impact do the management concepts of job description, authority, and responsibility have on the activities of a buying center?

How important is a company's corporate culture in the establishment of buying centers? What type of corporate culture would contribute most to the establishment of effective buying centers?

Suppose an organizational structure identifies profit centers. What impact might they have on organizational buying?

How might purchasing agents with different levels of need for achievement, need for power, and need for affiliation (as explained by McClelland's need theory) differ in their organizational buying behavior?

Gatekeeper Role The role of collecting and passing on information—or withholding it—is known as the gatekeeper function.

What theories of communication within organizations help explain this function?

Basic Concepts about Goods, Services, and Ideas

LEARNING OBJECTIVES

After you have studied this chapter, you will be able to . . .

1) Define *product* and explain why the concept of the *total product* is important for effective marketing.

2) Differentiate among convenience products, shopping products, and specialty products.

3) Categorize organizational products.

4) Explain the difference between product lines and product mixes.

5) Understand brand-related terminology, including *brand, brand name, brand mark, trademark, manufacturer brand, distributor brand,* and *family brand*.

6) Discuss the characteristics of effective brand names.

7) Analyze the importance of packaging in the development of an effective product strategy.

8) Discuss the role of customer service in product strategy.

9) Discuss the nature of a service product and explain the four basic characteristics of services.

10) Discuss product strategies for services.

For pre-adolescent kids, carrying the wrong lunchbox to school can be as traumatic as wearing no-name sneakers or having a home haircut. Some kids might go so far as to feign illness if Mom and Dad didn't spring for the latest, hippest Hercules or Barbie box.

Though sneakers carry the most status in school-yards today, kids still attach a certain amount of importance to the ol' lunchbox. And Oscar Mayer has discovered a way to tap into those lunchbox dollars with Lunchables.

When Lunchables was first introduced in 1989, Oscar Mayer was simply extending the company's lead in luncheon meats by adding bread and condiments necessary to complete the meal. The basic idea for Lunchables was to provide convenient meal solutions for mothers and kids. This product concept was successful for several years. However, when sales began to flatten out, Oscar Mayer went to its target market, 6-to-12-year-olds, and asked for input. The result was product modification and the introduction of Lunchables Fun Packs, which added juice, candy, and games.[1]

Of course, to reach the market, many marketing functions other than product development must be performed. But let's stick with the product itself. Oscar Mayer successfully launched Lunchables by developing a total product concept. To begin with,

its brand name, Lunchables, is easy to say and remember. It is descriptive. The tag below the name—"lunch combinations"—tells consumers that this is more than just lunch meat.

The package's hip graphics tell that this is a fun pack. Fun is built into the food. Other brand names, such as Kraft cheddar cheese, CapriSun juice drink, and Skittles candy, also appear on the package. Brain teasers and games often appear on the back of the package. Contests such as "Jam with the Pros" offer kids a chance to win a visit to their school by an NBA star.

Aside from the tangible things, the buyer of a Lunchables Fun Pack purchases intangible things, such as the Oscar Mayer name and reputation. The name Oscar Mayer is associated with the best lunch meats in the world. Consumers associate Oscar Mayer with quality.

A Lunchables is more than a food item; it is a bundle of satisfactions—the particular bundle of benefits that constitutes this Oscar Mayer product.

This is the first of two chapters dealing with product issues. It begins by explaining how marketers view products and product strategy. It then categorizes products using several different classification schemes and goes on to discuss the nature of product lines and product mixes. Next, it discusses the nature of branding, packaging, warranties, and customer service.

What Is a Product?

The product an organization offers to its market is not simply a bar of soap, a rental car, or a charitable cause. As with so many other marketing elements, there is more to the product than meets the eye. A product may be a thing, in the nuts-and-bolts sense, but it doesn't have to be. It can be a reward offered to those willing to pay for it: A mowed lawn is the payoff for someone who buys a lawn mower. To an organization, a product is a bundle of benefits. This customer-oriented definition stresses what the buyer gets, not what the seller is selling. For example, a Disney World resort hotel provides more than a place to stay. It offers sun and fun, relaxation and entertainment, and a sense of pride about being a good parent.

Defining the product in terms of benefits allows anything from a tangible item to a service to an idea to be identified as a product. Whether an organization's offering is largely tangible (a ship), largely intangible (financial counseling), or even more intangible (the idea of world peace), its offering is a product.

THE TOTAL PRODUCT

Because a product can have so many aspects and benefits, marketers think in terms of the **total product**—the broad spectrum of tangible and intangible benefits that a buyer might gain from a product once it has been purchased. Marketers view total products as having characteristics and benefits at two levels. **Primary characteristics** are basic features and aspects of the core product. These characteristics provide the essential benefits common to most competing products. Here, consumers expect a basic level of performance.[2] A quarter-inch drill bit, for example, is expected to provide quarter-inch holes. **Auxiliary dimensions** of a product provide supplementary benefits and include special features, aesthetics, packaging, warranty, instructions for use, repair service contract, reputation, brand name, and so on. Each auxiliary dimension is part of the *augmented product*. Together, these two groups of features fulfill the buyer's needs. Any one of many benefits may be important to a particular buyer. Effective marketers build strategies emphasizing those benefits that are most meaningful to the target markets.

Exhibit 9-1 uses Close-Up toothpaste to illustrate the nature of a core product and the associated auxiliary dimensions. The essential benefits of any toothpaste are cleaning teeth and preventing tooth decay. Close-Up's package (a tube with a flip-cap) also benefits the consumer by making the product convenient to store

Total product
The wide range of tangible and intangible benefits that a buyer might gain from a product after purchasing it.

Primary characteristic
A basic feature or essential aspect of a product.

Auxiliary dimension
An aspect of a product that provides supplementary benefits, such as special features, aesthetics, packaging, warranty, repair service contract, reputation, brand name, or instructions.

The core product for a hotel is a room to sleep in. However, there are many auxiliary dimensions to this service product. Hotel personnel who provide speedy, friendly personal service and who go out of their way for hotel guests are product characteristics that provide competitive advantage.

The Core Product and the Augmented Product

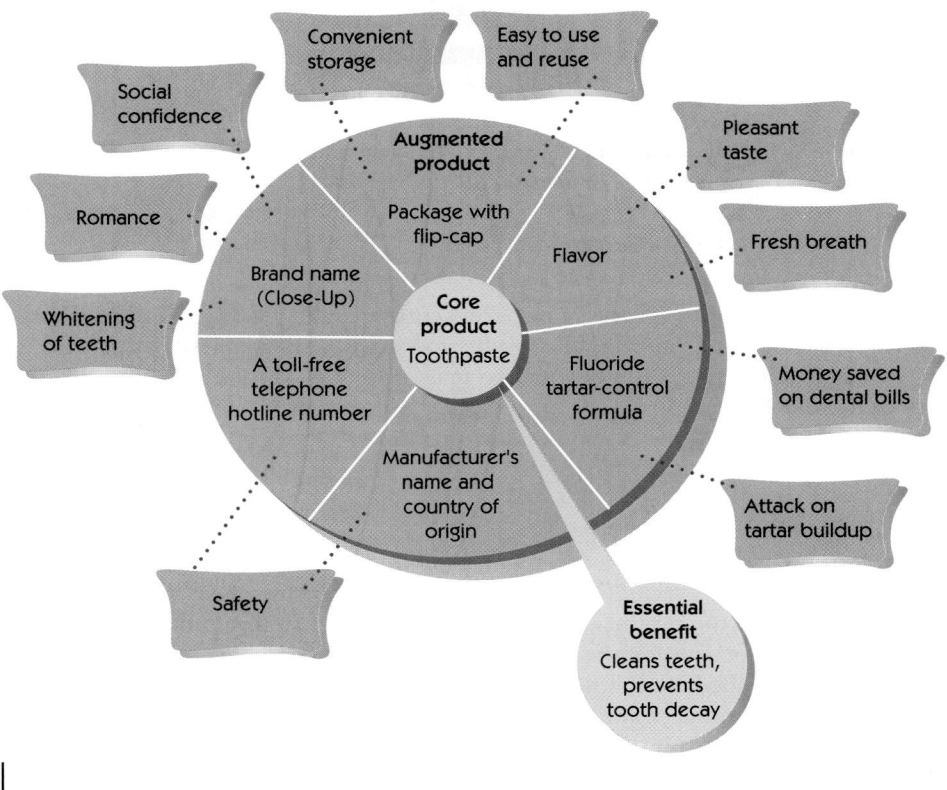

and easy to use. The brand name Close-Up suggests social confidence and romance. The printing of the manufacturer's name, the country of origin, and telephone hotline number on the package provides a safety benefit. Each auxiliary dimension adds a benefit that may be important to a buyer.

PRODUCT STRATEGY AND THE PRODUCT CONCEPT

Product strategy involves planning the product concept and developing a unified mix of product attributes. Successful product strategy requires that all aspects of the product be analyzed and managed in light of competitive offerings. Deciding which product features and which consumer benefits to stress is the creative dimension of product strategy.

The **product concept** (also called the *product positioning concept*) defines the essence, or core idea, underlying the product features and benefits that appeal to the target market. The product concept reflects the marketing strategist's selection and blending of a product's primary characteristics and auxiliary dimensions into a basic idea or unifying concept. In short, it provides a reason for buying the product. The product concept often is described in the same terms used to characterize the competitive market position that the product is expected to occupy in consumers' minds. For example, Go-Gurt is yogurt packaged for kids

> The product concept reflects the marketing strategist's selection and blending of a product's primary characteristics and auxiliary dimensions into a basic idea or unifying concept.

Product strategy
The planning and development of a mix of the primary and auxiliary dimensions of a product.

Product concept
The end result of the marketing strategist's selection and blending of a product's primary and auxiliary dimensions into a basic idea emphasizing a particular set of consumer benefits; also called the *product positioning concept.*

On many airlines, quality meals are becoming a thing of the past. Recognizing that their business guests/air passengers are going to be hungry in-flight, several upscale hotels are offering departing guests gourmet brown-bag meals to eat on airplanes. This auxiliary benefit is very meaningful to the hotel's customers.

in a toothpaste-like tube. There's no spoon required. The product concept is for kids to have fun eating yogurt while on the go—anytime, any place. For parents, Go-Gurt is positioned as a fun new way to make sure kids get the nutrition of yogurt. Some widely used product concepts are "Our product has the most advanced technology"; "We build the highest-quality product"; "Our product is made in the USA"; and "Ours is a basic, no-frills product; it's the best value."

PRODUCT DIFFERENTIATION

Product differentiation
A strategy that calls buyers' attention to aspects of a product that set it apart from its competitors.

Calling buyers' attention to aspects of a product that set it apart from its competitors is called **product differentiation**. To differentiate their product, marketers may make some adjustment in the product to set it apart from other similar products. Or they may promote one or more of the product's tangible or intangible attributes. For example, an automobile battery with a selector dial that switches on a supplemental booster battery when the primary battery fails to hold a charge will be more competitive than an ordinary battery. This product feature is a tangible difference that provides a functional benefit.

What differentiates one product from others need not be a scientifically demonstrable improvement. Stylistic and aesthetic differences accomplished through changes in color, design, and shape, as well as technological differences, can play a role in product differentiation. Party Animals, for instance, are "adult crackers" baked in animal shapes to set the brand apart visually from competitors, such as Ritz. If consumers see such variations as important, then the variations differentiate the product from its competitors.

Classifying Consumer Products

Many factors influence a buyer's decision-making process. One of the strongest is the product itself, because the product includes so many physical, psychological, and purchase-behavior dimensions. For this reason, marketing managers have developed some widely accepted product classifications that describe both products and, more importantly, buyers' perceptions of them. We will discuss consumer products here and then consider organizational products in the next section.

Furniture, appliances, groceries, hardware—a seemingly infinite number of categories of consumer products can be identified. The great number and diverse nature of products offered for sale make consumer product classification a complex task. Products may be classified on the basis of many criteria. We will discuss two widely accepted systems: classification by tangibility and durability and classification by consumers' buying behavior. (See Exhibit 9-2.)

TANGIBILITY AND DURABILITY

Products may be classified according to tangibility and durability—whether they are goods or services and, if goods, whether they are durable or nondurable.

Widely Accepted Classifications for Consumer Products

Classification by Tangibility and Durability

Classification by Consumers' Buying Behavior: Their Willingness to Expend Effort

Goods have a tangible, physical form, whereas **services** are tasks, activities, or other intangibles. **Durable goods** function over an extended period. Consumers use durable goods, such as automobiles and refrigerators, many times. **Nondurable goods**—which are quickly consumed, worn out, or outdated—are consumed in a single use or a few uses. Chewing gum, paper towels, and hand soap are examples of nondurable goods.

The distinction between goods and services is meaningful, but remember that services, like the physical, tangible items we call goods, should be referred to as *products*. This is especially important now because the service industry accounts for more than half of personal consumption expenditures.[3] If government is included as a service, the proportion of personal consumption accounted for by services is even greater. Because services are so important, this chapter ends with a special discussion of strategies for the marketing of services.

For now, however, if you think about a restaurant's product, you will realize that it is difficult to separate goods from services entirely. This reality has led some marketing experts to array products along a continuum from pure good to pure service. A barbecue grill is obviously a tangible good; an employment agency clearly provides a service. But a restaurant provides both a good (the food it prepares) and a service (the cooking and serving of the food, as well as convenience, atmosphere, and other aspects of its total product offering). Thus, you will find a restaurant in the middle of the goods–services scale in Exhibit 9-3.

CONSUMER BEHAVIOR

One of the first product classification systems to be developed is the most widely recognized and the most useful for answering questions regarding marketing mix decisions. This is the consumer product classification scheme developed by Melvin T. Copeland in 1924. Copeland suggested three general classifications of consumer products: convenience, shopping, and specialty.

Three important points should be made about Copeland's scheme. First, the plan applies to consumer products, not organizational products. Second, and most significant, the classes are primarily based not on the products themselves but on consumers' reasons for buying, their need for information, and their shopping and

Service
A task or activity performed for a buyer or an intangible that cannot be handled or examined before purchase.

Durable good
A physical, tangible item that can be used over an extended period.

Nondurable good
A physical, tangible item that is quickly consumed, worn out, or outdated.

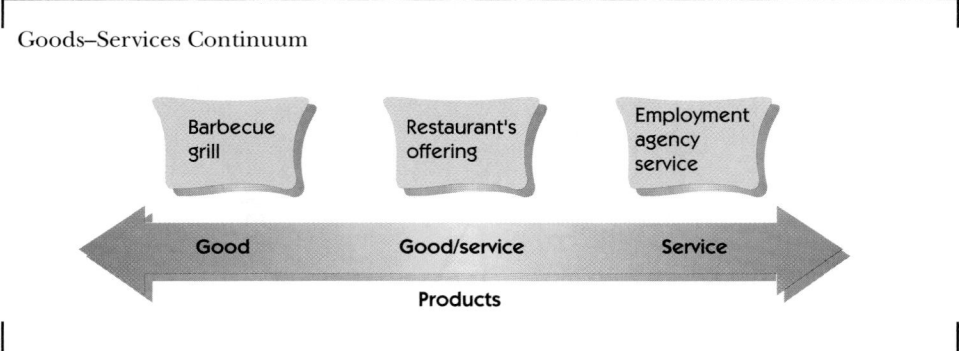

Goods–Services Continuum

purchase behaviors. The reason Copeland's plan has remained popular for so long is that it is consumer-oriented. Third, the classifications are somewhat generalized; they are based on a "typical" consumer's reasons for buying. The categories are less useful when applied to specific shoppers, especially very poor or very rich ones.

Convenience product
A relatively inexpensive, regularly purchased consumer product bought without much thought and with a minimum of shopping effort.

Convenience Products   The first of Copeland's categories is **convenience products**. Bic disposable ball-point pens are convenience goods; so are shoelaces. In most cases, so is gasoline. What do these items have in common? They are relatively inexpensive; they are purchased regularly and repeatedly; and they are bought almost reflexively, without a great deal of thought. In fact, they are bought with a minimum of consumer shopping effort. Buyers of a particular gasoline brand may be loyal, but their loyalty is not very deep. If they are running low on gas, most drivers will settle for a brand similar to their regular brand rather than drive a few extra miles to get their preferred brand. In short, consumers want to buy products such as these at the most convenient locations. How far out of your way would you go to buy, say, a quart of a particular brand of milk? The answer to such a question provides a guide to determining whether any given product is a convenience product.

Because shoppers rarely expend much shopping effort to obtain convenience products, distribution is a key element in the marketing mix. The object is to make the product available in almost every possible location. For example, thousands of retailers in every large city sell soft drinks and candy bars. These convenience goods are also common vending machine items. Convenience items that are purchased largely on impulse, such as candy bars, are sold in drugstores, discount stores, convenience outlets, and college bookstores. In individual stores, impulse items that are purchased on the spur of the moment are usually placed at the most convenient spots, such as near the checkout counter.

In the convenience goods classification, one brand is fairly easily substituted for another of its type, and retailers seldom, if ever, make extensive personal selling efforts. Therefore, extensive advertising by the manufacturer or service provider may be appropriate. The heavy advertising expenditures of Coca-Cola and Pepsi-Cola attest to the importance of extensive advertising.

Shopping product
A product for which consumers feel the need to make comparisons, seek out more information, examine merchandise, or otherwise reassure themselves about quality, style, or value before making a purchase.

Shopping Products   **Shopping products**, the second of Copeland's classifications, include products for which consumers feel the need to make product comparisons, seek out additional information, examine merchandise, or otherwise reassure themselves about quality, style, or value before making a purchase. In other words, prospective buyers of these products expect to benefit by shopping around. Decisions about shopping products are not made on the spur of the moment, in part because shopping goods are generally priced higher than convenience goods, and consumers are more involved with the purchases.

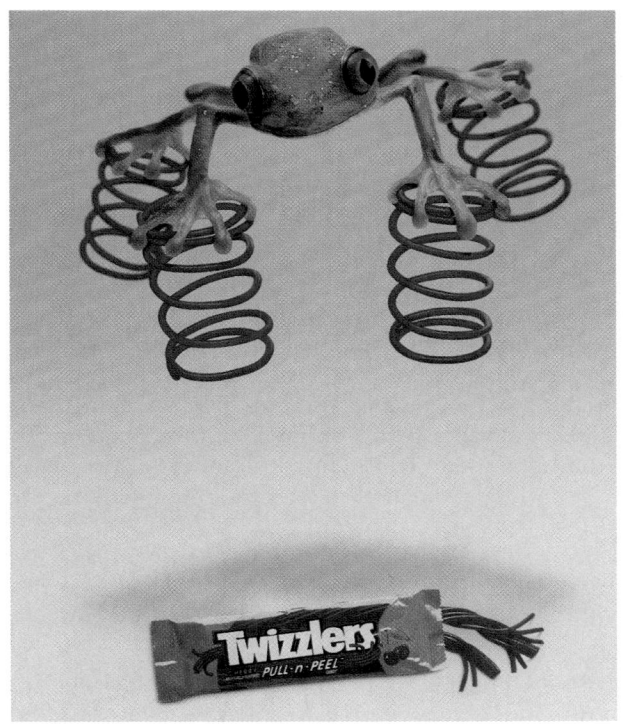

Candy bars are convenience products. They are purchased repeatedly and almost reflexively, without a great deal of thought. On the other hand, silverware and dinnerware, such as Oneida brand, are shopping products. Consumers feel the need to reassure themselves about such products' quality, style, or value before making a purchase.

There are two types of shopping products. If consumers evaluate product alternatives as similar in quality and features but different in price, these products are *homogeneous shopping products.* For homogeneous shopping products, such as washing machines and undershirts, obtaining the lowest price is the primary reason for making comparisons. *Heterogeneous shopping products* have identifiable product differences. These products tend to be subject to the whims of fashion and are more likely to be noticed by the shopper's family and friends. Thus, the risks, both monetary and social, associated with heterogeneous shopping products are fairly high. Clothing, shoes, furniture, and everyday tableware are examples of heterogeneous shopping products.

Buyers of heterogeneous shopping products are willing to search for the styles, brand names, or quality they want. Furthermore, they may wish to purchase the products in a particular store. You may have heard a friend say, "I got this suit at the Ivy League Shop." But people seldom say, "I got this Doublemint gum at the 7-Eleven." Thus, the distribution problem differs from that associated with convenience goods. Because people are willing to shop around, the idea is not to place the product everywhere but to place the product in the proper spots. The best distribution strategy becomes one of selective distribution. Within a store, shopping products probably will not be placed up front. Furniture can be placed in a distant area of a department store because customers are willing to seek it out.

Marketing mix elements shift somewhat in relative importance when we move from convenience products to shopping products. Product characteristics, including quality, become more important. Price will be a consideration for consumers, but with heterogeneous products it need not be as uniform among competing brands as in the case of easily substituted convenience products. Retail marketers, however, may stress the price of heterogeneous products because they are competing with other retailers of the same brands or similar brands.

Specialty Products   In some cases, consumers know exactly what they want. They have selected the brand in advance and will not accept substitutes. For example, they may insist on having Woody at A Cut Above the Others style their hair because they see his service as unique. At the moment of purchase, they no longer need to make shopping comparisons among alternatives. They have thought about their purchase. They regard the brand as having a particular attraction other than price. Products that are the object of this type of consumer preference fall into Copeland's third category, **specialty products**.

Many specialty products are seldom-purchased items, such as stereo equipment, pianos, wedding receptions, and expensive cars. Potential buyers may gather a great amount of information before making the purchase decision. They may go so far as to buy and read books or magazines dealing with the product class. At the time of purchase, they may spend considerable time and effort to get to the appropriate store, but they no longer need to make shopping comparisons; their minds are made up.

Brand insistence can be strong. A shopper may have decided, after considerable thought, that only Wedgwood china and Waterford crystal will do for the dining room. Sales personnel or additional advertising will not sway such a shopper. This brand preference is important to retailers.

The marketer of a specialty product may develop a marketing mix that includes exclusive distribution of the brand. Dealers stocking S-type Jaguars are few and far between, in part because a potential buyer of such an expensive car will travel a considerable distance to purchase one. Advertising the brand's uniqueness and pricing the cars at a level suitable to, and supportive of, the brand's image are appropriate tactics for the marketer.

As mentioned earlier, Copeland's scheme is a generalized portrayal of consumer goods for the majority of consumers. Unsought purchases, such as the purchase of ambulance services in an emergency, may not fit neatly into this scheme. Furthermore, a particular individual may view some products very differently from most other consumers. Nevertheless, marketers who identify which description best fits their products may use these generalizations to choose appropriate retail outlets and plan other elements of the marketing mix.

Classifying Organizational Products

Organizational products can be categorized in much the same way as consumer products. As Exhibit 9-4 shows, the most commonly used classification system breaks **organizational products** into capital products, production products, and operating products.

CAPITAL PRODUCTS

Capital products consist of installations and accessory equipment. Installations are major capital items necessary to the manufacture of a final product. Buildings and facilities, assembly lines, heating plants, and other such major purchases are included in this category. Many of these products are made to order, such as an

Specialty product
A consumer product that is not bought frequently, is likely to be expensive, and is generally purchased with great care.

Organizational product
A product or service that is used to produce other products and/or to operate an organization.

In Germany, Stover Pommes Frites is McDonald's supplier of french fries. The company purchases capital products to perform its production operations.

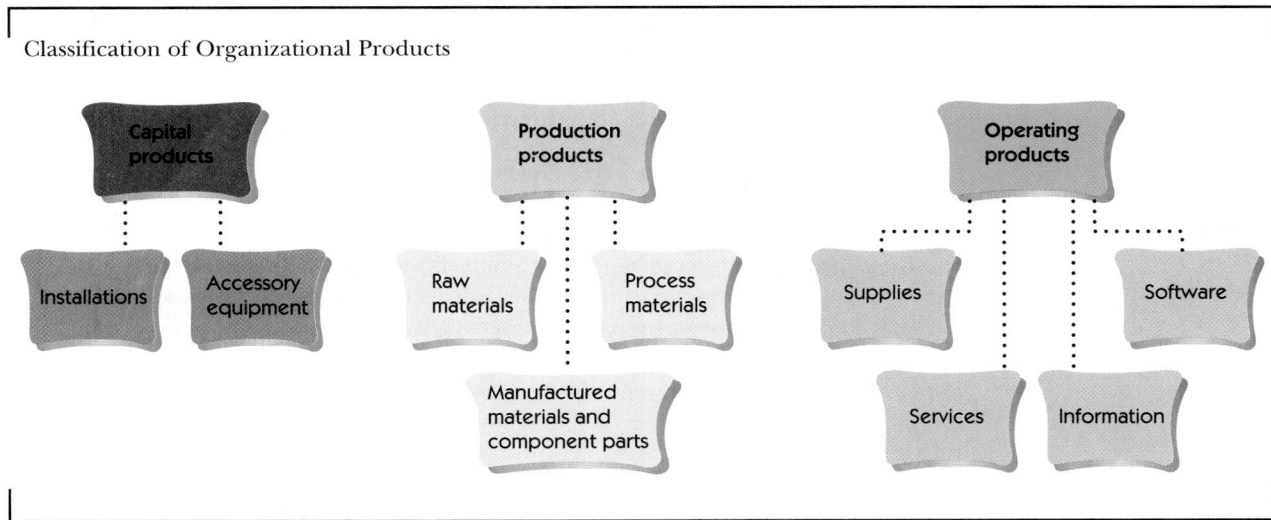

Classification of Organizational Products

air-conditioning system for a factory. Accessory equipment facilitates an organization's operations. Generally included in this category are such things as pickup trucks, forklifts, desktop computers, and copying machines. These items, as a rule, do not involve as large a capital outlay as installations. They are not generally thought of as being specially built to do only one job, although a product such as a pickup truck can be modified to handle specialized tasks.

PRODUCTION PRODUCTS

Production products can be subdivided into raw materials, manufactured materials and component parts, and process materials. Raw materials are organizational products that are still very close to their natural states—that is, they have undergone almost no processing. Bars of aluminum, chunks of granite that will be made into statuary, and trees to be made into lumber or paper are good examples. Manufactured materials and component parts are a step above raw materials in the processing chain. Manufactured materials, such as fabric, thread, and yarn, are created by transforming raw materials. Manufactured materials are used as basic ingredients for producing a company's products. Component parts have been processed even more. They include screws, computer chips, and parts of all sorts that end up in a finished product. To a lawn-mower manufacturer, spark plugs, wires, and bushings are all component parts. Notice that unlike raw materials, manufactured materials and component parts have undergone considerable processing. Process materials are used in making finished products but do not become part of these products. An example is an acid used to soak dirt and grime off machine parts.

OPERATING PRODUCTS

Operating products are the closest thing to a convenience good in the organizational products classification scheme. Operating supplies include paper, pencils, brooms, envelopes, light bulbs, and other short-lived stock items that an organization routinely buys and uses up as it operates. Software refers to standard computer packages that can be used by any organization. Microsoft PowerPoint, Adobe Illustrator, and Shockwave are examples. Services may be broadly defined as work provided by others. Thus, operating services include everything from janitorial services and machinery maintenance to the services of lawyers, accountants, and medical providers. Information consists of news, data, and knowledge pertinent to the operation of the business.

At first glance, this system may appear to be more product-oriented and less buyer-oriented than Copeland's plan. However, the categories do reflect buyer concerns as major business purchases, such as the acquisition of a new factory building or a computerized assembly system, involve different problems and buyer concerns than do purchases of brooms and sweeping compounds. In this sense, the categories of organizational products are buyer-oriented.

The Product Line and the Product Mix

In discussing consumer and organizational products, we have treated each product type separately, as if a given organization offered just one **product item**—that is, one particular version of a specific good or service. In reality, most organizations market more than one product. Even an industrial cleaning company, whose product would appear to be simply "cleaning," offers an array of services. Does the client want a daily cleanup or a weekly one? Did the client hire the company to do a once-a-year major cleaning or to clean up after some remodeling work? Does the customer want the windows washed? What the cleaning firm has to offer is, in fact, a product line.

From a marketing perspective, then, a firm's **product line** is a group of products that are fairly closely related. At Procter & Gamble, for example, products in a line perform some particular function; product lines include a food products line, a paper products line, a cleaning products line, and a cosmetic products line. Alternatively, a product line may be identified as a group of products that are sold to the same customer groups. A few years ago, Black & Decker, a company that

dominates the mass market for power tools sold in stores like Kmart, found it was losing ground at residential construction sites, where crew members use more profitable, high-end, durable tools. So Black & Decker introduced its DeWalt professional and industrial power-tool line, which consists of 30 drills, saws, and sanders to appeal to this market. Yet another way a product line may be identified is by price or

quality. Kraft's pizza division divides its packaged pizza products into three lines based on price. Its cheaper Tombstone brand products are distinct from its middle-tier DiGiorno brand and its more expensive California brand. The phrase *depth of product line* refers to the number of different product items offered in a product line. For example, Louis Rich's food product line has grown to include several variations: turkey franks, turkey bologna, turkey pastrami, and several other lunch meats made of turkey. All these items are closely related, because they are all in the same product category. A line such as this has considerable depth.

The products that constitute a company's various product lines may be similar only in a broad sense, such as **product class**. Clairol's hair-coloring line is somewhat different from its shampoo and conditioner line and certainly different from its line of hair dryers, curlers, and other appliances.

A really diversified marketing organization may offer several product classes and define its various product lines in many ways. A **product mix** encompasses all offerings of the organization, no matter how unrelated they may be. General Motors Corporation manufactures and sells large, medium, and small cars, as well

Product item
A specific version of a particular good or service.

Product line
A group of products that are fairly closely related. The number of different items in a product line determines the depth of the product line.

Kraft's pizza product line includes Tombstone, DiGiornio, and California pizza brands.

Product class
A broad group of products that differ somewhat but perform similar functions or provide similar benefits—for example, all automobiles made for personal use.

Product mix
All the product offerings of an organization, no matter how unrelated. The number of product lines within a product mix determines the width of the product mix. A wide mix has a high diversity of product types; a narrow mix has little diversity.

Quidel Corporation Walk into an Osco drugstore, and on a shelf near the ovulation testing kits you'll find Conceive brand pregnancy tests. A cherubic infant smiles at you from the pink box. Price: $9.99.

A little farther down the aisle, and near the condoms, you'll find another pregnancy test, called RapidVue. The package features no smiling baby, just brick-red lettering against a mauve background. Price: $6.99.

Both tests are products of San Diego–based Quidel Corp.—and they are identical except for the packaging. What's different is the market. "The market definitely divides between the women who want babies and those who don't," explains Quidel Chief Executive Steven Frankel. He explains why the smiling baby sells for more than the plain-wrapper product: "It's like what Charles Revson said about cosmetics: People buy hope. In our case, they pay more for hope than for possible relief."[4]

as buses, Army tanks, locomotive engines, and a wide range of parts and other products. Other organizations are similarly diversified. The phrase *width of product mix* is used to identify the extent of the product lines associated with one firm, no matter how diverse or narrow they may be. You might be surprised to discover just how varied the product mix of a firm like Chesebrough-Ponds, Beatrice Foods, or Procter & Gamble really is.

The Marketer's Product Portfolio

Just as the investor or financial advisor seeks to assemble a group of stocks or other investments that form a sound total package, so the marketing manager can view the product mix as a collection of items to be balanced as a group—a **product portfolio**. A balanced product mix might contain some good old standby products, some new products that have already shown promise, and some products in R&D that may be a bit risky but have a high payoff potential. The marketing manager considers the interrelationships and cash flows for the complete mix of products rather than concentrating on the isolated problems of the individual members of that mix. Evaluation of a company's or strategic business unit's product mix is called product portfolio analysis.

> The marketing manager considers the interrelationships and cash flows for the complete mix of products rather than concentrating on the isolated problems of the individual members of that mix.

Product portfolio
A collection of products to be balanced as a group. Product portfolio analysis focuses on the interrelationships of products within a product mix. The performance of the mix is emphasized rather than the performance of individual products.

PRODUCT PORTFOLIO ANALYSIS

Product portfolio analysis as envisioned by the Boston Consulting Group is illustrated in Exhibit 9-5. The horizontal scale depicts the market share as high or low. On the vertical scale, the same words refer to the market growth rate. The combinations of these variables yield four quadrants:

High-market-share product in a high-growth market

High-market-share product in a low-growth market

Low-market-share product in a high-growth market

Low-market-share product in a low-growth market

To put this in perspective, let's assign some picturesque names and familiar products to each of the matrix cells. The market for software products that process streaming media is high growth, and RealPlayer has a high market share.

The Product Portfolio

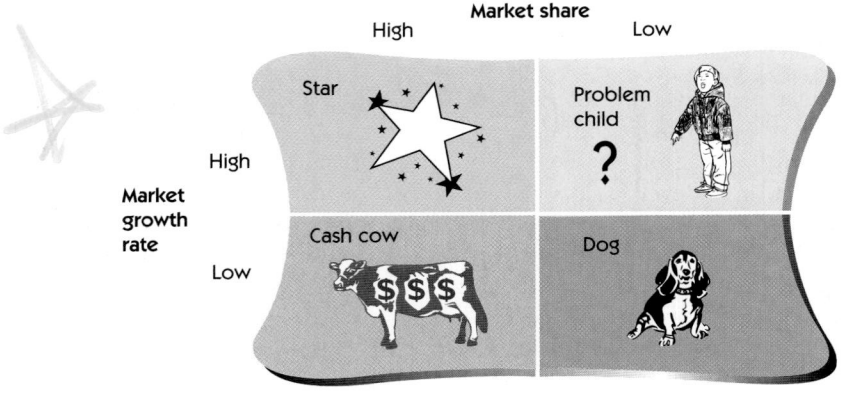

It is a **star**. The canned-meat market is low growth, and Spam has a high market share. It is a **cash cow**. The market for DVD players is growing rapidly, and Aiwa has a low market share. A product in a high-growth market that seems to be having trouble picking up market share is, for its marketers, a **problem child**, or a question mark. The facial-soap market is low growth, and Palmolive has a low market share. It is a **dog**.

Clearly, every company would like to market a star. But cash cows also have their value. Although Spam may not be part of an exciting and growing market, for example, it does make a lot of money for Hormel. This product and other cash cows are likely to have been popular for years and to generate cash flow. Excess monies generated by the cows can be used to finance the growth of products the organization hopes will become stars or to correct problems causing a product to be a problem child.

Some marketing experts believe organizations should get rid of dogs to free themselves to concentrate on more profitable projects, but such an approach cannot work for every organization. Not every product can be a star, and dogs can have their uses. They might be profitable in the sense that they contribute to meeting overhead and administrative expenses. Furthermore, products with low shares of low-growth markets may continue to appeal to customers who have special needs or who buy primarily on the basis of price. Many brewers, for example, continue to market low-priced beers that appeal to bargain hunters. The investment made in marketing these products is small. If there are no advertising costs and no expenses incurred in improving the product, the brand that is simply placed on the shelf for sale may be profitable. A dog may occupy a safe and secure market niche in which there are few challenges from competitors.

LIMITATIONS OF PRODUCT PORTFOLIO ANALYSIS

The product portfolio concept does have limitations. The first is that it may give the inexperienced student of marketing an unjustified feeling of security. Simply placing the names of products in the appropriate quadrants on a chart is not appropriate application of the portfolio concept; that merely helps to describe the portfolio. When the matrix has been formed, the marketing manager's difficult

Star
A high-market-share product in a high-growth market.

Cash cow
A high-market-share product in a low-growth market.

Problem child
A low-market-share product in a high-growth market.

Dog
A low-market-share product in a low-growth market.

decisions are only beginning. If you have a star, is competition desperately trying to knock it down? Probably. So what steps come next? If you have a cash cow, how vulnerable is it to competition? Wouldn't the competitors like to have a cow of their own? They certainly would. How about the dogs? Should you sell them off? Who would buy them? Should you hold on to them because no competitor seems to be addressing their limited target markets? How can that be done so as to maximize the cash flow? How much are you willing to spend trying to make the problem child into a star?

A second overriding problem that the portfolio concept only begins to address is the reality of the marketplace and of human nature. On the surface, the portfolio suggests that the marketing manager should work hard either to turn problem children into stars or to develop stars in some other way. However, keeping up a steady flow of stars is difficult, to say the least. The Etch-A-Sketch has been the staple of Ohio Art's toy line for more than 40 years. Although Ohio Art has a cash cow, the company has not been very successful in developing additional items in the star category, and its profits have been declining in recent years. Many organizations and their marketing managers are tempted to build up the cows to make sure they retain a high market share. Often, however, competition or other environmental forces may block the development of stars with money produced by cash cows.

Branding—What's in a Name?

According to legend, the practice of branding products originated when an ancient ruler decided that products should bear some sort of symbol so that, if something should go wrong, buyers and the authorities would know who was to blame. Forced to identify their products with themselves, the story goes, producers began to take greater pride in their products and to make them better than those of their competitors, thus reversing the negative intent of the king's order. Whether the story is true or not, it makes the point that branding serves many purposes, both for the buyer and for the seller.

Branding helps buyers to determine which manufacturers' products are to be avoided and which are to be sought. Without branding, a buyer would have difficulty recognizing products that have proved satisfactory in the past. Many consumers are not able to analyze competing items strictly on the basis of physical characteristics. They rely, therefore, on a brand's or firm's reputation as an assurance that the product being purchased meets certain standards. For example, the computer chip marketer's "Intel Inside" stickers on personal computers offer consumers reassurance when they feel confusion and anxiety about making a computer purchase.

> A brand that has earned a reputation for high quality may pave the way for the introduction of new products.

Branding helps sellers to develop loyal customers and to show that the firm stands behind what it offers. A brand that has earned a reputation for high quality may pave the way for the introduction of new products. Part of the attraction of Kellogg's Honey Crunch Corn Flakes, for example, is its connection with the original Kellogg's Corn Flakes, a branded product with a long record of public acceptance.

In large measure, the free enterprise system, with its accent on letting the market decide which firms will succeed and which will fail, depends on branding. Even societies that have tried to do away with branding, such as China, have found that citizens somehow determine which products are good and which are bad, even if they have to use product serial numbers or other bits of information to differentiate among products.

Brand
An identifying feature that distinguishes one product from another; more specifically, any name, term, symbol, sign, or design, or a unifying combination of these.

Brand name
The verbal part of a brand—the part that can be spoken or written.

Brand mark
A unique symbol that is part of a brand.

Logo
A brand name or company name written in a distinctive way; short for logotype.

Trademark
A legally protected brand name or brand mark. Its owner has exclusive rights to its use. Trademarks are registered with the U.S. Patent and Trademark Office.

Despite the common practice of speaking of brands, brand names, and trademarks as if all these terms meant the same thing, there are some technical differences among them.

Brands   A **brand** is any name, term, symbol, sign, design, or unifying combination of these. A **brand name** is the verbal part of the brand. For example, Sega, Cover Girl, and America Online are brands. When these words are spoken or written, they are brand names. Many branded goods and services rely heavily on some symbol for identification. Merrill Lynch, a stockbroker, makes considerable use of an image of a bull, and Microsoft Windows is represented by a window that materializes out of an expanding pattern of rectangles floating to its left. Such unique symbols are referred to as **brand marks**. A brand name or company name written in a distinctive way—for example, *Coca-Cola* written in white script letters on a red background—is called a **logo**, short for *logotype*.

Trademarks   A brand or brand name can be almost anything a marketer wants it to be, but it does not have any legal status. A **trademark**, on the other hand, is a legally protected brand name or brand mark. The owners of trademarks have exclusive rights to their use. Thus, the word *trademark* is a legally defined term. Either a brand name is a registered trademark or it is not.

The registered trademark gives a marketer proprietary rights to exclusive use of a symbol or name. The NBC peacock is a registered trademark. So is the name Coca-Cola, the script style in which it is written, and the product's distinctive bottle design. Since the holder of a trademark has exclusive rights to use the trademarked name or symbol, a certain amount of protection is provided to the trademark holder. The name Ball Park Frankfurters is a registered trademark, so

Mercedes' star symbol is a brand mark that is strongly associated with the company's products. Because the symbol is so powerful, this advertisement features only the brand mark and a single word tied to the Mercedes brand. Use of the word *Mercedes* is not necessary.

http://www.mercedes-benz.com

Innovation

Pizza Hut had not changed its brand mark for many years. When the pizza restaurant decided to update its brand mark, it realized the importance of capitalizing on its unique "red roof" symbol. The new brand mark symbolically communicates the casual and enjoyable eating experience provided at Pizza Hut. The vibrant green and yellow colors are intended to reflect freshness and fun.

Service mark
A symbol that identifies a service. It distinguishes a service in the way a trademark identifies a good.

Generic name
A brand name so commonly used that it is part of everyday language and is used to describe a product class rather than a particular manufacturer's product.

no other franks with that name are likely to appear on the market. There is even some protection against similar names, if a legal authority can be induced to agree that the similarity is great enough to constitute an infringement of the original trademark. That's why a small grocery store with a coffee cart called Federal Expresso heard from lawyers representing Federal Express.

Service Marks **Service marks** provide the same identifying function for services that trademarks provide for goods. Like brands, they can be legally protected by registration. The NBC chimes and GM's Mr. Goodwrench are thus legally protected. Service marks may also include slogans like "Fly the Friendly Skies of United."

GENERIC NAMES

Some words are so obviously part of everyday language that no one should be permitted to use them exclusively. These **generic names** describe products or items in terms that are part of our standard vocabulary—for example, *flower* and *cat food*. Other words and terms, such as *nylon, kerosene, escalator, cellophane,*

e-commerce | Changing Everything

Simply registering an address on the Internet does not establish the owner's right to receive trademark protection. According to the Ninth Circuit U.S. Court of Appeals, a domain name must be used publicly to sell goods or services in order to be protected.

Brookfield Communications, which sells entertainment news to the film industry, took legal action against West Coast Entertainment, a video rental chain with more than 500 stores. West Coast registered the domain name Moviebuff.com in 1996, more than 18 months before Brookfield used the name to market a software database providing information about the film and television industries. Even though West Coast had used the name first, Brookfield claimed it had the right to Moviebuff.com. It argued that West Coast's use of the domain name failed to satisfy a requirement under trademark law that a trademark be used to promote a service or good. The Ninth Circuit ruled that trademark rights are not conveyed through mere intent to use a name commercially.

The decision means that West Coast may not use the domain name Moviebuff.com to promote its Web site offering movie reviews, news, and industry commentary. The ruling provides crucial guidance to the countless companies that are aggressively building online identities. Companies generally obtain the right to do business under a given name by being the first to use it. But the three-judge panel's decision on the requirements for establishing an online brand goes further. "Registration . . . does not in itself constitute 'use' for purposes of acquiring trademark priority." Federal law "grants trademark protection only to brand names that are used to identify and to distinguish goods or services in commerce—which typically occurs when a brand name is used in conjunction with the actual sale of goods or services."[5]

and *formica*, were originally invented to name particular products but have become legally generic through common usage. Therefore, the 3M Company can call its tape Scotch brand cellophane tape but can no longer claim that it is the one and only cellophane tape. In many instances, a brand name becomes a generic term when a judge determines that a word, such as *formica*, is in such common usage that the original formulator of the word can no longer hold the right to it.

It is because valuable brand names can and do become legally generic that Muzak advertisements stress that there is only one Muzak, with a capital M. Rollerblade advertisements call attention to the fact that Rollerblade is a brand name and it is technically incorrect to use "rollerblading" as a verb. Coca-Cola exerts every effort to make certain that you do not get a Pepsi when you ask a waiter for a Coke. Vaseline, Kleenex, Frisbee, and other commonly used names—names that are in fact employed to mean a generic product class—may one day be legally declared generic.

One clever marketer of waterproof, all-purpose sealing tape turned the generic issue around. An executive at Manco recognized that most customers pronounced the generic *duct* tape as "duck" tape. So the company registered the trademark Duck brand tape and used a friendly yellow duck as its brand symbol. Today, it is the market leader for this product.

WHAT MAKES A "GOOD" BRAND NAME?

What constitutes a good brand name? Instant Ocean, a synthetic sea salt for use in aquariums, has a good brand name. It is easy to remember. It is easy to say. It is pronounceable, at least in English, in only one way. It has a positive connotation. And it suggests what the product is supposed to do. Irish Spring deodorant soap, Orange Crush soda, and QuickSnap cameras from Fuji are also excellent names in that they associate the product with an image that is meaningful to consumers. Brand names also are often useful in reinforcing an overall product concept. Brands like Land O' Lakes butter, L'Eggs, Duracell, Moist and Easy, and Nature Made may communicate product attributes far better than any other variable in the marketing mix.

Notice that brand names and symbols say something about the product. Jiffy cake mix is quick. Ocean Freeze fish are fresh-frozen. Toast 'Em Pop-Ups tells both what they are and how to cook them. Spic and Span, Dustbuster, and Beautyrest tell what to expect from these products. But brand names also say something about the buyers for whom the products are intended. Right Guard Xtreme Sport is a deodorant for active young guys who try to realize their per-

periods when a high cost of living puts pressure on household budgets, many no-frills products make gains in supermarket sales, particularly in such product categories as fabric softeners, canned green beans, and facial tissues. Even among some products for which brand identity is a major factor influencing purchases, such as cosmetics and beer, generics have had a modest success. Many of the same factors that encourage manufacturers to supply distributors with private brands encourage them to produce generic goods.

FAMILY BRANDS AND INDIVIDUAL BRANDS

Family branding, or *umbrella branding,* involves using a single brand name, like Hunt's, Del Monte, or Campbell's, over a whole line of fairly closely related items. The idea of family branding is to take advantage of a brand's reputation and the goodwill associated with the name. Introduction of a new product, such as Snickers Cruncher, is easier because of Snickers's strong brand recognition. Family branding is used by Levi Strauss, General Electric, MCI, and a host of other corporations.

Use of a family branding strategy does not guarantee success in the marketplace. In what was a relatively rare occurrence, a Campbell's product failed despite the Campbell's name. The product was Campbell's Very Own Special Sauce, a prepared spaghetti sauce. Although there may have been many reasons for its failure, the fact that Campbell's name is strongly associated with prepared "American" foods, such as franks and beans, probably was a factor. Most prepared spaghetti sauces on the market bear names like Mama Rosa's and Prego.

Although the failure of its "special" sauce did no serious damage to Campbell's reputation, a product that proves to be dangerous or of poor quality can hurt an organization's overall image. A company's other brands may suffer greatly because of problems with a product of the same name. This is one reason why some firms use individual brand names rather than family brand names. An **individual brand** is not shared by other products in that line.

Besides the motive just mentioned, marketers adopt the individual branding strategy for several other reasons. For one, the products produced by a company might differ substantially from one another. Kraft Foods markets Maxwell House regular coffee, as well as General Foods International flavored instant coffees. An organization may believe that its products are different enough that not much can be gained by identifying the products with one another.

Some organizations practice the individual branding approach because they wish to market several products that appeal to different market segments. There are, for example, many individual brands of detergents within the detergent lines of Procter & Gamble, Lever Brothers, and Colgate-Palmolive. Some contain bleaching crystals; some have fabric softeners; some have extra whitening power; some have extra strength; some have low suds; and so on.

Often, the reason a firm markets many individual brands in a product category is the belief that it is better to lose business to another of its own brands than to

Family branding
The practice of using a single brand name to identify different items in a product line; also known as *umbrella branding.*

Individual brand
A brand that is assigned to a product within a product line and is not shared by other products in that line.

As described in Chapter 7, VeriSign is a "trust services" company. It's digital certificates verify that people or digital communications are who or what they claim to be, allowing for safer communication and e-commerce activities where security and access control are needed. Over 150,000 Web sites have purchased the company's digital certificates, and nearly 4 million individuals have been issued certificates for use in online surfing and buying. All Fortune 500 companies with a Web presence and all of the top 40 electronic commerce Web sites use VeriSign digital certificate services.

Digitalme is a new identity management technology, developed by Novell, that brings a new level of convenience, freedom, and control to the Web for individual consumers. Digitalme empowers consumers to take control of how their personal information is shared, used, and maintained on the Net.

Working together, VeriSign and Novell are offering consumers a co-branded Digitalme member card linked to a VeriSign digital certificate. The combination of VeriSign's recognized trust services and the convenience of Digitalme enables consumers and businesses alike to share, use, and maintain personal information on the Internet with confidence. This new service is enabling consumers and businesses across the Internet to build authenticated and trusted online communities.[7]

lose business to another company's brand. The Mars Company, for example, offers Snickers, Milky Way, Three Musketeers, M&Ms, and many other candies. The matter of shelf space comes into play here. A retailer may have room to display only 25 individual brands of candy bars. If 15 of them are Mars brands, the chances that a customer will select a Mars product are obviously much improved.

Marketers sometimes use a combination of family branding and individual branding strategies. The Kellogg's name is featured on Apple Jacks, Frosted Mini Wheats, Rice Krispies, and many other cereals whose brand names differ. The Willy Wonka name and brand mark appear on packages of candies with more exotic names, including Everlasting Gobstopper, Oompas, Dinasour Eggs, Mix-ups, and Volcano Rocks. Some marketers refer to these as *sub-brands*.

CO-BRANDING

Co-branding
The use of two individual brands on a single product.

Co-branding is the use of two individual brands on a single product. For example, Kraft Foods combines its Oscar Mayer Lunchables brand with the Taco Bell brand for tacos and nachos. General Mills' Count Chocula cereal package features the Hershey's brand name because the cereal is made with real Hershey's cocoa. In credit card marketing, MasterCard does almost 30 percent of its business with co-branded cards, many of which are affinity programs. An *affinity program* targets individuals who are inclined to behave in similar ways because they share an interest or a common background, such as alumni of Southern Illinois University. Co-branding partners should be carefully evaluated to make sure their combined effect will be positive rather than negative.

Co-branding is the use of two individual brands on a single product. Pillsbury's Moist Supreme cake with Jell-O Pudding in the mix is an example of co-branding.

http://www.pillsbury.com

BUTTER RECIPE CAKE MIX
with Artificial Butter Flavor
Pillsbury MOIST Supreme®
JELL-O® Pudding in the Mix
Irresistibly MOIST
1 LB. 2.25 OZ. (517g)

LICENSING

A product's greatest strength may be an intangible quality or the symbols associated with it. Binney and Smith, for example, has learned that its brand name Crayola and the Crayola logo are valuable assets that other companies may want to use. When a brand name like Crayola, Harley-Davidson, or Disney adds value to a product,

FAO Schwarz

it is said to have brand equity. **Brand equity** means that market share or profit margins are greater because of the goodwill associated with the brand.

Brand equity may be a company's strongest asset. High brand equity often indicates that the brand can be effectively used on other products. Thus, the company may enter into a **licensing agreement** with another firm so that the second firm can use the company's trademark. The proliferation of Garfield, South Park, and other trademarks from newspapers, movies, and television programs is the result of licensing.

Packaging

A package is basically an extension of the product offered for sale. In fact, the package is often more important than the product it contains. Consider the Glue Stic and IncrEdibles, frozen macaroni and cheese in microwaveable cylinders, similar to push-up ice cream packages. These packages are more than simple containers. They offer considerable consumer benefits.

Packages perform many functions. They contain a product and protect it until the consumer is ready to use it. Beyond this, packages facilitate the storage and use of products. (Think again about the Glue Stic container.) Thus, packages should be designed for ease of handling.

Consumers often identify products by their packages. Because distinctive packages on a shelf can attract attention, they can play a major part in promotional strategy. For example, the Good Stuff company markets oval pieces of cedar that help keep moths away from woolen clothing in closets and drawers. The wood chunks are called Sweater Eggs and are packaged in egg cartons. The packaging lends charm to the product and reinforces the brand name. A package on the retailer's shelf may be surrounded by ten or more other packages competing for consumers' attention. In these days of self-service, every package design must attract attention and convey an easily identifiable image. The package must have *shelf impact*. It must tell consumers what the product is and why they should buy it.

Today, environmental considerations may also strongly influence packaging decisions. Packaging waste is piling up, and many industries, such as the fast-food industry, try to make all packaging biodegradable or easy to recycle.

In summary, **packaging** provides a containment function, a protection-in-transit function, a storage function, a usage facilitation function, a promotion function, and an ecological function. Designing packaging thus involves making many decisions, including decisions about labels, inserts, instructions for use, graphic design, and shipping cartons, as well as decisions about the sizes and types of physical containers for individual product items within the outer package.

LABELING—TELLING ABOUT THE PRODUCT

The paper or plastic sticker attached to a can of peas or a mustard jar is technically called a **label**. But as packaging technology improves and cans and bottles become less prominent, labels become incorporated into the protective aspects of the package. In the case of a box of frozen broccoli, for example, a good portion of the vegetable's protection comes from the label, which is more properly called, in this case, the *wrapper*.

Whether the label is a separate entity affixed to a package or is, in effect, the package itself, it must perform certain tasks. It carries the brand name and information concerning the contents of the package, such as cooking instructions and information relating to safe and proper use of the product. A label may also carry instructions for the proper disposal of the product and its package, or at least a plea to consumers to avoid littering. The label must contain any specific nutritional information, warnings, or legal restrictions required by law. Some labels, such as those of Procter & Gamble, also give a toll-free telephone number that customers with ideas or complaints can use. Consumers' calls are a major source of Procter & Gamble's product improvement ideas.

Most consumer packaged goods are labeled with an appropriate **Universal Product Code (UPC)**, an array of black bars readable by optical scanners. The advantages of the UPC—which allow computerized checkout and compiling of computer-generated sales volume information—have become clear to distributors, retailers, and consumers in recent years.

GLOBAL IMPLICATIONS AND LEGAL GUIDELINES FOR PACKAGING

Package designers are relatively free to develop package designs. However, when the package will be used in several countries, marketers must determine whether to use a single package with one language, a single package with two or more languages, or multiple packages tailored to the separate countries. Decisions about use of colors and symbols, protection in transit over long distances, and other aspects of package design should be made only after local culture and usage patterns have been considered.

In particular, a company must follow the legal guidelines and requirements of each country where its product will be marketed. For example, the European Union requires that 90 percent of packaging waste by weight be recoverable through recycling or other uses. In the United States, package designers must follow state and local laws, such as those requiring that soft drink bottles be clearly labeled as returnable. In Germany, recyclable packages display a green dot, signifying that these packages can be disposed of in special recycling bins issued by the government.

Many countries have laws about deceptive packaging. Packages intentionally designed to mislead consumers, labels that bear false or misleading information, or packages that do not provide required warnings soon draw the attention of the Federal Trade Commission, some other official body, or consumer groups.

Product Warranties

A **product warranty** communicates a written guarantee of a product's integrity and outlines the manufacturer's responsibility for repairing or replacing defective parts. It may substantially reduce the risks the buyer perceives to be associated with the purchase.

Unfortunately, consumers often find that warranties are difficult-to-understand documents written in legal jargon. Several manufacturers have made use of this fact by offering warranties advertised as simple, short, plain-English documents. Marketers who have not taken this approach may not realize that terms like *fully guaranteed, unconditionally guaranteed,* and *lifetime guarantee* don't mean much to many buyers, especially buyers who have been disappointed with the service received on other guaranteed products.

Some of the difficulties associated with warranties were resolved by the **Magnuson-Moss Warranty Act** of 1975. This law requires that any guarantees provided by sellers be made available to buyers prior to purchase of the product. It also grants power to the Federal Trade Commission to specify the manner and form in which guarantees may be used in promotional material. Further, the act stipulates that a warranty must use simple language and disclose precisely who the warrantor is. The warranty must indicate clearly what products or parts of products are covered by the terms of the warranty and which are excluded. The act also specifies what the warrantor is obliged to do in the event of a product defect, how long the warranty applies, and what obligations the buyer has.

A warranty is part of the total product; the seller should not view it as a nuisance. Effective marketers use the warranty as an opportunity to create satisfied customers and to offer an intangible product attribute that many buyers desire.

As a result of the increase in lawsuits, some labels carry warnings that seem silly. The purchaser of a Batman or Superman costume may read the following warning: "Cape does not enable user to fly."

Magnuson-Moss Warranty Act
Federal law requiring that guarantees provided by sellers be made available to buyers before they purchase and that the guarantees specify who the warrantor is, what products or parts of products are covered, what the warrantor must do if the product is defective, how long the warranty applies, and the obligations of the buyer.

Customer Service
Our earlier discussion identified customer service as one element of the product mix. Effective marketers, knowing that marketing does not end with the sale of goods, may create a competitive advantage by emphasizing the amount and quality of customer services. For example, Southwestern Bell offers Internet Services DSL technical support by phone (1-800-NET-HELP) 24 hours a day, 7 days a week. Customers can talk with a staff of experts about technical issues, system status, and other problems.

Delivery services, gift wrapping, repairs, and other customer services all help marketers compete. These services, as auxiliary dimensions of the product, create and maintain goodwill. They provide an opportunity to enhance consumer satisfaction with the total product. The following sections provide a complete discussion of the product strategies for pure services and for tangible goods with a high service component.

Services Are Products Too!
At the beginning of this chapter, we defined a product as a bundle of benefits. This definition holds as well for services as for tangible goods. Services are tasks or activities performed for buyers or intangibles that cannot be handled or examined before purchase.

Services differ in their nature and in the reasons consumers purchase them. Consumers purchase *instrumental services*—typically, work performed by others—to achieve a goal without direct involvement in the task. For example, a lawn care company provides an instrumental service. In contrast, a store that rents videotapes of movies provides a *consummatory service;* the consumer is directly involved and immediately gratified by use of the service. Taking a skiing lesson may be both instrumental and consummatory. The ski instructor performs an instructional task for the student, and the student receives gratification as the service is consumed.

Characteristics of Services

Both instrumental and consummatory services have the following characteristics: (1) intangibility, (2) perishability, (3) inseparability, and (4) heterogeneity. Marketing strategies associated with each of these service characteristics are discussed next.

INTANGIBILITY

Services are intangible, even though the production of a service may be linked to a tangible product. (The transportation service an airline provides is tied to its fleet of airplanes, renting a videotaped movie is tied to the temporary use of the videocassette, and so on.) The element of intangibility makes the marketing of services different from the marketing of tangible goods. **Intangibility** means that buyers normally cannot see, feel, smell, hear, or taste a service before they conclude an exchange agreement with a seller. Because of this intangibility, consumers may misunderstand the exact nature of a service. For most of us, the idea of something intangible is harder to grasp than something tangible, and evaluating the quality of something intangible is difficult. To help consumers understand and evaluate the nature of their services, marketers often employ a marketing strategy to make the intangible tangible.

It can be argued that because of a service's intangibility, customers purchasing a service purchase promises of satisfaction.[8] Thus, implementing a strategy to make a service tangible requires stressing symbolic clues or providing supplemental tangible evidence to indicate that promises about a service's quality will be kept. This can be done in a number of ways. It may be as simple as polishing the brass railings on the bar to symbolically enhance a restaurant's atmosphere. Prominently displaying a brand name and logo on the organization's letterhead, facilities, and equipment or highlighting them in advertising and sales promotion efforts are other subtle ways to associate a tangible symbol with a service. Celebrity spokespersons are sometimes used to create confidence that the service marketer is committed to the promise of satisfaction. Promotional messages also often portray the people who provide the service to make the service more tangible. Allstate's slogan "You're in good hands with Allstate" promotes the idea that the people and the company are reliable. You can see for yourself that these are good people, the ads imply; if they promise something, you can rely on the promise being fulfilled. And as the Mr. Goodwrench campaign for GM's service illus-

Intangibility
The characteristic of services referring to the customer's inability to see, hear, smell, feel, or taste the service product.

Customers—who cannot taste, feel, or smell an intangible service in advance—purchase promises of satisfaction. The Chicago Cubs organization makes its service tangible by stressing symbolic clues, such as the familiar entrance to the "friendly confines" of Wrigley Field, and by providing supplemental tangible evidence, such as free baseball caps on special promotional days.

http://www.cubs.com

trates, an entire marketing program may be developed to provide tangible symbols that the promise of good service will be kept. Effectively marketing intangibles, then, relies on developing a symbolic appearance of competency and credibility. Consumers should believe that what is promised will be delivered.

The strategy of creating tangibility through symbols is typically implemented with branding and through the promotion mix. However, service marketers often tie physical goods to their services to provide additional tangible evidence of the promised service. A health club membership comes with a membership card, for example, and a dentist's gift of a toothbrush is evidence that a dental service has been performed.

e—commerce Changing Everything

When you think about it, establishing a service relationship online isn't all that different from starting a dating relationship. The problem is that a lot of Internet companies approach their first date with a list of 20 questions: "Could you please fill out this three-page form about your income, family history, and medical background?" Imagine if that were the first question that a prospective romantic interest asked you! It's absurd to expect people to respond to such questions before you've established a certain level of trust with them.

Instead, what if you started by asking a customer three or four little questions? After establishing that this potential "date" is interested in what you have to offer, you and this customer could begin sharing information back and forth. . . . A San Francisco startup called myplay is wooing customers with a similar approach. The site is an online personal storage locker for customers' favorite music. When you first sign up, myplay sends you a few preliminary questions. Then, using your answers to those questions, it customizes your locker. The site asks you a few more questions each time it contacts you. Over time, the company gets to know you, and you get to know—and to trust—the company.

It's Human Psychology 101, and the rules are no different in the Internet space from what they are anywhere else. You must establish a certain level of trust: You need to prove to me that you're not going to misuse any of my information, and then you need to show me that you'll deliver service and value in return—and then I'll tell you more.[9]

PERISHABILITY

Leo Burnett, the founder of a major advertising agency, said, "All our assets go down the elevator every evening." He was referring to the fact that services are perishable; services provided by humans cannot be stored. Thus, if the ability to produce a service exists, but this productive capacity goes unused because demand for the service is low, units of the intangible offering "perish." Consider, for example, an airplane flying from Atlanta to Charleston with half its seats empty. Every minute the plane is in the air, it produces a transport service, which is consumed by the passengers on board. The airline cannot store the service equivalent of the empty seats on that particular flight for later sale. Similarly, no-shows at a dentist's office, empty seats in a movie theater, and a slow night at a restaurant represent cases where all or part of a service supplier's productive capacity has been lost because of **perishability.**

Since perishable services cannot be inventoried, service marketers plan and implement demand management strategies (also called *capacity management strategies*). Demand management involves managing a service's supply so that it is in line with demand. For example, restaurants often hire extra part-time employees to work during peak times and offer price reductions during slow times to even out demand. An effective **demand management strategy,** then, requires the accurate forecasting of the need for services. Because service marketers can't store their products for sale at some other time, they must pay special attention to price adjustments. When prices fall, a dentist's services cannot be warehoused until prices rise again. A hotel owner in Florida cannot suspend operations without considerable cost while waiting for customers to return during the winter season. The service marketer must keep busy and, unlike the marketer of goods, cannot keep busy by building inventory. Pricing strategy provides an important tool for leveling the service marketer's demand.

To adjust for losses from perishability, service marketers often implement **two-part pricing.** The user of or subscriber to the service pays a fixed fee (for example, membership initiation) plus a variable usage fee (for example, tennis court time). Many hotels, restaurants, and airlines sell their services in advance or require reservations to avoid problems associated with perishability. Airlines are

Perishability
The characteristic of services that makes it impossible to store them for later use.

Demand management strategy
A strategy used by service marketers to accurately forecast the need for services so that supply is in line with demand; also called a *capacity management strategy.*

Two-part pricing
A pricing strategy in which the marketer charges a fixed fee plus a variable usage fee, in order to adjust for losses resulting from a service's perishability.

known for overbooking flights, because not all travelers are on time for their flights. When everyone does show up, the airlines offer free tickets or a monetary incentive to individuals willing to take a different flight.

INSEPARABILITY

In marketing tangible goods, the producers (for example, industrial engineers or assembly line workers) need not come in direct contact with those who buy the goods. Because it is possible to separate production from consumption in exchanges involving tangible products, distinct selling and marketing departments evolved naturally to handle the activities aimed at consummating these exchanges. This type of separation is often impossible in marketing intangible services. In many cases, services are inseparable from their producers. **Inseparability** means that producer and consumer must be present in the same place at the same time for the service transaction to occur.

Inseparability changes the sequence of events usually involved in a marketing exchange. In goods marketing, the product is first produced, then sold, and then consumed. Usually, then, producers of tangibles can produce and show or display their offerings. Suppose however, that a patient is to be operated on by a surgeon. Delivering the promised service requires the simultaneous presence of both surgeon and patient. If either is absent, the other is likely to suffer. If the surgeon does not appear, the patient's problem may have to continue for a time, or an unfamiliar surgeon may have to perform the operation. If the patient fails to show up, the surgeon is left with unproductive time and therefore may lose some income. Exhibit 9-7 portrays the different orders for typical goods exchanges and typical service exchanges.

Essentially, inseparability constrains service suppliers' flexibility in designing their offerings, because the amount of service they can produce depends largely on the amount of time they have available. Neither a surgeon nor a hairdresser nor a rock singer can squeeze more than a certain number of operations, haircuts, or live concerts into a given day or month. Inseparability, because it often demands personal contact between buyer and seller, also can cause many distribution problems. Thus, most channels of distribution for services are direct channels in which the service provider markets the product directly to the consumer or organizational user. An accountant, for example, deals directly with a client. (However, it is possible to have intermediaries in the distribution of a service. We discuss such intermediaries in Chapters 11 and 12.)

Because of inseparability, service organizations have been extremely production-oriented in their approach to distribution. For instance, hospitals traditionally had a single location, and their clients were expected to visit the "factory."

Inseparability
A characteristic of services referring to the fact that production often is not distinct from consumption of a service—that is, the producer and the consumer of a service must be together in order for a transaction to occur.

exhib 9-7

The Effect of Inseparability on the Exchange Process

Tangible Products

Production — Sale — Consumption

Time ·················>

Intangible Products

Sale — Production / Consumption

Time ·················>

Today, under more competitive conditions, hospitals realize the need for convenient, multiple locations, emergency care centers, and ambulatory care centers that supplement the main hospital. Similarly, universities traditionally were located in small rural towns, and students came to the service facility to purchase the service. Today, however, universities offer extension programs, telecommunication programs, and classes in urban business centers.

By looking beyond its core service, air transportation, British Airways redefined its view of what an airline does. The company recast its first-class transatlantic service to emphasize what passengers really want—which is to eat and then to sleep. After dining (either on the ground in the first-class lounge or once they get on board), premium flyers can slip into BA pajamas if they wish, put their heads on real pillows, curl up under a small blanket, and then enjoy an interruption-free flight. On arrival, first-class flyers can have breakfast, use comfortable dressing rooms and shower stalls, and even have their clothes pressed before they set off for business.[10]

This production orientation means service providers tend to see themselves more as creators or producers of an offering than as marketers. They tend to accent the pride, technical difficulties, and other elements involved in production instead of understanding the need to satisfy consumers. In other words, many service providers are production-oriented rather than customer-oriented. Overcoming this orientation problem leads to a strategy in which the production process is considered a marketing activity. Thus, managing personnel becomes a marketing activity, because the standards for personnel effectiveness and efficiency must be based on consumers' perceptions, not on assembly line standards.

This leads us to a consideration of the **service encounter**—the period of time during which a consumer interacts with a service provider. A consumer's evaluation of a service offering often depends on evaluation of the physical surroundings and the behavior of the front-line employees during the service encounter. This is true even though production of the service often requires a great deal of time beyond the service encounter. For example, accountants may spend ten times as many hours working on a tax return as they do interacting with the client. But an accountant who accurately computes a client's taxes and then smokes a cigarette during the service encounter with the nonsmoking client may find the client does not return the next year. The tax work was acceptable, but the smoking was not.

Service encounter
A period during which a consumer interacts with a service provider.

Most services are delivered by people. The quality of contact between customers and front-line staff provides a competitive edge, so employees are the key to success. The service marketer must therefore consider employees part of the service offering. The doctor's bedside manner and the personality of a lawyer's receptionist are part of the product offered to consumers. Competent employees must be hired and then trained so that they perform the service properly. They need to know the organization's marketing goals and be trained to serve well and respond to any complaints.

HETEROGENEITY

Because many intangible offerings are closely tied to the supplier's personal performance, there can be great variability, or **heterogeneity,** among the services provided. Standardizing services—that is, reducing service heterogeneity—is difficult. It is not possible to deliver equal amounts of smiling by all employees at a service outlet, medical care of equal quality by several doctors at the same time, or even care of equal quality by the same doctor all the time. When purchasing a service—say, in the form of an airline ticket—the customer can know only in a very general way what to expect from the pilot and flight attendants. Knowing precisely what to expect ahead of time is impossible. Heterogeneity leads service marketers to choose one of two alternative strategies: standardization or customization.

Heterogeneity
The characteristic of services referring to the fact that the quality of delivered services can vary widely.

It's easy to tell employees to do whatever it takes to satisfy a customer, as long as there is no cost. However, Ritz-Carlton's employees are really empowered. The Ritz-Carlton Hotel's employees can spend up to $2,000 to redress a guest grievance. They have permission to break from their routine for as long as needed to make a guest happy. Expensive, perhaps—but customers who have had problems resolved are more loyal than those who didn't have a problem at all.[11]

The Strategy of Standardization   Because of the heterogeneous nature of services, mass marketers may expend a great deal of effort to standardize the services they offer. For example, although a hotel room at the San Francisco Hyatt Regency may be slightly different from a hotel room in the San Antonio Hyatt Regency, the company has made a great attempt to standardize its services. At McDonald's restaurants, all customers receive nearly the same courteous treatment.

In certain situations, it is possible to standardize services by using machines. Thus, automated car washes and electronic funds transfer systems ensure that service quality does not vary.

In general, standardization strategies require strict quality control. Standardization emphasizes careful personnel selection and extensive personnel training. It also emphasizes marketing research to discover if service falls below established standards.

The Strategy of Customization   In contrast to standardization, a customization strategy requires modifying, or customizing, a service for each individual customer. A yacht may be chartered to visit any destination chosen by the customer, for example. A health club's fitness program may be customized to suit the customer's desires and individual physical condition.

The Total Service Product

Earlier in this chapter, we explained that a product should be thought of as consisting of a core product and several auxiliary dimensions. The total product concept applies to goods and services equally well. However, service marketers often face product decisions somewhat different from those facing goods marketers. Service marketers consider participants, physical evidence, and process of service delivery to be the key auxiliary dimensions associated with the marketing of their core services.

For example, the core service marketed by Hertz, a rental car company, is transportation—the temporary use of a car. But Hertz knows its augmented product is

what went right?

KitchenAid   If the customer service representatives answering calls about KitchenAid's mixers seem a little more knowledgeable than the average toll-free talker, it may be because they were actually building the units right before they picked up the phone.

Six of KitchenAid's 30 customer service lines are located at the Greenville, Ohio–based factory where the baking equipment is assembled. Employees who have good work records, pleasant speaking voices, and, no doubt, lots of patience, work 4 hours of their shift on the assembly line and 4 hours operating the help line.

Plant workers who've staffed the phones report feeling better about their own jobs after having made contact with customers who really value the fruits of their labor.

KitchenAid isn't using the assembly line folks in its marketing efforts yet, but it may do so in the future. Who knows? Maybe the workers could start offering up their favorite chocolate chip cookie recipes along with operating instructions.[12]

what differentiates the company from its competitors, so it carefully manages the auxiliary dimensions just mentioned. The attractiveness, dress, and demeanor of participants, such as the rental car counter personnel with whom the customer interacts, are an important part of the marketing mix. Physical evidence—including a modern counter near the baggage claim area, yellow counter signs with the Hertz brand name, the Hertz Number One Club membership cards, and the easy-to-read rental agreement—are other aspects of the marketing mix that can influence perception of the total product. An important auxiliary dimension, process of service delivery, refers to how a service is delivered as opposed to the technical activities required for performance of the core service. Do customers have to wait in long lines or take a crowded shuttle bus before they are given the keys to the car? Problems like these relate to the process of service delivery.

The Role of the Internet in Providing Customer Services

Technology is playing an ever bigger role in the ways customers communicate with businesses. For many organizations, the Internet has revolutionized the nature of customer services. Technology can replace what a human does. For example, in the past, if you wanted to know if your bank had processed one of your checks, you had to call the bank. Today, you can access the bank's Web site to learn your bank balance, which of your checks have been processed, and whether you need to move money from your credit line into your checking account. But in using technology to perform tasks that humans could perform, effective marketers make sure that Internet technology provides an opportunity for service enhancement, not service replacement. For example, the Gateway Computers Web site allows customers who are waiting for their custom-made computers to check the status of their orders as often as they want, any time of the day or night. Offering easy, round-the-clock access enhances Gateway's customer service.

Internet-based customer service can give customers control over all aspects of their interaction with a company through a user-friendly Web site.[13] A FAQ (Frequently Asked Questions) list can be one of the most beneficial customer services on a Web site. Butterball Turkey's Web page provides information about perfect turkey preparation, lists the ten most frequently asked questions about turkey preparation, and—for those who need more help—offers an e-mail address where they can ask a home economist a question. This Internet service sure beats getting a busy signal or holding for a customer service representative on Thanksgiving Day.

> Effective marketers make sure that Internet technology provides an opportunity for service enhancement.

The Internet allows customer service to be personalized. For example, Yahoo! offers a service known as MyYahoo!, a customizable version of the popular portal. When a visitor logs on to MyYahoo!, he or she gets local weather reports, sports scores for teams that are of personal interest, and prices for stock portfolios that the visitor has entered into MyYahoo!'s database.

The speed of customer service can be greatly enhanced by using e-mail. E-mail is an inexpensive way of responding to a complaint or answering a specific consumer question. In addition, many organizations use e-mail to provide other customer services. CNET, which covers the technology industry, sends a daily e-mail listing of headlines and special features to its thousands of subscribers. The Internet news site tries to build brand loyalty by making sure that its readers get the news highlights as quickly as possible.

Internet customer services may both enhance customer service and save the company money. By transferring its package tracking system to the Web, FedEx increased customer satisfaction while significantly reducing expenses. The company saves money by using fewer customer service representatives and spending less on traditional support services such as its telephone service center. A customer can learn about shipments or drop-off locations at his or her own convenience and obtain printed records instantaneously.

Summary

The term *product* refers to both goods and services in the consumer and organizational marketplaces. Products should be broadly defined to include their intangible, as well as their tangible, aspects.

1) Define product and explain why the concept of the total product is important for effective marketing.

Products can be goods, services, ideas, or any other market offering. The total product concept recognizes the many benefits, both tangible and intangible, that each product incorporates. This total product view permits marketers to identify market segments according to benefits received and to adjust products to appeal to those segments.

2) Differentiate among convenience products, shopping products, and specialty products.

Consumer products can be categorized as convenience, shopping, or specialty products. Convenience products are typically inexpensive and are purchased at a convenient location with little shopping effort. Shopping products are purchased after buyers have compared price, quality, and other product attributes. Specialty goods are products for which buyers will accept virtually no substitutes and which they will go to great lengths to obtain.

3) Categorize organizational products.

The three classes of organizational products are capital products, production products, and operating products. Capital products include installations and accessory equipment. Production products include raw materials, manufactured materials and component parts, and process materials. Operating supplies, conventional software, services, and information comprise the operating products category.

4) Explain the difference between product lines and product mixes.

A firm's product line is a group of products that are fairly closely related. The phrase *depth of product line* describes the number of different product items offered in a product line. A firm's product mix encompasses all offerings of the organization, no matter how unrelated they may be. The marketing manager can view the product mix as a product portfolio to be balanced as a group. The product portfolio concept uses relative market share and market growth to identify whether a product is a star, a cash cow, a problem child, or a dog.

5) Understand brand-related terminology, including brand, brand name, brand mark, trademark, manufacturer brand, distributor brand, and family brand.

A brand is a name, term, symbol, sign, or design that distinguishes one product from competing products. A brand name is the verbal part of the brand. A brand mark is a unique symbol used by an organization to identify its product. A trademark is a legally protected brand name or brand mark. Manufacturer, or national, brands are the property of manufacturers; distributor, or private, brands are the property of wholesalers or retailers. A family brand is carried by a group of products with the same brand name.

6) Discuss the characteristics of effective brand names.

Most effective brand names are easy to remember and pronounce, short, and distinctive. They suggest positive associations and images, reinforce the product concept, and communicate product benefits. They may also say something about the user. Finally, they avoid linguistic traps. Proposed new brand names must be researched for market acceptability and possible trademark infringement.

7) Analyze the importance of packaging in the development of an effective product strategy.

Packaging provides a containment function, a protection-in-transit function, a storage function, a usage facilitation function, a promotion function, and an ecological function. In some instances, packages may be as important as the products they contain.

8) Discuss the role of customer service in product strategy.

Marketers can create a competitive advantage by emphasizing the amount and quality of customer services. Delivery, gift wrapping, repair, and other customer services all can be important aspects of a product strategy to create competitive advantage.

9) Discuss the nature of a service product and explain the four basic characteristics of services.

A service is a task or activity performed for buyers or an intangible that cannot be handled or examined before purchase. The four basic characteristics of services are (1) intangibility—buyers cannot normally see, feel, smell, hear, or taste a service before agreeing to buy it; (2) perishability—unused productive capacity disappears in the sense that the provider's time cannot be used again if a customer does not make use of the service; (3) inseparability—the producer and consumer generally must be present at the same time and place, and the provider of the service cannot be separated from the service provided; and (4) heterogeneity—providers of services vary widely in their skills, and even a single provider cannot perform in the same way on every occasion.

10) Discuss product strategies for services.
Service providers cannot store their products for future use, so forecasting and managing demand are

of key importance. Such strategies as altering prices to attract customers during off-season or off-hour times and two-part pricing (using fixed and variable usage fees) exemplify demand management strategies. Standardization strategy attempts to control the inherent heterogeneity of services by such means as automation or strict controls on service-providing personnel. Customization strategy involves modifying the service to fit individual buyers' needs.

Key Terms

auxiliary dimension (p. 226)
brand (p. 238)
brand equity (p. 245)
brand mark (p. 238)
brand name (p. 238)
cash cow (p. 236)
co-branding (p. 244)
convenience product (p. 230)
demand management strategy, or capacity management strategy (p. 249)
distributor brand, or private brand (p. 242)
dog (p. 236)
durable good (p. 229)
family branding (p. 243)
generic name (p. 239)
generic product, or generic brand (p. 242)

heterogeneity (p. 251)
individual brand (p. 243)
inseparability (p. 250)
intangibility (p. 248)
label (p. 246)
licensing agreement (p. 245)
logo (p. 238)
Magnuson-Moss Warranty Act (p. 247)
manufacturer brand, or national brand (p. 241)
nondurable good (p. 229)
organizational product (p. 232)
packaging (p. 246)
perishability (p. 249)
primary characteristic (p. 226)
problem child (p. 236)
product class (p. 234)
product concept (p. 227)

product differentiation (p. 228)
product item (p. 234)
product line (p. 234)
product mix (p. 234)
product portfolio (p. 235)
product strategy (p. 227)
product warranty (p. 246)
service (p. 229)
service encounter (p. 251)
service mark (p. 239)
shopping product (p. 230)
specialty product (p. 232)
star (p. 236)
total product (p. 226)
trademark (p. 238)
two-part pricing (p. 249)
Universal Product Code (UPC) (p. 246)
world brand (p. 242)

Questions for Review & Critical Thinking

1. What is the product concept for each of the following brands?
   a. America Online
   b. Domino's Pizza
   c. Pillsbury Toaster Strudel
   d. MicroSoft Office97
   e. Pelonis Safe-T-Furnace
2. What characteristics distinguish convenience, shopping, and specialty products?
3. Evaluate the following brand names.
   a. Match Light charcoal
   b. Arm & Hammer Pure Baking Soda
   c. Almost Home cookies
   d. Scotch brand videocassettes
   e. Kwik-Kopy printing
   f. Sun-Maid raisin bread
   g. Diehard batteries
   h. Handi-Wrap
4. What are the characteristics of an effective brand name?

5. When is it a good idea to use family branding? Individual brands?
6. What is the service element in each of the following and what are its important characteristics?
   a. A city zoo
   b. Avis car rental
   c. A shoeshine
   d. A taxicab ride
   e. New false teeth from a dentist
7. In what ways do inseparability and intangibility affect marketing planning for the following organizations?
   a. A church
   b. Your local public school board
   c. A ski resort
8. Are there any products that have no service components? Why or why not?
9. Service workers often work in teams. The following questions will help you gain a better understanding of your orientation to work in a

group. Respond either Y (yes) or N (no) to each of the following statements:

a. I usually feel uncomfortable with a group of people that I don't know.
b. I enjoy parties.
c. I do not have much confidence in social situations.
d. I am basically a shy person.
e. I like going on job interviews.
f. I usually feel anxious when I speak in front of a group.
g. Large groups make me nervous.
h. I would rather work on a group project than an individual project.
i. I am basically a loner.
j. I find that groups bring out the best in me.

Scoring: Give yourself 1 point for each of your responses that match the following answer pattern:

a = Y, b = N, c = Y, d = Y, e = N, f = Y, g = Y, h = N, i = Y, j = N. Total your score.

Interpretation of score: If your score is 8 or higher, you probably prefer to avoid most group situations. This means you are a *group avoider.* If you have a score of 2 or lower, you probably seek out group situations and activities and are thus a *group seeker.* Unfortunately, it is not always possible to choose your preferred situation. When people get into situations that conflict with their orientation, they may not function as well as they would otherwise. Try to match your activities with your group preference style.[14]

10. After completing the questionnaire above, form a small group as directed by your instructor and discuss how the scores of the group members differ.

---

e—exercises | http://zikmund.swcollege.com

1. Go to the JRC&A home page at http://www.JRCandA.com. Select Strategic Branding. What recommendations are offered for global branding?
2. BitLaw is a comprehensive Internet resource on patent, copyright, trademark, and Internet legal issues. Visit the Web site at http://www.bitlaw.com and report on what you find.
3. To learn more about warranties, go to A Businessperson's Guide to Federal Warranty Law at http://www.ftc.gov/bcp/online/pubs/buspubs/warranty.

Address Book (Useful URLs)

U.S. Patent and Trademark Office	http://www.uspto.gov
Tradename	http://www.tradename.com
U.S. Consumer Product Safety Commission	http://www.cpsc.gov

Ethically Right or Wrong?

Smith & Wesson and the federal government made a deal that ended local and federal lawsuits against the company. Smith & Wesson promised to build additional safety locks into new guns, develop guns that cannot be operated by children, and deny guns to purchasers unless they complete a background check. As part of its deal with the federal government, Smith & Wesson agreed to establish certain rules for retailers of its products. Gun dealers are upset about the following details of the agreement:

- Only one handgun can be purchased in a 14-day period.
- One can't buy a firearm without passing a safety test.
- No one under 18 is permitted to enter a gun store without an adult.
- Dealers can't sell legal semiautomatic rifles and certain ammunition magazines.[15]

These rules apply to all guns in the store, not just to Smith & Wesson's. Many gun dealers say they'll discontinue carrying Smith & Wesson products because they don't believe the manufacturer has the right to dictate what should occur at the retail level. They believe the deal will only hurt legitimate gun owners.

QUESTIONS

1. Should Smith & Wesson have fought expensive lawsuits it believed it could have won?
2. Is it right for a manufacturer to take actions that many of its dealers do not agree with?
3. Should guns be outlawed?

TAKE A STAND

1. According to government studies, most home accidents involve bicycles, stairs, doors, cleaning agents, or tables. What does this list say about product safety? If a child eats a spoonful of Tide, where does the fault lie? Establish some criteria that a marketer of push scooters (or motorized scooters) should use to ensure that its product is safe.
2. It has been estimated that 50 percent of all "Indian" arts and crafts sold in the United States are not hand-made tribal goods at all. These souvenir goods are factory-produced in Asia and South America and have no association with Hopi, Zuni, or any other indigenous tribes. Is it right to market fake tribal jewelry?
3. A doctor's bedside manner is part of the service offered to patients. Discuss this product strategy from an ethical perspective.
4. A restaurant customer asks the waiter if the fish on the menu is fresh. Although the fish was frozen, the waiter answers yes, because he knows it tastes great and the customer will love the chef's sauce. Take a stand.
5. A small percentage of people suffer from allergies, asthma, or sensitivity to perfumes or other chemicals. Even a whiff of certain chemicals can cause respiratory problems, memory loss, or dizziness. Should there be perfume-free sections in restaurants and other service establishments?

VIDEO CASE 9-1
Ben & Jerry's (B)

Ben & Jerry's Homemade, Inc., the Vermont-based manufacturer of ice cream, frozen yogurt, and sorbet, was founded in 1978 in a renovated gas station in Burlington, Vermont, by childhood friends Ben Cohen and Jerry Greenfield, with a $12,000 investment ($4,000 of which was borrowed).[16] They soon became popular for their innovative flavors, made from fresh Vermont milk and cream. The company currently distributes ice cream, low fat ice cream, frozen yogurt, sorbet, and novelty products nationwide, as well as in selected foreign countries, in supermarkets, grocery stores, convenience stores, franchised Ben & Jerry's scoop shops, restaurants, and other venues.

In 1988 Ben & Jerry's Homemade, Inc. created a document called the Statement of Mission. The company is dedicated to the creation and demonstration of a new corporate concept of linked prosperity. Its mission consists of three interrelated parts that address product, economic, and social goals.

Ben & Jerry's gives away 7.5 percent of its pre-tax earnings in three ways: through the Ben & Jerry's Foundation, through employee Community Action Teams at five Vermont sites, and through corporate grants made by the Director of Social Mission Development. The company supports projects that are models for social change—projects that exhibit creative problem solving and hopefulness. The Foundation is managed by a nine-member employee board and considers proposals relating to children and families, disadvantaged groups, and the environment.

PRODUCT STRATEGY

Ben & Jerry's product strategy is to differentiate its super premium brand from other ice cream brands. The brand image reflects high quality, uniqueness, and a bit of amusement. Its all-natural flavors have unique names. For example, "Chubby Hubby" has chunks of chocolate-covered peanut-butter-filled pretzels in a rich vanilla malt ice cream with deep ripples of fudge and peanut butter. Other names in the company's line of ice creams include Cherry Garcia, Bovinity Divinity, Dilbert Totally Nuts, New York Super Fudge Chunk, Chunky Monkey, and From Russia with Buzz.

The new product development process and flavor naming process are a top priority at Ben & Jerry's. For example, Phish Food ice cream was developed as a unique product with a fun name associated with the band Phish. Ben Cohen had been a neighbor of members of Phish since the band's early years as favorites on the local music scene. When Ben & Jerry's suggested mixing up a Phish ice cream to celebrate their shared Vermont roots, the band agreed. So Ben & Jerry's concocted a chocolate ice cream with chewy marshmallow nougat, a thick caramel swirl, and a school of fudge fish in every pint. Most marshmallow variegates disappear into nothingness. The company took great pains to make sure that the marshmallow was the way it was meant to be. With Phish Food you can see, taste, and feel the white streaks of marshmallow. The Phish Food package is a departure from Ben & Jerry's traditional graphics. The pint container is designed with images from Phish's concert light show, featuring Phish band members Trey

Anastasio, Mike Gordon, Jon Fishman, and Page McConnell on the pint lid along with Ben and Jerry.

QUESTIONS

1. Does Ben & Jerry's use an individual or a family branding strategy?
2. What are the characteristics of a good brand name? How do you rate Ben & Jerry's flavor names based on these criteria?
3. What role does marketing research play in new product development and brand name development?

VIDEO CASE 9-2

Boyne USA Resorts (A)

Boyne USA, the fifth largest ski operator in the United States, operates skiing, golf, and lodging properties thoughout the nation. Its skiing operations include Big Sky in Montana, Crystal Mountain in Washington, Brighton in Utah, and two ski resorts in Michigan. The services marketing company owns lodging and golf resort properties in Florida, Tennessee, and Michigan.

Boyne USA began operations in Michigan where in addition to its two ski resorts, Boyne Mountain and Boyne Highlands, it operates the Bay Harbor resort. Bay Harbor includes a five-star hotel and golf course.

For half a century, Boyne USA's founder, Everett Kircher, has devoted his life to developing destination resorts that embody his love and passion for the great outdoors. His comprehensive vision and design for each was carefully planned, not just to ensure the well-being of the natural surroundings and their inhabitants, but to embellish and build upon those resources. He wanted guests to experience the wonders of the "Boyne lifestyle."

The Boyne lifestyle—luxurious surroundings, impeccable service, and outstanding amenities in a pristine setting—is a lifestyle shared by people of like minds who want the best that life can offer. Whether it be a day on a championship golf course, mountain biking in the back country, a quiet day on the beach, or an even quieter day interrupted only by the spontaneous excitement of landing a trophy fish out of your favorite river, a Boyne resort can provide it.

For example, the Inn at Bay Harbor is the centerpiece of Bay Harbor Village, which is set along the water's edge. The Inn at Bay Harbor's architectural design rekindles the heritage and style of the great turn-of-the-century northern Michigan inns. It provides luxurious accommodations. The inn features 131 one-, two-, and three-bedroom suites, the Bay Harbor Beach Club, the Spa at the Inn at Bay Harbor (a full-service spa), pool, conference facilities accommodating groups from 15 to 270, plus a spectacular lakefront restaurant. The Inn at Bay Harbor affords guests breathtaking views of Lake Michigan and the surrounding coast.

QUESTIONS

1. What are the most important characteristics of the service that Boyne USA markets?
2. How important is employee interaction with customers at a resort?
3. Service quality involves meeting customer expectations. How might the staff at the Bay Harbor resort improve service quality?
4. If a customer has a problem or is dissatisfied with a service, how should the customer's problem be handled?

Strategies for New Products and the Product Life Cycle

LEARNING OBJECTIVES

After you have studied this chapter, you will be able to . . .

1) Define product newness and explain the chances of success and failure for new products.

2) Identify general characteristics of successful new products.

3) Characterize the stages of new product development.

4) Identify some of the most common reasons for new product failures.

5) Describe the product life cycle and characterize its stages.

6) Describe the new product diffusion process and list the groups of adopters to which marketers must direct their appeals.

7) Identify strategies for modifying existing products.

8) Explain the total quality management process for goods and services.

9) Understand how marketers manage product lines.

10) Identify some ethical questions associated with product strategy.

In March of 1999, Philips and TiVo fired the first shot in a revolution that will see TV viewing habits undergo a radical change. The two collaborating companies were the first to offer a digital recording system and product category now known as a personal video recorder (PVR).

What radical change are PVRs bound to have on TV viewing? Within a few years, these "uberVCRs" will be able to record up to 100 hours of programming. Just as important, viewers will be able to skip over the ads. As a result, TV ad viewing will be cut nearly in half. So says a recent Forrester Research report that envisions an era of ubiquitous pay TV as broadcast, cable, and satellite networks scramble to replace dwindling ad dollars. Welcome to the 21st century!

What is the fuss all about? Just what is a PVR? The heart of the personal TV system is a Philips receiver: a modem-equipped set-top box that accepts television programming from any source, including satellite, cable, and antenna. Inside the box is the guts of the system, a hard drive capable of digitally recording either 14 hours ($499) or 30 hours ($999) of programming.

However, the brains of the box, TiVo's intelligent search engine and user interface, enable much more than mere time shifting. Because the unit is always recording, viewers can pause, rewind, or instant-replay broadcasts in real time. They can also establish a "preference profile" that instructs the unit to record their favorite programs and to recommend similar material as it automatically sifts through more than 100,000 broadcast listings each week.

There are three subscription options: $9.95 per month, $99 per year, or $199 for a lifetime deal. For their money, viewers receive content via TiVo's Broadcast Center, including material from Showtime, E! Entertainment Television, FLIX, HBO, Style, The Weather Channel, The Movie Channel, and ZDTV, as well as daily program recommendations, entertainment and sports-oriented editorial content, and new service updates and features.

Forrester Research's analysis of the PVR market indicates that "the two main features that drive TV sales are choice and convenience. First there was the convenience of the remote control, and then the choices offered by cable and satellite networks. The PVR puts you right in the middle of the two so you can watch whatever you want whenever you want."

The Forrester team interviewed Replay PVR beta users and discovered most didn't look at ads anymore. "With Replay and other PVRs, you can skip ahead 30 seconds very easily. People can start watching prime time shows at 9 and see three hours of shows in two hours just by skipping the ads."

Personal video recorders use an intelligent interface and an internal hard drive to record programs digitally. With features like instantaneous fast-forward and reverse, the ability to pause live broadcasts, and easy-to-create viewer profiles, PVRs will broaden viewers' options by offering, at any given moment, a menu of recorded programs based on their preferences.[1]

TiVo's digital recording system—which allows viewers to watch the shows they want, when they want—is amazing. And this new product is still in its infancy. This chapter begins by addressing the nature of new products and the characteristics associated with new product successes. It goes on to describe the new product development process and to discuss the fact that most new products fail. Then the focus shifts to the product life cycle, an extremely influential concept in the planning and marketing of a product from its birth to its death. The adoption and diffusion processes, discussed next, help explain a product's acceptance over the course of its life cycle. The chapter then addresses issues related to the marketing of products that have been on the market for some time and discusses strategies for expanding product lines and withdrawing or eliminating goods or services that no longer enjoy adequate market demand. Finally, ethical issues associated with product strategy are considered.

What Is a New Product?

New product
The meaning of this relative term is influenced by the perceptions of marketers and consumers. In general, it refers to a product new to a company or any recently introduced product that offers some benefit that other products do not.

The TiVo personal video recorder discussed at the beginning of the chapter certainly appears to be a new product. Before reading further, however, pause for a second to decide in your own mind what a **new product** is. Think of an example or two, and try to identify what makes them new. Is the egg-shaped video camera that plugs into your desktop computer's USB port really a new product? Is Logitech's Cordless MouseMan Wheel that uses radio frequency truly different from the first mouse? Does the ingenious, and highly practical, voice-activated word-processing software qualify as really new?

To some marketers, a new product may be a major technological innovation. The first computers were introduced in the 1940s. Though primitive by today's standards, at that time they were altogether new to the market. At one time or other, so were microwave ovens, radial tires, adjustable rate mortgages, and automatic teller machines. To other marketers, new products might be simple additions to an otherwise unchanged product line, such as new shades of lipstick or hair coloring introduced by Revlon or Clairol.

Even a "me, too" item, developed in imitation of a competitor's successful product, is a new product to the imitating company. Furthermore, a product may be new because it offers some benefit that similar products do not. For example, Velcro tabs on paper diapers, which allow parents to check for wetness and reseal the diaper securely, make these diapers different from those that reseal with ordinary adhesive tape. The marketing concept, after all, tells marketers to consider a product as a bundle of tangible and intangible benefits. If the bundle of benefits offered by a product differs from the bundle already available, then the product can be said to be new.

From the buyer's point of view, a product may be new if it is something never before purchased, even if it has been on the market for years. In international marketing, old products may become "new" again, especially when a manufacturer's established product is being offered to people in a less-developed country. There are, for example, places in the world where VCRs and color televisions are new to most people. It is clear, then, that the term *new* and the related term *novel* are used in a relative sense. They are influenced by perceptions, whether you are a marketing manager or a consumer. Let's begin by taking the manager's perspective.

Management's Perspective on New Products

Managers may consider a product new if it is new to the market or simply new to the company. Products can be either new-to-the-world products, product category extensions, product line extensions, or product modifications. Companies have considerable experience marketing product modifications but far less experience with products in the first three categories.

- *New-to-the-world products* are inventions that create an entirely new market. These are the highest-risk products, because they are new to both the company and the market. The technology for producing these innovative products, which is itself new to the company, is often the result of a large investment in research and development.
- *Product category extensions* are new products that, for the first time, allow a company to diversify and enter an established market for an existing product category. These products are not entirely new to the market, but the company has had no previous technological or marketing experience with them. If these products imitate competitive products with identical features, they can be described as "me, too" products.
- *Product line extensions* are additions to an existing product line that supplement the basic items in the established line. Line extensions include enhanced models, low-price economy models, and variations in color, flavor, design, and so on. These new products may be family branded or marketed under a new brand name, perhaps a private label that appeals to a different market segment.
- *Product modifications* include product improvements, cost reductions, and repositionings. "New and improved" versions replace existing products and are intended to provide improved performance, enhanced features, or greater perceived value. Cost reductions replace existing products by providing similar performance at a lower cost. Repositionings may modify existing products by targeting new market segments, offering a new benefit, or assuming a different competitive position. The marketing task for these products often is to communicate the benefits of product modifications to consumers who do not see the products as unique or strikingly different from past offerings.

The Consumer's Perspective on Newness

From a consumer perspective, new products vary in degree of newness. There are three types of innovations: discontinuous, dynamically continuous, and continuous, as shown in Exhibit 10-1.

DISCONTINUOUS INNOVATION

Discontinuous innovations are pioneering products so new that no previous product performed an equivalent function. As a result of this near-complete newness, new consumption or usage patterns are required. The lithium battery pacemaker implanted in heart patients was a discontinuous innovation. The fax machine was

Discontinuous innovation
A product so new that no previous product performed an equivalent function. Such a product requires the development of new consumption or usage patterns.

e x h i b 10-1

The Continuum of Newness

Discontinuous innovation
- New function not performed by any previous product
- Need for behavior changes

Dynamically continuous innovation
- Improvement of performance
- Similar consumption pattern

Continuous innovation
- Variation of existing product
- Same consumption pattern

Breakthrough   Major change   Ongoing alteration

another. These products, once new to the world, did things no products before them had done, and to use them properly, people had to make extensive behavior changes. Artificial hearts and a drug to cure AIDS are still in their developmental stages, but once perfected and made available, they, too, will be discontinuous innovations.

DYNAMICALLY CONTINUOUS INNOVATION

In the newness continuum, somewhere between the breakthrough achieved with the perfected artificial heart and the commonplace newness of the *new and improved* consumer product, is the **dynamically continuous innovation**. New products in this middle range represent changes and improvements that do not strikingly change buying and usage patterns.

The hybrid gasoline engine/electric motor car is an example of a dynamically continuous innovation. The buying habits of those purchasing cars and fuel may be altered by successful and appealing hybrid gas/electric automobiles, but virtually all driving behavior will remain as it is. Compare this situation with the way the Model T Ford affected society. Similarly, although TiVo's personal video recorder system, mentioned in the opening story, is genuinely new, its effect on buyers and users is nothing like the effect of the first videotape recorder.

CONTINUOUS INNOVATION

A **continuous innovation** is a commonplace change that is part of an ongoing product modification effort, such as a minor alteration of a product or the introduction of an imitative product. The flat-panel computer monitor is an example of a continuous innovation. This new product is an improvement over existing monitors because it takes up less space. Although the product has a new form, it is used in the traditional manner, so consumers do not have to change their con-

Dynamically continuous innovation
A product that is different from previously available products but that does not strikingly change buying or usage patterns.

Continuous innovation
A new product that is characterized by minor alterations or improvements to existing products and that produces little change in consumption patterns.

The Rocket eBook is an electronic reader that can hold about 10 books. It allows users to bookmark pages, underline passages, or look up words in a built-in dictionary. To use the eBook, consumers must change their behavior—but not extensively. It is a dynamically continuous innovation.

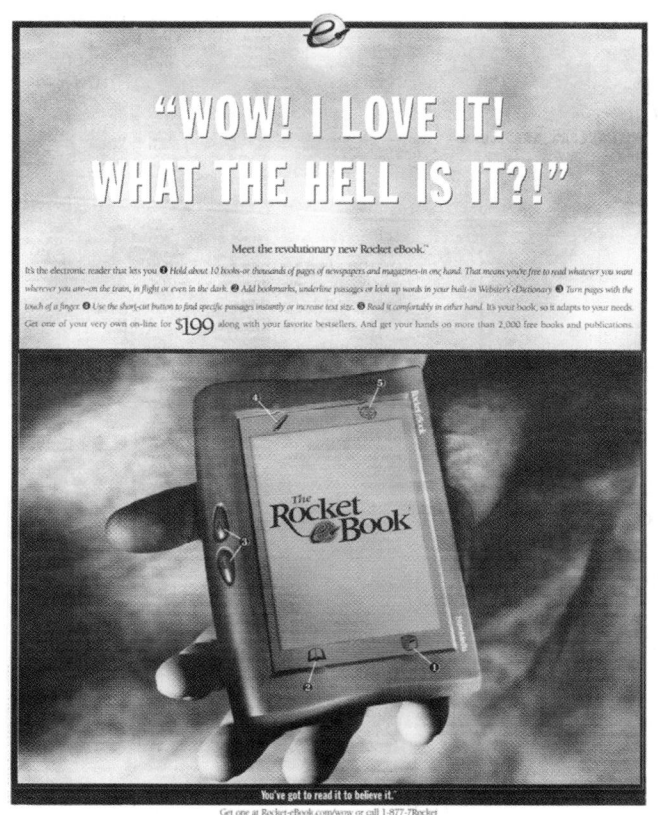

sumption behavior. This is a key characteristic of a continuous innovation. Marketers constantly strive to improve products, because even minor improvements, such as reducing calories or salt, can provide a competitive advantage. Although this approach may be viewed as fine-tuning the product, the new product is an innovation of a sort.

The Slim Chances of Success

Product success is both difficult to define and difficult to achieve. It is problematic to determine the number of new product successes and failures because, like newness, success is so hard to define. How much of a success must a new product be before it is truly "a success"? It is a widely accepted belief that relatively few new product ideas become commercial successes. But because most organizations would rather not talk about their failures, this belief is based largely on estimates. Moreover, some product ideas wither in their developmental stages, and documentation of ideas that were suggested but never made it to market is seldom available. For our purpose, failure occurs when a product does not meet the organization's expectations.

Several estimates of new product failure rates are available. Some of these suggest that 80 percent of new product ideas do not become commercial successes.[2] Once a new product has actually appeared on the market, the success rate is much higher because of the research, planning, and effort that have gone into its introduction. It is estimated that there is a one-in-three failure rate among new product introductions.

Clearly, failure and success rates vary from organization to organization. In general, the failure rate is higher for consumer products than for organizational goods. In the consumer package-goods market, for instance, the failure rate is likely to be far higher than in the organizational electrical components field. This difference is due to the dynamic nature of the consumer marketplace and the fact that consumers often cannot tell marketers exactly what new products will satisfy them. In contrast, the organizational buyers of electrical components are able to give detailed information to component manufacturers. No wonder, then, that new product failure and success rates vary greatly.

The Characteristics of Success

Five characteristics influence a new product's chances for success in the marketplace: relative advantage, compatibility with existing consumption patterns, trialability, observability, and simplicity of usage.[3] When a product lacks one or more of these characteristics, the others may be used effectively to make up for the deficiency. Nonproduct elements of the marketing mix—price, promotion, and

The Olympus Stylus Epic Zoom 80 camera is the smallest all-weather 35mm zoom camera. Consumers do not need to change their consumption behavior to use this "new and improved" pocket-sized camera. It is a continuous innovation.

distribution—must be developed and adjusted with these same characteristics in mind.

RELATIVE ADVANTAGE

Relative advantage
The ability of a product to offer clear-cut advantages over competing offerings.

Products that offer buyers clear-cut advantages over competing offerings are said to have **relative advantage**. In organizational markets, relative advantage often arises when new products perform exactly the same functions less expensively or faster than existing products. Experience and improved technology, for example, may make it possible to replace metal parts with cheaper and lighter plastic ones. In other cases, relative advantage arises from totally new technology. Computer systems that use spoken words as input obviously have a relative advantage over earlier generations that require typed input. In contrast, some new products prove to have no relative advantage over their competitors. When the Miller Brewing Company test-marketed its Clear Miller Beer, the company quickly learned that its colorless beer didn't look or taste like beer. This new product had no relative advantage.

COMPATIBILITY WITH EXISTING CONSUMPTION PATTERNS

Everything else being equal, a new product that is compatible with existing patterns of consumption stands a better chance of market acceptance than one that is incompatible. This is true even when the newer item has some relative advantage.

Consider, for example, Specialized Bicycle's Armadillo anti-puncture tires. A layer of Kevlar (a super-strong polymer used to make bullet-proof vests) allows the tires to repel thorns, nails, and glass. The new tire is completely compatible with the behavior of people who ride bikes; and because it has a relative advantage, it should achieve rapid market acceptance. On the other hand, it will take time for the market to accept the Handwriter for Windows, a digital pad on which a computer user writes or draws with a pen. The pad converts handwritten characters into computerized text and gives the pen mouselike pointing capabilities with Windows programs. However, the thin pad is quite different from a keyboard or a mouse and requires a departure from existing usage patterns.

TRIALABILITY—THE OPPORTUNITY FOR BUYER TESTING

Trialability
The ability of a product to be tested by possible future users with little risk or effort.

Trial sampling
The distribution of newly marketed products to enhance trialability and familiarity; giving away free samples.

A new product has **trialability** when possible future users can test it with little risk or effort. Dove Nutrium Bar, a dual-formula soap that "goes beyond cleansing and moisturizing to replenish skin's essential nutrients," has trialability. Clorox Disinfecting Wipes are premoistened and treated towels that kill 99.9% of bacteria; they are not expensive, and the buyer need not invest in special equipment to use them. A product's trialability may be enhanced by coupons in newspapers, magazines, and the mail. New shampoos and laundry products are made available in small, inexpensive packages to encourage consumers to try them with little monetary risk. When companies give away free samples to possible buyers, bringing trialability to perhaps its highest level, the process is termed **trial sampling**. Sending computer discs and offering 50 or 100 hours of unlimited Internet and online service is America Online's major means of generating new customers.

Divisibility
The ability of a product to be sampled in small amounts by consumers.

Effective marketing management demands careful consideration of steps that may encourage buyer sampling of a new product. For example, marketers arranged for new flavors of Kellogg's Nutri-Grain cereal bars to be given to passengers flying on Southwest Airlines. In such a situation, there is a high probability that consumers will try the product. Items intended to be sold in cases or six-packs, like juices, sodas, and other drinks, might first be offered in single-drink packages or be given away by the cupful in shopping malls. Customers who are reluctant to buy 12 of a given product may be willing to try just one. Trialability is more appropriately referred to as **divisibility** when it refers to the opportunity to try a small amount.

OBSERVABILITY—THE CHANCE TO SEE THE NEWNESS

Some new products enter the marketplace with attributes or characteristics that are visible to the customer. Kyocera's VisualPhone is a mobile phone that can send and receive images of callers. The new product has a video screen and a small camera embedded in its upper right-hand corner. The gadget has a relative advantage over regular mobile phones, and that advantage is easy to see. Kyocera's VisualPhone is a product with **observability**.

Other products possess definite relative advantages that are not observable or so easily grasped. A new brand of allergy tablets with an advanced formula that relieves allergy symptoms without causing drowsiness has an advantage that is not observable by most buyers. Advertisements for products with hidden qualities frequently feature experts or credible users who attest to the products' worth, making hidden qualities observable.

Observability
The ability of a product to display to consumers its advantages over existing products.

SIMPLICITY OF USAGE

A complex product—or one that requires complex procedures for storage or use—starts out with a disadvantage. Digital cameras, at their introduction, were viewed by consumers as phenomenal. However, because it was difficult for the average person to understand the technical mechanism inside the cameras, the cameras themselves were designed for easy operation. The **simplicity of usage** offsets the complexity of the product itself. Makers of early digital cameras carefully trained salespeople to explain the new product to people who found it difficult to grasp the system and arranged for newspaper and magazine columnists to try it so that they could explain it to their readers.

Simplicity of usage
Ease of operation. This product benefit can offset any complexity in the product itself.

New Product Development

What is the source of product innovations? How are new product ideas generated? There is no one answer to these questions. Some innovations are discovered by accident or luck, such as the vulcanization of rubber (discovered when a rubbery mixture was spilled on a hot stove) and Ivory's floating soap (first made when a mechanical mixer was left on overnight and whipped raw soap materials into a lightweight cleanser). Necessity, it seems, was the mother of invention for the ice cream seller in St. Louis who ran out of paper cups and rolled pancakes into serving cones—the first ice cream cones. On occasion, the amateur inventor working in a basement comes up with an innovation that goes on to achieve great success. However, these days, when innovations require sizable financial investments and other resources for support and commercialization, most innovations come from serious research and development efforts undertaken with the support of formal organizations. For example, the TiVo personal video recorder mentioned at the beginning of this chapter was introduced only after years of research and development.

The new product development process can be quick, the result of a sudden flash of insight. But in many cases, such as in the development of space satellites, telecommunication systems, and other highly technical products, the

The U.S. Mint is changing the face of money (from George Washington to Sacagawea) with its new dollar coin. Because the Susan B. Anthony dollar coin failed to gain public acceptance when it was introduced 20 years ago, the Mint is promoting the new dollar coin's simplicity of usage and compatibility with existing vending machines.

http://www.usmint.gov/goldendollar

process can take years. The development process may be lengthy not because of technical problems but because it takes time to research and understand potential market resistance to a new product. Even when a new product has a technological advantage, customers may not accept it.

Exhibit 10-2 shows the five general stages in the new product development process: idea generation, screening, business analysis, development, and commercialization. Products pass through these stages at varying rates. A product may stall for a time in one, for example, and pass through another so quickly that it appears to have skipped it entirely.

IDEA GENERATION

Idea generation stage
The stage in new product development in which a marketer engages in a continuing search for product ideas consistent with target market needs and the organization's objectives.

In marketing-oriented organizations operating in dynamic environments, **idea generation**—the exploration stage of new product development—is less a period of time than an ongoing process. Thus, the idea generation stage involves a continuing search for product ideas that are consistent with target market needs and with the organization's objectives.

In many organizations, particularly those in industries with complex technology, generating ideas and searching for technological breakthroughs are likely to be the tasks of the research and development (R&D) department. R&D personnel may focus creative thinking on transferring a technology from an existing product category to a new product, on miniaturization, or on basic research to create new-to-the-world products. For example, for years healthcare workers have experienced skin rashes, hives, itching, runny noses, itchy eyes, coughing spells, difficulty breathing, and other allergic reactions from exposure to the natural rubber latex used in gloves and wraps for splints, sprains, and protective dressings. 3M recognized this problem and used its R&D technology to create a new product: synthetic rubber, latex-free, self-adherent wrap that does not release the proteins that cause allergic reactions.

Although a large proportion of new product ideas flow from technology-driven research departments, other sources should not be ignored. New product suggestions may come from customers. Sales representatives may uncover or be told about new product opportunities. Marketing research can yield new product sug-

what went right?

Palm and Nokia Palm Computing wants to collaborate with consumer electronics and cellular handset companies by incorporating its operating system into new wireless products. Recently, the handheld computing company took a big step in that direction by signing a licensing deal with Nokia, the giant Finnish corporation. The two companies will work together to develop a pen-based smart phone that Nokia will sell worldwide.

Mark Bercow, vice president of strategic alliances and platform development at Palm Computing, said, "It's not like we're picking them at the exclusion of others, but clearly Nokia is interesting because they're the number one handset maker in the world."

Palm Computing will receive ownership of any intellectual property created during the development of the new phone. Palm Computing will license these new technologies to other would-be smart phone makers.

Nokia, which will market the phone, expects product development to take about two years. The digital phone will appear initially in North America, followed by an overseas rollout. The inclusion of the Palm OS in the phone should eliminate the need for a QWERTY keyboard, because users will be able to use the pen-based Graffiti language instead.[4]

The General Stages in the Development of New Products

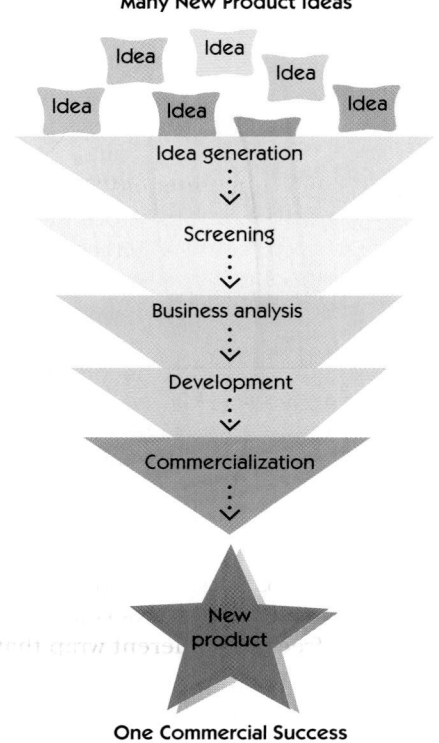

gestions. An employee, a supplier, or a distributor may come up with a good—or even brilliant—idea.

Companies can stimulate the generation of ideas by encouraging employees to think about new products that could address consumer complaints, make a task easier, add benefits to existing products, or provide new uses for existing products. Many organizations have instituted reward systems to encourage employee suggestions. The focus at this stage is on encouraging creativity rather than on evaluating suggestions. The organization wishes to generate ideas, not kill them.

SCREENING

The **screening stage** of the product development process involves analyzing new ideas to determine which are reasonable, compatible with the organization's goals, and appropriate to the organization's target markets. This step is extremely important, because the underlying assumption of the entire product development process is that risky alternatives—possibilities that do not offer as much promise for success as others—should be eliminated from consideration. Resources can then be concentrated on the best prospects so that market failures can be avoided.

The screening stage is also important because it is the first stage at which alternative ideas are sorted. New ideas may now be rejected. From time to time, of course, any management team is likely to reject some ideas that they later wish they had accepted. Because mistakes will be made, managers must screen ideas with caution. In fact, because an idea rejected at this stage is eliminated from further consideration,

Screening stage
The stage in new product development in which a marketer analyzes ideas to determine their appropriateness and reasonableness in relation to the organization's goals and objectives.

Thoughts of talking automobiles conjure TV images of either *My Mother the Car* or K.I.T.T. from *Knight Rider,* both fine vehicles that knew how to hold a conversation. Recently, automakers and high-tech industry players have made strides to bring talking cars to life.

In January, IBM and Motorola announced they were joining forces to introduce wireless and Web-based services into drive time. Part of IBM's contribution concerns speech recognition, which would allow drivers to keep their hands on the wheel and their thoughts on email. A demo video for the speech-enabled car features a "Blair Witch," up-the-nose shot of a driver calling out commands, seemingly to himself. "Run diagnostic check," he says. The car answers moments later in a soothing female voice: "Temperature above safe range. Pull over as soon as it's convenient." In addition to announcing engine trouble in motherly tones, the on-board computer features hands-free dialing, a speakerphone, and dictation capability.

Although voice-enabled autos won't contain the more exciting gadgets showcased on television—flamethrowers, torpedo launchers, and ejector seats, for example—at least they'll roll off the assembly line soon. According to Roger Matus, vice president of marketing at speech-recognition company Dragon Systems, fitting cars with Internet access and auditory technology is the next big item on automaker checklists. "Speech and e-commerce in cars is a natural," he says. "After all, it's very difficult to use a keyboard when you're driving down the interstate. You shouldn't even be using your cell phone."[5]

some companies prefer to allow a marginal idea to progress further rather than risk rejecting it too early in the process. However, at later stages, the costs of analysis and evaluation are substantially increased. Balancing the costs of additional investigation against the loss of a viable product idea is one of management's most delicate tasks.

BUSINESS ANALYSIS

A product idea that survives the screening process enters the **business analysis stage**, at which point it is expanded into a concrete business recommendation. This recommendation includes both qualitative and quantitative means of evaluation. The qualitative evaluation seeks such specifics as a listing of product features, information on resources needed to produce the product, and a basic marketing plan. Creativity and analysis come together at this stage.

Although qualitative evaluations of the product and its likely success are important, business analysis requires quantitative data—facts and figures. The new product idea is evaluated with increasingly detailed quantitative data on market demand, cost projections, investment requirements, and competitive activity. Formal buyer research studies, sales and market forecasts, break-even analyses, and similar research efforts are undertaken. In short, the business analysis is a review of the new product from all significant organi-

Business analysis stage
The stage in new product development in which the new product is reviewed from all organizational perspectives to determine performance criteria and likely profitability.

Balancing the costs of additional investigation against the loss of a viable product idea is one of management's most delicate tasks.

When a product, such as the wearable computer, moves from product concept to product prototype, it enters the development stage of new product development. At this stage, research evaluates how well a wearer/computer user can perform computing tasks while walking or engaging in other activities.

http://www.media.mit.edu

zational perspectives. It emphasizes performance criteria and chances for success in the marketplace.

DEVELOPMENT

A new product idea that survives the preliminary evaluative stages is ready for the fourth stage, development. In the **development stage**, the proposed new product idea is transformed from a product concept to a product prototype. The basic marketing strategy is developed, and decisions are made about the product's physical characteristics, package design, and brand name, as well as about market segmentation strategy. Specific tactics within the product strategy are also researched during this stage.

In the development stage, paper-and-pencil concepts become demonstrable products. Research and development or production engineers give marketers a product that can be tested in customer usage studies, sold in test markets, or investigated in other limited ways. This is not to say that the product is in its final form. For example, if soft drink marketers convene a panel of consumers to taste-test a new formulation and the product is not well accepted, it might be reformulated or its package might be changed. The product can be retested until the proper set of characteristics has been discovered. We discuss three popular forms of testing here.

Concept Testing   **Concept testing** is a general term for many different research procedures used to learn consumers' reactions to a new product idea. Typically, consumers are presented with the idea—illustrated in graphic form or described in writing—and asked if they would use it, if they like it, if they would buy it, and so on.

Concept testing helps to ensure that product concepts are developed with the needs of the consumer or user in mind. For example, General Electric's design engineers are sent out to talk with dealers and customers about new product concepts to ensure that market feedback goes where it can do the most good—to the engineers who design the products. GE wants design engineers to get their directions from customers. GE's objective is to bring the technology and consumer demand together.

Test Marketing   **Test marketing** is an experimental procedure in which marketers test a new product under realistic market conditions in order to obtain a measure of its potential sales in national distribution. Test markets are cities or other small geographical areas in which the new product is distributed and sold in typical marketplace settings to actual consumers. No other form of research can beat the real world when it comes to testing actual purchasing behavior and consumer acceptance of a product.

Development stage
The stage in new product development in which a new product concept is transformed into a prototype. The basic marketing strategy also develops at this time.

Concept testing
Research procedures used to learn consumers' reactions to new product ideas. Consumers presented with an idea are asked if they like it, would use it, would buy it, and so on.

Test marketing
A controlled experimental procedure in which a new product is tested under realistic market conditions in a limited geographical area.

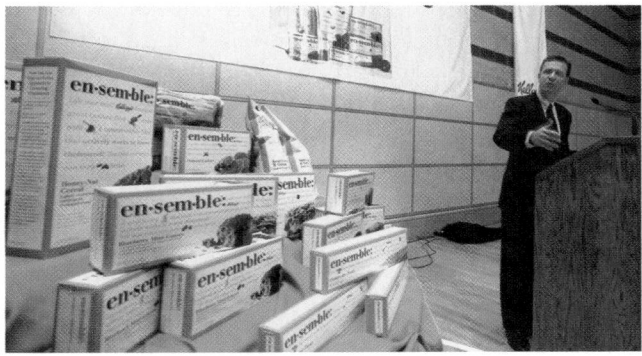

There is a growing trend toward functional foods—foods that offer a specific health benefit beyond basic nutrition. Kellogg developed and test-marketed Ensemble, a line of nutritionally enhanced cereals, cookies, lasagna, and other foods, to capitalize on this trend. Unfortunately, like most new products, Ensemble lasted less than a year on store shelves.

Note that test marketing involves scientific testing and controlled experimentation, not just trying something out in the marketplace. Simply introducing a product in a small geographical area before introducing it nationally is not test marketing.

Test marketing serves two important functions for management. First, it provides an opportunity to estimate the outcomes of alternative courses of action. Managers can estimate the sales effect of a specific marketing variable—such as package design, price, or couponing—and then select the best alternative action with regard to that variable. Second, test market experimentation allows management to identify and correct any weaknesses in either the product or its marketing plan before making the commitment to a national sales launch, after which it is too late to make changes.

Test marketing investigates how consumers react in actual marketplace settings. Pepsi and Frito-Lay are testing consumer reactions to a vending machine that sells both soft drinks and snacks-in-a-can.

In selecting test markets, the marketer must choose cities that are representative of the population of all cities and towns throughout the United States.[6] Test market cities should be representative in terms of competitive situation, media usage patterns, product usage, and other relevant factors. Of course, no single test market is a perfect miniature of the entire United States. Nevertheless, it is important to avoid selecting areas with atypical climates, unusual ethnic composition, or uncommon lifestyles, any of which may have a dramatic impact on the acceptance of a new product. Some of the most popular test markets are mid-sized cities where costs won't be prohibitive, such as Tulsa, Oklahoma; Charlotte, North Carolina; Green Bay, Wisconsin; Odessa, Texas; Nashville, Tennessee; Omaha, Nebraska; and Portland, Maine.

Test marketing is expensive. Developing local distribution, arranging media coverage, and monitoring sales results take considerable effort. The cost of test marketing a consumer product can be several million dollars. However, if a firm must commit a substantial amount of money to investments in plant and equipment to manufacture a new product, the cost of test marketing may be minimal compared with the cost of a possible product failure. The marketer, then, must balance the cost of test marketing against the risk of not test marketing.

Beta Testing   Marketers of new software or Internet products wish to avoid selling poor-quality programs that have "bugs." *Beta testing* is the second and final phase of bug-catching in the development of software. Customers who are representative users receive free copies of the initial software. They run the new application on their computer systems to check for any bugs and incompatibilities with hardware or other software and report back to the software organization. In exchange for their efforts, they are the first to receive the final version of the software, thereby getting a head start in using the new product.[7]

COMMERCIALIZATION

After passing through the filtering stages in the development process, the new product is ready for the final stage of **commercialization**. The decision to launch full-scale production and distribution entails risking a great deal of money, because commercialization involves a serious commitment of resources and managerial effort. This stage is the last chance to stop the project if managers think the risks are too high. Many successful marketing firms, such as Procter &

Commercialization
The stage in new product development in which the decision is made to launch full-scale production and distribution of a new product.

Gamble, remain willing to stop a project right up to the last moment. Although a lot of money may have been spent in reaching the commercialization stage, any amount is small compared with the sums that full commercialization will demand.

Even when marketers use great caution, product failures still occur. It is not difficult to find products that should have been killed before commercialization. For example, the Dow Chemical Company developed a compound of resins and methanol to be sprayed on car tires to increase their ability to maintain traction on ice. The product, Liquid Tire Chain, truly did work, as proved by in-use testing. Not surprisingly, however, buyers stored the pressurized cans of the product in the trunks of their cars. When the aerosol containers froze in winter weather, the material within them solidified, making the product useless. The in-use tests Dow had undertaken somehow missed this factor. Unfortunately for Dow, the product failed after commercialization. Had testing been more complete, this failure could have been avoided.

Why Do New Products Fail?

New product failures and near-failures occur with some regularity, as we pointed out earlier. Furthermore, it is not just small, inexperienced organizations that have new products fail. Consider that Pillsbury's Oven Lovin', a cookie dough loaded with Hershey's chocolate chips, Reese's Pieces, and Brach's candies in a resealable tub, failed after millions of dollars had been spent in the new product development process. After researching the Oven Lovin' concept by surveying consumers, the company skipped the test marketing stage, in an effort to save money, and launched the product nationally. Consumers, based on limited experience during the survey, said they liked the Oven Lovin' resealable tubs. Unfortunately for Pillsbury, however, at home many shoppers found they ended up baking the entire package at once—or gobbling up leftover dough raw instead of saving it—eliminating the need for the pricier packaging. The product failed within two years of its introduction.[8]

In introducing Benefit, a high-soluble-fiber cereal made with psyllium, General Mills stressed the cereal's ability to reduce cholesterol levels. When sales did not meet expectations, the company learned that although consumers understood the role of oat bran in reducing cholesterol levels, they were confused about the term *soluble fiber*. The final blow to the product came when a barrage of publicity questioned whether Benefit with psyllium was a drug or a cereal.

What are the most common reasons for product failures? Following are several:

- *Insufficient product superiority or uniqueness.* If a "me, too" product is merely an imitation of products that are already on the market and does not offer the consumer a relative advantage, the product may be doomed from the start. Although the Everlast brand has been around boxing for years, Everlast sports drink was not much different from Gatorade. It took only a short time for the product to fail.
- *Inadequate or inferior planning.* Many product failures stem from failure to conduct proper marketing research about consumers' needs and failure to develop realistic forecasts of market demand and accurate estimates of the acceptance of new products. Overly optimistic managers may underestimate the strength of existing competition and fail to anticipate future competitive reactions and the need for sizable promotional budgets. Too often, the enthusiastic developer of a product is surprised to find that it takes more time and effort than expected to launch the product successfully or that the market for the product is not as substantial as forecasts suggested. When Colgate-Palmolive, anxious to beat its rivals to market, commercialized Fab 1 Shot without test marketing, it

quickly learned that the single-packet detergent and fabric softener was not cost-effective for large families. Colgate-Palmolive learned its lesson in the marketplace, while Procter & Gamble and Clorox learned the same thing in test markets.

- *Poor execution.* No matter how good the plans are for commercializing a product, adequate resources must be allocated so that strategies can be properly executed. Many new products fail because managers who think the product is so good it will sell itself do not provide adequate resources to commercialize the product. For example, Pillsbury failed with Appleeasy because, in response to increasing apple prices, the company reduced the amount of apples in its recipe rather than increase the production budget. Sometimes a new product fails because the organization lacks the expertise to carry out production or marketing activities.
- *Technical problems.* Problems may stem from the product itself—failures in production or design. For example, Hot Scoops, a microwavable hot fudge sundae, left the consumer with a mess rather than a sundae if the microwave timer wasn't set exactly right.
- *Poor timing.* The market may change before the new product is introduced, or the company may enter the market too early or too late in the product life cycle. For instance, if a new luxury product is introduced just as a downturn in the economy occurs, the product's chances for success are substantially reduced.

All managers planning new product introductions have one thing in common: They must attempt to predict the future. The product designed in 2001 but commercialized in 2003 is likely to meet an environment somewhat different from the one that existed when the product was being designed. Hence, marketing plans may not work as well as expected. New product marketing deals with forecasting. As the wry adage goes, "Forecasts are dangerous, particularly those about the future."

The Product Life Cycle

The **product life cycle** is a depiction of a product's sales history from its "birth," or marketing beginning, to its "death," or withdrawal from the market. Generally, a product begins its life with its first sale, rises to some peak level of sales, and then declines until its sales volume and contribution to profits are insufficient to justify its presence in the market. This general pattern does vary from product to product, however. Products such as salt and mustard have been used for thousands of years. Arm & Hammer baking soda has been used for over 150 years. Cellular phones and fax machines are mere youngsters by comparison. Some products, such as Topp's Talking Baseball Cards, fail at the very start of their lives. But whether a product has a very short, short, long, or very long life, the pattern of that life may be portrayed by charting sales volume.

Traditionally, the product life cycle has been thought of as reflecting the life of a product class or product category as a whole—for example, the life of hand-held video games as a group, without regard to model or brand. However, marketing managers also use the product life cycle idea in evaluating specific brands of products, because most brands, as well as most products, have limited market lives.

The product life cycle is illustrated in Exhibit 10-3. A product's life, as suggested earlier, typically flows through several distinct stages as sales volume is plotted over time. These stages are introduction, growth, maturity, and decline. As illustrated in

General Pattern of the Product Life Cycle

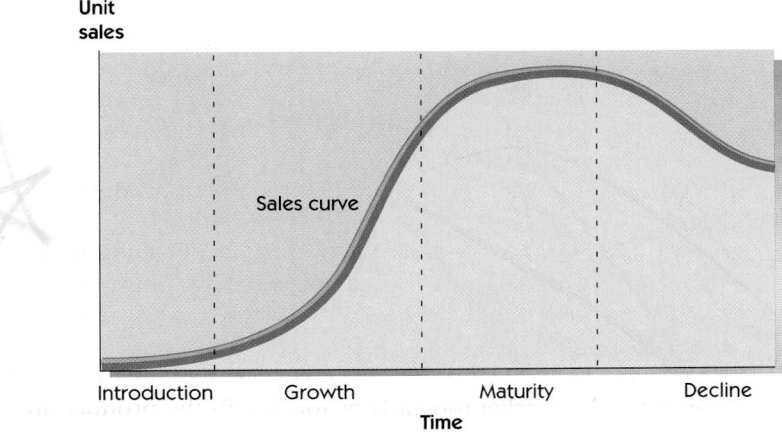

Exhibit 10-4, both sales volume and industry profit change over the course of the life cycle. Exhibit 10-4 also shows the period of product development, which precedes the introductory stage. During this period, no sales are made, but investments are made in the belief that subsequent profitable sales will justify them.

The product life cycle, which is helpful for visualizing the stages of market acceptance, has its greatest practical use as a planning tool. Many successful marketing companies build their strategies around the concept, graph financial and market data against product life cycles, and develop long- and short-range plans for each stage.

THE INTRODUCTION STAGE

During the **introduction stage**, the new product is attempting to gain a foothold in the market. Sales are likely to be slow at the start of the period because the product is, by definition, new and untried. It takes time to gain market acceptance. Sales volume and sales revenues are still low relative to the high expenses associated with developing the product and the marketing mix necessary to introduce the product to the market. In most cases, profits are negative.

The marketing effort in the introductory stage is focused not only on finding first-time buyers and using promotion to make them aware of the product but also on creating channels of distribution—attracting retailers and other intermediaries to handle the product. It is also a time for attempting to recoup most of the research and development costs associated with the product. However, during this period, product alterations or changes in manufacturing may be required to "get the bugs out" of the new market offering. Thus, the introduction stage is typically a high-cost/low-profit period. Although it is an exciting time, it is also a time of uncertainty and anxiety about the new product's ability to survive.

Selecting strategies appropriate to the introductory stage is an important matter, yet organizations differ widely in their choices. Some companies believe that being a pioneer and risk taker is the best approach—the greater the risk, the greater the reward. Thus, in many industries, such as tires and aircraft, the same

Introduction stage
The stage in the product life cycle during which the new product is attempting to gain a foothold in the market.

Industry Profit and the Product Life Cycle

Unit sales/investment
profit (dollars)

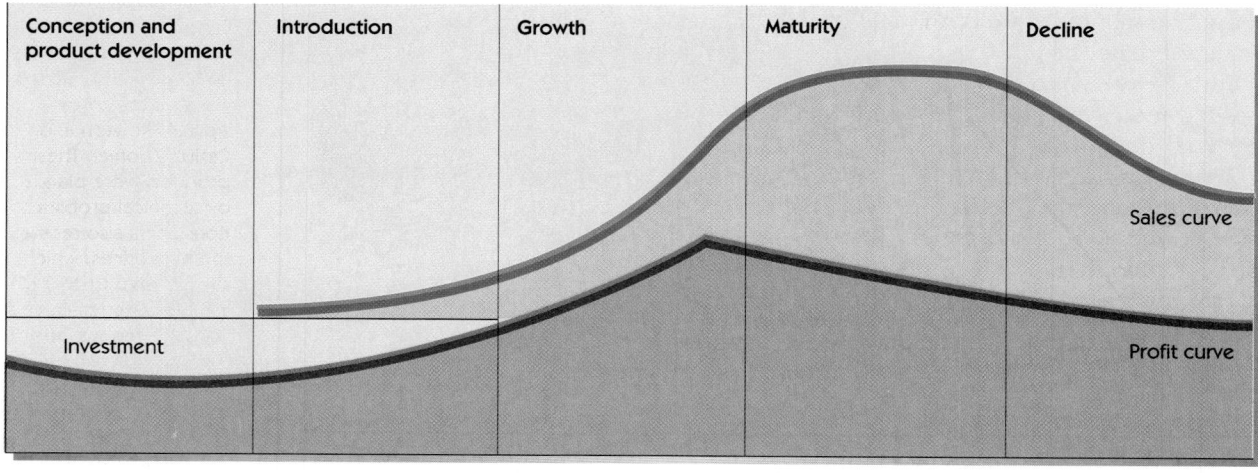

Sales	Low	Rapid growth	Slow growth, peak sales	Declining
Profits	Nonexistent or negligible because of high production and marketing costs	Reach peak levels as a result of high prices and rising demand	Increasing competition reduces profit margins and ultimately cuts into total profits	Declining volume pushes costs up to levels that lower profits
Competition	None of importance	Growing	Many rivals competing for a piece of the pie	Few competitors, with a rapid shakeout of weak members
Customers	Innovative	Mass market	Mass market, differentiated	Laggards

companies are the leaders in new product development over and over again. Other companies quickly follow the pioneer's lead, jumping into the market during the introductory stage. Still others hold back, waiting to see whether the new product will actually take off into a growth period. Each approach has obvious advantages and risks that management must weigh.

The length of the introductory stage varies dramatically. Personal computers and home video games gained market acceptance rapidly. Laser discs, on the other hand, took years to reach a modest level of popularity and experienced rapid decline as soon as the CD-ROM entered its growth stage. Another product category, concentrated laundry detergent, presents a further example of slow market acceptance. The first serious effort to introduce a product that cleans a full load of wash with only a quarter-cup of powder was made in 1976, when Colgate-Palmolive introduced Fresh Start, a powder in a plastic bottle. But rapid sales growth for the category did not occur until 1990, when two other brands, Ultra Tide and Fab Ultra, were successfully introduced. Their marketers succeeded, in part, by stressing the environmental advantage of small packages.

THE GROWTH STAGE

If a product earns market acceptance, it should, at some point, enter a period of comparatively rapid growth. The classic product life cycle portrays this **growth stage** as a period when sales increase at an increasing rate. In other words, sales grow slowly at first but increase at a faster rate later on.

When the product enters its growth stage, profits can be expected to be small. As sales continue to increase during this stage, profits increase, partly because sales increase but also because the start-up expenses encountered earlier diminish. As a rule, profits peak late in the growth period.

A product that has entered the growth stage has shown that it may have a future in the marketplace. As a result, the number of competitors and the level of marketing activity can be expected to increase. Pioneering firms are often required to alter their products because competitors, having had the opportunity to learn from the pioneer's mistakes and the time to study the market, may have improved on the original. Competition also increases because of the industry's recognition of an untapped potential market. Competing firms seem to feel that there is enough profit to go around and that they may be able to grab a sizable market share without taking away from each other (as they must do during the maturity stage).

Products that are currently in their growth stages include digital phones, digital cameras, and wireless information and shopping services. During their growth stages, the profits associated with these products will rise (although not for every company), peaking at the end of the period. Distribution costs will be brought under control as channels become more organized and able to perform their tasks routinely. Product quality will be stressed and improved. Persuasive efforts to create brand preference will become the emphasis of promotion. Promotion expenses will be adjusted as rising sales and profits indicate the product's potential.

THE MATURITY STAGE

As the product approaches the end of its growth period, sales begin to level off. A change in the growth rate—a decrease in the rate at which sales are increasing—heralds the end of the growth period and the beginning of the **maturity stage**. As Exhibit 10-4 showed, profits level off and then fall in the maturity stage. This is to be expected as competing firms try to operate within a static or slow-growth market. When the growth rate slows down, the product requires marketing strategies and tactics appropriate for the maturity stage. Later in this stage, for reasons such as diminished popularity, product obsolescence, or market saturation (which occurs when most target customers own the product), the product begins to lose market acceptance.

Business people who travel need some way to maintain addresses and phone numbers, keep appointment schedules, perform basic computations, and, more recently, communicate electronically. AT&T's Personal Communicator 440 was the first personal digital assistant on the market; it was followed by Apple's Newton and Casio's Zoomer. These products were plagued by technical problems. Consumers also resisted the high prices, which ranged from $1,599 to $2,999. As a result, unit sales volume was too low for the companies to hold out until the market matured. The lessons that Palm and other later market entrants learned from the first movers' mistakes kept personal digital assistants from disappearing from the market.

http://www.palm.com

Growth stage
The stage in the product life cycle during which sales increase at an accelerating rate.

Maturity stage
The stage in the product life cycle during which sales increase at a decreasing rate.

what went wrong?

Levi's in Maturity   After riding a wave of success for much of the '90s, Levi Strauss & Company is getting bloodied by the likes of the Gap, Tommy Hilfiger, and Fubu. And though Levi's is still synonymous with blue jeans, it has lost touch with many of its customers, including teenagers, who view its staple straight-legged denims as something their baby-boomer parents and even grandparents would wear.

"Everyone has a pair of Levi's, including their parents," said Jill Kilcoyne, an associate research director with Teenage Research Unlimited. "There are so many other jeans available that give them the fashion look that [teenagers] want. Teens want to own their own brand; they want the newest and the coolest." Fickle youth probably accounts for a good portion of the sales drop. But Levi Strauss also has missed marketing opportunities, bungled a string of buyouts, and experienced higher production costs at its U.S. plants.

Although Levi's SilverTab jeans and Dockers casual pants are still hot brands, overall the manufacturer's star is clearly slipping. Sales steadily climbed from $4.9 billion in 1991 to $7.1 billion in 1996 but began to taper off. The company's revenues fell 3 percent to $6.9 billion in 1997 and then dropped another 13 percent to $6 billion. In 1999, Levi Strauss, which began making blue jeans for gold miners more than a century ago, said it would close 11 of its 22 North American plants and lay off 5,900 workers.

In surveys by Teenage Research Unlimited, teenagers ranked Levi's as one of their three favorite brands until 1998, when the manufacturer tumbled to No. 8. The seeds of Levi Strauss's troubles were planted in the early 1990s when the company, still enjoying booming sales, began missing trends. First, it didn't predict the popularity of baggy jeans. Then, it didn't foresee the low-rise, hip-hugging denims now found in many girls' closets. Several years after the Gap put hip-huggers on its shelves, Levi still doesn't have them.

The Levi of the '90s, analysts say, has failed to market itself aggressively enough to win back youthful consumers, even as hot new jeans makers continue to bite into its market share. The company for a long time also refused to follow the lead of other clothing makers who moved their manufacturing operations abroad, leaving themselves with higher costs. In addition to closing domestic facilities, Levi is working to design more stylish brands. It also plans to add computer kiosks, which will allow consumers to design their own pair of Levi's, to several department stores.

It has been estimated that Levi's share of the denim market has declined from almost 50 percent in 1990 to about 25 percent. Gaining ground were Vanity Fair's Lee and Wrangler brands, designers such as Donna Karan New York, and department store labels including JCPenney Co.'s Arizona Jeans.[9]

Most products on the market are in the maturity phase. During this stage, competition is likely to be intense. After all, one of the goals of effective marketing is to achieve brand maturity and to maintain it for as long as the market supports the product. Further, because a product in the maturity stage has achieved wide market acceptance, the primary means for any one company to increase its market share is to take market share away from competitors. For example, in the mature automotive business, strategies to maintain market share and defend against inroads from foreign competition are common.

One strategy to increase market share is to produce private brands for distributors. Thus, private labels emerge in the maturity stage. An organization selling a mature product may pick up new business in the price-conscious segment of the market as other, less competitive companies withdraw. Persuading existing users to use more of the product may also be a major objective for marketers of mature brands. Many food companies advertise recipes that require their product as an ingredient in order to foster increased usage of that product.

Organizations in mature markets have solved most of the technological problems encountered early in the product life cycle. The products require little technological improvement, and changes become largely a matter of style. CD players, for example, are now offered in tiny sizes and in big sizes, with tape decks and without, with belt clips for joggers and with handles for toting them down the street. They run on house current, batteries, and solar power. Fashionable designs and model variations become important during a product's maturity.

Although Exhibit 10-4 showed that industry profits generally peak near the end of the growth stage, many individual firms in mature market situations are very profitable. A major reason for this continuing profitability is the experience gained during the earlier stages. Economies of scale also play a part. Organizations in mature markets whose brands are profitable typically use the funds these brands generate to support other items in the product mix. The laundry detergent industry is certainly in its mature stage, but industry leader Procter & Gamble uses the sizable profits generated by Tide and Cheer to pay for the development and introduction of new product items and lines.

Successful marketing managers, recognizing the onset of maturity, investigate the causes of that maturity. If a product is in the mature stage because it has become—and remains—widely used (like roofing supplies or tires), sales volume is likely to remain stable. In contrast, if an alternative product or brand has become popular owing to some environmental change, sales may have peaked. The effective marketer needs to know why a product is in its maturity stage, not just that it is there.

THE DECLINE STAGE

The **decline stage** in the product life cycle is marked by falling sales and falling profits. There is likely to be a shakeout in the industry, decreasing the number of firms as managers become aware that the product has entered the decline stage. Survivor firms compete within an ever-smaller market, driving profit margins lower still. Ironically, the last surviving firm or

firms may, as individual organizations, enjoy high profits at this point when the industry's profits are declining. This is because most competitors have withdrawn from the market, leaving what is left to one or two suppliers. Makers of parts for Edsel and De Lorean automobiles are neither large nor numerous, yet they can survive by catering to car collectors. Brylcreem, Ovaltine, Good & Plenty, and blacksmiths are not as common as they once were, but they still survive. Nevertheless, profits for the industry will be low, because only one or two producers are left. Eventually, the decline stage ends with the disappearance of the product from the market.

Exhibit 10-5 summarizes the typical marketing strategies used over the course of the product life cycle.

DO ALL PRODUCTS FOLLOW THE SAME LIFE CYCLE?

All products follow a product life cycle. All products are introduced, and most eventually disappear. But the shapes of the product life cycles, the rates of change in sales and profits, and the lengths and heights of the cycles vary greatly. As Exhibit 10-6 (page 281) shows, some products, like peanut butter, seem to be firmly preserved in the maturity stage forever, whereas others, such as novelty items like talking baseball cards, have very short life cycles.

Decline stage
The stage in the product life cycle during which the product loses market acceptance because of such factors as diminished popularity, obsolescence, or market saturation.

The humble black phonograph record, a mainstay of the music industry for nearly a century, is a virtually extinct species. Because of consumer preferences for audiocassettes and runaway enthusiasm for the compact disc, conventional record albums now account for just a tiny portion of U.S. sales of recorded music (down from 30 percent of the market in 1985). Faced with this drastic decline, music marketers are thinking about what was once unthinkable—the prospect of a recording industry that doesn't sell records. Vinyl records are at the end of their life cycle.

10-5 Typical Marketing Strategies during the Product Life Cycle

STAGE OF LIFE CYCLE	OVERALL STRATEGY	PRODUCT	PRICES	DISTRIBUTION	PROMOTION
Introduction	Market acceptance: foster product awareness and trial purchase	Basic design with competitive advantage	High, to recover some of the high costs of launching	Selective, as distribution is slowly built up	Informative, to generate brand awareness
Growth	Market penetration: persuade mass market to prefer the brand; expand users and use	Product improvements; expanding product line	High, to take advantage of heavy demand	Intensive, using few trade discounts, since dealers are eager to stock the product	Persuasive, to create brand loyalty and product differentiation
Maturity	Defense of brand position: prevent competition from making inroads	Product differentiation; full product lines	What market will bear; important to avoid price wars	Intensive, using heavy trade allowances to retain shelf space	Extensive, to retain key existing customers and stimulate brand switching
Decline	Reduction of expenses: prepare for removal of product from market; squeeze all possible benefits from the product	Minimal changes to product; product line reduced to best sellers	Low enough to permit quick liquidation of inventory	Selective, as unprofitable outlets are slowly phased out	Minimal to none

Indeed, marketers may expect specific brands to have short lives. Cereals, snack foods, and toys, for example, may gain considerable profits as fad items. Teenage Mutant Ninja Turtles cereal and Jurassic Park Raptor Bites candy were expected to be only short-term successes. Similarly, General Foods used carbonated confection technology to produce several fad bubble gum and candy items, including Increda Bubble, Pop Rocks, and Space Dust. These fad candies, as well as some more familiar products, are marketed on a cyclical basis reflecting a belief that their faddish nature does not justify year-round marketing expenditures. Other products are brought back in essentially unchanged form once a new generation of buyers has replaced the old. Many stories in Walt Disney comic books and movies on videotape are reissued once an age cohort of readers and viewers has been replaced by a new group. These sorts of products have short lives. Marketers aware of this can develop strategies appropriate for short product life cycles.

The shapes of the product life cycles, the rates of change in sales and profits, and the lengths and heights of the cycles vary greatly.

IS THERE LIFE AFTER DECLINE?

Occasionally, a product life cycle changes slope, reversing the downward trend associated with the late maturity and decline stages. Some products and brands approach extinction, only to suddenly achieve a new-found popularity. Such a turn

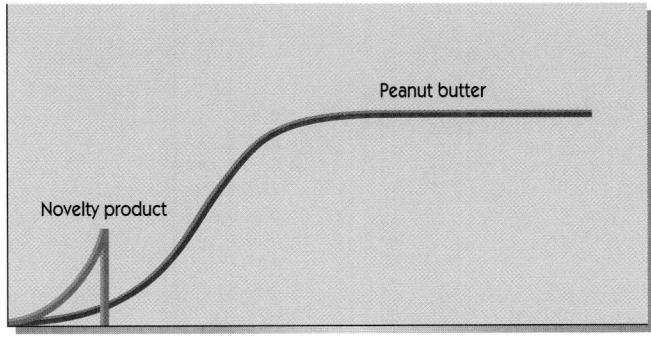

Long and Short Product Life Cycles

of events may be due to nostalgia or to the sudden realization that an old, familiar brand or product was really pretty good after all. A change in the marketing environment may bring this about.

In the last decade, for example, considerable medical attention has been given to proper nutrition and exercise as means of maintaining good health. Consumers have begun to recognize the importance of fiber in the diet. Some new products appeared in response to nutrition-related concerns, and certain old products—Granola, soups, and natural sweeteners such as honey, among others—were suddenly more in demand and were marketed accordingly. Similarly, the increased concern with physical fitness helped the sales of jogging shoes, jump ropes, bicycles, and exercise machines.

The Adoption and Diffusion Processes

At all stages of the product life cycle, but especially during the introduction stage, organizations are concerned with who will actually buy, use, or in some other way adopt the product. Marketers who understand why and when customers accept new products are able to manage product strategy effectively over the course of a product's life cycle. This understanding requires familiarity with the related processes of adoption and diffusion.

A person who purchases a product he or she has never tried before may ultimately become an adopter. The mental and behavioral stages through which an individual adopter passes before actually making a purchase or placing an order constitute the **adoption process**. These stages are awareness, interest, evaluation, trial, and—finally—adoption.

Not all potential buyers go through the stages of the adoption process at the same rate of speed. Some pass through them very quickly and are the first to adopt the new product. Others take longer to become aware of the product and to make up their minds to purchase it. Still others take a very long time to accept

> Not all potential buyers go through the stages of the adoption process at the same rate. Some pass through them very quickly and are the first to adopt the new product. Others take longer.

Adoption process
The mental and behavioral stages through which a consumer passes before making a purchase or placing an order. The stages are awareness, interest, evaluation, trial, and adoption.

The Diffusion Process

Unit sales and
percentage
of adopters

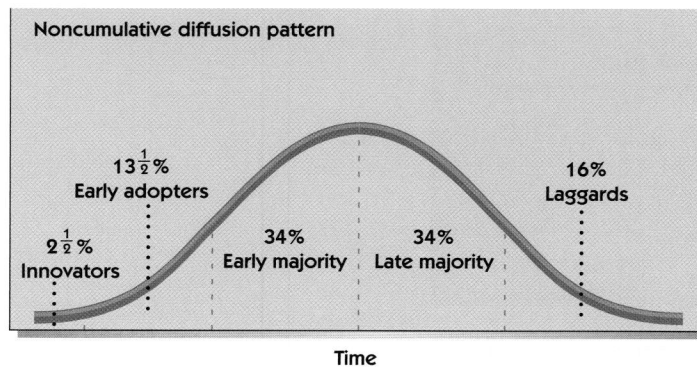

Cumulative
percentage
of adopters

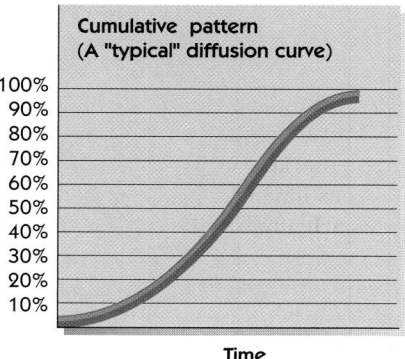

and adopt the product. This spread of the new product through society is called the **diffusion process**. The stages in the diffusion process can be charted, as shown in Exhibit 10-7. As the exhibit shows, the cumulative pattern of adopters closely follows the shape of the product life cycle.

To remember the difference between the adoption process and the diffusion process, keep in mind that individuals go through the various psychological stages involved in adoption, while it is the new product that is diffused through the social system as it is purchased by the various groups of adopters.[10]

Diffusion process
The spread of a new product through society.

INNOVATORS—BEING VENTURESOME

Innovators—the consumers most likely to try something new—are the first to buy a new product. These people are venturesome, willing to be daring and different. They are the customers most confident about thinking for themselves and most likely to deviate from their local community's established way of doing things. Innovators, because they are eager to try new ideas, are extremely important in getting a new product accepted in the market. As Exhibit 10-7 shows, this venturesome group is small in number. As might be expected, members of this group are likely to be younger and better educated than the average consumer. They are generally higher-income buyers or financially stable individuals, who can afford to take a chance on something new.

Innovator
A member of the first group of consumers to buy a new product.

EARLY ADOPTERS—FOLLOWING THE LEAD

A larger group than the innovators, but a somewhat less adventurous one, is the early adopter group. Many characteristics of the innovator group are also found among the early adopters, since to be an **early adopter** often requires the income, self-confidence, and education to use a product that has still not gained wide acceptance. A major difference, however, is that unlike innovators, who adopt the product during the introduction stage of the product life cycle, most early adopters buy the product during the growth stage.

Early adopters read more magazines than the average person and have high usage rates in the product category in which the innovation falls. Although mem-

Early adopter
A member of the group of consumers who purchase a product soon after it has been introduced, but after the innovators have purchased it.

bers of this group follow the lead of the innovators, they are more integrated into their local communities. Early adopters are conceived of as opinion leaders, who help to determine which new products later adopters will find acceptable. Early adopters can be expected to influence their friends and coworkers and thus to contribute greatly to a new product's progress. Developers of new products therefore spend considerable time and resources in identifying and reaching this group. They are a significant target for advertisements and other promotions aimed at creating a market where none existed before.

EARLY AND LATE MAJORITIES—RIDING THE BANDWAGON

The early and late majorities, taken together, constitute approximately 68 percent of the overall group that adopts a new product (see Exhibit 10-7). They make up the mass market on which many products depend. The two halves of this market are seen as having similar characteristics in differing degrees.

The **early majority** is usually made up of solid, middle-class consumers, who are more deliberate and cautious in making purchasing decisions than are early adopters. Once this group adopts a new product, late in the growth stage, the product's acceptance and its diffusion throughout the social system are well established. In general, members of the early majority are of average socioeconomic status.

As time goes by and more and more consumers adopt an innovation, it is perceived to less risky. At this time, the product has reached maturity, and the late majority adopts the innovation. Members of the **late majority** are slightly less educated and financially stable than members of the early majority. They also are older, more conservative, and more traditional. They tend to be skeptical about new product ideas and reluctantly adopt innovations only when the products no longer carry the risk associated with newness. Social pressure also may force late adopters to purchase a product.

LAGGARDS—BRINGING UP THE REAR

Laggards, or final adopters, make up the last group to adopt a product. These people see a need for the product but for economic, social, or educational reasons have been slow to accept it. Innovations are not welcome to this older group, which is lowest in socioeconomic status. Laggards resist challenges to past fashion and traditions. The laggard group is especially easily identified when the product in question is clothing. Frequently, a new clothing design is adopted by innovators, early adopters, and members of the majority groups, who then drop it as the laggard group begins to wear the style.

NONADOPTERS—HOLDING OUT

No matter what the innovation, there are always some individuals who never buy the new product or adopt the new style. These people are known as **nonadopters**.

USE OF THE ADOPTER CATEGORIES

Planners about to introduce a new product should give close consideration to the diffusion process and the various adopter categories. Characteristics of the various adopter groups may provide the basis for market segmentation efforts. As you have seen, youth, economic resources, adventurousness, and other possible segmenting variables are usually not spread evenly among the adopter groups. Research and analysis of the characteristics of adopters can help the new product on its way and will surely pay off for marketing managers. As the target marketing and positioning focus shifts from early adopters to the early majority and late majority, promotional and other marketing plans, including pricing and distribution strategies, should be altered. Indeed, even the product strategy should be modified.

Early majority
A group of consumers, usually solid, middle-class people, who purchase more deliberately and cautiously than early adopters.

Late majority
A group of consumers who purchase a product after the early majority, when the product is no longer perceived as risky.

Laggard
A member of the group of final adopters in the diffusion process.

Nonadopter
A member of the group of consumers who never buy a particular new product or adopt a particular new style.

Strategies for Modifying Existing Products

New products should be carefully designed to appeal to well-researched target markets. However, most products and brands enjoy limited lives because of the dynamic nature of competition within target markets. Product strategy does not end with the design of the product; its role is ongoing. Dynamic markets must be monitored and researched so that appropriate strategies can be devised to keep old customers, to attract new ones, and to extend the product life cycle. Developing strategies for modifying existing products and managing the product mix is an important aspect of product management.

As we have stressed time and time again, no single facet of the marketing mix stands alone. Each facet must be viewed in light of what it contributes to the total mix, and each must be consistent with—and supportive of—the other variables. Despite these strong interrelationships, many marketing strategies have been developed that are specifically aimed at the product variable in the marketing mix. It is to these that we now turn our attention.

Product modification

The altering or adjusting of the product mix, typically influenced by the competitive nature of the market and by changes in the external environment.

The marketer's decision about **product modification**—that is, the altering or adjusting of the product mix—is typically influenced by the competitive nature of the market (such as design changes made by competitors) and by changes in the external environment (such as the discovery of a new technology). For example, when Braun noticed a trend toward greater consumption of gourmet coffees in coffee shops like Starbucks and at home, the company conducted a scientific study of what makes coffee flavors different from one another. It then introduced a new coffee maker that allows a user to select where the water will flow through the coffee grounds and how long it will have contact with them, thus controlling the bitterness or robustness of the coffee flavor.[11] Blaupunkt's DigiCeiver is an improvement on the traditional automobile radio because it produces a much cleaner sound by eliminating the static in automobile radios. When an analog signal comes in, the DigiCeiver converts it to a digital signal and gets rid of the noise. Most product modification decisions attempt to create a competitive advantage, through such means as product differentiation or reducing costs. We will discuss three general strategies for modifying existing products: cost reduction, repositioning, and total quality management strategies.

COST REDUCTION STRATEGIES

Cost reduction strategy

A product strategy that involves redesigning a product to lower production costs.

As new competitors, perhaps global competitors with factories in newly industrialized countries, enter the market, profits may be squeezed. The company with a product in the maturity or decline stage may choose to introduce a **cost reduction strategy**. This product strategy requires redesigning the product and working with production experts to lower factory costs or operating costs. For example, Chrysler is working on perfecting a plastic car body that would consist of only 6 big pieces instead of the typical 80 parts. The plastic parts need no paint and could halve the price of a car.

Implementing a cost reduction strategy may require moving production to another country. Stanley Works, a company that 35 years ago produced all its tools in New England, now operates a factory in Puebla, Mexico, to make its sledgehammers and wrecking bars. Low-cost labor was essential to compete with inexpensive imports from China.

Often, a company elects to produce a stripped-down version of the initial product with less expensive materials, aimed at price-conscious market segments. Shuttle by United, which United Airlines initiated to compete with low-fare airlines like Southwest, is an example. The cost reduction strategy need not mean a reduction in quality.

PC WEEK became eWEEK because its content changed over the years to focus on Internet-based solutions and not just personal computers.

REPOSITIONING STRATEGIES

A **repositioning strategy** changes the product design, formulation, brand image, or brand name so as to alter the product's competitive position. Reformulating a soft drink to use NutraSweet instead of sugar, for example, may be intended to change the product's major benefit (from a sweet treat to weight control). Repositioning strategies usually include a corresponding change in promotion strategy.

A change in the market environment or an initial mistake in brand name selection may mean that a name or symbol has to be changed to reposition the brand. The original brand name may have been a bad choice that grew worse over time. This was the case with Heartwise cereal, whose name was changed to Fiberwise after the Food and Drug Administration argued there was no evidence that the cereal was good for the heart. In other instances, a brand name or trademark symbol may serve long and well but become inappropriate as the brand ages and times change.

Around the world, organizations are repositioning themselves to adapt to changes resulting from merger, diversification, or international interests. Southwestern Bell, which became SBC Corporation, changed its name because it is no longer just a regional marketer in the Southwestern United States—it is a global marketer. As international trade becomes ever more important, companies are adding words like *International* and *Worldwide* to their official names. However, each name change, especially when the original name is well established, involves many risks. Goodwill may be lost if customers fail to realize that the new company is the same as the old one.

Repositioning strategy
A product strategy that involves changing the product design, formulation, brand image, or brand name so as to alter the product's competitive position.

TOTAL QUALITY MANAGEMENT STRATEGIES

Total quality management strategies emphasize market-driven quality as a top priority. Chapter 2 indicated that for many years some U.S. corporations did not keep pace with the product quality offered by a number of overseas competitors. Today, with intense levels of global competition, most companies must adopt a total quality management philosophy. Total quality management involves properly implementing and adjusting the product mix (and procedures within the entire organization) to ensure customers' satisfaction with product quality. It is a strategy

Total quality management strategy
A product strategy that emphasizes market-driven quality; also called a *quality assurance strategy*.

based on the conviction that if an organization wishes to prosper, every employee must work for continuous quality improvement.

What is quality? Organizations once defined quality by engineering standards. Most marketers today don't see quality that way. Some marketers say that quality means that their good or service conforms to consumers' requirements—that the product is acceptable. Effective marketers subscribing to a total quality management philosophy, however, believe that the product's quality must go beyond acceptability for a given price range. Rather than having consumers pleased that nothing went wrong, effective marketers want consumers to experience some delightful surprises or reap some unexpected benefits. In other words, quality assurance is more than just meeting minimum standards. Total quality management requires continuous improvement of product quality, enhancement of products with additional features as the products age, or both.

Managers continuously improve product quality to keep their brands competitive. Obviously, a Bentley from Rolls-Royce does not compete with a Geo Storm from General Motors. Buyers of these automobiles are in different market segments, and their expectations of quality differ widely. Nevertheless, marketers at both Rolls-Royce and General Motors try to determine what quality level their target market expects and then attempt to market goods and services that continually surpass expectations.

Product enhancement
The introduction of a new and improved version of an existing product, intended to extend the product's life cycle by keeping it in the growth stage.

Marketers expect **product enhancement**—the introduction of a new and improved version of an existing brand—to extend a product's life cycle by keeping it in the growth stage. The Gillette Company is a master at this strategy. Exhibit 10-8 depicts the product life cycle for Gillette razors.

Notice how the company has managed to keep its basic product alive by steadily improving blades and razors. In 1990, Gillette introduced Sensor, a razor with a new suspension system. It provides a cleaner, smoother, and safer shave and has proved very successful. In 1994, Gillette upgraded the Sensor with SensorExcel, a razor that features rubber "microfins" (designed to stretch the skin for a closer shave) and a larger lubricating strip. Next, Gillette introduced the Mach3, a new, more advanced shaving system with three blades, in 1998.

e   x   h   i   b   10-8

Gillette Razor Blades' Product Life Cycles

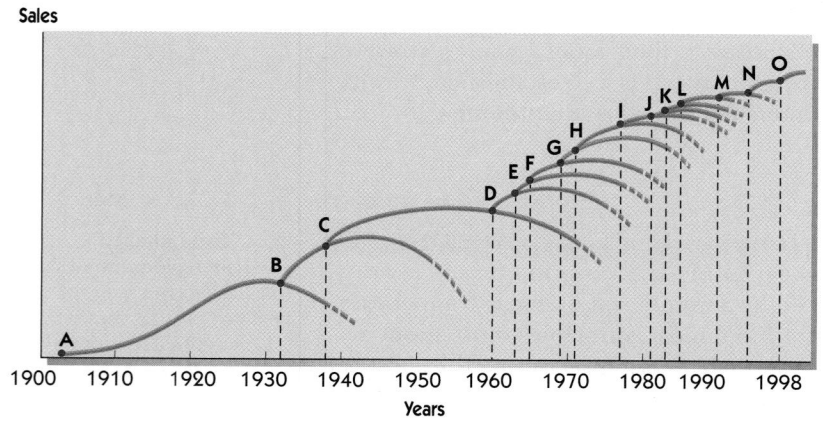

Blade	Year Introduced
A. Original Gillette blade	1903
B. Blue blade	1932
C. Thin blade	1938
D. Super blue blade	1960
E. Stainless steel blade	1963
F. Super stainless steel blade	1965
G. Platinum-plus blade	1969
H. Trac II	1971
I. ATRA	1977
J. Good News	1981
K. Good News Pivot	1983
L. ATRA Plus	1985
M. Sensor	1990
N. SensorExcel	1994
O. Mach3	1998

Gillette's strategy heavily emphasizes improving product performance—how well the razors remove whiskers. Product performance, however, is only one aspect of quality. Consumers perceive other dimensions of product quality, as defined in Exhibit 10-9. (The special aspects of service quality will be described in Chapter 11.)

Many of the dimensions of quality listed in Exhibit 10-9 are influenced by the quality of raw materials, production technology, and quality control at the factory. Although middle-level marketing managers have some influence in these areas, they do not have the primary decision-making responsibility for these activities. To ensure production quality, therefore, top management must communicate the consumers' needs to those who have production authority.

Top managers often have people from different functional areas of the company, such as finance, production, and marketing, work as a team to establish the appropriate processes for total quality management. Individuals in these cross-functional teams are empowered to organize their work and make decisions. They share a common goal and jointly design and develop processes so that the organization runs smoothly, efficiently, and effectively, without "bureaucratic red tape" and barriers that give functional managers exclusive control over certain operations. Cross-functional teams operate under the assumption that employees actively involved in the quality process have valuable insight about ways to improve customer-driven quality.

1 We've been on a roll for 67 years.

2 So we've popped up with another big idea. It's an ingenious dispensing system that pops up strips of tape – pre-cut, one at a time, right into your hand. Scotch™ Pop-up Tape Strips make gift wrapping easier, especially when you've got your hands full. We're making tape even more handy, because we make the leap *from need to...*

3M *Innovation*

©3M 1999   For more information, call 1-800-3M-HELPS, or Internet: http://www.3m.com

Scotch brand tape has evolved during the product life cycle of "cellophane" tape. 3M is an innovative company that understands how product enhancement extends a product's life.

http://www.3m.com

Quality Dimensions for Goods[12]

Performance	How well does the product perform its core function? (How well does a razor remove whiskers?)
Features	Does the product have adequate auxiliary dimensions that provide secondary benefits? (Does a motor oil come in a convenient package?)
Conformity to specifications	What is the incidence of defects? (Does a vineyard sell spoiled wine?)
Reliability	Does the product ever fail to work? Does the product perform with consistency? (Will the lawn mower work properly each time it is used?)
Durability	What is the economic life of the product? (How long will a motorcycle last?)
Aesthetic design	Does the product's design look and feel like that of a high-quality product? (Is a snowmobile aerodynamic?)
Serviceability	Is the service system efficient, competent, and convenient? (Does a computer software company have a toll-free telephone number and a technical staff to answer questions quickly?)

Design and style can be used to differentiate a product from its competition. This Macintosh laptop computer is ergonomically designed for portability. The functional design is reinforced by the aesthetic design and bright colors, which evoke user-friendly advanced technology.

http://www.apple.com/imac

Product design
A product's configuration, composition, and style. This characteristic influences most consumers' perceptions of product quality.

Style
A distinctive execution, construction, or design in a product class.

Fashion
A style that is current or in vogue.

Fad
A passing fashion or craze that interests many people for only a short time.

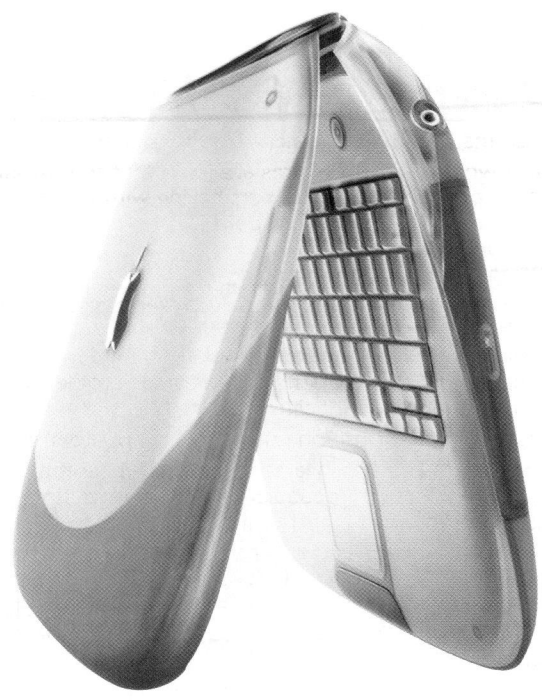

Product Design Product design—that is, a product's configuration, composition, and style—influences most quality dimensions. Marketers must work with engineers on product design to achieve quality goals. Assuring that a product design is aesthetically pleasing and fashionable often requires considerable consumer research, artistic creativity, and product planning.

Often, consumers' perceptions of quality are influenced by a noticeable aspect of product design or formulation. For example, the sound quality of stereo speakers can be difficult to assess, so many consumers believe that the larger the speaker, the better the sound. Consumers of tomato juice equate thickness with quality. With automobiles, a solid sound when the door closes symbolizes good construction and a solid, safe body.

Color contributes to the way people perceive products. When a Windex competitor tested a colorless window cleaner against the market leader, consumers did not perceive the new (and improved) cleaner to be better. However, when the product was tinted blue, consumer evaluation of product quality improved dramatically. When Igloo Products Corporation wanted to boost sales of its coolers, the company brought in a color consultant. She turned up her nose at Igloo's prosaic red and blue coolers and advised the company to add turquoise- and raspberry-colored products to the line. After the new shades hit the shelves, sales jumped 15 percent. Igloo currently offers its coolers in purple, tangerine, and lime green, as well as in traditional red and blue.

The design of a building, an evening gown, a piece of furniture, or any other product may be influenced by what is currently in fashion. The terms *style*, *fashion*, and *fad* refer to specific concepts. **Style** refers to a distinctive execution, construction, or design. For example, paintings might be in the classic, impressionist, or modern style. A **fashion** is a style that is current or in vogue. A **fad** is a passing fashion or craze in which many people are interested for a short time. A fad item is purchased because of its novelty. For example, Tiger's Giga Pets, Tamagotchi's Virtual Pets, and Playmates' Talking Nano—digital "animals" on key chains—were fad items in 1997. The perceived quality of many products—especially clothing, such as a T-shirt from the Beastie Boys' latest concert tour—is intertwined with consumers' feelings about fashion and fads. Marketers spend considerable effort trying to understand how styles, fashions, and fads influence perceived product quality.

Implementing a Total Quality Management Strategy As we have pointed out, underlying total quality management is the assumption that the voice of the consumer has to be brought into the quality improvement process. Thus, marketing research—specifically, customer satisfaction surveys—is an integral part of a total quality management strategy. Managers of quality assurance programs have found that companies that do not measure quality are less likely to improve product quality than companies that regularly measure quality against established standards.

STAGE	IMPLEMENTATION STEPS
Commitment Stage	Establish that it is the customers, not the organization, who define quality.
Exploration Stage	Discover what product features are important to customers: • What problems are customers having with the product? • What aspects of product operation or customer service have disappointed customers? • What is the company doing right?
Benchmarking Stage	Establish quantitative measures that can serve as benchmarks or points of comparison for evaluating future efforts: • Initial measures of overall satisfaction • Measures of the frequency of customer problems • Quality ratings for specific attributes Identify the brand's position relative to competitors' quality positions.
Initial Quality Improvement Stage	Establish the quality improvement process within the organization. Translate quality issues into the internal vocabulary of the organization. Establish performance standards and expectations for improvement.
Measurement Stage—Wave 1	Conduct Wave 1 to measure trends in satisfaction and quality ratings. Determine if the organization is meeting customer needs as specified by quantitative standards.
Continuous Quality Improvement Stage	Through quality improvement management, allow employees to initiate problem-solving behavior without a lot of red tape. Initiate proactive communications with consumers.
Measurement Stage—Wave 2	Conduct Wave 2 to track quality and compare results with earlier stages.
Continuous Quality Improvement Stage	Continue quality improvement efforts.

Exhibit 10-10 illustrates the stages in the implementation of a total quality management strategy. The process begins with making a commitment to total quality assurance through a program that measures performance against consumers' standards, not standards determined by quality engineers within the company. All changes in the organization are oriented toward improvement of consumers' perceptions of product quality. Exhibit 10-10 indicates that establishing consumer requirements, quantifying benchmark measures, setting objectives, conducting marketing research studies, and making adjustments in the organization to improve quality go hand in hand. Total quality management is an ongoing process for continuous improvement.

The steps described in Exhibit 10-10 work for both goods and services. However, service products and customer services offered along with goods have some distinctive aspects.

Matching Products to Markets—Product Line Strategy

The ultimate goal of the marketing manager is to develop a total product offering that satisfies the desires of target customers. Because most markets have heterogeneous needs, an organization ideally would develop a series of products so that each target market's needs and desires would be mirrored by a product offering. However, as discussed in Chapter 8, in reality a firm must select meaningful market segments that will be profitable. The **product line strategy** involves matching product items within a product line to markets.

The options an organization faces may be described in the following terms:

- The **full-line**, or **deep-line**, **strategy** means offering a large number of variations of a product.
- The **limited-line strategy** entails offering a smaller number of variations.

Product line strategy
The strategy of matching items within a product line to markets.

Full-line strategy
A product line strategy that involves offering a large number of variations of a product; also called a *deep-line strategy.*

Limited-line strategy
A product-line strategy that involves offering a smaller number of product variations than a full-line strategy offers.

Single-product strategy
A product line strategy that involves offering one product item or one product version with very few options.

- The **single-product strategy** involves offering one product item or one product version with very few model options.

The product line strategy is influenced by the diversity of the market and the resources available to the company. In general, the deeper the product line, the higher the cost. Customers have more selection with a deep line, and this gives the marketer more opportunities to make a sale. However, offering too many product items may involve an economic penalty to the organization. Conversely, a sparse line may not match the market's demands, and the company may lose sales. However, high volume of one or a few items usually results in production and distribution economies of scale that increase profit margins.

A major product strategy question to consider is this: How many variations on a product can be presented to the market before the extra customer satisfaction achieved is no longer worth the expense to the company? The product line strategy alternatives must be evaluated in terms of the market addressed.

STRATEGIES FOR EXPANDING THE PRODUCT LINE OR THE PRODUCT MIX

Interpreting the market's needs often leads organizations to develop new product items that are very similar to existing products. These may be product line extensions or product category extensions.

Product line extension
An item added to an existing product line to create depth; also called a *line extension.*

Product category extension
A new item or new line of items in a product category that is new to the company.

Brand extension
A product category extension or product line extension that employs a brand name already used on one of the company's existing products.

A **product line extension** (or line extension) is an item added to an existing product line to provide depth. For example, when Uncle Ben's Inc. added Uncle Ben's Calcium Plus rice, it created a product line extension. A **product category extension** is a new item or new line of items in a product category that is new to the company. For example, Ultra Slim-Fast, which began as a diet drink (a meal replacement shake), expanded into microwavable meals and frozen desserts.

A product category extension may be called a brand extension if products in the new category use a brand name already used on one of the company's existing products. That is what Ultra Slim-Fast did. The term **brand extension**, however, may also refer to a product line extension. This can be a bit confusing. However, if you remember that the term *brand extension* involves the use of a brand name and may be used for either a new item in an existing product line or an item in a new product category, you will find the terminology easier to understand.

The concept of brand equity, introduced in Chapter 9, helps explain the reasons for brand extensions.[13] When a brand name like Weight Watcher's, Disney, or Harley-Davidson adds value to a product, the name is said to have brand equity. Market share or profit margins are greater because of the goodwill associated with the brand. Brand equity gives a brand higher financial value if the company is sold and also if the brand is used on other products. Brand equity is especially useful for brand extensions in similar product categories.

Cannibalize
To eat into the sales revenues of another product item in the same line.

Sometimes a product line extension will **cannibalize** sales from other items in the product line—that is, eat into the sales revenues from those items.[14] For example, Gillette's Mach3 shaving system, the result of a multi-year development project, was intended to lure customers away from inexpensive disposable razors, which had achieved a 60 percent share of the market. Mach3 did indeed take sales away from competitors' brands. However, it also cannibalized sales from Gillette's other razor brands. Gillette has a tradition of creating incremental technological advancements that lead to product line extensions. When Mach3 was introduced in 1998, Gillette knew it would take sales away from SensorExcel, but the company also knew it would improve overall company profits.

PRODUCT MODIFICATIONS FOR INTERNATIONAL MARKETS

The home-based international marketer must decide how much to adjust a product and its domestic marketing strategy for each foreign market. Similarly, the globally oriented multinational must determine the extent to which market variations necessitate marketing adjustments.

A marketer adopting a **globalization strategy**, or standardization strategy, standardizes its product mix and promotion mix around the world. This strategy assumes that, in our modern era of global communication, the behavior of many consumers throughout the world has become very similar. For example, this strategy assumes that around the globe, members of market segments that can afford Panasonic videotape recorders desire the same features and buy for the same reasons. It also assumes that cost savings from production and marketing economies of scale will more than offset any sales lost because the organization's product and promotional strategies have not been adapted to local conditions. Using this strategy, a company will sell the same product, with no adjustments, in all markets. This works well for some products but not for others. Products vary in sensitivity to environmental conditions such as economic, cultural, and social factors. Industrial products, for example, may be used in much the same way in all markets in the world. Therefore, their use (and thus their marketing) is not sensitive to the peculiarities of separate cultures and economies.

At the opposite extreme are certain food items, whose use and acceptance vary among countries. Other products that are highly sensitive to local conditions are not likely candidates for extension to foreign markets. Post-It Notes provides a good example. Post-It Notes are big sellers in the United States and Japan. In Japan, however, the shape of the paper is long and narrow to accommodate the vertical orientation of Japanese writing. Many situations call for a customization strategy.

A **customization strategy** adapts the product strategy to each country where the good or service is marketed. There are two basic approaches to a customization strategy. The company may sell the same product, adapted to a specific market, or it may sell a new product invention in a market.

Many products are best marketed with some sort of adaptation to local conditions. For example, Stanley Tools found that—despite the fact that the European Union offers the potential for a unified market for many of its products—the English and the French disagree on whether a handsaw should have a wooden or a plastic handle. Sometimes adjustments are required because of government regulations. For instance, when Mentor O&O, a small manufacturer of surgical equipment used in eye care, decided to market one of its testing devices in Germany, the company had to modify its equipment to meet design specifications established by the German government. The Mentor testing device sold in the United States, which meets the rigorous standards of the U.S. government, has an alarm bell with an on-off switch. The German specifications required that the on-off switch be removed and dictated just how loud the alarm bell must sound.

Product invention requires the development of a new product for the international market. A company may opt to use *backward invention* (re-creating or reintroducing a product that is obsolete in the domestic market in another market) or *forward invention* (creating a new product for the different market conditions). Forward invention is the costliest and riskiest product strategy, but the potential for rewards is also the greatest.

The general approach taken by many marketers is to maintain a global corporate strategy with tactical adjustments where local conditions warrant them. If there were no strategic continuity of approach, the company would not gain a solid and cohesive global identity. Instead, its identity would consist of a patchwork of the fragmented efforts in its various markets. There is value in coordinating and standardizing strategic planning worldwide.

ELIMINATING OLD PRODUCTS

Many products that were once winners eventually become losers. However, managers, while stressing new product development efforts, often neglect product elimination efforts. Profits can be enhanced by eliminating certain costs associated with products in the later stages of the product life cycle, as well as by increasing the productivity of the resources released when older products are

Globalization strategy
A plan by which a marketer standardizes its marketing strategy around the world; also called a *standardization strategy*.

Customization strategy
A product line extension strategy that involves making a product in relatively small lots for specific channels of distribution or specific customers.

phased out. Hence, elimination of products is a strategic move that product managers should consider. The products may either be dropped entirely or be replaced by other products that better satisfy changing market requirements. Marketing managers should devote systematic attention to the elimination of products that are no longer profitable, although this is sometimes a painful process necessitating the realignment of company personnel and other assets. Every organization works with a limited pool of talent and resources. Expending these on products that are in the final period of the decline stage detracts from efforts to pursue new opportunities.

Ethical Considerations Associated with Product Strategy

When product strategy is viewed from a macromarketing perspective, it becomes apparent that marketers have certain responsibilities. For example, many laws require that marketers be accountable to customers, competitors, and the general public. This section discusses consumers' right to safety, their right to be informed, and their concerns about quality of life and ecology. It also addresses the issue of product obsolescence.

THE RIGHT TO SAFETY

Consumers have many expectations when they buy a product. They want it to work properly, to last a certain amount of time, and so on. But probably the most basic expectation is that a product will be safe. Although most of us are willing to take certain reasonable risks, we do not want our use of a product to place us unnecessarily in danger.

The makers of Sudafed 12-hour capsules faced a safety problem when some packages of that product were found to contain deadly cyanide. The manufacturer did not place the cyanide in the capsules. However, was the company negligent in failing to package Sudafed in tamper-proof bottles so that no one else could put poison in the capsules? Should ketchup, mayonnaise, and milk all be in tamper-proof containers to guard against any similar attempts?

Clearly some reasonable risks must be taken. Most would agree, however, that consumers should be protected against products that are hazardous to life or health. The modern emphasis on the **right to safety** is a move away from *caveat emptor* ("let the buyer beware") to a philosophy that holds sellers responsible for their products.

Right to safety
The right to expect the products one purchases to be free from unnecessary dangers. Consumers assume they are entitled to this right.

THE RIGHT TO BE INFORMED

After the Food and Drug Administration investigated Calegene Incorporated's genetically engineered "Flavr Savr" tomato gene, the agency concluded that it is a safe food additive. Critics, who contend the new genes that go into these tomatoes may be medically and environmentally unsafe, want genetically engineered tomatoes to be labeled. They want the **right to be informed**.

Most of us would agree that the consumer should not be given grossly misleading information or exposed to deceptive advertising, fraudulent labeling, or other deceitful practices. The consumer has the right to the facts needed to make an informed choice. The right to be informed is reflected in laws and practices involving the inclusion on labels of information on nutritional content, product content, country of origin, and quality. Requirements relating to truth in lending and package design also point out the importance of this right.

Right to be informed
The consumer's right to have access to the information required to make an intelligent choice from among the available products.

QUALITY OF LIFE AND ECOLOGY

As the United States, Canada, and certain other nations have become more affluent, the values of their citizens have changed. People are increasingly concerned with

Around the world there is a growing concern for quality of life among consumers. Many consumers will use only products that do not harm the environment.

quality of life. This term, although difficult to define precisely, reflects a lessening concern with being economically well-off and an increasing concern with well-being.

This shift translates into a feeling on the part of consumers that organizations should be expected to be more than economically efficient. Customers call on business organizations also to preserve the environment and to conserve natural resources.

Issues of quality of life spring from the idea that citizens have certain rights that no organization can be permitted to violate. Meeting quality-of-life expectations while fulfilling other missions has caused organizations many problems. Yet most consumers are interested in both quality-of-life issues and the demands of the law. So organizations that wish to meet customers' demands must address these expectations.

A major quality-of-life issue involves ecological problems and the protection of the environment. Many people believe that organizations, as important members of society, have a responsibility not to tamper with or damage the environment. However, this issue is complex, because people want other things as well. Environmental issues are loaded with trade-offs:

- People want low-priced electricity. Yet marketers of electric power are told that nuclear plants are disruptive to ecosystems and very dangerous. And many people do not want electric companies to burn coal in order to generate electricity, because burning causes air pollution. Coal mining too can create pollution and can leave the land permanently scarred.
- Nonreturnable cans and bottles create litter problems and damage the environment in other ways. But people do not like the bother and expense associated with returnables and often just throw them away.
- People want clean air, but they do not want to car pool or take buses to work.

That marketing has a social responsibility to preserve the environment is obvious. What is not obvious is how that responsibility will be met. Who will pay—in dollars and inconvenience—for a cleaner environment? Are consumers willing to pay higher prices for products that reduce pollution? Does society place a higher value on lower-priced automobiles or on clean air?

A cleaner environment can be achieved in part through producers' efforts to recycle waste products to make new products. Recycling efforts by both businesses and individual consumers can reduce trash and litter and conserve natural resources.

Quality of life
The degree to which people in a society feel a sense of well-being.

Product obsolescence
The process by which an existing product goes out of date because of the introduction of a new product.

Physical obsolescence
The breakdown of a product due to wear and tear.

Planned obsolescence
The practice of purposely causing existing products to go out of date by introducing new products at frequent intervals.

Right to choose
The consumer's right to have viable alternatives from which to choose.

The issue of **product obsolescence**—which occurs when an existing product becomes out of date because of the introduction of a new product—is another ethical concern. Some critics have said it is inappropriate for marketers to strive to make existing products obsolete, or out of date—especially when the obsolescence is related to a change in fashion rather than technology.

To be sure, no product lasts forever. When a product breaks down because of wear and tear, as when a lawn mower stops working after six years, the problem is **physical obsolescence**. **Planned obsolescence** is more controversial. Because new products yield the greatest profits, marketers plan product obsolescence to help maintain an adequate profit level and ensure corporate survival. Many products, then, are designed not to last a long time.

Although it may sound paradoxical, this planned obsolescence is generally an attempt to satisfy consumer needs. For most consumers, purchasing a $450 lawn mower that lasts for six summers is preferable to spending $1,900 for one that lasts 30 years. Furthermore, individuals in our culture find new styles of apparel, extra gadgets on appliances, and the latest automobile models more attractive. Although these style changes may not improve the performance of a product, they satisfy a number of psychological and social needs.

Product obsolescence is part of a broader issue that has been called the consumer's **right to choose** within a free enterprise system. Some argue that planned obsolescence violates consumers' right to have alternatives from which to choose; they suggest that consumers are being manipulated. Others argue that although the macromarketing system has occasionally failed to observe consumers' right to choose, if a company offers a poor product or makes one obsolete unnecessarily, competitors usually take advantage of the situation by offering customers the products they demand.

The free enterprise system, with rare exception, does serve the consumer's right to choose, and serves it well. The consumer's right to choose is interrelated with the need for competition in a free market. The Interstate Commerce Commission Act, the Sherman Act, the Clayton Act, the Federal Trade Commission Act, the Robinson-Patman Act, the Wheeler-Lea Act, and the Celler amendment to the Clayton Act all protect consumer choice.

Marketers of haute couture are sometimes criticized for planning fashion obsolescence.

Summary

Products differ in their degree of newness and in their chance of succeeding in the marketplace. Marketers must understand what is involved in developing and introducing new products. They must also understand the product life cycle and plan strategies to enable their products to succeed throughout the life cycle.

1) Define product newness and explain the chances of success and failure for new products.

Managers and consumers view newness differently. Managers classify new products on the basis of newness to the company and newness to the market. Consumers distinguish products on a continuum of newness that includes discontinuous innovations, dynamically continuous innovations, and continuous innovations. A new product's chances for commercial success are generally low. The failure rate is ordinarily greater for consumer products than for organizational goods, because the consumer market is more dynamic and organizational buyers are better able than consumers to express their needs to marketers.

2) Identify general characteristics of successful new products.

Five characteristics influence a new product's chances for success in the marketplace: (1) relative advantage, a clear-cut improvement over existing products; (2) compatibility with existing consumption and usage patterns; (3) trialability, which allows buyers to test the new product with little effort or risk; (4) observability, which allows buyers to see and understand the product's advantages over existing products; and (5) product simplicity, which allows the consumer to understand and operate the product.

3) Characterize the stages of new product development.

New product development involves five processes: (1) idea generation, the search for a new idea; (2) screening, the evaluation of an idea's suitability to the organization and target markets; (3) business analysis, the detailed study and testing of the new idea; (4) development, the construction and testing of the actual product; and (5) commercialization, the full-scale production and marketing of the new product.

4) Identify some of the most common reasons for new product failures.

Some of the most common reasons for new product failures are insufficient product superiority, inferior or inadequate planning, poor execution, technical problems, and poor timing.

5) Describe the product life cycle and characterize its stages.

The product life cycle charts the sales history of a product from introduction to withdrawal. The life-cycle stages are introduction, growth, maturity, and decline. The introduction stage is characterized by large expenditures, an intensive marketing effort, and low profits. In this stage, the marketer must generate product awareness and create channels of distribution. The growth stage involves large expenditures and increasing competition, as well as rapid sales growth. The marketer must create brand preferences and promote differential features. During the maturity stage, sales growth decreases, reflecting intense competition. The goal is to maintain or expand market share. Decreasing profits and decreasing expenditures mark the decline stage. Introducing a new and improved product may reverse declines in sales, but termination is typically the final phase.

6) Describe the new product diffusion process and list the groups of adopters to which marketers must direct their appeals.

Not all buyers adopt a new product at the same time. The path is blazed by innovators, followed by early adopters, members of the early and late majorities, and finally laggards. Members of the first groups tend to be younger, more adventurous, better educated, and wealthier than members of later groups. Each group has characteristics and concerns that the marketer must address.

7) Identify strategies for modifying existing products.

Developing strategies for modifying existing products is an important aspect of product management. These strategies include cost reduction, repositioning, and total quality management. Decisions to modify products are typically influenced by the degree of competition in the marketplace and by changes in the external environment.

8) Explain the total quality management process for goods and services.

Total quality management programs measure quality from the customer's perspective and adjust product strategies accordingly. Implementing a total quality management strategy involves discovering what customers want, establishing quantitative measures to serve as benchmarks, establishing the quality improvement process within the organization, measuring customer satisfaction with the improvements, and so on, in a continuous process of quality improvement.

9) Understand how marketers manage product lines.

The product line strategy, which attempts to match product items to markets, is influenced by the diversity of the market and the resources available to the company. Marketers must ask themselves how many variations of a product can be offered before the extra customer satisfaction achieved is no longer worth the expense to the company.

10) Identify some ethical questions associated with product strategy.

Ethical issues associated with product strategy include those involving consumers' right to safety, consumers' right to be informed, and quality of life. The issue of whether product obsolescence, and especially planned obsolescence, is ethical is part of the broader issue of consumers' right to choose.

Key Terms

adoption process (p. 281)
brand extension (p. 290)
business analysis stage (p. 270)
cannibalize (p. 290)
commercialization (p. 272)
concept testing (p. 271)
continuous innovation (p. 264)
cost reduction strategy (p. 284)
customization strategy (p. 291)
decline stage (p. 279)
development stage (p. 270)
diffusion process (p. 282)
discontinuous innovation (p. 263)
divisibility (p. 266)
dynamically continuous innovation (p. 264)
early adopter (p. 282)
early majority (p. 283)
fad (p. 288)
fashion (p. 288)

full-line, or deep-line, strategy (p. 289)
globalization strategy (p. 291)
growth stage (p. 277)
idea generation stage (p. 268)
innovator (p. 282)
introduction stage (p. 275)
laggard (p. 283)
late majority (p. 283)
limited-line strategy (p. 289)
maturity stage (p. 277)
new product (p. 262)
nonadopter (p. 283)
observability (p. 267)
physical obsolescence (p. 294)
planned obsolescence (p. 294)
product category extension (p. 290)
product design (p. 288)
product enhancement (p. 286)
product life cycle (p. 274)

product line extension (p. 290)
product line strategy (p. 289)
product modification (p. 284)
product obsolescence (p. 294)
quality of life (p. 293)
relative advantage (p. 266)
repositioning strategy (p. 285)
right to be informed (p. 292)
right to choose (p. 294)
right to safety (p. 292)
screening stage (p. 269)
simplicity of usage (p. 267)
single-product strategy (p. 290)
style (p. 288)
test marketing (p. 271)
total quality management strategy (p. 285)
trial sampling (p. 266)
trialability (p. 266)

Questions for Review & Critical Thinking

1. What is your definition of a new product?
2. Classify the type of innovation represented by each of the following products.
   a. A wristwatch from Samsung that also functions as a cell phone
   b. An identity checker for use by banks and organizations that need to control who enters the premises. The product verifies a person's identity in seconds, using magnetically coded cards and electronic sensors to check people's fingerprints.
   c. A chainless bicycle. Instead of a chain, a shaft device (an axle located between the pedal and the wheel) transforms pedal movements into wheel rotation.
3. For the products in question 2, identify key product features that might speed acceptance.
4. Identify the steps in the new product development process. What takes place in each?
5. What are the main reasons new products fail?

6. What are the benefits and limitations of test marketing?
7. At what stage of the product life cycle would you place each of the following products?
   a. Cigars
   b. Lawnmowers that mulch
   c. Digital personal assistants (stylus-activated personal computers)
   d. Theme amusement parks
   e. Tennis balls
   f. Slide rules
8. Trace the product life cycle for a particular brand, such as the Sony digital camera.
9. Identify some typical marketing mix strategies used during each stage of the product life cycle.
10. Does marketing grow in importance as a product matures and moves from the introductory stage through the growth stage and into the maturity stage? Explain.

11. What are the most prominent characteristics of each adopter group in the diffusion process?
12. What guidelines would you suggest for rejuvenating old brands in the mature stage of the product life cycle?
13. How important is brand equity to a line extension strategy?
14. Some home builders are marketing houses with cable setups so that new owners can install computer terminals. What product strategy does this reflect?
15. SNOT (Super Nauseating Obnoxious Treat), Wurmz'n Dirt, and Bubble Tongue are names of some recently introduced novelty candy items. Now it's your turn to come up with some new ones. Form groups as directed by your instructor.

Step 1: Take 10 minutes to do some brainstorming to generate new product ideas for novelty candies. Do not evaluate the ideas, just generate as many as you can.
Step 2: In the next 10-minute period, evaluate the ideas and decide which products should be considered for business analysis.
Step 3: Discuss as a class how the groups' ideas emerged and whether each group was able to come to a consensus about which products were best.

---

e—exercises | http://zikmund.swcollege.com

1. Go to The New Products Showcase & Learning Center Web site at http://www.showlearn.com/. Click on The Product Showcase and then on Hits & Misses. Discuss an example of a failed product and a successful product.
2. Go to http://www.3m.com and click on 3M Innovation to read numerous stories about innovative products developed by 3M.

Address Book (Useful URLs)

Hot Product News	http://www.newproductnews.com
ZDNet Product Reviews	http://www.zdnet.com/products
Invention Facts and Myths	http://www.ideafinder.com/history/of_inventions.htm

---

Ethically Right or Wrong?

Coffee is a product in the mature stage of its life cycle. It has been served for hundreds of years.

McDonald's franchisees are required to prepare coffee at very high temperatures because McDonald's coffee consultants say hot temperatures are necessary to fully extract the flavor during brewing. McDonald's operations and training manual says coffee must be brewed at 195 to 205 degrees and held at 180 to 190 degrees for optimal taste. Coffee made at home is normally 135 to 140 degrees.

An Albuquerque woman bought a 49-cent cup of coffee at the drive-in window of a McDonald's and, while removing the lid from the top of the foam cup to add cream and sugar, spilled it, causing third-degree burns of the groin, inner thighs, and buttocks. She was in the hospital for over a week. Her lawsuit claimed the coffee was "defective" because it was so hot.

A jury awarded $2.9 million to the woman, who claimed McDonald's Corporation served dangerously hot coffee.[15]

1. If you had been on the jury for this case, what stand would you have taken?
2. If you owned a fast-food franchise other than McDonald's, at what temperature would you serve your coffee?

TAKE A STAND

1. What arguments are given by critics who say that it is inappropriate for marketers to strive to make perfectly good products obsolete?
2. Pet owners complain that a new flea and tick spray is making their dogs sick. Should the marketer take the product off the market?
3. A pajama manufacturer has developed a new fire-resistant chemical that will not wash out of children's pajamas until they have been washed more than 100 times. Should the pajamas be marketed as fire resistant?
4. Marketers introduce hundreds of new consumer package goods products every year. One year, 31 baby foods, 123 breakfast cereals, and 1,143 beverages were introduced. Does society need all these new products?
5. Is it ethical to initiate a cost-reduction strategy that requires closing a U.S. factory and opening a factory in an underdeveloped nation?

|case|

VIDEO CASE 10-1
Etec (B)

Etec was founded by an inventor and a former police officer. The company markets AutoCite, which is short for Automatic Citation Issuance System. Using this handheld computer and printing device, a police officer can write and record traffic violations much more efficiently. Today, AutoCite is used by police departments in more than 350 cities, municipalities, and college campuses. However, Etec sold only three units in its first two years of operation.

AutoCite is durable and works in all types of weather. A police officer who gives multiple tickets in a given location does not have to reprogram location information into the AutoCite. This allows the officer to produce more tickets in a given time period.

QUESTIONS

1. What are AutoCite's primary product characteristics and auxiliary dimensions?
2. How important are customer service and customer training for a product such as AutoCite?
3. In what stage of the product life cycle is AutoCite?
4. Products in the electronics industry often become obsolete because of new technology. How should AutoCite's marketing strategy deal with the issue of obsolescence?

cross-functional insights

Many theories and principles from other business disciplines can provide insights about the role marketing plays in an organization. The questions in this section are designed to help you think about integrating what you have learned in other business courses with the marketing principles explained in Chapters 9 and 10.

Trademarks   A trademark is a legally protected brand name or brand mark. The owners of trademarks have exclusive rights to their use.

What is the legal process required to obtain a trademark?

What can a marketer do if someone uses a trademark or patent without permission?

Warranty   A product warranty communicates a written guarantee of a product's integrity and outlines the manufacturer's responsibility for repairing or replacing defective parts.

According to U.S. law, what is an express warranty? What is an implied warranty?

New Product Development   New product development is the lifeblood of an organization. The process for developing new products starts with screening ideas and ends with commercialization of the new products.

How do the need to make a large investment in research and development for a new product and a financial manager's knowledge of net present value influence the decision to go ahead with the project?

How important is capital budgeting in new product development?

Should marketers expect higher rates of return on new-to-the-world products or on line extensions?

Can PERT (Program Evaluation and Review Technique) charts be used for new product development?

Product Life Cycle   The product life cycle is a depiction of a product's sales history from its "birth," or marketing beginning, to its "death," or withdrawal from the market. Products go through the stages of introduction, growth, maturity, and decline.

How does the return on investment (ROI) of a new product influence decision making? What is the relationship between ROI and net present value over the course of a product life cycle?

It is said that product life cycles are one of the justifications for the economic theory of comparative advantage. How is this so?

What role does ISO 9000 play in modifying products for the European market?

Which is more important to product managers during the growth stage of the product life cycle: financial accounting or managerial accounting?

Does the Occupational Safety and Health Act (OSHA) have any influence on product strategy?

Product Portfolio Analysis   Evaluation of a company's or a strategic business unit's product mix is called *product portfolio analysis*. Product portfolio analysis involves a matrix. The horizontal dimension of the matrix depicts relative market share on a scale from high to low. On the vertical scale, the same words refer to market growth rate. The combinations of these variables yield four quadrants: high-market-share product in a high-growth market, high-market-share product in a low-growth market, low-market-share product in a high-growth market, and low-market-share product in a low-growth market.

How are cash flow and product portfolio analysis related?

The Nature of the Supply Chain and Distribution

11

chapter

After you have studied this chapter, you will be able to . . .

1) Explain the general purpose of distribution and logistics in the marketing system.

2) Evaluate the role of the supply chain and physical distribution in the marketing mix.

3) Show how distribution managers can make physical distribution provide maximum satisfaction to buyers while reducing costs.

4) Explain the total cost approach to physical distribution.

5) Understand why all marketers—even not-for-profit and service organizations—engage in distribution.

6) Characterize the functions of channel intermediaries.

7) Identify the major channels of distribution used by marketers.

8) Describe the major vertical marketing systems.

9) Differentiate among channel cooperation, channel conflict, and channel power.

The French-born founder of Sole Technology Inc. chose to crack a tough niche market—shoes for skateboarders. But it appears he's brought to his new endeavor the success he garnered as a skateboard champ during the 1980s.

Sole has become one of the leading makers of skateboard shoes in just seven years. And the company has managed to grow its market share without becoming "uncool." *Uncool* may not be a word found in too many business plans. However, it's an important consideration in this business, and one on which founder Pierre Andre Senizergues has built his company's marketing strategy. That strategy is aimed at keeping the company's hard-core audience happy while it expands into larger distribution channels.

Some companies tend to lose focus as they get bigger. At Sole they believe it's the other way around. The more the company grows, the more money they invest at the core level. Sole stays cool by limiting the distribution of its product lines. Sole's eS and Emerica shoes sell only through skate shops, while its best-selling line, etnies, also sells in shopping centers.

Some retailers find the strategy frustrating. Pacific Sunwear, a chain of stores located in shopping centers, carries the etnie but isn't allowed to sell the other lines. Although Pacific Sunware would like to sell the entire line, Sole is sticking with its distribution strategy so that it doesn't become uncool.[1]

As sales at Sole Technology Inc. continue to climb, its founder remains committed to a distribution strategy that keeps the company cool.

This chapter provides an overview of the purpose of the distribution element of the marketing mix. It defines logistics, physical distribution, and channels of distribution. It explores the functions that intermediaries perform and the many alternative channels of distribution for goods and services. It addresses the major decisions managers make in planning a distribution strategy. It discusses how the implementation of a distribution strategy may create channel conflict, and, finally, it describes some of the legal and ethical issues related to channels of distribution.

Distribution Delivers a Standard of Living to Society

The major purpose of marketing is to satisfy human needs by delivering products to buyers when and where they want them and at a reasonable cost. A key element in this statement of marketing's mission is *delivery*—the movement of products from the point of production to the point of consumption. In many ways, all marketing effort is meaningless unless products are placed in the hands of those who need them. Thus, distribution is of overwhelming importance in any discussion of marketing functions. Distribution is estimated to account for about one-quarter of the price of the consumer goods we buy. Most would agree that this is a cost well worth bearing. Distribution creates time utility and place utility.

Distribution of products among the members of a society becomes necessary once the idea develops that efficiency can be gained—even in a primitive economy—if one person specializes in, say, hunting and another person specializes in fishing or farming. In a primitive economy, distribution is fairly straightforward; but in today's global economy, it is far more complex. For example, products shipped into Baltimore may ultimately be sold in Oregon, and Washington state apples may be consumed in Florida. The basic function of distribution, however, remains the same. In one way or another, the distance between the grower or producer of a product and the final user of that product must be bridged. The distance to be covered can be quite long, as when Mexican oil ends up in Australia. Or it can be quite short, as when a farmer at a roadside stand sells the watermelon that grew just a few yards away. Whatever distance a product must be moved, society relies on the marketing function of distribution to do the job—to provide products in the right place at the right time.

Supply Chain and Logistics Defined

Logistics describes the entire process of moving raw materials and component parts into a firm, moving in-process inventory through the firm, and moving finished goods out of the firm. Effective marketers create and maintain long-term relationships with a chain of organizations to perform this logistics function. The term **supply chain** is used to describe all the organizations that regularly supply a marketing company and all members of the marketer's channel of distribution. The ideal supply chain is a collaborative arrangement in which all organizations see themselves as partners working together to increase logistical efficiency.

Logistics
The activities involved in moving raw materials and parts into a firm, moving in-process inventory through the firm, and moving finished goods out of the firm.

Supply chain
All the collaborating organizations that help supply a marketing company and help distribute the marketer's products. The supply chain always includes the channel of distribution.

Physical distribution involves the flow of products from producers to consumers. Computerization, automation, and information technology assist with the management of physical distribution. These technologies have helped marketers to accelerate order fulfillment and minimize costs.

Supply chain management, or *logistics management*, thus involves planning, implementing, and controlling a chain of organizational relationships to assure the efficient flow of both inbound materials and outbound finished products.

Clearly, the term *supply chain management* is broad in scope because it encompasses planning and coordinating the physical distribution of finished goods and managing the movement and storage of raw materials and supply parts needed during the procurement and production processes. **Materials management** is concerned with only part of this process: bringing raw materials and supplies to the point of production and moving in-process inventory through the firm. General Motors Corporation wants to get to the point where every time a dealer sells a Cadillac, Firestone or Goodyear automatically sends another set of tires to one of GM's plants. This goal illustrates the importance of materials management and how a flexible company can coordinate logistical activities to react to the market faster.

Supply chain management deals with the "big picture" of an organization's distribution process. **Physical distribution** involves the flow of finished products from the end of the production line to the consumer. Exhibit 11-1 shows the interrelationship between materials management and physical distribution.

Physical distribution consists of several identifiable concerns and activities:

- *Inventory management.* For example, a retailer determines how many Arizona Diamondbacks baseball caps is an adequate number and when to order them.

Supply chain management
The planning, implementing, and controlling of a chain of organizational relationships to assure the efficient flow of both inbound materials and outbound finished products; also called *logistics management.*

Materials management
The activities involved in bringing raw materials and supplies to the point of production and moving in-process inventory through the firm.

Physical distribution
The activities involved in the efficient movement of finished products from the end of the production line to the consumer.

e x h i b 11-1

The Flow of Materials in the Supply Chain

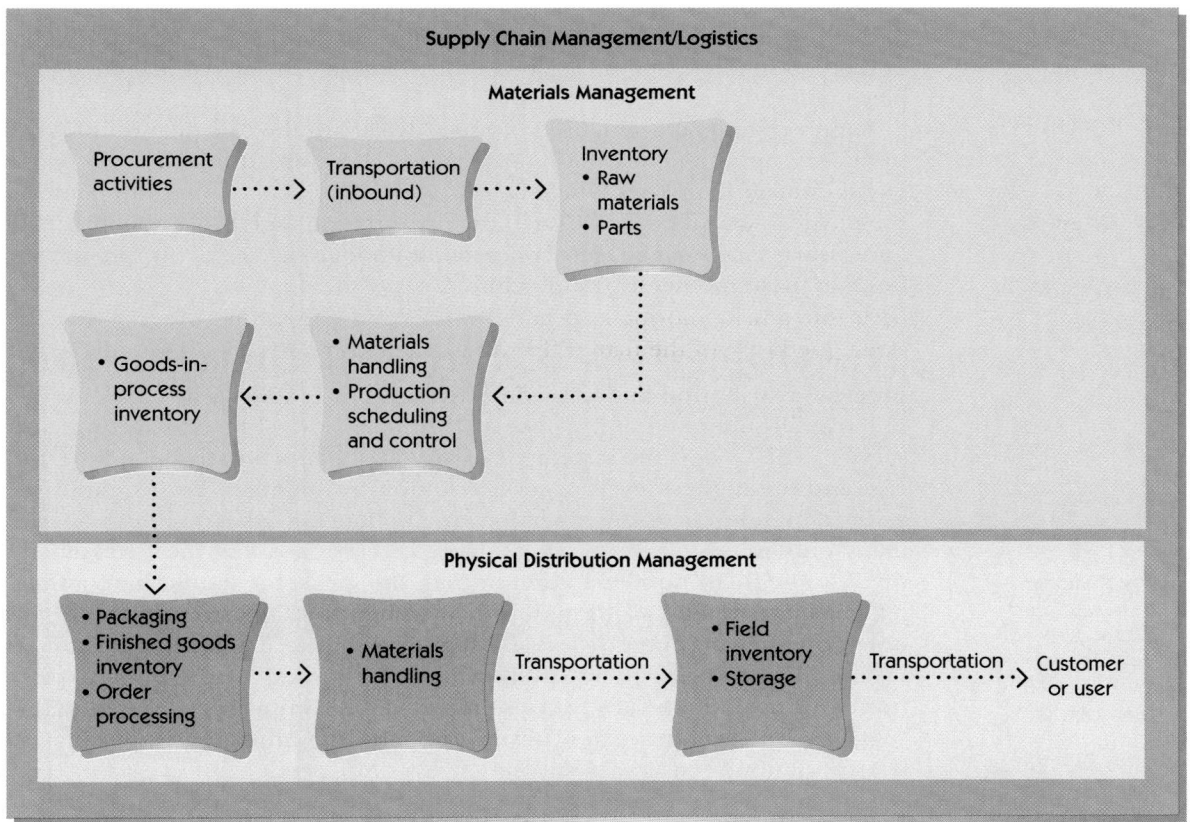

Webvan.com is an Internet grocery service. It seeks a competitive advantage via a consumer-oriented logistics strategy that involves a sophisticated computerized order processing, inventory management, and distribution system. Packers load groceries onto automated conveyor belts, which transfer the groceries to vans. The vans are custom designed with separate storage boxes for frozen and refrigerated items. Deliveries are made within a 30-minute window selected by the customer.

- *Order processing.* Sales office personnel or computers receive customers' orders and then arrange for the requested merchandise to be shipped and for the customer to be billed.
- *Warehousing and storage.* Producers of seasonal goods, such as air conditioners, bathing suits, and mittens, hold products in storage for distribution as needed through the seasons.
- *Materials handling.* Forklifts, conveyor belts, and other means are used to move merchandise into, out of, and within warehouses, retail stores, and wholesaler's facilities.
- *Protective packaging and containerization.* For example, sheets of paper for photocopiers are bound into packs of 500 sheets, the packs are placed in cardboard boxes containing ten packs, and the boxes are placed on pallets.
- *Outbound transportation.* For example, automobiles made in Japan are loaded on ships sailing to the United States and then transported by rail and/or truck to dealers around the country.

Physical distribution, then, deals with the flow of products from producers to consumers. Its major focus is on the physical aspects of that flow rather than the institutional activities involving changing title, facilitating exchanges, and negotiating with intermediaries. (These topics, which involve activities within channels of distribution, are discussed later in this chapter.) As part of the "place" portion of the overall marketing mix, physical distribution activities contribute time and place utility.

Supply chain management, or *logistics,* deals with the "big picture" of an organization's supply and distribution processes. Therefore, it relies heavily on demand estimation or sales forecasting to achieve the goal of smoothly controlling the physical flow of goods through the organization and its distribution channels. Forecasting enables managers concerned with logistics to synchronize the activities that make up the distribution effort.

The Objectives of Physical Distribution

Physical distribution has many objectives. All of them can be condensed into one overall statement of purpose: to minimize cost while maximizing customer service. This goal is the statement of an ideal. Unfortunately, the lowest total cost and the highest levels of service seldom go together. For example, to achieve high-level customer service, an appliance marketer should operate many warehouses, each carrying a large inventory so that local customers' orders can be filled rapidly. In lieu of that, the marketer should have a fleet of jet transports ready at all times to fly merchandise to customers within a few hours of receiving their orders. Both approaches to maximizing customer service are likely to prove inconsistent with the other half of the physical distribution objective, which calls for minimizing cost. Minimizing cost generally suggests few warehouses, low inventories, and slow, inexpensive means of transportation.

The twin goals of maximum service and minimum cost, while not necessarily contradictory, can rarely both be met. Some compromise usually is necessary.

Thus, physical distribution managers, while striving for the ideal, must work toward realistic objectives, performing a sort of balancing act in the process.

In many cases, organizations can establish competitive advantages over rivals through more effective physical distribution. This is especially true in industries in which the products of one organization are essentially the same as those of competitors, as in the coal and the steel industries. Marketers experience difficulty in establishing competitive advantages through price differentials or product superiority in such industries, but physical distribution offers an avenue to develop an advantage. Providing more reliable delivery or faster delivery, avoiding errors in order processing, and delivering undamaged goods are all potential areas of competitive advantage.

Manufacturers selling directly to consumers perform the physical distribution function on their own. However, many physical distribution functions are carried out by intermediaries within a channel of distribution.

What Is a Channel of Distribution?

Channels of distribution were briefly discussed in Chapter 1. A channel of distribution may be referred to by other names, and terms vary from industry to industry. But whether *channel, trade channel,* or some other variant of the term is used, the functions performed remain the same. The term *channel of distribution* has its origins in the French word for canal, suggesting a path that goods take as they flow from producers to consumers. In this sense, a channel of distribution is defined by the organizations or individuals along the route from producer to consumer. Because the beginning and ending points of the route must be included, both producer and consumer are always members of a channel of distribution. However, there may be intermediate stops along the way. Several marketing institutions have developed to facilitate the flow of the physical product or the transfer of ownership of (or title to) the product from the producer to the consumer. Organizations that serve as marketing intermediaries specializing in distribution rather than production are external to the producing organization. (In the past, intermediaries were called *middlemen.*) When these intermediaries join with a manufacturer in a loose coalition aimed at exploiting joint opportunities, a channel of distribution is formed.[2]

A **channel of distribution**, then, consists of producer, consumer, and any intermediary organizations that are aligned to provide a means of transferring ownership (title) or possession of a product from producer to consumer. The channel of distribution can also be seen as a system of interdependent relationships among a set of organizations—a system that facilitates the exchange process.

All discussions of distribution channels assume that the product in question has taken on its final form. The channel of distribution for an automobile

The main business of the Hollywood movie studios once was simply making films—that is, production. Today, the crucial factor determining a studio's profitability is film distribution. Major U.S. film studios produce only about half the movies they distribute. They purchase many films from independent studios. The large studios concentrate on distribution and other marketing functions and are compensated for these efforts through a fee system, usually 25 to 30 percent of a film's rentals. Film distribution itself has also changed in recent years. Supplying films to theaters is no longer enough. Home Box Office, Showtime, and other cable systems, as well as TV networks, independent stations, and videocassette marketers, are now critical in the film marketing process. Distribution is the name of the game in Hollywood.

Channel of distribution
The complete sequence of marketing organizations involved in bringing a product from the producer to the ultimate consumer or organizational user.

begins with a finished automobile. It does not include the paths of raw materials (such as steel) or component parts (such as tires) to the automobile manufacturer, which is an industrial user in these other channels. It should be emphasized that the channel's purpose in moving products to people is more than a simple matter of transportation. The channel of distribution must accomplish the task of transferring the title to the product as well as facilitating the physical movement of the goods to their ultimate destination. Although title transfer and the exchange of physical possession (transportation) generally follow the same channel of distribution, they do not necessarily need to follow the same path.

All but the shortest of channels include one or more intermediaries. A distinction may be made between **merchant intermediaries**, which take title to the product, and **agent intermediaries**, which do not take title to the product. Although agent intermediaries never own the goods, they perform a number of marketing functions, such as selling, that facilitate further transactions in the exchange process.

Most intermediaries are independent organizations tied to the producers they deal with only by mutual agreement; they are not owned by the producers. Some intermediaries are owned by producers, such as the company-owned sales branches and sales offices that sell NCR point-of-sale systems. However, these company-owned sales branches and offices are clearly separate from the production facilities operated by the company.

In service marketing, it sometimes appears that there is no channel of distribution. When a beautician delivers a product, such as a haircut or make-up advice, he or she deals directly with the customer. But even in these shortest of distribution channels, involving no intermediaries, marketing functions are being performed. The required activities are simply performed by the provider of the service (or, in a self-service environment, by the ultimate consumer).[3]

When identifiable intermediaries are present, the channel members form a coalition intended to act on joint opportunities in the marketplace. Each channel member, from producer to retailer, must be rewarded or see some opportunity for continued participation in the channel. The coalition between channel members may be a loose one resulting from negotiation or a formal set of contractual arrangements identifying each party's role in the distribution process. The **conventional channel of distribution** is characterized by loosely aligned, relatively autonomous marketing organizations that have developed a system to carry out a trade relationship. In contrast, formal vertical marketing systems are more tightly organized systems in which the channel members are either owned by a manufacturer or a distributor, linked by contracts or other legal agreements such as franchises, or informally managed and coordinated as an integrated system through strategic alliances. Vertical marketing systems are discussed in greater detail later in this chapter.

Not included in the channel of distribution are transportation companies, financial institutions, and other functional specialists selling services that assist the flow of products. They are *collaborators*, playing a specialized role by providing a limited facilitating service to channel members.

Marketing Functions Performed by Intermediaries

Perhaps the most neglected, most misunderstood, and most maligned segment of the economy is the distribution segment. Retailers are seen by some as the principal cause of high consumer prices, simply because retailers are the marketers with whom consumers most frequently come into contact. Retailers collect money from consumers, so even though much of that money is passed to other distributors or

---

Merchant intermediary
A channel intermediary, such as a wholesaler or a retailer, that takes title to the product.

Agent intermediary
A channel intermediary that does not take title to the product. Agent intermediaries bring buyers and sellers together or otherwise help complete a transaction.

Conventional channel of distribution
A channel of distribution characterized by loosely aligned, relatively autonomous marketing organizations that have a system for carrying out trade relations.

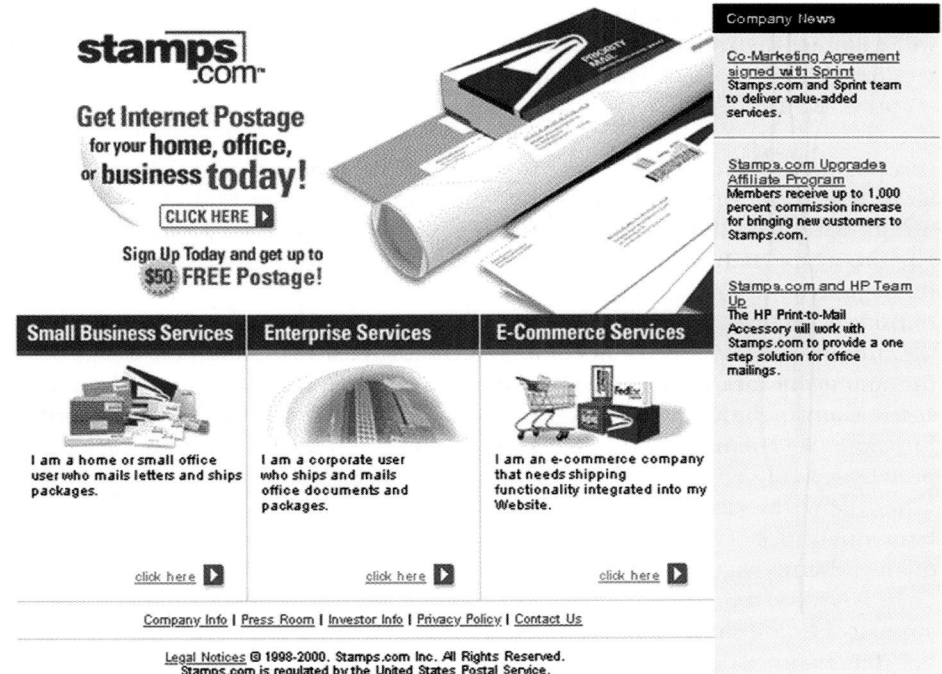

manufacturers, retailers often bear the brunt of customers' complaints. Wholesalers are also seen as causing high prices, perhaps because much of what they do is done outside the view of consumers. In either case, many suggest "cutting out the middleman" as a means of lowering the prices of consumer goods. For thousands of years, the activities of those who perform the distribution function have been misunderstood, and this viewpoint persists today.

> A company can eliminate intermediaries, but it cannot eliminate the functions they perform.

Students of marketing should understand that an efficient distribution system must somehow be financed. Most of the time, "eliminating the middleman" will not reduce prices, because the dollars that go to intermediaries compensate them for the performance of tasks that must be accomplished regardless of whether an intermediary is present. In other words, a company can eliminate intermediaries, but it cannot eliminate the functions they perform.

Nevertheless, it is not impossible for a marketer to develop a process to perform distribution functions more efficiently without an intermediary. As will be explained later in this chapter, using the Internet and/or other new information technologies in some instances can alter the economics of distribution and lower the cost of transactions so that a marketer is more competitive without an intermediary. However, we first need to discuss how intermediaries fit into the channel of distribution.

HOW INTERMEDIARIES FIT INTO DISTRIBUTION CHANNELS

Chapter 1 outlined a conventional channel of distribution consisting of a manufacturer, a wholesaler, a retailer, and the ultimate consumer. Not all channels include all of these marketing institutions. In some cases, a unit of product may pass directly from manufacturer to consumer. In others, it may be handled by not just one but two or more wholesalers. To show why these many variations exist, we will examine the role of intermediaries in marketing channels.

Consider this conventional channel of distribution:

Manufacturer → Retailer → Ultimate consumer

It is possible, as shown here, to have a channel of distribution that does not include a separate wholesaler. A manufacturer can choose to sell directly to retailers, in effect eliminating the wholesaler. However, the marketing functions performed by the wholesaler must then be shifted to one of the other parties in the channel—the retailer or the manufacturer. For instance, with the wholesaler out of the picture, the manufacturer may have to create a sales force to call on the numerous retailers. If the manufacturer assumes some or all of the marketing functions, they are said to have been shifted backward in the channel. If the retailer assumes them, they are said to have been shifted forward in the channel. For example, the manufacturer may decide to perform the function of breaking bulk by sending comparatively small orders to individual retail customers. On the other hand, the retailer may be willing to accept truckload lots of a product, store large quantities of it, and perform the activity of breaking down these larger quantities into smaller quantities.

In any case, the functions performed by the eliminated wholesaler do not disappear; they are simply shifted to another channel member. The channel member that assumes these functions expects to be compensated in some way. The retailer may expect lower prices and higher margins for the extra work performed. The manufacturer may expect larger purchase orders, more aggressive retail promotion, or more control over the distribution process.

The key to setting the structure of a channel of distribution is to determine how the necessary marketing functions can be carried out most efficiently and effectively. Certain variables, such as price, the complexity of the product, and the number of customers to be served, can serve as guides to the appropriate channel structures. However, the functions to be performed should be the primary consideration in the marketing manager's distribution plans. Let us consider some of the major functions performed by intermediaries: physical distribution, communication, and facilitating functions.

PHYSICAL DISTRIBUTION FUNCTIONS

Physical distribution functions include breaking bulk, accumulating bulk, creating assortments, reducing transactions, and transporting and storing.

Breaking Bulk   With few exceptions, intermediaries perform a bulk-breaking function. The **bulk-breaking function** consists of buying in relatively large quantities, such as truckloads, and then selling in smaller quantities, passing the lesser amounts of merchandise on to retailers, organizational buyers, wholesalers, or other customers. By accumulating large quantities of goods and then breaking them into smaller amounts suitable for many buyers, intermediaries can reduce the cost of distribution for both manufacturers and consumers. Consumers need not buy and store great amounts of merchandise, which would increase their own storage costs and the risks of spoilage, fire, and theft. Manufacturers are spared the necessity of dividing their outputs into the small order sizes retailers or consumers might prefer.

Accumulating Bulk   In the majority of cases, it is the task of the intermediary to break bulk. However, an intermediary may also create bulk, buying units of the same product from many small producers and offering the larger amount to buyers who prefer to purchase in large quantities. These intermediaries are performing a **bulk-accumulating function**. An intermediary performing this function is called, not surprisingly, an **assembler**. The classic examples of assemblers are in agricultural and fishing businesses. A maker of applesauce, such as Mott's, or a

---

Bulk-breaking function
An activity, performed by marketing intermediaries, consisting of buying products in relatively large quantities and selling in smaller quantities.

Bulk-accumulating function
An activity, performed by marketing intermediaries, consisting of buying small quantities of a particular product from many small producers and then selling the assembled larger quantities.

Assembler
A marketing intermediary that performs a bulk-accumulating function.

The Bulk-Breaking and Bulk-Accumulating Functions

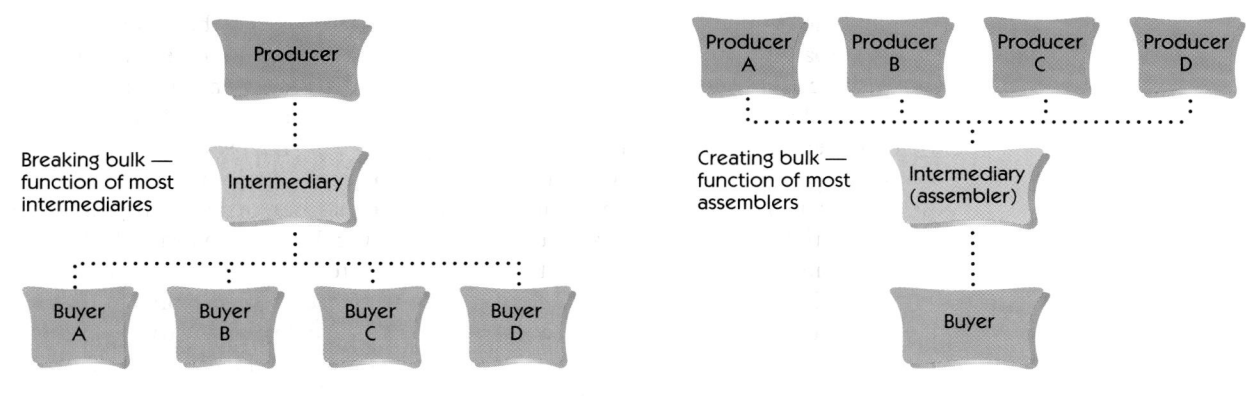

fish canner, such as Bumble Bee, would probably not want to have to deal with many small farmers or independent owners of fishing boats. Assemblers gather large quantities of apples or tuna or other products attractive to large buyers. Exhibit 11-2 contrasts the operation of assemblers with that of bulk-breaking intermediaries.

After accumulating bulk, marketers of agricultural products and raw materials typically perform a **sorting function**, which involves identifying differences in quality and breaking down the product into grade or size categories. For example, eggs are sorted into jumbo grade AA, large grade AA, and so on.

Creating Assortments   Another function that intermediaries perform is the creation of assortments of merchandise that would otherwise not be available. This **assorting function** resolves the economic discrepancy resulting from the factory operator's natural inclination to produce a large quantity of a single product or a line of similar products and the consumer's desire to select from a wide variety of choices. Wholesalers that purchase many different products from different manufacturers can offer retailers a greater assortment of items than an individual manufacturer is able to provide.

Consider how magazine publishers and retailers use intermediaries to solve a very big assorting problem. There are tens of thousands of magazine titles available from U.S. publishers. No newsstand operator or other retailer carries anything like that number; a series of intermediaries is used to sort these many titles into appropriate groupings for individual stores. National wholesalers, such as Hearst ICD and Select Magazines, move the thousands of titles to hundreds of local wholesalers. Their reward

Sorting function
An activity, performed by marketing intermediaries, consisting of classifying accumulated products as to grade and size, and then grouping them accordingly.

Assorting function
An activity, performed by marketing intermediaries, consisting of combining products purchased from several manufacturers to create assortments.

Intermediaries perform a variety of physical distribution functions. The extensive assortments created by supermarkets are a major reason consumers shop at these stores.

http://www.safeway.com

for fulfilling this huge task is about 6 percent of the magazines' retail prices, out of which they must pay all expenses involved. The local distributors continue the task of breaking bulk, moving the magazines to countless supermarkets, newsstands, drugstores, and other retail spots. But there is more to the local wholesaler's task than simply breaking bulk and making delivery. The local wholesaler must select, from among the 30,000 available titles, the ones that are appropriate for the individual retailers' operations. Then, this assortment of titles must be assembled in the proper numbers for each retailer. The local wholesaler is paid about 20 percent of the cover prices.

Reducing Transactions   There is one underlying reason why intermediaries can economically accumulate bulk, break bulk, and create assortments. The presence of intermediaries in the distribution system actually reduces the number of transactions necessary to accomplish the exchanges that keep the economy moving and consumers satisfied.

As Exhibit 11-3 indicates, even if only four suppliers of grocery items attempt to transact business with just four supermarket buying headquarters, the number of interrelationships necessary is far greater than the number needed once an intermediary, such as a food wholesaler, is added to the system. Channel intermediaries, in their dual roles as buying agents for their customers and selling agents for the manufacturers with which they deal, simplify the necessary transaction process considerably. (Of course, channels of distribution can become too long. Such channels are common in Japan.) Intermediaries not only reduce the number of transactions but also reduce the geographic distances that buyers and sellers must travel to complete exchanges and spare manufacturers the trouble of locating and contacting individual potential customers. These are some of the ways wholesalers and retailers can reduce costs. If manufacturers and consumers had to perform all these activities themselves, they would have to bear the costs involved.

e   x   h   i   b   i   t 11-3

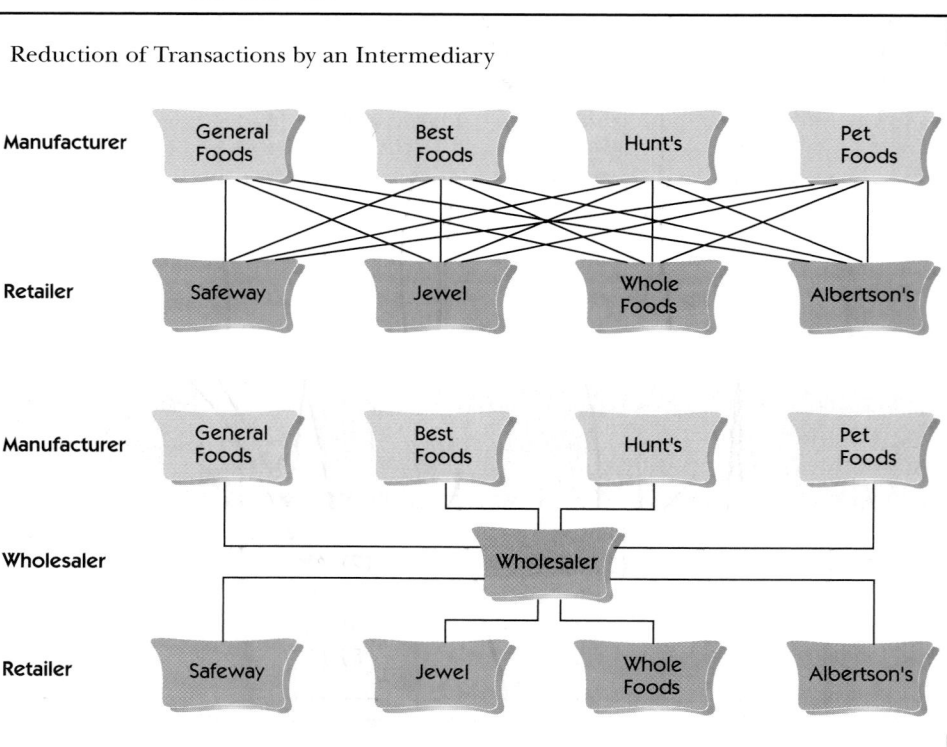

Reduction of Transactions by an Intermediary

Transportation and Storage   Intermediaries, in most cases, perform, manage, or collaborate with two other physical distribution functions: transportation and storage. Merchandise must be physically moved from points of production to points of consumption. Storage of inventory at various locations along the way often is necessary.

Transportation   Transportation decisions involve selecting the specific mode that will be used to physically move products from a manufacturer, grower, wholesaler, or other seller to the receiving facilities of the buyer. The major alternative modes of transportation are railroad, motor carrier, air freight, water transportation, and pipeline.

There are several cost trade-offs to consider when selecting modes of transportation. The first consideration is always the needs of the buyer. If it is extraordinarily difficult or expensive to satisfy a need (e.g., immediate delivery), the seller should investigate the buyer's willingness to bear the extra costs involved. Transportation considerations include the nature of the product (bulk, perishability, weight, fragility), the necessary speed and dependability of delivery, and the cost and availability of transportation methods and storage space. Alternative modes of transportation may be evaluated in terms of these variables. A general comparison of transportation alternatives appears in Exhibit 11-4.

Rail transport demonstrates its comparative advantage over other transportation modes when the freight to be hauled consists of heavy and bulky items. These can be moved by rail over long distances at low cost. Shippers may find that unit costs of transporting smaller shipments are lower if the goods are shipped by truck. However, as shipment size increases, the economies of rail transport come to equal, and then exceed, those of truck shipment.

The major disadvantages of rail transport are that it is relatively slow and that it can be used only where tracks are located. In addition, the industry has both a reputation for **damage in transit** and an unreliable delivery record. However, in recent years, some rail lines have attempted to modernize operations and have become more competitive with other means of transportation. For example, some lines provide **diversion in transit** privileges, which permit a shipper to direct a shipment to a destination that was not specified at the start of the trip. A fruit and vegetable shipper may send California oranges or artichokes to the east coast and then, when the products are approaching that part of the country, divert them to the particular eastern city where prices are highest or demand greatest. Railroads have introduced this and other services and special rates in an attempt to offset some of the advantages offered by their competitors, especially truckers.

Rail transport
The shipment of products by train over railways.

Damage in transit
Breakage, spoilage, or other injury to products that occurs while the products are being transported.

Diversion in transit
Direction of a rail shipment to a destination not specified at the start of the trip.

General Comparison of Attributes of Various Transportation Modes

e x h i b 11-4

LOW COST	SPEED	RELIABILITY OF DELIVERY	ABILITY TO DELIVER TO MANY GEOGRAPHICAL AREAS	REPUTATION FOR DELIVERING UNDAMAGED GOODS
(1) Pipeline	(1) Air	(1) Pipeline	(1) Motor	(1) Pipeline
(2) Water	(2) Motor	(2) Air	(2) Rail	(2) Water
(3) Rail	(3) Rail	(3) Motor	(3) Air	(3) Air
(4) Motor	(4) Pipeline	(4) Rail	(4) Water	(4) Motor
(5) Air	(5) Water	(5) Water	(5) Pipeline	(5) Rail

Note: These comparisons are of a very general nature intended only to show the trade-offs involved when cost of use is compared with other attributes of modes of transportation.

Motor carrier
A member of the trucking industry or another carrier, such as Greyhound's package service, that transports products over roads.

Air freight
The shipment of products by air carrier.

Water transportation
The shipment of products by ship, boat, or barge.

Pipelines
Systems of pipes through which products such as oil and natural gas are transported.

Motor carriers include trucks as well as far less important operations like Greyhound's package service, which uses buses as carriers. Despite the fact that trains can move greater quantities of products at lower prices, most marketers—especially marketers of products boxed in cartons—prefer motor carriers over rail transport. One reason is that damage in transit is less likely than when rail transport is used. Furthermore, trucks are more accessible and more flexible than railroads, and they are generally more reliable in terms of delivery deadlines. Although they are most efficient at moving comparatively small shipments over short distances, they also are effective for long distances.

The primary advantages of **air freight** are its speed and distance capabilities. For many shippers, these advantages compensate for the high costs associated with air transportation. There are other advantages as well. Fast transportation permits inventory reductions and savings in warehousing costs. Air freight has a record of seldom damaging goods in transit. In remote areas inaccessible by truck or railroad, it may be the only transportation choice available. Traditionally, air transportation has been used primarily to move goods of high unit value, perishable goods, and emergency orders. The growth of international trade has contributed to a dramatic increase in the use of air transport during the past two decades, however. Today, manufacturers, especially producers of high-technology products, often choose to ship goods on demand via air freight rather than incur the costs of carrying inventory. Indeed, the use of air freight, electronic interchanges, and strategic alliances is causing a shift away from use of regional warehouses and trucks to an instant, or "just-in-time," supply cycle.

As a rule, **water transportation** offers a very low-cost means of moving products. It is most appropriate for bulky, low-value, nonperishable goods such as grain and coal. It is also appropriate for some fairly expensive items (such as automobiles being sent from Germany or Japan to U.S. or Canadian markets) if they can be properly protected from damage during transit. Goods are transported on inland bodies of water, such as the Great Lakes and the Mississippi River, as well as on oceans. However, major problems, such as the closing of some routes and ports by ice during winter, may arise on inland waterways. Water is also the slowest mode of transportation. However, when time constraints are not great or when bulk and low unit value will not justify faster, more expensive transportation, water transportation is employed extensively.

Pipelines are the most specialized transportation means because they are designed to carry only one or two products. They are used mainly to transport natural gas and crude petroleum from wells to storage or treatment facilities. Most pipelines are owned by the companies that use them, such as gas and oil producers. Pipeline shipping is generally less expensive than rail but more expensive than waterway transportation. A big part of the expense is incurred during construction of the pipeline itself. Once in place, however, pipelines are a low-cost and reliable method of transportation.

In many instances, an *intermodal service*, which combines two or more modes of transportation, provides advantages. Many such services involve transporting loaded truck trailers or other large containers to some location from which they can be moved to local destinations by trucks. For example, railroad flatcars may carry the containers to the first location, where the containers are transferred onto trucks. This intermodal service combines the long-distance hauling attractions of the railroad with the local delivery flexibility of trucks. Similar intermodal methods involve transporting loaded containers first by ship, barge, or airplane and then by truck.

Storage and Inventory Control Storage consists of holding and housing goods in inventory for a certain time period. It is necessary because of the almost inevitable discrepancies between production and consumption cycles. Consider this

what went wrong?

KLM Royal Dutch Airlines You're one of the world's biggest airlines, and a shipment of live squirrels has broken open. You can't send them on, and the shipper won't take them back. What do you do? Don't put them in a shredder. That was the lesson learned the hard way by KLM Royal Dutch Airlines, which did just that, inciting animal lovers and touching off civil and criminal investigations. The 440 ground squirrels, which are a hot pet in some countries, had been flown to Amsterdam from Beijing in nine cardboard boxes. KLM is a leader in live cargo shipping and operates an Animal Hotel, where the squirrels checked in before the final leg of their journey, which was supposed to end in Athens.

But the shipper had not provided a health certificate showing they had no diseases. And because they were not in proper cages, 30 escaped. KLM said this occurred when its employees tried to feed them; animal-rights groups said the squirrels were so hungry they turned to cannibalism and some gnawed their way out in desperation. One of them got on a plane, which had to be searched and then disinfected. About 15 remained at large. Those were the lucky ones. The rest were dumped alive into a shredder, which KLM said was the most humane way to destroy them. An uproar ensued, fueled by a headline that included the Dutch word for "meat grinder."

As if that weren't enough, it emerged that KLM keeps the shredder on standby at the pet hotel. The airline said it is used mainly for destroying chicks that die in transit. But animal-rights groups said KLM whistle-blowers report the shredder has been used for live turtles and tropical birds, and maybe even apes and opossums. The airline said it is investigating and issued an effusive apology, saying it "made a grave mistake on ethical grounds." Sandra C. Maas, a KLM spokeswoman, said the airline had been operating under instructions from the Ministry of Agriculture, but added, "We should have been civilly disobedient."[4]

---

extreme example: The materials needed to operate Midwestern steel mills come from the northern Great Lakes via ship or barge. But shipment is impossible in the winter because the lakes freeze. Therefore, the materials must be stored at accessible locations. Such storage diminishes the effects that an uneven production cycle, caused by a cyclical supply of raw materials, would have on the steel business. In other cases, marketers have more goods than they can sell at one time. Products of a seasonal nature, such as air conditioners, class rings, skis, and wedding gowns, can be manufactured throughout the year, but there is a seasonal demand. Storage permits the makers of these items to operate a steady production stream.

The need for storage is one of the primary reasons for using intermediaries. Intermediaries of all types, including retailers, frequently store goods until they are demanded by customers further along in the channel of distribution. Hence, a fundamental concern of intermediaries is control of inventory levels. Inventory control involves decisions concerning the size of inventories. It weighs the benefits of overstocking inventory against the dangers of costly stock-outs—which occur when the product desired by the customer is not on hand. The ideal inventory level is one that provides adequate service to customers while keeping suppliers' costs as low as possible. The presence of these twin goals, set at cross-purposes, complicates inventory decisions.

Valuable guidance on questions of inventory control can be found in sales forecasts. Also useful are facts such as how much inventory was needed in past planning periods, how much was left over at the ends of past periods, the inventory turnover rates of individual warehouses, the value of the inventories, and the inventory carrying costs.

New technologies, such as global positioning systems, are changing the face of logistics. Many coast-to-coast trucking organizations use two-way satellite data communications links between a computer at the company's headquarters and each of its tractor trailer trucks. These GPS systems improve customer service and automate routing.

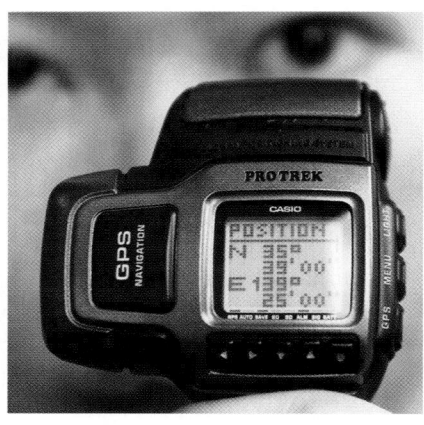

Systems concept
The idea that elements of a distribution system (or another system) are strongly interrelated and interact to achieve a goal.

Total cost concept
In relation to physical distribution, a focus on the entire range of costs associated with a particular distribution method.

Integration of the Physical Distribution Functions Breaking physical distribution down into components permits us to concentrate on individual aspects of a complex subject. However, this approach is somewhat misleading because it suggests that the parts operate separately, without interacting. It is important to understand that the components are parts of a system. The **systems concept**—the idea that elements may be strongly interrelated and may interact toward achieving one goal—is of special value in distribution. Even the casual observer can see that a warehouse is of no meaningful use unless it fills and empties as part of a system intended to achieve some distribution goal. No shipment of merchandise via railroad or plane is of real value unless it is taken from the carrier and moved to where it is actually needed. Marketing managers can use each part of a distribution system to help satisfy customer demands at reasonable cost, but only within the context of a system.

The key ideas inherent in the systems approach to physical distribution have contributed to the development of the **total cost concept.** Marketing managers who have adopted this concept see the answer to the distribution problem as a system—a system aimed at reducing total physical distribution cost.

Let's consider the case of an organizational good, a file cabinet, produced in California and intended for sale in New Hampshire. A relatively slow means of transportation from west coast to east coast, such as ship or train, would reduce the cost of the transcontinental shipment. But if the purchaser of the file cabinet could not wait for a slow shipment, the distributor would have a problem. A large inventory might be warehoused on the east coast. This would involve high costs for paperwork, inventory handling, and local taxes, but the cost in terms of lost sales could be even greater if the inventory was not available. Could the problem be solved simply by using a more expensive means of transportation directly from the west coast, eliminating the need for an east coast warehouse? Using air freight likely would reduce problems of storage and handling at both ends of the transaction and would probably lessen the total cost. Inexpensive transportation, then, could prove more costly in the long run.

Minimizing the costs associated with only one or two steps of a multistep process can result in increasing the cost of the whole process. Systems-oriented managers make trade-offs, increasing the cost of some parts of the system to produce even greater cost reductions in other parts of the system, thus reducing the total cost.

Total cost is an important measure that was not always appreciated. At one time, shippers selected their transportation modes in a one-dimensional way. If management thought a product required quick delivery, the fastest mode of transportation was chosen. If quick delivery was thought not to be a major concern, the cheapest means of transportation, within reason, was selected. Looking back, we may wonder why

> Systems-oriented managers make trade-offs, increasing the cost of some parts of the system to produce even greater cost reductions in other parts of the system, thus reducing the total cost.

transportation experts frequently did not attempt to determine whether it was possible to lower the total cost of distribution, even if that meant using a more expensive means of transportation; but this approach was uncommon until relatively recently.

Sometimes the customer's satisfaction may be more important than a dollars-and-cents cost reduction. One possible payoff of increasing some system costs may come in the form of greater buyer satisfaction. Unfortunately, it is easy for distribution managers to become so concerned with dollars that they neglect customer costs and payoffs.

COMMUNICATION AND TRANSACTION FUNCTIONS

Intermediaries perform a communication function, which includes buying, selling, and other activities involving gathering or disseminating information. The ultimate purpose of the communication link between the manufacturer and the retailer or between the wholesaler and the retailer is to transfer ownership—that is, to complete a transaction that results in an exchange of title.

Wholesalers and retailers may perform an important promotional function for manufacturers when they provide product information and price quotes. Most frequently, this communication is carried out by a sales force. However, intermediaries also use advertising and such sales promotion tools as retail displays. In other words, intermediaries perform a **selling function** for the manufacturer, often providing a sales force or other promotional efforts that they can supply more efficiently than the manufacturer can. The wholesaler provides a **buying function** for retailers, organizational users, and other customers. A wholesaler's contact with numerous manufacturers allows it to evaluate the quality of a wide assortment of goods from competing manufacturers. Thus, retailers and other customers are freed of the burden of evaluating every manufacturer's product assortments. This allows them more time to specialize in the retailing and merchandising of products.

Intermediaries further serve as channels of communication by informing buyers how products are to be sold, used, repaired, or guaranteed. They can even explain new product developments. (In fact, retailers should pass along more of this information to their customers; unfortunately many retail salespeople are not trained to provide information of this sort.) Because intermediaries typically deal with a number of manufacturers or other suppliers of goods, they are in a unique position to serve as conduits of information.

Intermediaries, being "in the middle," are well placed not only to pass information from producers to other channel members but also to collect information from channel members or retail shoppers and return it to producers. For example, suppose a retailer receives serious consumer complaints about a product or some product-related matter such as repair service. The retailer should pass this information backward in the channel to the wholesaler, who can bring the matter to the attention of the producer. *Should* is the key word here. Too often, whether because of apathy or the fear of somehow being blamed for a problem, intermediaries fail to perform this potentially valuable service. Marketers at all levels should encourage communication throughout channels of distribution, because the satisfaction of all channel members and consumers is at stake.

FACILITATING FUNCTIONS

The transportation and storage functions of channel intermediaries are their most obvious contributions to the operation of the marketing system. However, intermediaries perform additional, so-called facilitating functions, which are not quite so apparent to observers of a channel in operation. Because the tasks of a channel intermediary can be so varied, it is nearly impossible to list all the facilitating functions a channel member might perform. However, three major categories of facilitating functions should be mentioned specifically: providing extra services, offering credit, and taking risks.

Extra Services   Channel members, particularly intermediaries, can and do provide a range of extra services that increase the efficiency and effectiveness of the

Selling function
Activities, performed by intermediaries, that are associated with communicating ideas and making a sale and thus effecting the transfer of ownership of a product.

Buying function
Activities, performed by intermediaries, that are associated with making a purchase and thus effecting the transfer of ownership of a product.

Service function
Activities, performed by intermediaries, that increase the efficiency and effectiveness of the exchange process. Repair services and management services provided by intermediaries are examples.

channel; intermediaries thus perform a **service function**. For many products, the availability of a post-sale repair service is an absolute necessity. Office photocopiers, for example, always seem to need either routine maintenance or minor or major overhauls. Wholesalers and retailers of such machines usually offer repair services on either a contract or an emergency basis. They also carry necessary supplies like paper. Other products—such as personal computers and cellular telephones—are not so prone to breakdowns, yet buyers like to know that repair service is available should it ever be needed. Technical support is critical for many Internet and software companies. Honoring manufacturers' guarantees can be another responsibility of intermediaries.

Channel intermediaries can also provide a variety of management services. In the food industry, for example, wholesalers offer such services as computerized accounting and database systems, inventory planning, store site selection, store layout planning, and management training programs. The extra services offered are good business for the wholesalers in that (1) they attract customers and (2) they help their food retailer customers to stay in business and to remain successful.

Payment and Credit Services A system of payment is required for the transfer of ownership. A buyer may pay in cash or use credit provided by a channel member or a third party. Most intermediaries perform a **credit function** by offering credit service of one kind or another. Although some wholesalers and retailers operate exclusively on a cash-and-carry basis, promising to pass related savings on to their customers, they make up a relatively small proportion of the millions of intermediaries operating in the United States.

Credit function
Provision of credit to another member of a distribution channel.

Wholesalers and other nonretailer channel members may provide credit in a number of ways. Intermediaries in many fields routinely offer 30, 60, or more days to pay for merchandise ordered. Often, the days do not start "counting" until the goods are delivered to the buyer's place of business. In effect, such a service permits the buyer to make some money on a product before having to pay for it.

Companies engaged in e-commerce may have encrypted online payment and/or credit systems that provide secure electronic transactions for their customers.[5] Software wallets, Internet security, and other relevant online payment issues are discussed elsewhere in the book.

Risk Taking In almost everything they do, channel intermediaries perform a **risk-taking function**. When purchasing a product from a manufacturer or supplier of any type, intermediaries run the risk of getting stuck with an item that has fallen out of favor with the buying public because of a shift in fashion or the death of a fad. It is also possible for a product to spoil while it is in storage or be lost through fire or some other disaster. Intermediaries bear these risks in addition to market risk.

Risk-taking function
Assumption of the responsibility for losses when the future is uncertain.

Intermediaries run obvious risks in offering credit to the individuals and organizations to which they sell. They take legal risks in that intermediaries, not just manufacturers, can be held responsible for problems caused by faulty products or misleading claims.

Typical Channels of Distribution

We have already suggested that not all channels of distribution are alike. In fact, the variety of distribution channels is extensive indeed. That is because marketers are constantly seeking new ways to perform the distribution function. Both manufacturers and intermediaries have developed all sorts of variations on the basic theme of distribution. Each variation was developed in an effort to perform the distribution function better and thereby attract business.

Channels may be distinguished by the number of intermediaries they include; the more intermediaries, the longer the channel. Some organizations choose to sell their products directly to the consumer or organizational user; others use long channels that include numbers of wholesalers, agents, and retailers to reach buyers.

This discussion focuses on the most common of the numerous channels of distribution available. Exhibit 11-5 shows the primary channels for consumer and business-to-business products.

CHANNELS OF DISTRIBUTION FOR CONSUMER GOODS AND SERVICES

Exhibit 11-5 gives examples of typical channels for the distribution of consumer goods and services.

The Direct Channel for Consumer Goods and Services   A good example of the direct channel is supplied by the neighborhood bakery, which converts flour, water, and other raw materials into baked goods and then retails these products, providing any other functions that might be necessary to complete the transaction. The direct channel is also familiar as the distribution method used by many marketers of services and not-for-profit groups that solicit donations.

Marketers of consumer goods and services that promote their products through mail-order catalogs, telemarketing (telephone sales), and toll-free numbers listed in advertisements and that distribute directly to consumers through the mail or a delivery service are also using direct channels. The strategies of these direct marketers, which do not use retail outlets or contact customers in person, rely largely on data-based management and certain direct-response promotional strategies. We will discuss direct marketing further in Chapters 12, 13, and 14.

The Manufacturer (Producer)– Retailer–Consumer Channel   The *manufacturer–retailer–consumer channel* is commonly employed when the retailer involved is a sizable organization, such as a discount chain like Wal-Mart. This type of retail marketing organization may prefer to deal directly with manufacturers to be able to order specially made merchandise or obtain discounts or other benefits. Generally, the benefits must be important enough to make the retailer willing to perform many wholesaling functions. However, in an effort to please large retail customers, the manufacturer may agree to perform wholesaler functions. The efficiencies a manufacturer gains from the large orders placed by Sears or Wal-Mart can more than offset the wholesaling costs the manufacturer may have to absorb.

Service producers also use this channel of distribution. HBO's Visitor Information Network (VIN) is a tourism channel that provides continuous programming for hotel

In the United States, Gevalia Kaffe's fine coffees of Europe are available only by express home delivery. The company's distribution strategy is to use a direct channel of distribution.

http://www.gevalia.com

Typical Channels of Distribution

The Primary Channels of Distribution

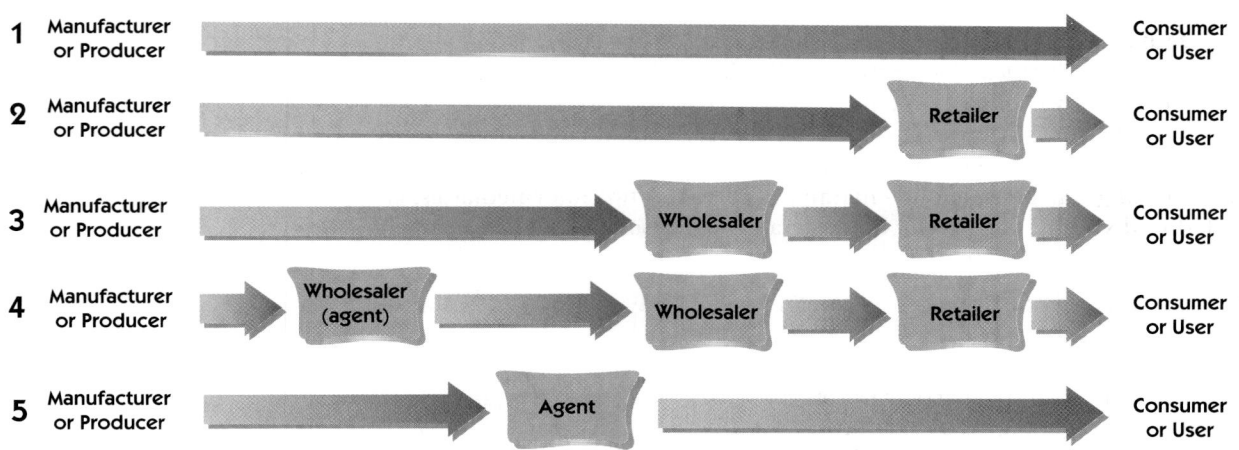

Consumer Examples

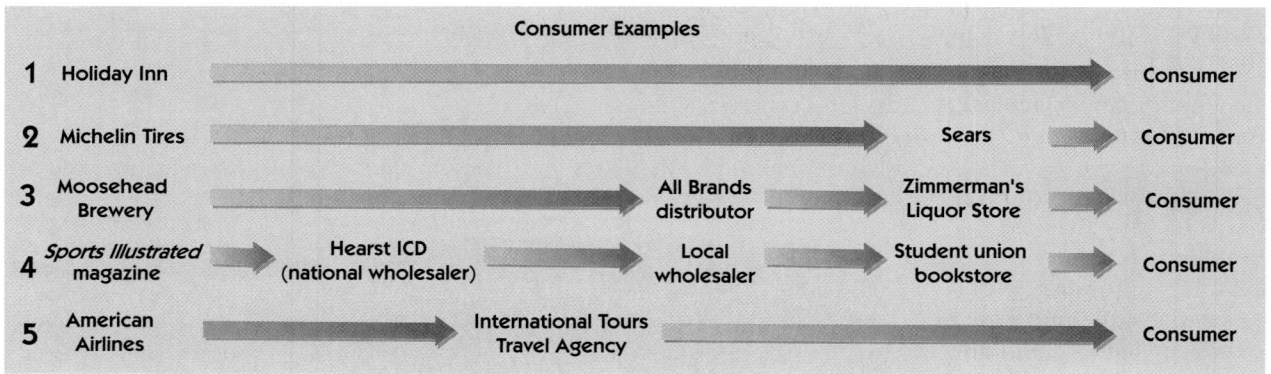

Business-to-Business Examples

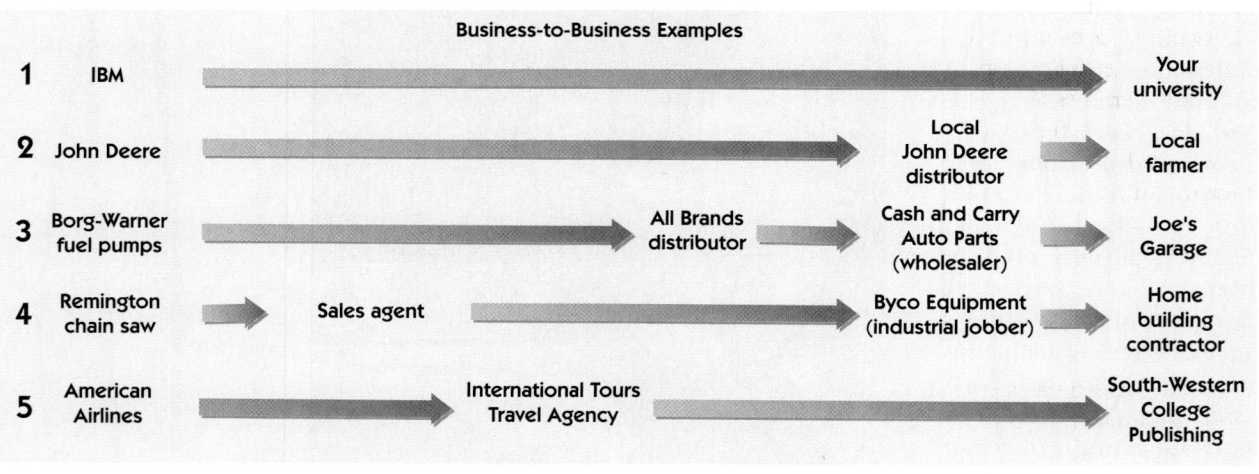

rooms, highlighting local attractions, dining, and shopping. The channel of distribution for this service is VIN–hotel–consumer, or producer–retailer–consumer.

Many other service marketers use a producer–retailer–consumer channel when consumers can benefit from the location, product information, or other services a retailer offers. For example, many dry cleaners have their customers' suede clothing dry-cleaned by companies specializing in the dry-cleaning process rather than in retailing.

The Manufacturer–Wholesaler–Retailer–Consumer Channel   The *manufacturer–wholesaler–retailer–consumer channel* of distribution is the most commonly used structure for consumer goods. This is because most consumer goods are so widely used. It would be virtually impossible for the Wrigley Company, for example, to deal individually with every retailer stocking chewing gum, let alone every consumer of gum. Thus, a long channel, with at least two intermediaries, is needed to distribute the product. Wholesalers can also be used in the distribution of services.

Channels That Include Agents   A familiar type of agent is the real estate agent. Consumers marketing their homes (or other used goods) often lack time and marketing skills, so they hire agents. Manufacturers, especially those lacking expertise in marketing a particular product line, may choose to permit manufacturers' agents or selling agents to handle the marketing of their products. Such agents do not take title to the goods they sell and usually earn commissions rather than a salary.

In marketing channels for consumer goods, agents may, depending on the circumstances and the product they offer, sell to retailers or wholesalers. The *manufacturer–agent–wholesaler–retailer–consumer channel* is widely used in the marketing of consumer products, especially convenience goods.

It might seem that travel agents used by airlines function as retailers. Technically, however, they are part of a channel involving an agent. The service producer–agent channel is common in marketing of consumer services. Ticketmaster provides such services for sports teams like the Chicago Bulls and the Chicago Cubs.

CHANNELS OF DISTRIBUTION FOR BUSINESS-TO-BUSINESS MARKETING

Business-to-business marketers use channels that are similar to those used by the marketers of consumer products. The primary channels are illustrated in Exhibit 11-5.

The travel agent is the traditional intermediary in the purchase of airline tickets. However, a growing number of travelers are using the Internet to purchase tickets directly from the airline service provider.

The Direct Channel in Business-to-Business Marketing

The name "business-to-business" suggests the importance of the direct channel in the marketing of organizational products. Indeed, the direct channel is the one most commonly used in the marketing of organizational goods. Direct organizational sales of industrial machinery such as escalators, power-generating machinery such as turbine engines, metals such as titanium, and many other products require well-informed salespersons, and perhaps engineers, who can help the buyer fit the product into its organizational facility or manufacturing process. Otis Elevator, for example, is a business-to-business marketer that uses a direct channel.

Many business-to-business marketers now use the Internet for electronic commerce. This constitutes a direct channel.

The Manufacturer–Wholesaler–Organizational User Channel

Because, by definition, retailers deal with consumers, there is no distribution channel for organizational goods that directly parallels the manufacturer–retailer channel. However, there is a trade channel for organizational goods that relies on just one wholesale intermediary, which performs a function much like that of a retailer. This is the *manufacturer–distributor–organizational user channel*. The names for this type of wholesaler vary from industry to industry; among the most common terms used are *jobber* and *distributor*.

Snap-On Tools, maker of socket wrenches and other hand tools, uses distributors who, working out of well-stocked vans, call directly on Snap-On's customers, professional mechanics. Distributors selling to organizational users may also operate store-like facilities that buyers such as electricians or plumbers may patronize. In either format, organizational distributors perform storage and communication functions. They may, as in the Snap-On example, provide delivery, and they may also supply credit or perform other functions. The organizational distributor is classified as a merchant intermediary, because this distributor takes title to the goods. Channels of distribution for organizational goods sometimes include more than one merchant wholesaler. This arrangement is most common in international marketing.

Business-to-Business Marketers Also Use Agents

The *manufacturer–agent–organizational user channel* is commonly used in business-to-business marketing by small manufacturers that market only one product to many users. The wide range of customers to which agents sell suggests the main attraction of agents for manufacturers: flexibility. One type of agent intermediary, the broker, can be used on an occasional basis, as needed. No continuing relationship—and therefore no continuing financial remuneration or other obligation—is necessary. Similarly, manufacturers' agents operate on a commission basis within fixed geographic territories. Therefore, they appeal to small organizations whose limited financial resources make it difficult for them to fund their own sales forces. Manufacturers' agents are also attractive because they can be employed in "thin" market areas or in foreign countries where potential sales do not seem to justify a manufacturer's forming its own sales force.

icollector allows shoppers to find items they desire for their collections. The company works with over 300 top auction houses, antique dealers, and art galleries online. Customers can track down an item, check its value, and then place a bid. Like other brokers, icollector is an agent intermediary, receiving compensation for putting buyers and sellers in touch with each other.

DISINTERMEDIATION

A shift in many channels of distribution is currently under way because of the dramatic impact of e-commerce on business-to-consumer and business-to-business distribution. Because the Internet allows direct communication with customers and online selling, many channels are being disintermediated. **Disintermediation** refers to the compression, or "shortening," of marketing channels because one or more intermediaries have been eliminated. When IBM decided that it would market its Aptiva computers directly, on the Internet, and no longer sell them in stores, it disintermediated a portion of its distribution system.

Remember, however, that eliminating a "middleman" does not eliminate the need for that intermediary's function. When a manufacturer decides to disintermediate, it must itself perform those distribution functions previously performed by the intermediary. Alternatively, it may choose to outsource some distribution functions. For example, it may contract with UPS or FedEx to provide transportation and storage services.

One of the most revolutionary changes resulting from disintermediation is the growth of *infomediaries*, providing a new form of intermediation.[6]

INFOMEDIARIES AND VERTICAL EXCHANGES

The communication function of intermediaries has always been important, because buyers and sellers need information to make decisions. In some situations, buyers also need to search out organizations or individuals that are marketing the product they desire. In the past, a consumer might read a copy of *Consumer Reports* to reduce the time spent searching for information and to learn experts' evaluations of products. The consumer would then go to a store to purchase the desired item.

In today's digital world, a new form of intermediary has emerged. An **infomediary** serves as an electronic information broker, providing shopping services or information buying assistance to help buyers and sellers find each other.

> Infomediaries can offer sophisticated and highly specific information searches at a very low cost.

Infomediaries can offer sophisticated and highly specific information searches at a very low cost. Auto-By-Tel, for example, supplies its customers with the names of local automobile dealers that will provide the exact car the buyer wants at a rock-bottom, no-negotiation price. Auto-By-Tel's role as an intermediary is to provide information. The physical transaction takes place elsewhere.

In addition, another new breed of intermediaries is emerging to facilitate business-to-business e-commerce. These new intermediaries are online trading communities that specialize in vertical markets. (*Vertical markets* focus on specific industries, such as chemicals, or specific business processes, such as food processing. *Horizontal markets* offer products, such as office supplies, that a wide range of companies across industries use.[7]) Such e-commerce intermediaries have been called *aggregators, vertical market makers, vertical marketplaces, vortals, butterfly markets,* and several other names; however, we prefer the term *vertical exchanges.*[8] A **vertical exchange** specializes in using the Internet to connect and assist numerous buyers and numerous sellers in a vertical market. Vertical exchanges provide portals or electronic hubs that function as electronic marketplaces, administer Web-based procurement systems that allow for the transfer of title, and provide customized services such as online tracking of shipments.

Most of the vertical exchanges operating these Web-based marketplaces do not take title to the products or physically handle them. They are just pure information and Web-service intermediaries. They create value several ways. The greatest benefit is created by bringing together a critical mass of buyers and sellers and by *aggregating* information from buyers and sellers. By aggregating information for a vertical market, the vertical exchange allows a buyer to compare many suppliers simultaneously. Buyers benefit because they have more choices. Sellers benefit because they have access to more buyers. Geographical barriers and the need for extensive travel are minimized. Overall, a vertical

Disintermediation
The compression, or "shortening," of marketing channels because one or more intermediaries have been eliminated.

Infomediary
An intermediary that serves as an electronic information broker.

Vertical exchange
A business-to-business intermediary that specializes in using the Internet to connect and assist numerous buyers and numerous sellers in a vertical market.

what went right?

VerticalNet Barely four years old, VerticalNet, a creator of online vertical trading communities, is a company whose CEO, Mark Walsh, proudly proclaims it is "the least sexy site on the Internet."

In an age when many Internet properties are valued largely for their flash or the loftiness of their business model, VerticalNet makes money paving new sales avenues and creating communities for 41 unglamorous industries, such as food ingredients, paints and coatings, and adhesives.

"We're doing what the Net is supposed to do—expand your buying community and drive transactions," Walsh says. In doing so, VerticalNet has become a model for business-to-business vertical exchange success. Each of VerticalNet's arcane-topic portals serves as a hub for the denizens of the trade. At http://www.solidwasteonline.com, people interested in solid-waste management can read pithy news stories, product reviews, and recommendations and visit storefronts from hundreds of vendors.

VerticalNet is essentially a portfolio of over 40 vertically focused exchanges. The company is bringing entire industries online that heretofore couldn't even spell the word Internet. Buyers at VerticalNet portals know that all the vendors presented are in their field of interest, and by virtue of the store's placement, nearly every lead the seller gets is a qualified one.

These thousands of storefronts account for 65 percent of VerticalNet's revenues. About a quarter of revenues come from sponsorships, and about 10 percent come from commissions on transactions enabled by VerticalNet.

The company charges $6,000 per year to host the storefront. VerticalNet has a 90 percent renewal rate among customers of its storefronts. Its salespeople can barely keep up with the vendors begging them to put a "buy this now" button next to their products. The storefronts have also proven successful as low-cost sales operations, allowing companies to reach buyers in geographic areas or industries in which they have no sales force.

A VerticalNet-sponsored survey following up on people who left sales leads in storefronts found that 15 percent bought the product from the manufacturer, and 25 percent said the product was still under significant consideration. Fifty percent of the time, these purchases were made from a company the buyer had never done business with before. The average dollar volume of the transaction? $25,000.[9]

exchange improves matching for both buyers and sellers.[10] In addition, operating a standardized system, perhaps a business-to-business online auction, reduces search and information transfer costs. Vertical exchanges create value because the costs related to doing business on the Internet are "shared" by all participants and thus reduced for any particular member of the vertical exchange's trading community.

Consider an example. Chemdex is a vertical exchange for the life sciences research industry.[11] Through its Chemdex Marketplace, it exhibits 250,000 products from more than 120 suppliers, including biological chemicals and reagents like antibodies, enzymes, and organic and inorganic chemicals. Buyers are biotech and pharmaceutical companies, as well as academic and research institutions. Buyers can access the marketplace via the Chemdex Web site and search for specific products. Chemdex's primary function as an intermediary is to provide information and e-commerce solutions. Supplier companies, such as SmithKline Beecham and Genetech, are connected to potential buyers through the Chemdex portal, which contains an electronic catalog, a search engine, and an easy-to-use ordering system. Once a transaction occurs between trading partners, Chemdex provides services that support order fulfillment and other after-the-sale activities.

Vertical Marketing Systems

In many industries, such as the fast-food restaurant industry, the dominant distribution structure is the vertical marketing system. The concept of a vertical marketing system emerged with the need to manage or administer the functions performed by intermediaries at two or more levels of the channel of distribution.

Vertical marketing systems, or vertically integrated marketing systems, are networks of vertically aligned establishments that are professionally managed as centrally administered distribution systems. Central administration is intended to provide technological, managerial, and promotional economies of scale through the integration, coordination, and synchronization of transactions and marketing activities necessary to the distribution function. There are three types of vertical marketing systems: corporate systems, contractual systems, and administered strategic alliances.

Vertical marketing system
A network of vertically aligned establishments that are managed professionally as centrally administered distribution systems.

CORPORATE SYSTEMS—TOTAL OWNERSHIP

The **corporate vertical marketing system** connects two or more channel members through ownership. It is exemplified by a retailer, such as Sears, that integrates backward into manufacturing to assure quality control over production and corporate control over the distribution system. A manufacturer may obtain complete control of the successive stages of distribution by vertically integrating through ownership. Sherwin-Williams administers a corporate vertical marketing system by owning more than 2,000 retail paint outlets.

Corporate vertical marketing system
A vertical marketing system in which two or more channel members are connected through ownership.

CONTRACTUAL SYSTEMS—LEGAL RELATIONSHIPS

In a **contractual vertical marketing system**, channel leadership is assigned not by ownership but by a contractual agreement. In such a channel, relationships are spelled out so that there is no question about distribution coordination. The relationship between McDonald's franchise holders and McDonald's headquarters is a contractual one wherein the rights and responsibilities of both parties are clearly identified. The idea behind such an approach to distribution is that if all parties live up to the agreement, the system will work smoothly and well. In the main, this has certainly been the case for McDonald's, although the secret of McDonald's success is not merely the employment of a contractual vertical marketing system but also the hard work required to make it succeed.

There are three subtypes of contractual systems: retailer cooperative organizations, wholesaler-sponsored voluntary chains, and franchises. A **retailer cooperative organization** is a group of independent retailers, such as Certified Grocers, that maintains a centralized buying center to perform a wholesaling function. These retailers have combined their financial resources and their expertise to more effectively control their wholesaling needs. By capitalizing on economies of scale, they lower wholesaling costs with their cooperative effort. At the same time, they retain independence.

Contractual vertical marketing system
A vertical marketing system in which channel coordination and leadership are specified in a contractual agreement.

Retailer cooperative organization
A group of independent retailers that combine resources and expertise to control their wholesaling needs through use of a centralized wholesale buying center.

Wholesaler-sponsored voluntary chain
A vertical marketing system, initiated by a wholesaler, that links a group of independent retailers in a relationship with the wholesale supplier.

Franchise
A contractual agreement between a franchisor and a franchisee by which the franchisee distributes the franchisor's product.

The **wholesaler-sponsored voluntary chain** is similar to a cooperative organization except that the wholesaler initiates and manages the collaborative effort so that it has a strong network of loyal retailers. The independent retailers served agree to use only this one wholesaler, while the wholesaler agrees to service all the organized retailers. Ace Hardware is a voluntary chain. Each of the stores uses the common name and receives marketing support that helps the independent retailer compete with chain stores.

A **franchise** is a contractual agreement between a franchisor, typically a manufacturer or a wholesaler, and a number of independent retailers, or franchisees. The franchise agreement often gives the franchisor much discretion in controlling the operations of the small retailers. In exchange for fees, royalties, and a share of the profits, the franchisor offers assistance and, often, supplies. Franchise assistance may take the form of marketing research information or strategic marketing planning aids (for example, new product planning) from franchisor experts. The franchisee is usually responsible for paying for insurance, property taxes, labor, and supplies.

The franchise has been popular and successful in the fast-food industry. Subway, Wendy's, Boston Market, and many other familiar fast-food restaurants are franchises. Subway is one of the fastest-growing fast-food franchise operations. Franchising is prominent in the service industry as well. Consider such familiar names as Brakeman, Midas, Mail Boxes Etc., and Century 21.

One of the main advantages of the franchise system, as well as some other contractual marketing systems, is that it offers brand identity and a nationally recognizable storefront for a retail outlet. Ethan Allen Carriage Houses, Holiday Inns, Burger Kings, and other franchise operations have strong identities. The person driving down the highway has a very clear conception of what products or services will be found at the franchise outlet.

ADMINISTERED STRATEGIC ALLIANCES—STRONG LEADERSHIP

Administered strategic alliance
A vertical marketing system in which a strong channel leader coordinates marketing activities at all levels in the channel through planning and management of a mutually beneficial program.

The third major type of vertical system is the **administered strategic alliance**. Here, a strong position of leadership, rather than outright ownership, may be the source of influence over channel activities. The "administrator" may be any channel member large enough or with enough market clout to dominate the others. Alternatively, a strategic alliance may be built on a commitment to establish a long-term relationship based on collaborative efforts.

Caterpillar's dealerships are all independently owned, but the heavy equipment manufacturer considers its dealers as vital partners. Caterpillar is as concerned about dealers' performance as the dealers are, because the company's enormous and loyal dealer network is one of its major competitive advantages. According to Caterpillar's president, "We have a tremendous regard for our dealers. We do not bypass or undercut them. Some of our competitors do and their dealers quit. Caterpillar dealers don't quit; they die rich."[12] Caterpillar's strong focus on administering the strategic alliances leads the company to offer a range of support and consulting services aimed at helping dealers boost their profitability. One Caterpillar service ensures that dealers' inventories are at the right level. An extranet connects all dealers to the Caterpillar ordering system so that they can order any part they need for next-day delivery. "When you buy the iron, you get the company," Caterpillar literature says.

Administered systems generally are constructed around a line of merchandise rather than the complete manufacturing, wholesaling, or retailing operation. For example, a manufacturer wishing to ensure that wholesalers and retailers follow its comprehensive program of marketing activities might use an administered strategic alliance to coordinate marketing activities and make them attractive to all parties (perhaps by offering discounts or financial assistance). Administered strategic alliances may include arrangements to share or pool inventory information or exchange other databases so that purchase orders are executed automatically by computers. Examples of strong channel leadership through administered strategic alliances may be found in companies such as O. M. Scott and Sons Company (a producer of lawn products) and Baxter Healthcare. The position of leadership can be held by a wholesaler or a retailer as well as by a manufacturer.

Planning the Channel of Distribution

Distribution strategy requires two major decisions. The first involves the structure of the channel of distribution. The second concerns the number of intermediaries that will be used, or the extent of distribution.

DETERMINING THE STRUCTURE OF THE CHANNEL

What determines whether a channel of distribution should be short or long? The selection criteria are influenced by the other elements of the marketing mix strategy, by organizational resources, and by a number of external environmental factors.

The Marketing Mix Strategy   In selecting the channel of distribution, an organization must consider other elements of the marketing mix. For example, an organization's long-term strategic pricing plan may determine whether it will distribute a product through high-margin outlets or through high-volume outlets appealing to price-conscious consumers. The product's characteristics, especially its tangible characteristics, may also play an important role in channel selection. For instance, if live Maine lobsters are to be sold in Tokyo, the channel of distribution will be largely dictated by the perishability of the product. Many products require after-sale service; hence, an intermediary's technical repair service often is an important consideration in selecting a channel of distribution. The size, bulk, and weight of a product will determine whether short channels are necessary to reduce transportation and handling costs. Other product considerations, such as the product's technical complexity, the replacement rate, the gross margin, and the image of the product, also influence the type of channel selected.

Organizational Resources   Arm & Hammer Heavy Duty Detergent is marketed by Church & Dwight, a small company in comparison to Procter & Gamble and Colgate, its competitors. Church & Dwight works with 80 food brokers to market its product in supermarkets, whereas Procter & Gamble has the luxury of employing its own sales organization.

Utilizing one or more marketing intermediaries, as Church & Dwight does, disperses the responsibility for the performance of the distribution function. Thus, an organization that is unable or unwilling to devote financial resources to supporting its own sales force, storing a large inventory, or providing other distribution functions may use wholesalers or retailers to provide the resources or managerial expertise to handle these activities.

A company's existing channels of distribution for its other products are a tremendous resource—they may be the main determinant in the selection of a channel of distribution. Clearly, it made sense to market calcium-enriched V8 Splash through the same channel as regular V8 and other Campbell Soup Company products. Relationships within this channel had already been established. Allowing one distribution channel to carry several items may lead to certain economies of scale.

External Environmental Factors   Many elements of the external environment can affect channel selection. We will discuss market characteristics, consumer preferences and behavior, the nature and availability of intermediaries, and several other factors.

Market Characteristics The number of customers and the amount of the average purchase influence the length of the channel of distribution selected. If the market consists of a few large purchasers, channels are likely to be short. Conversely, if there are many small customers, channels are likely to be long.

Consumer Preferences and Behavior Customers' past behavior and preferences as to purchase location are major criteria that influence the selection of a distribution channel. Perhaps ultimate consumers prefer to buy a certain product in a wholesale club, such as Sam's. If Sam's prefers to purchase directly from manufacturers rather than through wholesalers, this preference has a dramatic impact on channel selection. At each market level, customer preferences must be considered. Furthermore, if a manufacturer finds that some of its buyers prefer to purchase its product in drugstores and others prefer to buy the product in discount stores, multiple channels of distribution may be necessary.

The Nature and Availability of Intermediaries In many cases, capable intermediaries are either unavailable or unwilling to handle a product. When the Levi Strauss Company tried to market its Tailored Classic men's suits, a high-quality, medium-priced product, the company found retailers resistant to handling the wool and wool-blend line because of customers' traditional association of Levi's with more casual clothing. Retailers insisted on displaying the Levi's suit and sport-coat line next to low-priced clothing and demanded price reductions. Furthermore, many retailers would not carry the line because their store images contrasted with the image of the traditional Levi product line. When the preferred intermediary is unavailable, a manufacturer may have to alter its channel of distribution, possibly by eliminating the wholesaler and going directly to the ultimate consumer in a certain territory.

Other Environmental Factors Any of the environmental forces discussed in Chapter 3 or Chapter 4 may have an impact on the channel of distribution. For example, the wholesaling and retailing structure in Japan is strongly influenced by political and legal factors. An organization must carefully consider all possible environmental forces before making a decision about a channel of distribution.

THE EXTENT OF DISTRIBUTION: HOW MANY OUTLETS?

Once the structure of the distribution channel has been determined, the manufacturer is faced with the problem of deciding on the intensity of distribution at each level within the channel. Selecting the number of wholesalers and the number of retail outlets is an important decision that will determine the number of outlets where potential customers can expect to find the product. The various strategies, based on the degree of distribution intensity, are (1) intensive distribution, (2) selective distribution, and (3) exclusive distribution.

Intensive distribution
A distribution strategy aimed at obtaining maximum exposure for a product at the retail level or wholesale level.

Intensive Distribution The strategy of **intensive distribution** seeks to obtain maximum product exposure at the retail level. When consumers will not go out of their way to purchase a particular product or will readily accept substitutes when that brand is not available, the appropriate strategy is to saturate every suitable retail outlet with the brand. Gasoline, chewing gum, and other convenience goods normally receive intensive distribution. Intensive distribution at the wholesale level allows almost all appropriate wholesalers to carry the product.

Products that are distributed intensively may be presold through mass media advertising or other means. Coca-Cola, for example, needs little personal selling and may be distributed in vending machines, supermarkets, drugstores, restau-

what went wrong?

Specialized Bicycle It all sounded so simple and so true. "Grow or die." "You must be virtual." "Go global." "Capital is easy." "Everybody is an entrepreneur." "Technology makes life easier." "You must be on the Web in a big way."

The New Economy of the '90s buzzed with such mantras of the moment. A chorus of business gurus proclaimed, "Everything you know is wrong." Seasoned company owners and artless upstarts alike were persuaded to set aside experience and common sense in favor of the trend du jour.

If you were swept off your feet by the catchy slogans above . . . well, let's just say you were not alone. Some of the smartest CEOs around were also caught up by the hype swirling around these new business imperatives. Mountain bike pioneer Mike Sinyard thought he saw the future rolling toward him.

Specialized Bicycle Components—the company Sinyard founded in 1974—had always catered to a hard core of cross-country racers and "enduro" riders like Sinyard himself. But the builder of mountain bikes knew there were only so many enthusiasts out there.

"The market was consolidating and we decided we needed critical mass," recalls Sinyard. To compete, he figured he had better grow the company into a big, national brand. Sinyard realized he needed to enter the mass marketplace if he wanted to really grow. So in the fall of 1995, Specialized rolled out a separate brand, FullForce, and placed it in numerous discount sporting-goods chains.

"We thought we'd have a niche brand and a mass-market brand," he says.

But the new strategy aroused the wrath of the company's core customer: the independent bicycle-shop dealers. Their only competi-tive advantage in the war against the Wal-Marts of the world was to serve the enthusiast with better products that were unavailable elsewhere. With Specialized cropping up in the aisles of the enemy, they felt betrayed.

"We were hell bent on growing, and we went away from our root value of 'don't be bigger, be better,'" Sinyard says. "Our customers became very hot with us and told us point blank they didn't like what we were doing."

It didn't go over well with employees, either; they felt it went counter to the culture that Sinyard had created. Even Sinyard himself was troubled when he went into a super-store one day and saw his product lumped in with an aisle of alcoholic beverages.

So just eight months after getting into the mass market, Sinyard and Specialized got out. The experience proved a costly one for the Morgan Hill, Calif., company.

"It was a huge loss and a big lesson," says Sinyard. The company ended up losing several million dollars in developing the brand, ramping up, and registering the logo.

But Sinyard immediately applied the lesson. In his new mission statement he committed to serving "full-service dealers and discerning cyclists." Specialized's CEO also personally composed a letter to dealers that was printed in the trade press—an embarrassing but healing public atonement.

"Competitors called it 'Mike's mea culpa letter,'" Sinyard recalls.

Specialized has since regrouped and even grown within its niche: sales have gone from $150 million in 1995 to approximately $170 million today. No longer worried about being consumed by someone bigger, Sinyard is confident in the power of his small but agile company: "I say, bring 'em on, we're ready."[12]

rants, and many other outlets. Pennzoil intensively distributes its motor oil in service stations, as well as in Kmart and Target stores and other mass merchandising outlets, where more than half of U.S. car motor oil is sold. To increase the intensity of its distribution, Pennzoil purchased a large share of Jiffy-Lube International, the leading oil-change-while-you-wait franchise.

Selective Distribution At the retail level, a strategy of **selective distribution** restricts the sale of a product to a limited number of outlets. The manufacturers of

Selective distribution
A distribution strategy in which a product is sold in a limited number of outlets.

High-quality, prestigious brands such as Chanel No. 5 often use selective distribution strategies. Each store Chanel selects must meet certain standards and appeal to Chanel's target market.

http://www.chanel.com

Tommy Hilfiger shirts focus their marketing efforts on certain selected outlets with the desired store image. Each store must meet the company's performance standards while appealing to a specific target market. As distribution becomes more selective, the manufacturer may expect a greater effort on the part of the retailer (such as a willingness to hold a larger inventory). Because retailers benefit from limits on the number of competitors, they are expected to be more willing to accept the manufacturer's suggestions and controls on the marketing strategy—for example, by supporting the list price.

Selective distribution is much more commonly used for specialty and shopping goods than for convenience goods. However, Noxell Corporation, marketer of the Noxzema and Cover Girl brands of make-up and skin cream, selectively distributes its products in chain stores such as Kmart and Woolco. It lets its competitors vie for distribution in the more prestigious department and specialty stores. Its selective distribution strategy reaches its target market.

Exclusive Distribution   We mentioned earlier that Caterpillar maintains a strong network of exclusive dealers. When a product requires aggressive personal selling, a complete inventory of the product line, repair service, or other special efforts, an intermediary may be granted an exclusive area. Generally, a manufacturer or wholesaler that grants a retailer **exclusive distribution** expects a maximum sales effort or expects to gain something from the prestige or efficiency of the retail outlet. Exclusive distribution agreements often involve contractual arrangements. Suppliers typically have written agreements with exclusive distributors stipulating certain responsibilities that are too important to be left to a mutual understanding. Contracts outline tenure of appointment, trading area, sale conditions, warranty considerations, and extent of product line coverage. However, exclusive dealing may not be legal if it tends to lessen competition in a particular geographical area.

Note that the extent of distribution must be determined at each level in the channel. For example, a manufacturer like Coca-Cola may execute an intensive distribution strategy at the retail level and an exclusive distribution strategy at the wholesale level.

Exclusive distribution
A distribution strategy in which only one outlet in a given area is allowed to sell a product.

Issues Surrounding Channel Relationships

Because the actions of one channel member may greatly influence the performance of another channel member, the relations among channel members are of considerable interest. The retailer relies on the manufacturer to create an adequate sales potential through advertising, product development, and other marketing strategies. An exclusive dealer's welfare is in jeopardy if a manufacturer's marketing strategy is not successful. A manufacturer may depend on the successful performance of a small number of wholesalers, which cannot be left to sink or swim on their own merits. In the following sections, we examine several issues related to relationships among interdependent channel members.

CHANNEL COOPERATION

The objectives and marketing strategies of two channel members—for example, a manufacturer and a retailer—may be in total harmony. Both parties may recognize that their tasks are linked and that by working together they can jointly exploit a marketing opportunity. The manufacturer promptly delivers a high-quality product with a good reputation; the retailer prices the product as expected and carries an inventory of the full product line. **Channel cooperation** exists when the marketing objectives and strategies of two channel members are harmonious.

CHANNEL CONFLICT

Channel conflict exists when channel members have disagreements and their relationship is antagonistic. Channel conflict often results from the absence of a clearly identified locus of formal channel power.[14] Channel members may disagree about the channel's common purpose or the responsibility for certain activities. The behavior of one channel member may be seen as inhibiting another channel member from attaining its goals. (Channel conflict describes vertical conflicts among members of the same channel of distribution.[15] It should not be confused with economic competition between two like intermediaries at the same level in a channel, such as Macy's and Bloomingdale's, which is sometimes referred to as *horizontal conflict*.)

Consider the following instance of channel conflict. In 1992, Goodyear began selling its products to Sears—something it had not done before. In fact, for more than 60 years, Goodyear tires could be purchased only on new cars or from the company's exclusive network of independent dealers. Then in 1993, Goodyear started selling replacement tires to Discount Tire Company, a big independent tire retailer. These alignments with Sears and Discount caused considerable channel conflict. Goodyear's independent dealers expressed anger and feelings of betrayal. They protested that Goodyear's actions had eroded their competitive positions. Many dealers retaliated by taking on competing brands, especially private brands.

Vertical conflict can also arise when a wholesaler is frustrated because the manufacturer bypasses it and sells directly to larger accounts. Another typical source of conflict is a situation in which a dealer wishes to minimize its investment in inventory but cannot do so because the distributor does not maintain the proper inventory level and thus cannot be relied on to guarantee speedy delivery. Vertical conflict may occur when sales are down and, consequently, manufacturers accuse dealers or distributors of failing to promote aggressively. Conflict can also arise if manufacturers, wholesalers, or retailers believe that they are not making enough money on the product line.

> Channel conflict often results from the absence of a clearly identified locus of formal channel power.

CHANNEL POWER

An organization that is able to exert its **channel power** and influence over other channel members is referred to as the **channel leader** or *channel captain*. A channel

Potential channel conflict is a problem for manufacturers desiring to sell directly to consumers through the Internet. Traditional retailers don't want their suppliers to undercut retail prices, thereby allowing the retailers' business to be cannibalized. Procter & Gamble, a leading mass marketer of cosmetic and personal care brands, has adopted a distribution and branding strategy that will avoid channel conflict caused by selling to Internet shoppers. P&G created an entirely new, higher end, online-only cosmetics brand, which has no existing retailers to offend. Reflect.com will not sell existing P&G brands, but rather a line of custom-blended beauty products available only through the Web site.

http://www.reflect.com

Channel cooperation
Coordinated efforts by distribution channel members whose marketing objectives and strategies complement each other.

Channel conflict
Antagonism between distribution channel members.

Channel power
The extent to which a channel member is able to influence the behavior of another channel member.

Channel leader
A distribution channel member that is able to exert power and influence over other channel members; also known as a *channel captain*.

Clinique, the cosmetics company, was surprised to find in a survey it conducted on the Web that 80 percent of the people logging on to its informational site said they would like to buy the products online. Clinique considered the fact that channel conflict could arise if the company created a virtual store.

Its executives were at first reluctant to sell its cosmetics online, nervous about its crucial department-store relationships. Some stores wouldn't like the idea of a manufacturer's selling on its own Web site. Mindful of this, when Estée Lauder, Clinique's parent, decided to take the plunge, it contacted its distribution outlets and explained what it was trying to do. At the same time, Clinique offered to help department stores in setting up their own sites. The company managed to convince the stores that consumers were not facing an either/or situation.

As it turned out, Clinique's new Happy perfume is the No. 1 seller on its Web site and at Macy's Web site. Clinique believes if consumers come to its site, they should be able to buy. But if they're at Macy's Web site buying a sweater and also want Clinique's perfume, they shouldn't have to switch sites. Clinique is now enjoying a higher margin on Web sales than it does in department stores. The company has also been surprised at how little cannibalization has actually occurred. It has learned that at least 20 percent of its online buyers are new customers and 41 percent of purchases are of products customers have never used before. Thus, Clinique finds its new Web site is adding to, not detracting from, the brand's overall sales.[16]

leader has mutually agreed-on authority to reward, punish, plan, coordinate, or otherwise dictate the activities of channel members. For instance, Home Box Office is the channel leader for the distribution of movies on pay TV. HBO virtually dictates how much it will pay for a film. Furthermore, HBO finances film production; in recent years, it has become a major source of financing for independent movie producers.

There are several sources of channel power. Because of the size of its purchases, a large retailer such as Wal-Mart may be able to dictate marketing strategy to less powerful channel members. In placing an order for a private-label brand, Wal-Mart may insist on certain product specifications, prices, or delivery dates. A small manufacturer may be so dependent on the Wal-Mart order that it changes the specifications on its own brand so that it can economically produce a product that meets Wal-Mart's specifications.

Reverse Distribution

Backward channel
A channel of distribution for recycling, in which the customary flow from producer to ultimate user is reversed.

In recent decades, the recycling of waste has become an important ecological goal. The major problem in recycling is determining who is responsible for the "reverse distribution" process it involves. The macromarketing task is to establish a **backward channel** of distribution, one in which the ultimate consumer who seeks to recycle waste materials must undergo a role change.

The distribution channels for marketing automobiles are changing. More and more car buyers are doing their shopping at Web sites. Using the Internet, consumers can compare the specifications of various models and learn their retail and wholesale prices. Auto-By-Tel, a computerized broker service, allows Internet shoppers to buy a car without price haggling or psychological pressure. It's no surprise that these services have contributed to a shift in channel power.

http://www.autobytel.com

By recycling your old newspapers or metal cans, you become a "producer" of a usable product that has some economic utility. Thus, in this backward channel, the consumer is the first link in the process rather than the last. The backward channel in this case is likely to be run by traditional manufacturers of paper or cans. Yet the flow of goods is the reverse of what most descriptions of marketing operations suggest.[17]

Ethical Forces in Distribution Management

You might think of recycling as involving certain ethical issues as well as issues of distribution. Indeed, several ethical issues arise in connection with distribution and its macromarketing role. One of the most controversial issues is the cost of distribution.

As mentioned earlier, a commonly heard cry is "eliminate the middleman!" But as we have explained, eliminating the intermediary does not eliminate the functions intermediaries perform. Thus, a manufacturer that eliminates wholesalers will have to perform the wholesaling function itself. This may cost more than using independent wholesalers if the wholesalers were better at their job than the manufacturer could or would be.

A critic might note that some individual aspects of the distribution system are nonessential. Yet it has been shown repeatedly that "nonessentials" such as convenience are important to consumers. The success of 7-Eleven, Quick-Trip, and similar stores proves that consumers want—and will pay for—convenient location and quick service. The customers decide the trade-offs in this case, agreeing to pay a little more money to avoid paying with their time. People can quickly and profoundly influence the distribution system simply by where they shop. It is arguable that distribution is the aspect of marketing that is most responsive to consumer demands.

Summary

Distribution is a necessary but often misunderstood marketing function. The common desire to "eliminate the middleman" shows that the general public has little appreciation for the role played by a channel of distribution.

1) Explain the general purpose of distribution and logistics in the marketing system.

A channel of distribution makes it possible for title or possession of a product to pass from producer to consumer. By common agreement, channel members share the responsibility for performing the basic functions of marketing. Distribution provides time and place utility to buyers by delivering the right products at the right time in the right place. It bridges the gap between manufacturers and final users. In effect, distribution delivers a standard of living.

2) Evaluate the role of the supply chain and physical distribution in the marketing mix.

The term *supply chain* is used to describe all the organizations that regularly supply a marketing company and all members of the marketer's channel of distribution. *Logistics* describes the entire process by which materials, in-process inventory, and finished goods move into, through, and out of the organization. *Supply chain management* (logistics management) involves planning, implementing, and controlling the efficient flow of both inbound materials and outbound finished products. Physical distribution, one aspect of logistics, provides time and place utility by moving products from producer to consumer or organizational user in a timely and efficient manner.

3) Show how distribution managers can make physical distribution provide maximum satisfaction to buyers while reducing costs.

The central objective of physical distribution is to keep costs down while keeping the level of service up. Yet improved service raises costs, and reduced costs lower levels of service. Distribution managers must balance these two goals. The marketing concept suggests that managers should determine what level of service will fit buyers' needs and what prices are acceptable to them.

4) Explain the total cost approach to physical distribution.

The total cost concept takes a systems approach to physical distribution. By placing emphasis on controlling total cost, the manager focuses on how the parts of the distribution system can be used to keep total costs down. Raising expenditures in one part of the system may reduce total costs; lowering expenditures in one part of the system might raise total costs.

5) Understand why all marketers—even not-for-profit and service organizations—engage in distribution.

All marketers, including not-for-profit, service, and for-profit concerns, engage in some form of distribution because there is always some gap between the marketer and the customer that must be bridged.

6) Characterize the functions of channel intermediaries.

Channel intermediaries perform a variety of functions, including breaking bulk, accumulating bulk, sorting, creating assortments, reducing transactions, transporting, storing, communicating, financing, providing management services, and other facilitating functions.

7) Identify the major channels of distribution used by marketers.

The major distribution channels for consumer goods are (1) producer to consumer, (2) producer to retailer to consumer, (3) service producer to agent to consumer, (4) producer to wholesaler to retailer to consumer (the most commonly used consumer goods channel), and (5) producer to wholesaler (agent) to wholesaler to retailer to consumer. The major organizational products channels are (1) producer to user, (2) producer to wholesaler to user, and (3) producer to agent (wholesaler) to user. There are numerous variations on these basic channel models, many of which involve specialized intermediaries.

8) Describe the major vertical marketing systems.

In a corporate vertical marketing system, the members are owned outright by the controlling organization to ensure cooperation and increase effectiveness. In a contractual vertical marketing system, the members are linked to the channel leader by formal contract. An administered strategic alliance is made up of organizations that follow the lead of the dominant member of the system or engage in a collaborative effort. In all cases, the purpose of the vertical marketing system is to ensure cooperation among channel members, and the goal is increased effectiveness of the channel.

9) Differentiate among channel cooperation, channel conflict, and channel power.

Channel cooperation occurs when channel members share harmonious marketing objectives and strategies. Channel conflict is present in channels of distribution in which there is some disharmony. Conflict should not go unmanaged. Channel power is the ability of one organization in a channel of distribution to exert influence over other channel members. The most powerful organization is the channel leader.

Key Terms

administered strategic alliance
   (p. 324)
agent intermediary (p. 306)
air freight (p. 312)
assembler (p. 308)
assorting function (p. 309)
backward channel (p. 330)
bulk-accumulating function
   (p. 308)
bulk-breaking function (p. 308)
buying function (p. 315)
channel conflict (p. 329)
channel cooperation (p. 329)
channel leader (p. 329)
channel of distribution (p. 305)
channel power (p. 329)
contractual vertical marketing
   system (p. 323)

conventional channel of
   distribution (p. 306)
corporate vertical marketing system
   (p. 323)
credit function (p. 316)
damage in transit (p. 311)
disintermediation (p. 321)
diversion in transit (p. 311)
exclusive distribution (p. 328)
franchise (p. 324)
infomediary (p. 321)
intensive distribution (p. 326)
logistics (p. 302)
materials management (p. 303)
merchant intermediary (p. 306)
motor carrier (p. 312)
physical distribution (p. 303)
pipelines (p. 312)

rail transport (p. 311)
retailer cooperative organization
   (p. 323)
risk-taking function (p. 316)
selective distribution (p. 327)
selling function (p. 315)
service function (p. 316)
sorting function (p. 309)
supply chain (p. 302)
supply chain management (p. 303)
systems concept (p. 314)
total cost concept (p. 314)
vertical exchange (p. 321)
vertical marketing system (p. 323)
water transportation (p. 312)
wholesaler-sponsored voluntary
   chain (p. 324)

Questions for Review & Critical Thinking

1. What might happen if wholesaler intermediaries for the following brands were eliminated?
   a. Izod Lacoste shirts
   b. Cutty Sark Scotch whiskey
   c. Weyerhauser lumber

2. Outline the macromarketing functions performed by wholesalers and retailers.

3. At a national bottlers' meeting, the vice president of marketing for the Dr Pepper Company said, "No matter how good a job we do, [consumers] can't get Dr Pepper unless you [bottlers] have made the sale to retailers." Why would the vice president say this?

4. Several years ago, Airwick professional products division, which sells a variety of disinfectants, cleaning agents, insecticides, and environmental sanitation products, sold its products through a network of 65 distributors and 10 branch sales offices. The company decided to drop its sales branches. What circumstances might lead to such a change in channel strategy?

5. Only recently have medical professionals started to realize that they, like manufacturers, must give thought to their distribution systems. What distribution decisions might hospitals, dentists, and pediatricians have to make?

6. How will the decision of Sam's Wholesale Club, Price Club/Costco, and similar stores to sell food affect Procter & Gamble's distribution system?

7. If you were the manufacturer of the following products, what channels of distribution would you select?
   a. Fax machines
   b. Automobile mufflers
   c. MP3 music software
   d. Mobile telephones
   e. Dolls

8. Outline the channel of distribution for the following.
   a. An airline
   b. A bakery
   c. A pizza restaurant

9. What advantages do vertical marketing systems have over conventional marketing systems?

10. Would you use exclusive, selective, or intensive distribution for the following products? Why?
   a. Dr Pepper
   b. Lexus automobiles
   c. Panasonic VCRs
   d. Ethan Allen furniture
   e. Fieldcrest Mills towels
   f. Michelin tires

11. What environmental forces might shape international distribution strategies?

12. Identify the possible sources of conflict in a channel of distribution.

13. What macromarketing functions do intermediaries perform for society at large?

14. Form groups of six people, and in each group have two students represent a supermarket retailer, two students represent a grocery wholesaler, and two students represent a manufacturer of packaged foods. Identify at least three issues over which channel conflicts might arise. Each channel member team should state its position on these issues.

 **e—|exercises|**   http://zikmund.swcollege.com

1. Traditionally, travel agents have played a key role in the distribution system for travel services. As use of the Internet continues to expand, however, radical changes are taking place in the travel services distribution system. Using a search engine such as Yahoo!, enter "Airlines—Reservation Systems" as a subject. Select a document and read it to get information about using the Internet to purchase airline tickets. Then answer the following questions and bring your answers to class for discussion.
   a. What are the best ways to make airline reservations using the Internet?
   b. Who is most likely to use the Internet as the distribution system for airline tickets?
   c. Who will not be served by this distribution system? What alternative channel will best reach the unserved group?
   d. Is there potential for channel conflict? Explain your answer.
   e. What is the future of this distribution system for airline tickets? For other travel services? Why?
2. FreeMarkets.com is a vertical exchange. Go to http://www.freemarkets.com and describe its services.
3. The Rainforest Company (http://www.the-rainforest-co.com) is both a manufacturer and a wholesaler. What type of products does the company distribute? Why does it have information about rainforests on its home page?

Address Book (Useful URLs)

Logistics Business	http://www.logistics.co.uk/
United States Council for International Business	http://www.imex.com/uscib

Ethically Right or Wrong?

A manufacturer of construction equipment historically has marketed its product only in the eastern United States, where it uses wholesalers to sell to construction contractors. The company plans to expand into the western United States, using agents to sell to wholesalers until the volume of its business is large enough to make it feasible to hire its own sales force in the new market. Arrangements are made with several agents to sell the product. The company, however, does not mention its plans to hire its own sales force after the agents have established a wholesale distribution system. Is this ethical?

TAKE A STAND

1. A liquor wholesaler wishes to purchase five cases of a small California winery's vintage Cabernet Sauvignon (a red wine), which has received favorable reviews. The winery says this wine is in short supply, and it ships five-case orders only to wholesalers that also purchase five cases of its Chardonnay (a white wine). The Chardonnay is rated as a very ordinary wine, and the wholesaler sells many comparable brands. What should the wholesaler do?
2. A supermarket sells many products packaged in aluminum cans and glass bottles. It does not offer any recycling facility or service. Is this a responsible policy?
3. Wal-Mart notifies manufacturers that it will no longer deal with intermediaries. Its intentions are to deal directly with manufacturers. The move squeezes independent wholesalers and brokers out of the picture. Is this right?

VIDEO CASE 11-1

Burton Snowboards (B)

Since 1992, Burton Snowboards has been leading the industry from its factory in Burlington, Vermont. Burton markets snowboards and snowboarding equipment and nothing else. Its products include snowboards, bindings, boots, gloves, hats, and snowboarding clothing. Video case 1-1 described the entrepreneurial history of Burton.

Burton employs a selective distribution strategy. All of its retail dealers sign a franchising agreement requiring them to provide quality displays and premium service to their retail customers. Burton ships snowboards from its factory in Vermont to a warehouse in upstate New York and then ships products to dealers via truck transport companies, such as Roadway and Yellow Freight, and parcel delivery companies, such as UPS.

Burton's sales force calls on its dealers several months before the snowboarding season begins. Dealers reorder throughout the season. However, because Burton uses a just-in-time inventory system, the company goal is for dealers to order the ideal amount of merchandise. Burton strives to ensure that dealers do not order excess inventory. They don't want dealers to be forced to mark down prices during after-the-season sales. Lower prices could affect Burton's quality image.[18]

QUESTIONS

1. Outline Burton's channel of distribution.
2. Why would Burton Snowboards choose a strategy of selective distribution?
3. What should Burton expect of its dealers? What should the dealers expect of Burton?
4. Is relationship marketing important to a company like Burton? How would relationship marketing influence Burton's promotional stategy?
5. Do you think the 80/20 principle (mentioned in Chapter 8) would apply to retail sales in the snowboarding industry? Why or why not?

Retailing, Direct Marketing, and Wholesaling

12

chapter

There she is, hair as big as all outdoors, smiling supremely as she steps to the podium to announce her reunion tour. Yes, it's diva Diana Ross. But the footage, complete with video montages and music, isn't playing on your TV.

No, it's streaming into a small box at the center of your computer screen. And while Miss Ross beams amid a hail of popping flashbulbs, the lower left corner of your computer screen serves up info about the Supremes' Detroit hometown and history, while at the lower right, an array of Supremes-, Motown- and music-related products for sale has begun scrolling into view.

All of it—video, audio, text and commerce—is as tightly orchestrated as an early Supremes performance itself. And all of it, from the original electronic press kit to the online programming to the history and e-commerce tie-in, has been produced by Centerseat, a New York-based digital media and commerce company.

Centerseat has built an archive of more than 100,000 hours of classic TV and films dating back to 1908—which is currently being cleansed, digitized and audio- and color-corrected—much of which Centerseat will be able to distribute offline on broadcast, cable and satellite TV as well.

In the meantime, Centerseat and its 85 staffers have been making deal after deal, signing on big names to both back up its business—Terry Baker, formerly a senior producer for *Good Morning America* now serves as VP of news and information programming—as well as front its shows—former CNN and NBC reporter Mary Alice Williams is already developing and hosting several shows for the company.

And Centerseat is offering more than 1 million products online.[1]

Centerseat brings point of interest simultaneously together with point of purchase. Is this innovative Web site performing a retailing function? It certainly seems so, but it is hardly a traditional one. The Internet is changing the face of retailing. This chapter deals with retailing and how retailing adapts to changes in the environment. The chapter begins by addressing the importance of retailing and classifying retailers according to several criteria. It then describes a theory proposed to explain the historical patterns of change in retail institutions. Next, it discusses retail management strategies, focusing on merchandise assortment, location, atmospherics, customer services, and data-based management. It then turns to wholesaling, examining types of wholesalers, their importance to the U.S. economy, and the strategies they use to market goods and services.

Retailing and Its Importance

Retailing consists of all business activities associated with the sale of goods and services to ultimate consumers. Retailing involves a retailer—traditionally a store or a service establishment—that deals with consumers who are acquiring goods or services for their own use rather than for resale. Of course, Wal-Mart, The Gap, Best Buy, and other familiar organizations offering products for sale to consumers are retailers. However, the definition of retailing includes some less-than-obvious service marketers, such as hotels, movie theaters, restaurants, and ice-cream truck operators. And even if an intermediary calls itself a "factory outlet," a "wholesale club," or a "shopping channel," it is a retailer if its purpose is to sell to the ultimate consumer.[2] Furthermore, Amazon.com and many other new "dot-com" companies that sell on the Internet are retailers. Because these retailers are e-commerce firms, they are often called **e-tailers.**

Viewed in the context of the channel of distribution, retailers are the important final link in the process that brings goods or services from producers to consumers. Poor marketing on the part of retailers can negate all the planning and preparation that have gone into other marketing activities.

In the United States, there are more than 1.5 million retailing institutions accounting for about $2 trillion in sales.[3] About 15 percent of U.S. workers are employed in retailing.

Retailing Institutions— Toward a System of Classifications

Retailers are a diverse group of businesses. In the distribution of food there are supermarkets, convenience stores, restaurants, and various specialty outlets. Merchandise retailers may be department stores, apparel stores, consumer electronics stores, home improvement stores, pet shops, or various types of retailing systems for home shopping. Service retailers, such as movie theaters and banks, are as diverse as the types of services offered for sale.

Retailing is dynamic, and retail institutions evolve constantly.[4] For example, institutions such as "mom and pop" grocery stores are at the end of their life cycle. Individual companies like Sears, which began in the late 1880s as a mail-order retailer of watches and jewelry, are continually transforming themselves into new types of retailers. Warehouse clubs and interactive shopping on the Internet are but two retailing innovations that have developed in recent decades. In the next 20 years, retailers will inevitably adjust to their changing environments by transforming themselves further.

> Retailing is dynamic, and retail institutions evolve constantly.

In light of this constant change, and of the very large number of retailers in the United States, how can retail institutions be sorted into more easily analyzed groups? Two commonly used methods classify retailers on the basis of ownership and prominent strategy.

CLASSIFYING RETAILERS BY OWNERSHIP

One popular method of categorizing retailers is by ownership. Most retailers are **independent retailers**, operating as single-unit entities. Independent operations may be proprietorships, partnerships, or corporations, but they are usually owned by one operator, a family, or a small number of individuals. They are not generally integrated into a larger corporation. These retailers are often thought of as small, but some are quite sizable. Taken together, they are an important part of the U.S. retailing scene.

An independent retailer that owns the merchandise stocked but leases floor space from another retailer is a **leased department retailer**. A leased department—for example, a branch bank, a jewelry department, or a pharmaceutical department—operates independently from the lessor retailer (the retailer that rents out the floor space), although it often operates under the lessor's name. The lessor grants leased department retailers this degree of independence because they have special expertise in handling the particular product line, will increase total store traffic, or are necessary to the lessor because consumers expect to find the departments' merchandise in the store.

If a retail establishment is not independent, it is classified as either a chain or an ownership group. The more familiar of these classifications is the **chain store**—one of a group of shops bearing the same name and having roughly the same merchandise assortment and store image. Chain-store systems consist of two or more stores of a similar type that are centrally owned and operated.

Chains have been successful for a number of reasons, but one of the most important is the opportunity they have to take advantage of economies of scale in buying and selling goods. Conducting centralized buying for several stores permits chains to obtain the lower prices associated with large purchases. They can then maintain their prices, thus increasing their margins, or they can cut prices, attracting greater sales volume. Unlike small independents with lesser financial means, chains can also take advantage of promotional tools, such as television advertising, by spreading the expense among many member stores, thus stretching their promotional budget. Other expenses, such as costs for computerized inventory control systems, may also be shared by all stores.

Chains vary in size. The Tattered Cover with its 2 bookstores, Hansen Galleries with its 6 art gallery outlets, and Kmart with its more than 2,500 stores are all chain stores. The number of stores in a chain can make a big difference in the way the business operates.

According to the U.S. Department of Commerce, the term **corporate chain** is used for chains with 11 or more stores. Typically, as the number of units in a chain increases, management becomes more centralized, and each store manager has less autonomy in determining the overall marketing strategy. Although corporate chains possess many advantages over independents, some analysts say independents and smaller chains are more flexible. They may be better able to apply such marketing techniques as segmentation than are bigger operations, whose appeal must be more general.

Retail franchise operations are a special type of chain. Although the broad marketing strategy in such chains is centrally planned, the retail outlets are independently owned and operated. Franchises provide an excellent example of the evolution of retail institutions to fit the American culture. Midas Muffler Shops, Arby's, and other nationwide franchise chains are now found in nearly every population center. Thus, as the country's mobile citizenry moves from place to place, a familiar Midas shop or Arby's is "waiting" for them when they arrive. Each new franchise benefits from the company's experience, reputation, and shared resources.

The other type of retailing organization is the **ownership group**—an organization made up of various stores or small chains, each having a separate name, identity, and image but all operating under the ultimate control of a central owner.

Independent retailer
A retail establishment that is not owned or controlled by any other organization.

Leased department retailer
An independent retailer that owns the merchandise stocked but leases floor space from another retailer, usually operating under that retailer's name.

Chain store
One of a group of two or more stores of a similar type, centrally owned and operated.

Corporate chain
A chain consisting of 11 or more stores.

Ownership group
An organization made up of stores or small chains, each with a separate name, identity, and image but all operating under the control of a central owner.

Typically, the members of such groups are former corporate chains bought out by much larger ownership groups. Target, Federated Department Stores, and B.A.T. Industries are ownership groups that operate stores with different names. Bloomingdale's, Lazarus, Burdines, Rich's, Jordan Marsh, The Bon Marché, Abraham & Straus, and Stern's are owned by the Federated Department Stores ownership group.

CLASSIFYING RETAILERS BY PROMINENT STRATEGY

Retailers can also be classified based on their most prominent retail strategies. The decision as to whether to market products and services with an in-store retailing strategy (also called a bricks-and-mortar strategy) or a direct marketing (non-store) retailing strategy is such an important discriminating factor that these two major groupings will be discussed separately. Exhibit 12-1 shows these groupings and their subcategories.

In-Store Retailing   Many fundamental strategies differentiate in-store retailers. The variety of products they sell, store size, price level relative to competitors, degree of self-service, location, and other variables can be used to categorize retailers. Each strategy has its particular advantages and disadvantages, and each fits particular markets and situations. Try to envision the following store classes as responses to particular marketing opportunities.

Specialty store
A retail establishment that sells a single product or a few related lines; also called *single-line retailer* or *limited-line retailer*.

Specialty Stores   **Specialty stores**, also called *single-line retailers* or *limited-line retailers*, are differentiated from other retailers by their degree of specialization—that is, the narrowness of their product mixes and the depth of their product lines. These traditional retailers specialize within a particular product category, selling only items targeted to narrow market segments or items requiring a particular selling expertise, such as children's shoes, automobile mufflers, or clocks. The major reason for their success is the development of considerable expertise in their particular product lines. Wallpapers to Go, for example, offers free wallpapering lessons to instruct consumers on what wallpapering techniques to use and what to buy. Service establishments, such as restaurants and banks, are often classified as specialty retailers. These retailers do not try to be all things to all people.

Department store
A departmentalized retail outlet, often large, offering a wide variety of products and generally providing a full range of customer services.

Department Stores   **Department stores** are typically large compared with specialty stores. They carry a wide selection of products, including clothing, furniture, home appliances, housewares, and—depending on the size of the operation—a good many other products as well. These stores are "departmentalized" both physically and organizationally. Each department is operated largely as a separate entity headed by a buyer, who has considerable independence and authority in buying and selling products and who is responsible for the department's profits. Independent department stores do exist, but most department stores are members of chains or ownership groups.

Most Americans turn to the right when they enter a building. So airports put gift stores on the right and food outlets on the left, reasoning that hungry people will go against their natural rightward tendency to grab a bite to eat.

MAJOR GROUP	RETAILER CLASSIFICATION	BRIEF DESCRIPTION
IN-STORE RETAILING	Specialty store	Narrow variety, deep selection within a product class, personalized service; makes up large bulk of all retailing operations
	Department store	Generally chain operations, wide variety, full range of services
	Supermarket	Wide variety of food and nonfood products, large departmentalized operation featuring self-service aisles and centralized checkouts
	Convenience store	Little variety, shallow selection, fast service
	General mass merchandiser	Wide variety, shallow selection of high-turnover products, low prices, few customer services
	Catalog showroom	General mass merchandiser that uses a catalog to promote items
	Warehouse club	General mass merchandiser that requires membership if customers wish to shop; store goods warehouse-style
	Specialty mass merchandiser	Less variety but greater depth than general mass merchandiser, low prices, few customer services
	Off-price retailer	Specialty mass merchandiser that sells a limited line of nationally known brand names
	Category superstore	Specialty mass merchandiser that offers deep discounts and extensive assortment and depth in a specific product category
DIRECT MARKETING	Mail-order/direct response retailing	Generally low operating costs, emphasis on convenience; often uses computerized databases; includes mail order, television home shopping, and telephone sales
	Door-to-door selling	High labor cost, image problems; popularity is decreasing in the United States, increasing in less-developed countries
	e-tailing	Consumer initiates contact with retailer via computer and the Internet
	Vending machines	High-turnover products, low prices

Most department stores are characterized by a full range of services, including credit plans, delivery, generous return policies, restaurants, and a host of other extras such as fashion clinics, closed-door sales for established customers only, and even etiquette classes for customers' children. Such services, as well as the need to carry a wide variety of merchandise and maintain a large building, increase store operating costs and necessitate higher prices than those at discount stores. Some consumers seek the service and atmosphere of the department store but then make actual purchases at a discount store. In short, discounters and other types of store operators are formidable competitors for traditional department stores.

Supermarkets and Convenience Stores   Today's **supermarket** is a large departmentalized retail establishment selling a variety of products, mostly food items but also health and beauty aids, housewares, magazines, and much more. The dominant features of a supermarket marketing strategy are large in-store inventories on self-service aisles and centralized checkout lines. Often, supermarkets stress the low prices resulting from self-service. The inclusion of nonfood items on supermarket shelves was once novel, in that it represented the stocking of items that did not traditionally belong in the supermarket's group of offerings.

Supermarkets were among the first retailers to stress discount strategies. Using such strategies, large self-service retail establishments sell a variety of high-turnover

Supermarket
Any large, self-service, departmentalized retail establishment, but especially one that sells primarily food items.

products at low prices. A good part of a retailer's ability to hold prices down stems from the practice of offering few services. Other than the costs of the goods they sell, most retailers find that personnel costs are their largest financial outlay. Thus, by eliminating most of the sales help, having no delivery staff, and hiring stock clerks and cash-register operators rather than true salespeople, discounters are able to take a big step toward reducing their prices. Buying in large volume also reduces the cost of goods sold.

Convenience stores are, in essence, small supermarkets. They have rapidly developed as a major threat to their larger cousins. 7-Elevens, Quick-Trips, and other imitative convenience stores have sprung up and multiplied across the United States. These stores carry a carefully selected variety of high-turnover consumer products. As their names generally imply, the major benefit these stores provide to consumers is convenience—convenience of location and convenience of time. By choosing handy locations and staying open 15, 18, or 24 hours a day, 7 days a week, convenience stores offer extra time and place utility. Consumers must pay for these conveniences and seem quite willing to do so. Managers of these stores price most of their "convenience goods" at levels higher than supermarkets, to provide high profit margins. Convenience stores are unusual among retailers because they have both a high margin and a high inventory turnover.

Mass Merchandisers   **Mass merchandise retailers,** sometimes called *mass merchandise discount stores* or *superstores,* sell at discount prices to achieve high sales volume. Mass merchandisers cut back on their stores' interior design and on customer service in their efforts to reduce costs and maintain low prices. Supermarkets were the forerunners of mass merchandisers. In fact, the term *supermarket retailing* has been used to describe Target, Wal-Mart, and many other stores that have adopted the supermarket strategy, incorporating large inventories, self-service, centralized checkouts, and discount prices. Using supermarket-style discount strategies helps mass merchandisers to offer prices lower than those at traditional stores.

Mass merchandisers can be classified as general or specialty. *General mass merchandisers,* such as Wal-Mart, carry a wide variety of merchandise that cuts across product categories. They may sell everything from drug and cosmetic items to electrical appliances to clothing, toys, and novelty items. The wide variety of goods general mass merchandisers offer at low prices means that they usually cannot afford to carry a deep selection of goods in any product line. Retailers usually carry either a wide variety or a deep selection, but not both. The expense associated with having many kinds of goods and many choices of each kind makes the two possibilities largely mutually exclusive. (Indeed, small retailers can often compete with giant mass merchandisers on the basis of selection.)

In contrast with general mass merchandisers, *specialty mass merchandisers* carry a product selection that is limited to one or a few product categories. For example, some specialty mass merchandisers sell only clothing.

We will discuss two types of general mass merchandisers, catalog showrooms and warehouse clubs, and two types of specialty mass merchandisers, category superstores and off-price retailers.

Catalog showrooms, like Service Merchandise, publish large catalogs identifying products for sale in the store. Typically, these are high-margin items. The catalog—or an accompanying price list—shows the "normal" retail price of the item and the catalog discounter's much lower price. Often, the discounter's price is printed without a dollar sign in the form of an easily decipherable "code" to let the buyer know that a special deal—not available to just anyone—is being offered. Catalog discounters, like other discounters, do not offer customer conveniences or salesperson assistance. Service is slowed by the need to wait for purchased products to be delivered from a storage place. However, this successful formula permits lower prices.

Some discounters operate a special sort of store called a **warehouse club** or a *closed-door house.* At Sam's Wholesale Club and Price Club, customers are asked to

---

Convenience store
A small grocery store stressing convenient location and quick service and typically charging higher prices than other retailers selling similar products.

Mass merchandise retailer
A retailer that sells products at discount prices to achieve high sales volume; also called a *mass merchandise discount store* or a *superstore.* There are two basic types of mass merchandise retailers: general mass merchandisers and specialty mass merchandisers.

Catalog showroom
A general mass merchandise outlet where customers select goods from a catalog and store employees retrieve the selected items from storage.

Warehouse club
A general mass merchandise outlet at which only "members" are allowed to shop; also called a *closed-door house.*

become "members" and are issued cards that permit entry to the store. Some closed-door houses require that customers already be members of some specific group, such as a labor union or the civil service. While these operations run the risk of being seen as discriminating against persons not in the target customer group, the membership idea has been found by some retailers to be an effective way to build store loyalty. Moreover, if in building its membership base the club develops an actual list of customers, direct-mail advertisements can be sent to these people, eliminating, to a large extent, other forms of advertising with their large proportions of waste circulation. Warehouse clubs combine wholesaling and retailing functions. For these marketers, the showroom facility doubles as a storage place, or warehouse, allowing the retailer to hold far greater amounts of stock than traditional retailers retain. Furthermore, when they sell to service organizations or business members, such as schools, restaurants, and day-care centers, the clubs are actually wholesalers. However, many members who purchase as small-business customers also use these stores for personal shopping, and these are retail sales.

Warehouse clubs focus on sales volume and often sell in bulk. This requires that manufacturers change their packaging strategy. For example, Kellogg's, which initially refused to package in bulk, now provides dual packages of its cereals and Pop-Tarts for warehouse clubs.

Off-price retailers are specialty mass merchandisers that aggressively promote nationally known brand names of clothing at low prices. Dress Barn and Gordmans stores are typical examples. Off-price retailers can purchase brand name goods such as apparel or footwear at below-wholesale prices (even below prices paid by traditional mass merchandisers) because they typically do not ask for promotional allowances, return privileges, extended payment terms, or the highest-quality merchandise. They also keep their costs low by offering few services. Off-price stores have evolved because many name-brand manufacturers that once sold exclusively to retailers such as Saks Fifth Avenue, Neiman-Marcus, and Bloomingdale's are now more willing to sell seconds, overruns, discontinued items, or out-of-season merchandise to large-volume retailers, even when retail prices are below suggested levels. When a manufacturer owns and operates an off-price store, the store is called a *factory outlet.*

Toys "Я" Us, Petsmart, and Sportsmart are specialty mass merchandisers that apply the supermarket format to the marketing of toys, pet food and supplies, and sporting goods. A mass merchandise discounter specializing in a certain product category is called a **category superstore** or *category killer.* Sportsmart, which sells 100,000 different items, provides an example. It is radically different from the typical independent sports store because it stocks virtually all competing brands of soccer balls, baseball gloves, sports team jackets, and the like, rather than carrying a single brand, as most sports stores do. Category superstores apply a

www.bluefly.com℠
the outlet store in your home™

deep discount strategy, setting prices even lower than those of general mass merchandisers, and offer the most extensive assortment and greatest depth in the product lines they carry. This retailing strategy is designed to attract most of the local business for the product category and to eliminate ("kill") the competition.

Direct Marketing: Retailing without a Bricks-and-Mortar Store   **Direct marketing** involves the use of advertising, telephone sales, catalogs, the Internet, or other communications to elicit a direct response from consumers. Direct marketing in a retailing context has also been called *nonstore retailing* and *direct-response retailing*. The many means of direct marketing include mail-order sales, door-to-door selling, vending machines, and e-tailing on the Internet. Whether direct marketing uses the telephone, catalogs, letters, other print media, television, or the Internet to reach consumers, it always calls for a direct response, generally an order by mail, telephone, or the Internet.

Mail-order retailing through catalogs is one of the oldest forms of direct marketing. Sears, Roebuck and Company began in the mail-order business and moved on to other types of marketing. Today, the famous Sears "wish book" catalog no longer exists. However, companies such as Banana Republic and Sharper Image still combine catalog advertising with both mail-order and in-store retailing. Others, like Sundance, are exclusively committed to direct marketing operations. Consumers perceive mail-order buying as more risky than in-store shopping. In fact, catalog buying is among the shopping methods perceived as riskiest by consumers. Those who have had a favorable experience with this nonstore shopping method are more favorably inclined toward it.

Catalog retailers and some other mail-order marketers make extensive use of data-based marketing, discussed in Chapter 5. They buy computer-generated mailing lists from companies that specialize in developing them, or they compile lists themselves. As mentioned in the discussions of data-based marketing and relation-

Direct marketing
Marketing in which advertising, telephone sales, or other communications are used to elicit a direct response, such as an order by mail or phone; also called *nonstore retailing* and *direct-response retailing*.

Lands' End's "Your Personal Model" is an interactive feature that enables Internet shoppers to build and store a three-dimensional model of themselves. They can even—in a virtual sense—try on clothing selections online. The software allows shoppers to select clothing that is flattering to their size and shape.

http://www.landsend.com

USER GUIDE
LANDSEND.COM
ACCOUNT

Your Personal Model from Lands' End

Welcome!

Our site has a brand new look. We hope this makes your shopping experience better than ever. Here are just some of the new features of Your Personal Model:

- Build your 3-D model using exact measurements.
- Receive personalized fashion goals for your model.
- Try clothing on with a single click.

This is the spot where you can begin to create Your Personal Model, the interactive shopping tool that helps you build a wardrobe based on your shape and your lifestyle. Feel free to browse!

▶Create your
 Lands' End account

▶Sign-in*

▶Stay anonymous

ship marketing, the lists can be narrowly focused on selected groups—teens, homeowners, newlyweds, and so on.

Advertising in magazines and other print media may call for a direct response and thus may constitute direct marketing. Certain target customers may be reached effectively by such marketing efforts. Purveyors of vitamins and other health aids for senior citizens, for example, conduct a brisk business through advertisements placed in such magazines as *Modern Maturity*.

Direct marketers that advertise on television and fill orders by mail or express delivery services have multiplied rapidly. They now hawk everything from cutlery to Elvis Presley memorabilia. The familiar television campaigns that urge viewers to write or call a toll-free number are good illustrations of this approach to retailing.

Television home shopping is a direct marketing innovation developed with the advent of cable TV. Viewers tuning in to a cable shopping channel see a "show" where products are demonstrated by a "host." Consumers can call the host while the show is on the air to ask questions about the product or to purchase it.

Telemarketing, the selling of retail merchandise by telephone, is a growing aspect of direct marketing. It involves both database management and personal selling.

What most attracts consumers to the various forms of direct marketing is convenience. Shopping at home, especially at such hectic times of the year as the Christmas holidays, provides an undeniable attraction. So does the fact that many direct marketers will ship gift-wrapped orders directly to the person for whom the merchandise was bought, thus freeing the customer from wrapping and delivery chores. Direct marketing may attract retailers because it offers many opportunities to reduce operating costs. No in-store salespeople need to be hired, trained, or paid. Often businesses may be headquartered in rural areas or unattractive industrial parks that ordinary retailers would avoid. Indeed, the retailer that conducts business out of the consumer's view can cut many corners.

On the other hand, direct marketing retailers face certain special expenses. The catalog retailer incurs considerable expense in the preparation and mailing of catalogs, for example. Effective direct marketing retailers concentrate on fulfillment operations to make sure that goods are shipped promptly so that customers receive their orders quickly and in good condition. In part to overcome the sense of unease some feel about buying merchandise they cannot examine, many direct retailers offer liberal return policies.

Door-to-Door Selling   Cutlery, vacuum cleaners, magazines, and cosmetics are among the many products successfully sold door-to-door. This kind of retailing is an expensive method of distribution. Labor costs, mostly in the form of commissions, are quite high. Yet many consumers enjoy the personal in-home service provided by established companies like Cutco, Fuller Brush, and Avon. In general, products sold door-to-door are of the type that particularly benefit from demonstration and a personal sales approach. Vacuums and carving knives are among the many products that lend themselves to such demonstrations.

In-home retailing is often performed by organizations with outstanding reputations, including the Girl Scouts, Mary Kay, and the several Tupperware-style "party" merchants. Unfortunately for the many legitimate companies practicing this form of retailing, the image of the door-to-door approach has been tarnished by some unethical salespeople. A number of laws make door-to-door selling difficult. For example, Green River ordinances, in effect in many local areas, put constraints on the activities of door-to-door salespeople by limiting the hours or neighborhoods in which they may call or by requiring stringently controlled licenses.

It is interesting to observe that while door-to-door retailing is decreasing in importance in the United States, it is growing in some less-developed countries. Avon, for example, has a major door-to-door organization in China, and Tupperware parties are popular in many countries.

Vending Machines   The coin-operated *vending machine* is an old retailing tool that has become increasingly sophisticated in recent years. For the most part, items dispensed through vending machines are relatively low-priced convenience goods.

There is a vending machine for about every 40 people in the United States. Vending machines can be found almost everywhere—and this is a big part of their appeal to the marketers that use them. Cigarettes, gum, and other items can be sold in hotels, college dormitories, and church basements without an investment in a store or in personnel. Items sold through vending machines are generally small, easily preserved, high-turnover goods such as candy and soft drinks. Technological improvements in vending machines have allowed machines to dispense airline tickets, traveler's insurance, customized greeting cards, and breathalyzer tests.

e-tailing on the Internet

The newest development in nonstore retailing is **e-tailing**, or computer-interactive retailing on the Internet. Consumers can shop from their homes or offices by using personal computers to interact with retailers via the Internet. For example, Egghead.com sells consumer electronics products and computer software. Travelocity.com allows owners of personal computers to book airline flights and hotel reservations on-line. E*Trade makes it possible for investors to buy and sell stocks via the Net. The number of Internet Web sites, or "store fronts," where products can be ordered has been growing very rapidly. And the operations of e-tailers are expected to continue expanding dramatically. Two years ago, Amazon.com was only an Internet bookstore, but today shoppers can find thousands of items ranging from toys to kitchenware to consumer electronics products at the Amazon.com site. Its slogan, "Earth's Biggest Selection," communicates the message that no physical store could possibly offer the variety and depth of merchandise available at Amazon.com.

An Internet retailing strategy is not limited by the geographical location of a physical store. An e-tailer can market to customers everywhere. An e-tailer must maintain a Web site, which requires high-speed computers and sophisticated software, but it does not have to maintain physical stores or employ sales clerks and other store personnel. In some cases, e-tailers do not even hold any inventory. Hence, marketing costs can be relatively low. Savings from operations may be passed on to customers.

Interactivity is a fundamental and vital aspect of an Internet retail strategy. Shoppers visiting an Internet store use hyperlinks to narrow their search efforts or to get additional details about a product. When consumers provide information about their unique needs, marketers can address their specific requirements on a one-to-one basis. For example, customers who return to a Web site can be greeted by name and offered product recommendations based on their past purchases and their specific tastes.

> An Internet retailing strategy is not limited by the geographical location of a physical store.

In addition to interactivity, e-tailing offers many other advantages for consumers. Internet shopping at home is convenient. No travel is required, and consumers have access to e-tailers 24 hours a day, 7 days a week (24/7). Prices are often lower than prices at bricks-and-mortar stores. Priceline.com, Buy.com, and numerous other e-tailers offer rock-bottom prices—some even let you name your own price. The Internet allows many retailers to offer broader and deeper product lines than they could in bricks-and-mortar stores or through printed catalogs. Shelf space does not limit the number of items in a product line. For example, Amazon.com offers an assortment of 3,500 video games, three times the selection of a typical electronics store. Because going from one Web site to another is a simple task, comparison shopping can be done relatively easily.

Several companies provide automated shopping programs known as "shopbots" to make shopping easier for their customers. **Shopbots** are smart agent software programs designed to perform shopping tasks for buyers.[5] Once shopbots learn a user's preferences, they can perform four basic tasks, as summarized in Exhibit 12-2: Search, Alert, Compare, and Negotiate. For example, Saleseeker.com and Bottomdollar.com provide lists of items and prices available at various Web site stores. MySimon.com locates goods and services based not only on price but also on certain policies (e.g., merchandise return and technical support policies), shipping time, and overall quality of the marketers. Respond.com connects buyers and sellers via email. Mercata.com uses a shopbot to aggregate buyers and use the power of volume purchasing to drive down prices. The more people who want to buy the same item, the lower the price.

New Web site shopping malls and other innovative retailing approaches are being created as Internet shopping evolves. For example, The Della & James Web site contains an online gift registry, combining the convenience of the Internet, the opportunity to choose among brands that customers know and trust, and lists of local retailers' in-stock merchandise.

Shopping on the Internet is not without its disadvantages. The most obvious disadvantage is that a shopper cannot touch, pick up, or carefully examine a product. Although Furniture.com and other companies make furniture available online, consumers cannot sit on a couch without visiting a bricks-and-mortar store. Another disadvantage is that consumers who purchase goods online must wait for delivery. (However, there are exceptions. For example, software and digital music can be purchased and downloaded from the Internet extremely quickly). Finally, a major disadvantage of Internet shopping for many consumers is potential problems with privacy. Many are reluctant to provide credit card numbers online, even though credit card fraud on the Internet is no more likely than credit card fraud in other retail situations.

e-commerce | Changing Everything

What's a bot? In short: A bot is a software tool for digging through data. You give a bot directions and it brings back answers.

The word is short for "robot," of course, which is derived from the Czech word *robota*, meaning work. The idea of robots as humanoid machines was first introduced in Karel Capek's 1921 play *R.U.R.*, in which the playwright conceived Rossum's Universal Robots. Sci-fi writer Isaac Asimov made them famous, beginning with his story "I, Robot" (1950) and continuing through a string of books known as the Robot Series.

On the Web, robots have taken on a new form of life. Since all Web servers are connected, robot-like software is the perfect way to perform the methodical searches needed to find information.

For example, Web search engines send out robots that crawl from one server to another, compiling the enormous lists of URLs that are the heart of every search engine. Shopping bots compile enormous databases of products sold at online stores.

The term *bot* has become interchangeable with *agent*, to indicate that the software can be sent out on a mission, usually to find information and report back. Strictly speaking, an agent is a bot that goes out on a mission.[6]

Shopbot
A smart agent software program that performs shopping tasks for online shoppers.

Automated Shopping Tasks Performed by Shopbots

e x h i b 12-2

FUNCTION	WHAT THE BOT DOES
Search	Searches for products available for sale online
Alert	Alerts shopper to new releases or recommends new purchases based on past purchase behavior
Compare	Acts as a comparison shopper, collecting information about price and availability from competing e-tailers
Negotiate	Buys, sells, and bargains with other bots based on price or other criteria set by the user

Respond.com is a new online shopping service connecting buyers with sellers. An online shopper simply types in a request for any product or service, and Respond.com goes to work contacting the appropriate sellers. Buyers get personal responses to their requests from sellers via e-mail. Compared to traditional ways of shopping and getting information, logging on to Respond.com gets buyers exactly what they want with less effort. For sellers, Respond.com is a reliable source of highly targeted customer leads.

http://www.respond.com

The Internet, with its worldwide "audience," is dramatically changing the nature of retailing. Its impact is so great that we will examine other aspects of Internet strategy in our section on key issues in retail strategy. And because the Internet is a communication medium as well as a retail transaction medium, many aspects of Internet retailing strategy and tactics are interrelated with the design of the organization's Web site. We will discuss Web site design in Chapter 14.

The Wheel of Retailing

Many types of retailing institutions have been developed over the last century. Many more will evolve as retail marketing continues to respond to changes in its environment. Several patterns of retail development have been observed, but the best-known hypothesis relating to retail institutional development is called the **wheel of retailing.** This theory states that new retailing institutions enter the marketplace as low-status, low-margin, low-price operations and then move toward higher status, margin, and price positions. The formulator of the theory viewed this process as the spinning of a wheel, as shown in Exhibit 12-3. The emergence of discount stockbrokers like Charles Schwab illustrates the entry process. These brokers made an impact on the marketplace by charging low commission fees; however, they did not provide investment advice as traditional "full-price" brokers do. And, with the emergence of Internet brokers such as E*Trade, the wheel continues to turn.

Retailing scholars have observed that a pattern of "trading up" does exist. As time goes by, retailers that started out small with inexpensive facilities begin to operate businesses far larger and fancier than those with which they began. One

Wheel of retailing
The theory that new forms of retail institutions enter the marketplace as low-status, low-margin, low-price operations and then gradually trade up, opening a market position for a new low-end retailer.

Some Positions on the "Wheel of Retailing" in Order of Decreasing Markups

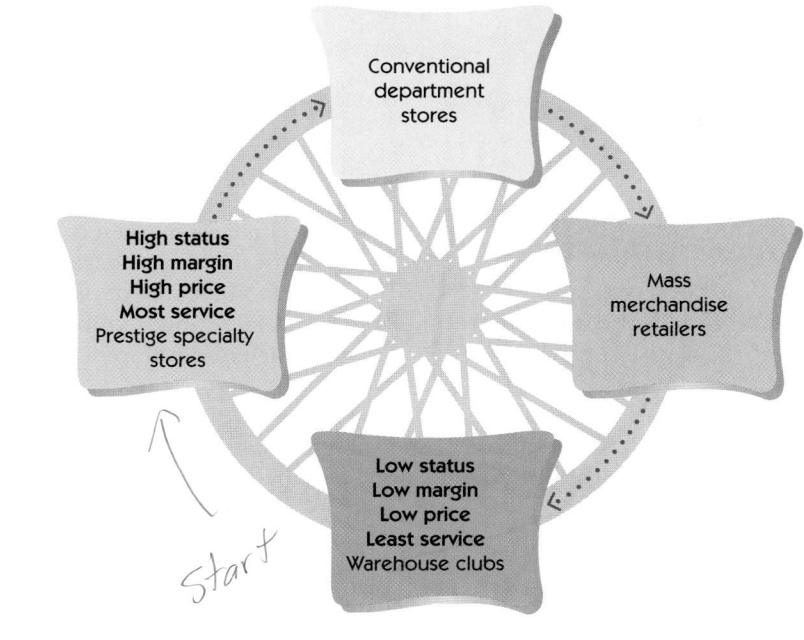

cause of this trading up is the American tradition of competing, at the retail level, more on the basis of nonprice variables than on the basis of price variables. Americans do not have a tradition of haggling over prices. Instead, retailers tend to compete with one another by such nonprice means as offering free services, frequent-purchaser programs, and more attractive stores. These things tend to drive up margins and prices. Whatever the causes of trading up, the end result, with respect to the wheel of retailing theory, is the same: A low spot on the wheel, once occupied by a low-margin retailer that has traded up, is left open for an innovative retailer that can operate at a margin lower than those earned by existing retailers. The lower margin should attract customers. The innovator is thus tempted to snatch that lower spot, and the evolutionary process continues. Many of the discounters of the 1930s and 1940s followed this pattern and eventually ended up much like the department stores from which they sought to differentiate themselves. The discounters then became vulnerable to the newer, low-margin, low-price retailers such as warehouse clubs and category superstores.

> With respect to the wheel of retailing theory, a low spot on the wheel, once occupied by a low-margin retailer that has traded up, is left open for an innovative retailer that can operate at a margin lower than those earned by existing retailers.

The wheel hypothesis has much intuitive appeal and has been borne out in general by many studies of retail development, but it only reflects a pattern. It is not a sure predictor of every change, nor was it ever intended to describe the development of every individual retailer. There are many nonconforming examples of retail managers who, for whatever reasons, have not traded their stores up from the positions they originally occupied.

Years ago, health food stores were small and unpretentious. Now, supermarket-sized health foods stores, such as Whole Foods and Wild Oats Market, are evolving to serve consumers' increased attention to, and knowledge of, nutrition. The big health foods stores pose a major competitive threat to traditional health foods stores, which tend to have between 2,000 and 5,000 square feet of floor space and higher prices.

Retail Management Strategies

Retailers, like all marketers, create marketing strategies. They analyze market segments, select target markets, and determine the competitive position they wish to occupy.

Like all marketers, retailers must develop a marketing mix. The concept of the marketing mix is essentially the same in all applications of marketing. Exhibit 12-4 shows some of the decision elements retail marketers face in developing a retail marketing mix.

No single chapter can discuss all aspects of the retail marketing environment. Here we will address six problem areas of special importance. These are merchandise assortment, location, atmospherics, customer service, database management, and Internet strategy.

exhibit 12-4

Elements of the Retail Marketing Mix

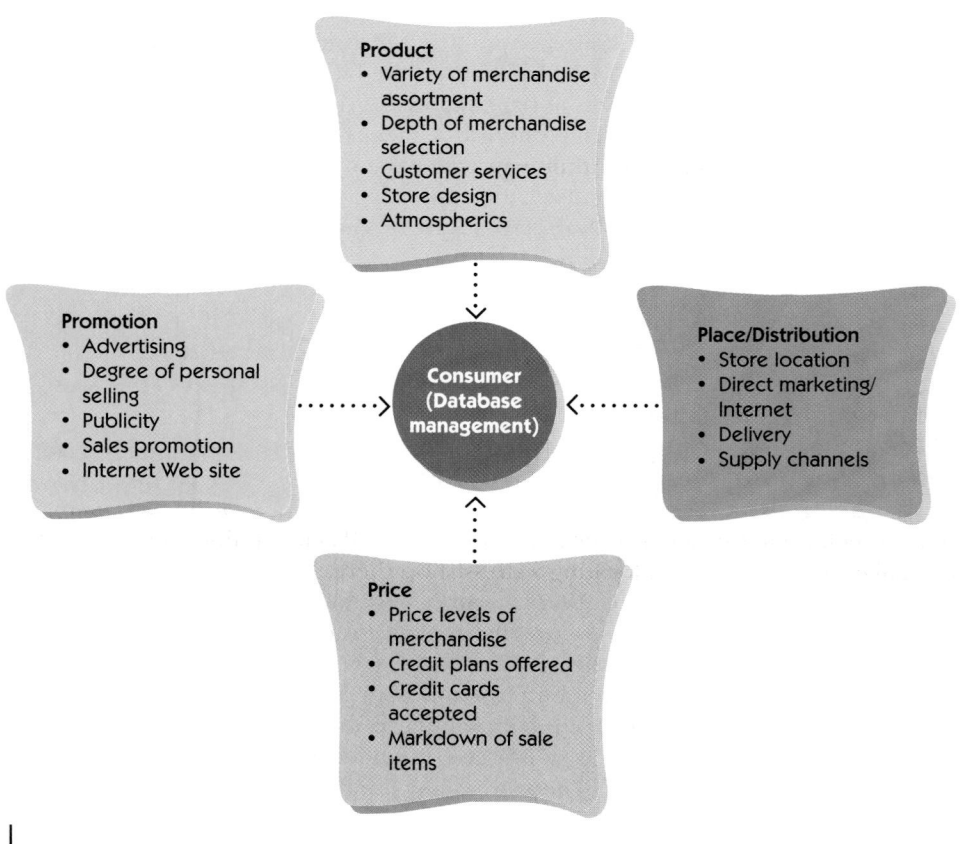

Product
- Variety of merchandise assortment
- Depth of merchandise selection
- Customer services
- Store design
- Atmospherics

Promotion
- Advertising
- Degree of personal selling
- Publicity
- Sales promotion
- Internet Web site

Consumer (Database management)

Place/Distribution
- Store location
- Direct marketing/Internet
- Delivery
- Supply channels

Price
- Price levels of merchandise
- Credit plans offered
- Credit cards accepted
- Markdown of sale items

MERCHANDISE ASSORTMENT

One image that comes immediately to mind when the word "store" is mentioned is a physical place where merchandise has been assembled for sale. Of course, direct marketers have changed our notion of the meaning of the word *store*. Nevertheless, one of the prime retailing functions is to provide a product assortment for customers. Stated in different terms, retailers perform an *assorting function*—they build desired assortments of varied goods so that manufacturers and customers don't need to. It is clearly in the interests of both consumers and producers to allow retailers to perform this service and to reward them for it.

From the individual customer's perspective, a major advantage of one retailer over a competitor is merchandise assortment. Other things are important, of course, but no shopper will patronize a store unless he or she feels that there is some chance that the merchandise sought will be found there. How does a retail marketer decide what merchandise assortment to carry? Information and suggestions are available from manufacturers and from intermediaries. Trade magazines and newspapers may offer useful insights. But most importantly, the retailer must carefully consider the target market's needs and wants and match the merchandise selection with those desires. This truth is elemental in effective retail marketing. Yet retailers frequently make buying mistakes, the costs of which must be absorbed through markdowns or other means. Buying errors cannot be totally avoided, but marketing research and careful planning can minimize them. The means of aligning merchandise offerings with customer desires cannot be detailed here, but it is important to note that marketing—not guesswork—must be the basis of all decisions in this area.

LOCATION, LOCATION, AND LOCATION

There is an old saying that the three most important factors in successful retailing are *location, location,* and *location*. This is not absolutely true—an out-of-the-way location can be compensated for by other means, especially huge selections and low prices. Nonetheless, the adage makes a point. Retailers are justifiably concerned about locating in the right part of the right town. They must monitor changes that may affect the suitability of an existing location or make another site more attractive.

The right location depends on the type of business and the target customer, not on any formula or rule of thumb. As with merchandise assortment questions, the answer lies in careful marketing planning. Experience dictates certain guidelines, however. Toys "Я" Us, for example, has several specific guidelines for store location. In the United States, it requires that its outlets be placed in metropolitan areas with populations of at least 100,000 people, of which an established percentage must be children. Ideally, the selected location is a free-standing building near a major mall. Toys "Я" Us, which operates as a global retailer, has other criteria for other countries around the world.

Retail site selection experts note that an important attribute of any intended site is the other types of outlets around it.[7] Obviously, Toys "Я" Us expects major shopping malls to generate traffic near its toy store locations. More specifically, many retailers seek what are called *complementary businesses*. Placing a diner near a gas station makes more sense than locating a dress shop there. The nature of the retailer's business operations may affect whether the number or the nature of nearby businesses is important, however. Catalog discounters, for example, can rely on their customers to do some preshopping using the catalogs. This, plus lower prices and the immediate gratification of being able to take items home from the store, reduces the need for store locations in expensive, high-traffic areas. In contrast, the traffic generated by a shopping center is far more important to a Docktor Pet Center, a Sharper Image electronics store, or an Orange Julius shop.

Shopping centers are important locations for many retailers. As you are well aware, there are several kinds of shopping centers. Older versions are often long strings of stores set in a parking area. This design is called a *strip*. A design that features stores built around a central area, in which shoppers can stroll, is called a *mall*.

You undoubtedly have also noticed that shopping centers come in different sizes, essentially small, medium, and large. The official size designations, however, are *neighborhood, community,* and *regional.* The neighborhood shopping center is likely to be a small strip containing such shops as a drugstore, a dry cleaner, and a supermarket. The community center is larger, with perhaps a mass merchandiser, clothing store, or small furniture dealer. The regional center is the largest, with 100 or even 200 stores, serving a large population and drawing customers from a wide geographic area.

The downtown area is—or at least used to be—a shopping center. For any number of reasons, including parking, crime, and a lack of public transportation, downtowns, or central business districts, have declined greatly in retailing importance since the post–World War II exodus of population to the suburbs.

The flight to the suburbs and the movement of retailers to suburban malls are difficult to overcome. Nevertheless, some city governments have successfully revitalized downtown areas. In some cities, "downtown malls" have been built to rekindle interest in downtown-based activities. Inner-city shopping malls such as the ones located in the rejuvenated Jax brewery in New Orleans, Boston's Faneuil Hall marketplace, and Chicago's Watertower Plaza are thriving.

ATMOSPHERICS

Atmospherics

Physical characteristics of a store's environment, such as appearance, layout, and displays.

Retail strategy includes managing every aspect of the store property and its physical characteristics to create an atmosphere conducive to buying. **Atmospherics** are physical characteristics of the environment, such as the store's exterior and interior appearance, layout, and displays, that contribute to a shopper's mental impression of what the store is. Store atmosphere may influence store image, increase store traffic, influence the amount of time shoppers spend in the store, or encourage shoppers to make impulse purchases.[8]

Exterior atmospherics can exert a strong influence on new customers' willingness to enter a store. The building's architecture, parking facilities, storefront, and other outside features may either encourage or discourage patronage by communicating a certain message. The architectural motif of a Taco Bell, for example, makes an impression on the consumer and communicates a message about the restaurant's product line.

The longer a shopper remains in a store, the more he or she will purchase.[9] And the amount of time a customer spends in a store depends on its atmosphere and how enjoyable the shopping experience is. Planning the interior design and layout to influence the movement and mood of the customer is a primary concern of retailers. Atmospherics, such as lighting, music, colors, and the perception of uncrowded space, are used to foster favorable customer attitudes. Disney stores' layouts are designed to communicate the fun and excitement of Disney theme parks and characters. They are also designed to get customers to walk to the back wall; a large video screen at the back of every store shows animated features, accompanied by familiar songs. The chances are good that customers will return to the front by a different route and see additional merchandise.

> Retail strategy includes managing every aspect of the store property and its physical characteristics to create an atmosphere conducive to buying.

CUSTOMER SERVICE

The customer services a retailer offers may be as important as—or even more important than—the merchandise offered for sale. The courteous personal service

Retail marketers create and maintain a store atmosphere as part of their marketing strategy. In the Warner Brothers Studio Store shown here, a life-sized Bugs Bunny entertains the store's smallest customers. The store is filled with icons of Daffy Duck, Tweety Pie, the Roadrunner, Elmer Fudd, and, of course, that wascally wabbit Bugs. Walk into a Warner Brothers store and you are reminded of the characters you grew up with. The atmosphere shouts "fun!"

and information provided by a salesperson may make the difference between success and failure in a retail setting. Maintaining convenient store hours, providing parking facilities, and offering product information are essential to the operation of many retail operations. Other services, such as delivery, alterations, repair, credit, return privileges, and gift wrapping, supplement the retailer's merchandise offerings. In some cases, the service offering (such as Domino's Pizza's in-home delivery) is the primary reason for selecting one retailer over another.

Development of the retailer's marketing mix thus requires decisions about the **service level**, or the extent of extra services that will be provided to consumers. Service-level strategies are often interrelated with pricing strategies. An organization that wants to be competitive in price will typically match competitors' service levels. Retailers that emphasize nonprice competition may be full-service organizations that provide extra services to create a competitive advantage. The level of service consumers expect is also a major determinant of service level. Many retailers regularly survey consumers to determine the amount and quality of services they expect.

Service level
Extent of extra services provided to customers. Service level is often related to price.

DATABASE MANAGEMENT

Retailers, as the final link in the distribution channel, have always had direct contact with their customers, and in many cases one-on-one relationships with individual customers. The local butcher knew when a customer walked into the shop how she wanted her steaks and chops trimmed. The jewelry store salesperson would often send a note to a male customer just before his wife's birthday. So it should come as no surprise that retailers, especially direct marketers, have recognized that customer databases can be used to better serve customers and to develop customer loyalty.

Retailers are in the ideal situation to build proprietary databases. When a consumer makes a purchase, information about it can be automatically entered into and stored on the store's or direct marketer's computer. When that purchase can be linked to the customer's name, phone number, or other information (such as demographic information) and to other purchases, the retailer has extremely useful information. For example, Helzberg Diamonds, which has 191 stores in 28 states, uses its database to identify customers who responded to special sales promotions in the past. The company then mails letters and brochures encouraging these customers to visit the store when similar promotions are occurring. Supermarkets have learned from their databases that married men who purchase diapers between 6 p.m. and 8 p.m. are also likely to purchase beer. Data like these

what went right?

Wal-Mart Pharmacies Pharmacies have changed a lot in the past two decades, but one thing remains constant: the large burden on staff to stock all those little bottles, jars, and boxes in perfectly straight rows in aisle after aisle. Every time a customer picks something up to read the label, you're guaranteed that the thing needs to be straightened or turned so it faces front. It's a lot of work. Not long ago Wal-Mart tried an experiment: it began replacing traditional shelves with a system of bins. Instead of facing a shelf of aspirin bottles, say, the shopper saw a blowup of the aspirin bottle's label. Under that blowup was the bin, into which the aspirin bottles had been dumped. That made an enormous difference.

First, it solved the problem of stocking—a clerk could just roll a trolley of merchandise to the aisle, open the bin, dump in the goods, and move on. No more straight lines. The shoppers liked it better, too—instead of facing a row of bottles with tiny print, they saw a large, easy-to-read version of the label. It was much easier on the eyes, especially for elderly shoppers. Wal-Mart's main concern in making the change was whether shoppers would perceive the bins as being somehow cheaper and lower in quality than the shelves. In fact, just the opposite was true—shoppers said they thought the bins were an upgraded display system—a very elegant solution.[10]

about past purchases and frequency of purchase have immense consequences for retailers. Data-based marketing is an important part of contemporary retailers' marketing efforts.

INTERNET STRATEGY

Amazon.com, Garden.com, eToys, and many other new e-commerce companies were founded to conduct retail business exclusively on the Internet. Many other retailers view their businesses as traditional bricks-and-morter operations, and their strategy does not involve any Internet activity. However, using the Internet does not have to be an all-or-nothing substitute for an in-store retailing strategy. Many bricks-and-mortar retailers view the Internet as an additional means of communicating with customers. Eddie Bauer uses several retail strategies: catalogs, retail stores, and e-tailing. So does Victoria's Secret. Victoria's Secret began in the mail-order business using catalogs and then moved to retail stores and later to the Internet. Using this clicks-and-mortar strategy, both organizations have experienced tremendous growth in the Internet portion of their businesses.[11] The effective retailer will consider its organizational mission, its target market's needs, and other strategic issues to determine to what extent the Internet should be part of its business.

Sometimes a traditional store will acquire another company or collaborate with another organization as part of its Internet strategy. Petsmart decided to partner with idealab!, a leading Internet incubator of companies such as eToys, to help with its Internet operations. Petsmart saw its core competencies as store operations and warehousing, not Web site development. Drugstore.com has an alliance with Rite-Aide because slow delivery can be a problem when prescriptions are purchased on the Internet. This e-tailer/bricks-and-mortar collaboration allows Drugstore.com customers to pick up prescriptions at Rite-Aide stores. Microsoft and Radio Shack have formed an alliance to operate a "store within a store." As many as 7,000 Radio Shack stores will have part of their floor space devoted to demonstrating Microsoft's high-speed Internet connections, software products, and other services. In turn, Microsoft's MSN Web portal will refer visitors to the newly launched RadioShack.com.

Nordstrom operates traditional department stores. It also operates Nordstromshoes.com, which it promotes as the world's biggest shoe store, telling readers to "Make room for shoes. Get rid of everything else." For a retailer on the Internet, merchandise selection is not limited by geography or physical space, as in a bricks-and-mortar store.

http://www.nordstrom.com

Many new e-commerce companies currently engaged in retailing on the Internet seek the "first-mover advantage." eToys established its Internet store before Toys "Я" Us or Zany Brainy and thus gained the advantage of being positioned in consumers' minds as "the" Internet toy store. If your first Internet purchase was a book from Amazon.com, it is likely that you will return to the Internet store where you had a satisfactory experience. The hope of every first mover is to get big fast so that it will be difficult for competitors to get a large share of the Internet sales. The goal of Amazon.com has been to be faster, bigger, cheaper. Its strategy was to start out with low-priced books, expanding to music on CDs and then to a wide merchandise assortment. Once Amazon gets to know its customers, it uses smart agents to recommend books, music, or other products that are similar to past purchases.

Wholesaling

A wholesaler neither produces nor consumes the finished product. A **wholesaler** is a marketing intermediary that buys products and resells those products to retailers, other wholesalers, or organizations that use the products in the production of other goods or services. A wholesaler's primary function is facilitating either the transportation of products or the transfer of title to them.

Wholesalers have much in common with retailers; both of these types of marketers act as selling agents for their suppliers and as buying agents for their customers. Both are creators of time and place utility. Both must carefully evaluate the needs of their customers and deliver an appropriate total package of goods and services if they are to succeed in business. And both have developed ways of performing marketing functions that specially suit market conditions.

Wholesaler
An organization or individual that serves as a marketing intermediary by facilitating transfer of products and title to them. Wholesalers do not produce the product, consume it, or sell it to ultimate consumers.

what went wrong?

Levi Strauss   This online sales thing is tougher than it looks. That's the conclusion that Levi Strauss came to when marketing executives decided to stop selling Levi's and Dockers products directly to consumers through its Web site.

Instead, it began allowing two retailers—Macys.com and JCPenney.com—to sell the products online. Levi's had previously forbidden its retailers from competing with it on the Internet.

Selling online had proved more difficult, and less profitable, than the company had hoped. During its Internet efforts, Levi learned that it's costly to run a world-class e-commerce business. When the company evaluated its priorities for the year 2000, it decided this was a great time to allow its retailers to offer its products. Instead of competing with retailers, Levi is now using its money and resources to help channel partners sell online.

Levi's' traditional business has been struggling somewhat, which may have prompted it to be more attentive to retailers in its primary channels. Some analysts conclude that Levi's may have realized that while selling directly on the Internet seems at first glance to be more efficient, it may not be the best route toward profits for all bricks-and-mortar companies.[12]

Classifying Wholesalers

The functions of all intermediaries, including wholesalers, were discussed in Chapter 11. This section describes the different types of wholesaling establishments and institutions in the United States. Intermediaries performing wholesaling functions are traditionally divided into two groups—merchants and agents. The only distinction between these categories lies in whether the intermediaries take title to the goods they sell. Merchant intermediaries take title; agent intermediaries do not. This has nothing at all to do with physical possession of goods. Some merchants take possession of merchandise and others do not; some agents take possession of the goods they sell, but most do not. Taking title to goods means that the merchant intermediary owns that merchandise and must be prepared to handle any risks associated with ownership—including getting stuck with merchandise that, for whatever reason, turns out to be unsellable.

A recent *Census of Wholesale Trade* reported that there were 453,470 wholesale trade establishments in the United States.[13] Of these, 376,330 were merchant wholesalers, and they accounted for almost 60 percent of wholesale sales volume. There were 29,305 manufacturer's sales branches, and they accounted for slightly less than a third of the wholesale sales volume. The 47,835 agents and brokers accounted for approximately 11 percent of wholesale sales volume.

MERCHANT WHOLESALERS

Merchant wholesaler
An independently owned wholesaling concern that takes title to the goods it distributes.

Merchant wholesalers are independently owned concerns that take title to the goods they distribute. Merchant wholesalers represent about 80 percent of all wholesaling concerns in the United States.[14] Valley Media, for example, is a top wholesale distributor of music and video products, such as CDs, DVDs, videocassettes, and video games. It distributes products to more than 6,000 bricks-and-mortar retailers, such as Best Buy, Wherehouse Entertainment, and Sears. However, its customers also include CDnow, Amazon.com, and more than 100 Internet retailers.[15]

Not all merchant wholesalers operate on a national basis. Small merchant wholesalers often restrict their business to a limited geographical area. They may cover single cities or areas stretching only 100 or 200 miles from the main office. This allows them to replace retailers' inventory quickly. It also reduces or eliminates the need for overnight trips by trucks or sales personnel and so holds down expenses.

Merchant wholesalers may be classified in terms of the number and types of services they provide to their customers. In this regard, they provide perfect examples of how marketing firms adjust their total product offerings of goods and services to reflect the demands of particular situations and market segments.

Full-Service Merchant Wholesalers   As their name suggests, **full-service merchant wholesalers** provide their customers with a complete array of services in addition to the merchandise they offer. Such services include delivery, credit, marketing information and advice, and possibly even such managerial assistance as accounting aid or other nonmarketing aid. Full-service wholesalers are also called *full-function wholesalers*.

Within this category, three subsets of wholesalers are identifiable by lines of goods offered: **general merchandise wholesalers**, which sell a large number of different product types; **general line wholesalers**, which limit their offerings to a full array of products within one product line; and **specialty wholesalers**, which reduce their lines still further. A coffee and tea wholesaler or a spice wholesaler exemplifies this last class.

Wholesalers determine how wide or narrow a line to carry by carefully considering the customers they serve and the industry in which they operate. When the target customers are operators of general stores, the decision to be a general merchandise wholesaler is logical. In some industries, however, traditional marketing practices may require some degree of specialization. Occasionally, the specialization is required by law, as in the case of beer wholesalers, which in many states are not permitted to deal in any other alcoholic beverage.

Limited-Service Merchant Wholesalers   Regardless of the product line carried, full-service merchant wholesalers provide an essentially complete line of extra services. However, some customers may not want—or may not want to pay for—some of those services. They may prefer to sacrifice services to get lower prices. Thus, a group of **limited-service merchant wholesalers**, or *limited-function wholesalers*, has developed.

Cash-and-Carry Wholesalers   Buyers who are not willing to pay for and who do not need certain wholesaler services, such as delivery and credit, may choose to patronize **cash-and-carry wholesalers**. Such intermediaries eliminate the delivery and credit functions associated with a full-service wholesaler and permit buyers to come to the warehouse or other point of distribution to pick up their merchandise and to pay cash. The resulting savings are passed on to buyers, who are, after all, performing several functions normally associated with wholesalers.

Truck Wholesalers   **Truck wholesalers**, also called *truck jobbers*, typically sell a limited line of items to comparatively small buyers. Most of these merchant wholesalers sell perishable items. Their mode of operation, selling from a truck full of merchandise, can be justified by the increased freshness immediate delivery offers. Some truck wholesalers sell items that are not particularly perishable but that face keen competition. They might, for example, sell snack items to tavern owners. Although truck jobbing is an expensive means of distributing relatively small amounts of merchandise, it is an aggressive form of sales and provides instant delivery to buyers.

Direct-Marketing Wholesalers   **Direct-marketing wholesalers** operate in much the same way as mail-order catalog retailers and other direct marketers. Traditionally they used catalogs and direct mail, took phone and fax orders, and then forwarded merchandise to buyers via mail or a parcel delivery service. These wholesalers have been most important in reaching remote rural locations where market potential is low. However, in recent years, many types of wholesalers, such as office supply wholesalers, have made strategic decisions to focus on direct marketing via the Internet.

Full-service merchant wholesaler
A merchant wholesaler that provides a complete array of services, such as delivery, credit, marketing information and advice, and managerial assistance; also called a *full-function wholesaler*.

General merchandise wholesaler
A full-service merchant wholesaler that sells a large number of different product lines.

General line wholesaler
A full-service merchant wholesaler that sells a full selection of products in one product line.

Specialty wholesaler
A full-service merchant wholesaler that sells a very narrow selection of products.

Limited-service merchant wholesaler
A merchant wholesaler that offers less than full service and charges lower prices than a full-service merchant wholesaler; also called a *limited-function wholesaler*.

Cash-and-carry wholesaler
A limited-service wholesaler that does not offer delivery or credit.

Truck wholesaler
A limited-service wholesaler that sells a limited line of items (often perishable goods) from a truck, thus providing immediate delivery; also called a *truck jobber*.

Direct-marketing wholesaler
A limited-service wholesaler that uses catalogs or the Internet, mail or telephone ordering, and parcel delivery.

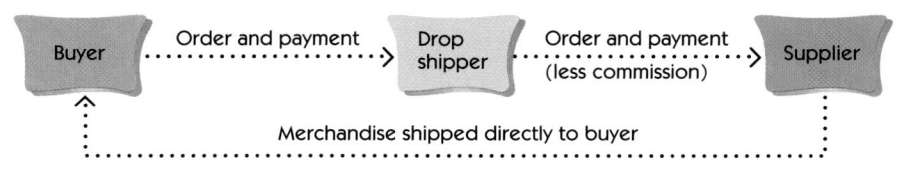

Operation of a Drop Shipper

Drop shipper
A limited-service wholesaler, often dealing in bulky products, that takes customer orders and arranges for shipment of merchandise from the producer directly to the customer; also called a *desk jobber.*

Rack jobber
A limited-service wholesaler that contracts with a retailer to place display racks in a store and to stock those racks with merchandise.

Agent
A wholesaler that does not take title to goods. Agents sometimes take possession of goods but function primarily to bring buyers and sellers together or otherwise help consummate a marketing transaction.

Broker
An agent intermediary whose major role is placing buyers and sellers in touch with one another and assisting in contractual arrangements.

Drop Shippers　**Drop shippers** are merchant wholesalers that take title to goods but do not take possession of the goods or handle them in any way. Drop shippers accept a buyer's order and pass it on to a producer or supplier of the desired commodity, which then ships the product directly to the buyer. (See Exhibit 12-5.) The big advantage of this system is that the product need not be loaded and unloaded several times. Also, it goes directly to where it is needed, which lowers transportation costs. These advantages are especially important when the product is bulky, unwieldy, and comparatively inexpensive. Thus, drop shipping is most commonly used for products such as coal, cement, building blocks, and logs.

Because the drop shipper does not physically handle any products, no investment in warehousing facilities or equipment is required. In fact, so little equipment of any sort is required that these wholesalers can often get by with little more than a small office, a desk, and a telephone. For this reason, they are also called *desk jobbers.*

Rack Jobbers　**Rack jobbers** are a type of merchant wholesaler that came to prominence in the 1930s when supermarket operators began to practice scrambled merchandising and started selling cosmetics and other items they had not previously carried. To do this easily, they contracted with wholesalers willing to come to the store, set up a display rack, stock and replenish it, and give the supermarket operator a percentage of the sales. Now rack jobbers sell many different product lines, such as work gloves, paperback books, magazines, toys, cosmetics, and panty hose.

The attraction of this system for the store operator is the chance to stock and sell certain items at little risk. The great attraction for the rack jobber is the chance to place merchandise in a high-traffic supermarket location. Like most relationships between members of a channel of distribution, theirs is a mutually beneficial one.

AGENTS

Agents, the second general category of wholesalers, may take possession of goods they deal in but do not take title to them. Agents, as a rule, do not carry an inventory or extend credit, but they may provide physical facilities for conducting business. They may help to arrange for delivery or credit as part of their services, which can be generally described as bringing buyer and seller together. Agents typically receive commissions based on the selling prices of the products they help to sell. The commission percentage varies tremendously depending on the industry. Agents are expected to be familiar with their products and with who wants to sell and who wants to buy them. In short, they are expected to have an expert knowledge of the market in which they operate.

Brokers　Traditional **brokers** are agent intermediaries who receive a commission for putting sellers in touch with buyers and assisting with contractual negotiations.

Brokers generally portray themselves as "neutral" in their selling process, working for both buyers and sellers. Brokers are found in many fields. Such commodities as coffee, tea, crude petroleum, and scrap metal are frequently brokered. So are the financial instruments handled by the familiar stockbroker. Effective brokers are experts in the market for the products in which they deal. In effect, they sell their expertise. They have relatively low expenses. Their commissions are also small, likely to be 6 percent or less of the selling price.

Use of brokers holds particular appeal for sellers because brokers work strictly on commission and do not enter into long-term relationships with the companies that use them. A broker can be used only when needed and does not tie sellers to continuous expenses the way a full-time sales force does. Chapter 11 mentioned that the Internet has created infomediaries, which serve as electronic information brokers that help buyers and sellers find each other. Of particular importance are the vertical exchanges emerging as online trading communities for B2B (business-to-business) e-commerce. These new intermediaries serve as electronic hubs that provide an online brokering function.

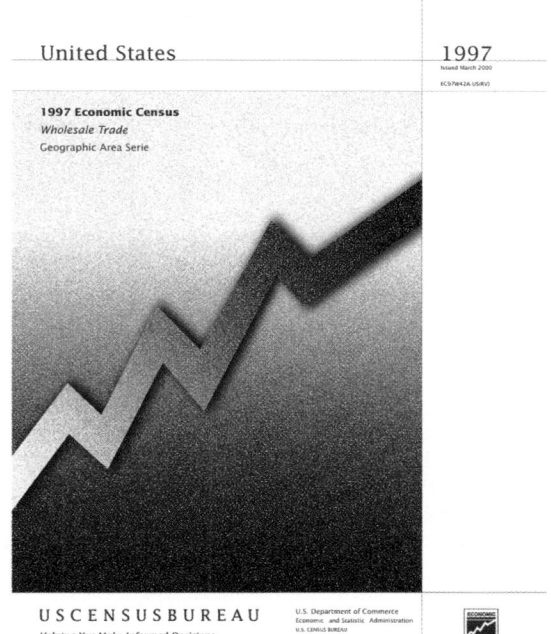

United States 1997

1997 Economic Census
Wholesale Trade
Geographic Area Serie

USCENSUSBUREAU
Helping You Make Informed Decisions

U.S. Department of Commerce
Economic and Statistic Administration
U.S. CENSUS BUREAU

The U.S. Department of Commerce conducts its Economic Census every five years. Just about any statistic about wholesaling you could imagine can be found in the *1997 Economic Census: Wholesale Trade*.

http://www.census.gov/ epcd/ www/97EC42.htm

Commission Merchants

The **commission merchant** is an agent intermediary similar to a broker. Unlike brokers, however, commission merchants are usually given certain powers by sellers. They might be empowered, for example, to attempt to bid up the selling price or to accept a selling price as long as it is above a previously agreed-on floor. Commission merchants thus perform a pricing function and more clearly work in league with the seller than do most brokers. They are most commonly found representing producers of agricultural products. Commission merchants, despite the name, are like other types of agents in that they do not take title to the goods they sell. However, they often take possession of those goods so that potential buyers can inspect them. Once a sales agreement has been reached, the commission merchant deducts a commission from the selling price and returns the balance to the producer.

Commission merchant
An agent intermediary similar to a broker but having certain additional decision-making powers, such as the power to make price adjustments.

Auction Companies

Auction companies are agent intermediaries that perform valuable services in the buying and selling of livestock, tobacco, and other commodities, as well as artwork and used mechanical equipment. In a sense, many of these companies take possession of the goods they deal in, because frequently they provide some special place in which the auction can be held. The auction company receives a commission based on the final, highest bid offered for an item or product, provided that this bid is above a minimum agreed-on figure.

The products sold through auction could be sold in some other manner, but auction companies offer a certain convenience in that they bring buyers together in one spot and expedite a bidding process that might otherwise take a long time. Some industries, such as the tobacco industry, have traditionally used auction companies and continue to do so for that reason.

Auction company
An agent intermediary that brings together buyers and sellers. Auction companies often assemble merchandise for sale in a central location and sell it by means of a bidding process.

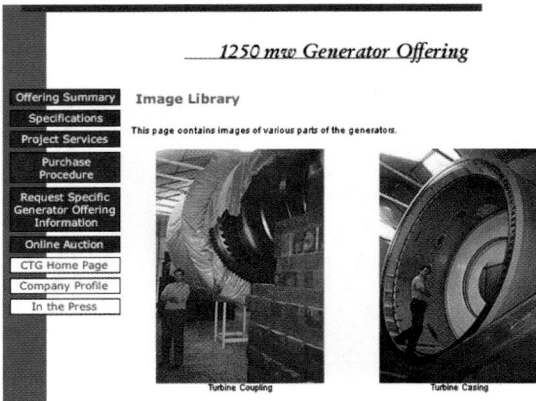

1250 mw Generator Offering

Offering Summary
Specifications
Project Services
Purchase Procedure
Request Specific Generator Offering Information
Online Auction
CTG Home Page
Company Profile
In the Press

Image Library

This page contains images of various parts of the generators.

Turbine Coupling   Turbine Casing

The operation of the auction system provides some less-than-obvious advantages: (1) products can generally be examined by potential buyers; (2) sellers and buyers may, if they choose, remain anonymous; and (3) buyers may enjoy the thrill of the auction and savor their victory over other bidders. This last factor may not be important to a tobacco buyer, but it is to a patron of art auctions.

Auction companies are beginning to appear on the Internet. For example, FastParts is an online auction site for overstocked electronic parts. An auction on the Internet has the advantage of appealing to a greatly expanded geographical market.

Manufacturers' agent
An independent agent intermediary that represents a limited number of noncompeting suppliers in a limited geographical area; also called a *manufacturers' representative*.

Manufacturers' Agents and Selling Agents   **Manufacturers' agents**, also called *manufacturers' representatives*, are independent intermediaries that specialize in selling and are available to producers that do not want to perform sales activities themselves. These agents operate in geographically limited areas, such as a few states or a portion of a state, representing two or more noncompeting producers and spreading selling costs among them. Suppose a maker of photocopying equipment wants to employ a sales force only in major markets, not in smaller cities or rural areas. It might decide to hire a series of manufacturers' agents to cover areas with low market potential and to let the company's own sales force take the more important markets. The existence of markets with low market potential is not the only good reason to use manufacturers' agents. Their familiarity with local markets is often an advantage. Another reason is that the producer may lack the interest or expertise to perform sales and marketing functions. Still another is finances: A company that has relatively few financial resources is more likely to use an agent because the agent need not be paid until a sale is made.

Selling agent
An independent agent intermediary similar to a manufacturers' agent but representing a given product in every area in which it is sold, rather than in a limited geographical area.

Selling agents are also paid a commission and are expected to be familiar with the products they handle and the markets they serve. However, they differ from manufacturers' agents in one major respect. They sell the products manufactured by the producers they represent not in a single geographical area but in all the areas in which the products are sold. Because, in effect, they function as sales and marketing departments, they are often given more responsibility than manufacturers' agents. They may be permitted to handle the advertising and pricing of the products sold and determine any conditions of sale to be negotiated. The manufacturer that uses a selling agent obtains what might be called an external marketing department.

Exhibit 12-6 gives an overview of the various wholesalers in the two basic classifications.

MANUFACTURERS THAT DO THEIR OWN WHOLESALING

Throughout this section, we have been considering wholesaling as if it were performed entirely by independent organizations other than manufacturers. Actually, although the various agent and merchant intermediaries are extremely impor-

MERCHANT WHOLESALERS		AGENT WHOLESALERS	
Merchant wholesalers take title to goods and earn profits		Agents do not take title, but some may take possession of products; they receive a commission based on the product selling price; they usually do not extend credit.	
Full-service merchant wholesalers	Take title; take possession; deliver goods; extend credit; provide marketing information; provide managerial assistance	Brokers	
		• Traditional	Assist in contractual negotiations; bring buyers and sellers together
Limited-service merchant wholesalers		• Vertical exchanges	Bring buyers and sellers together electronically on the Internet
• Cash-and-carry wholesalers	Do not provide delivery or credit	Commission merchants	Perform pricing function for sellers
• Truck wholesalers	Have a limited product line; deliver goods	Auction companies	Offer convenience in bringing buyers and sellers together
• Direct-marketing wholesalers	Use catalogs and the Internet; are important in rural locations	Manufacturers' agents	Help manufacturers, often in "thin markets," to sell products
• Drop shippers	Don't physically handle products; generally deal in bulky products	Selling agents	Like manufacturers' agents, specialize in selling but also act as an external marketing department
• Rack jobbers	Deal in a wide variety of small products; are responsible for stocking products		

tant, especially in particular lines of trade, many manufacturers perform the wholesaling functions themselves. Some manufacturers have become disenchanted with wholesalers for a number of reasons. They believe that wholesalers handling the products of many manufacturers cannot promote any one manufacturer's product as that producer feels it should be promoted.

When manufacturers do their own wholesaling, whether to retailers or to industrial users, they may use sales offices, sales branches, or both. (The U.S. Department of Commerce classifies sales branches and sales offices as wholesalers even though, according to our definition, they are not independent intermediaries.) **Sales offices** and **sales branches** are wholesaling establishments maintained by producers of the products sold, and both may serve as headquarters for "outside" salespeople or as offices for "inside" salespeople. The central difference between the two is that the sales branch carries an inventory of products whereas the sales office does not. The bulk of the product, the need for fast delivery, the technical aspects of the product, and the opportunity to sell a standardized product rather than a custom-made one all contribute to the decision as to whether to use offices or branches.

The reason manufacturers choose to do their own wholesaling can be expressed in one word: control. The maintenance of sales offices and branches permits manufacturers to control more effectively the flow of goods to their customers, the training and selling activities of their salespeople, and the flow of information returned to headquarters by a staff that is actually out in the field.

WHOLESALERS THAT DISTRIBUTE SERVICES

Some wholesalers specialize in the distribution of services. For example, your college library may use the services of BRS (Bibliographical Retrieval Service),

Sales office
A wholesaling establishment that is maintained by a manufacturer for its own product and does not carry an inventory of the product.

Sales branch
A wholesaling establishment that is maintained by a manufacturer for its own product and carries an inventory of the product.

Lexis/Nexis, or the Dow-Jones News Retrieval Service. These organizations are wholesalers that market information services.

Chapter 5 discussed worldwide information systems, but not in the context of wholesaling and retailing. However, as you can now see, information and other services flow through channels of distribution. As the 21st century unfolds, interactive media will become even more prominent, and distribution channels for information and entertainment services will become even more significant.

Wholesale Management Strategies

Wholesalers, like all marketers, create marketing strategies. They analyze market segments, select target markets, and determine the competitive position they wish to occupy. To a great extent, the wholesaler's strategy is dominated by physical distribution concerns, the subject of Chapter 11. However, two other aspects of strategy have dimensions that deserve special attention, and we discuss them here. They are (1) selecting target markets and creating assortments and (2) developing strategic alliances.

SELECTING TARGET MARKETS AND CREATING ASSORTMENTS

We have seen that wholesalers sell to three basic classes of customers: retailers that resell the product, other wholesalers that resell the product, and organizations in the business market that use the product. Each of these customers has different needs. The wholesaler must determine which target markets to serve and what product mixes to offer. Further, the depth of the product lines offered must be matched to the needs of the target market. Consider this wholesaling strategy. Frieda's Finest is a produce grocery wholesaler that specializes in marketing uncommon fruits and exotic foods, such as tamarinds, babaco, and purple potatoes, to retailers. Its success with kiwi fruit is typical. Once the pioneering company succeeds in gaining market acceptance for the product, larger produce companies like Chiquita enter the market with their brands and become such formidable competitors that Frieda's Finest must exit the market. Then it once again attempts to pioneer the wholesaling of another rare food.

ORGANIZATIONAL COLLABORATIONS FOR LONG-TERM RELATIONSHIPS

A wholesaler and its customer determine the extent to which the wholesaler will be involved in the operation of the customer's business. The customer expects the wholesaler to have an inventory of products in sufficient quantity to make rapid delivery possible. But in many situations, the wholesaler goes on to form a strategic business alliance with its customer.

A strategic business alliance is a commitment between a wholesaler and its customer to establish a long-term relationship. Such alliances may include arrangements to share or pool inventory information or interchange other databases so that purchase orders are executed automatically by computers. Vertical marketing systems are, of course, the strongest type of strategic alliance. However, wholesalers that are not part of such systems may also concentrate on building long-term relationships with their customers. For example, Fleming Foods offers many managerial services to grocery retailers because it considers them "partners." This wholesaler provides computer programs and other assistance to determine supermarket locations, design store layouts, and maintain the proper levels of on-shelf inventory.

Regulation of Retail and Wholesale Distribution

In the United States, in other countries, and in international trade agreements, dealings in the area of distribution may be subject to numerous restrictions. For example, a manufacturer's ability to exercise power over wholesalers and retailers is often regulated in an attempt to preserve the independence of intermediaries and to assure that the distribution system does not encourage unfair competition.

The Sherman Antitrust Act, the Clayton Act, the Federal Trade Commission Act, and other laws dealing with antitrust policy are the bases for much U.S. legislation influencing distribution. In the United States, the three main legal issues concerning wholesale and retail distribution are exclusive dealing, exclusive territories, and tying agreements.

EXCLUSIVE DEALING

Exclusive dealing refers to a restrictive arrangement by which a supplier prohibits intermediaries that handle its product from selling the products of competing suppliers. A manufacturer may wish to deal only with those distributors that will agree to market only its brand. Would such an arrangement be legal? The answer to this question depends on whether the arrangement abuses the intermediary's right to act independently or the rights of other business competitors to succeed.

If a manufacturer restricts an intermediary from selling products that compete with that manufacturer's products, the activity is illegal if it tends to restrict competition. A new brand of automobile engine oil would never reach the marketplace if all makers of oil already in the market enforced exclusive dealing agreements with their wholesalers and retailers. Such arrangements, in blocking entry of a new product, would appear to be restricting competition.

An exclusive dealing arrangement is likely to lessen competition if (1) it encompasses a substantial share of the market, (2) the dollar amount involved is substantial, or (3) it involves a large supplier and a smaller distributor, in which case the supplier's disparate economic power can be inherently coercive. Exclusive dealing arrangements generally are legal if it can be shown that the exclusivity is necessary for strategic reasons, such as a franchisor's need to protect a product's image. Exclusive dealing may also be legal if the supplier's own sales are restricted because of limited production capacity.

EXCLUSIVE TERRITORIES

A manufacturer that grants a wholesaler or retailer an **exclusive territory** may be performing an illegal act. The key point, as in so many legal matters relating to business, is restriction of competition. If the granting of exclusive territories does not violate the statutes relating to this point, then limiting the number of outlets within an area or assigning exclusive territories may be considered proper. Again, in many cases, this evaluation must be made by the legal system.

What about Cadillac? This organization attracts dealers in part by promising that other dealers will not be set up within the same areas. A number of defenses might be offered on behalf of organizations engaged in this sort of practice. It might be argued that the investment expected from new dealers is so great that dealers could not be recruited unless they were offered some sort of exclusive territory. In this case, the defense is that the nature of the business demands such exclusivity. It also might be argued that the image associated with the product offered demands some exclusivity. Cadillac, for example, is portrayed as a luxury product. Excellent sales and service people are thus necessary. Cadillac dealers and mechanics are carefully selected and trained. If some exclusivity of territories were not maintained—if anybody could be a Cadillac dealer—then the quality of products and services might diminish. If Cadillac dealerships were allowed to open on every other street corner, this might destroy the elite image Cadillac Motor Division is trying to create.

TYING CONTRACTS

Tying contracts require a channel intermediary or a buyer to purchase lines of merchandise that the seller sees as supplementary to the merchandise the purchaser actually wants to buy. The seller tells the buyer, in effect, "If you want to have this

Exclusive dealing
A situation in which a distributor carries the products of one manufacturer and not those of competing manufacturers.

Exclusive territory
An area defined by geographical boundaries or population and assigned to a retailer, wholesaler, or other dealer with the understanding that no other distributors will be assigned to operate in that area.

Tying contract
An agreement tying the purchase of one product to the purchase of another. The buyer who wishes to purchase a certain product is required by the seller to purchase additional products, whether the buyer wants to purchase those products or not.

product (say, a printing press), you must also buy my other product (paper)." Thus, two or more products are tied together. The Clayton Act appears to make tying contracts illegal, but whether a particular agreement is, in fact, a tying contract is open to debate. Certain tying agreements can be legal, but, as with the complex issues discussed above, the legal system usually must make a determination.

LEGALITIES OF INTERNATIONAL DISTRIBUTION

The many restraints, limits, and problems associated with domestic retailing and wholesaling are compounded in the international marketplace. Domestic laws, the laws of the country to which goods are being shipped, the laws of the nations through which goods are being shipped, and the general conventions associated with international trade must all be obeyed. The many-faceted aspects of international constraints on distribution are beyond the scope of this chapter, but the immense problems that flow from them should be recognized by all students of marketing.

Summary

Retailing and wholesaling are the major distribution institutions that make the marketing system work.

1) Describe the function of retailing and wholesaling in the distribution system.

Retailers deal with ultimate consumers, people who buy products for their own use. Wholesalers deal with institutions that acquire products for organizational use or for resale. Both types of intermediaries buy, sell, and help to physically distribute products through the economy.

2) Categorize the various types of retailers by ownership and prominent strategy.

Retail establishments in the United States may be classified by ownership as independents, leased departments, chains, franchises, or ownership groups. They may also be classified by retail strategy as in-store retailers or retailers engaged in direct marketing. In-store retailers may be further classified as specialty stores, department stores, supermarkets, convenience stores, general mass merchandisers, or specialized mass merchandisers. Discount department stores were the first general mass merchandisers. Catalog showrooms and warehouse clubs are among the more recent forms. Specialty mass merchandisers include off-price retailers and category superstores. Direct marketing by retailers includes mail-order selling, direct marketing via television, telemarketing, in-home retailing through computers, door-to-door selling, and selling from vending machines.

3) Understand the key elements of retailers' marketing strategies.

Retail marketers of all types must develop effective marketing mixes aimed at attracting and satisfying target markets. Merchandise assortment, location, atmospherics, customer service, database management, and Internet strategy are of special importance to retailers.

4) Explain the impact of the Internet on retailing.

e-tailing is the name for interactive retailing on the Internet. Consumers can shop from their homes or offices by using personal computers to interact with retailers via the Internet. The number of Internet Web sites, or "store fronts," where products can be ordered has been growing very rapidly. An Internet retailing strategy is not limited by the geographical location of a physical store; an e-tailer can market to customers everywhere. The variety and depth of merchandise available from e-tailers are often much greater than a physical store could offer. Shoppers visiting an Internet store use hyperlinks to narrow their search efforts or to get additional details about a product. When consumers provide information about their unique needs, marketers can address their requirements individually. Internet shopping at home is convenient. No travel is required, and consumers have access to e-tailers 24 hours a day, 7 days a week. Several companies provide automated shopping programs known as shopbots to make shopping easier for their customers. Shopbots are smart agent software programs designed to perform shopping tasks for buyers.

5) Distinguish between merchant wholesalers and agents and describe their functions in the distribution system.

Independent wholesalers are either merchants or agents. Merchants take title to the goods they sell; agents do not. The wholesaler's primary function is facilitating transfer of products or title to them.

6) Show how full-service and limited-service merchant wholesalers contribute to the marketing system.

Full-service merchant wholesalers can perform credit and delivery functions and provide managerial assistance and market information. Limited-service wholesalers perform some, but not all, intermediary functions, eliminating those that particular buyers do not require. These intermediaries can therefore lower their costs of doing business and the prices they must charge their customers.

7) *Identify the marketing contributions of agent intermediaries such as brokers, auction companies, and selling agents.*

Agent intermediaries such as brokers, auction companies, and selling agents may offer expert knowledge of the marketplace, provide physical facilities for doing business, give advice to buyers and sellers, and help bring buyers and sellers together. They therefore play important roles in exchanges without actually taking title to the products.

8) *Understand the key elements of wholesalers' strategies.*

To a large extent, the wholesaler's strategy is dominated by physical distribution strategies. However, selecting target markets, creating assortments for customers, and developing strategic alliances are also important aspects of wholesale strategy.

9) *Describe some of the legal concerns associated with the development and management of channels of distribution.*

The macromarketing role of distribution raises several issues that have been addressed by laws. Exclusive dealing arrangements can be seen as stopping the distribution of competitors' goods or services and are thus sometimes illegal. So are exclusive territorial arrangements, which may restrict free trade. Tying agreements, which tie purchase of one product to purchase of another, are in almost all cases illegal.

Key Terms

agent (p. 358)
atmospherics (p. 352)
auction company (p. 359)
broker (p. 358)
cash-and-carry wholesaler (p. 357)
catalog showroom (p. 342)
category superstore (p. 343)
chain store (p. 339)
commission merchant (p. 359)
convenience store (p. 342)
corporate chain (p. 339)
department store (p. 340)
direct marketing (p. 344)
direct-marketing wholesaler (p. 357)
drop shipper (p. 358)
e-tailers (p. 338)

e-tailing (p. 346)
exclusive dealing (p. 363)
exclusive territory (p. 363)
full-service merchant wholesaler (p. 357)
general line wholesaler (p. 357)
general merchandise wholesaler (p. 357)
independent retailer (p. 339)
leased department retailer (p. 339)
limited-service merchant wholesaler (p. 357)
manufacturers' agent (p. 360)
mass merchandise retailer (p. 342)
merchant wholesaler (p. 356)
off-price retailer (p. 343)

ownership group (p. 339)
rack jobber (p. 358)
retailing (p. 338)
sales branch (p. 361)
sales office (p. 361)
selling agent (p. 360)
service level (p. 353)
shopbot (p. 347)
specialty store (p. 340)
specialty wholesaler (p. 357)
supermarket (p. 341)
truck wholesaler (p. 364)
tying contract (p. 363)
warehouse club (p. 342)
wheel of retailing (p. 348)
wholesaler (p. 355)

Questions for Review & Critical Thinking

1. Give some examples of retailers in your area that fit the following categories:
   a. Warehouse club
   b. Specialty store
   c. Chain store
   d. Catalog showroom
2. Which of the following retailers would tend to use free-standing locations? Why? Why would the others not use such locations?
   a. Kmart
   b. McDonald's
   c. A local department store
   d. A popcorn shop
3. What are the advantages of direct marketing?
4. What are some of the disadvantages of using vending machines as retail outlets?

5. How can a small retailer use the Internet to market its products?
6. What trends do you predict in retail marketing on the Internet?
7. Find out about furniture marketing in the United States, and discuss the evolution and development of retailing in this industry.
8. What are the key elements of a retailer's marketing mix? Provide examples.
9. Do you think executives in small independent retail organizations have the same growth orientation and business philosophy as executives in large corporations? Why or why not?
10. Find local examples of the following:
    a. Cash-and-carry wholesaler
    b. Rack jobber

c. Manufacturer's sales office

d. Auction company

11. What is the major difference between agents and merchant wholesalers?

12. What are the advantages and disadvantages for each of the following businesses of using manufacturers' agents?

a. New company marketing voice synthesizers for computers

b. Large established company marketing truck axles

c. West Virginia coal company selling coal in Pennsylvania

13. Form small groups as directed by your instructor. Each group is to function as a department store buying center for women's casual fashions for either the upcoming winter season or the upcoming spring season. The group should come to a consensus and make a buying recommendation.

14. Under what conditions is exclusive dealing legal?

15. Under what conditions are exclusive territories legal?

---

e—exercises   http://zikmund.swcollege.com

1. Go to http://www.faoschwarz.com for the F. A. O. Schwarz toy store on the Internet. Then go to http://www.amazon.com and enter Toys. Evaluate the toy stores' Web sites. Which is a better marketing tool? Why?
2. Go to http://www.mallofamerica.com for the Mall of America and take a virtual tour. Is the shopping center's layout typical of most malls?
3. To learn about a number of companies' strategies for international retailing, visit Michigan State University's International Retailing Web site at http://www.msu.edu/~hed/internationalretailing/. Spend some time looking at the companies' options. Do you think it would be difficult to understand international retail markets? Why?

Address Book (Useful URLs)

Corporate Intelligence on Retailing	http://www.cior.com
International Council of Shopping Centers	http://www.icsc.org
iMALL	http://www.imall.com
Retail Futures	http://www.retailfuture.com

Ethically Right or Wrong?

A Utah ice-cream maker planned to market a new frozen novelty item in a 30-store California chain, until the chain demanded $20,000 to put the product in its freezers. This *slotting allowance* (also known in the grocery industry as a *stocking allowance,* an *introductory allowance,* or *street money*) is an admission fee that many packaged-goods marketers—large and small—must pay to squeeze their brands onto crowded supermarket shelves.

Retailers say they need the slotting allowance to compensate them for entering new product information into the computer, finding space in the warehouse, redesigning store shelves, and notifying individual stores about the latest entries. They also want to turn their buying efforts into new sources of profit. Is it ethical to charge a slotting allowance?

1. A Wal-Mart moves into a small town, and many small retail establishments go out of business within a year. Is this right?
2. A major chain store has six supermarkets in a certain city but none on the poor side of town, where many minority consumers live. Should the store open a new branch on the poor side of town?
3. A wholesaler refuses to carry a lawn-mower manufacturer's product line because the wholesaler already represents a competitor's line. Is this legal? Ethical?
4. A manufacturer of office equipment used a manufacturers' agent on the west coast to sell to wholesalers for 6 years. The agent did a good job, and sales volume reached $1 million in the territory. When this happened, a sales representative was hired to replace the agent, and the long-standing relationship between manufacturer and agent was terminated. What obligation does the manufacturer have to the agent?

VIDEO CASE 12-1
Hudson's

The Dayton-Hudson Corporation, headquartered in Minneapolis, is the fourth largest general merchandise retailer in the United States. It operates Target, Mervyns, and a department store division that includes Dayton's, Hudson's, and Marshall Fields. Historically, Hudson's has been a department store marketing clothing, cosmetics, fragrances, jewelry, and other dry goods to middle-income households.

The Somerset Collection is a shopping center located in an affluent suburb of Detroit. Prior to a major expansion in 1995, the mall contained many elegant specialty stores as well as upscale department stores Neiman Marcus and Saks Fifth Avenue. When the Somerset Collection decided to expand the number of stores in its mall, it made retail store space available to both Hudson's and Nordstrom. Seattle-based Nordstrom, one of the nation's leading fashion retailers, is renowned for its services, its quality merchandise, and generous size ranges for the entire family. Nordstrom accepted the offer from the Somerset Collection.

Although Hudson's had other stores in the Detroit area, it also accepted the offer from the Somerset Collection. The decision was made in part because a refusal to lease the space would have opened the opportunity to another retailer competitor. Hudson's, however, realized that the typical Somerset Collection shopper was more prosperous and had different expectations than the middle-income customers it had been serving for years. It offered an opportunity to target a different type of shopper.

QUESTIONS
1. How important would marketing research be to a Hudson's in its opening of a new store in the Somerset Collection mall?
2. What impact will competing retail stores in the Somerset Collection, such as Nordstrom, have on Hudson's? Should Hudson's alter its marketing strategy (customer service, merchandise, layout, etc.) for the Somerset Collection location? If so, how? If not, why not?
3. What type of store layout and atmospherics should Hudson's have in the Somerset Collection location?

cross-functional insights

Many theories and principles from other business disciplines can provide insights about the role of marketing in an organization. The questions in this section are designed to help you think about integrating what you have learned in other business courses with the marketing principles explained in Chapters 11 and 12.

Distribution Delivers a Standard of Living to Society   The major purpose of marketing is to satisfy human needs by delivering products of various types to buyers when and where they want them and at a reasonable cost.

How does the economic concept of scarcity relate to the distribution of a standard of living?

Channel Conflict   Channel conflict refers to a situation in which channel members disagree and their relationship is antagonistic. Disagreements may relate to the channel's common purpose or the responsibility for certain activities. The behavior of one channel member may be seen as inhibiting the attainment of another channel member's goals.

How are conflicts between channel members similar to conflicts that an organization's cross-functional teams experience? Can similar techniques be used to reduce these conflicts?

Retailers   Retailing consists of all business activities involving the sale of goods and services to ultimate consumers.

Are most retailers entrepreneurs? What characteristics of entrepreneurs would help them become successful retailers?

What stages of company growth would be typical for a successful retail business started by an entrepreneur?

If an entrepreneur were starting a retail business, what form of ownership would be best: a sole proprietorship, a partnership, or a corporation?

What would the typical small retailer's balance sheet look like?

What should a retailer know about teamwork? What types of teams might a retailer utilize?

What type of inventory cost system should a retailer have?

Merchant Wholesalers and Agent Wholesalers   Channel members may be merchant wholesalers, which take title to the goods, or agent wholesalers, which do not take title to goods.

Who may be a legal agent?

How is agency authority in a channel of distribution created?

How is an agency relationship in a channel of distribution ended?

How does the Uniform Commercial Code apply to the relationship between manufacturers and merchant wholesalers?

Logistics   Logistics describes the entire process of moving raw materials and component parts into a firm, moving in-process inventory through the firm, and moving finished goods out of the firm. Supply chain management thus involves planning, implementing, and controlling the efficient flow of both inbound materials and outbound finished products.

What factors should a company consider when determining locations for factories and company-owned warehouses? How important are logistics and physical distribution in this decision?

How do labor unions influence logistics management and physical distribution functions?

Integrated Marketing Communications

LEARNING OBJECTIVES

After you have studied this chapter, you will be able to . . .

1) Discuss the three basic purposes of promotion.

2) Define the four major elements of promotion.

3) Describe the basic model for all communication processes, including promotion.

4) Explain the hierarchy of communication effects.

5) Explain how the elements of promotion can be used to support one another in a promotional campaign.

6) Describe the general promotional strategies known as push and pull strategies.

7) Discuss promotional campaigns and provide examples.

chapter

Lee jeans were way off the cool meter with young consumers. The company didn't want to alienate loyal buyers—women 35 and over—but it had to shed its "mom's jeans" image to appeal to kids. How could Lee Apparel Company connect with 15-to-34-year-olds who think Lee is, like, totally unhip?

Early rounds of focus groups found that kids under 17 changed their minds daily on what was cool to wear, while adults in their late 20s and early 30s felt comfortable in their broken-in Levi's. The 17-to-22 segment, however, seemed open to new brands, a finding reiterated in a large-scale study by the Cambridge Group and Roper Starch Worldwide. The study divided consumers into 11 psychographic profiles, among them "Fit Me/Fit My Lifestyle." That segment included a number of 17-to-22-year-olds who were style leaders, influential among their peers. If Lee could grab them, their friends would follow. The study also confirmed that people thought Lee jeans were more durable than other jeans, and that didn't necessarily mean uncool. The success of Timberland and Doc Martens had shown that functional brands could still be fashionable. Additional focus groups revealed that 17-to-22-year-olds wanted their jeans to give them the confidence to do anything, whether it was playing basketball on the court or watching it on TV. Lee needed to connect its durable image with the indestructibility that the target market craved.

A truly break-out campaign was needed—something that would set Lee apart on the rack. Perhaps, Fallon McElligott suggested, there were icons buried in Lee's archives that would click with today's savvy young consumers and link unmistakably back to the brand. In interviews with target buyers, three "antiques" grabbed the spotlight. A slogan from the 1940s, "Can't Bust 'Em," had a retro appeal that also suggested strength and qual-

ity. The word *dungarees*, resurrected from an earlier line, lent a James Dean authenticity. And then there was the Buddy Lee doll, an all-but-forgotten icon from the 1920s. Buddy Lee reflected the target market's idealized view of that era—and he was cool, like Bart Simpson.

The iconography study also influenced product design for the Lee Dungarees line. Researchers had a radical proposal: Dump the signature leather patch and pocket stitching. Kids said the details reminded them of their parents' jeans. Lee leaders gulped, but gave the go-ahead. Tapping into the retro vein, designers incorporated styling similar to that of jeans circa the 1920s.

The media strategy was anything but vintage. Tests of various creative concepts found that those "Fit Me/Fit My Lifestyle" 17-to-22-year-olds considered themselves cool hunters: They needed to discover Lee Dungarees before everyone else did. Posters of Buddy Lee were plastered around cities like New York and Los Angeles to pique the interest of early adopters. After a run of commercials on cable TV that introduced Buddy Lee, "Man of Action," the pint-size hero hit the mainstream in spots during primetime shows like *Dawson's Creek*.

Initial retail orders of Original Straight-Leg Dungarees, the line's flagship product, hit 1.3 million units, 300 percent more than anticipated. Roughly 26 percent of 17-to-22-year-olds thought Lee was cool before the rollout. Four months into the campaign, that figure reached 42 percent.[1]

Lee's use of research to develop a new advertising campaign to inform and amuse its target market is one example of how marketing communication is instrumental to an organization's success. Advertising, public relations/publicity, personal selling, and sales promotion are all elements of the fascinating world of promotion, the subject of this chapter. The chapter begins by describing the three purposes of promotion and how the four basic promotional elements help accomplish promotion's purposes. It explains the new media that have emerged because of the revolution in digital technology and how these new media are dramatically influencing the promotional mix. It next examines the theory of communication and the hierarchy of communication effects. Then it discusses selecting a promotional mix. After describing some strategies for promotional campaigns, the chapter ends with a discussion of the ethics of persuasion in our society.

Reminding customers may be a promotional objective for marketers with loyal customers. In this advertisement, computer graphics remind consumers of the familiar shape of the Coca-Cola bottle.

http://www.cocacola.com

Promotion: Communication with a Purpose

Effective marketers know that the old adage "Build a better mousetrap and the world will beat a path to your door" contains a basic flaw. If the "world" doesn't find out that there is a better mousetrap, the manufacturer will be a very lonely person, indeed. Having a great product is not enough. People must be made familiar with the product's benefits. Some form of promotion is necessary to make consumers, and other publics with which an organization interacts, aware of the existence of a product.

> Having a great product is not enough. People must be made aware of the existence of a product.

Promotion is applied marketing communication. Marketers use it to communicate both factual information and persuasive messages to prospective buyers. In the marketing mix, promotion serves three purposes:

- *To inform.* Promotion provides a great deal of factual information about products and places of business, such as where a store is located and whether it accepts credit cards.
- *To persuade.* Persuasion that encourages purchases or changes in attitude is, of course, a primary goal of promotion. In fact, a popular definition of promotion is "persuasive communication."
- *To remind.* Promotional messages may be aimed at reminding a brand's current consumers why they should continue to buy it.

New Communication Media Are Shaping Promotion

Advertising, personal selling, and publicity are among the traditional forms of promotion. Technical definitions of each will be provided in the following section. However, new media have emerged because of the revolution in digital technology. The availability of these new media has dramatically influenced the elements of promotion and how they are defined in our information age.

The traditional 20th-century view broke media into two categories: *mass media*, in which there was no interaction between the marketer and the audience, and *personal media*, such as personal selling, which involved a dialogue between buyer and seller. Today, because of computers' capacity to interact with consumers, advances in digital technology have made this distinction outdated.

For our purposes, we will use a simple threefold classification of media: mass media, personal media, and electronic interactive media. Exhibit 13-1 shows the individual promotional media in each of these classifications.

MASS MEDIA

Mass media are means of communication that reach large audiences without personal contact or instantaneous interaction between the marketer and the receiver of the message. Messages in print media, such as newspapers and magazines, and broadcast media, such as radio and television, are targeted at a general group of people rather than at any particular individual. When people think of advertising, they traditionally envision messages in mass media, but, as you will see, the nature of advertising is changing.

Mass media
Advertising media, such as television, radio, newspapers, and magazines, that reach a broad audience from many market segments and involve no personal contact or instantaneous interaction between the marketer and the target of the message.

e x h i b 13-1

Three General Media for Marketing Communications

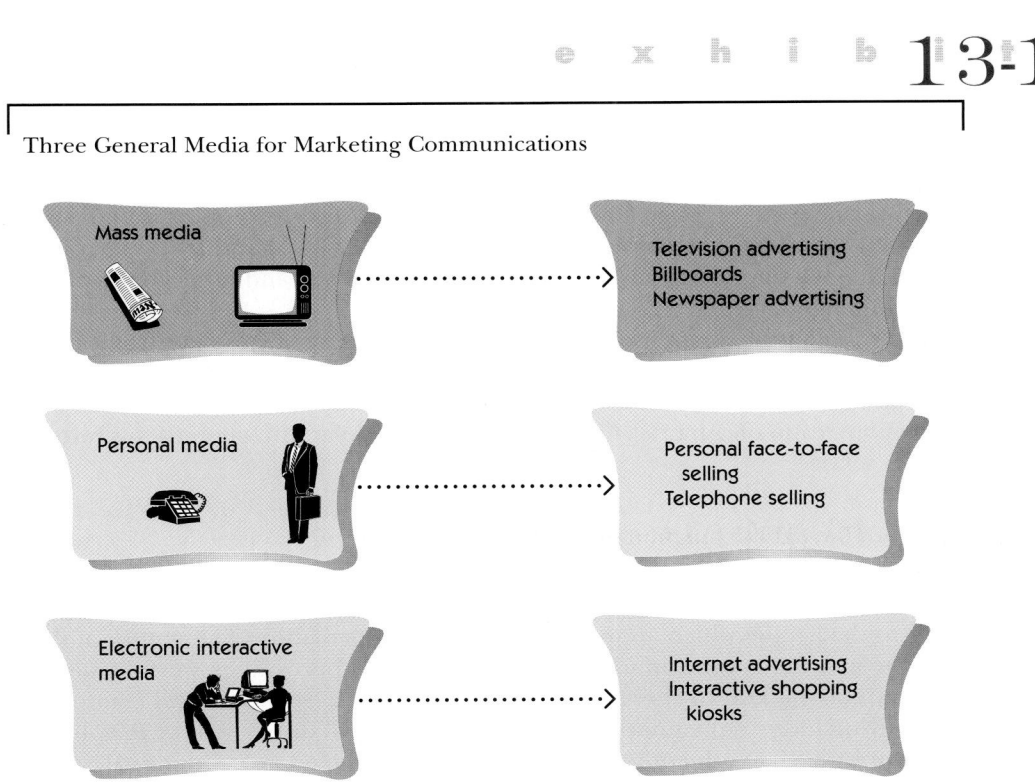

Mass media — Television advertising / Billboards / Newspaper advertising

Personal media — Personal face-to-face selling / Telephone selling

Electronic interactive media — Internet advertising / Interactive shopping kiosks

Magazine advertisements are classified as mass media because they reach a broad audience. However, they can be aimed at specific target markets. This advertisement for Boeri helmets symbolically communicates the company's persuasive message.

PERSONAL MEDIA

Personal media
Personal forms of communication involving face-to-face interaction and person-to-person interaction (as by telephone).

When two people have a conversation, human interaction takes place. The medium is personal. When **personal media** are used for communication, the messages are directed at a particular individual (or a small group), who has the opportunity to interact with another human being. When they think of the traditional role of personal selling, most people envision two people engaged in a face-to-face dialogue or a telephone conversation.

ELECTRONIC INTERACTIVE MEDIA

Electronic interactive media
Media, such as the Internet, touch-tone telephone systems, and online information services, that allow marketers to reach large audiences with personalized individual messages and that provide an opportunity for immediate interaction.

As mentioned in Chapter 3, digital technology is having a profound impact on society in general and marketing in particular. Its greatest impact is in the creation of new forms of media.

Electronic interactive media allow marketers to reach a large audience, to personalize individual messages, and to provide the opportunity for immediate interaction. To a large extent, electronic interactive media are controlled by the users themselves. Users are not passive audience members—they are actively involved in two-way communication.

The Internet, a medium that is radically altering many organizations' promotional strategies, provides a prominent example of the new electronic interactive media. Consumers determine what World Wide Web information they will be exposed to and for how long. Although the Internet is the most sophisticated new medium, electronic interactive media also include CD-ROM and DVD materials, touch-tone telephone systems, interactive kiosks in stores, and other forms of digital technology.

Today, a consumer can use an interactive medium to converse electronically via computer with another consumer, an advertiser, or an information content provider. One well-used means of conducting interactive conversations is the MTV discussion group on America Online—the most popular attraction of this information service.

The Elements of Promotion

The four main subsets of promotion are personal selling, advertising, publicity (as part of a public relations effort), and sales promotion. It is up to the marketer to determine which approach is best for each situation. The nature of the message and the context in which it is to be delivered provide powerful clues about which method to choose. Few organizational buyers would feel comfortable buying industrial equipment solely on the basis of direct mail or telephone communication. On the other hand, few consumers need help from a salesperson to choose a certain brand of canned peas; they are content to rely on advertising for most product information.

PERSONAL SELLING

Personal selling is a person-to-person dialogue between buyer and seller. The purpose of the interaction, whether face-to-face or over the phone, is to persuade the buyer to accept a point of view, to convince the buyer to take a specific course of action, or to develop a customer relationship. Personal selling is the most flexible means of delivering a promotional message. Questions can be answered, pauses can be taken at appropriate spots to allow an idea to sink in, and responses can be tailor-made to address particular customer objections or reluctance to complete a purchase.

e—commerce | Changing Everything

Walter Fredrick Associates used to use a sales team to solicit new accounts for its architectural equipment and computer supplies business. When the company created a Web site to sell its products, sales were discouraging. Then, Fredrick's copied the approach of e-commerce giants like Amazon.com and created a virtual sales force—by establishing an affiliate program. Every time a prospect links to inkjetexpress.com from an affiliated Web site and buys something, the affiliate gets a 5% commission. In less than a month, the affiliates increased Fredrick's site traffic from five visitors per day to an average of 182.[2]

ADVERTISING

Advertising includes any informative or persuasive message carried by a nonpersonal medium and paid for by a sponsor whose product is in some way identified in the message. Traditional mass media, such as television and magazines, are most commonly used to transmit advertisements. However, the direct mailing of catalogs, electronic media advertisements featuring computerized ordering, and other direct-response vehicles are becoming increasingly popular. Thus, contemporary definitions of advertising recognize that it can be carried by mass media or via interactive electronic media.

The ability to communicate to a large number of people at once is the major benefit of advertising. Because it is indirect and nonpersonal, advertising allows marketers to send a uniform and unvarying message with great frequency. You may see a soft drink commercial several times as you watch a basketball game on TV. You would never ask a salesperson to repeat a message over and over again.

Mass media advertising is not without disadvantages. Even though the cost per person may be low, a large absolute dollar expenditure is often required to reach the target audience through a medium such as national television. This expense tends to restrict all but the larger, better-financed organizations from using national advertising. Mass media advertising, unlike personal selling, does not allow the message to be personalized and tailored to the prospect. Immediate, direct feedback from a prospect is rare when mass media are utilized. In contrast, when marketers advertise on electronic interactive media, the audience has the opportunity to "customize" the nature of the information they receive and to interact with the marketer through the medium. Advertising via mass media and interactive media is the subject of Chapter 14.

PUBLICITY/PUBLIC RELATIONS

Advertising is a form of message delivery in which the sender pays to send the message. Publicity is similar to advertising in that it may use the same mass media. The difference between the two is that **publicity** involves a message that is not paid for and whose content is determined by the communication medium. When information about a company, a product, or an event is considered newsworthy, mass media may communicate that information "for free." Thus, the organization being publicized neither pays for the message directly nor is identified as the message sponsor. The Internet is a new medium for publicity that has, in many cases, increased the speed of message diffusion.

Personal selling
Person-to-person interaction between a buyer and a seller wherein the seller's purpose is to persuade the buyer to accept a point of view, to convince the buyer to take a course of action, or to develop a customer relationship.

Advertising
An informative or persuasive message carried by a nonpersonal medium and paid for by an identified sponsor whose organization or product is identified in some way.

Publicity
A message about a product, organization, or event carried by a nonpersonal medium but not paid for by a sponsor. Publicity involves a third party who determines whether the message is newsworthy enough to transmit and what the nature of the transmitted message will be.

When information about a business-sponsored sporting event is considered newsworthy, mass media will communicate that information for free. The fact that publicity is free does not mean that it goes unmanaged. Coca-Cola and Fuji are experts at carefully orchestrating publicity.

Although publicity is "free" in the sense that mass media are not paid to communicate the message, this does not mean that publicity should go unmanaged. For instance, you can be certain that every year the Neiman-Marcus Christmas catalog will generate a great deal of publicity. The organization manages to get this publicity by its time-honored tradition of featuring spectacular "his and hers" Christmas gifts. One year, Neiman-Marcus offered a set of wooden mosaic desks in the form of seven-foot-long ranch animals. For "him" the desk was a steer with authentic 42-inch horns. For "her" the desk was a custom-made likeness of a horse. The Christmas catalog is a carefully orchestrated annual publicity event.

Marketers may expend considerable time and effort in getting news releases and interviews with company spokespersons placed in newspapers and on broadcasts to promote a favorable organizational image. When an organization systematically plans and distributes information in an attempt to manage the nature of the publicity it receives, it is engaged in public relations. The purpose of *public relations* is to actively manage publicity (and sometimes other promotional elements) to establish and maintain a positive organizational image or to ensure that the public understands an organization's policies.

SALES PROMOTION

Sales promotion
Promotional activities other than personal selling, advertising, and public relations that are intended to stimulate buyer purchases or dealer effectiveness over a specific time period.

Marketers use the term **sales promotion** to categorize a variety of promotional activities that are something other than personal selling, advertising, or public relations. Sales promotions are usually intended to induce buyers to make purchases or to stimulate dealer effectiveness in a specific time period. Sales promotions add value to the product offering or provide an incentive for certain behavior.

Nike's television advertising portrayed a number of "cliffhanger" situations (such as a runner crashing into a glass door during a footrace) that ended with "continued at whatever.nike.com." Visitors to the Web site could choose among several endings. Combining advertising and a Web site promotion is an example of an integrated marketing communication effort.

http://www.nike.com

Thus, special offers of free goods, coupon deals, display items for store use, training programs, in-store demonstrations, and vacation trips for top salespeople are sales promotions. With a few exceptions, these are not routine events but special, out-of-the-ordinary occurrences. Although they typically involve programs paid for by an identified sponsor, they are distinguished from ad-

	PERSONAL SELLING	ADVERTISING*	PUBLICITY	SALES PROMOTION
Mode of communication	Direct and personal	Indirect and personal	Indirect and nonpersonal	Indirect and nonpersonal
Regular and recurrent activity?	Yes	Yes	No—only for newsworthy activity	No—short-term effort
Message flexibility	Personalized and tailored to prospect	Typically uniform and unvarying	Beyond marketer's direct control	Uniform and unvarying
Direct feedback possible?	Yes	No—if placed in the mass media	No	No
Marketer controls message content?	Yes	Yes	No	Yes
Sponsor identified?	Yes	Yes	No	Yes
Cost per contact	High	Low to moderate	No direct costs	Varies

*Internet advertising is somewhat different from mass media advertising.

vertising because they are temporary offers of a material reward to customers, salespeople, or sales prospects.

Sales promotion programs amplify or bolster the advertising and personal selling messages offered by an organization. More often than not, these effects occur at the point of purchase. For instance, advertising may create an awareness of a new product like Listerine Pocket Pak, but the cents-off coupon is the enticement that gets the first-time buyer to try the mouthwash delivered via dissolvable strips.

The main purpose of sales promotion is to achieve short-term objectives, such as a first-time trial of a product. The characteristics of the four elements of promotion are summarized in Exhibit 13-2.

Integrated Marketing Communications— The Promotional Mix

The effective marketer recognizes that each of the four elements of promotion has certain strengths. The combination of elements a marketer chooses is the marketer's **promotional mix**. Some organizations, like the San Diego Zoo, emphasize advertising and public relations efforts in their promotional mixes. Others, especially those engaged in business-to-business marketing, make personal selling the main ingredient. No matter what the promotional mix, marketers should strive to blend the elements effectively, integrating and uniting the appropriate elements to accomplish their promotional objectives. The term **integrated marketing communications** is used to remind managers that all elements of the promotional mix should be coordinated and systematically planned to be in harmony with each other. Later in this chapter, we discuss what specific factors marketers consider when choosing a promotional mix. Before we do, however, we will consider how communication occurs.

The Communication Process

Communication is the process of exchanging information with and conveying meaning to others. The goal of communication is a common understanding. That is, the goal is to have the **receiver** of the information understand as closely as possible the meaning intended by the sender, or **source**, of the message.

Promotional mix
An organization's combination of personal selling, advertising, publicity and public relations, and sales promotion; its total promotional effort.

Integrated marketing communications
Marketing communications in which all elements of the promotional mix are coordinated and systematically planned so as to be harmonious.

Communication
The process of exchanging information with and conveying meaning to others.

Receiver
In communication theory, the one at whom a message is aimed.

Source
In communication theory, the one who sends a message.

One communication theorist described communication as "who says what to whom through which channels with what effect."[3] In slightly different terms, he was saying that to achieve the desired effect, the marketer must consider the source, the message, the channel, and the receiver.

Exhibit 13-3 summarizes the communication process graphically. In considering the exhibit, remember that it describes all types of communication—words, gestures, pictures, and so on. The model may be used to describe an advertisement, a telephone sales call, a point-of-purchase display, or any promotional communication.

> To achieve the desired effect, the marketer must consider the source, the message, the channel, and the receiver.

ENCODING THE MESSAGE

Evaluate the Blazer advertisement shown in Exhibit 13-4 in terms of the model in Exhibit 13-3. Who says what to whom? The communication source (the advertiser) wishes to communicate the notion that the Blazer is a durable, high-quality product that helps drivers enjoy driving in rugged terrain. This idea—not an easy one to get across—is the message of the advertisement. The message is communicated primarily in a visual and symbolic way, through the intriguing image of a Blazer easily negotiating a gravel road in the mountains. The sender's idea has been encoded by means of this picture. **Encoding** is the process of translating the idea to be communicated into a symbolic message consisting of words, pictures, numbers, gestures, or the like. Encoding is a necessary step—there is no way to send an idea from one person to another without encoding it.

As in the Blazer advertisement, nonverbal messages and nonrational symbolism are essential to the encoding process, because words can be hopelessly inadequate to express emotions. "There are just no words to express the various nuances of sensation and feeling, to express such things as mood and aesthetic impression. Try to describe to a child how a strawberry tastes compared to a raspberry, how a carnation smells, why it is pleasurable to dance, what a pretty girl looks like."[4] The emotional definition of a situation or the precise meaning of human feelings may be determined almost entirely from facial expressions; from movements of the body, such as the gestures of a traffic officer; from expressions of excitement, such as weeping, blushing, or laughter; or from sounds, such as whistling, singing, or involuntary exclamations.

In Exhibit 13-4, the word *Chevrolet* appears only in the Internet address shown in very small print. However, the company's nameplate symbol communicates that the Blazer is part of the Chevrolet family of cars.

Encoding

In communication theory, the process by which a sender translates an idea to be communicated into a symbolic message, consisting of words, pictures, numbers, gestures, or the like, so that it can be transmitted to a receiver.

e x h i b 13-3

A Basic Model of the Communication Process

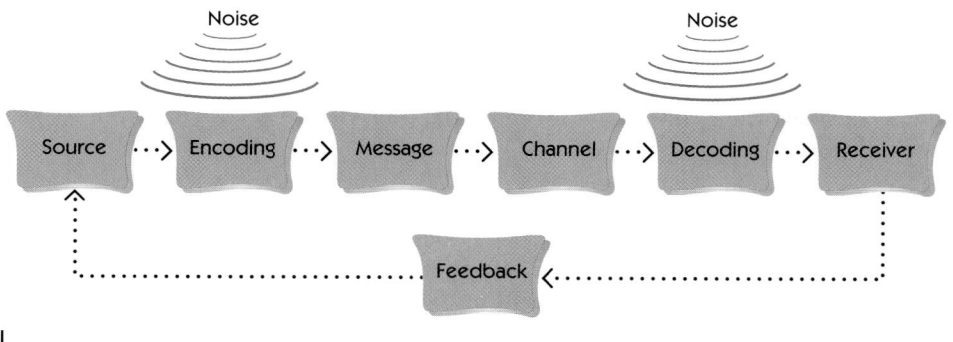

What Is Communicated in This Advertisement?

TRANSMITTING THE MESSAGE THROUGH A CHANNEL

Once the sender has created the message by encoding an idea into a transmittable form, it must be somehow conveyed to the receiver: It must be sent through a *channel of communication*, such as a magazine or other medium. Even people's casual conversations are sent through a channel, though the medium is the less obvious one of vibrating vocal cords, which send sound through air.

The message arrives at the receiver via the channel of communication. But some receivers will be more receptive than others. For example, some receivers of the communication about the Blazer will be consumers who for one reason or another (their age, their dislike of the outdoors) have little interest in a rugged vehicle that facilitates driving in mountains and rough terrain. It is the sender's job to pick the medium that will reach a maximum number of target receivers and a minimum number of nontarget receivers.

DECODING THE MESSAGE

The message arrives and is viewed, heard, or otherwise sensed by the receiver. But in order for communication to occur, the receiver must decode it. **Decoding** is the mental process by which the receiver interprets the meaning of the message. A difficulty encountered at this stage of the communication process is that receivers may interpret the message in different ways, given their particular biases, backgrounds, and other characteristics. That is, selective perception operates as the

Decoding
In communication theory, the process by which the receiver of a message interprets the message's meaning.

message is decoded. People interpret messages and give them meaning based on their personal experiences and backgrounds (see Chapter 5). An advertisement for cigarettes may be viewed differently by different people, for example. Nonsmokers may pass over the message entirely; antismokers may be angered by it; smokers satisfied with another brand may note the advertisement only casually. Some who see the advertisement may not "get it" at all; for whatever reason, the intended imagery may escape them completely.

In the Blazer advertisement, if the receiver interprets the message "like a rock" to mean that Blazers are tough, sturdy, and long lasting, the communication has worked.

FEEDBACK

Feedback
Communication of the receiver's reaction to a message back to the source.

Often, the communication process includes **feedback**, communication of the receiver's reaction that goes back to the source of the message. In a personal selling situation, the feedback may be direct and immediate, as when the customer raises questions about the product or states why he or she will not purchase it. Indeed, as mentioned, the great attraction of personal selling is that there can be a two-way conversation, which ensures greater understanding between the people involved.

Feedback about advertising, sales promotions, or publicity and public relations is in most cases slower and less direct. For instance, advertisers may conduct surveys, count coupon redemptions, or evaluate letters and telephone calls from consumers to learn the audience's reactions. Although advertisers can get delayed

Visual explanations are the sole basis for this communication, which explains how to set up a Bose Wave Radio audio system. Because there is no text, the poster can be used in any country around the world. Do you think the sender and the receiver will share a common sense of meaning?

http://www.bose.com

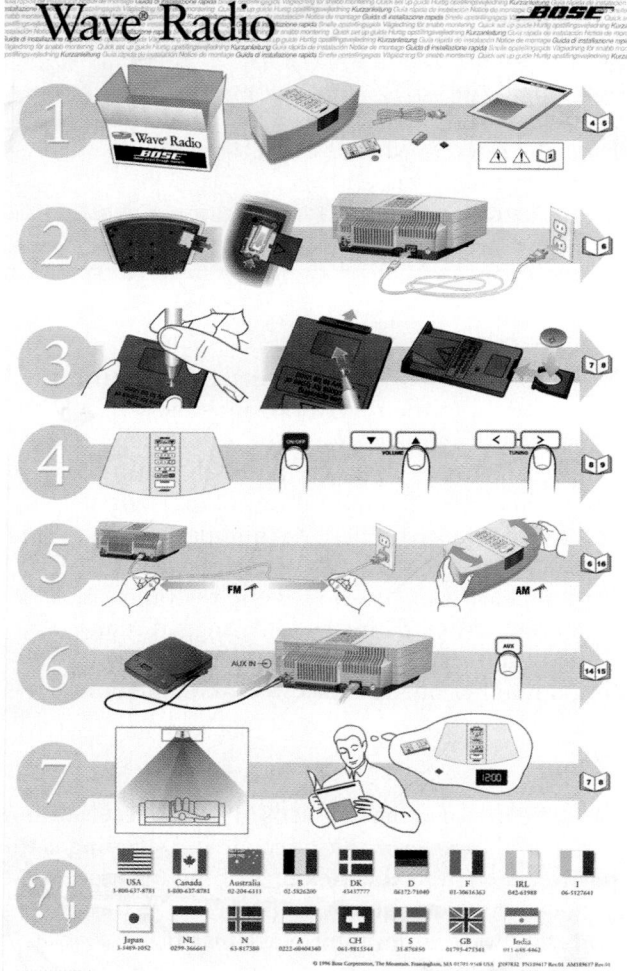

feedback about an advertisement's effectiveness, the feedback rarely provides all the desired information about the receivers' responses to the message.

Ideally, in perfect communication, the message that was decoded and entered the mind of the receiver would be exactly the same as the one the sender had in mind, encoded, and transmitted. If the sender and the receiver share a common social background and have similar needs, they are more likely to similarly interpret the meaning of the words and symbols in the message. Perfect transmission, though, is never possible. In many cases, however, the sender can develop messages that will be decoded by the target audience to communicate approximately the message the sender had in mind.

It is likely—perhaps even inevitable—that any communication process will be interrupted or distorted by factors that communication experts term "noise." **Noise** is interference or distraction, and it may disrupt any stage of the communication process. Noise may come in the form of conflicting messages, misunderstood terminology, inadequacies in the channel of communication, and so on. A listener might not hear a radio advertisement because of loud traffic noises outside the car. In a cigarette advertisement, the Surgeon General's warning (a conflicting message) is noise. The sources of noise may be external to the individual, such as traffic noises, or internal, such as daydreaming that prevents a listener from concentrating on a sales presentation. Many advertising messages cause people to think of a competing product. Brand loyalties and past learning are internal distractions that may interfere with the decoding process.

Noise
In communication theory, any interference or distraction that disrupts the communication process.

The Hierarchy of Communication Effects

Ford has extolled the virtues of its "built to last" theme thousands of times. McDonald's has made hundreds of different advertisements for its burgers. Why are there so many commercials for the same products? Creativity aside, the main reason is that a single communication, no matter how cleverly designed and implemented, may not be enough to persuade a customer to change an attitude or make a purchase. Promotion, as a rule, becomes more effective with repetition. Promotion usually seeks to change people, and people tend to change very slowly. Habits and beliefs developed over long periods of time will not be altered quickly by just a few messages. The presentation of a message may be varied, as in the McDonald's example, because the effectiveness of a promotion wears out as the repetitive presentation becomes boring.

> A single communication, no matter how cleverly designed and implemented, may not be enough to persuade a customer to change an attitude or make a purchase. Promotion, as a rule, becomes more effective with repetition.

Marketers have come to expect various responses to their communications. To understand the different effects that promotion may bring about, it is useful to think of the promotion process as a staircase, or series of steps in a hierarchy.

Promotion can be thought of as a force that moves people up a series of steps called the hierarchy of communication effects.[5] This promotion staircase is shown in Exhibit 13-5.

1. On the bottom step stand potential purchasers who are completely unaware of the existence of the product in question.
2. Closer to purchasing, but still a long way from the cash register, are those who are merely aware of the product's existence.

Promotion Moves Customers Up the Seven Steps in the Hierarchy of
Communication Effects

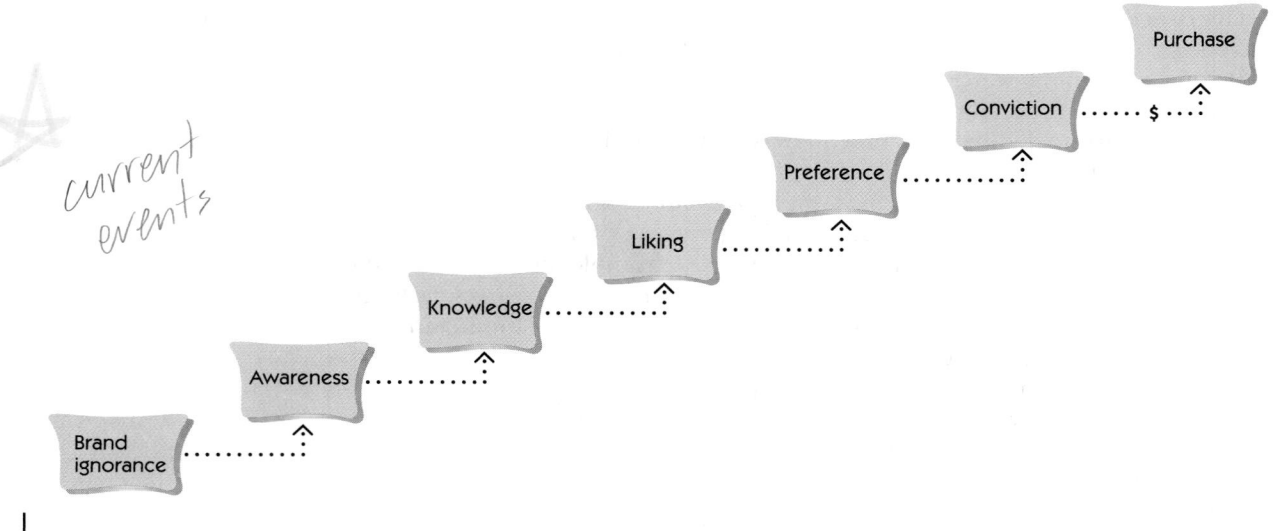

current events

3. Up one step are prospects who know what the product has to offer.
4. Still closer to purchasing are those who have favorable attitudes toward the product—those who like the product.
5. Those whose favorable attitudes have developed to the point that they prefer the product in question over all other possibilities are up still another step.
6. Even closer to purchasing are consumers who couple preference with a desire to buy and the conviction that the purchase would be wise.
7. Finally, of course, is the top step, where consumers translate this intention into an actual purchase.

According to this somewhat idealized portrayal, consumers may move through the seven-step hierarchy, from total ignorance of a brand's existence to purchase of that brand. When the purchase decision leads to a reward, the result is a satisfied, or reinforced, customer.

The hierarchy model shown in Exhibit 13-5 suggests that communication may not be a one-step process. Marketers use promotion to induce buyers to change— that is, to move up the staircase. Communication may be aimed at any step, depending on the objective of the communication. The question is "What step should the marketer aim at?"

Part of the answer comes from the nature of the product. Marketers of a totally new product such as the Flashback electronic recorder—a miniature device that uses no tape, has no moving parts, and records sound digitally onto a flash-memory chip—face a different set of communication problems than marketers of Windex. Windex's communication need not include an extensive discussion of the fact that the product provides fast, easy, streak-free cleaning. Most consumers are already aware of Windex's benefits. In contrast, the seller of a near-revolutionary product may need to devote considerable effort to explaining what the product is, how it works, and even that it works.

Whatever the product, the nature of the market is the most important consideration in deciding what step to aim at. The organization seeking to create an effective promotional message must begin with one of marketing's most basic rules: Identify the target market or, in this case, the target audience.

As discussed earlier, the whole communication process must be built around the intended receiver of the message. A key question, then, is "What is the target audience's psychological state?" If the marketing organization is attempting to influence those who are currently on the Awareness and Knowledge steps, a primary promotional objective will be to provide factual information. For example, according to many petroleum companies, most citizens are totally unaware of how oil company revenues are allocated. Thus, some of these companies spend a good portion of their advertising budgets in an effort to inform people of the true nature of the oil business. They demonstrate that a large portion of revenues are spent on additional exploration, on the development of products that enhance the lives of consumers, and on protecting the environment.

Appealing to consumers who are on the Liking and Preference steps calls for promotional messages aimed at encouraging existing favorable feelings toward the good or service offered. For example, advertisements for many cosmetics, fashion items, soft drinks, and airlines emphasize the fun or sophistication associated with the products. The target audiences in these cases already know about the brands and probably know that the company is a respected manufacturer or service provider. Thus, the advertisements stress emotional feelings toward the product offered.

Prospective customers who are on the Conviction step of the model are very close to action, but they may need a little shove to get them to act. A bit of encouragement may be all that is required. Being reminded that now is the time to buy, warned that prices may go up, or notified that a two-for-one coupon is available may motivate these consumers to move up the staircase to the final step, the purchase.

As you saw in Chapter 6, the sale is not the end of the line. The marketer may continue to use promotional messages to reinforce the buyer's belief that he or she made a

An American visitor to Chinese cities such as Shanghai and Beijing will see fleets of bicycles crowding the streets. So when Intel wanted to build awareness of its brand of computer chip in China, the company decided to use an inexpensive sales promotion. Intel distributed almost one million bike reflectors with the glow-in-the-dark message "Intel Inside. Pentium Processor."

http://www.intel.com

good buy or, later on, to remind the customer of the product and its value or effectiveness. For example, the advertisers of frequently purchased products like tomato sauce often remind buyers how satisfied they have been with the product. A promotion for an infrequently purchased durable good might advise the buyer to tell a friend about the purchase or to remember that the company sells other fine products. Such efforts often reduce consumers' post-purchase dissonance.

Sophisticated consumer behavior research suggests that some consumer purchasing decisions, especially those made when consumers have low involvement with the product, do not follow the steps in the hierarchy of communication effects. Nevertheless, this approach is useful in understanding how many promotions work.

THE HIERARCHY OF EFFECTS AND THE PROMOTIONAL MIX

As you have just seen, not all consumers are on the same step of the promotion staircase. Consumers on different steps will respond to different sorts of appeals.

Promotion can be thought of as a force that moves people up a series of steps called the hierarchy of communication effects. If the marketing organization is attempting to influence those who are in the Awareness and Knowledge steps, a primary promotional objective will be to move them to the Liking and Preference steps. Promotional messages for many products in the mature stage of the product life cycle, such as this one for Stetson fragrance, stress emotional feelings toward the product so as to reinforce liking and preference for a product customers already are familiar with.

http://www.stetson.com

This suggests that different elements of the promotional mix may be more effective with different consumers.

To some extent, they are. Exhibit 13-6 illustrates, in general terms, the relative importance of advertising and personal selling at different steps in the hierarchy of effects, classified as pre-transaction, transaction, and post-transaction stages of the buying process. (The transaction may be roughly defined as the period in which the exchange agreement or the negotiation of the terms of sale becomes final.)

In the pre-transaction stage, the consumer becomes aware of a brand, acquires knowledge, and formulates likes, dislikes, and preferences. The purpose of promotion at this stage is to inform, and advertising generally plays a larger role than personal selling. In the transaction stage, personal selling is important because the consumer must be persuaded to make a positive evaluation, develop a conviction, and actually make the purchase. In the post-transaction stage, advertising reminds and reassures consumers about their satisfaction.

These relationships are strongly influenced by the many forces that contribute to the purchase decision. The characteristics of the marketplace, the state of the economy, the nature of the product, and the seller's overall marketing strategy vary from case to case, but these general statements illustrate the roles advertising and personal selling play at each stage.

Push and Pull Strategies

The prime target of a promotional strategy may be either the ultimate consumer or a member of the distribution channel. Using the target as a basis for classification, we can identify the basic strategies of push and pull. No single strategy is purely one type or the other—but, in general, the strategies can be described as follows and illustrated as shown in Exhibit 13-7.

A **push strategy** emphasizes personal selling, advertising, and other promotional efforts aimed at members of the channel of distribution. Thus, the manufacturer of a product heavily promotes that product to wholesalers and other dealers. The wholesalers then promote the product heavily to retailers, which in turn direct their selling efforts to consumers. Not infrequently, the wholesalers and retailers are offered strong price incentives or discounts as part of this process. The term *push* comes from the fact that the manufacturer, with the help of other channel members, pushes the product through each level in the channel of distribution. The push strategy may be thought of as a step-by-step approach to promotion, with each channel member organizing the promotional efforts necessary to reach the channel member next in line.

In contrast, the manufacturer implementing a **pull strategy** attempts to stimulate demand for the product through promotional efforts aimed at the ultimate consumer or organizational buyer. The goal is to generate demand at the retail level in the belief that such demand will encourage retailers and wholesalers to

Push strategy
A promotional strategy whereby a supplier promotes a product to marketing intermediaries, with the aim of pushing the product through the channel of distribution.

Pull strategy
A promotional strategy whereby a supplier promotes a product to the ultimate consumer, with the aim of stimulating demand and thus pulling the product through the channel of distribution.

The Relative Importance of Advertising and Personal Selling Related to the Job to Be Done

	Steps in hierarchy of effects	Stage in consumer decision-making process	General purpose of promotion	Relative importance of advertising and personal selling
Pre-transaction	• Awareness • Knowledge • Liking • Preference	• Problem recognition • Search	Information to aid in recognition and understanding Information to create a positive feeling or affect	Personal selling Advertising
Transaction	• Conviction • Purchase	• Evaluation • Choice	Persuasion	Advertising Personal selling
Post-transaction		Post-purchase satisfaction	Reminder and reassurance	Personal selling Advertising

stock the product. If the customer is pulled into the store, each channel member will "pass the demand back" through the channel. In other words, the demand at the buyer end of the channel pulls the product through the channels of distribution.

Marketing organizations need not limit themselves to using only a push or only a pull strategy. Effective marketing often makes use of a combination of push and pull.

Promotional Campaigns

Throughout this chapter, we have considered the individual aspects of promotion while emphasizing that the parts of the promotional effort must fit together and complement each other. For example, a trade magazine mailed to owners of automobile muffler shops may do more than simply promote itself to potential buyers of advertising space as the place to advertise to reach target customers. The magazine's management may sponsor race cars or make awards to outstanding people in the muffler business, thereby building the magazine's image as a major force in the trade. All of these activities fit together into a unity of presentation that could be called the magazine publisher's total promotional effort or promotional mix.

Chapter 1 noted that military terminology is commonly used in football and in business. This tendency is evident in the term **promotional campaign**. A promotional campaign is a part of a firm's promotional mix, just as a military campaign is a portion of a total war effort. Thus, a promotional campaign is a series of promotional activities with a particular objective or set of objectives.

Promotional campaign
A series of promotional activities aimed at achieving a specific objective or set of objectives.

Flow of Promotional Dollars and Effort in Push and Pull Strategies

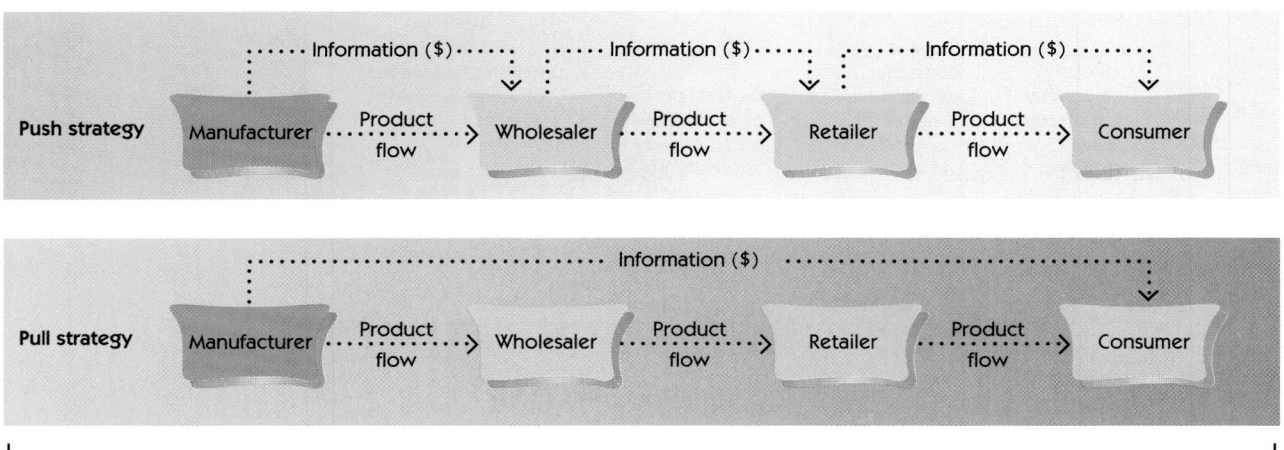

The phrase "particular objective" is important here, because it is this objective that indicates the goal to be reached. The campaign must be constructed to achieve that goal. The task of introducing a new product requires a promotional campaign considerably different from one intended to increase the sales of an established or widely recognized product.

Because most products are in the mature stage of the product life cycle, this section focuses primarily on promotional campaigns for these products. However, aspects of these strategies can also be applied to product introductions or to products in the growth stage. There are four major approaches to developing a promotional campaign for a mature product: image building, product differentiation, positioning, and direct response.

IMAGE BUILDING

The product or brand image is an individual's net impression of what the product or brand "is all about." It is the symbolic value associated with the brand. Buyers frequently prefer one product or brand over another because of its image. Thus, they often purchase or avoid brands or products not because of what they cost or how they work but because of what they say about the buyer-user—how they symbolize that person's personality or lifestyle. Marketers are properly concerned with this symbolic value or image. Thus, many promotional campaigns are aimed at **image building**.

Holiday Inn is one of the most recognized brands in the hotel/motel industry. However, over the years, many of the chain's hotels and motels had been neglected. Holiday Inn properties were often perceived as old, rundown, roadside motels with coffee shops. Today, the company is trying to replace its tarnished image with a more colorful, contemporary one, which communicates that it is a reinvigorated company. The message communicated in its advertising is "On the way. Every Holiday Inn as good as the best Holiday Inn."

Not-for-profit organizations are also concerned with image building. Consider the image of a Girl Scout, which has traditionally been one of dependability, trustworthiness, and honesty. In the MTV era, many young girls had come to see this positive image as being too squeaky-clean. Girl Scout membership had been dropping, especially in the 8–11 age group. Focus group research showed that these preteens perceived Girl Scouts as childish. So the organization's marketers de-

Image building

A promotional approach intended to communicate an image and generate consumer preference for a brand or product on the basis of symbolic value.

cided that the Girl Scouts had to move away from the uniformed, goody-goody image and show that Girl Scout meetings were a fun, mature, cool place to be.

To overcome its image as an organization that was "locked in time," the Girl Scouts used a promotional campaign aimed at making the organization more relevant to the older age group while emphasizing the activities available to all girls who join. The new image portrayed Girl Scouts as more action-oriented. For example, cookie packages showed Girl Scouts engaged in outdoor games such as volleyball. The not-for-profit organization developed an image-building advertising campaign that portrayed a hipper, more active organization. Using MTV-style graphics, TV advertising incorporated rap music and fantasy images, such as scenes of windsurfing, skiing, and parachuting, to suggest that the Scouts could offer girls a lot of fulfilling activities. One television ad closed with the line "The Girl Scouts. As great as you want to make it."[6]

In general, image-building promotional campaigns do not focus on product features but emphasize creating impressions. These may be impressions of status, sexuality, masculinity, femininity, reliability, or some other aspect of the brand's character thought to be alluring to target customers. Most advertisements for perfumes (such as Chanel No. 5 and Obsession) and clothing (Calvin Klein and Guess?) concentrate almost entirely on creating impressions.

PRODUCT DIFFERENTIATION

A promotional campaign aimed at developing **product differentiation** focuses on some dimension of the product that competing brands or competing products do not offer or accents some way in which using the product provides the solution to a consumer problem. For example, in its Piggyback suitcase advertising, Samsonite tries to persuade frequent flyers that they should think of this suitcase with wheels and a telescoping handle as a luggage cart that doubles as a suitcase. The advertising shows how sturdy construction and tie-down straps, which allow customers to pile on several other carry-on bags, make the Samsonite Piggyback suitcase different from regular bags. The promotional campaign focuses on attributes of the product, not its image or price.

Product differentiation and related promotional efforts often take the form of the **unique selling proposition (USP)**. As the name suggests, the basic idea of the USP is to identify and promote an aspect of the product that the competition

Product differentiation
A promotional approach in which the marketer calls buyers' attention to those aspects of a product or brand that set it apart from its competitors.

Unique selling proposition (USP)
A unique characteristic of a product or brand identified by the marketer as the one on which to base a promotional campaign. It is often used in a product-differentiation approach to promotion.

Beautyscene is an e-commerce business that markets cosmetics, fragrances, and health supplements. One of its advertisements shows a beautiful woman wrapped in the cord of a computer mouse. This one shows a woman's back being massaged with a component of a computer's central processing unit. These advertisements are part of an image-building campaign. Beautyscene wishes to create a strong image that blends beauty and technology together.

http://www.beautyscene.com

in the future, beauty will be more than skin deep

beautyscene.com
the future of beautiful

does not offer or, because of patents or other reasons, cannot offer easily. Energizer batteries were the first to have an "on-battery tester." Initially, Eveready and the Coppertop had no such feature and no such benefit. The on-battery testing feature provided Energizer with a unique selling proposition around which a promotional campaign was built. The USP tells buyers that if they buy the product, they will receive a specific, exclusive benefit.

Generally, mature products are not truly unique, especially from the point of view of performance. Yet *parity products*—those with ingredients nearly identical to those of competitors' brands, such as Tylenol's brand of acetaminophen—are often promoted as if they were special. This can be done because aspects of a product other than the strictly functional ones can be promoted as effectively as functional features. This fact is illustrated in the classic statement "Don't sell the steak, sell the sizzle." Keep in mind, though, that the point stressed in the unique selling proposition, whatever it is, must be meaningful to the potential buyer. It is possible to "sell the sizzle" only if the sizzle means something to the buyer—that is, if it satisfies a need. If buyers do not care about the USP, it does not influence the purchasing decision.

POSITIONING

You may recall that a brand's *competitive position* is the way consumers perceive it relative to its competition. The positioning approach, which promotes a brand's competitive position, is often the focal point of promotional campaigns. The campaign objective is to get consumers to view the brand from a particular perspective. When the National Football League launched the World League of American Football in Europe, the game was positioned and promoted somewhat differently than it is in North America. In Europe, American football is marketed as a fun outing for the family, not as the gladiatorial spectacle that it is in the United States. The focus of the promotions is to bring the family out to have an enjoyable afternoon. Emphasizing pregame festivities and postgame parties is part of the marketing effort.

In launching a positioning campaign, the marketer assumes that consumers have so much information about other brands and similar products that the campaign must create a distinct position for the brand in the prospect's mind. Xerox, long thought of as "the copier company," today positions itself as "the digital documents company," involved in faxing, scanning, copying, and printing. It wants to hold a position unoccupied by other competitors, who merely make photocopiers. Wild Oats Markets positions itself as an alternative to regular supermarkets. Its promotions communicate the message that Wild Oats is an organic community market working with artisan companies.

How do marketers go about positioning their brands? Exhibit 13-8 shows that there are many positioning strategies. It also suggests that brand image campaigns and product differentiation campaigns can be thought of as ways to position a product. Positioning strategies often communicate what a product does. Such strategies may promote a single product attribute—"the car dealer with the lowest prices in town"—or multiple attributes—"the high-performance luxury car." Sometimes the promotional campaign positions a brand in terms of its users— "for the working woman." In general, the important point about positioning is not what "selling point" is used as the basis of positioning but the idea that promotion can be used to position a brand relative to the competition. Note, too, that promotional campaigns that stress positioning are highly interrelated with the market segmentation strategy and the overall positioning strategy.

DIRECT-RESPONSE CAMPAIGNS

Recall our discussions in earlier chapters about direct channels of distribution, in which the manufacturer of a good or the producer of a service deals directly with the customer. The purpose of this "direct marketing" is to obtain a direct response, such as a sale.

FOCUS OF POSITIONING STRATEGY	EXAMPLE
Image of user	Volkswagen Passat: Drivers wanted
Image of quality	Hallmark: When you care enough to send the very best
Value/price	Suave: Beautiful hair doesn't have to cost a fortune
Product attribute	Heinz's rich and thick, slow-out-of-the-bottle ketchup is positioned as the "rude ketchup."
Product benefit	Florida Department of Citrus: Orange juice helps fight cancer, heart disease, colds and flu
Use or application	Arm & Hammer Baking Soda: Try adding Arm & Hammer along with your laundry detergent for a cleaner, fresher wash
Product class	Raid Baits: There's no better way to kill bugs dead
Competitor	Visa: The Olympics don't take American Express

A **direct-response campaign** is conducted specifically to elicit a direct, measurable response, such as an order, a donation, an inquiry, or a visit to a store or Web site. For example, a direct marketer such as L. L. Bean engages in a direct-response campaign by sending out its catalog. Of course, most personal selling (discussed in more detail in Chapter 15) fits in this category. However, the growing availability of highly targeted computerized databases and the rapid expansion of Internet shopping have brought increased prominence to direct-response promotions conducted via mail, telephone, and other media.

A direct-response campaign, like the other major promotional campaigns, may be used in conjunction with other strategies. The advertising and personal selling tactics associated with direct-response campaigns will be addressed in the next two chapters.

Direct-response campaign
A promotional approach intended to elicit a direct, measurable response, such as an order.

The Ethics of Persuasion

Of all the macromarketing issues involving promotion, the use of persuasion has attracted the most attention. The most common target of critics of promotion is persuasion in advertising, but every element of promotion has been criticized at one time or another.

An important aspect of this issue is the difference between informative and persuasive promotion. Most people would grant that some advertising or other promotion is needed; otherwise, consumers wouldn't know where to buy a product they wanted, whether a gas station would accept a credit card, or what freeway exit leads to a motel. Thus, critics often maintain that informative advertisements are fine. They argue, however, that it is not right to use marketing skills, psychology, and expensive commercials to persuade consumers to buy a product, vote for a particular candidate, or give to a certain charity. For example, many would argue that all cigarette advertising should be banned because it promotes an unhealthful product. In summary, the basic argument is that persuasive advertisements are wasteful and manipulative.

A common defense against such criticism is that advertisements for an inferior product are almost certain to sell the product only once. Even the richest companies with the best sales records sometimes lose millions of dollars introducing products that fail in the marketplace. In fact, the quickest way to kill a poor product is to promote it aggressively. People will find out about its inferior nature just that much more quickly.

Your own answer to questions about the proper use of persuasion will be influenced by your view of whether people are—or should be—able to exercise freedom of choice. Are consumers able to control their own destinies? Do you ever not

what went right?

IBM e-business To position itself as a company on the cutting edge of electronic commerce, IBM developed an advertising campaign that promotes the notion of "e-business." The term was new when the campaign began; however, since then it has been widely used in stories by the news media and in the marketing campaigns of other companies. The IBM ad campaign has featured customers of all kinds, from body-pierced Web designers to corporate titans. Its implicit message is that the Internet is not about just putting up a Web site—it is the technological starting point for a complex re-thinking of how business is done. The ads say, in effect, "Trust us, we're IBM, we know more about business and complex technology than anyone else."[7]

buy products you see advertised? Have you ever said no to a salesperson? Why? Rethinking the earlier discussions of the hierarchy of needs, selective perception, and other aspects of consumer behavior should help you to make a decision on this issue. Chapters 14 and 15 address several specific issues involved in the ethics of advertising, personal selling, sales promotion, and public relations.

Summary

Promotion consists of four elements: personal selling, advertising, publicity (as part of a public relations effort), and sales promotion. All must be integrated into the promotional mix.

1) Discuss the three basic purposes of promotion.
Promotion is communication designed to inform, to persuade, and to remind buyers about the existence and benefits of a good, service, or idea. Without promotion, buyers would have less information on which to base their buying decisions.

2) Define the four major elements of promotion.
Personal selling occurs when a seller communicates a persuasive message directly to a buyer. Advertising includes any persuasive message carried by a non-personal medium and paid for by an identified sponsor. Publicity involves a message that is not paid for and has no identified sponsor, delivered

through a mass medium. Sales promotion consists of nonroutine, temporary promotional efforts designed to stimulate buyer purchases or dealer effectiveness in a specified time period.

3) Describe the basic model for all communication processes, including promotion.
The communication process occurs when a source encodes a message and sends it through a channel to a receiver, who must decode it and may respond with feedback. Noise may interfere. Each element in the process plays an essential role in the transference of a message from the source to the receiver.

4) Explain the hierarchy of communication effects.
Consumers often move through a seven-step hierarchy in relation to a product: ignorance, awareness, knowledge, liking, preference, conviction, and purchase. Consumers at different steps have different communication needs.

5) Explain how the elements of promotion can be used to support one another in a promotional campaign.

The effective marketer integrates all the elements of promotion—advertising, personal selling, publicity/public relations, and sales promotion—into a promotional mix. Such a mix is planned to meet the information requirements of all target customers. Each element of the mix performs a task. Some elements may be aimed at the target customer at a lower stage of the hierarchy of communication effects; others may be aimed at potential customers near the top of the staircase. Advertising's strength is in creating awareness and spreading information to a wide audience. Personal selling is best at moving buyers from liking to conviction to purchase.

6) Describe the general promotional strategies known as push and pull strategies.

A push strategy is directed toward members of a channel of distribution. A pull strategy is directed toward consumers in order to stimulate demand for the product.

7) Discuss promotional campaigns and provide examples.

A promotional campaign consists of promotional activities designed to achieve specific objectives. An image-building approach stresses the symbolic value associated with the product. A product-differentiation approach emphasizes unique product features. A positioning approach promotes a brand in relation to competing brands. A direct-response campaign seeks a direct measurable response.

Key Terms

advertising (p. 375)
communication (p. 377)
decoding (p. 379)
direct-response campaign (p. 389)
electronic interactive media (p. 374)
encoding (p. 378)
feedback (p. 381)
image building (p. 386)
integrated marketing
  communications (p. 377)

mass media (p. 373)
noise (p. 381)
personal media (p. 374)
personal selling (p. 375)
product differentiation (p. 387)
promotional campaign (p. 385)
promotional mix (p. 377)
publicity (p. 375)
pull strategy (p. 384)
push strategy (p. 384)

receiver (p. 377)
sales promotion (p. 376)
source (p. 377)
unique selling proposition (USP)
  (p. 387)

Questions for Review & Critical Thinking

1. Identify the type of promotion being used in each of the following cases, and comment on its effectiveness.
   a. A Chicago Cubs announcer wears a Budweiser jacket during a televised game.
   b. A TV ad says, "CNN Headline News: If you don't have it, [tell] your cable operator to get it."
   c. A Special Olympics representative telephones at 8:15 p.m. while you are watching your favorite TV show and asks you to make a donation.
   d. As a forward receives the basketball, the announcer says, "Here comes the Windex man."
   e. At the supermarket, a banner announces a scratch-and-win bingo game.
   f. During a corporate takeover attempt, a corporate raider invites television reporters from major cities to question him during a live satellite news conference. Reporters are allowed to splice in video of themselves for the evening news so that it appears that each local reporter has spoken to the corporate executive in an exclusive interview rather than via a satellite hookup.

2. What is sales promotion? Give some creative examples of sales promotion.
3. Using the communication model shown in Exhibit 13-3, give examples of the encoding and decoding that might take place during the personal selling process.
4. What is noise in the communication process?
5. How does selective perception enter into the communication process?
6. How does a push strategy differ from a pull strategy?
7. Comment on the following: "Promotion mirrors the values and lifestyles of the target consumers."
8. For each of the following brands, indicate whether the primary promotional strategy is likely to be image building, positioning, or a unique selling proposition.
   a. Mountain Dew soft drink
   b. MTV
   c. SnackWell cookies
   d. BMW convertibles
9. Form small groups as directed by your instructor. Outline a promotional campaign for your college or university in general or for the business department or school in particular.

1. The promotional mix and promotional strategy should be an integrated marketing communication. Take a look at Mama's Cucina, an Internet site at either http://www.eat.com or http://www.ragu.com.

   This Web site is constantly changing. However, you should find selections such as Mama's New Sauces, Mama's Italian Cookbook, Goodies from Mama, Learn to Speak Italian, and Family Room. Select several options from the menu, and evaluate Ragú's promotional efforts. Answer the following questions, and bring your answers to class:
   a. Why does a spaghetti sauce company need a site on the Internet?
   b. Why does Ragú have recipes on this Web site?
   c. Why did Ragú use the personality of Mama rather than the authority of the company?
   d. Explain the messages communicated on the Ragú Web page in terms of the communication model presented in Exhibit 13-3.
2. Go to http://www.adage.com to learn the advertising news of the day. Write a short summary of an article you read.
3. Go to the PR Newswire Web site at http://www.prnewswire.com, and select two news releases. What do they have in common?

Address Book (Useful URLs)

Integrated Marketing Communications, Inc.	http://www.intmark.com
Communications Arts Magazine	http://www.commarts.com

Ethically Right or Wrong?

A London advertising agency created a television commercial showing a disheveled streeet person walking into a liquor store with a handful of panhandled coins. Asking for "the usual," he is served a brown-paper package. When he removes the contents, the viewer sees not a bottle of cheap whiskey but instead a jar of Heinz Salad Cream, a flavored mayonnaise of the Miracle Whip variety. What happens next is startling: The homeless man walks a few steps to a trash can and starts picking through it for discarded food. Next the viewers hear an announcer's voice: "Any food tastes supreme with Heinz Salad Cream."[8]

This advertisement gets the viewer's attention by presenting a shocking situation. However, is it ethical to poke fun at the plight of the homeless?

TAKE A STAND

1. Because showing a brand in a movie offers promotional benefits, some movie studios charge fees to feature products. For example, a studio might charge $20,000 simply to show the product, $40,000 to show the product and have an actor mention the brand name, and $60,000 to have an actor actually use the product. Is this policy ethical?
2. A tobacco company hands out free samples of a smokeless tobacco (snuff) at a college football game. Is this ethical?
3. Public television stations don't allow commercials, but they mention the names of program sponsors at the ends of the programs. Should this practice be stopped?
4. H. G. Wells claimed that "advertising is legalized lying." Do you agree?
5. Every Sunday afternoon on the campus of a New Jersey college, the admissions office becomes the center of promotional activity. Eight students, paid an hourly wage, call college prospects, who are not expecting the calls, and promote the virtues of the college from a student's point of view. The student telemarketers are trained and supervised like any other sales force. If an applicant is accepted, a faculty member in his or her major field calls the new student to talk about the course schedule. Should colleges engage in activities like this?

VIDEO CASE 13-1
Boyne USA (B)

Boyne USA, the fifth largest ski operator in the United States, operates skiing, golf, and lodging properties thoughout the nation.

Boyne Mountain and Boyne Highlands, two neighboring ski areas close to Petoskey, Michigan, are typical of Boyne's ski resorts. They offer similar lift capacities, but Boyne Highlands has slightly more advanced terrain than Boyne Mountain. Night skiing is available on weekends, holidays, and on Tuesday evenings throughout the season. Boyne Highlands' base village is the larger of the two, accommodating up to 900 guests and incorporating three heated outdoor pools. An excellent deal for kids—free skiing up to age 9, then a scale of generous discounts right up to age 19—is offered at both areas.

The first North American resort to install a six-seater chair lift, Boyne Mountain's 41 runs are up to a mile long over a 500-foot vertical. Although the trails predominantly suit beginners and intermediates, 3 percent of the trails are rated "experts only." Snow making equipment can cover 100 percent of the slopes. The base village can accommodate up to 600 guests; facilities include a new warm outdoor pool and a huge hot tub, as well as ice skating, a sauna, massage, gym, and beauty parlor. There are several restaurants, cafés, and bars.

Northern Michigan is recognized as America's Summer Golf Capital. The six championship courses at Boyne Mountain and Boyne Highlands are among the country's finest. Nestled among the scenic golf courses and ski slopes at Boyne Highlands, the Country Club of Boyne offers classic luxury and a showcase of amenities. This is golf at its world-class best. Members may play on all seven Boyne championship 18-hole courses, including some designed by Robert Trent Jones, Sr., Donald Ross, and Arthur Hills.

Bay Harbor Village is another Boyne resort in Michigan. It includes lodging at the Inn at Bay Harbor and the Bay Harbor Golf Course, which is one of the ten best in the United States.

Promoting Destination Resorts and seasonal golf and skiing activities is an important marketing activity at Boyne. The company targets corporate customers holding conventions and sales meetings at the resorts and individual consumers seeking recreation and vacation activities. The organization uses advertising, public relations, event marketing, sales promotions, an Internet Web site, and personal selling. One of Boyne's communications goals is to promote individual resorts yet to have a common corporate identity. It strives to achieve integrated marketing communications.[9]

QUESTIONS
1. Is it possible to promote many individual resorts and the corporation at the same time?
2. What is integrated marketing communications? How could advertising, public relations, event marketing, sales promotions, a Web site, and personal selling be coordinated at Boyne?

Advertising and Public Relations in an e-commerce World

14

chapter

Internet entrepreneurs are forever obsessing about strategies that will keep their customers coming back. AllAdvantage.com, a fast-growing startup with more than 3 million members after its first eight months, has come up with a new solution: Put them all on your payroll. In a recent month, the company sent checks to its members totaling more than $8 million.

Rich LeFurgy, chairman of the Internet Advertising Bureau and a partner in a venture firm backing AllAdvantage, claims the company is starting a revolution in media-audience relations. "The television industry would happily pay audiences to watch commercials if it could monitor consumer reaction," LeFurgy argues. The Net, on the other hand, enables advertisers and viewers to have that direct dialogue, and AllAdvantage hopes to broker the value of consumer attention.

At first blush, AllAdvantage's business model resembles that of NetZero, GoToWorld.com, ePIPO, and a growing legion of other Net companies that reward users for watching ads on the Web. To sign up for AllAdvantage, consumers fill out a short form that asks for name, postal address, e-mail address, and age. Then they download the software. Dubbed the Viewbar, the software occupies an inch-high block on the screen—users elect whether to place it above or below the browser—that streams banner-style ads whenever the PC is connected to the Net. AllAdvantage targets these ads to users based almost entirely on their surfing habits; while age and zip code are also key filters used for ad serving, the company does not solicit other personal data or depend on consumer surveys.

The Viewbar comes installed with a money light. Keep surfing and the green light stays on. Leave your computer idle for long and the light turns red, indicating that you're no longer earning money. The Viewbar can be clicked into oblivion at any point; just remember, unmetered browsing means you're leaving money on the table. Not that the cash flows interminably anyway. The company pays 50 cents for each hour a member is zipping around online, up to a maximum of 25 hours a month, or $12.50.

But it's not technology alone that distinguishes AllAdvantage from its cash-for-eyeballs competitors. AllAdvantage has surged ahead of the pack, thanks to a marketing scheme that transforms its core members into rabid recruiters. AllAdvantage members earn money from ads watched by everyone they refer. While members are limited on the money they earn for their own browsing time, they ring up an additional 10 cents for each hour their friends surf. And if these direct referrals go on to sign up their own friends, the original Adam or Eve earns an additional nickel for each hour these "expanded referrals" browse.

Scoff at nickels and dimes if you will, but one month the highest earning AllAdvantage member pulled in nearly $5,500, while another 44 members were sent checks for more than $1,000. Not bad for chump change.[1]

AllAdvantage is pioneering the use of the Internet as a new advertising medium. The story behind AllAdvantage illustrates the fascinating, ever-changing world of advertising. Whether a marketer is advertising on the Internet or in traditional media, the power of advertising can be amazing.

This chapter explores the captivating world of advertising. The chapter begins with a general discussion of the purpose of advertising. Next, it outlines the stages in an advertising campaign and describes each stage. It examines communication goals and advertising objectives, creative strategy, media strategy, and the use of research to evaluate these strategies. Finally, the chapter closes with a consideration of ethics.

The Nature of Advertising

Chapter 13 defined advertising as a message carried by a nonpersonal medium and paid for by an identified sponsor. This definition indicates two basic parts of advertising: the message and the medium. The two work together to communicate the right ideas to the right audience.

Advertising promotes goods, services, and ideas in mass media, such as television, radio, newspapers, and magazines, to reach a large number of people at once. It serves as a substitute for a salesperson's talking to an individual prospect. Mass media advertising is one-way communication and, unlike a salesperson, cannot receive direct feedback and immediately handle objections.

Advertisers, who must pay the mass media to present their advertisements, or commercials, control the exact nature of the one-way message that will be communicated to the target audience. The impersonal nature of advertising also allows marketers to control the timing and degree of repetition. These features often provide benefits that far outweigh the disadvantages associated with lack of feedback.

Marketers of soft drinks, cosmetics, soaps, and many other products that do not require direct and immediate feedback often rely heavily on advertising. For these marketers, the challenge is to present messages effectively to an audience that may not be interested in seeing or hearing them. They must contend with readers who quickly turn the magazine page or viewers who tape-record television programs and then fast-forward through commercials. They must cope with competitors that use advertising to compare brands. Because of these demands, advertising is often highly creative and innovative.

We all recognize and appreciate creative advertising. You probably remember a humorous Diet Pepsi commercial or dramatic Nike commercial that grabbed your attention. You may even have talked to your friends about some advertising you liked. Creative advertising can stimulate people to talk about products, services, and ideas. This word-of-mouth communication may be one of the most effective means of communicating a message to prospective customers. Advertising's power to influence word-of-mouth communication can be a great asset to a marketer.

Advertising supports other promotional efforts. It may communicate information about a sales promotion or announce a public relations event. Advertising helps the salesperson "get a foot in the door" by preselling prospects. A salesperson's job can be made much easier if advertising informs prospects about unique product benefits or encourages prospects to contact a salesperson. Without advertising, the salesperson's efforts may be hindered by the prospect's lack of knowledge about the company or its products.

Advertising can be subdivided into many different categories. A very basic scheme classifies advertising as product advertising or institutional advertising.

PRODUCT ADVERTISING

Product advertisement
An advertisement promoting a specific product.

Advertisements for E*Trade, Garth Brooks concerts, Hilton hotels, Lego building blocks, and many other brands are clearly intended to persuade consumers to purchase a particular product—indeed, a particular brand. These are **product advertisements**. An advertisement for Ford trucks that declares "Ford trucks—the best never rest" and suggests that viewers go down to the local Ford dealership is a product advertisement because it features a specific product.

If the Ford advertisement goes on to recommend that viewers go to the showroom for a test drive during an inventory reduction sale—that is, if it suggests an immediate purchase—it is also a **direct-action advertisement**, or *direct-response advertisement*. Many television advertisements and many direct-mail efforts are of this type. Those that include both direct-action advertising and a direct channel of distribution are a popular form of direct marketing. For example, companies in the recording industry frequently urge consumers to order special albums by calling a toll-free number and using a credit card. The Book-of-the-Month Club mails announcements of its latest offering to club members' homes and includes a return envelope so that the customer can order the latest selections. Direct-action advertisements, in general, utilize coupons, toll-free telephone numbers, or invitations to call collect in order to facilitate action and encourage people to "buy now." Much retail and Internet advertising emphasizes direct action.

Less assertive forms of product advertising are designed to build brand image or position a brand for an eventual sale rather than to sell merchandise right this minute. For example, consider an advertisement portraying the romance and adventure of Jamaica. The advertiser knows that the consumer is not going to run directly to a travel agency after seeing such an advertisement. The objective is to provide information so that the next time the family is considering a vacation, Jamaica will be among the spots considered. Such so-called **indirect-action advertisements** use a soft-sell approach calculated to stimulate sales in the long run.

INSTITUTIONAL ADVERTISING

Institutional advertisements aim to promote an organizational image, to stimulate generic demand for a product category, or to build goodwill for an industry. "Baseball fever . . . catch it" is an institutional advertising slogan. So are DuPont's "Better things for better living" and United Artists' "Escape . . . to the movies." These institutional advertising slogans do not stress a particular ball team, brand, or movie. Instead, they accent the sponsoring institutions. The baseball advertisement, for example, attempts to build demand for the sport as a whole. The advertisements paid for by DuPont and United Artists stress how wonderful, responsible, or efficient those companies are. Contrasting the "baseball fever" slogan with such team slogans as "Royals baseball. You've got a hit on your hands" or "Wrigley Field—there's no place like it" makes the difference between institutional advertising and product advertising quite clear.

Planning and Developing Advertising Campaigns

Developing an effective advertising campaign requires a stream of interconnected decisions on such matters as budgeting and media, as well as a strong creative strategy. The process followed in planning and developing an advertising program is shown in Exhibit 14-1.

Ahh, the power of Cheese.
www.ilovecheese.com

Direct-action advertisement
An advertisement designed to stimulate immediate purchase or encourage another direct response; also called a *direct-response advertisement*.

Indirect-action advertisement
An advertisement designed to stimulate sales over the long run.

Institutional advertisement
An advertisement designed to promote an organizational image, stimulate generic demand for a product, or build goodwill for an industry.

The purpose of this institutional advertisement is to encourage increased consumption of cheese. The goal of America's Dairy Farmers is to stimulate generic demand for all cheese brands rather than demand for a particular brand of cheese.

http://www.ilovecheese.com

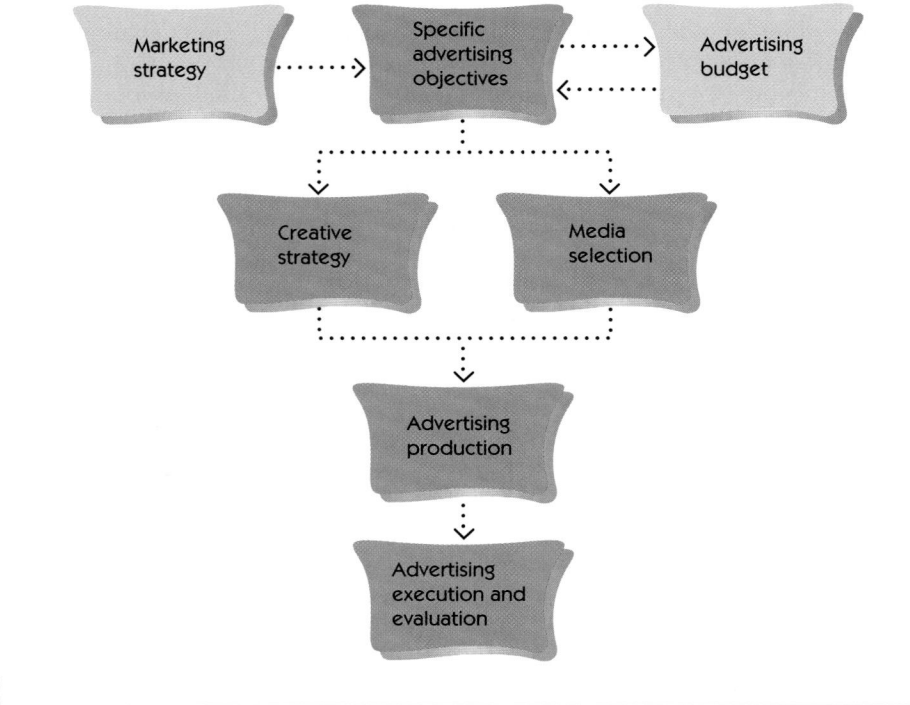

Advertising Planning and Development

Before developing a single advertisement, management must ask what the advertising is expected to do. Of course, advertising is supposed to sell the product. That statement, however, is too broad to be truly useful to marketing planners.

COMMUNICATION GOALS FOR ADVERTISING

What are appropriate goals for advertising? Because advertising is a method of communication, objectives directly related to advertising should be **communication goals**. In general, advertisers want to accomplish four broad communication goals: Advertisements are expected to generate attention, to be understood, to be believed, and to be remembered. These goals relate to selling the product, but they are primarily matters of communication.

If these broad communication objectives are not considered and met, more specific objectives will not be met either. For example, if no one pays attention to an advertisement, the advertisement cannot achieve its more specific objective of, say, enhancing a romantic brand image. Likewise, an advertisement must be understood and believed if it is to reinforce or change perceptions and attitudes about a brand's characteristics. And if it is not remembered, an advertisement will have little effect on buyer behavior. With these broad objectives in mind, marketers developing advertising campaigns can set more specific objectives.

SPECIFIC ADVERTISING OBJECTIVES

Encouraging increased consumption of a product by current users, generating more sales leads, increasing brand awareness, increasing repeat purchases, and supporting the personal selling effort are typical specific objectives for advertisements. As Exhibit 14-1 illustrates, these objectives are developed from the marketing strategy and provide the framework for creative strategy and media selection.

Communication goals
In the context of marketing, what the marketer wants a promotional message to accomplish: to gain attention, to be understood, to be believed, and to be remembered.

Many advertisements have disappeared from the media, even though "everybody liked them," because they did not contribute to accomplishment of specific objectives. For example, almost everyone who saw it enjoyed a unique television advertising campaign featuring a fictitious (off-screen) giant armadillo that rambled across the Lone Star State, terrorizing Texans in its quest to satisfy its unquenchable thirst for Lone Star beer. Texans loved to talk to friends about the exploits of the state's favorite animal. However, the advertisements, while humorous and attention-getting, did not sell the product. Because the ultimate objective is to sell the product, the advertisements were changed. A "great" advertisement that does not contribute to success in increasing market share, introducing a new product, or the like is only great in the creative sense. In the business sense, it is far from great.

> Advertisements are expected to generate attention, to be understood, to be believed, and to be remembered.

Opportunities in the marketplace, competitors' advertising campaigns, and prior marketing strategy decisions, such as selection of a target market segment, all influence the development of specific advertising objectives. An important influence is the product's stage in the life cycle.

ADVERTISING OBJECTIVES AND THE PRODUCT LIFE CYCLE

Advertising objectives change with environmental conditions, as do all other aspects of marketing. Marketing is dynamic; advertising, as one of its most visible components, must be especially reflective of change.

Once again, the concept of the product life cycle can be used to illustrate the changes. Exhibit 14-2 shows how advertising objectives change over the course of a product's life. During the introductory stage of the cycle, developing consumer brand awareness and getting customers to try the product are normal advertising objectives. Trade advertising, which is aimed at attracting distributors and interesting them in carrying the product, is equally important, although less obvious, during this stage. Additional trade advertising may be developed later, with the objective of increasing the numbers of distributors and retail outlets.

At the start of the product life cycle, it may be necessary to develop **primary demand**, or *generic demand*, for the product—that is, demand for the product class as a whole. This kind of advertising, which often must be so basic as to explain what a product is and how it works, is called **primary demand advertising**. It seeks to introduce the product rather than to make brand comparisons. Advertising of this sort is also called *pioneering advertising*.

Primary demand
Demand for a product class as a whole, without regard to brand; also known as *generic demand*.

Primary demand advertising
Advertising aimed at stimulating primary demand; also known as *pioneering advertising*.

Advertising for a mature brand, such as French's mustard, may be aimed at regular, brand-loyal users. Its purpose is substantially different from that of advertising used to introduce a new product. Promotion to loyal customers requires a campaign designed to remind them of the product's image and of their satisfaction with the product; regular buyers do not need detailed information about the product. In the case of mature products, then, advertisers give relatively little emphasis to explaining product features. Messages become

e—commerce Changing Everything

With the Comet Cursor, Comet Systems, Inc. has created a new form of online advertising. This rich media technology lets Web advertisers display a customized graphic or animation in place of the conventional "arrow" cursor. Comet Systems' technology is now used on over 50,000 Web sites; licensees include Warner Bros. Online, AT&T WorldNet, Comedy Central, Mattel, and Universal Studios Online.

Objectives Change over the Product Life Cycle

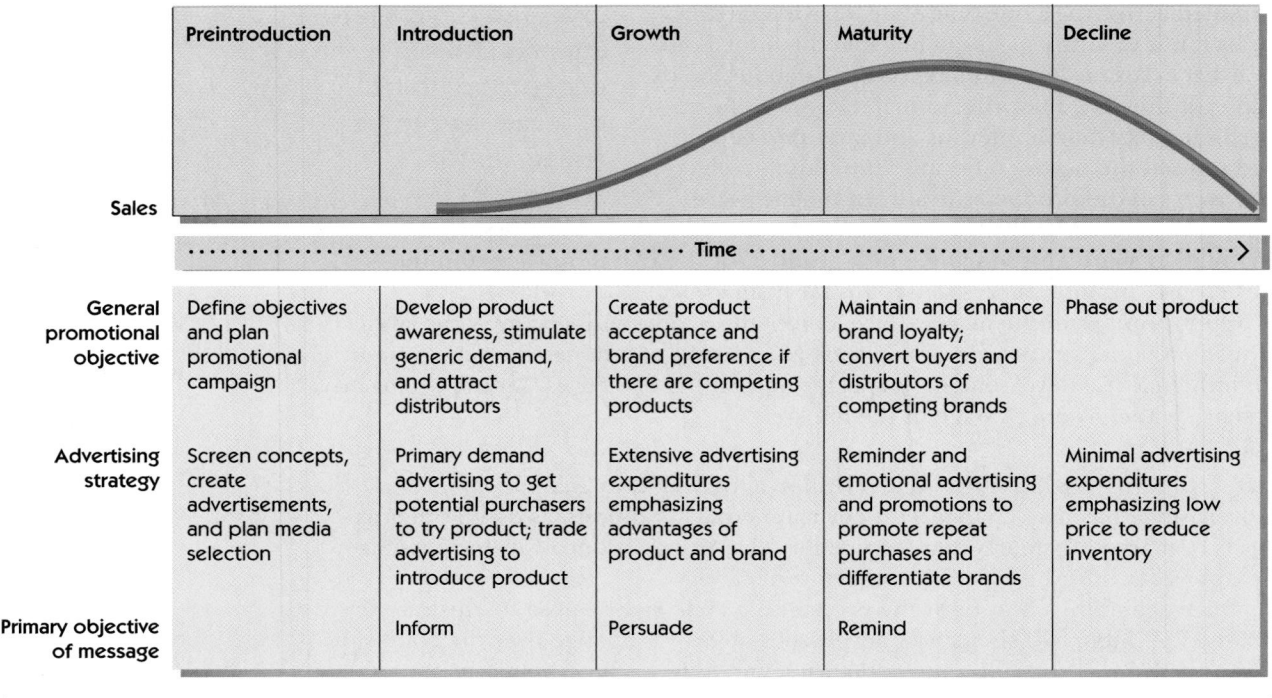

	Preintroduction	Introduction	Growth	Maturity	Decline
General promotional objective	Define objectives and plan promotional campaign	Develop product awareness, stimulate generic demand, and attract distributors	Create product acceptance and brand preference if there are competing products	Maintain and enhance brand loyalty; convert buyers and distributors of competing brands	Phase out product
Advertising strategy	Screen concepts, create advertisements, and plan media selection	Primary demand advertising to get potential purchasers to try product; trade advertising to introduce product	Extensive advertising expenditures emphasizing advantages of product and brand	Reminder and emotional advertising and promotions to promote repeat purchases and differentiate brands	Minimal advertising expenditures emphasizing low price to reduce inventory
Primary objective of message		Inform	Persuade	Remind	

increasingly symbolic as the product "ages." Partly, this reflects the fact that mature products have found their niche in the marketplace. They have been positioned, either by marketers or by the competitive forces of the market itself, to appeal to smaller and more specialized market segments than when they were new and lacked intense competition.

An advertising campaign for a product in the maturity stage of the product life cycle may not explain anything about the characteristics of the product. Often the advertisements reflect the psychological or emotional dimensions of the brand or the situations in which it is consumed. For example, the essence of Campbell Soup's advertising is the emotional aspects of nurture and nourishment. One of its television commercials portrays a young girl arriving at her new foster home. Overwhelmed, the child withdraws within herself—unable to speak until her foster mother brings her a steaming bowl of Campbell's soup. "My mommy used to fix me this soup," the child says quietly. The foster mother, fighting back tears, responds, "My mother used to make it for me too." The commercial closes with the woman and the child sharing memories.[2] Because most products on the market are in the maturity stage, much advertising uses psychological benefits to differentiate brands. Such advertisements stress the reasons a brand is better than its competitors, instead of emphasizing the newness or uniqueness of the generic product, as is done at the start of the product life cycle. Advertising of this kind is called **selective demand advertising**.

The most commonly encountered advertising objectives for mature products may be summarized as follows:

1. Increase the number of buyers
   - Convert buyers of competing brands
   - Appeal to new market segments

Selective demand advertising
Advertising aimed at stimulating demand for a particular brand.

- Reposition the brand
2. Increase the rate of usage among current users
   - Remind customers to use the brand
   - Inform regular consumers of new uses
   - Enhance brand loyalty and reduce brand switching among current customers

After determining the advertising campaign's objective, marketing managers begin to develop a creative strategy and to select advertising media. These activities are interrelated. In fact, the interrelationship between advertisement and medium is so strong that it is often impossible to tell whether the selection of the medium or the development of the advertisement comes first. For the purposes of our discussion, we will first examine how marketers create and produce advertisements and commercials.

L'original

As lower-priced bottled waters flood the market, Evian uses its advertising to position itself as "L'original." This ad, featuring a beautiful woman bathing in a tub filled with Evian, is based on an urban legend that the elite bathe in Evian. In other ads, a woman treats her goldfish to the French water and a bartender mixes a cocktail from small and large bottles of Evian. The series is a good example of an advertising campaign for a mature product. The advertisements reflect the psychological and emotional dimensions of the brand and consumers' enthusiasm for the product.

http://www.evian.com

Creative Strategy

In advertising, the generation of ideas and the development of the advertising message or concept make up the **creative process**. Actually, creativity is necessary to all aspects of the marketing mix, but the term has come to be particularly associated with the work of the people who actually develop and construct advertisements. Whether creative activity is based on information gathered by marketing research or on analysis by management, the basic thrust of an advertising message is developed primarily by the creative departments of advertising agencies.

Discussing creativity is a difficult task. It is possible to outline schematically the steps involved in the creative process, as illustrated in Exhibit 14-3. The role played by that elusive something called "creativity," however, can only be shown as a "creative spark." Advertising objectives provide a framework for creative efforts, but the creative spark is probably what makes an advertisement persuasive.

Advertising copy writers, art directors, and other creative people are responsible for the task of answering two questions: "What to say?" and "How to say it?" These questions reflect the two basic parts of the creative strategy.

WHAT TO SAY—THE APPEAL

The central idea of an advertising message is referred to as the **advertising appeal**. The purpose of the appeal, and of the advertisement, is to tell potential buyers what the product offers and why the product is or should be appealing to them. Thinking about advertisements you have seen will bring to mind the many kinds of appeals advertisers employ. It may be that the product has sex appeal, is compatible with the target customer's lifestyle (or desired lifestyle), or solves some particular problem such as "morning mouth," "medicine breath," or the need for healthy gums. Commercial messages that make firm promises, like "Never again will you have to weed your lawn, thanks to Jiffy Kill," are not uncommon. Many

Creative process
In the context of advertising, the generation of ideas and the development of the advertising message or concept.

Advertising appeal
The central theme or idea of an advertising message.

Creativity Is an Important Aspect of the Advertising Process

advertisers believe that specifically describing the answer to a problem in this manner is the most effective approach. Other advertisements, such as those for cosmetics, beer, and hotels, are built around less straightforward appeals that stress brand image.

When the same advertising appeal is used in several different advertisements to provide continuity in an advertising campaign, it is referred to as an **advertising theme**. The U.S. Army, for example, uses the theme "Be all that you can be" in its advertising to both high school dropouts and college graduates.

"What to say?" and "How to say it?" These questions reflect the two basic parts of the creative strategy.

To get a feel for how creative advertising appeals vary across an industry, it is useful to consider several brands of the same product and the advertisements developed for each.

The Visa credit card is positioned and advertised as the most widely accepted card. Advertising communicates the message that, because Visa is accepted at more places, it is "Everywhere you want to be."

MasterCard takes a different approach, advertising itself as a smart payment method associated with success and accomplishment. For instance, one MasterCard commercial shows a father and a son at a baseball game. It explains that tickets cost $28 and hot dogs, popcorn, and soda cost $18, but "real conversation with an 11-year-old [is] priceless." The ad concludes: "There are some things money can't buy. For everything else there's MasterCard."

The Discover card's appeal is different in that it stresses the fact that there is no annual fee for using Discover and that cardholders receive cash-back bonuses on purchases. Discover advertises, "People who really know money use the Discover Card. It pays to Discover." Discover promotes its notification-via-e-mail feature, which lets a cardholder know when the card's credit limit has been exceeded. Discover's television commercial communicates the message that using a Discover card with this feature will save a diner from being embarrassed by a waiter's announcement that his credit limit has been exceeded.

American Express reminds customers that its cards "Do more." Its Blue Card includes a smart card feature that stores data.

The important thing to note here is that the advertisements for these products, as well as those for many others, feature different appeals. If every credit card company simply said, "Our credit card is more convenient than paying with cash," no brand's advertising would be unique or memorable. Creativity is responsible for this uniqueness.

But there's more to creativity than that. Many advertising appeals, such as the appeals for credit cards just described, are part of positioning promotional campaigns.

Advertising theme
An advertising appeal used in several different advertisements to give continuity to an advertising campaign.

Advertisers create these appeals so that consumers will perceive their brand as holding a distinctive competitive position. This strategy may be so successful that perfectly true claims made by the producer of one brand are not believable because of the competitive positions other brands hold in consumers' minds. Creativity, then, is more than an advertising tool. It is a competitive tool.

HOW TO SAY IT—
EXECUTION OF THE APPEAL

Even when a copy writer or artist has an important and meaningful message to relate, its effect can be lost if it is not presented in the right way and in the right context. Marketing research can help in this regard. For example,

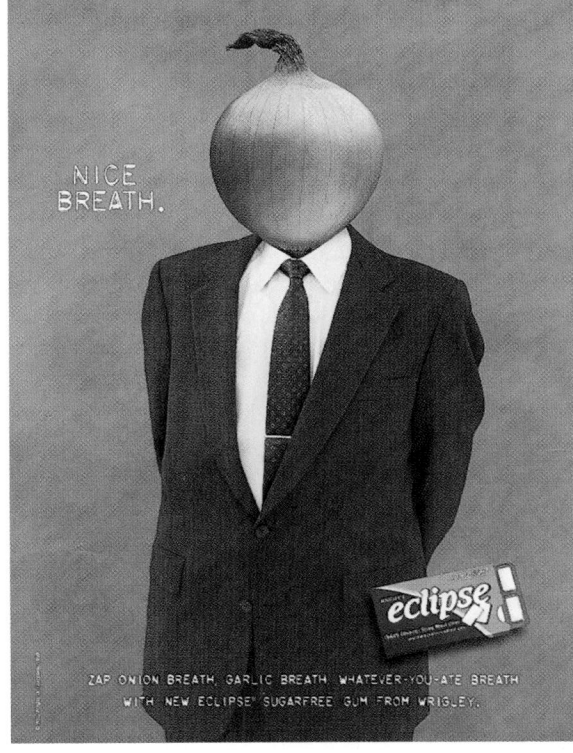

In advertising, how you say it is equally important as what you say.

http://www.wrigley.com

an advertising agency's research indicated that many women who buy frozen dinners lead hectic lives and, because of time constraints, have trouble coping with both work and everyday problems. So far so good. On this basis, the agency developed an advertisement for Swanson frozen dinners showing a rundown woman flopping into a chair just before her family is to arrive home demanding dinner. Suddenly realizing that she has a problem, the woman gets the bright idea of cooking a frozen dinner.

The problem was real enough, but the appeal was wrong. The last thing harried women want is to be reminded of how tired they are. Television viewers are fond of pointing out that married women in commercials are almost always peppy and well groomed, even when they are doing the laundry or washing the floor. Advertisers use such images to focus the target customer's attention on the solution to a problem without making her feel like cursing the laundry or the dirty floor. Realizing this, Swanson changed its advertising appeal.

How to say something is as important as—and sometimes more important than—what to say. This is perhaps doubly true in advertising. The person delivering the message, the emotional tone, and the situation in which the action takes place all influence the effectiveness of the advertisement.

Although some advertisements are simple, straightforward statements about the characteristics of a product, creating advertisements that grab the intended audience's attention often requires some embellishment. Advertisements must say things to people both with and without words, and the creative spark clearly is vital to accomplishing this goal. The Suzuki motorcycle slogan "Suzuki—The ride you've been waiting for" tells the target customer something about the excitement of Suzuki motorcycles. "I'm stuck on Band-Aid, and Band-Aid's stuck on me" is a catchy phrase. The Energizer pink bunny is a symbol rich in meaning; so are the Marlboro man's cowboy hat and horse. One mark of the talent and success of creative individuals is that much of their work is so powerful that it can be used effectively in advertisements for decades. Many slogans, pictures, and other components of advertisements can be immediately identified with particular products by generations of consumers. Success depends on the creative person's ability to capture a feeling or fact with just the right phrase and the right symbols. Compare these common advertising phrases with the way they might have been written:

"Are you a saltaholic?"
"Is it possible that you ingest undesirable levels of salt?"

"Michelin—because so much is riding on your tires."
"Michelin tires are safe."

Creative platform
The style in which the advertising message is delivered; also known as the *execution format*.

How an advertisement says something is its **creative platform**, or *execution format*. The creative platform is influenced by the medium that is used to convey the message. Obviously, a newspaper advertisement cannot duplicate the sound of a railroad train, but that sound might be used effectively in a radio advertisement. Determining how to communicate the message, then, is interrelated with selecting advertising media. Nevertheless, advertisers can present or creatively implement a basic appeal in a number of ways.

One Energizer battery commercial generates attention with a digitally reincarnated Elvis Presley filling his Cadillac convertible with gas late at night. When the gas station attendant tries to take a photograph of Elvis, he finds the camera's battery is dead. In an Outpost.com commercial, an executive fires a gerbil from a cannon, splatting it against a wall. These two creative platforms are quite different. Decision making by the people assembling the advertisements about what creative platforms to select and how to use those creative platforms is part of the creative process.

Storyline creative platform
An advertising creative platform that gives a history or tells a story about a product.

If Groucho Marx was before your time, now you have a second chance to appreciate him. Twenty-five years after his voice made famous the slogan "That's the best tasting pickle I've ever heard," the comic is back—or, at least, his inimitable delivery is. After searching its archives to find material for a new ad campaign, Vlasic decided to bring back an animated 1974 pickle ad featuring the Vlasic stork, voiced by Marx. "Groucho has a quirky sense of humor that seems to work well with pickles," says a Vlasic spokesperson.[3]

http://www.vlasic.com

Looking at some of the major creative platforms used in advertisements, especially TV commercials, helps put the creative strategies behind advertisements into perspective. The major creative platforms include storyline, product use and problem solution, slice of life, demonstration, testimonial and spokesperson, lifestyle, still life, association, jingle, and montage.

Storyline The **storyline creative platform** gives a history or tells a story about the product. For example, initial advertising for the Saturn automobile told the story of how a town, a company, and its employees were changed when General Motors made the decision to build a new kind of automobile. Similarly, certain European vacation spots are shown in all their historical glory from the Middle Ages to the present.

In television commercials that use the storyline creative platform, an unseen announcer (in a technique called *voice-over*) often narrates a story with a recognizable beginning, middle, and end. Some copy writers attempt to make the product the "hero" of the story.

Product Use and Problem Solution Straightforward discussion of a product's uses, attributes, benefits, or availability is a creative platform frequently utilized in advertising. A unique selling proposition, discussed in Chapter 13, is the central focus of such an advertisement. Comparatively simple advertisements for products ranging from Crest toothpaste to Texaco gasoline explain uses of the product and how the product can solve a problem. Crest toothpaste fights tooth decay. Texaco gas stops your car from "pinging." A maker of exercise equipment may point out that being fat and out of shape is a problem ("Your chest doesn't belong on your stomach") and may show that its product is a solution to the problem.

Slice of Life The **slice-of-life creative platform** dramatizes a "typical" setting wherein people use the product being advertised. Most of these commercials center on some personal, household, or business situation—for example, an attractive neighbor going next door to borrow some Taster's Choice coffee, friends phoning a fellow football fan and asking "Wuzupppppppppp?" or two homemakers talking about a laundry problem.

The slice-of-life commercial often begins just before a character discovers an answer to a problem. Whether the trouble is dandruff, bad breath, or not being home for a holiday, emotions are running high. The protagonist may know of the problem or may be told about it by another character. The product is then introduced and recommended, and the needy person gives it a try. Just before the end of the commercial, we are told—and, indeed, we can see for ourselves—that the new user of the product is now a more satisfied, happier person. This creative platform is most common in TV commercials, but similar real-life stories can be developed in print media through the use of a series of pictures and in radio advertisements through the use of character voices. The slice-of-life creative platform is essentially a dramatized variation on the problem-solution creative platform.

Demonstration Certain products lend themselves to a **demonstration** creative platform. For example, a Master Lock advertisement in which bullets are repeatedly fired into a lock that does not open is suspenseful and self-explanatory. The demonstration creative platform makes its sales pitch by showing a clear-cut example of how the product can be used to benefit the consumer. It does this by either dramatically illustrating product features or proving some advertised claim. The Master Lock advertisement certainly seems to prove that product's claim to toughness.

Unusual situations, occasionally bordering on the fantastic, can draw attention to product benefits. A mosquito sucks a Tabasco eater's blood and then explodes in a television commercial for E. McIlhenney's Tabasco Sauce. In another, fireballs devastate the earth when God misses his plate with Tabasco. These novel situations draw viewers' attention and illustrates that Tabasco sauce is hot stuff.

Slice-of-life creative platform
An advertising creative platform that dramatizes a "typical" setting wherein people use a product.

Demonstration
An advertising creative platform in which a clear-cut example of product superiority or consumer benefits is presented.

The Hummer is no ordinary sports utility vehicle, which would require a bridge to cross 30 feet of water. Bridges are for mere mortals. Hummer advertising demonstrates that the Hummer can go places and do things impossible in any other wheeled vehicle.

http://www.hummer.com

Many demonstrations occur in infomercials. **Infomercials** are television commercials, usually 30 minutes long, that have the appearance of regular programs, such as cooking shows or talk shows. The product, such as a George Foreman grill, is repeatedly demonstrated on the infomercial. Often, a telephone number flashes on the screen so that the viewer can order the item.

Comparative advertising, which directly contrasts one brand of a product with another, is a form of demonstration advertising. In a comparative advertisement, the sponsor's product is shown to be superior to other brands or to Brand X in a taste test, laundry whiteness test, toughness test, or other appropriate contest. This creative platform is somewhat controversial on two counts.

First, some advertisers believe that calling attention to another company's brand helps that competing product by giving it free exposure. Certainly, the competing brand receives some attention, but this fact itself can be advantageous. Brands that do not have a high market share are intentionally compared with the best-known products to suggest that the two brands are equal. Pepsi, the challenger, thus urges comparisons with market leader Coke. For example, in one television commercial, delivery-truck drivers for both Coca-Cola and Pepsi-Cola order a meal at a diner. The Coca-Cola driver offers his competitor a sip from his Coke can. The Pepsi driver takes a sip, returns the Coke can, and then offers the Coke driver a sip of his Pepsi. After the Coke driver takes a single sip of Pepsi, he wants more. He refuses to return the Pepsi, causing a commotion at the diner.

This commercial suggests a second point of controversy: Some people do not feel that such comparisons are fair or sporting. On the whole, however, advertisements using the direct-comparison creative platform have been increasing in number in recent years. The Federal Trade Commission, believing that honest comparisons will help the consumer to make choices, has supported this trend.

Testimonial **Testimonials** and endorsements show a person, usually a prominent show business or sports figure, making a statement establishing that he or she owns,

ALL MY VEGETABLES HAVE BEEN GOOD THIS YEAR

uses, or supports the brand advertised. The idea is that people who identify with the celebrity will want to be like that person and use the same product. Alternatively, the advertiser hopes that consumers will see the endorser as an honest person who would not lend his or her name to a product that is not good. Testimonials may also use speakers who, by virtue of their training or abilities, are seen as "experts" on the products being advertised.

A variation on the testimonial appeal is the use of a **spokesperson**. The spokesperson represents the company and addresses the audience members directly, urging them to buy the company's product. Paul Reiser is a spokesperson for AT&T. AT&T hopes that people who admire and trust Reiser will associate his personable, warm, and humorous manner with its long-distance savings program. The spokesperson, often the commercial's central character, need not be a real person. The Poppin' Fresh Dough Boy, the Jolly Green Giant, and the Keebler elves are well-known animated spokespersons.

Lifestyle   The **lifestyle creative platform** combines scenes or sequences intended to reflect a particular target market's lifestyle. Soft-drink and fast-food advertisements, as well as those for many other consumer goods, frequently show product users in a sequence of daily activities. Young people might be shown enjoying some extreme sports activity and topping off a perfect day with a Mountain Dew. Thus, the enjoyable aspects of teenage life are shown in association with product usage. Important to such advertisements are the sorts of people actors portray.

Mountain Dew advertisements often show young people engaging in extreme sports such as skateboarding. The lifestyle creative platform combines scenes or sequences intended to reflect a particular target market's lifestyle.

Still Life   The **still-life creative platform** portrays the product in a visually attractive setting. The product or package is the focal point of the advertisement. Reminder advertising often uses a still-life creative platform because the most important purpose of the message is to reinforce the brand name. Absolut vodka has used this creative platform with great success.

Association   The **association creative platform** concentrates on an analogy or other relationship to convey its message. This creative strategy often "borrows interest" from another, more exciting product or situation. Thrilling activities, such as skydiving or windsurfing, and scenes of beautiful places, such as the coast of Maine or a mountain wilderness, are associated with a product in some way. The purpose of such analogies, which are often accompanied by music, is to create an emotional mood. Burger King, for example, has used popular tunes of the '60s and '70s as the primary element in commercials about its menu items. The commercials link Burger King to the good feelings associated with the music. The psychological benefits of the product are communicated through the associations drawn by the viewer. More everyday analogies are used to make a product and its benefits easier for the consumer to understand. For example, Lysol uses an analogy when it says, "It's like having a brush in a bottle."

Fantasy is a special associative creative approach. The long-lived series of advertisements for Chanel perfume is a perfect example of the use of the **fantasy creative platform**. The fantasy appeal seeks to associate the product not merely with a glamorous setting but with the target buyer's wildest dreams and hopes. This creative platform allows audience members to fantasize about themselves in the position of the rich, famous, or adventurous.

Jingle   "My bologna has a first name . . . it's O-S-C-A-R." Can you remember the rest of this jingle? What restaurant do you think of when you hear "For the seafood lover in you"? What does one have to do if one wants to "Reach out, reach out and touch someone"? Commercial **jingles**, many of them written by well-known composers, have what is termed "memory value." You literally cannot get them out of your head. You may find yourself thinking of them—or, at least,

Lifestyle creative platform
An advertising creative platform that reflects a target market's lifestyle or hoped-for lifestyle.

Still-life creative platform
An advertising creative platform that makes the product or package its focal point, emphasizing a visually attractive presentation and the product's brand name.

Association creative platform
An advertising creative platform that uses an analogy or other relationship to stimulate interest and convey information.

Fantasy creative platform
In the context of advertising, a type of association creative platform used to link a product with the target buyer's wildest dreams and hopes.

Jingle
A song or other short verse used in an advertisement as a memory aid.

able to remember them almost word for word once your memory is jarred—years after they have been withdrawn from the market. People often remember product names, phone numbers, and addresses in jingle form. Thus, jingles serve best as a memory aid; they can have a significant effect on product recall.

Montage

An advertising creative platform that blends a number of situations, demonstrations, and other visual effects into one commercial to emphasize the array of possibilities associated with product usage.

Montage   The **montage** creative platform blends a number of situations, demonstrations, and other visual effects into one commercial. The effect may be one of a swirl of colors or an exciting array of possibilities associated with product usage. Typical of such a creative platform are travel advertisements for places like Jamaica. In these TV spots, the varied sights and sounds of an island paradise are strung together not only to show the many activities that are to be found there but also to suggest the excitement of the place and the sense that there is so much to do that the trip will surely be worth the investment. Several of Pepsi's GenerationNext advertisements use this creative platform.

Other Creative Platforms   This short list of advertising creative platforms is far from exhaustive. Pure information, humor, sex appeal, computer graphics, and special effects, for example, have not been mentioned. However, the discussion should help you to think of other advertising creative platforms and of the ways they work in an effective marketing program.

Producing an Effective Advertisement

Advertisements can consist of verbal elements, graphic elements, and auditory elements. The exact combination of these elements depends on the people who design the advertisement—and, as suggested, their choices are strongly influenced by the advertising medium to be used. However, the ultimate consideration is that an advertisement must reflect the advertising objectives. The promotional mix should be a unified whole, employing all appropriate means of delivering a message. Thus, many TV, radio, and print advertisements for a product advance virtually the same message or appeal, even though each is constructed to fit the appropriate medium.

COPY—THE VERBAL APPEAL

The term **copy** refers to the words in an advertisement. The words may be printed or they may be spoken by a character in a commercial or by an announcer. In certain advertisements, such as radio advertisements, the copy makes the biggest contribution to the advertisement's effectiveness. Even in a visual medium, such as television, copy is likely to retain its supremacy, because many of the claims an advertiser makes must be supported by the comments of the announcers or the characters. For example, advertisements for laundry detergents may show two piles of wash, but it is the copy that assures viewers that the pile washed in Cheer is the whitest.

Copy
Any words contained in an advertisement.

ART—THE VISUAL APPEAL

The term **art** is used broadly to mean all aspects of an advertisement other than its verbal portions. Thus, drawings, photographs, computer graphics, graphs and charts, layout (the arrangement of the graphic elements), and even white space fall in the category of art.

The function of pictures in an advertisement is to illustrate a fact or an idea or to attract attention. White space and layout have more subtle purposes. Layout can be used effectively to focus the viewer's attention on the picture of the product. It can also be used to draw attention to the brand name, the price, the place a product is sold, or the written portion of the ad. White space can be used in similar ways, but it is more commonly used to suggest high quality. Notice that many newspaper and magazine advertisements employ considerable white space to accent the product. A great deal of white space says that the pictured item is special, probably expensive, and certainly high quality. It implies that the product deserves the spotlight given it by a plain field that accents its appeal.

Art
Any aspect of an advertisement other than copy, including pictures, layout, and white space.

COPY AND ART WORKING TOGETHER—THE AIDA FORMULA

Most advertisements, with the exception of radio advertisements, feature both copy and art. The two elements must work together to accomplish the communication objectives set by management. To ensure that copy and art complement each other, most advertisers follow a hierarchy of effects model known as the AIDA formula. **AIDA** stands for *attention, interest, desire,* and *action*.

AIDA
An acronym for *attention, interest, desire,* and *action*. The AIDA formula is a hierarchy of communication effects model used as a guideline in creating advertisements.

Attention   David Ogilvy, a famous advertising executive, once said, "When you advertise fire extinguishers, open with fire." He was speaking about getting the prospect's attention. An effective advertisement must draw the viewer's or listener's attention from the very first glance or hearing. Whatever follows will prove of little use if the member of the target audience has not first been influenced to pay attention to the message. Copy can be used to accomplish this, as when radio advertisements start out sounding like soap operas or mystery stories to draw attention. The copy can be enhanced by illustrations. Often people representing the target customers are shown in situations that make the viewers wonder, "What's going on here?" or "What happened to these people?" For example, to attract the attention of luggage users, the Samsonite luggage company has for years run advertisements showing suitcases falling out of airplanes or suitcases supporting automobiles that have flipped over on top of them. Humor is another attention-getting device.

> When you advertise fire extinguishers, open with fire.

Interest   After the target consumer's attention has been attracted, arousing interest is next. If the attention-getter is powerful enough, interest should follow fairly automatically. However, it may be necessary to focus the viewers' or listeners' attention on how the product or service being advertised actually pertains to them.

what went right?

Chevy Trucks There are good ideas. And then there are the kind of ideas that can lift a multibillion-dollar-a-year international corporation out of its doldrums. Ideas that can rebuild not just an image and a product but the morale of the army of employees who produce it as well.

This is the story of one of those ideas, and how it transformed the image of Chevy trucks with three notes and three words from a minor hit record by Bob Seger. The words are now legendary in the world of advertising and in the hallways of General Motors.

There, "Like a Rock" is not only the song that propelled one of the most successful and longest-lasting campaigns in automobile advertising, it's a three-word mission statement for the entire truck division.

When the ads began in 1991, you probably didn't think of Chevy trucks as being at all like a rock. Chances are pretty good you do now.

In that first ad, there were just 60 seconds of Chevy trucks being abused by heavy loads, muddy roads, bad weather, construction crews, ranchers, and a 1,500-pound prize bull. And, of course, Seger with his throaty, quarter-million-miles-of-wear-and-tear vocals proclaiming, "I was strong as I could be, nothin' ever got to me. . . . Like a rock."

The spot contained no performance stats, no product sell, and barely a mention of the vehicle it was pitching. But things have been looking up for Chevy trucks ever since. "Stood there boldly. . . ."

Yet had it not been for an old record collection, a mysterious autoworker in a Detroit restaurant, and a California carpenter known only as "Fred," it might never have happened.

[In 1990], Chevrolet was "in a battle for our very survival," says the company's Jeff Hurlburt. Sales were down, factories were shutting. Don Gould of Campbell-Ewald Advertising had to find a way to bolster the Chevy truck line,

which accounts for well over half of all Chevrolet sales. The research said that Chevy trucks performed well and were viewed as good-looking, but wimpy. "We were perceived as the least dependable, least durable," says R. M. "Mac" Whisner, manager of Chevy truck advertising. "We sought to reverse that."

Gould and his colleagues had two advertising campaigns ready to test, but he didn't like either. Desperate, he spent a weekend hunting through his music collection looking for inspiration.

"I was lying on my family room floor," he says. "I had this old tape of Seger's. . . . Right on the cover, it said, Like a Rock, and I thought, 'That is exactly what we need.'"

Gould patched together a mock-up commercial using old videotape with the song and rushed it to California for a focus group test, which is where Fred comes in. In the taped interviews before the presentation, Fred is the most vocal critic of American trucks. He considers them shoddy. After viewing the commercial, though, Fred is a changed man. "You got me!" he shouts.

He and the rest of the group say there is no way they could ever buy another truck without at least looking at a Chevy. "Good old Fred sold this," says Gould. "When he talked about goosebumps, we knew we had a hit."

They got the same response from every test they did. They didn't just have a great commercial, they had one that was making audiences stand up and cheer. The only problem was they didn't have the right to air it. In the rush to put the test commercial together, there had been no time to acquire the rights from Seger, and when they asked he turned them down. Flat. "That was a crazy time," says Gould. "We tried to get an audience with him . . . and nothing was working."

Seger, a work-a-day rocker with blue-collar Michigan roots, had not lasted to age 50 in

Desire Immediately following the arousal of interest is the attempt to create a desire for the product. In a TV commercial for ChemLawn, the viewer first sees a homeowner carrying tools and bags of lawn chemicals. One of the bags breaks, and the exhausted do-it-yourselfer looks on helplessly. The viewer at home sees, however, that the unfortunate fellow's neighbor has a very nice-looking lawn but does not look harried or sweaty. Certainly he has no piles of spilled lawn-care products around his

the music business by bending easily nor doing anything that smacked of "selling out." "For the first six months, we just said, 'No!'" Seger says now. "We just didn't want to do any commercials."

Finally, Gould convinced Seger's manager, Punch Andrews, to watch the ad. After 15 seconds Andrews was convinced. "Punch came to me and said, 'I know I've been bringing you these commercials for years and you have always said no,'" recalls Seger. "But he said he thought this one made sense. 'This is trucks,' he said. 'You drive them. It's very American.'"

But Seger was not swayed until one night when he was dining with his wife at a place called the Venue on Detroit's Woodward Avenue—once famous for drag races, burger joints, and rock clubs. An autoworker came up to the table and politely asked Seger to do something to help the auto industry.

"I had just read about how GM had lost over $1 billion in a single quarter, and I thought if I could do something to help I would. My dad worked at Ford for 19 years. I worked a little while in the plants making transmissions," says Seger. The next day he called Andrews and told him to accept. But not before first checking to make sure the autoworker was legitimate, and not working for the advertising agency. No one will discuss the terms of the deal, though experts say a total of $500,000 to $1 million would not be unusual. "Felt like number one . . ."[4]

ROOM FOR YOU AND FOUR OF YOUR SIDEKICKS.

Round 'em up and head 'em out in style. In a Chevy Full-Size Extended-Cab, there's plenty of room and comfort to go around. So check your boots and climb in.

Chevy
The most dependable, longest-lasting trucks on the road.

Chevy Trucks
LIKE A ROCK

property. The viewer is interested in this story: Why is one fellow miserable while his neighbor smilingly pities him? The contented homeowner is a subscriber to the ChemLawn service, of course. The viewer is treated to some scenes of the ChemLawn man applying liquid lawn chemicals in one easy step. The ChemLawn people know what and when to spray—another load off the homeowner's mind. Thus, interest in and desire for the product are established in nearly simultaneous steps.

Action   Action is the last part of the AIDA formula. In the ChemLawn example, the commercial ends with a call to action. In effect, the advertisement urges viewers to phone their local ChemLawn dealer for an estimate of what it will take to make them as happy as the man who has been able to get a nice lawn with no effort. Thus, the means to act is provided. Usually, the advertiser makes the action seem as effortless as possible by giving a phone number or closing with a note that credit cards are accepted.

How the AIDA Formula Works   The AIDA formula is based on a consumer behavior theory that closely parallels the hierarchy of communication effects model discussed in Chapter 13. The formula describes consumers' behavior and serves as a guideline for creating advertising. AIDA makes good sense as an advertising tool and is widely known and followed.

Understand that it may not be possible for every advertisement to move the reader or viewer through the four stages to action with a single exposure. Repetition is usually necessary so that the advertisement's message can "sink in." Repetition also increases the chance that the target customer will see or hear the message at a time when there are no distractions. Finally, repetition recognizes the buyer's changing environment. An advertisement that he or she has seen before may be perceived in a different light by the target buyer who has just been paid or has received a tax refund. Eventually, if the advertisement is an effective one aimed at the proper people, buyers are likely to move psychologically through the AIDA stages and then act.

As we have already seen, developing a creative strategy and developing a media selection strategy are interrelated processes, and the planning of these activities occurs simultaneously. We now turn our attention to the selection of media.

An effective advertisement draws attention immediately. Novel or humorous situations are proven attention-getters.

http://www.wallcoverings.org

Everyone knows that children love the Cartoon Network. What is not well known is that one-third of the Cartoon Network audience is 18 years old or older. The Cartoon Network appeals to certain distinct demographic and psychographic market segments. An objective of a media selection strategy is to choose media that reach the desired segment.

http://www.cartoonnetwork.com

Media Selection

Suppose you are about to open a retail store. You have already decided to have a Yellow Pages advertisement but are undecided about whether to use radio, television, or newspaper advertising as well. This choice is a matter of selecting a communication channel for your message. In making the choice, you are determining a **media selection strategy**, which must take into account the message you wish to transmit, the audience you want to reach, the effect you want to have, and the budget you have to support this effort.

Developing a media strategy requires answering two questions: "Which media will get the message to the desired audience efficiently?" and "What scheduling of these media will neither bore people with too-frequent repetition of the message nor let too many people forget the message?" Before we address these questions, let's look briefly at what the term *media* includes.

WHICH MEDIA?

The various media lend themselves to specific tasks. If we assume, for the moment, that budget considerations can be set aside, certain factors become dominant in choosing the medium to carry a sales message. If demonstration or visual comparison of one brand with another is the goal, television becomes the most logical contender. If a lengthy explanation of sales points is required, print advertisements (magazines and newspapers) and the Internet come to mind. If consumers need a message to remind them of package identification or convey a short sales idea, outdoor advertising (billboards) makes sense. Thus, before a marketing planner starts thinking about what medium to use, he or she must know what is to be said. Once the marketer has decided what is to be said, attention can turn to which medium

Media selection strategy
Plan for determining which media are most appropriate for an advertising campaign

can best say it. Ultimately, several different media may be selected to carry the multiple messages the marketer wants to communicate.

Several media may appear to be able to do a particular job. When this is so, the marketing planner can narrow the choice by considering which media will hit the all-important target market. At this point, the media expert becomes a market expert. Knowing the target market—who the heaviest buyers are, what their demographic and psychographic characteristics are—leads to a determination of which media will deliver the message to these prospects. For example, a media planner in the insurance industry may be trying to target young males between the ages of 18 and 34; a European airline may be targeting well-educated, high-income men and women between the ages of 25 and 49; the primary customers for a sun-block cream may be youthful, fashion-conscious women. What media will reach each of these targets most effectively?

MASS MEDIA

Most products can be related to a demographic profile. Data pertaining to mass media are geared to that same profile information. Thus, if the target audience includes men and women and it has been decided that television will do the best job and that the media budget permits such an expensive choice, the media planner may go for prime-time television—from 8 p.m. to 11 p.m. or 7 p.m. to 10 p.m., depending on the time zone. The next question is "Which television shows have audiences whose profiles most clearly match those of the target customers?"

Careful analysis of any organization's marketing communication efforts might show that what appears to be the most appropriate advertising medium is, in fact, inappropriate. Where should one advertise a product like children's crayons? Saturday morning television shows, with their excellent demographics and their ability to show happy children drawing and coloring, would seem to be an obvious choice. But when Crayola's marketing managers discovered that mothers were the prime factor in the purchase of crayons, they shifted a large portion of their advertising budget out of children's TV and into women's magazines, the Disney

what went wrong?

Channel, and family-oriented programming. *The Crayola Kids' Adventures*, a family-oriented television program, was used to reach children and parents at the same time. The copy theme they developed to appeal to parents' nostalgia, "There is only one childhood. And only one Crayola," reflected the shift in audience and the new media strategy.

ELECTRONIC INTERACTIVE MEDIA

It has been said that "Computing is not about computers anymore. It is about living."[7] This observation certainly holds true with respect to the media people use to gather information and entertain themselves. This discussion of electronic interactive media will focus on advertising on the Internet, but the same principles apply to other media.

Interactive media allow an individual to seek information, ask questions, and get answers without the direct assistance of a human being. We will focus our attention on Web sites.

A *company Web site* is one of the most common forms of Internet advertising. For instance, The World of Clinique Web site offers online consultations about skin type. Consumers can find answers to frequently asked questions about color and makeup and get tips on such topics as sun protection. As the consumer interactively learns about skin care, she, of course, also learns which Clinique cosmetic products are appropriate for her situation. A company Web site is an ideal way to reach consumers who want details about specific products, as interactive media can provide large amounts of information.

Of course, just because a company creates a Web site does not mean people will visit the site. When a content provider, such as *Business 2.0* magazine, publishes on the Web, it faces three challenges: how to get viewers to the Web site, how to get viewers to stay long enough to view the content, and how to get viewers to return to the site.[8] (If a Web site has the ability to retain visitors, it is said to be *sticky.*) A Web site should create an overall experience that satisfies the visitor's need for information and interaction. It should be easy to use, have a logical flow, and have a graphic look that creates a positive feeling of interest in the organization or product featured.[9] Of course, the marketing objective will determine whether the Web site is packed with advice or full of full-motion video images. However, the best Web site designs give the visitor a reason to return to the site.

One way to get people to visit a Web site is to advertise on another Web site. *Advertising banners*, another form of Internet advertising, are much like mass

What is the difference between a café and a subway station? People seek out reasons to spend time in cafés, but they pass through subway stations as quickly as possible. A Web site in which banner ads fly by Internet users who are just trying to get to their destination is like a subway station. Effective marketers design their Web sites to be like cafés, where customers linger and feel as if they belong.[10]

media advertising in the sense that a company puchases "space" on a search engine or on the commercial Web site of an information provider. A typical objective for a banner ad is to increase brand name recognition. However, banners can go beyond achieving brand awareness, because they are hypertext links to the advertiser's Web site. For example, a marketer of garden tools might work out an arrangement with the Yahoo! search engine company to display its banner—which consists of a small flag-like rectangle—at the top of the results page whenever a user enters the word "garden" as a search term. The advantage of this type of Internet advertising is that the audience has self-selected the topic, so the marketer's message reaches an involved, highly targeted market.

> **Streaming ads may prove to be more effective than current ad banners.**

Pop-up boxes (interstitials) like the one shown in Exhibit 14-4 are *windows*, a refined version of banner advertising. A visitor to the *Fortune* magazine Web site, for example, might find that a window providing subscription information pops up after the Web page loads. The viewer typically has to close the window or enter a response to the advertisment.

Streaming Media   Certain software, such as RealNetworks' RealPlayer and Apple's QuickTime, allows Internet users to access multimedia content such as audio or video without downloading it first. When visitors to a site use such software to view a program or an advertisement, they are said to be viewing **streaming media**. Streaming ads may eventually prove to be more effective than current ad banners. One study co-sponsored by Intel and Excite@Home found that streaming-media advertisements provided 22 percent higher recall and 35 percent more click-throughs (to the advertiser's Web site) than banner ads.[11]

Today, three-dimensional computer-generated video can create photo-realistic results,[12] which users can either watch linearly or interact with. Interactive animated environments will take advertising on the Internet to a whole new level. However, it will be some time before all Internet users have access to these technologies. With live ad insertion capabilities, streaming-media ads are expected to become more prevalent as broadband technology with increased bandwidth be-

Streaming media
Multimedia content, such as audio or video, that can be accessed on the Internet without being downloaded first.

e x h i b **14-4**

Banners and Pop-up Boxes Are Internet Options

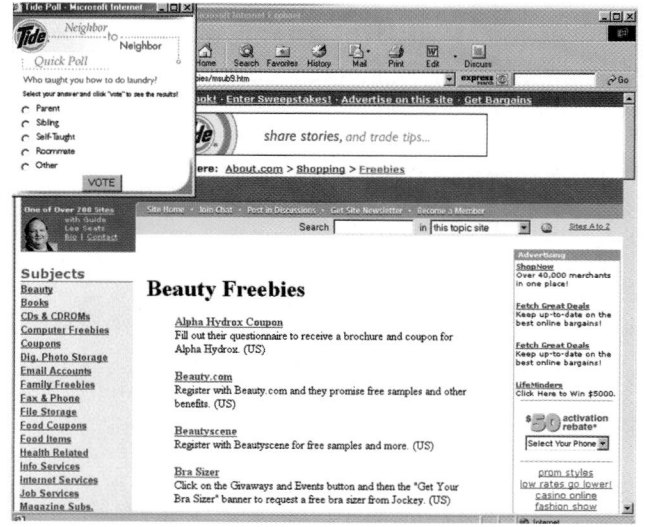

come more available. (*Broadband* refers to technology that allows for the high-speed transfer of data over media such as the Internet.)

Using Smart Agent Software to Reach Highly Targeted Audiences   Chapter 3 discussed how information technology can be used to deliver personalized content to a viewer's desktop. Computer software programs known as *smart agents*, or *intelligent agents*, find information without the user's having to do any searching; they then store that information—sometimes entire Web sites, complete with images and links—on the user's computer for later viewing.[13] Smart agent software that learns a user's preferences and searches out information is making advertising on the Internet and other interactive media more targeted and effective. Firefly (http://www.firefly.com) makes recommendations about music, movies, and books by comparing one user's interests to the interests of his or her "nearest neighbors," other Firefly users who have similar demographics and interests. Firefly also utilizes smart agents to make its selling of advertising space more attractive to its clients. Advertisers can have certain banners delivered to some target audiences, while other banners are served up to other users. An ad will appear only when someone with the appropriate demographics and entertainment preferences uses the service.

DIRECT MARKETING WITH DATABASES

Direct-marketing media, such as direct mail, can be very selective and can reach a clearly defined market, such as all families within a certain zip code area or all holders of American Express cards. But direct mail can also end up in the wastepaper basket.

Direct mail has been in existence for more than a century; however, advances in digital technology have changed the nature of direct marketing in recent years. In particular, modern computer technology has improved the selectivity of this medium. Now computers can access databases to customize materials sent to different market segments and to personalize the message any individual consumer or household receives. For example, a personalized greeting may appear on a letter that, in addition to conveying an advertising message, indicates the name of a local retailer that sells the brand being advertised. If the database records the ages of the children in households, an advertiser using direct marketing can send coupons only to those households with, say, children in diapers. Furthermore, if the database also indicates the brand of diapers a consumer regularly purchases, an advertiser like Huggies can limit the mailing list to consumers who are loyal to Pampers or other competing brands.

E-MAIL AS AN ADVERTISING MEDIUM

Williams-Sonoma Inc., a retailer of cookware and other household goods, uses e-mail as a medium to promote its new online bridal registry, as well as to draw customers into its stores. In a promotional experiment, 5 percent of customers contacted by e-mail went to a local Williams-Sonoma outlet. A subsequent test was twice as successful. In both cases, the response rate far exceeded the rate for the company's direct-mail campaigns. Williams-Sonoma believes that the key is communicating with customers in the channel they want.[14]

The use of *e-mail advertising* as a promotional medium is growing because it has the advantages of speed, personalization, and interactivity. Advertising via e-mail has many things in common with traditional direct-mail campaigns: Database management and data mining are extremely important, as they allow marketers to create customer profiles and tailor messages and products to them. In addition, use of e-mail permits an advertiser to determine whether the customer responds to the communication and thus measure the effectiveness of a particular ad.

A major disadvantage of e-mail advertising is that the receiver of the message may not read it because he or she considers it *spam*, which is the term for unsolicited and unwanted e-mail. Furthermore, if a company sends too many e-mails to a customer, it may actually drive the customer away. Effective marketers send e-mail only to customers who ask for it. Some have called this approach "permission marketing," because the consumer consents to receive e-mail from the marketer. An executive at Williams-Sonoma explained the logic of permission-based e-mail this way: "Our fall catalog can cost us a dollar. E-mail doesn't cost us anything, but it can cost us the relationship if we mail customers too much."[15]

The general rule is to let the customer control what he or she receives. This means that, in addition to asking for permission to send e-mail advertising, marketers should provide an easy way for customers to opt out if they no longer wish to receive e-mail.

EACH MEDIUM HAS ADVANTAGES AND DISADVANTAGES

Newspapers have the advantages of mass appeal within selected geographical markets, a general respect in the community, and a short lead time (that is, newspaper advertisements can be inserted, withdrawn, or altered quickly). Magazines have relatively long lead times but offer the advantages of selectivity of audience and far better reproduction of print and pictures than can be found in newspapers. Radio provides geographic and demographic selectivity because the programming of different stations attracts different sorts of listeners. Its lead time is short, and its usefulness in exposing listeners to frequent messages is obvious.

Television reaches a mass audience. However, specialization by type of show is possible. For example, the World Wrestling Federation *Smackdown* appeals to boys and young men; *Friends* appeals to a range of young to middle-aged adults. Television allows advertisers to "show and tell," because television ads can involve sight, sound, movement, cartoons, actors, and announcers. The strengths of television may be outweighed by its expensiveness. Cable television, with advertising rates lower than network television's, can be a good alternative for many products because it offers the advantage of greater psychographic selectivity. Even when the advertising rates for a particular program or station are relatively low, however, the costs to develop and produce a commercial keep many potential users away from TV.

Exhibit 14-5 highlights the general characteristics of several media. Today, U.S. advertisers spend more than $200 billion per year to place advertisements in various media.[16]

what went wrong?

Sony A software flaw allowed advertisers to view the e-mail addresses of subscribers to Sony Music Entertainment Corporation's Infobeat service.

The roughly 2.5 million users who subscribe to Infobeat get a daily e-mail update of music and entertainment news. The newsletter contains advertisements that give special URLs for interested consumers.

"By clicking on select advertisements, certain advertisers had the ability to obtain the e-mail address of the user who clicked on the link," the company said in a letter to subscribers.

Sony said it had recently been informed of the error and had fixed the problem, but advised subscribers to set up passwords for their accounts.

The company said it contacted its advertisers, who "confirmed that they did not collect or use any of this information."[17]

MEDIUM	ADVANTAGES	DISADVANTAGES
Newspapers	Geographic market selectivity Flexibility—easy to insert and change ads Editorial support (newspapers may write stories about paying advertisers)	Lack of permanence of advertising message Poor print/production quality Limited demographic orientation
Magazines	Demographic/psychographic selectivity Possibility of long life for ad Good print/production quality Editorial support	Lack of flexibility—difficult to make last-minute changes Expensive, especially for color ads
Radio	Geographic and demographic market selectivity Flexibility—easy to change Relatively inexpensive	Lack of permanence of advertising message "Clutter"—message may become lost in a group of several ads Lack of visual support Limited impact—radio is a background medium
Television	Advertiser can "show and tell"— demonstration is possible Geographic market selectivity Good market penetration because of large viewing audience	Lack of permanence of advertising message Expensive for national audience on major network Clutter Consumers videotape and skip ads
Direct mail/Catalogs	Highly selective Easy to measure results Lengthy copy possible Reader governs exposure	Expensive, especially on a cost-per-person basis Little or no editorial support Limited reader interest
Internet/e-mail	Easy to measure audience/response Lengthy copy possible Readers read and interact with what interests them Readers can request additional information Inexpensive, especially on a cost-per-person basis	Not everyone has Internet access—cannot reach consumers who are not online Not always possible to gain advance knowledge of audience Unsolicited e-mail may be considered spam
Point-of-purchase materials	Promotes impulse buying "Sells" in nonpersonal selling environment Ties together product and ads	Difficult to obtain desired placements Clutter Limited creative possibilities
Directory (the Yellow Pages)	Permanence of ad High reach and frequency potential	Limited customer usage Market coverage limited to phone customers
Outdoor (billboards)	High reach and frequency potential Market selectivity High impact because of size Inexpensive	Message must be brief Image of billboards is poor in some markets Location choices may be limited

WHAT SCHEDULING?

The **media schedule** is a time schedule identifying the exact media to be used and the dates on which advertisements are to appear. Media planners select not only the general media category (such as magazines and cable television) but also the specific media vehicles (such as *Sports Illustrated* and *Star Trek: Voyager*). Selecting the specific media vehicles requires advertisers to consider reach, frequency, and timing.

Reach—that is, the percentage of people exposed to an advertisement in a given medium—is an important factor in determining which media to use. Obviously, the advertiser wishing to reach the largest number of people in the target audience must take costs into consideration. A major aspect of the media selection job is making cost comparisons—evaluating whether, for example, *Sports Illustrated* has a lower cost per thousand readers than *The Sporting News*.

Media schedule
A document identifying the exact media to be used and the dates on which advertisements are to appear; also known as the *media plan*.

Reach
The number of people exposed to an advertisement carried by a given medium.

Frequency
The number of times an advertisement is repeated in a given medium within a given time period, usually 4 weeks.

You could read this whole magazine, or just call the new Jenny Craig.

NEW!
ABC
Program™
Jenny Craig®
1-800-448-6109

Another factor with cost implications is the repetition, or frequency, of the advertising message in a given medium within a given time period, typically 4 weeks. **Frequency** reflects the average number of times an average individual is expected to be exposed to an advertiser's message. An advertiser may decide to trade off reach for frequency. Placing two advertisements in *Forbes*, for example, may be more cost-effective than placing a single advertisement in *Fortune*.

Although cost is an important issue, strategy considerations may be equally important in choosing between reach and frequency. For example, frequency may be more important than reach when repetition will help the audience learn something new. If the advertising objective for a new brand is to establish awareness or to communicate a new product feature, the benefits of high frequency may outweigh the benefits of wide reach. Because the trade-off between reach and frequency is a complex issue, marketing managers often use marketing research to help them choose the best media schedule.

Measuring the Effectiveness of Advertising

An advertiser about to commit more than $2,000,000 for a 30-second television commercial to be aired during the Super Bowl or for the development of a series of advertisements created especially for the Christmas season will want some way to measure the effectiveness of those advertisements. Measuring the effectiveness of advertisements in terms of the sales dollars generated is difficult. Despite that fact, several approaches to measuring effectiveness have been developed. These research techniques do not provide exact measures of effectiveness, but they do provide a systematic way of developing and testing advertisements to determine whether they are accomplishing the intended objectives. Advertising research may be divided into two phases: (1) the pretesting stage of developing and refining advertising and (2) the posttesting stage of evaluating its effectiveness.

DEVELOPING MESSAGES AND PRETESTING ADVERTISEMENTS

Effective marketers are reluctant to spend large sums of money running advertisements that have not been carefully pretested. Before advertisements are put on TV or in magazines, they may have gone through several stages of testing. The purpose of **pretesting** is to limit—or, even better, to eliminate—mistakes.

Pretesting may be conducted in the earliest stages of the development of an advertisement, and it may continue virtually until the advertisement is printed or broadcast. First, the basic appeal of an advertisement or of the concept around which it will be built may be tested. Then a headline, picture, or slogan may be tested. A "rough" version of the advertisement, featuring still photos in the case of

Pretesting
In the context of advertising, research carried out beforehand on the effectiveness of an advertisement. It begins at the earliest stages of development and continues until the advertisement is ready for use.

a television commercial or a story acted out by nonprofessional actors in the case of a radio advertisement, can be assembled rather inexpensively and shown to a sample audience to measure appeal and believability. It does no good to create a funny, clever, or dramatic advertisement unless the impact of the advertisement comes through to the people it is supposed to affect.

Many of the marketing research tools discussed in Chapter 5 are used to pretest advertisements. Focus group discussions with consumers can be especially helpful.

POSTTESTING ADVERTISEMENTS

Once an advertisement has been developed and has run in the chosen media, **posttesting** should be done to determine if it has met the objectives set by management. Posttests usually measure brand awareness, changes in attitudes toward the product, or the number of inquiries generated about the product.

Measuring Brand Recall and Recognition Because advertisers must gain the attention of buyers and have them remember the names of brands or the stores in which they can be found, many posttests are designed to evaluate recognition or recall.

Recall tests can take many forms. For example, a telephone survey may be conducted during the 24-hour period following the airing of a television commercial to measure day-after recall. In such studies, the telephone interviewer first poses a question such as this:

> "Did you watch *Monday Night Football* last night?"

If the answer is positive, the next question might be

> "Do you recall whether there was a commercial on that program for an automobile?"

If the answer is again positive, the interviewer might ask

> "What brand of automobile was that?"

To this point, what has been measured is **unaided recall.** The interviewer gives no clue as to the brand of car advertised. In an **aided recall test,** the questions might be phrased differently, as in these examples:

> "Do you recall the brand of automobile advertised? Was it an American sports car?"
> "I'm going to read you a list of automobile brand names. Can you pick out the name of the car that was advertised on the program?"

While aided recall is not as strong a test of attention and memory as unaided recall, it still provides valuable information. After all, remembering the brand and model of car when you see it on the automobile dealer's lot may be all that is necessary.

Aided recall is similar to recognition. One way to measure recognition is to show an advertisement to a respondent and simply ask whether the respondent remembers having seen it before. If the answer is yes, the respondent is asked questions about particular portions of the advertisement.

Measuring Changes in Attitudes about a Product Effective advertisements can contribute to changing consumers' attitudes toward a brand. To measure and evaluate attitude change,

Posttesting
In the context of advertising, testing that takes place after an advertisement has been run, to determine whether it has met the objectives set for it by management.

Recall test
In the context of advertising, a research tool used to determine how much people remember about an advertisement.

Unaided recall test
In the context of advertising, a test of consumers' memories of an advertisement, in which no clues are provided as to the specific material to be remembered.

Aided recall test
In the context of advertising, a test of consumers' memories of an advertisement, in which clues about the specific material to be remembered are provided.

The ACNielsen Company rates the popularity of television shows by means of mechanical observation. Its "peoplemeter," a recording device attached to a family's television, uses a microprocessor to identify which family members are watching the television, when they are watching, and what station is being watched.

http://www.acnielsen.com

researchers must record buyers' attitudes before they are exposed to the relevant advertisement and after exposure. Thus, a two-part, before-and-after study must be undertaken.

For example, suppose a new Neutrogena advertisement states that Neutrogena hand cream has great powers to heal badly irritated skin on hands and feet. The effectiveness of Neutrogena's new advertisement could be measured by before-and-after surveys among target buyers. The result of the first survey might show that few consumers know the product heals hands and feet. Next, advertisements could be shown to a sample of these target buyers. A second survey would be conducted after the advertisement was run. If the results of this survey showed increased recognition of the product's healing properties, the ads would be credited with some measure of success in changing attitudes.

Generating Inquiries about the Product   In certain situations, such as evaluation of one direct-mail piece versus another, the generation of inquiries is a good measure of an advertisement's effectiveness. Many advertisements, especially for organizational products, include a phone number readers can call or a coupon they can return for additional information. Advertisers of organizational products often count the number of inquiries generated by one magazine advertisement versus another to measure advertising effectiveness. Internet advertisements often provide hyperlinks to a company's Web site. Counting "hits" is similar to inquiry analysis.

SALES AS A MEASURE OF ADVERTISEMENT EFFECTIVENESS

After noting some of the ways in which marketers try to measure the effectiveness of their advertising, you might ask, "Why not just use sales figures?" Unfortunately, this is easier said than done. Advertisers have difficulty using sales as a direct measure of advertising effectiveness because many factors other than advertising influence sales. It is nearly impossible to separate the effect of the economy, the price, retailer activity, and so on from the effects of advertisements. Nevertheless, most marketers examine this measure, even if sales changes cannot be scientifically "proven" to result from advertising.

Test marketing research and laboratory experiments designed to simulate sales behavior are the most sophisticated research tools available to evaluate advertising effectiveness when sales volume is the primary criterion. However, because advertising's effect on sales may not be immediate, even the most elaborate research may not establish a relationship between advertising and sales.

Public Relations

One defining characteristic of publicity is that it always involves a third party, such as a newspaper reporter or editor, who has the ultimate power to determine the nature of the message. Because the marketer does not pay for space in a newspaper or time on a TV program, publicity is "free." However, because favorable publicity can have the same impact as advertising, effective marketers plan publicity with as much care and consideration as they give to the rest of the promotion mix. This is often the responsibility of the organization's public relations department.

Public relations is the managerial activity that identifies, establishes, and maintains favorable relationships between an organization and the publics on whom its success or failure depends. The purpose of **public relations** is to actively manage publicity (and sometimes other promotional elements) to establish and maintain a positive organizational image and to provide the public with information about an organization's products, policies, or personnel.[19]

Public relations
The activities involved in actively seeking to manage the nature of the publicity an organization receives.

PUBLICITY

Publicity, when properly managed, can serve many purposes. Marketers often wish to attract the public's attention or maintain public visibility. Many organizations wish to provide consumers or other public interest groups with useful information. Others use public relations to change attitudes or to combat negative publicity from another source. Here are some examples:

- Nissan Motor Company, a company that recently developed a fuel-efficient engine combining an electric motor with a gasoline engine, may use publicity to attract attention to its hybrid electric engine system that cuts exhaust emissions dramatically.
- Political candidates routinely use "photo opportunities" to maintain visibility among apathetic voters.
- The Surgeon General of the United States uses publicity to inform the public about the dangers of teenage smoking.

In general, no matter what the marketer's purpose, the information offered must be timely and interesting—that is, newsworthy—if it is to result in publicity for the marketer. Usually, the more engrossing and captivating the material, the more likely it will be publicized. Celebrities are often asked to work with charity organizations because their fame and personalities help get the much-needed "free" publicity. Information offered by public relations departments often takes the form of news releases and press conferences, but it may take many other forms as well, as illustrated in Exhibit 14-6.

News Releases   Marketers may spend considerable time and effort in getting news releases and interviews with company spokespersons placed in newspapers

The Scope of Public Relations

General Purpose	Means	Target Audience
Corporate visibility/image • Industry news • Financial progress reports • Company policy changes • Personnel news • Event sponsorship • International developments	News releases (Publicity) Press conferences (Publicity) Lobbying (Personal selling) Annual reports (Advertising)	Consumers General public Employees Government officials and legislators
Product information • New products • Product improvements • New advertising • Price changes • Product usage information	Event sponsorship (Sales promotion) Web site (Publicity)	Stockholders

and on broadcasts, to foster a favorable corporate image. Suppose, for example, that you are in charge of public relations for 3M Corporation and your company has just entered into a joint venture with NEC Technologies, Inc. to develop a "smart" airbag system. Your publicity objective may be to provide information about the new product's characteristics and potential benefits and to make the public aware that it will be on the market in the near future. You might issue a **news release**—a relatively brief typewritten statement explaining that although airbags save lives in vehicle crashes, they have one drawback: they can be lethal to children and small adults.[20] The news release might go on to say that 3M and NEC are working together to develop a "smart" airbag system with an occupant-sensing feature that determines whether there is an adult, a child, or something else on the passenger seat. The new product will signal the passenger airbag not to deploy if there is not an adult in the seat. The news release might further state that the goal of the NEC and 3M relationship is to develop sensor assemblies for a wide range of vehicle seats that are easy to install, comfortable, and durable. 3M will design and manufacture the antenna subassembly for NEC, using its expertise in adhesives, converting, precision coating, and connector technologies.

Well-executed news releases are written in a form that a newspaper, magazine, or broadcast editor can easily incorporate into a news story. Photographs, films, and videotapes often are distributed to the media to accompany news releases. For example, videotapes of company operations and interviews with company spokespersons often are distributed to television broadcasters.

Press Conferences   The **press conference** is another form of publicity that can create goodwill and positive relations between an organization and the public. When an organization wishes to make a specific announcement, it may notify the mass media that it has scheduled a press conference where a statement will be made and reporters can ask questions. For example, the professional football team with the worst record in football will inevitably call a press conference to announce the signing of its recently drafted Heisman Trophy winner. The organization's public relations department thus seeks to promote next year's team via publicity.

Appearances   Talk shows are known for guests who promote their books, recordings, and concerts. The entertainment business is one of the most extensive users of public relations. Performers' appearances are usually part of well-planned marketing strategies. For example, Tony Bennett's singing career, which dates to

News release
A brief written statement sent to the press or others, describing a new product, a product improvement, a price change, or some other development of interest. The release is intended to be newsworthy.

Press conference
A meeting called by an organization to announce a newsworthy event to the press.

what went wrong?

Beatles Road Sign Ban   The city of Liverpool planned to put up brown and white signs reading "Liverpool—birthplace of the Beatles" on the busy M6 motorway. Unfortunately, the plan to use road signs to promote Liverpool as the home of the Beatles was rejected by British authorities as a hazard for motorists. The Department of the Environment, Transport and the Regions ruled that the signs would distract motorists because they also contained information about other tourist attractions in the city. An official explained, "Drivers have just four seconds to assimilate information (from signs). There is a limit on the number of words allowed. It comes down to safety grounds—it was too distracting." The ruling against the public relations effort produced a howl of protests from the port city's politicians. One Liverpool councilor questioned why Liverpool's signs had been rejected as a distraction while the town of Stratford-upon-Avon, once home to William Shakespeare, was allowed to use road signs describing itself as "Shakespeare Country."[21]

the 1950s and 1960s, has been revitalized because of a savvy public relations effort by his son and manager. Bennett's appeal to young audiences—fans of alternative rock—was enhanced by careful exposure of the entertainer with guest appearances on programs such as *The Simpsons* and *The David Letterman Show*. He also appeared with one member of the Red Hot Chili Peppers on an MTV awards show, shared concert bills with groups such as Smashing Pumpkins, and recorded an *MTV Unplugged* show.

Not only entertainers but also sports figures, politicians, environmentalists, and activists for social causes use their guest appearances on television programs to promote their agendas. **Person marketing** is a term sometimes used to describe marketing when the "product" is a person. If basketball star Shaquille O'Neal wishes to promote his image, appearances are a very cost-effective medium for doing so. Further, the public does not view appearances as formal advertisements.

Company Web Sites   Many organizations provide considerable company, product, and service information on company Web sites. Internet visitors may find information about the organizational mission, company history, investor relations, financial statements, and other company news. A company Web site is a perfect repository for recent, and even old, articles and press releases about the company. Customer service and e-mail features may also be incorporated into the company site. The company Web site provides a golden opportunity for public relations.

EVENT SPONSORSHIP

Sponsorship of sporting events and charitable causes can be very effective for marketers who wish to generate publicity or to reinforce a certain image with a tie-in to a special event. A company collaborating in the sponsorship of an event or cause provides financial resources, personal services, equipment, or facilities to obtain an alliance with the event or the charitable organization. In return, the company obtains direct exposure to the public targeted by the event and the ability to transfer the event's or organization's image to its products.

For example, MasterCard was a major sponsor of the first World Cup soccer games held in the United States. The MasterCard logo was prominently displayed behind the goal, where an estimated two billion fans could see it as they watched Brazil win the championship, beating Italy in a penalty-kick shootout. Sponsors of televised sporting events such as the World Cup must rely on the TV camera to show their banners and signs. The lack of complete control over promotional efforts is a disadvantage of event sponsorship. However, sponsors of a global event such as the Wimbledon Tennis Championship, the PGA Championship, or the World Series can expect to receive media coverage and considerable publicity around the world.

When a marketer such as The Country Music Association actually creates a special event to sponsor, such as the Fanfare Festival in Nashville, the company is the *title sponsor* and the activity is called **event marketing.** You can probably see that event sponsorship can be an integrated marketing communication that is both a public relations effort and a sales promotion effort.

Person marketing
The use of marketing techniques, especially promotion, when the product is a person.

Event marketing
A public relations effort that involves creating an event to sponsor.

Public Relations Goes beyond Publicity: An Integrated Marketing Communications Approach

Although management of an organization's public image through publicity is the cornerstone of public relations, all forms of promotion may influence an organization's relationship with the general public. Thus, managers should not overlook the coordination of public relations efforts with other promotional efforts. Many of the objectives of publicity are the same as the objectives for other promotions.

Indeed, all of these activities may be carried out by a public relations department. For example, the Macy's Thanksgiving Day parade is a sales promotion event that enhances Macy's public image. And the lobbying effort by the Friends of Kuwait is a form of personal selling, even though the public relations workers involved have titles other than sales representative. (The term *public relations* may be used in preference to the term *sales* by government officials, who would rather go to lunch with a lobbyist than with a salesperson, or by a charity that prefers to discuss its fund-raising as something other than a sales promotion.)

As Exhibit 14-6 illustrated, public relations to enhance organizational image and to communicate product information includes more than just publicity. The exhibit also illustrated that public relations efforts have various target audiences—not just consumers but also stockholders, government bodies, environmental groups, and the like—which can be reached in various ways.

Public relations campaigns—like all promotional campaigns—should use an integrated marketing communications approach. Each promotional element should be employed so that its unique characteristics help communicate a unified message. Because integrated marketing communication is so important, large public relations companies such as Hill & Knowlton and Ketchum PR are as familiar with using advertising as they are with using publicity to tell a company's story.

CRISIS MANAGEMENT

Crisis management
A public relations effort that involves disseminating information during an emergency.

Sometimes a tragic event, such as an airplane crash, or some other occurrence, such as criticism from an activist group like Greenpeace, creates a public relations crisis. **Crisis management** is a public relations effort to manage an emergency that urgently requires dissemination of information.

Public relations specialists believe managers should make themselves available to journalists as quickly as possible after a crisis strikes. In the case of a plane crash or a tire recall, the public has an urgent need for information. Thus, the company should not delay—it should respond immediately.

Another guideline for crisis management is that top executives should be visible when a crisis occurs. Top executives can be very effective as company spokespersons. Public relations efforts during a crisis should use these executives to communicate important information about company policy. Experience shows that it is vital that the executives tell the truth rather than using subterfuge to postpone dealing with the problem. It is also wise for them to apply the K.I.S.S. formula—which stands for "keep it short and simple" (or "keep it simple, stupid")—to their remarks. A message that is too complicated for the public to understand can defeat the purpose of crisis management.

Sometimes, rumors about a company's operations or products reach near-crisis proportions. When the company wants to cope with untrue rumors, it should develop a plan of action for rumor control. The following steps are recommended:[22]

1. Create a rumor center and appoint a person to be responsible for its operation on a constant basis. Have the rumor center trace the rumors' origins.
2. Send out the correct facts. Don't just deny the rumors; demonstrate the truth to dispel them.
3. Hold press conferences when appropriate.
4. Ask a respected third party, such as an outside expert, to comment on the rumors.
5. Deal with rumors locally when appropriate.

INTERNAL MARKETING AND EMPLOYEE RELATIONS

One of an organization's most important publics consists of its managers and employees. Employees who feel that they are important parts of a worthwhile activity, who identify themselves with the creation of good products for others, who take pride in the delivery of outstanding service, and who understand the workings of the organization are likely to be satisfied employees. Giving employees a sense of identification and satisfaction with the company should thus be a priority for every organization. The term **internal marketing** is often used by marketers when referring to public relations efforts aimed at their own employees.

Internal marketing may be especially important for employees who have contact with ultimate consumers or who have a direct effect on ultimate consumers' satisfaction with the product. The objective of internal marketing directed toward these employees may be to help them recognize their role in the organization's effort to create customer satisfaction; these employees should understand that the level of service they provide is essential to the firm's existence.

When Delta Airlines created its "We love to fly and it shows!" advertising campaign, the company combined advertising with an internal marketing effort. Consider one ad in this campaign: a television commercial for Delta Airlines that portrays the soldiers of the U.S. Army's "Company B." The ad opens with a troop of soldiers in the pouring rain being dismissed by a stern sergeant. Whooping with joy, the men stampede to the nearest telephone booth. "Even when Company B heads for the telephone," says an announcer, "it's no problem for Gail Godfrey." Godfrey, a real Delta reservationist, keeps her cool as the phone is passed from one soldier to another. Hailing from all over the country, they're all anxious to fly home. As the last soldier hangs up, a fellow reservationist asks Godfrey if she's answered many calls that afternoon. "One," Godfrey replies, looking a little sheepish.

This advertisement was designed to communicate what Delta believes is its unique competitive advantage: the service provided by its frontline personnel. The advertisement illustrates how Delta employees go beyond the call of duty. Delta realized that before it aired the ad campaign, internal marketing would be necessary to ensure that its employees would deliver on the promise. Delta produced an employee video for the campaign, and every employee got a cassette explaining how important he or she was to the campaign's success.

International Public Relations

Throughout this book, the importance of understanding local cultures has been stressed. As you can imagine, in public relations, understanding the language, norms, values, religious traditions, government regulations, and other dimensions of the culture is absolutely vital. This topic is complex, and we cannot deal with it here in any depth. However, it should be emphasized that any multinational organization should consider employing public relations consultants with experience in local areas.

Evaluating and Monitoring Public Relations

Public relations managers should not rely solely on their own intuition about what the public thinks of their companies. A manager who really wants to know what people think about the company's reputation should systematically gather information from the public. Marketing research should be used to learn the opinions of both customers and noncustomers. Focus groups and surveys are common ways of gathering information about the public's attitudes toward the company image. In most image research, attitudes toward competitors also are measured and used as a benchmark. That way, the company knows, for example, whether it is seen as more socially responsible or less socially responsible than the competition. Monitoring newspaper, television, and radio news coverage is another means to learn what the public is thinking. Press clippings and videotapes are often systematically analyzed to quantify the content of these communications.

Internal marketing
Marketing efforts aimed at a company's own employees.

Ethical Issues in Advertising

Social commentators frequently debate ethical issues concerning advertising.[23] We will discuss three of these issues: deceptive practices, public standards, and promotions aimed at children.

DECEPTIVE AND MISLEADING PRACTICES

Our society grants consumers the right to be informed and prohibits deceptive practices and promotions that intentionally mislead consumers. For example, consumers have the right to know how likely it is that they will win a contest or sweepstakes. State and federal regulations now require that the odds of winning such sales promotions be conveniently available to potential participants.

Misleading or deceptive advertising
Advertising that leads consumers to inaccurate conclusions. Intentionally making false statements is an extreme case of deceptive advertising.

Misleading Advertising   Because of its direct effect on buyers, one area of particular concern is **misleading or deceptive advertising**. People feel strongly about this issue, largely because in almost all societies the truth is revered and lying is considered wrong. In the United States, the Federal Trade Commission Act of 1914 makes it illegal to run dishonest advertisements. Thus, laws and court cases aimed at ending the worst abuses have long been part of the American business scene.

Identifying what comprises misleading or deceptive advertising is not always easy. Although people disapprove of blatant deception and the legal system forbids it, hard-and-fast rules are difficult to develop and enforce. Consider the use of the terms "ozone-friendly," "biodegradable," "photodegradable," "recycled," and "recyclable" in advertising messages. When can a marketer honestly say that a product is conveniently recyclable? What constitutes proof of a claim that no chemical will migrate to the stratosphere and cause unnatural and accelerated deterioration of the ozone layer? Many contend that these terms, if used in advertisements, should conform to legal requirements.

Bait and switch
An advertising technique, usually associated with retailers, in which a product is offered at an extremely low price to attract customers, who are then told the product is unavailable and are "switched" to a more expensive, higher-margin product.

Bait and Switch   Advertising that attempts to employ the tactic known as **bait and switch** offers another example of the difficulty in determining what is deceptive. The bait-and-switch technique involves advertising a product at an amazingly low price. Consumers, drawn to the store by the advertising, are "switched" to another, higher-priced item by salespeople who claim that the advertised item is, for some reason, no longer available.

Although this tactic is clearly deceptive, proving intentional deception is difficult. Would anyone claim that a salesperson should not try to sell an item that was not mentioned in the store's advertisement? What about the common sales tactic of trading up, whereby the salesperson tries to interest the customer in an item priced higher than the one the customer first mentioned? Because the marketing concept stresses honest attempts to create customer satisfaction, a salesperson might in good conscience point out a better, more expensive item. The question of the ethics of switching revolves around intentions and the actual availability of the product. Bait and switch occurs when a consumer cannot purchase the product because the marketer had no intention of selling it.

Puffery
The practice of exaggerating a product's good points in advertising or selling.

Puffery   Another gray area involves puffing. **Puffery** is the practice of stating opinions or making slight exaggerations, a practice that society in general considers harmless. Movie producers often publicize their films and publishers sometimes advertise their books by using puffery—who hasn't heard "the most exciting movie ever!" and "the funniest book you'll ever read"? Even though these are not provable statements, most would not favor banning them. But where does puffing stop and lying begin? Often, the Federal Trade Commission or a judge is required to make the final decision.

PUBLIC STANDARDS

Matters of law and ethics are frequently decided on the basis of public standards, or beliefs about what is right and proper. Even more often, they are decided on the basis of what somebody thinks are public standards. Certain advertisements, such as the Calvin Klein perfume advertisements showing nude men and women in provocative poses, cause a stir because they challenge public standards or someone's ideas about public standards. But public standards are not always obvious. Try to decide what public standards dictate in regard to these marketing questions, for example:

- Should liquor advertising be allowed on television?
- Should minorities be portrayed in menial roles in television commercials?
- Should lawyers be allowed to send direct-mail materials to accident victims or their families in personal-injury and wrongful-death cases a week after the accident?

The public's sense of decency, then, is a tricky thing to deal with. Television networks are often accused of offering too much sex and violence. Groups condemn shows ranging from *The X-Files* to *South Park*. Other groups condemn the self-proclaimed TV watchdogs, saying no one should tell the American people what to do and "if you don't like it, you don't have to look at it."

Questions of public standards raise philosophical issues marketers must consider. Although the issues can be difficult, marketers can and do make choices. In many cases, marketers may decide to offend one market segment in order to satisfy the needs of another. Consider, as a case in point, the marketing of products such as Preparation-H. Clearly, many people find mass media advertising of this type of product offensive. Other segments of the population find the advertising perfectly acceptable. If the advertising for some product offends you, ask yourself if it would be acceptable to adults in another market segment who need the product.

PROMOTIONS AIMED AT CHILDREN

Marketing to children has always been an area of controversy.[24] Critics argue that advertising aimed at children fosters materialism, amplifies status inequalities, encourages the consumption of foods high in sugar and low in nutritional value, and induces conflict within families. They also maintain that children are especially susceptible to persuasion and that special protection should therefore be provided for them.[25] Others argue that children understand the purpose of commercials and must learn to be consumers. Marketing helps socialize them into the consumer role. Further-more, parents—the ultimate arbitrators—have considerable influence on children, which they can choose to use to counteract marketers' influences.

Because of their importance to growth and health, food products sold to children are the focus of special concern. When, in a test market, General Mills advertised Mr. Wonderful's Surprise as "the only cereal with a creamy filling," consumer groups complained that the product, like other sweetened cereals, was not high in nutritional value. The cereal contained 30 percent sugar and 14 percent fat. General Mills argued, however, that the product should be considered as part of the child's total diet, not as an item "out of context."

We began this chapter by saying that advertising is a captivating topic. Now that you have read the chapter, you should recognize that marketers employ many different strategies and hold diverse opinions about how to manage advertising activities. This diversity exists in large part because advertising relies heavily on creativity. Careers in the advertising field can be fascinating indeed.

Summary

Advertising is the promotional activity in which the art of marketing is most visible.

1) Understand the purpose of product advertising, direct-action advertising, and institutional advertising.

Product advertising promotes the attributes, benefits, uses, and images of specific products. Direct-action advertising encourages immediate action. Institutional advertising promotes an organization or industry as a whole, stressing goodwill, image, and contributions to society, or stimulates generic demand for a product category.

2) Differentiate between primary demand and selective demand advertising.

Primary demand, or generic demand, advertising promotes a product category without stressing particular brands. Selective demand advertising accents a particular brand.

3) Discuss the stages in the development of an advertisement.

Advertisements are developed in five basics steps: (1) setting objectives consistent with the marketing strategy and the advertising budget, (2) determining a creative strategy, (3) developing the advertising message, (4) formulating a media selection strategy, and (5) running the advertisements and measuring their effectiveness. Creativity is important throughout the process.

4) Analyze the role of communication objectives in the advertising process.

Because advertising must communicate with target markets, its communication goals must be clearly defined. Effective advertisements must gain attention, be understood, be believed, and be remembered.

5) Show how advertisements for a product are likely to change over the course of the product's life cycle.

In the introductory stage, advertisements must help to develop primary demand for the product category by explaining what the product is and how it works, with little stress on brand name. In the growth stage, they seek to develop selective demand for particular brands and models. In the maturity stage, they stress product images or features that set the product apart from its competitors in order to maintain market share and enhance brand loyalty. During the decline stage, advertising efforts help phase out the product.

6) Define advertising appeal and describe several commonly used creative platforms.

The advertising appeal conveys information about product benefits to the target audience. After deciding what to say, the marketer must decide how to say it. Creative platforms include storyline, which features a story about the product or tells its history; product use and problem solution, which shows how a product can be employed to solve a problem; slice of life, which dramatizes how the product solved a particular problem; demonstration, which shows how the product is used; testimonial, in which spokespersons attest to the product's worth; lifestyle, which links the product to the target customer's own lifestyle (or one the customer aspires to); still life, which focuses on visual aspects of the product; association, which draws an analogy to convey a message; jingle, which is especially effective as a memory aid; and montage, which blends a number of visual effects.

7) Compare the advantages and disadvantages of various advertising media.

Each medium has advantages and disadvantages. Magazines and newspapers, which permit the consumer to reread a message, are suitable for longer, more complicated messages. Magazines can reproduce pictures more clearly than newspapers. Radio seems best suited for reminders or other short messages for specific target groups. Television permits the use of music, motion, and color. Outdoor advertising is appropriate for short messages but may be limited in its reach. Direct mail and e-mail can be personalized. Streaming media on the Internet are dramatically changing the nature of advertising on the Web. The appropriate mix of advertising media depends on the advertising budget and the advertiser's objectives.

8) Explain how advertising effectiveness is measured.

Pretesting evaluates effectiveness before an advertisement is placed in the mass media; posttesting determines if the finished version of the advertisement achieved its objectives. Sales are the ultimate measure of effectiveness, but the relationship of advertising to sales is difficult to measure.

9) Describe the nature of public relations and explain how publicity should be managed.

Public relations is the managerial activity that identifies, establishes, and maintains beneficial relationships between an organization and its publics. Its specific purposes are to enhance the organizational image and to convey information. Favorable publicity can have the same impact as advertising. Hence, effective marketers plan publicity with as much care and consideration as they give to the rest of the promotional mix.

10) Discuss several ethical issues involving advertising.

Our society grants consumers the right to be informed and prohibits deceptive practices and promotions that intentionally mislead consumers. Hence, deceptive advertising is illegal; but it may be difficult to identify. Questions about what public standards should be used in advertising may also present ethical dilemmas for marketers. Another issue involves advertising to children. Children are a special public, and there is disagreement about whether advertising aimed at this public is ethical.

Key Terms

advertising appeal (p. 401)
advertising theme (p. 402)
AIDA (p. 409)
aided recall test (p. 421)
art (p. 409)
association creative platform (p. 407)
bait and switch (p. 428)
communication goals (p. 398)
comparative advertising (p. 406)
copy (p. 409)
creative platform (p. 404)
creative process (p. 401)
crisis management (p. 426)
demonstration (p. 405)
direct-action advertisement (p. 397)
event marketing (p. 425)
fantasy creative platform (p. 407)

frequency (p. 420)
indirect-action advertisement (p. 397)
infomercial (p. 406)
institutional advertisement (p. 397)
internal marketing (p. 427)
jingle (p. 407)
lifestyle creative platform (p. 407)
media schedule (p. 419)
media selection strategy (p. 413)
misleading or deceptive advertising (p. 428)
montage (p. 408)
news release (p. 424)
person marketing (p. 425)
posttesting (p. 421)
press conference (p. 424)
pretesting (p. 420)

primary demand (p. 399)
primary demand advertising (p. 399)
product advertisement (p. 396)
public relations (p. 422)
puffery (p. 428)
reach (p. 419)
recall test (p. 421)
selective demand advertising (p. 400)
slice-of-life creative platform (p. 405)
spokesperson (p. 406)
still-life creative platform (p. 407)
storyline creative platform (p. 404)
streaming media (p. 416)
testimonial (p. 406)
unaided recall test (p. 421)

Questions for Review & Critical Thinking

1. Indicate the advertising objective in each of the following instances:
   a. Macy's holds its Fourth of July sale.
   b. Sega advertises that its Dreamcast 128-bit console would make a nice Christmas gift.
   c. "There is Hertz and not exactly."
   d. The California raisin growers promote raisins as a snack food.
2. When does advertising stimulate primary demand? When should it?
3. Watch several TV commercials, and determine the advertising objective of each one.
4. Identify three institutional advertisements and explain their purpose.
5. Identify some credit card advertisements other than those mentioned in the book, and compare them with the ones discussed in the book.
6. Does the AIDA formula have more relevance for the writing of advertising copy or the graphic aspect of advertising?
7. Describe the steps in developing a creative strategy.
8. What type of spokesperson would you hire to do a testimonial advertisement for each of the following?
   a. Campaign against alcohol abuse
   b. Campaign to encourage cigar smoking
   c. Campaign for high-quality luggage
9. Suppose you are the creative director for an advertising agency that has just landed the Cleopatra Soap account. You will be introducing the new brand to the market. Suggest a creative advertising strategy.
10. What advertising media would you select for each of the following? Why?
    a. Local zoo
    b. Local amusement park
    c. Local clothing store
    d. National soft drink
11. What products are most suited for advertising in mass media? Direct-marketing media? Interactive media?
12. What are some reasons for pretesting and posttesting specific advertisements? What are the best ways to do the testing?
13. Discuss how a political candidate for a national office might develop strategies for both advertising and public relations.
14. Provide some examples of unethical advertising and public relations efforts. Why are they unethical?
15. Form small groups as directed by your instructor. Suppose an urban university is planning to advertise its educational programs in local newspapers and perhaps on radio. What creative strategy would you utilize? Be specific. Discuss as a class what decisions each group made.

1. Go to http://www.usatoday.com and visit *USA TODAY's* Ad Track Index. Select the most current date and see if you agree with their ratings of commercials.
2. Go to the Leo Burnett Web site at http://www.leoburnett.com, the BBDO Web site at http://www.bbdo.com, the J. Walter Thompson Web site at http://www.jwtworld.com, or the Web site of another advertising agency you find using a search engine such as Yahoo!. What is the agency's mission, and what business activities does it perform for its clients?
3. The Commercial Archive at http://www.commercial-archive.com offers a random selection of television commercials from the past and present, in both streaming and downloadable video formats. Select a commercial, perhaps one that aired during the last Super Bowl, and identify its creative platform.
4. The Web site of the Department of Advertising at the University of Texas (http://advertising. utexas.edu/research/slogans/) lists numerous advertising slogans. Review this list, pick a particular slogan, and explain why it is good advertising copy.
5. Go to http://www.mypoints.com to see a system for earning redeemable points while using the Internet. How does this differ from the typical frequency marketing program, such as an airline frequent flyer program?

Address Book (Useful URLs)

Adcritic	http://www.adcritic.com
Clio Awards	http://www.clioawards.com
Advertising Research Foundation	http://www.arfsite.org
American Association of Advertising Agencies	http://www.aaaa.org
Sweepstakes Online	http://www.sweepstakesonline.com
Publicity Club of Chicago	http://www.publicity.org
Public Relations Society of America	http://www.prsa.org

Ethically Right or Wrong?

A large computer company was downsizing its operation by offering employees early retirement and telling some people that they would be laid off if they did not accept the retirement package. At the same time, the company spent almost a quarter of a million dollars to construct a Rose Bowl float that was used for only a few hours during the New Year's Day parade. Was this public relations effort proper, in light of the company's financial problems?

TAKE A STAND

1. Bid.com runs advertising focusing on a seminude model who urges you to "shop naked." Is this approach appropriate?
2. A consumer advocate wishes to create a center for the study of commercialism because the public needs to be aware of the insidious nature of advertising. "The whole emphasis of our society has become 'buy, buy, buy,'" she claims. Do you agree?
3. While visiting in Kentucky, an outdoor advertising executive saw a billboard for a car dealer that claimed "We'll beat the pants off any deal in town." The billboard featured a mannequin with undershorts down around its ankles. The executive decided to use a mannequin with its pants down and the same

lowest-price-in-town theme for an automobile dealer located in another state. Is this ethical?

4. Superstar athletes are used to advertise a basketball shoe priced at over $150. Poor inner-city teenagers are frustrated because they cannot afford the shoes their heroes wear. Is this situation good for society?

5. A retailer of roller skates uses the attention-getting headline "Kick some asphalt" and an action shot of a helmeted skater. Is this advertisement decent?

6. A business-to-business marketer holds a sweepstakes that requires visitors to its booth at an industry trade show to fill out a form. The marketer does not use a random drawing, but picks as the winning company a company that is a good prospect for future business.

7. A prankster writes a phony Miscrosoft press release that says the computer software giant is planning to buy the Catholic Church. Microsoft says the story has no truth to it. The person starting the rumor just wanted to have some fun. Was this wrong?

|case|

VIDEO CASE 14-1
W. B. Doner Advertising Agency

In 1973, Red Roof Inn started building economy lodging motels along interstate highways in the midwest. Its basic strategy was to give travelers a clean, comfortable room at a great price. Red Roof's promotional effort emphasized the slogan "Sleep Cheap." Its media plan used highway billboards to communicate the "sleep cheap" concept.

During the 1970s and early 1980s, Red Roof Inn's business grew rapidly. There was little competition in the economy segment of the lodging market. Gradually, however, this lucrative segment began to draw increased competition from Hampton Inn, Budget Inn, and others. Occupancy at Red Roof Inns began to decline as sophisticated new competition using aggressive advertising began to take some of the company's business away.

Red Roof began searching for a new advertising agency. W. B. Doner, an advertising agency with headquarters in Southfield, Michigan and Baltimore, Maryland, won the account for Red Roof's business. W. B. Doner clients at the time included Chiquita International and British Petroleum.

The advertising agency analyzed customer research and concluded that although the "sleep cheap" slogan communicated the idea that Red Roof Inns were economical, many people not familiar with the motels had a negative perception. For them, the slogan brought to mind an image of a run-down motel. The agency's analysis also suggested that the typical Red Roof Inn customer was a business traveler, often a sales representative, on a per diem expense account.

QUESTIONS
1. What factors are critical if an advertising agency is to win a client's business?
2. What type of creative strategy for Red Roof Inn should the advertising agency recommend?
3. What type of media and integrated marketing communications strategy would you suggest?

Personal Selling, Sales Management, and Sales Promotion

LEARNING OBJECTIVES

After you have studied this chapter, you will be able to . . .

1) Describe the role of personal selling and relationship management in the marketing process.

2) Identify marketing situations in which personal selling would be the most effective means of reaching and influencing target buyers.

3) Show how the professional salesperson contributes to a modern marketing firm.

4) Outline the steps involved in making a sale.

5) Explain why the marketing process does not stop when the sale is made.

6) Characterize the major aspects of the sales manager's job.

7) Classify the various forms of sales compensation.

8) Identify some of the ethical issues facing sales personnel.

9) Identify the purposes of sales promotion and explain how the major sales promotion tools work.

"I see them everywhere, and I have come to understand that they are among the bravest of us. They face on a daily basis what we all dread the most: flat, cold rejection. Even the best of them hears 'No' more than he hears 'Yes'. . . . Yet all of them get up each morning and go out to do it again." So says Bob Greene, describing salespeople in his book *American Beat*. Probably many of us share Greene's image of what salespeople's lives are like.

But salespeople don't just make sales. For many, if not most, salespeople, servicing accounts—working with existing customers—is a big part of the job. That means they hear questions like "Can you help me solve this?" as often as simple "Yes" and "No" answers. To prosper, most salespeople need to know more than the customer about some aspects of the customer's own business. Today's salesperson is often a cross between a consultant and a vendor.

Christine Sanders, a top sales representative for Eastman Kodak copiers, typifies today's successful salesperson. Selling and leasing machines that cost from $18,000 to $105,000, Sanders may spend up to 6 months closing a sale. Her commission ranges from a few hundred to a few thousand dollars. The sales she feels best about are the ones "you earn because you really understood a customer's applications or because you worked hard or were persistent in the face of a lot of competition," she says.

At Northwestern University, Sanders earned a bachelor's degree in a special program that combined economics and communications. She didn't plan on a sales career, but she effectively trained for one through extracurricular activities that often involved fund-raising.

After recruiting her in a campus interview, Kodak sent Sanders through a 10-week training program that included classroom work, real and simulated sales calls, and many sessions probing the innards of the copiers she would eventually sell. The training was "intense," she recalls, "good preparation for the real world."

Sanders shone in the suburban Chicago territory she was given and quickly advanced, eventually to a territory that includes a handful of major accounts in downtown Chicago. Forty-hour work weeks are uncommon for Sanders; the job typically demands 50 to 60. "Whatever it takes to satisfy the customer," she says.

Companies that buy or lease Kodak copiers get a package of services along with their hardware. Training is one of these services, and if a customer with 24-hour administrative operations needs to conduct late-night training sessions, a Kodak sales representative may oblige. For one such session, Sanders got up at 4 a.m. and drove to the customer's office. No trainees appeared that morning. "But I was there," she says, "and the customer will never forget that."

Her advice to newcomers in the sales profession is to know their product, their competitors' products, and their customers. That way, they can sell the benefits of their product without slamming a rival firm. A salesperson may need to understand what bothers a prospective customer about a competing product, Sanders says, "but you don't need to harp on that. I'd rather sell the benefits of my company and myself than ever bad-mouth the competition, because I think it's unprofessional and it doesn't really buy you anything—and it could come back to haunt you."[1]

Christine Sanders, the saleswoman introduced in the opening story, is a member of a profession that remains vital even in the age of e-commerce. This chapter begins by explaining the nature of personal selling in organizations and its importance in our economy. It discusses the various types of personal selling jobs and then describes the creative selling process and the tactics that order-getting salespeople use in each stage of this process. After describing the basic principles of sales management, it addresses some ethical issues facing both salespeople and sales managers. The chapter ends with a discussion of sales promotion.

Personal Selling Defined

Personal selling, as noted in Chapter 13, is a person-to-person dialogue between the prospective buyer and the seller. Thus, it consists of human contact and direct communication rather than impersonal mass communication. Personal selling involves discovering and communicating customer needs, matching the appropriate goods and services with these needs, communicating benefits, and developing customer relationships.

The salesperson's job may be to remind, to inform, or to persuade. In general, the salesperson's responsibility is to keep existing customers abreast of information about the company's products and services and to convey a persuasive sales message to potential customers. Salespeople are also expected to be aware of changes in the markets they serve and to report important information to their home offices. Professional sales personnel are vitally important as a direct link to the company's customers. Salespeople communicate a company's offering and show prospective buyers how their problems can be solved by the product. They finalize the sale by writing orders.

Many different businesses—farms, factories, retailers, banks, transportation companies, hotels, and other enterprises—use personal selling. Each business faces personal selling tasks that are unique. Various methods of personal selling may be used to accomplish these tasks.

We are all familiar with **retail selling**—selling to ultimate consumers. In business-to-business transactions, field selling, telemarketing, and inside selling are the three basic methods of personal selling. **Field selling** is performed by an "outside" salesperson, who usually travels to the prospective account's place of business. **Telemarketing** involves using the telephone as the primary means of communicating with prospective customers. **Inside selling** is similar to retail selling by store clerks; a salesperson using this approach sells in the company's place of business and deals with customers face to face. For example, the typical plumbing wholesaler employs inside sales personnel to assist customers—plumbers—who travel to the wholesaler's place of business to obtain fixtures, tools, or parts.

Retail selling
Selling to ultimate consumers.

Field selling
Business-to-business selling that takes place outside the employer's place of business, usually in the prospective customer's place of business.

Telemarketing
Using the telephone as the primary means of communicating with prospective customers. Telemarketers often use computers for order taking.

Inside selling
Business-to-business selling in the salesperson's place of business.

The Characteristics of Personal Selling

Two basic characteristics that contribute to the importance of personal selling are its flexibility and its value in building relationships. We will look more closely at these characteristics and then discuss the disadvantages of personal selling.

PERSONAL SELLING IS FLEXIBLE

Perhaps the key word to describe personal selling's advantage over other means of promotion is *flexibility*. Flexibility means that the salesperson can adapt a sales presentation to a specific situation. When a sales prospect has a particular problem or series of problems to solve, the professional salesperson can adjust the presentation to show how the product or service offered can solve these problems and satisfy the individual needs of the potential customer. Similarly, the salesperson can answer questions and overcome objections. The salesperson can even "read" the customer. Sensing that the client agrees with a certain aspect of the presentation or is not interested in a given point, for example, the salesperson can shift gears and move to another consumer benefit or otherwise adjust the presentation of the sales message.

All this is possible because personal selling entails a two-way flow of communication and elicits direct and immediate feedback. Consider the following examples of how feedback allows the salesperson to gather as well as provide information.

- The salesperson discovers in casual conversation that potential buyers have problems that no products on the market can solve.
- A customer suggests how existing products can be modified to better suit client needs.
- A customer provides the salesperson with new sales leads by mentioning other firms that could use the salesperson's merchandise.

Personal selling also is flexible because it allows the carrier of an organization's message to concentrate on the best sales prospects. In contrast, a television advertisement might be seen by just about anyone, including many people who will never be interested in the product offered for sale. This "waste circulation," as marketers call it, can be reduced or even eliminated by effective personal sellers. With personal selling, large-volume buyers can be visited or called frequently. Personal selling allows efforts to be concentrated on the profitable accounts, because it is a selective medium.

PERSONAL SELLING BUILDS RELATIONSHIPS

Throughout this book, we have emphasized that the relationship between marketer and buyer does not end when the sale is made. Long-term success often depends on the ability of the sales force to build a lasting relationship with the buyer. This is especially true in business-to-business marketing. For many business-to-business marketers, the relationship intensifies after the sale is made. How well the marketer manages the relationship becomes the critical factor in what buying decision is made the next time around.

The term **relationship management** refers to the sales function of managing the account relationship and ensuring that buyers receive the appropriate services. The goal of relationship management is to help customers expand their own organizational resources and capacities through the relationship. The salesperson is the key in relationship management, for it is the salesperson who makes sure the product solves the customer's problems and contributes to the success of the customer's organization.

Relationship management The sales function of managing the account relationship and ensuring that buyers receive appropriate services.

SOME LIMITATIONS OF PERSONAL SELLING

Our emphasis on the advantages of personal selling as an effective communication tool should not overshadow its major limitations. Personal selling cannot economically reach a mass audience and therefore cannot be used efficiently in all marketing situations. Face soaps, such as Ivory and Dove, may be used by tens of millions of people; millions more are potential users. However, reaching these target customers by personal selling would be too expensive. Advertising via mass media is the appropriate tool for products like these because it can reach a mass audience economically. (Personal selling does, however, play a role

An old business adage says "It costs six times as much to get a new customer as it does to keep an old customer." Although the figures vary industry by industry, the point is valid. Cost-effective marketers work to retain customers by managing relationships with them.

in marketing these products when sales representatives call on the major retailers and wholesalers that distribute them.)

Personal selling is expensive because it involves one-on-one communication. The cost per thousand viewers and cost per sale for a high-priced TV advertisement are quite small, since the ad is seen by a vast audience. In contrast, the average cost per call for personal selling exceeds $300 for many organizational products. The high cost results from the fact that recruiting, training, and paying salespeople costs the marketer a great deal. Each salesperson, because of the nature of the job, talks to only one or a few people at a time and may spend many hours driving to and from appointments and waiting in reception rooms. When you realize in addition that many sales calls may be needed to generate a single sale, you can see that the cost per sale can be tremendously high. The advantages of personal selling, however, often offset the high cost per sale. In some cases, as in selling custom-made machinery, personal selling is the only way a sale can be made.

The Types of Personal Selling Tasks

The importance of personal selling varies considerably across organizations. Some organizations may rely almost entirely on their sales forces to generate sales, while others use them to support a pull strategy based on advertising. Some organizations employ salespeople who do little professional selling, such as store clerks at SportsTown and Kmart, while others employ engineers and scientists as technical sales representatives. Clearly, these two types of sales representatives are not comparable.

Because of this diversity, it is useful to differentiate among selling tasks. The marketing manager must do this, for example, in deciding which selling skills and job descriptions are appropriate to the sales objectives to be accomplished. To assign a highly skilled salesperson to a task that could be accomplished just as efficiently by a less skilled individual or an interactive data-based marketing system would waste an important resource.

ORDER TAKING

Millions of people are employed in sales jobs of a routine nature. These people, who do very little creative selling, are called **order takers.** They write up orders, check invoices for accuracy, and assure timely order processing. The term *order taking* is appropriate here because the customer decides on the products and then tells the salesperson what the order is to be. The order taker's job is to be pleasant and helpful and to ensure that the order truly satisfies the customer's needs. The order taker may engage in **suggestive selling** by suggesting that the customer purchase an additional item ("Would you like French fries with your hamburger?").

In general, order-taking salespeople are divided into the "inside" sales group and the "outside," or field, sales group. Inside order takers are exemplified by auto parts salespeople. The customer looking for auto parts comes to the shop seeking the parts; the salesperson does not seek out the customer. The inside salesperson may provide some advice on product quality or installation and may even suggest that additional parts or tools would make the job easier or that the customer might as well change the oil filter while handling the other repairs. However, the order taker typically does not substantially modify the basic order presented by the customer.

Telemarketing is becoming a major activity of many inside order-taking sales representatives. Telemarketing involves the use of telephone selling in conjunction with computer technology, which is used for order taking. Of course, all salespeople telephone prospects and customers, and telephone selling is an important part of many order-getting sales jobs. However, we will use the term *telemarketing* to mean using the telephone as the primary means of communication.

Outside, or field, salespeople may also be order takers. Manufacturer or wholesaler representatives selling such well-known products as Campbell's soups find

Order taker
A salesperson who is primarily responsible for writing up orders, checking invoices, and assuring prompt processing of orders.

Suggestive selling
Suggesting to a customer who is making a purchase that an additional item or service be purchased.

themselves in this position. The question they ask their customers is essentially "How much do you want?" Some sales representatives in positions of this sort do a better job than others in enlarging order size, tying the product to special sales promotions, and so on. Such efforts are likely to be rewarded with a promotion or a bonus.

ORDER GETTING

In **order getting**—also called *creative selling*—the sales job is not routine. Order getters must seek out customers, analyze their problems, discover how the products for sale might solve those problems, and then bring these solutions to the customers' attention.

Creative selling calls for the ability to explain the product and its auxiliary dimensions in terms of benefits and advantages to the prospective buyer and to persuade and motivate the prospect to purchase the right quality and volume of products or service. Whereas the order taker's job is to expedite the sale, the order getter's job is to make the sale. Put another way, the primary function of the creative salesperson is to generate a sale that might not occur without his or her efforts. Creative salespeople generally invest far more time and effort in making a sale than do order takers. And, while it is possible to engage in creative selling in either an inside or a field environment, it is far more common for creative salespeople to go to the customer's place of business to evaluate the needs to be addressed. This process can take a very long time. An IBM salesperson attempting to demonstrate that a particular computer networking system is the best available to meet the needs of a state government, for example, can spend years preparing to make a sale.

Order getters may specialize in certain types of selling. For example, some organizations have sales personnel, often called **pioneers,** who concentrate their efforts on selling to new prospects or selling new products. Selling an established product or service for the first time to a new customer or selling an innovative product new to the market to an existing customer generates new business for the organization. In contrast, **account managers** concentrate on maintaining an ongoing relationship with existing customers and actively seek additional business for reorders or for other items in the product line. Although pioneering and account management activities may be specialized in some organizations, in many instances the creative salesperson may be involved in both.

An order-getting salesperson's primary responsibility is, of course, selling. However, order getters, especially account managers, may spend a great deal of time engaged in other activities. Exhibit 15-1 classifies the job activities of order getters.

SALES SUPPORT AND CROSS-FUNCTIONAL TEAMS

Many salespeople hold jobs whose titles suggest that they are involved in special selling situations. One commonly encountered salesperson of this sort is the so-called **missionary.** Pharmaceutical manufacturers, for example, employ missionaries, called *detailers,* to call on doctors and provide them with information on the latest prescription and nonprescription products. Detailers do not take orders; sales occur only when the doctor prescribes medication for patients. Missionary sales

Order getting
An adaptive selling process that tailors sales efforts and product offerings to specific customer needs; also known as *creative selling*. An order getter is primarily responsible for developing business for the firm. Order getters seek out customers and creatively make sales.

Pioneer
A salesperson who concentrates on selling to new prospects or on selling new products.

Account manager
A salesperson who concentrates on maintaining an ongoing relationship with existing customers.

Missionary
A salesperson who visits prospective customers, distributes information to them, and handles questions and complaints but does not routinely take orders. Missionaries really serve as customer relations representatives.

Forget the mythical lone-wolf star salesman; today's salespeople tend to work in teams. The traditional sample case? It's more likely to hold spreadsheets than widgets, and the team member hauling it around probably regards herself as a problem solver, not a vendor.

Activities of Order-Getting Salespeople[2]

GENERAL ACTIVITY	SPECIFIC ACTIVITIES
Selling	Prospect for and qualify leads; prepare sales presentations; make sales calls; overcome objections; follow-up
Working with orders	Enter orders; expedite orders; handle shipping problems
Servicing the product	Test equipment; teach safety guidelines; supervise installations; minor maintenance
Information management	Receive feedback from clients; provide feedback to superiors
Servicing the account	Perform inventory control; set up point-of-purchase displays; stock shelves
Conferences/meetings	Attend sales conferences; set up exhibitions, trade shows
Recruiting/training	Recruit new sales representatives; train new sales representatives
Entertaining	Take clients to lunch, sporting events, golfing, tennis, etc.
Traveling	Visit prospects in other cities, regions
Working with distributors	Establish relations with distributors; extend credit; collect past-due accounts

Cross-functional sales team
The sales representative and those who support his or her efforts in making sales and servicing accounts. Support personnel may include technical specialists and missionary salespeople.

Account service representative
A sales employee at company headquarters or at a branch office who corresponds with clients and provides customer service to established accounts; sometimes called a *sales correspondent.*

personnel in fact rarely take or actively seek orders; their primary responsibility is to build goodwill by distributing information to customers and prospective customers and by "checking in" to be sure that buyers are receiving satisfactory service from company representatives and other relevant channel members such as wholesalers.

Even missionary salespeople working for consumer goods companies and calling on retailers do not sell anything directly. If a retailer insisted on placing an order, the missionary would not refuse to accept it but would simply pass it on to the salesperson who regularly handles the retailer's account. Missionaries are, in effect, employed by the manufacturer to perform a public relations function.

Other specialized sales support people are found in industries in which scientists and engineers serve as technical specialists to support the regular field sales force. The credentials and expertise of these sales engineers, applications programmers, and other technical support personnel are often helpful in concluding sales of complicated products such as nuclear reactors, computer installations, and advanced jet engines.

In many organizations, the salesperson in contact with the customer is supported by a **cross-functional sales team.** A creative salesperson who successfully closes a deal has perhaps called on a technical specialist in engineering or logistics or a more experienced salesperson for aid. Perhaps the path to a successful selling experience was made easier by a missionary salesperson. After the sale, the missionary may play a further role in keeping the buyer content and certain that the best choice was made. Order takers, whether in the field or at the home office, may see to it that orders are handled promptly and without error. The customer may be provided with the name and phone number of an **account service representative,** someone at company headquarters who can answer questions about delivery, post-sale service, installation, and repair parts when the salesperson is away from the home office. A toll-free number also may be provided.

The effective cross-functional sales team is a good illustration of the marketing concept in action. It reflects an effort to satisfy customers, not just sell products. Many people in the organization, from accountants to engineers, engage in a unified effort to build relationships.

The Creative Selling Process

As you have seen, in some selling jobs the salesperson does little true selling. Perhaps the least creative selling situation involves the "canned presentation." Here, the salesperson memorizes a descriptive or persuasive speech and is directed to give that speech to any and all potential customers without variation. Such an approach is common in many telephone selling situations.

Except perhaps for the canned-sales-talk deliverer, all salespeople can benefit from knowledge of the **creative selling process.** This series of steps provides guidelines for the salesperson. It suggests that professional selling is an adaptive process that begins with the identification of specific potential customers and tailors the sales dialogue and product offering to each prospect's needs. The ultimate goal is customer satisfaction.

Professional selling is an adaptive process that begins with the identification of specific potential customers and tailors the sales dialogue and product offering to each prospect's needs.

Creative selling process
The seven-step process by which creative selling is carried out: (1) locating qualified prospects, (2) preapproach planning, (3) approaching the prospect, (4) making the sales presentation, (5) handling objections, (6) closing the sale, and (7) following up.

The creative selling process includes the following steps: (1) locating qualified prospects (2) preapproach planning, (3) approaching the prospect, (4) making the sales presentation, (5) handling objections, (6) closing the sale, and (7) following up. These steps are portrayed in Exhibit 15-2. Again, the steps represent a guideline that helps salespeople to think about the tasks they face. Unlike the canned sales presentation, they are not to be followed slavishly.

STEP ONE: LOCATING QUALIFIED PROSPECTS

An established sales representative may rely on regular customers for a certain amount of business, but a successful salesperson is not content to service only

e x h i b 1 5-2

The Creative Selling Process

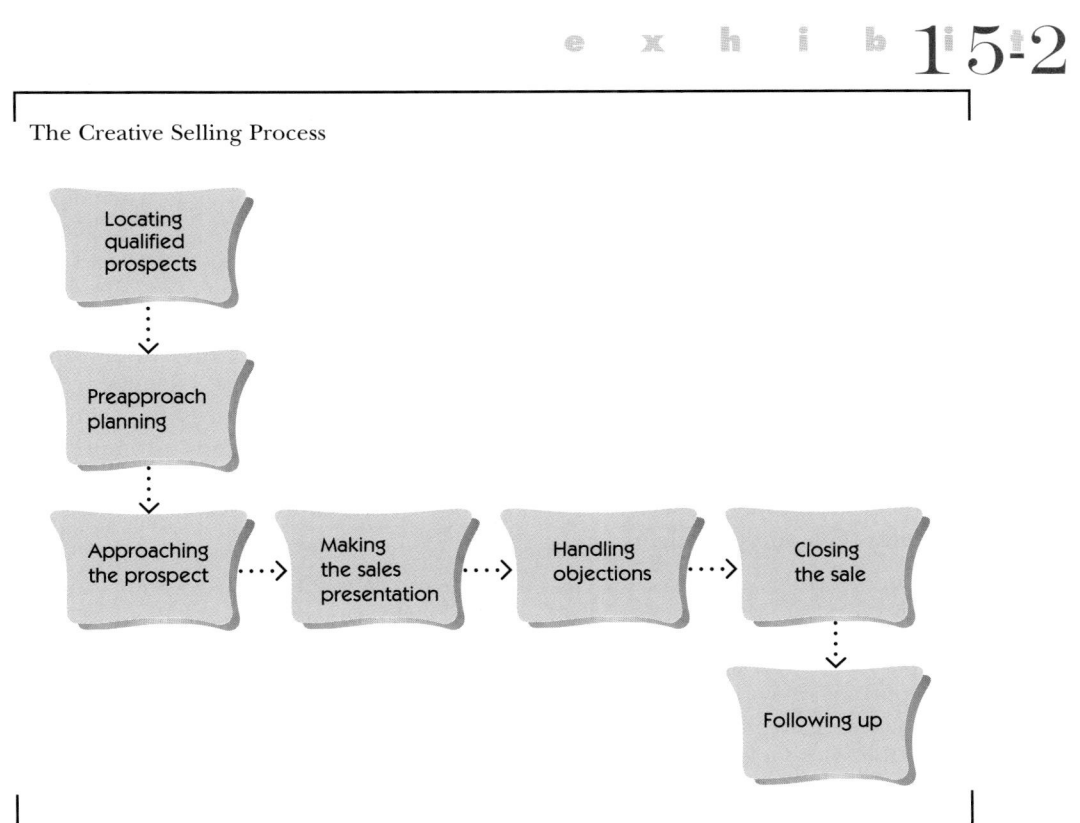

existing accounts. Sales calls to regular customers are only part of the sales job. New customers must be sought. However, making a sales presentation to someone who has no need for the product, who cannot pay for it, or who is not empowered to purchase it is not an efficient use of time. The salesperson must thus identify likely customers, or prospects.

Prospecting
Identifying likely customers. In prospecting, the salesperson may search lists of previous customers, trade association lists, government publications, and many other sources.

Locating prospects is called **prospecting.** Lists of previous customers, referrals, trade lists, advertising inquiries (such as postcards or coupons returned to the sales office by interested parties), records of visitors to company Web sites, and other sources may all provide the names of prospects. While each industry or line of business has its traditional means of generating "leads," such as membership lists published by trade associations, good salespeople are prepared to dig harder for prospects. Government publications providing breakdowns of business patterns in particular countries, states, and cities can be used, and perhaps even cross-referenced with other sources, to develop lists of likely buyers. The number of prospecting tools is nearly unlimited.

Identifying prospects is only the beginning. Prospects must need the product, must be able to pay for it, and must be in a position to make, or at least contribute to, the buying decision. Determining that these conditions are met is called **qualifying** the prospect. Another consideration in the qualifying process is determining whether the prospective buyer's order will be of sufficient size—that is, whether the account has an adequate sales potential.

Qualifying
Evaluating a prospect's potential. Key questions are whether the prospect needs the product, can pay for it, and has the authority to make—or at least contribute to—a decision to buy.

STEP TWO: PREAPPROACH PLANNING

Preapproach planning involves gathering and evaluating information about the prospect's situation. The information gained during this step lays the foundation for planning the other steps in the selling process.

Before making the sales call, the salesperson should learn what member of an organization should be contacted—it is important to know who has the authority to make the purchase decision. Who else strongly influences the purchase decision? A plant superintendent may be in charge of production, but calling on the superintendent only is the wrong tactic if the vice-president makes all the buying decisions.

In addition to learning what roles different individuals play in the buying center, the salesperson should learn the prospect's requirements and any other relevant information that might help in making the sale. Many salespeople find that checking the prospect's home page on the Internet is an ideal way to learn about the company. In other circumstances, the salesperson can search company databases to find existing customers whose situations are similar to the prospect's. For example, Hallmark now recognizes that the same mix of greeting cards should not be sold to every store. Hallmark's sales teams use data derived from bar codes that appear on all Hallmark cards; when a card's bar code is scanned at the checkout counter, information about the sale goes into Hallmark's database. Sales teams can retrieve merchandising information about greeting cards and then plan a unique presentation that tailors card selections, displays, and promotions to a retailer's demographics.

Once the salesperson has done enough homework on the prospect, he or she prepares the approach.

STEP THREE: APPROACHING THE PROSPECT

Approach
The step in the creative selling process wherein the salesperson makes initial contact and establishes rapport with a prospect.

The **approach** involves making an initial contact and establishing rapport with a prospect. If the prospect is already familiar with the salesperson and the company, the approach may be as simple as making a telephone call to request an appointment or knocking on the prospect's door with a friendly greeting. In other situations, the salesperson may have to be more creative in attracting the attention of the prospect. The salesperson may, for example, approach the prospect by mentioning an offer that can benefit the prospect. What better way to attract attention than to offer a benefit that will save money for the customer, make the customer's products more attractive to buyers, or add prestige to the customer's good name?

The approach is intended to make a good impression, attract the prospect's attention, and solidify the prospect's willingness to listen to the sales presentation.[3] The

importance of making a good impression during the first few seconds of the approach should not be underestimated. Experience is a great helper in this matter, but research and caution can serve the seller well, too. For example, smoking a cigar or cigarette in a nonsmoker's office may lose a sale before the presentation has even begun. Not wearing a hard hat in a location where protective gear is required may make the salesperson appear too unfamiliar with the situation in which he or she is supposedly going to solve a client's problem.

In many Asian countries, prospects view the approach as a pivotal phase in the selling process. Formal introductions and ritualistic exchange of business cards are expected in many places. Business is not conducted until a *personal relationship* is established.

STEP FOUR: MAKING THE SALES PRESENTATION

The **sales presentation** is the salesperson's attempt to persuasively communicate the product's benefits and to explain appropriate courses of action to the potential buyer. Typically, an effective sales presentation tells the product story.

The presentation begins by focusing the prospect's attention on the story. Some salespeople do this by producing some physical object, such as the product itself (if it is both portable and eye-catching), a model of the product, or something that relates to the product in an interesting or even humorous way. It is more common, however, to use an opening statement designed to attract attention. Thus, opening lines such as "I'm here to show you how we can save $5,000 a week in your factory" or "I've got a computer networking system that everyone in your organization will consider user-friendly" are frequently heard.

After focusing the prospect's attention, the salesperson must generate interest in the product being offered. An opening comment that the salesperson can save the client a great deal of money in income taxes may gain attention, but it must be followed by the development of interest in the product being sold as the means to save the tax money. Describing the product's benefits in an interesting way, explaining how it works, and demonstrating its use can all be part of an effective presentation.

Arousing interest in the product itself is still not enough to make a sale. A desire to purchase the product must also be generated. A scale model of an executive jet plane may be interesting, but it is of little use if it does not help bring about a desire to own the plane itself.

In assembling effective sales presentations, the salesperson may find visual aids such as PowerPoint graphics and video recordings effective ways to illustrate a product's benefits. In recent years, many salespeople have come to rely on computers in their presentations. They may use portable, laptop units to illustrate some aspect of the product or offer computer-generated data that answer the customer's "what if" questions. For example, a representative of an industrial robotics firm may bring a laptop computer into the prospect's office, ask for information

Sales presentation
The step in the creative selling process wherein the salesperson attempts to persuasively communicate the product's benefits and to explain appropriate courses of action.

such as production schedules, delivery requirements, and so on, and enter that information into the computer. Within minutes, the computer can yield output that shows exactly how the salesperson's product will affect the prospect's business operations.

Note that some of the communication in the sales presentation may not be verbal. Many successful salespeople use body language, seating arrangements, and clothing colors to communicate important nonverbal messages to their clients.

STEP FIVE: HANDLING OBJECTIONS

In most sales presentations, the salesperson does not make a one-way presentation while the customer passively listens. The customer, no matter how friendly or interested in the product, may have reservations about committing money or other resources in a purchase agreement. Questions or strong objections are likely to arise. Because objections explain reasons for resisting or postponing purchase, the salesperson should listen and learn from them.

Indeed, the sales call should be a dialogue or conversation in which questions are welcomed and direct feedback elicited. It is undesirable to have the prospect sit quietly until the end of the talk and then say "No" without any explanation. Effective salespeople encourage prospects to voice reasons why they are resisting the purchase. Even though the well-prepared sales presentation covers such topics as the quality of the product, the reputation of the seller, post-sale services, and the like, the objection or question reveals to the salesperson what points the customer views as most important.

There are many means of **handling objections.** When an objection indicates that the prospect has failed to fully understand some point that was made, the salesperson can comment on the area of uncertainty. A question about a product characteristic may mean that the prospect has not grasped how the product works or seen the benefits it can provide. A salesperson who encounters an objection of this type can go on to provide additional persuasive information, clarify the sales presentation, or offer the basic argument for the product in a different manner.

Experienced sales representatives can also turn objections into counterarguments. A stockbroker might say, "You are right, Dr. Jerpe. The price of this Internet stock has dropped 40 percent in the last six months. That is exactly why I am recommending it to you. At this low price, it is now underpriced and is an excellent buy, in the opinion of our analysts."

One tactic for handling objections is to agree with the prospect, as did the stockbroker mentioned above, accepting the objection with reservation. This is consistent with the marketing concept's prescription to sell the product from the customer's point of view. The salesperson's counterargument is intended to refute the objection. The purpose of this method of dealing with objections is to avoid getting into an argument with the prospect. If the customer says the price is high and the salesperson says it is low, the discussion goes nowhere fast. But if the salesperson responds, "Yes, it is priced higher than many, but our product quality is higher than the competitors', so you get more for your money," the salesperson has agreed and counterargued at the same time. More importantly, the seller has given a reason for the higher price.

The prospect's questions, objections, and other comments may reveal how close the prospect is to making a purchase decision. Good salespeople use such clues to determine whether they should attempt to enter the closing stages of the sales presentation.

STEP SIX: CLOSING THE SALE

Ultimately, salespeople must make the sale. In selling, the term **closing** indicates that the sale is being brought to a finish. The main advantage of personal selling over other forms of promotion is that the salesperson is in a position to conclude negotiations by actually asking for an order.

Handling objections
The step in the creative selling process wherein the salesperson responds to questions or reservations expressed by the prospect.

Closing
The step in the creative selling process wherein the salesperson attempts to obtain a prospect's commitment to buy.

what went right?

SOQ NOP   The senior regional sales manager from John Deere was wearing an odd tie tack. It was in the shape of a cross. The vertical letters spelled out DEERE, the horizontal SOQ NOP. When asked what the letters stood for, his reply was "Sell on quality, not on price." He added, "It's my toughest job, in down markets, to make my own people realize that the objective is to sell the benefits, not just resort to price. I tell them a story. I was going after a sale some years ago. It came down to two final contenders. The fellow making the buy called me in to give me one last chance. His message in a nutshell: 'You're just too high on the price side. No hard feelings, and we hope we can do business with you again in the future.' I was about to walk out the door, unhappy to say the least. Then I had an inspiration. I turned and said, 'Those are nice-looking boots you've got on.' He was a bit surprised, but said, 'Thanks,' and he went on to talk for a minute or so about those fine boots, what was unique about the leather, why they were practical as well as fine. I said to him, at the end of this description, 'How come you buy those boots and not just a pair off the shelf in an Army-Navy store?' It must have taken 20 seconds for the grin to spread all the way across his face. 'The sale is yours,' he said, and he got up and came around his desk and gave me a hearty handshake."[4]

Unfortunately, many salespeople are knowledgeable and convincing when making sales presentations, but they never get around to asking for the order. Sometimes this is due to the presenter's genuine belief in the product being offered—a belief so strong that he or she can barely stop talking about it. In other cases, worry about receiving a negative answer or misreading the client's willingness to deal may be the cause.[5] In any case, there comes a point when the presentation must be drawn to its logical conclusion.

Because closing the sale is so vital, experienced sales personnel constantly try to read prospects' reactions to the presentation for signs that a conclusion is in order. Signs revealing that prospects are ready to buy are called **closing signals.** For example, a comment such as "These new machines should reduce the number of breakdowns we've been having" may indicate a readiness to purchase. Should the prospect offer a signal like this, the sales representative should quickly respond and ask for the prospect's signature on the order.

When the prospect's willingness to close is not clearly revealed, the salesperson may utilize what is called the trial close. A **trial close** is a tactic intended to draw from the prospect information that will signal whether a sale is imminent. For example, the salesperson may attempt to focus the conversation on closing the sale by asking whether the customer prefers the standard model or the deluxe (thus narrowing the alternatives to a choice). If the customer indicates a preference in a positive way, the sale may almost be made.

Salespeople often use standard closing techniques such as the following:

- The direct, straightforward approach. The salesperson requests the order.
- The assumptive closing technique. The salesperson takes out the order forms or in some other way implies that an agreement has been reached, saying something like, "Let's see here, you'll need 20 units by the first of the month."
- The "standing-room-only" closing technique. Here the sales representative indicates that time is an important factor and supply is limited. A typical phrase used is "We've been selling a lot of these lately, and I want to make sure that you get what you need."
- The summative approach. Here, the salesperson summarizes, usually with pencil and paper, the benefits of buying the product, perhaps mentioning some

Closing signals
Signs from the prospect revealing that he or she is ready to buy.

Trial close
A personal selling tactic intended to elicit from a prospect a signal indicating whether he or she is ready to buy.

The communication revolution has freed sales representatives from the office. Computers enormously increase the amount of information a salesperson can gather about his or her customers. With cellular phones, fax machines, portable computers, and information systems, a sales representative can tap into company databases and transmit information from any remote location.

disadvantages that are overcome by the advantages. When the product's benefits have been summarized, the salesperson asks for the order.

STEP SEVEN: BUILDING RELATIONSHIPS—THE FOLLOW-UP

Marketers view the closing of the sale not as the end of a process but as the start of an organization's relationship with a customer. A satisfied customer will return to the company that treated it best if it needs to repurchase the same product at some time in the future. If a related item is needed, the satisfied customer knows the first place to look. The professional salesperson knows that the best way to get repeat business is to keep customers. And the best way to keep customers is to follow up with a telephone call, an e-mail, or a personal visit after the sale.

During the **follow-up**, salespeople make sure that everything was handled as promised and that the order was shipped promptly and received on schedule. Few things are worse than promising a delivery date and having the goods arrive weeks or months late. Sales personnel should also check with the customer to determine whether there were any problems such as missing parts or damage to the merchandise during shipping. The customer, once in possession of the product, may need additional help in integrating it into company operations. Post-sale services such as repairs or returns may also be necessary.

In a sense, how well the follow-up is performed differentiates between a simple selling job and marketing. After all, if customer satisfaction is not achieved or if the organization appears not to even try to achieve it, the company is unlikely to enjoy anything more than a one-shot sale. When the possibility of repeat purchase or expanded business seems strong, a single follow-up call after the transaction may not be enough. In many situations, the salesperson, with the help of others in the organization, must initiate a relationship emphasizing ongoing follow-up. Buyers—especially buyers of technically complex products—may expect salespeople and their companies to offer continuous, long-term help in solving problems and contributing to organizational success. If a marketer does not meet a buyer's expectations with excellent service, the buyer may terminate its relationship with the seller. And in many situations, if an account is lost, it is lost for good.

There are many ways a salesperson can foster an ongoing relationship; showing appreciation for an order, expediting delivery, and resolving complaints are but a few. Often, the salesperson engaging in relationship management obtains help from others in the organization. For example, BlackIce Defender has an extensive

Follow-up
The final step in the creative selling process, wherein the salesperson, after the sale has been made, contacts the buyer to make sure every aspect of the sale was handled properly.

sales support service that offers customers technical assistance with its firewall software via the Internet or by telephone.

Sales Force Automation

The application of digital and cellular technologies to personal selling is known as *sales force automation*. Cell phones, fax machines, e-mail, and voice messaging systems have changed the way sales representatives communicate with prospects and clients. Laptop computers, data-based marketing systems, mass customization systems, and the Internet have also dramatically changed the personal selling process.

Many aspects of relationship marketing have already been discussed. However, from the perspective of the sales force, the establishment and maintenance of mutually beneficial long-term relationships with customers is *relationship selling*. The goal of relationship selling is to earn the position of preferred supplier by fostering trust among key accounts.[6]

Sales representatives used to keep facts such as a client's birthday, whether she plays golf, and her favorite restaurants in their own notebooks; if the representative left the company, so did the client information. Today, this type of information, along with past purchasing history and responsiveness to promotions, is kept in the company's database. Data-based marketing software can help the salesperson personalize the sales call. In fact, data-based marketing systems can analyze customer and prospect data to provide the salesperson with a list of who should be visited in person, who should receive a phone call, and who should receive a customized letter. Product configurators are increasingly being used by sales representatives who sell complex products that have to be custom-tailored for a particular customer's situation. These software programs (often available on a company's intranet) configure and price products on the spot, reducing the time a sales representative spends working on a proposal.[7] Sales automation can also help with follow-up. The computer can be used to send e-mail to the sales representative to indicate that a shipment has been sent on time or that a delay can be expected and that a computer-generated letter has already been sent to the customer explaining the problem.

This discussion of sales automation has just scratched the surface of information about new technologies, but these examples should give you some insight into how much different the sales process in the 21st century will be from selling in the 20th century.

Salesforce.com is a Web site for salespeople and organizations. The Web site's tools help small and mid-sized organizations exploit the power of the Internet. Salesforce.com allows a company to easily access, manage, and/or share all its sales information—immediately, efficiently, and reliably—right from each salesperson's computer. There's no software, hardware, or networks to buy, and nothing to install or maintain—salesforce.com manages the site so a company's sales information is completely safe and secure, and available 24/7 from anywhere.

Dallas-based Aviall Inc. is a $400 million aviation parts distributor. A few years ago, Margaret Bouline, the Vice President of Information Systems at Aviall, got the CEO's approval for a $250,000 budget for a Web-based order-entry system. Little did Bouline know that her project's success would depend on a constituency far from the corner office: Aviall's 300 sales reps around the globe. Fearing their jobs were at stake, the sales representatives bad-mouthed the site to customers and told them not to use it. The executives were caught off-guard. They didn't take into account that the sales reps would view the Web-based order-entry system as a hostile move. Many sales representatives felt threatened and saw the action as the first step in eliminating their jobs. Bouline tried pitching the site as a boon for the salespeople, since letting customers take care of routine orders and quotes online would free the sales reps to develop deeper relationships and win new customers. Although the reps received commissions for orders placed over the Web, they still resisted the site. The company finally figured out why: Aviall's sales reps viewed the great customer service they offer as a way to distinguish the company from other distributors. What the information systems people were doing wrong was saying, "Here's this wonderful e-commerce system, and here's how it's going to benefit you and Aviall." They should have been saying, "Look at what a wonderful tool this is for your customer."

For the second phase of its e-commerce effort, Aviall took a much more cross-functional, customer-centric approach to rolling out an improved site. The company hammered out its new e-commerce strategy in conjunction with an overhaul of its overall sales strategy. The committee overseeing the sales/e-commerce strategy first identified target market segments. Next, they brought in customers and Aviall business people from those segments and asked them what problems they had and how e-commerce could help solve them. And the pitch to the sales reps also stressed the customer-service benefits. Every rep also received a kit explaining how to use the new Web site and what speaking points to use to sell it, along with a canned demo on a CD-ROM for reps who did not feel comfortable demonstrating the site themselves.[7]

Sales Management

Sales management is the marketing management activity dealing with planning, organizing, directing, and controlling the personal selling effort. Sales managers are responsible for a number of administrative tasks. The major activities involved in operating a sales force are shown in Exhibit 15-3.

Sales personnel, like most employees, require some degree of supervision and management. However, typical salesmen or saleswomen, especially those operating in a business-to-business setting, are responsible for setting priorities and managing their own time. Although they maintain contact with sales management and may ask for advice or other support, most of the time they work away from their direct supervisors. For this reason, the job of the sales manager differs significantly from that of other managers.

The sales manager's responsibilities also may include selling activities. After all, virtually every sales manager earned the job by per-

Sales management
The marketing management activity that deals with planning, organizing, directing, and controlling the personal selling effort.

forming well in the field. Sales managers may accompany less-experienced sales personnel during training periods or work with a veteran salesperson to sell a particularly significant account. Thus, while sales managers are responsible primarily for planning, organizing, directing, and controlling the sales force, they also have the opportunity to engage in the personal selling process.

SETTING SALES OBJECTIVES

All good managers, before setting out to accomplish a task, first give considerable thought to what that task should or must be. In other words, they set objectives. The reason a statement of sales objectives is so important is that much of sales management involves the assignment of resources. How can the manager know, for example, how many salespeople to hire unless the tasks to be accomplished are first understood?

Sales objectives
The specific objectives that an organization's sales effort will attempt to meet. Sales objectives should be precise and quantifiable, should include a time frame, and should be reasonable given the organization's resources.

Sales objectives should meet the criteria by which objectives generally are evaluated in the marketing world. They should be precise, be quantifiable, include a time frame, and be reasonable given the organization's resources, its overall promotional strategy, and the competitive environment in which it operates. If the objectives are not precise, neither managers nor salespeople will know what they are trying to accomplish. If they are not quantifiable, managers cannot know when an objective has been reached. If no time frame is included, the sales force has "forever" to reach the goals. If the objectives are not reasonable, time and effort will be wasted in a pursuit doomed to fail from the start.

Sales objectives can be expressed in many ways. Among these are sales totals in dollars, sales totals in units of products, increases over previous sales totals, market share, sales calls completed, sales calls on new customers, and dollar or unit sales per sales call made. An example of a sales objective stated in terms of sales volume is "to expand annual sales in the Virginia/West Virginia sales territory by 10 percent over last year's dollar volume." The sales forecast—which, depending on the organization, may or may not be the responsibility of the sales manager—strongly influences decisions about sales objectives.

ORGANIZING SALES ACTIVITY

Because nonretail sales forces typically must contact their customers either in person or by telephone, sales departments generally are organized so that sales personnel are responsible for certain accounts. Calling regularly on the same organizations and individuals leads to a better understanding of customers' problems and needs and provides the sales representative with an opportunity to develop a personal relationship with the client. The specific accounts and prospects assigned to a salesperson comprise the **sales territory.** A sales territory commonly is thought of as a geographical area. Territories are not always so defined, however. Sales territories may also be determined according to customer type or product line. Every method of creating territories has advantages and disadvantages. Whatever the method employed, the characteristics and needs of the customers to be served should always take precedence over the convenience of the sales force.

Geographically Based Sales Territories   Sales personnel frequently are assigned to particular geographical sales territories. Exhibit 15-4 shows an organization chart for a company using this approach. Notice that as an individual manager moves higher in the organizational scheme, he or she becomes responsible for

e-commerce | Changing Everything

Fisher Controls Inc., a St. Louis subsidiary of Emerson Electric Co. that builds valves and process-control systems, has close to 500 product lines, each with 4 million to 5 million possible configurations. Each configuration can be sold with every other product line, resulting in a staggering number of product possibilities. Before they began using configuration software, Fisher's salespeople—who typically required engineering backgrounds to do the work—would take days to figure out configurations and pricing by hand, then put together proposals and specification sheets. If they made mistakes, the difference came out of their commission.

Today, the process requires only a button click. Fisher uses a configurator and a pricing quote engine that evaluates customer requirements—including the pressures and temperatures the part will need to endure—and comes up with ideal configurations. The pricer automatically suggests discounts based on the customer's relationship with Fisher.[8]

Sales territory
The specific and prospective accounts assigned to a salesperson. They may be based on geographical divisions, customer types, or product lines.

The Managerial Activities of Sales Managers

MANAGEMENT FUNCTION	SALES MANAGEMENT ACTIVITY	EXAMPLE
Planning	Setting sales objectives	Determine specific sales objectives that reflect the organization's overall strategy.
Organizing	Organizing sales activity	Determine if sales territories should be based on geography, customer type, product line, or selling tasks
Directing	Recruiting and selecting personnel	Determine the best individuals to hire
	Training and developing personnel	Determine how much knowledge sales personnel need to have about customers' businesses
	Managing compensation	Determine if a straight commission, a salary, or some combination is the best compensation plan
	Motivating	Determine how much praise and reinforcement each salesperson needs
Controlling	Evaluating and controlling	Determine if sales quotas have been met

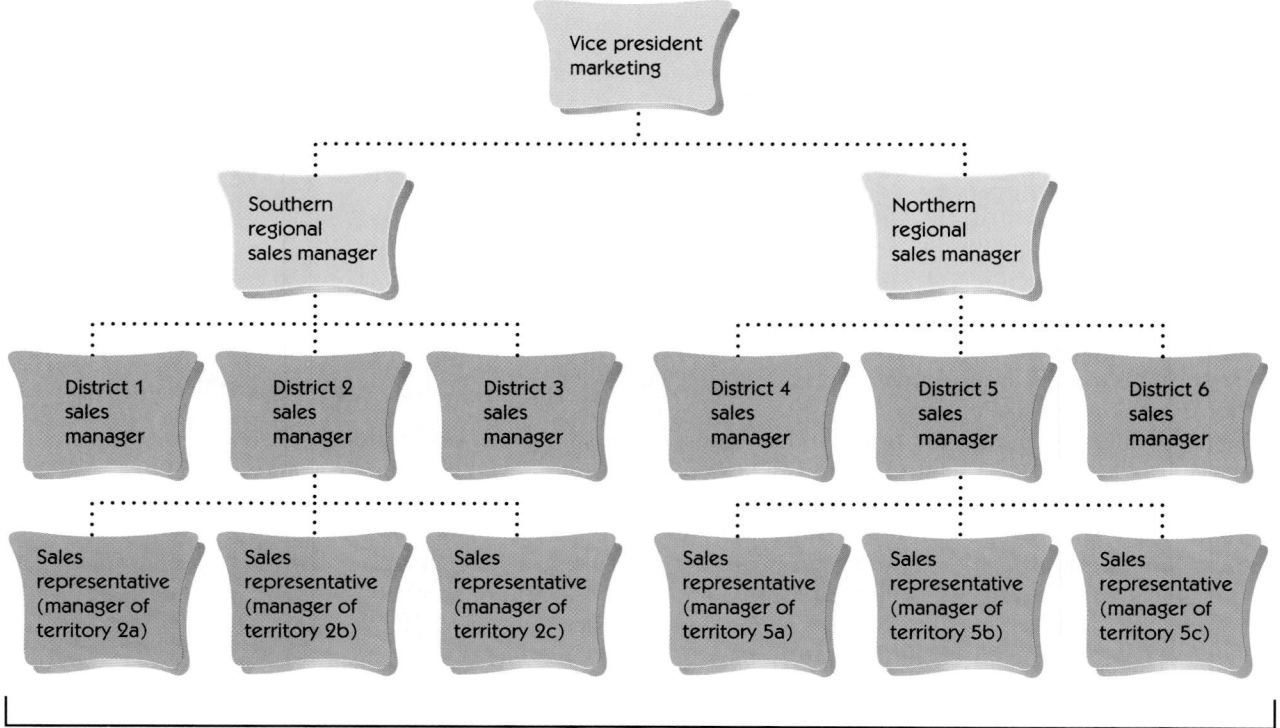

Example of a Geographic Sales Organization

increasingly larger territories, with the vice president for marketing ultimately responsible for the entire country, or even the world.

District sales managers and regional sales managers, who are held accountable for the activity of sales personnel operating within specific areas, are referred to as **field sales managers** because of their direct concern for salespeople out in the field. Their primary concern is management of the field sales personnel who report to them.

Much attention has been paid to the design of geographic sales territories. A number of variables should be considered as the market is being "cut up" into sections for assignment to individual sales representatives. Even though each company's situation is different, similar factors must be weighed. A major concern is creating territories that are roughly equal in terms of physical size, transportation within the territory, the number of current and potential customers within the territory, the general economic state of the territory, and the size of the territory's sales and sales potential. Personnel problems result when one salesperson gets a "bad" territory and another gets the "best" territory. Thus, equality and fairness are important goals in this process.

Organization by Customer Type   When a sales organization specializes by customer type, two or more salespeople may cover the same geographical area. For example, a chemical manufacturer may have one sales representative call on users of petrochemicals in the Southwest and another representative call on users of other chemicals in this region. Similarly, a textbook publishing company may cover the Midwest with one sales representative who calls on business and engineering professors and another who deals with professors in colleges of arts and sciences. Notice that in both cases more than one representative of the same com-

Field sales manager
A district or regional sales manager, so called because his or her main concern is the salespeople in the field.

pany may call on a single organization and the representatives may call on different individuals within these organizations. Obviously, the chemical company and the publisher both feel that the customer is better served by dealing with a salesperson who is a specialist rather than a generalist.

Even when salespeople are assigned by customer type, the matter of geography still enters the picture. The bookseller specializes by buyer type within a specific area, as do the chemical company's representatives. Thus, the sales force is organized by a combination of geography and customer type. In fact, the inescapability of the geographic factor makes a combination approach to the assignment of sales territories the most commonly employed.

Organization by Product Line   Within large, multiproduct companies, each corporate division or product line may have its own sales force. As with organization by customer type, the emphasis is on specialization. Multiline organizations often find that their salespeople must know a great many technical details about their products and customers. The need to remember too many products and too many details will almost certainly reduce the salesperson's ability to sell a product effectively.

RECRUITING AND SELECTING THE SALES FORCE

Two shoe salespeople were sent to a poverty-stricken country. The first cabled, "Returning home immediately. No one wears shoes here." The second, more optimistic salesperson cabled, "Unlimited possibilities. Millions still without shoes."[9] This apocryphal story illustrates one of the most important jobs sales managers perform: the personnel function. The personnel function starts with finding and hiring individuals for sales slots in the organization—people who are both interested in sales jobs and qualified to fill them. An important point here is that no salesperson, whatever his or her qualifications, is universally acceptable in all selling situations. Thus, the sales manager must decide what characteristics a given sales position requires. These requirements must be carefully thought out and matched with job candidates, not only for the sake of the sales organization but also for the sake of the individuals hired. The task at hand is to get the right person for the job.

Because selling situations vary tremendously, the analysis of a sales position should include a list of traits that an appropriate applicant should have. Some traits and accomplishments commonly considered in recruiting sales personnel are educational background, intelligence, self-confidence, problem-solving ability, speaking ability, appearance, achievement orientation, friendliness, empathy, and involvement in school or community organizations. These things do not guarantee that an applicant will be a successful sales representative. They may, however, be used as indicators of otherwise difficult-to-determine attributes. For example, a friendly and helpful personality may be considered a meaningful trait, and membership in clubs and service organizations may suggest that a job applicant has that trait.

One of a sales manager's more important activities is recruiting. Finding the right person for an open sales position can make other sales management tasks easier.

TRAINING THE SALES FORCE

After sales personnel have been recruited and selected, they must be trained. Training programs vary from company to company. Some companies use an apprentice-type system, sending the newcomer into the field with an experienced salesperson to "learn the ropes." Others put the recruit through an intensive training program at headquarters or at a regional office before putting him or her out in the field. A few organizations believe in a "sink or swim" method, whereby new people are sent out on their own to succeed or fail.

A typical sales training program for a recent college graduate hired by an office photocopier company is likely to cover the following areas: (1) company policies and practices, (2) industry and competitors' background, and (3) product knowledge and selling techniques. The graduate may receive several weeks of instruction at a center run by staff who specialize in training recruits. The instruction will probably feature guest lectures by both field salespeople and company executives. The next stage may require the graduate to work as an account service representative for several months, becoming familiar with customer needs and complaints and handling these by telephone or letter. The next phase may be on-the-job training that involves making sales presentations under the supervision and guidance of the sales manager or a senior salesperson. Programs like this usually are varied to suit the needs of the incoming employee. If the new person is experienced in sales, for example, less emphasis will be placed on selling skills than on company policies and product information.

In many successful sales organizations, training to develop the skills of sales personnel is an ongoing process. Most sales representatives can benefit from a refresher course, a few days learning about new products, or just a break from their regular schedules. Thus, ongoing training often is carried out at the home office, at sales conventions, or even at a local hotel or conference center.

COMPENSATING THE SALES FORCE

Sales work—unlike certain other business professions, such as accounting or personnel management—is generally highly visible. It involves the attempt to achieve quantifiable results: Did sales go up or did they fall? How many new accounts were opened? How many calls were made? For this reason, most sales managers feel that salespeople who achieve the highest performance in terms of some specific measure should receive the highest compensation. Financial incentives are not the only motivators, but they are important and deserve the sales manager's close attention.

what went right?

JCPenney Because shoppers expect good service at JCPenney, the company has a sales training program for its sales associates. The training covers a variety of tasks, such as understanding body language. The body language training showed associates how to mirror the behavior of customers. If the customer is in a hurry, the associate needs to be in a hurry. If the customer is indecisive or taking her time, so does the associate.

A few years ago, JCPenney also began rolling out a companywide CD-ROM system that offers self-paced instruction. New associates must complete an eight-hour "new hire and point-of-sale training program" on the computer before they go out on the floor. The program gives them the JCPenney philosophy of customer service. An in-company intranet—which provides employees with up-to-the-minute product information—was also rolled out that year.

Investment in all this technology quickly paid for itself. JCPenney stopped flying employees to Texas for training. It halted publishing, warehousing, and mailing training programs. It put those dollar savings into technology and recouped its investment in equipment within a year.[10]

What would be the ideal compensation plan for salespeople? It would be simple, so that disagreements over the size of paychecks and bonuses might be avoided. It would be as fair as possible to avoid arousing petty jealousies among the sales team members. It would be regular, so that salespeople would be able to count on a reasonable reward coming to them steadily. It would provide security to the salesperson as well as a degree of incentive to work harder. It would give management some control over the sales representative's activities. Finally, it would encourage optimal purchase orders by the customer. (For example, a heavily incentive-based plan might encourage salespeople to engage in extra-hard-sell activities, including selling customers items that they really do not need. This is not optimal ordering; ordering should promote the development of a long-term profitable relationship with clients.) Based on the sales manager's objectives and the nature of the selling job, management must select from among the following types of compensation plans.

Straight Salary or Wage　The **straight salary** method or an hourly wage plan offers the salesperson compensation that is not immediately tied to sales performance. Management has the greatest control over a salesperson's time and activity under this plan and the least uncertainty about selling expenses, because earnings are not tied to sales. Many creative salespeople dislike this plan, preferring to accept the risks of commission in the hope of achieving high earnings. However, there are some selling situations that require use of the straight wage or salary plan. The common denominator among these situations is management's desire to control a salesperson's time and activity. Straight salary is most likely when the job requires the salesperson to engage in nonselling activities. For example, retail sales personnel may be expected to arrange stock, clean up spills, feed the fish in the display tank, or fill in wherever an extra worker is needed. To pay these people on anything other than a straight wage or salary plan would reduce management's control.

Straight Commission　Unlike the salary plan, the **straight commission** plan rewards only one thing: sales performance. A clear-cut financial incentive is its prime advantage. On the surface, this plan would seem to have considerable appeal to most managers. However, the plan has a number of disadvantages. As suggested, salespeople paid this way cannot be expected to perform additional activities that do not lead directly to a sale. In other words, their activities are difficult to control. Furthermore, they may be reluctant to try to sell to new accounts that may develop slowly or to sell merchandise that is difficult to move, preferring instead to raise their short-term compensation by concentrating on products they know they can sell quickly. Management may decide to discourage this understandable behavior by lowering the commissions on easy-to-sell products and raising it on those harder to sell. This, however, destroys one of the straight commission plan's key advantages—simplicity. In addition, salespeople may resent changes that might reduce their incomes. Straight commission has other shortcomings, too. The salesperson has little security. If the economy slows down, or if sales fall off for some other reason beyond the salesperson's control, the incentive in the plan may be lost, because the sales representative may fail to achieve a satisfactory income over a period of a few weeks or more.

Quota-Bonus Plan　Under the **quota-bonus plan,** each salesperson is assigned a sales quota—a specific level of sales to be achieved over a specified period. The incentive is built in because a bonus is offered to salespeople who exceed their quotas. A base salary is related to the quota total, while the bonus provides a commission-like incentive. This plan attempts to provide aspects of both straight salary and straight commission.

Salary Plus Commission　As the name suggests, the **salary plus commission** compensation plan combines two pay methods by granting the salesperson a straight

Straight salary
Compensation at a regular rate, not immediately tied to sales performance.

Straight commission
Compensation based strictly on sales performance.

Quota-bonus plan
Compensation plan whereby a salesperson is paid a base salary related to achievement of a quota and a bonus for sales exceeding the quota.

Salary plus commission
Compensation consisting of a regular salary plus a commission based on sales performance.

salary or wage and a commission on sales. Typically, because a salary is provided, the commission is smaller than would be expected in a straight commission pay package. The intent of this plan is to allow management to ask salespeople to engage in nonselling work (since they are on salary) but also reward them for successful sales efforts (with a commission).

MOTIVATING THE SALES FORCE

Many salespeople work alone in the field, often at great distances from their home offices and far from direct supervision. This unique situation—the idea of working for oneself—draws many talented individuals into selling. But it can also create problems with respect to supervision.

Many salespeople are high achievers and may seldom require supervision from sales managers. For these people, the selling process itself is ample motivation. There is an intrinsic challenge in making the sale and a related challenge in trying to understand and solve customers' problems.

Despite all this, most salespeople need at least occasional support from management. Sales personnel often are subject to broad fluctuations in morale and motivation, from the lows that may accompany a string of customer rejections or a sense of being alone on the road to the highs of obtaining major orders, enjoying peaks of success, and earning substantial commissions and bonuses. Sales personnel, especially young trainees, may become discouraged if they are not given proper help, supervision, and attention to morale. Because sales personnel do need a "listening ear" as well as direction and advice, telephone contact is helpful to the sales manager in supervising the sales force.

> There is an intrinsic challenge in making the sale and a related challenge in trying to understand and solve customers' problems.

While experienced sales managers may know how, by words and actions, to properly reward and encourage salespeople to keep them fresh and interested in the job, many corporations use another element of their promotional mixes to help in this matter: the sales promotion. Sales contests, bonus plans, prizes and trips to be won, and sales conventions in exciting cities can all be of great help to the sales manager seeking to keep sales force motivation high. Periodic sales meetings also are useful, both for creating a feeling of group support and mutual interest and for providing a time for training and transmitting information.

Many sales organizations rely on sales meetings as the primary means of motivating the sales force. For example, the field sales manager of a New Jersey territory rented the Meadowlands football stadium. Corporate executives, family, and friends were assembled to cheer as each salesperson emerged from the players' tunnel. The electronic scoreboard bearing the salesperson's name and the cheering crowd motivated the salespeople to keep excelling at their jobs.

EVALUATING AND CONTROLLING THE SALES FORCE

An organization's overall marketing plan must be translated into a series of sales plans that specify regional, district, or territorial goals. Evaluation of a sales manager's or a sales representative's performance is based on whether he or she has met the appropriate goal or objective.

Objectives, especially those that a sales manager and a sales representative work out together, should be specific and measurable if they are to form the basis for reviewing the salesperson's performance and progress. The evaluation system must be fair and based on a mutual understanding of the performance standards and how they were determined. Note that the actual performance should be measured against predetermined standards, not standards set after the fact. It does little good to tell the sales representative that his or her performance this past year was "not too good" if the salesperson was given no indication of what was expected at the start of the year. To minimize misunderstandings, the salesperson often is assigned a sales quota. During progress reviews, actual sales can be compared with the quota.

To do their jobs properly and meet their own objectives or quotas, sales managers must develop instruments of control that provide feedback from salespeople in the field. This feedback is not always expressed in terms of sales generated but may involve measures of effort, such as increases in the number of sales calls made per week, increases in the number of orders per sales call (the sales "batting average"), or reductions in selling expenses. Feedback tells managers if they should proceed with plans as scheduled, change course, look into particular problems, or check in with local sales personnel to take corrective action. For example, a simple but fundamental aspect of the sales manager's job is to assure that each salesperson calls on an appropriate number of customers. In most companies, therefore, sales representatives keep a log, call report, or activity report that must be filed weekly or monthly and that indicates the number of calls made and relates special information about accounts. Sales managers evaluate this "paperwork" to determine whether the sales representative is working at an appropriate intensity level.

Ethical Issues in Sales and Sales Management

Salespeople may be regularly confronted with decisions involving ethical and legal issues. These issues can range from violations of price discrimination and antitrust laws to "little white lies" about a competitor's product. The sales job is one of personal interaction, and because the range of interactions is so broad, the ethical issues confronting salespeople are innumerable. The basic starting point is for the sales force to know the law. Yet this is not enough, and companies that have adopted the marketing concept usually communicate to the sales force what ethical behavior is expected of them.

Many organizations have codes of conduct for salespeople. At a very general level, most include statements similar to the following:

> Salespeople should be honest and straightforward with prospects. They should keep their promises. They should use factual information and avoid misrepresentation and deception. They should not make statements that lead inadvertently to implied warranties. They should neither provide bribes or valuable gifts nor solicit them for themselves. They should not conspire with competitors.

Sales Promotion

We turn now to the final topic of this chapter: sales promotion. The typical purpose of a sales promotion effort is to bolster or complement other elements of the promotional mix during a specific time period. Thus, a sales promotion program—say, a contest—may be used as an incentive to motivate the sales force, may play a part in company advertising, or may serve as the basis for a publicity campaign. Here are some examples of sales promotions aimed at achieving a variety of objectives at various levels of the marketing channel:

- Sales promotions may be used to encourage a wholesaler's sales force to sell more aggressively to retailers. For instance, the salesperson with the highest sales volume for a particular period might win a trip to Hawaii.
- A sales promotion may be conducted to obtain retailers' cooperation with a consumer-targeted promotion. A marketer of videotaped movies wishing to reach consumers at the retail level could provide a special promotional allowance to retailers who agree to place displays at key locations in their stores.

- A sales promotion's objective may be to draw attention to a company or a product. McDonald's may issue a press release indicating that Big Mac sandwiches and fries were served to more than 15,000 athletes, coaches, and officials participating in the Sydney 2000 Olympic Games.

In the remainder of this chapter, we examine sales promotions in two general categories: promotions geared toward wholesalers and retailers and promotions aimed at ultimate consumers.

SALES PROMOTIONS GEARED TOWARD WHOLESALERS AND RETAILERS

Sales promotions targeted at wholesalers and retailers are generally intended either to motivate these channel members to make special efforts to market a product (for example, by giving the product more shelf space) or to increase the number of distributors and dealers handling the product. The major forms of sales promotion at the wholesale and retail level are trade shows, contests, point-of-purchase displays, cooperative advertising and promotional programs, and allowances.

Trade show
A meeting or convention of members of a particular industry where business-to-business contacts are routinely made.

Trade Shows **Trade shows** are extremely important in business-to-business marketing. Industrywide conventions and trade association meetings are scheduled throughout the year at hotels and convention centers across the country. The typical trade show features many booths where producers, suppliers, and other marketers display and provide information about their products, in effect using the booths as temporary bases of sales operations. You may be familiar with boat and auto shows, where hundreds and even thousands of products and services are shown and demonstrated. Most trade shows are organized along the same lines. Usually trade shows are not open to the general public because marketers use these shows to distribute literature, obtain sales leads, and sell products to wholesalers, retailers, organizational buyers, and other members of the trade. The main purpose of a trade show is to serve as a central marketplace. Trade members, by making a single trip to the city in which the trade show is held, can view many products and discuss trends with many other professionals in the industry.

Contest
In the context of a wholesaler's or retailer's sales promotion, a means of motivating a sales force by offering bonuses or prizes for sales performance.

Contests **Contests** to motivate a manufacturer's sales force or a wholesaler's or retailer's sales force are very common sales promotion activities. The purpose of these contests is to increase sales levels by stimulating individual competition among salespeople. Competition is, of course, stimulated by the chance to win bonuses or prizes.

Sales contests add some excitement to regular activities and provide the opportunity for a salesperson to gain personal recognition as well as extra compensation and prizes. The major problem with sales contests is that the sales increases that result are often temporary. Furthermore, to improve their performance in a contest, salespersons often shift sales that would have occurred in another time period to the contest period.[11]

The main purpose of a trade show is to serve as a central marketplace where members of the trade can find many vendors.

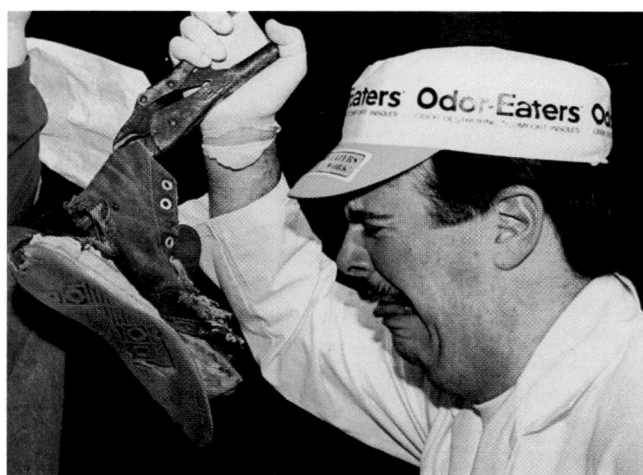

Odor-Eaters International sponsors an annual Rotten Sneaker Contest. The contestant with the smelliest old sneakers wins a $500 savings bond and a trophy. As you can imagine, the contest is newsworthy, and it generates a lot of publicity.

http://www.odor-eaters. com/rotten.html

Display Equipment and Point-of-Purchase Materials   Display equipment and other **point-of-purchase materials** are often provided to retailers and other members of distribution channels so that they can conveniently display or highlight the product to be sold. Such materials come in many forms. Convenience stores and bars almost always display clocks supplied by soft-drink or beer marketers, for example. Bookstore operators often receive new books in shipping packs that can be converted into book display racks.

Cooperative Advertising and Promotions   **Cooperative advertising** and other co-operative promotions are frequently used by manufacturers to increase promotional activity at local wholesale and retail levels. Programs vary, but the essence of all of them is that suppliers share promotional expenses with their customers. For example, suppose the manufacturer of La-Z-Boy chairs offers retailers a 50/50 co-op program. Half of the retailer's advertising expense will be borne by the manufacturer, so the retailer will pay just half of what an ad would ordinarily cost and will get to promote its own name as well as the La-Z-Boy brand name. The reward for the supplier who offers such a program is the active local support of dealers and the increased likelihood of immediate consumer purchases.

Allowances   An **allowance** is a reduction in price, a rebate, merchandise, or something else given an intermediary for performance of a specific activity or in consideration for a large order. For example, a manufacturer may offer free merchandise to retailers that feature its product in point-of-purchase displays.

SALES PROMOTIONS AIMED AT ULTIMATE CONSUMERS

Like other forms of promotion, sales promotion at the consumer level can inform, remind, and persuade. Specific objectives of sales promotions may be to attract more in-store attention to a product, to serve as a reminder at the point of purchase, to help break down loyalty to competing brands, to add value to the product in the consumer's eyes, to make short-term price adjustments, to encourage consumers to try a product for the first time, to offer an incentive for repeat purchases, or to induce large-volume purchases. The objectives of sales promotions are almost limitless, and their nature is bounded only by the marketer's imagination. For convenience, however, sales promotions can be grouped into these categories: product sampling, cents-off coupons, rebates,

> The objectives of sales promotions are almost limitless, and their nature is bounded only by the marketer's imagination.

Point-of-purchase materials
Promotional items intended to attract attention to specific products in the places where those products are purchased. Signs and displays in supermarkets are examples.

Cooperative advertising
Advertising paid for jointly by a supplier and a customer—for example, by the manufacturer of a product and a retailer.

Allowance
A reduction in price, a rebate, or the like, given to a marketing intermediary in return for a large order or the performance of a specific activity.

contests and sweepstakes, premiums, multiple-purchase offers, point-of-purchase materials, and product placements.

Product Sampling   The purpose of **product sampling** is to reach new customers by inducing trial use. A free trial or sample of the brand is given to consumers to stimulate product awareness, to provide first-hand knowledge about the product's characteristics, and to encourage a first purchase. Typically, miniature packages of the product are distributed to homes, on airplanes, in retail settings, or at public events. Product sampling is expensive, but good for new brands in mature markets where strong brand loyalties may exist.

Coupons   Coupons, which generally offer price reductions of some kind, are one of the most widely used sales promotions. Like other kinds of price reductions, coupons have an established record of increasing short-term sales. They attract new users to a brand, encourage brand switching, and stimulate increased purchases among existing users. It should be noted that cutting prices occasionally with cents-off coupons does not damage a product's long-term quality or value image—many price-conscious consumers always clip coupons.

Coupons have an attention-getting quality and are often found as portions of print advertisements or in inserts in newspapers. They may also be printed on packages or placed inside packages. Coupons are increasingly being distributed in stores and by direct mail. Innovative companies such as Surf4Savings.com have devised software that allows them to distribute coupons via the Internet. With the growth of data-based marketing, there have been changes in the nature of coupon distribution strategy. Coupons may be distributed selectively to consumers who are known to use particular competing brands or who are identified in a database as having certain purchasing behaviors of interest to the marketer. This helps minimize a major disadvantage of coupons: the fact that most coupon redemptions are made by consumers who already buy the brand.

Rebates   A **rebate,** like a coupon, is a price reduction designed to induce immediate purchase. However, with a rebate the consumer gets money back from the manufacturer rather than a price break at the retail level. Rebate offers often require that the consumer purchase multiple units (for example, three boxes of cereal). Typically, the consumer must then send in some proof of purchase, after which the company will send a check to the consumer. For many consumers, this time lag is less attractive than an immediate price reduction at the retail level. For the marketer, however, costs are lower, because rebate offers are typically printed on the packages or placed inside them and do not involve circulating materials by other means.

Contests and Sweepstakes

Contests and sweepstakes stimulate purchases by giving consumers a chance to be big winners. Certain types of consumers enjoy these exciting promotions. Contest partici-

---

Product sampling
A sales promotion in which samples of a product are given to consumers to induce them to try the product.

Rebate
A sales promotion wherein some portion of the price paid for a product is returned to the purchaser.

---

e-commerce | Changing Everything

iWon.com is a new Internet portal that offers users sweepstakes prizes of $10,000 a day, $1 million a month, and $10 million on tax day in exchange for users' registration information. By using any of iWon's features, including its search function, to send and receive e-mail, go shopping, and read the news, users automatically earn entries into the three sweepstakes. Drawings are made daily and posted onto the home page.

iWon has cultivated business collaborations with the likes of Inktomi, which makes search software for content and e-commerce, plus such content partners as Weather.com, Travelocity.com, Mail.com, AutoWeb.com, Apartments.com, Realtor.com, Gamesville.com, and HealthScout.com.

iWon views the sweepstakes as the cost of acquiring and retaining consumers. In other words, using sweepstakes to give away millions is considered a sales promotional expenditure. CBS obtained a majority ownership in iWon in exchange for $70 million in television advertising. The online portal relationship is consistent with CBS's strategy of swapping multi-year, multi-million dollar advertising and branding deals in exchange for stakes in popular Internet destinations, such as SportsLine.com and MarketWatch.com. iWon also has made deals with e-commerce partners, from whom it will receive cuts of transactions that iWon sends their way. Banner advertising and sponsorships also are in iWon's revenue model plans.[12]

what went right?

Cakebread Cellars Cakebread cellars of Rutherford, California, ranks as a small winery, producing 45,000 cases a year. But the brand, distributed by Kobrand Corporation of New York, has a steadfast following of 10,000 who receive its chatty food and wine newsletters. The quarterly routinely sings the praises of such offbeat pairings as peanut butter sandwiches and Cakebread Zinfandel. Through the mailing list, Vice President for Sales/Marketing Dennis Cakebread, son of winery founder Jack Cakebread, had no trouble rounding up 20 fans to go salmon fishing with him.

Cakebread and crew set off from San Francisco at 6 a.m., returning in the late afternoon. The outing wrapped up with a dinner of the day's catch at Aqua, a local seafood restaurant. "We were all exhausted," recalled Cakebread. "But we forgot that as we all sat down and clinked our first glass."

Cakebread, which also has attracted Californians with fly-fishing seminars, is planning an out-of-state event in Chicago, where the winery is sponsoring a mushroom-foraging trip, complete with an appropriately wined dinner of the finds. It's a lot of effort for small groups of people, Cakebread admitted. "But I think we earn customers for life," he said. "The people on our fishing trip should go back to where they work and spend all day Monday talking about the trip. Every time they order salmon, they should recount the trip. Every time they see a fishing boat, they should talk about the trip."[13]

---

pants have to complete some task, such as submitting a recipe to the Pillsbury Bake-Off, and are awarded prizes when their entries are judged to be among the best. Sweepstakes participants become winners based on chance. Sweepstakes are tied easily to repeat purchases of a brand when the chances of winning increase with each purchase. If sweepstakes promotions require the purchase of a unit of the product, however, state or local lottery laws may prohibit them.

Premiums and Self-Liquidating Premiums A **premium** is a product offered free or at a reduced price when another product, the key brand, is purchased. The premium, such as a Beanie Baby toy at an L.A. Dodgers game, is a giveaway; consumers see themselves as getting something for nothing. *Self-liquidating premiums* are special types of premiums that consumers obtain by using proofs of purchase, trading stamps, cash, or a combination of these.

Premium
A product offered free or at reduced charge with the purchase of another product.

Multiple-Purchase Offers Multiple-purchase offers, or two-for-one deals, are tied to price or to some other promotion. Offering four bars of Dial soap for the price of three is a typical example of a multiple-purchase offer; it encourages a bigger-than-normal purchase and helps maintain customer loyalty.

Point-of-Purchase Materials Banners, pamphlets, coasters, and similar materials may be used to provide information at the point of purchase. Point-of-purchase materials serve as reminders. Reminding a shopper of an appeal used in advertising may trigger a sale. In-store videos, shopping-cart videos that start electronically when the cart moves toward the aisle where the product is stocked, and other technological innovations are changing the nature of these sales promotions.

Product Placements A product or company that appears in a movie scene is exposed to millions of movie viewers. If a certain brand of soft drink is consumed or if a certain brand of clothing is worn by a celebrity actor in a movie or television show, a very positive message can be communicated in what most consider a noncommercial setting. In recent years, movie studios have come to recognize that

15-5 A Summary of Consumer Sales Promotions

ACTIVITY	DESCRIPTION	FEATURES	EXAMPLE
Product sampling	A sample of the brand is given to consumers	Expensive but good for new brands in mature markets where brand loyalties may exist	Dolphins and Friends crackers
Coupons	Most often, a temporary price reduction coupon is found in an advertisement, but it may be located in the store or the package	Cutting the price does not damage long-term quality or value image; many price-conscious consumers always clip coupons	Save $1 on Crest White-stripes
Rebates	Consumer is offered the opportunity to get money back from the manufacturer rather than receive a price break at the retail level	Lower cost than circulating coupons because rebate coupon is inside package and fewer consumers participate	Mail-in rebate of $10 on Black and Decker drill
Contests and sweepstakes	Consumer is given a chance to be a big winner	Some consumers like contests; they may be tied to repeat purchase of a brand	Safeway Bingo Game Sweepstakes
Premiums and self-liquidating premiums	Another product is offered free or at a reduced charge if the key brand is purchased	Consumers see themselves as getting something for nothing	Oscar Mayer wiener whistle given away with each pack of hot dogs
Multiple-purchase offers	Multiple purchases are tied to price or another promotion	Induces heavier-than-normal purchases and maintains customer loyalty	Four bars of Dial soap for the price of three
Point-of-purchase materials	Banners, pamphlets, coasters, and similar materials are used to provide information at the point of purchase	Reminders at the point of purchase may trigger a sale	Cardboard display for Stephen King's latest book
Product placements	Products appear in movies	Communicates a positive message in a noncommercial setting	Movie scene filmed inside a Taco Bell restaurant

Product placement
A promotional exposure resulting from a product's being shown in a movie or on a TV show.

selling these **product placements** in their movies can be a profitable side business. Marketers of widely used consumer goods and services often are willing to pay large fees for product placements. In some cases, the product placements are tied in to other promotional efforts.

Exhibit 15-5 summarizes the major forms of consumer sales promotions. As a final note we should mention that sales promotions can be overused. For example, a number of sales promotions, such as coupons, rebates, and premiums, lower the price of the product or similarly enhance the product offering. If these special incentives are used regularly or if consumers can predict their timing, then consumers may buy only during sales promotions. Marketers who continually use this type of sales promotion risk the loss of traditional sales to price-conscious consumers.

Tie-in
A collaborative effort between two or more organizations or brands that work as partners in a promotional effort.

Sales Promotion Tie-Ins   A **tie-in** involves a collaborative effort between two or more organizations or brands that work as partners in a promotional effort. Tie-ins generally borrow interest value from movies, sporting events, or other marketing efforts. When McDonald's sells a Happy Meal that includes a Isuzu Axiom secret vehicle toy, its sales promotion effort is based on a tie-in with the popular

Sky Kids movie. It expects its Happy Meals sales to benefit from the popularity of the movie.

The benefits of tie-ins with premiums are easily appreciated, but contests, sweepstakes, coupons, and other sales promotional elements can also benefit from a tie-in approach. For example, The Women's National Basketball Association (WNBA) and L'Oreal's tie-in collaboration includes providing makeovers and giving away free samples at some WNBA games.

Warner Brothers Studio is making a movie based on the Harry Potter stories. Fast food restaurants, apparel marketers, candy companies, and toy merchandisers will have promotional tie-ins with the movie about the popular boy wizard.

Summary

Professional selling is important to the success of most organizations. Selling is most effective when it is a flexible process involving identifying and fulfilling customer needs on an individual basis, thus reflecting the marketing concept. Sales promotion supports other elements of the promotional mix by stimulating sales over short periods of time.

1) Describe the role of personal selling and relationship management in the marketing process.

Personal selling occurs when a seller personally attempts to persuade a prospective buyer to purchase a product. A salesperson is a professional who can effectively communicate the benefits of a product or service. The sales message must be flexible—adapted to the individual needs of each prospective buyer. Relationship management refers to the sales function of managing the account relationship and ensuring that the buyer receives the appropriate services.

2) Identify marketing situations in which personal selling would be the most effective means of reaching and influencing target buyers.

Personal selling is effective because the salesperson can adjust the sales message on the basis of direct verbal and nonverbal feedback and close the sale. It works better than other forms of promotion for technical, expensive, innovative, or complex products and is effective in selling to organizational buyers. However, it is inefficient in reaching large numbers of consumers of frequently purchased products.

3) Show how the professional salesperson contributes to a modern marketing firm.

There are three kinds of selling tasks: order taking, order getting, and sales support. Order takers perform routine sales tasks. The professional order-getting salesperson must apply the marketing concept by identifying customers' problems and solving them individually with the organization's products, terms of sale, and other benefits. Sales support personnel engage in special activities such as providing service and expertise.

4) Outline the steps involved in making a sale.

The steps involved in making a sale are (1) locating and qualifying prospects, (2) preapproach planning, (3) making the approach, (4) making the sales presentation, (5) handling objections, (6) closing the sale, and (7) following up.

5) Explain why the marketing process does not stop when the sale is made.

Obtaining an order is the beginning of an organization's relationship with a customer. Satisfied customers provide repeat sales. To ensure an enduring buyer-seller relationship, sales personnel should follow up on orders to guarantee that they are delivered in proper condition on schedule and that post-sale services are provided.

6) Characterize the major aspects of the sales manager's job.

Members of the sales force must be managed so that their efforts are directed toward organizational goals. A sales manager is responsible for (1) setting sales objectives, (2) organizing the sales force, (3) recruiting and selecting sales personnel, (4) training the sales force, (5) developing an effective compensation plan, (6) motivating the sales force, and (7) evaluating and controlling the sales force.

7) Classify the various forms of sales compensation.

Sales personnel may be compensated by use of a straight salary method, a commission based on sales, or a combination of these plans, such as a quota-bonus plan or a salary plus commission.

8) Identify some of the ethical issues facing sales personnel.

The ethical issues facing sales personnel are numerous because of the broad range of human interactions involved. In general, companies expect salespeople to comply with the law and be honest and straightforward in all their dealings.

9) Identify the purposes of sales promotion and explain how the major sales promotion tools work.

Sales promotion programs support other promotional elements, which in turn support the sales promotion. At the wholesale and retail level, they include trade shows, contests, point-of-purchase displays, cooperative advertising, and allowances. Popular sales promotions at the consumer level are product sampling, cents-off coupons, rebates, contests and sweepstakes, premiums and self-liquidating premiums, multiple-purchase offers, and point-of-purchase materials.

Key Terms

account manager (p. 439)
account service representative (p. 440)
allowance (p. 457)
approach (p. 442)
closing (p. 444)
closing signals (p. 445)
contest (p. 456)
cooperative advertising (p. 457)
creative selling process (p. 441)
cross-functional sales team (p. 440)
field sales manager (p. 450)
field selling (p. 436)
follow-up (p. 446)

handling objections (p. 444)
inside selling (p. 436)
missionary (p. 439)
order getting (p. 439)
order taker (p. 438)
pioneer (p. 439)
point-of-purchase materials (p. 457)
premium (p. 459)
product placement (p. 460)
product sampling (p. 458)
prospecting (p. 442)
qualifying (p. 442)
quota-bonus plan (p. 453)
rebate (p. 458)

relationship management (p. 437)
retail selling (p. 436)
salary plus commission (p. 453)
sales management (p. 448)
sales objectives (p. 448)
sales presentation (p. 443)
sales territory (p. 449)
straight commission (p. 453)
straight salary (p. 453)
suggestive selling (p. 438)
telemarketing (p. 436)
tie-in (p. 460)
trade show (p. 456)
trial close (p. 445)

Questions for Review & Critical Thinking

1. For each of the following, tell whether you would expect the salesperson to be an order taker or an order getter.
   a. Selling satellite TV subscriptions to home-owners
   b. Selling industrial power tools to purchasing agents in the aircraft industry
   c. Selling blocks of Oakland A's season tickets to businesses that entertain customers at the games
   d. Selling paper products to office supply stores
2. How would you prospect for and qualify customer accounts if you were selling each of the following?

   a. Chain saws to hardware wholesalers
   b. Installation of cables for office computer networks
   c. Life insurance
   d. Executive jet aircraft
3. "Salesmen are born, not made." Do you agree? Why or why not?
4. What are the steps in the personal selling process? Which is the most important step?
5. As a salesperson, how would you handle the following objections?
   a. "The price is too high."
   b. "I don't have enough money. I'll have to wait a month or two."
   c. "I'm just not certain if I need one or not."

6. The sales volume of a person with 25 years of selling experience begins to slip. How would you motivate this person to work harder?

7. How have changes in technology changed the way salespeople do their jobs?

8. How could a sales manager determine the number of salespeople to hire? Be creative.

9. Over a 5-year period, a company keeps the same sales personnel in the same geographical territories. What problems might this policy create?

10. Why do most college students avoid careers in personal selling?

11. How important are personal appearance and proper dress in personal selling?

12. Many salespeople take clients to restaurants for lunch. What should a young salesperson be told about entertaining at lunch?

13. Some sales promotions are geared toward stimulating activity among wholesalers and retailers; others are geared toward influencing ultimate consumers. How do the objectives of these types of promotion differ?

14. Give your opinion on the likely effectiveness of each of the following sales promotion tactics:
    a. A rebate offer on a car battery
    b. A four-unit package of panty hose for the price usually charged for a three-unit package
    c. A sweepstakes contest for a regional airline
    d. A free screwdriver with a can of WD-40 oil

15. Form small groups as directed by your instructor. Each group should brainstorm for ideas about how a local restaurant or college bar could creatively use a sales promotion. After 10 minutes of brainstorming, the group should evaluate the ideas suggested and select three for presentation to the class.

16. Field sales representatives often work in teams. Describe some situations in which team selling is most likely.

 **exercises** http://zikmund.swcollege.com

1. Visit the Sales and Marketing Executives Web site at http://www.smei.org to find several articles about personal selling. What are some of the topics of these articles?
2. Go to http://www.mypoints.com to see a system for earning redeemable points while using the Internet. How does this differ from a typical frequency marketing program, such as an airline frequent flyer program?

Address Book (Useful URLs)

Sales and Marketing Executives Marketing Library	http://www.sell.org
National Association of Sales Professionals	http://www.nasp.com/ethics.html
Canadian Professional Sales Association	http://www.cpsa.com

Ethically Right or Wrong?

A sales manager tells the sales force that he is under a lot of pressure to increase sales for the quarter, which ends in a week. Afterward, a salesperson calls a prospect who has recently mentioned that she is almost ready to place an order for a competitor's product and arranges to take her to dinner at an expensive restaurant. At dinner, after ordering the best of everything, the salesperson says a number of negative things about the way the competitor does business. Some of these statements are not completely accurate. The salesperson normally would not be misleading but really wants to make a quick sale to help the sales manager out. Did the salesperson do the right thing?

1. Are the following sales activities ethical?
   a. A salesperson skips lunch but adds the typical $10 charge to her expense account.
   b. In a hotel bar, a salesperson recognizes a sales representative from a competing company, and they discuss each company's prices, discounts, and terms of sale.
   c. A salesperson gives a Christmas gift worth $50 to a purchasing agent responsible for buying for a major account.
   d. A salesperson offers a customer who is "difficult to deal with" a higher discount than the typical prospect.
2. A business-to-business marketer holds a sweepstakes that requires visitors to its booth at an industry trade show to fill out a form. The marketer does not use a random drawing, but picks as the winning company a company that is a good prospect for future business.

case

VIDEO CASE 15-1

Closing Techniques: Five Top Salespeople

Elaine Bailey sells a sophisticated computer network product called Connect. By adapting her sales presentations to fit different prospects, she has built a million-dollar career selling computer products.

Rick Brown is a National Sales Manager for Ben & Jerry's Ice Cream. He sells established flavors like Cherry Garcia and new products such as Peace Pops. Ben & Jerry's sells to wholesale distributors, which in turn sell to supermarkets and other retailers. The company stresses long-term relationships with its customers.

LeRoy Leale sells financial services for a full-service financial firm. Estate planning, insurance, and stocks are among the products he sells. He has been the company's national sales leader twice. He truly believes in his product. He seeks referrals and spends quite a bit of time developing qualified leads. He closes more than 50 percent of the sales presentations he makes.

Bob Hopkins sells a cash register that has a built-in vault. The notion of a theft-proof cash register is the primary benefit he sells. Many of his prospects are large organizations with many cashiers, like 7-Eleven, or banks with extensive teller operations. They are often concerned with the cost of the machines. Many of these prospects have video camera surveillance and/or hire an armored-car service to pick up money each evening.

Jim Kilcoyne sells heart-lung machines. In most situations he sells to more than one person at a medical facility.

Think about what these salespeople have in common.

QUESTIONS

1. In each of the selling situations mentioned above, what types of signals might indicate that a prospect was ready to buy?
2. What is a trial close? What type of trial close would be best for each of the salespersons mentioned above?
3. What should the above salespersons do when the prospect shows no interest?

cross-functional insights

Many theories and principles from other business disciplines can provide insights about the role of marketing in an organization. The questions in this section are designed to help you think about integrating what you have learned in other business courses with the marketing principles explained in Chapters 13 through 15.

Promotional Budget   After managers have planned a promotional mix, they must determine if the organization can afford it. Determining how much money to allocate to each promotional element is a matter of budgeting.

Should advertising be treated as an expense or a capital expenditure?

Advertising   Advertising includes an informative or persuasive message carried by a nonpersonal medium and paid for by a sponsor whose product is in some way identified in the message.

When is deceptive advertising considered to be fraud?

How does the organizational mission affect advertising?

What is the nature of the collaborative relationship between the advertiser and the advertising agency?

What is the Federal Trade Commission's primary function? What types of penalties can the FTC impose on marketers who have used deceptive or unfair advertising?

Personal Selling/Creative Selling   Personal selling is a person-to-person dialogue between buyer and seller.

What should a sales representative know about listening skills?

Is on-the-job training or classroom training more important for a sales representative?

How is information technology changing field selling?

Is diversity training necessary for sales personnel?

As a company becomes more involved in using sales teamwork, will the entire department come to be composed of self-managed work teams? Will the teams assume many of the tasks normally believed to be managerial functions, such as making decisions about job assignments, budgeting, scheduling, and hiring?

Sales Management   Sales management is the marketing management activity dealing with planning, organizing, directing, and controlling the personal selling effort.

What planning activities are required of sales managers?

What human relations skills are important to sales managers?

How much authority should a national sales manager delegate to regional sales managers?

What should a sales manager know about the reinforcement theory of motivation?

Write a job description, and give job specifications for the following: sales representative, regional sales manager, national sales manager.

What should a sales manager know about the Uniform Commercial Code for sales contracts?

What should an international sales manager know about the Foreign Corrupt Practices Act?

Integrated Marketing Communications   The term *integrated marketing communications* is used to remind managers that all elements of the promotional mix should be coordinated and systematically planned so that they are in harmony.

What management skills are helpful in developing integrated marketing communications?

How important to effective integrated marketing communications efforts is a company's management information system?

Introduction to Pricing Concepts

16
chapter

L E A R N I N G   O B J E C T I V E S

After you have studied this chapter, you will be able to . . .

1) Define price and discuss it.

2) Tell how price interacts with the rest of the marketing mix.

3) Analyze price's place in the economy.

4) Outline the fundamentals of pricing strategy.

5) Characterize the relationship between price and organizational objectives.

6) Relate the demand in a target market to the prices charged.

7) Understand that demand and cost considerations influence pricing.

8) Differentiate among price elasticity, price inelasticity, and price cross-elasticity.

Jimmy Orr of St. Louis is an unrepentant Internet auction addict. His watch alarm goes off when bidding starts. He plans evenings around auction closes. And he panics midday if he can't find a PC with Net access. "I think that it is slowly starting to consume my life," says Orr, who buys toys, rare photos, books, and other memorabilia on eBay.

Orr is not alone. Online auctions have created round-the-clock worldwide electronic garage sales that allow millions to instantly participate from their homes and offices. eBay—the first and, by far, the largest auction Web site—has seen its number of registered buyers and sellers explode from a cultish 1.3 million in 1998 to 7.7 million. Some 3 million items are up for bid, from collectibles like Beanie Babies, velvet Elvis paintings, and rare base-ball cards to DVD players, fine art, furniture, cars, designer clothing, meteorites, and a $175,000 Canadian island. Along the way, eBay pioneered a piece of the new "auction economy," in which prices fluctuate based on supply and demand at any given moment.

Eager to join the frenzy, hundreds of Web sites have added auction services, including heavy-weights such as Yahoo!, Amazon, Excite@Home, and Lycos. Sellers are generally consumers or small businesses who form a dizzyingly varied, real-time flea market.

Then there are business-run sites that specialize in a product line, such as computer equipment re-tailers OnSale.com and UBid.com. More diverse services, such as First Auction, offer a sort of Internet-based Home Shopping Channel.

A new breed of auction aggregators—including AuctionRover.com, AuctionWatch.com, and iTrack—let bidders hunt for items across several sites. The number of online auction buyers in the United States is expected to grow from 1.9 million in 1999 to 6.5 million in 2002, says Jupiter Communications.

The latest trend in Internet auctions involves people who have quit their jobs to buy and resell items on auction sites. They become small busi-nesses. Granny with the embroidered blankets can be Bob Smith selling made-in-China goods.

eBay's size gives it a Catch-22-like edge. Its wide selection draws so many buyers that most sellers want to list items there. To combat that, Microsoft, Dell Computer, Lycos, and Excite recently formed a network to share listings. eBay is ideal for sellers be-cause the large number of bidders drives up prices. As a result, shoppers sometimes find better deals at smaller sites. But many like eBay's variety: they're more likely to stumble across items that interest them.

Most auction sites show the current high bid, the number of bids, and the time an auction closes. Veterans say they typically wait until the last few mo-ments to bid, to avoid being "sniped," or outbid at the last minute.[1]

At eBay and other Internet auction sites—as at physical auctions—getting a good price is the goal of both buyers and sellers. This chapter focuses on the nature of price as a marketing mix variable and the role of price in the economy. The chapter provides a framework by examining the fundamental concepts underlying pricing strategy. It shows the interrelationship between overall organizational and marketing objectives and an organization's pricing objectives. In doing this, it addresses target market considerations, supply and demand, price elasticity, and the nature of costs.

What Is Price?

Value
The power of one product to attract another product in an exchange.

As you have seen, marketing involves exchanging things of value. **Value** is a quantitative measure of the power one good or service has to attract another good or service in an exchange. An auto mechanic could exchange four tuneups for two months of coffee and doughnuts from a nearby diner. Such a trade is possible because the tuneups, the coffee, and the doughnuts all have value. When products are exchanged for one another, the trade is called **barter**.

Barter
The exchange of products without the use of money.

While it would be possible to value every product in the world in terms of every other product, such a system would be complicated and unwieldy. It is far easier to express these many values in terms of the single variable of money. Price is thus a statement of value, because it is the amount of money or other consideration given in exchange for a product.

Price has many names. These names vary according to tradition or the interests of the seller. *Rent, fee*, and *donation* are terms used in specific exchange situations to describe price. Some sellers avoid using the word *price* in order to make what is offered for sale appear to be of a quality that price cannot fully describe. Thus, a student pays tuition, not a price, for education. A commuter pays a toll. A professor who gives an off-campus speech "accepts an honorarium." A physician charges a fee for professional services. Universities, governments, professors, and doctors all sell their services for a price, no matter what that price is called.

In brief, marketing involves exchanges of things that have value. The name most commonly used to describe this value is price. In the United States, price is most commonly expressed in dollars and cents.

Price as a Marketing Mix Variable

Price has a special significance in that it ultimately "pays" for all of a firm's activities. Because sales revenue equals price times unit sales volume, the price of a product is one of the prime determinants of sales revenues. If the price can be increased while unit volume and costs remain the same, revenues and profits will be increased. For this reason alone, pricing decisions are important. But price is important for another reason. Like other marketing mix variables, price influences unit sales volume. Thus, proper pricing of a product is expected to increase the quantity demanded. Price is perhaps the most flexible element of the marketing mix because it can be changed rapidly in response to changes in the environment.[2]

A list price functions as a communication tool by adding symbolic value to a good or service and by helping to position the brand in relation to competitors.

List price
The basic price quote, before adjustment.

In setting prices, many marketers start with a basic price quote, called a **list price**. Price adjustments may be made when the season changes, when a buyer purchases a large quantity of a good, or for other reasons. Many marketers adjust list price with discounts or rebates. For example, retailers often mark down, or reduce, the list price when merchandise is out of season or moving slowly.

A list price functions as a communication tool by adding symbolic value to a good or service and by helping to position the brand in relation to competitors. A

Price is a primary consideration in the selection of brands of shopping goods. During periods of recession, consumers look for value. Everyday low prices work best during periods when consumers are price conscious.

high price may suggest a high-status good, a low price may suggest a bargain, and a discount coupon or rebate may encourage purchases by people who would otherwise not buy the product. Entire positioning strategies may revolve around price. For example, Tiffany & Company, a chain of exclusive jewelry stores, maintains an image as a seller of products of the highest quality by stocking reliable products and providing special services and also by charging comparatively high prices. Wal-Mart and Price Club stress bargains and must therefore keep prices at the lowest levels.

Price is closely related to other marketing variables and cannot be discussed without simultaneous consideration of product, place, and promotion. Pricing strategies must be consistent with a firm's other marketing mix decisions and must support the firm's other marketing strategies. For example, the Maytag product strategy—ensuring that customers will have "ten years of trouble-free operation"—stresses the quality and reliability that are highlighted in its advertising strategy, which is compatible with its premium pricing strategy. Although mechanical problems with its product are infrequent, Maytag's strategy requires the proper distribution system, for both its product and its service technicians. The premium pricing strategy, which allows an adequate profit margin for intermediaries, helps support the distribution strategy.

Price bears a special relationship to promotion. One job of promotion is to show potential buyers that an item is worth the price demanded. We can all think of products we bought or services we used because we believed that we were getting a good deal, a bargain, or high-quality workmanship. But after a bit of thought, we might admit that our favorable perception of the price or the quality originated in a familiar advertisement or a television salesperson's convincing presentation. In such instances, the consumer more willingly pays the asked-for price because promotion has convinced him or her that the price is justified.

e-commerce Changing Everything

A growing number of Internet companies are trying to get people to pick their wallets: their e-wallets, that is. While consumers have hesitated to share credit card information with unfamiliar firms, banks and new e-commerce companies are jumping in to provide e-wallet systems, which securely store credit card information and share it on demand with online merchants. That way, a person can buy books at one site, auto parts at another, and flowers at a third—all without entering the same information over and over. The e-wallet helps consumers who want to shop online but find there are too many forms to fill out and too many member names and passwords to remember. Most e-wallets let users surf and shop many Web sites using a single password.

DoughNET (http://www.doughnet.com) offers a shopping portal for teens. Parents set up allowances for their children, who then can use that money at partner stores including Barnes & Noble, Delia's, Fossil, and CDNow.

CyberCash, which supplies e-wallet technology to retailers, has developed several ways to simplify payments. Its latest incorporates its "InstaBuy" e-wallet into online banner ads. Users of the e-wallet can click on a Web ad and make a purchase by entering their password. First USA, the largest MasterCard and Visa issuer, has started a shopping portal using the CyberCash system.

The companies providing e-wallets profit either from a share in the transaction, from software that enables the transaction, or from other fees paid by merchants included on the e-wallet provider's system.[3]

PRICE COMPETITION

The degree of **price competition** influences the nature of the marketing mix. Intensive price competition exists in many industries, especially those dealing with raw materials such as crude petroleum. Because competing products are not distinctive, price becomes the key marketing variable. In other product categories, price may be less important to the consumer than a distinctive product feature or a differentiated brand image. For products in these categories, the firm that emphasizes low price exclusively may find that competitors will meet this low price. Shortly after Tylenol was introduced, its maker, Johnson & Johnson, built strong brand-name recognition by emphasizing that acetaminophen is less irritating to the stomach than aspirin. Bristol-Myers introduced Datril as a "me too" brand. The gist of its advertising campaign was that Datril was lower in price than the leading brand, Tylenol. Unfortunately for Datril, when Tylenol marketers saw that Datril was becoming serious competition, Tylenol met Datril's price—thereby forcing Bristol-Myers to change all of the Datril advertising. The primary Datril strength, low price, was no longer an issue. Today, Datril itself is no longer an issue.

If price is the sole basis of competition, then competitors can easily take away a product's competitive advantage. Of course, if the low price is the result of technology and production efficiency that competitors cannot easily match in the short term, then a low-cost, lowest-price strategy may be effective.

PRICE AND MARKETING EFFECTIVENESS

As mentioned, in some competitive situations price may be less important than some other feature. Effective **nonprice competition** allows a marketer to charge premium prices. Indeed, price is often indicative of overall marketing effectiveness. Lego gets a price substantially above that of many of its competitors but nevertheless sells far more building-block toys than any of them. This is fairly substantial proof that Lego's overall marketing strategy produces a product, promotion, and distribution mix consistent with and supportive of its pricing strategy. Lego is thus better off than its competitors. The ability to maintain prices and sales volume in the face of relatively stiff competition certainly indicates an excellent marketing strategy and effective execution of that strategy.

Price in the Economy

The main function of price in our relatively free-market economy is to help allocate goods and services. Most items of value are distributed to those who demand them and have the means to pay for them. When products are scarce or in short supply, prices are high, and wealthier citizens are better able than poorer citizens to afford them. Thus, from a macro-marketing perspective, price allocates available goods and services within the economy by determining who will get them. Price also determines the quantity of goods and services that will be produced

Changes in Cleanings Demanded as Price Increases

Price	Cleanings per month
$ 10	4
$ 25	2
$100	0

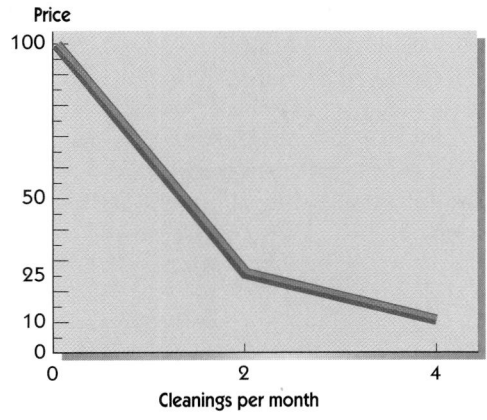

and marketed. An economist's explanation of demand and supply helps clarify the role of pricing in the economy.

DEMAND CURVE

Demand is the quantity of a product consumers are willing and able to buy at a given price. Usually, the quantity demanded changes as price changes. Thus, you might be willing to pay someone $10 to clean your untidy bedroom each week. But you might have the room cleaned only every two weeks if the price rose to $25, and not at all at a price of $100. At $100, you would either clean the room yourself or leave it dirty! This relationship can be shown either as a table or as a curve, as in Exhibit 16-1.

The **demand curve**, or *schedule of demand*, is a graphic representation of the relationship between the various prices sellers might charge for a product and the amount of that product that buyers will demand at each price. Clearly, it would be a great help to marketers to have access to a specific demand curve for their industry. While marketers seldom have an exact demand schedule showing how much they can sell at price 1, price 2, and price 3, they may have some demand information from marketing research. At the very least, when precise demand curves cannot be drawn, marketers make assumptions about demand. A demand curve is represented by the line labeled *D* in Exhibit 16-2. Note that as price declines, an increasing quantity of the product is demanded.

> Thus, from a macromarketing perspective, price allocates available goods and services within the economy by determining who will get them.

Demand curve
A graphic representation of the relationship between various prices and the amount of product that will be demanded at those prices; also called a *schedule of demand.*

SUPPLY CURVE

Supply is the quantity of a product that marketers are willing and able to sell at a given price in a given time period. A **supply curve**, or *supply schedule* (labeled *S* in Exhibit 16-2), graphically represents the amount of goods or services marketers will supply at various prices.

A supply curve shows that as prices become more attractive to suppliers (marketers), those suppliers will try to provide more of the product. Thus, in most

Supply curve
A graphic representation of the relationship between various prices and the amount of product that will be supplied at those prices; also called a *supply schedule.*

The Intersection of Supply and Demand

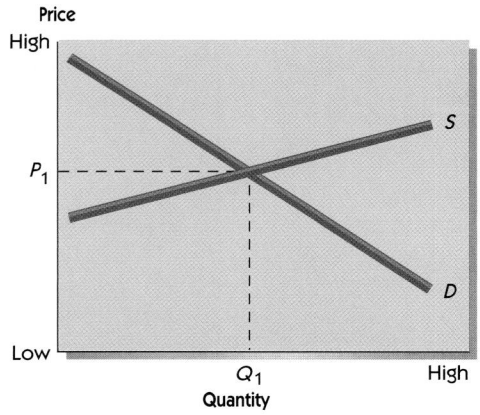

cases, as prices rise, suppliers are encouraged to supply more product; and as prices fall, they will prefer to supply less.

The intersection of the industry demand and supply curves establishes the market price (P_1) and the quantity produced (Q_1), or size of the market. Thus, economic theory shows how price determines how much will be produced and distributed to members of society.

We have focused here on price for an industry, not for an individual firm marketing a product. We now turn our attention to pricing strategy for a firm.

The Fundamentals of Pricing Strategy

Many mathematical tools can be used to determine the specific price that should be assigned to a particular product. Most marketing managers, however, would be reluctant to trust such an important matter as price setting exclusively to any mechanical technique. Company objectives, costs, and demand need to be considered. Further, managerial judgment, supported by marketing research, knowledge of competitors' actions, and an understanding of the target market's reaction to prices, plays an important role in pricing decisions. In setting prices, the following activities are essential

1. Determine your pricing objectives.
2. Know the importance of price to your target market.
3. Know the demand for your product.
4. Understand your costs.
5. Determine your pricing strategy.

Of course, like other marketing mix decisions, pricing decisions are also influenced by environmental forces. Competitive forces and legal influences are extremely important factors. This chapter discusses the first four items listed above. Chapter 17 focuses on pricing strategies and tactics, as well as the legal aspects of pricing.

Pricing Objectives

Pricing objective
The desired result associated with a particular pricing strategy. The pricing objective must be consistent with other marketing objectives.

Although we are concerned here with pricing, we should mention again that **pricing objectives** must be coordinated with the firm's other marketing objectives. These must, in turn, flow from the company's overall objectives. Thus, if Toshiba seeks to become the leader in developing and marketing high-technology electronics products, all of its marketing objectives, including its pricing objectives, must be consistent with that broad company mission. For example, the objectives associated with a high level of product differentiation at the overall marketing level would not generally be compatible with an objective of always setting prices below competitors' prices.[4] The relationship of pricing decisions to organizational objectives is diagrammed in Exhibit 16-3.

With organizational objectives firmly in mind, marketers pricing a good or service must determine what specific objectives are to be accomplished with the pricing strategy. Managers should know why certain prices are being charged, as well as why these prices might differ from buyer to buyer and from time to time. A firm may face any number of problems and opportunities, and these may give rise to many pricing objectives. Some possible objectives are shown in Exhibit 16-4, along with possible pricing steps to be undertaken for each objective. We discuss some of these objectives in the remainder of this section.

The important thing to note is that each pricing strategy—each type and level of price—has logic and reason behind it. Prices are set to help bring about a result. The hoped-for result is the pricing objective. Clearly, objectives narrow the range of pricing possibilities considerably and thus greatly facilitate the determining of price.

INCOME-ORIENTED OBJECTIVES

Organizations may focus on income-oriented pricing objectives because they find these goals compatible with the profitability dimension of the marketing concept. Although income-oriented objectives may be stated as short-term or long-term objectives, management should concentrate on the long run. In the short run, changes in the external environment, such as changes in a competitor's strategy, may hinder the achievement of an income target. Establishing a price that will ultimately achieve the desired profit level should remain the objective. Here, we discuss income-oriented objectives that involve achieving a target return on investment and maximizing profit.

e x h i b 16-3

The Relationship of Pricing Decisions to Company Objectives

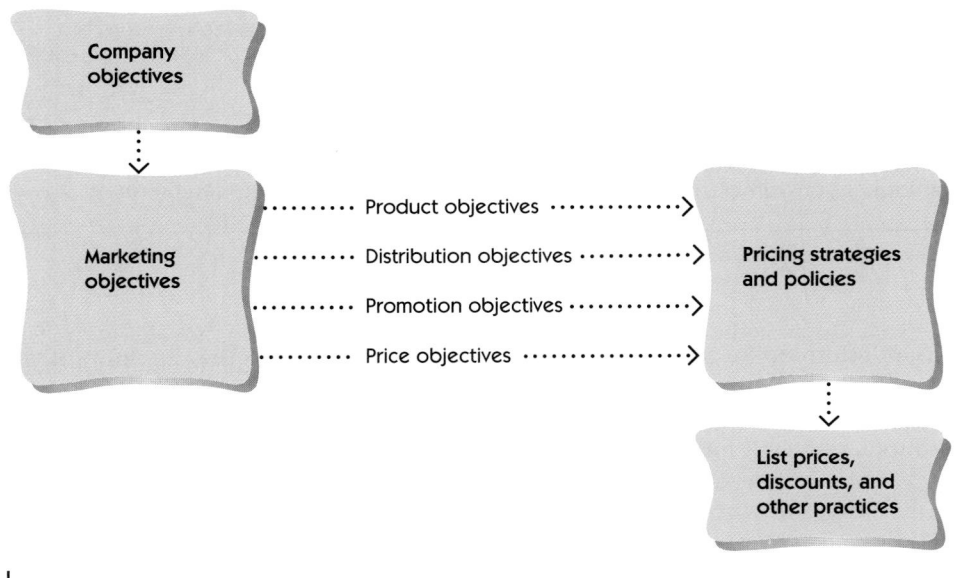

MAIN FOCUS OF OBJECTIVES	PRICING STEPS TAKEN*	WHY TAKE SUCH STEPS?
Income		
Achieve a target return on investment (ROI)	Identify price levels that will yield the required return on investment.	Firm may have a required return on investment and may drop product lines that cannot reach that return.
Maximize profits	Control costs and adjust prices to achieve profit maximization.	All companies would like to achieve profit maximization. Some come close to this goal, particularly for certain items in their product lines.
Increase cash flow	Adjust prices and discounts to encourage purchases and rapid payment.	The company may face a serious cash-flow problem and be unable to meet its obligations.
Survive/Keep a concern going	Adapt prices to permit the organization to "hold on" in periods of business downturns or until a buyer can be found.	The organization may be seeking to weather an economic storm or simply hold on for a few years. The organization may be for sale, and it is easier to sell a going concern than one that is out of business.
Sales		
Maintain market share	Assure that prices contribute to keeping sales in roughly the same position relative to those of competitors.	Many companies (such as Procter & Gamble in detergents) are long-time leaders and want to keep leadership positions.
Encourage sales growth	Adjust prices and discounts to encourage more purchases by existing buyers and to attract new buyers.	The firm may need a larger group of customers to ensure growth.
Competition		
Meet competition	Set prices about equal to those of competitors. Do the same with discounts offered.	Many firms avoid price competition and compete by means of nonprice competitive moves.
Avoid competition	Set prices at a level that will discourage competition in the firm's market.	A firm with a local monopoly might choose to keep prices low so that no new competitors will be attracted to its market.
Undercut competition	Set prices lower than the competition's.	The organization might undercut competition to project a bargain image or to draw customers away from competitors.
Social Concerns		
Behave ethically	Because of special considerations, set prices at levels lower than they would have been set on income, competition, or similar market factors.	A manufacturer of prescription medicines could charge almost any price for effective drugs but "does what's right," though this is partly to avoid government regulation.
Maintain employment	Set prices at levels that will maintain production and employment of workers.	An organization with strong community ties may seek to keep townspeople employed at least until a buyer for the company can be found.

*Notice that no consideration is given here to possible responses by competitors or shifts in demand.

Return on investment (ROI)

The ratio of profits to assets (or net worth) for an organization, a unit of an organization, a product line, or a brand; also called the *target profit*.

Target Return on Investment   **Return on investment (ROI)** is the ratio of profits to assets (or net worth) for an organization, an organizational unit (such as a division), a product line, or a brand. (See our Internet Appendix E, Financial and Economic Analysis for Marketers, at http://zikmund.swcollege.com for a discussion of how to calculate return on investment and other financial measures.) The ROI is also called the *target profit*. If management has determined that a certain ROI is needed from each product or product line, the prices for these must be set with the return objective in mind. Such a price is referred to as an *ROI price*.

Return on investment considerations are important to many pricing decisions because they provide a means to evaluate alternative marketing opportunities (or other investment options). Suppose two proposed products are expected to generate approximately the same sales volume, but one product can be priced to yield an ROI of 10 percent and the other an ROI of 30 percent. The latter product will be selected, unless a factor such as greater risk renders it less attractive. The choice between the two marketing opportunities is made easier because the ROI pricing method suggests a standard that the marketing manager can use for reference as the decision-making process continues.

Turnover (sales divided by average inventory) is an important factor in influencing the ROI of many organizations, especially retailers and wholesalers. Grocery store pricing strategies, for example, recognize that a higher return on investment may be generated if there is a rapid turnover of inventory. Thus, a grocery store might have a profit margin of less than 5 percent but a higher return on investment.

Profit Maximization   A form of pricing is suggested by the expression "all that the traffic will bear." Perhaps this is a distasteful idea, but in certain circumstances it works. Faced with a shortage of apartments in California's Silicon Valley, newcomers are willing to pay more rent than they had planned to pay rather than have no place to stay. Victims of cancer or other serious diseases frequently demonstrate that they will pay any price for a cure. In these and similar situations, sellers might try to raise their prices to the highest levels. This course of action is exemplified by the classic, but rare, monopolist that prices a good or service at the highest possible level. However, few, if any, businesses are free to behave in this manner, since legislation has restricted the extreme forms of profit maximization sometimes practiced by monopolies.

Aside from questions of ethics, an "all the traffic will bear" approach violates a major premise of the marketing concept: the idea that a consumer orientation and relationship building will lead to long-term profitability. Maximizing prices, even if it is tempting in the short run, can be disastrous if it results in threats, boycotts, bad public relations, or government action. Furthermore, a business charging a very high price over a short period runs the risk of being driven out of business by competitors willing to provide the same service or a substitute good at a more reasonable price. Given the realities of our market economy, then, effective marketers focus on maximizing profits over the long term and, accordingly, charge prices that will keep customers and the government comparatively content.

SALES-ORIENTED OBJECTIVES

Prices may be set to encourage sales growth or to maintain or increase market share. Sales-oriented pricing objectives are often intertwined with competitive objectives and with the company's commitment to the marketing concept, which emphasizes profitable sales volume. We limit our discussion here to objectives concerning market share.

Market share refers to the percentage of total industry sales accounted for by a particular firm. Caterpillar accounts for a large portion of the total sales in the excavator and road-building-tractor industry and thus has a large share of the market. In the soft-drink industry, the same is true of Coca-Cola. These companies, for financial reasons or for reasons of pride, seek to protect their impressive shares of the market. They keep their prices at reasonable levels even when it might appear that the popularity of certain items would permit them to raise prices without losing sales. The objective of this type of pricing is to maintain market share.

Price might also be used aggressively by firms seeking to enlarge market share. Such firms may cut prices drastically in an attempt to attract customers away from competitors. However, such a move can backfire. Competitors may begin to lower

Turnover
Sales divided by average inventory. Turnover measures the speed with which merchandise is sold.

Market share
The percentage of total industry sales accounted for by a particular firm or the percentage of sales of a given product accounted for by a particular brand.

their own prices, setting off a price war. Or customers may come to believe that the price reduction signals a cutback in the product's quality. Thus, price cuts are generally used to attract customers on a temporary basis. Coupons that expire on a certain date, rebates available for a short time, and January white sales are examples of temporary price cuts.

COMPETITION-ORIENTED OBJECTIVES

The effective marketer invariably tempers pricing judgments with considerations related to competition. Several situations in which competition is an issue in pricing decisions are discussed here.

Avoiding Competition   One pricing objective is to underprice goods and services to avoid attracting competitors. Businesses using this approach reason that it is better to own the only store in the neighborhood and make a reasonable profit than to make a large profit that attracts other marketers to the service area.

Meeting Competition   Businesses may find it necessary to price goods or services at approximately the levels charged by competitors. Indeed, unless the marketer is in the rare situation of holding an unbreakable patent on a product that is unique, difficult to copy, and in great demand, it is impossible to set prices without at least considering this strategy. Many goods are so similar that buyers can and do consider them to be virtually the same, forcing the individual firm to set its prices at the level established by competitors. New brands of coffee, for example, are generally priced at the going rate because one coffee is highly substitutable for another. Most consumers will not buy a brand of regular coffee that costs $3 more per pound than the others.

Where a brand is considerably more expensive than others, the higher pricing must be supported by other marketing strategies. These might include producing a genuinely better coffee blend, promoting the brand with an extensive advertising campaign, positioning it as a gourmet coffee, or packaging the coffee in attractive reusable containers.

Stabilizing Prices   A marketer may aim to match competitors' prices or maintain existing price differentials in order to avoid injurious price wars and help stabilize the general price level. This is a **price stabilization** strategy. It is fairly common, particularly in the retailing of gasoline and groceries. Though price wars in these fields are not unheard of, normally all gas stations in town charge roughly equal prices for fuel, and all grocery stores charge approximately the same price for milk. Thus, prices remain stable and predictable.

OBJECTIVES RELATED TO SOCIAL CONCERNS

Many organizations, especially not-for-profit organizations, set pricing objectives on the basis of social concerns. For example, zoos might be able to raise prices but refuse to do so because the organizational mission stresses public education above profit maximization. Pricing objectives for other organizations, especially sole proprietorships, might simply be to make enough to meet the payroll. Pricing objectives based on social concerns are highly interrelated with the ethical and legal aspects of pricing. We discuss this topic further in Chapter 17.

Target Market Considerations

Pricing decisions are affected by many factors. The most significant of these is demand from the organization's target market. Even when a competitor making the same product changes its price, target market considerations are important because the competitor's move may affect only the competitor's target market. In essence, the question the marketing manager faces is this: "Who are our customers and what do they want the price to be?" Many market segments are price-conscious. Recall that Pillsbury's Oven Lovin' cookie dough, loaded with

Price stabilization
A pricing objective aimed at avoiding widely fluctuating prices. The marketer with this objective sets prices to match competitors' prices or to maintain existing price differentials.

Hershey's chocolate chips, Reese's Pieces, and Brach's candies and packaged in a resealable tub, was a failure. One reason for the failure was that price-conscious shoppers didn't think the product was worth 20 cents more than the company's conventional tube of dough, especially since the new package was 10 percent smaller.

Nevertheless, the notion that the customer wants the lowest price is not always correct. Diamonds and Rolls Royce automobiles are expensive partly because people expect them to be expensive. A $100 bottle of perfume may contain only $10 to $20 worth of scent; the rest of the price goes to advertising, packaging, distribution, and profit. When consumers buy such perfume, they are buying atmosphere, hope, the feeling of being someone special, and pride in having "the best."

Coca-Cola Company is experimenting with a technology for temperature-sensitive vending machines. A software program will read the outside temperature and will raise prices when the weather gets hot.

http://www.cocacola.com

Even frequently purchased products can benefit from the customer's willingness to pay a higher price rather than a lower one. Most parents don't want to buy bargain-priced baby food for their infants, nor do most hosts want to offer their guests an inexpensive brand of whiskey to drink.

When targeting certain markets, then, marketers can expect to sell more at a higher price than at a lower one. However, most successful marketers do not employ high prices to appeal to buyers. Instead, they offer reasonably priced products that prove popular to target markets.

In essence, the question the marketing manager faces is this: "Who are our customers and what do they want the price to be?"

Know Your Demand

Marketers need to know how many people will buy their products. How many people are willing to buy and how much they will buy are primarily functions of price. Marketers use the concept of price elasticity to describe how sensitive demand is to price.

PRICE ELASTICITY OF DEMAND

Price elasticity measures the effect of a change in price on the quantity of a product demanded. Price elasticity refers to price sensitivity. Specifically, price elasticity measures what percentage change in quantity demanded is induced by a percentage change in price. Exhibit 16-5 illustrates the concept of *price elasticity of demand*.

Logic would lead us to predict that (1) a decline in the price of a product might lead to an increase in the quantity of it demanded and (2) the rate of increase might differ from case to case and from product to product. For example, we would expect that bread sales might increase as prices went down. However, the rise would be slight and would happen slowly, because bread is a common, unexciting product

Price elasticity
A measure of the effect of a change in price on the quantity of product demanded.

Demand Curve

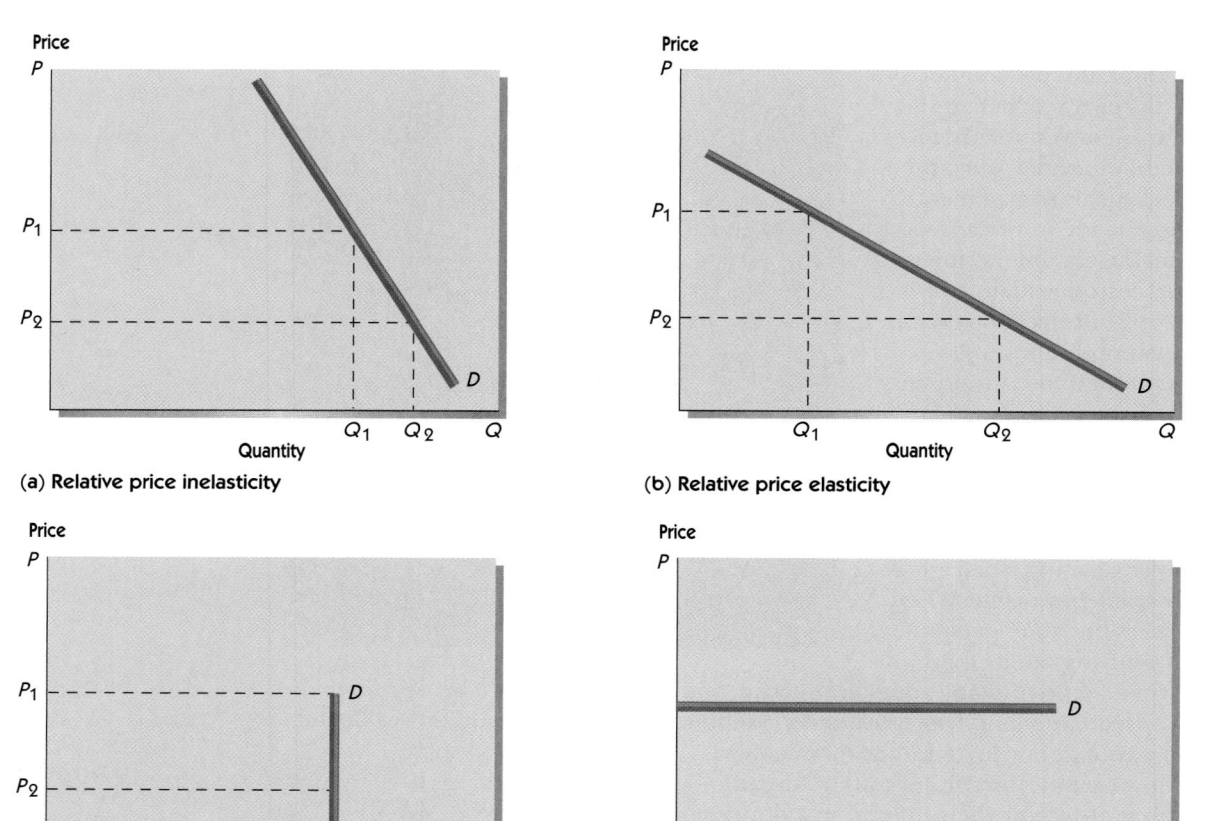

(a) **Relative price inelasticity**

(b) **Relative price elasticity**

(c) **Total price inelasticity**

(d) **Total price elasticity**

that most people can afford and are already buying. Demand increases are also limited by the fact that there is a limit to how much bread people can eat.

This situation is demonstrated in Exhibit 16-5(a). A decrease in price from P_1 to P_2 increases demand from Q_1 to Q_2. The gap between the two Qs is far less than the gap between the two Ps, illustrating *relative price inelasticity* of demand. That is, demand is not very flexible when price is changed. Thus, when price is raised from P_2 back to P_1, demand does not decrease rapidly; it is price inelastic.

The opposite situation is shown in Exhibit 16-5(b), in which a downward change in price does increase demand significantly. More than that, the increase in demand appears to be greater than the decrease in price might warrant. This curve might apply to, say, filet mignon. This product is very much in demand even though most families buy it in limited amounts because of its high price. The shopper who finds that the price of the steak has been reduced is likely to stock up. Thus, the demand for the product is highly flexible, or *elastic*, in terms of price.

If the slope of the demand (D) line in Exhibit 16-5(a) increases so that it becomes straight up and down as in Exhibit 16-5(c), the line shows absolute and complete inelasticity of demand. Regardless of the price charged, be it high or low, the same quantity is demanded. No change in price will affect demand. The classic example of this phenomenon is medicine sales. Suppose a patient needs one dose per day of a certain drug—say, insulin—to stay alive. If the price fell, the patient would not buy more than the prescribed amount. If the price became extremely high, the same single treatment would be demanded, even if the patient had to resort to drastic measures to meet the bill.

Another special case is shown in Exhibit 16-5(d). Here, the demand curve is perpendicular to the price axis. In this situation, there is a single price, and customers demand various quantities at that one price. Sometimes they demand no goods; sometimes they demand many units of goods. Whereas the vertical curve shows absolute price inelasticity, the horizontal line demonstrates *total price elasticity*—no change in price is needed to increase or decrease quantities demanded. The classic example of this situation involves the wheat farmer who grows a product that is nearly identical to that of all competitors and who is unable to influence market price. Such a farmer can only earn the going price and sell as much wheat as he chooses at that price.

The demand schedules for most products lie somewhere between the extremes of total price inelasticity and total price elasticity. It is the often-difficult task of the marketer to determine the nature of the demand curve for each product offered to the market. Information published by trade associations and information from other sources should assist in this chore. Experimenting with different price levels may also provide insights. Marketers experiment in this way every day. When items don't sell at one price, they charge a different price or offer a discount. They move, either consciously or unconsciously, to a new point on the demand schedule.

CROSS-ELASTICITY OF DEMAND

One other aspect of elasticity of demand should be mentioned here. Many products depend partially on cross-elasticity for their sales. **Cross-elasticity** describes how demand for one product responds to changes in the price of another product. The demand for laser printers, for example, is closely related to the demand for personal computers; they are complementary—they go together. Conversely, if the price of beef rises sharply, thereby reducing the demand for beef, the demand for lower-priced meat or for fish might increase. Effective marketers thus study not only their own product's demand schedule but also the demand schedules of substitute and complementary products.

Cross-elasticity
Elasticity in the demand for one product in relation to the prices of substitutable or complementary products.

Know Your Costs

Pricing methods based only on the seller's costs fail to include the all-important buyer in the pricing effort. Nevertheless, the seller's costs are a major area of concern. Although some products may occasionally be sold at a loss, cost must be recouped sooner or later. Cost thus provides the "floor" on which to build a pricing strategy.

Marketers often use **marginal analysis** in examining costs. This measure allows them to determine the costs and revenues connected with the production and sale of each *additional* unit of a product. The concept of marginal analysis can be demonstrated by example: If only one unit of a product or service is produced, all the costs of production and marketing must be assigned to that single unit. Thus, the cost associated with the very first brake repair job performed by a Brakeman franchise would be immense. All the fixed costs (that is, the expenses associated with entering the business) would have to be covered by that first repair job. However, each *additional* brake repair would take over some portion of these costs. When there were many brake repair jobs, only a small portion of the fixed cost would have to be allocated to each one.

The costs and revenues associated with the production of one more unit of a product are the marginal costs and marginal revenues. **Marginal cost** is the net addition to total costs created by the production of one more unit of a product.

Marginal analysis
A method for determining the costs and revenues associated with the production and sale of each additional unit of a product.

Marginal cost
The net addition to a firm's total costs that results from the production of one additional unit of product.

Airlines use special off-season fares to fill empty seats that would otherwise go unsold. They know that the costs and revenues associated with the production of "one more unit" of a product can be marginal when demand is low. Low off-season fares encourage more purchases by existing buyers and attract new buyers.

Marginal revenue
The net addition to a firm's total revenue that results from the sale of one additional unit of product.

Average cost
The total costs divided by the number of units produced.

Marginal revenue is the net addition to the total revenue of the firm from the sale of one more unit of a product. The basis of marginal analysis is the idea that these combine to create a point of maximum profitability for a firm. As shown in Exhibit 16-6, that point is where marginal cost equals marginal revenue.

Move a pencil point along the horizontal, or quantity, axis of Exhibit 16-6 and note the behavior of the variables shown. Begin by looking at **average cost**, which represents the total costs divided by the number of units produced. Moving from the extreme left, where the quantity produced and sold is zero, the average cost at

e   x   h   i   b   **16-6**

Behaviors of Costs and Revenues as Demand and Quantity Produced Increase

Price
(dollars)

Marginal cost   Average cost

Marginal revenue   Demand

Quantity

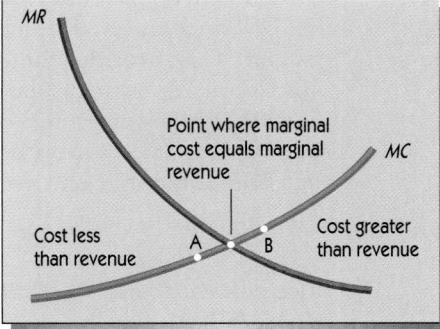

Intersection of Marginal Cost and Marginal Revenue Curves

Cost and
revenue (dollars)

MR

Point where marginal
cost equals marginal
revenue

MC

Cost less
than revenue

A   B

Cost greater
than revenue

Units produced and sold

first declines as quantity increases, because the cost of the first unit produced is far greater than the cost of the thousandth. The marginal cost also declines at first as we move along the quantity axis. In the case of the Brakeman franchise, this is because the same garage, using the same equipment and instruments, is handling an increasing number of cars. The marginal revenue declines because the revenue generated from each additional sale is an increasingly smaller portion of Brakeman's total income. The two cost curves eventually move upward because, after a certain level of output has been reached, production inefficiencies, such as overcrowding in the workplace, cause cost per unit to rise.

The important point is that *profit is maximized where marginal cost equals marginal revenue (MC = MR)*. Consider Exhibit 16-7, which shows only these two variables. Suppose a seller of a good or service discovered that the cost of producing one more unit was less than the revenue to be realized by producing that unit (in other words, suppose the firm was at point *A*). Management would logically decide to produce and sell that additional unit. That is, there would still be some profit to be made, because the cost would be less than the revenue to be gained. However, if management discovered its operation to be at point *B*, where cost per unit is *greater* than revenue, it would realize that the one more unit would cost *more* than it would bring in—that the company would take a loss on that unit. The sensible thing to do would be to cut back—not to point *A*, where the cost is still less than the revenue to be made, but to the point where cost and revenue levels come together; that is, production should be at the level where *MC = MR.*

Summary

Marketing involves the exchange of something of value. Value is generally represented by price. Price plays an important role in the marketing mix and in the attainment of marketing objectives.

1) Define price and discuss it.
Price represents value, which is the power of one product to attract another in an exchange. Price enables buyers and sellers to express the value of the products they have to offer.

2) Tell how price interacts with the rest of the marketing mix.
In an effective marketing mix, product, distribution, promotion, and price decisions must be consistent with and must support one another. For example, high price is consistent with high product

quality, an image-oriented promotion, and exclusive distribution in prestigious stores.

3) Analyze price's place in the economy.

Price plays a major role in the allocation of goods and services in market economies. In addition, price encourages or discourages demand; it often gives products a symbolic value that can easily be perceived by buyers; it helps achieve financial or market-share objectives; and it can be used in a rapid-response adjustment to environmental changes.

4) Outline the fundamentals of pricing strategy.

In setting prices, it is important to (1) determine your pricing objectives, (2) know the importance of price to your target market, (3) know your demand, (4) understand your costs, and (5) determine your pricing strategy.

5) Characterize the relationship between price and organizational objectives.

Organizational objectives are the basis for pricing strategies and are achieved partially as a result of those strategies. Price affects income generation, sales, competitive moves, and attainment of social objectives.

6) Relate the demand in a target market to the prices charged.

The price of a product must suit the target market. For example, the decision to target potential buyers of extremely expensive jewelry means that the prices charged can be high if they are supported by the appropriate product quality, promotion, and distribution choices.

7) Understand that demand and cost considerations influence pricing.

Marketers need to know how many people will buy their product and how much it will cost to meet this demand. Cost provides the "floor" on which to build a pricing strategy. Marginal analysis is a technique that helps marketers determine the cost and revenue associated with production and sale of each additional unit of a product.

8) Differentiate among price elasticity, price inelasticity, and price cross-elasticity.

Price elasticity exists when the change in quantity demanded exceeds the change in price that brought it about. Price inelasticity exists when the change in quantity demanded is smaller than the change in price. Cross-elasticity exists when price changes for one product affect demand for another, as when a rise in the price of beef contributes to an increase in the demand for fish.

Key Terms

average cost (p. 480)
barter (p. 468)
cross-elasticity (p. 479)
demand curve (p. 471)
list price (p. 468)
marginal analysis (p. 479)
marginal cost (p. 479)

marginal revenue (p. 480)
market share (p. 475)
nonprice competition (p. 470)
price competition (p. 470)
price elasticity (p. 477)
price stabilization (p. 476)
pricing objective (p. 472)

return on investment (ROI) (p. 474)
supply curve (p. 471)
turnover (p. 475)
value (p. 468)

Questions for Review & Critical Thinking

1. What are some other names given to price? Why are these names used instead of price?
2. What is the main macromarketing function of price in the economy? Differentiate between that function and the role of price as a micromarketing tool.
3. "A high price policy needs supporting policies." Explain.
4. Give examples of situations in which a low price might not suit other aspects of a firm's marketing plan.
5. Why does the consumer often view price as the most important part of a transaction?
6. Consumers can rent everything from houses, yachts, and luxury cars to televisions and other home appliances. What price-related advantages might renting bring to consumers? What aspects of buyer behavior are brought into play when a consumer compares renting a TV or refrigerator with buying the item?
7. Days Inn of America, a chain of hundreds of motels, adopted a slogan for use in its advertisements: "Inexpensive. But not cheap." What does this slogan say about Days Inn motels, their prices, and the target market Days Inn is trying to attract?

8. The price a firm charges for its goods or services often depends primarily on how the customer is expected to react to the price charged. In what situations have you, as a customer or seller, encountered this approach to pricing?

9. Differentiate among organizational objectives, marketing objectives, and pricing objectives.

10. Why must managerial judgment play a role in determining prices even though many mathematical techniques have been developed for that purpose?

11. How can target market considerations affect a firm's pricing policies?

12. Form small groups as directed by your instructor. Each person in the group should contact five people and pose the following question: "Suppose your favorite baseball team will be playing in the World Series. An acquaintance says he has two tickets to Game 4 that he cannot use. He asks you how much you would pay for the two tickets. How much would you offer to pay?" Meet as a group and plot the demand curve.

 **exercises** | http://zikmund.swcollege.com

Much pricing theory is related to economics. AmosWeb is A Guide to All Things Economic and the Home of Mr. Economy. Go to http://amosweb.com and you will find, among other things, the *AmosWorld Encyclopedic Glossary*. It is a searchable, cross-referenced database of economic terms. You should find it quite useful.

Address Book (Useful URLs)

The Economist newspaper	http://www.economist.com
The Conference Board	http://www.conference-board.org
The Professional Pricing Society	http://www.pricing-advisor.com

Ethically Right or Wrong?

1. Some Roses-Only stores import roses from South America. They sell imported roses at much lower prices than domestic roses. Some domestic rose growers believe that these low prices will increase the demand for roses and make roses widely available. They fear the market will become saturated and roses will lose their image as special flowers. Some suggest that the government should pass laws to restrict the importation of roses into the United States. How would you feel about this if you were an American rose grower? A retailer who imports roses from South America? A consumer who wants to buy roses for her mother's birthday?

2. Supply-and-demand theory suggests that prices should find their own level—that is, they should represent "all the traffic will bear." Is such pricing ethical? Is it good for society?

3. "Consumers want lower prices. If the marketing concept means being oriented toward the consumer, prices should be lowered." Comment.

VIDEO CASE 16-1
Toronto Blue Jays (B)

The Toronto Blue Jays major league baseball team began playing in the American League East on April 7, 1977. The Blue Jays defeated the Chicago White Sox that day, but at the end of its first season the team finished last in the division. The Blue Jays were the American League East Champions in 1985, 1989, 1991, 1992, and 1993, and both the American League and World Series Champions in 1992 and 1993. However, after the major league players went on strike in August 1994, which resulted in the cancellation of the 1994 World Series, the team experienced a period of losing. Attendance dropped to roughly 31,000 per game versus an average of 50,000 per game in the pre-strike years. While negative fan reaction about the players' strike and the poor team performance were factors influencing attendance decline, there was also increased competition for the entertainment dollar because of the formation of the Toronto Raptors and legalization of casino gambling.

After its losing streak, the team was again in contention by 1998. The Blue Jays finished second in the American League East. Carlos Delgado led the team with 115 RBI, and Jose Canseco recorded a team-high 46 homers. Roger Clemens won the Cy Young Award with a 20-6 record. Attendance picked up in the second half of the season. However, the team was losing money. Management identified two cost-related factors as the reason for the loss: escalating player salaries and weakness in the Canadian dollar. Ninety percent of Blue Jays revenue is in Canadian dollars yet 80 percent of expenses are in U.S. dollars. In 1998 the exchange rate made a Canadian dollar worth about 65 percent of the U.S. dollar. Management did not believe it could dramatically change either cost factor, so they looked to increasing revenue.

A large portion of a baseball team's revenues come from ticket sales to the games. The Blue Jays decided that they would have to raise prices to remain competitive.

The Blue Jays' marketing managers decided to use a value-added pricing approach that offers increased value to customers. The logic is that fans will gladly pay more for a really choice seat but won't pay too much for a cheap seat.

The Blue Jays play in the Sky Dome. The team offers fans a pricing structure in which better seats cost more. The best seats—closer to home plate—cost the most. The stadium has ten different seating areas:

Field Level Infield
Club Level Baselines
Field Level Bases
Field Level Baselines
SkyClub Outfield
SkyDeck Infield
100 Level Outfield
SkyClub Bleachers
SkyDeck Bases
SkyDeck Baselines
(These can be found at http://www.bluejays.com.)

In addition to ticket revenues, a baseball team obtains revenue from television and radio broadcasts, the sale of souvenirs, and the sale of food and drinks at the stadium.[5]

QUESTIONS

1. What role do supply and demand play in the price of baseball tickets? Is the demand for Field Level Infield seats more or less elastic than demand for SkyDeck Baseline seats?
2. If the Blue Jays raise prices, how can they increase the value of their product to justify higher ticket prices?
3. Is it the Blue Jays' social responsibility to offer very inexpensive seats so families can bring young children to the games?

Pricing Strategies and Tactics

By 2003, two historic ballparks, Tiger Stadium and Fenway Park, will be replaced. Dave Kindred, a *Sporting News* columnist, wonders if the last of the dinosaurs, Wrigley Field, will be next on the list. His concern about whether it will live much longer arises from the business side of sports. Major league baseball teams have become so desperate to increase revenue that little Wrigley Field, 85 years old, with 38,957 seats, is hard-pressed to meet the current demand, let alone what the future will bring.

Here, in his own words, is Kindred's solution:

Double the ticket prices. Don't build more luxury boxes, don't add an upper deck in the outfield. Just ask all Cubs fans to pay twice as much for a ticket as they're now paying. The bet here is, they'd do it. If any traffic anywhere will bear a 100 percent increase in ticket prices, the Chicago traffic will.

This double-the-price thought first occurred to me as an ironic joke. But now I think I'm serious. I mean, why not? Would you, dear Cubs fans, rather pay double and sit in the Friendly Confines or pay time-and-a-half to sit in a fancy-schmantzy Tribune Tower Ballyard? I say "time-and-a-half" because every new ballpark is reason to raise ticket prices, anyway, so the question becomes: Do we stay in Wrigley and pay $25 more, say, for a ticket, or do we go to a new place and pay $18.75 more?[1]

Dave Kindred's idea is clearly a creative one for the Cubs. Do you think this pricing strategy would work? How important is price to the average fan? What is the value of a game in the Friendly Confines? How important is the revenue from high-priced luxury boxes to a sports team? These questions involve pricing strategies, the subject of this chapter. The chapter begins with a discussion of common pricing strategies. It then focuses on techniques and methods of analysis for establishing a product's price and explains how marketers adjust list prices. The remainder of the chapter focuses on legal and ethical issues associated with pricing.

An Overview of Pricing Strategies

A wide range of pricing strategies are available to marketing managers, as shown in Exhibit 17-1. Managers may use several of these strategies to arrive at a price that reflects market realities, costs, consumer perceptions, and other considerations. Pricing strategies may be broadly categorized under five headings:

1. Differential pricing strategies
2. Competitive pricing strategies
3. Product-line pricing strategies
4. Psychological and image pricing strategies
5. Distribution-based pricing strategies

Differential Pricing Strategies

An organization that sells the same product to different buyers at different prices is using a **differential pricing strategy**. The type of industry strongly influences whether an organization uses differential pricing.

ONE-PRICE POLICY VERSUS VARIABLE PRICING

Determining whether to maintain a fixed price for all customers or to vary the prices from buyer to buyer is a basic pricing decision. Holding the price the same for all buyers is termed a **one-price strategy** (or a one-price policy, if it is routinely used for all pricing decisions).

In the United States, most retailers follow a one-price policy. Whether a billionaire or a child with only 50 cents enters the candy store, the price of the candy

Differential pricing strategy
A strategy whereby an organization charges different prices to different buyers of the same product.

One-price strategy
A strategy whereby an organization charges a single price for a product regardless of the circumstances surrounding the sale, the quantity bought, or any other unique aspect of the exchange.

e x h i b **17-1** The Basic Pricing Strategies

Differential pricing strategies	Product-line pricing strategies
Variable pricing	Total-profit pricing
Second-market discounting	Captive pricing
Skimming	Leader pricing
Periodic discounting	Bait pricing
Random discounting	Price lining
	Price bundling
Competitive pricing strategies	Multiple-unit pricing
Meeting the competition	
Undercutting the competition	**Psychological and image pricing**
Price leadership	**strategies**
Following the leader	Reference pricing
Penetration pricing	Odd and even pricing
Predatory pricing	Prestige pricing
Traditional pricing	
Inflationary pricing	**Distribution-based pricing strategies**
	F.O.B.
	Delivered pricing
	Zone pricing
	Uniform delivered pricing
	Basing-point pricing

bar is the same. Some marketers defend this strategy on the grounds that it is fair and democratic not to charge prices that might favor one customer over another.

A one-price policy provides the advantage of simplicity of administration, which leads, in turn, to lower personnel expenses. This is the main reason most retailers use it. Salespeople and clerks need not debate the price of a loaf of bread or a yard of cloth with each customer.

Among marketers that adopt a differential pricing strategy, the most popular is the **variable pricing strategy**, in which marketers allow customers to negotiate in an attempt to secure a favorable price. In many foreign markets, variable pricing is the rule. In the United States, automobile and real estate purchases often present such an opportunity. Variable pricing developed in the automobile industry as a response to

customers' desire to trade in their older models. When variable prices are used, each salesperson must be able to handle customers' questions, complaints, and attempts to have the price reduced. While the supermarket's one-price policy allows it to employ less experienced, lower-paid clerks, the automobile dealer must hire active salespeople—and pay them comparatively high commissions—to administer its variable price policy.

Where haggling is allowed, large companies usually find themselves in a better position than smaller firms to drive a hard bargain with suppliers. Federal legislation prohibits the use of variable pricing policies when they might give large or powerful organizational buyers competitive advantages over small organizational buyers. (This legislation, the Robinson-Patman Act, is discussed later in the chapter.) However, there are many situations in which seller and buyer engage in a bit of give and take. The variable pricing policy allows for this.

Internet auctions and *reverse auctions* on the Internet are a new form of variable pricing. Companies such as eBay (http://www.ebay.com) consider themselves online trading communities. Auctions on the Internet operate in a manner similar to the way traditional auctions work: When the auction closes, the highest bidder gets to purchase the good or service for sale. In a reverse auction, a buyer who wants to get the best price on an item indicates a willingness to buy and then allows sellers to compete for his or her business. Typically the buyer picks a maximum price he or she would pay for the item and does not accept sellers' bids higher than this price.

SECOND-MARKET DISCOUNTING

Second-market discounting is a differential pricing strategy designed to sell a brand at one price in the core target market and at a reduced price in a secondary market segment. For example, art museum memberships are often discounted to students and senior citizens. Theaters, airlines, and utilities may vary their prices among buyers. A theater's matinee price is ordinarily less than the evening price; a plane ticket is less expensive if one flies on a weekend; the industrial user generally pays less for electricity than the homeowner. The price differences are usually treated as "discounts" rather than price variants. They are not illegal under the Robinson-Patman Act because the groups of buyers are not considered to be in competition with one another.

Excess capacity is a requirement for a second-market discounting strategy. An organization exporting products to foreign markets may choose this strategy to make use of its excess capacity and to reduce its average production costs.

Variable pricing strategy
A differential pricing strategy whereby an organization allows customers to negotiate a price that varies from buyer to buyer.

Second-market discounting
A differential pricing strategy whereby a product is sold at one price in the core target market and at a reduced price in a secondary market.

SKIMMING

Skimming price
A relatively high price, often charged at the beginning of a product's life. The price is systematically lowered as time goes by.

A **skimming price** is a high price intended to "skim the cream off the market." It is best employed at the start of a product's life, when the product is novel and consumers are uncertain about its value. For example, compact disc players first sold at prices of about $800. Now they can be purchased for as little as $60. Similarly, in 1991, adding a first-generation sound card, a CD-ROM drive, and some speakers to a personal computer cost more than $1,000; today, this combination of devices costs less than $250.

This pattern—pricing high and systematically reducing price over time—allows companies to establish a flow of revenue that covers research and development expenses, as well as the high initial costs of bringing the product to market. A skimming strategy assumes the existence of a relatively strong inelastic demand for the product, often because the product has status value or because it represents a true breakthrough. Price is used as a means to segment the market on the basis of discretionary income or degree of need for the product. As the product life cycle progresses, prices are reduced in response to competitive pressures, and new market segments become the key targets.

Marketing managers are most likely to embrace a skimming strategy when production capacity limits output or when competitors face some barrier to market entry. For instance, during early stages of NutraSweet's product life cycle, when G. D. Searle and Company had a patent on the product, Searle charged the highest possible prices to soft-drink companies, the customers with the greatest need for the artificial sweetener. As it increased production capacity, and as other food manufacturers began to demand NutraSweet for diet versions of their products, Searle progressively lowered prices. In the 1990s, when its patent expired, it lowered its prices again and began heavily promoting the NutraSweet brand name to solidify brand loyalty.

PERIODIC DISCOUNTING

Periodic discounting
A pricing strategy whereby discounts are offered systematically and predictably.

Like skimming, **periodic discounting** uses price reductions that are predictable over time. The basic strategy is to price high and to discount systematically as time elapses. Summer fashion items are reduced in price in midsummer. Long-distance telephone calls are cheaper on weekends. The price changes associated with periodic discounting take place over shorter time periods than those associated with skimming. Further, prices may be expected to rise in subsequent periods.

RANDOM DISCOUNTING

Random discounting
A pricing strategy whereby discounts are offered occasionally and unpredictably.

On Valentine's Day, roses are no bargain. Florists charge a premium for Valentine's Day roses because prices tend to climb with demand, and Valentine's Day is the biggest rose day of the year. Lower prices for roses during the summer are quite predictable.

The **random discounting** pricing strategy involves lowering the price of a product randomly to entice new customers, perhaps by means of coupons or featured prices. It is designed so that customers do not anticipate the reduced prices and

therefore do not postpone purchases at the regular price. In its simplest form, the strategy is designed so that regular and high-income customers routinely buy at the normal (high) price and price-conscious shoppers purchase at the sale price. The key to implementing this strategy is to ensure that consumers can't predict the timing of the discounts.

Competitive Pricing Strategies

Competitive pricing strategies are used by organizations that have competitive pricing objectives.[2] Dominant firms may use pricing to exploit their positions. Weak firms may opt for the role of follower.

MEETING THE COMPETITION

Organizations concerned with meeting competition quite naturally set prices at levels equal to those of competitors—the going rate. Many U.S. firms choose a **meeting-the-competition strategy** to avoid price competition and price-cutting wars. This approach tends to shift competition to areas other than price. Setting prices for organizational products may be considerably different from setting prices for consumer products. An organizational buyer may solicit competitive bids, asking various suppliers to submit independent price quotations for a specific order. This permits the buyer to obtain the lowest possible price for products that meet certain predetermined specifications. When they must submit price quotes, many marketers adopt competitive pricing strategies.

For many custom-made products, the supplier may request a proposal from the buyer indicating the exact nature of the product or service that will be sold. Often, the buyer and the seller will then negotiate a price.

UNDERCUTTING THE COMPETITION

An **undercutting-the-competition strategy** emphasizes offering the lowest price among available choices. Marketers implementing this approach often use price as the focal point of the entire marketing strategy. For instance, most discount stores highlight undercutting the competition (traditional retailers). Their lower markup helps generate a higher volume of merchandise sales.

Many large organizations, especially those that compete in the global marketplace, also favor this strategy. Multinational organizations and others that price to undercut the competition often have certain advantages because of production costs. For example, many Asian electronics manufacturers pay relatively low wages, and their low labor costs allow them to undercut prices in many of their export markets. Organizations experienced in producing a product often find that their know-how and technical expertise provide economies of scale, which allow them to undercut competition with a discount strategy.

---

e—commerce Changing Everything

For a glimpse inside Jay S. Walker's universe, walk into his Stamford (Conn.) office. It looks like a rich man's playpen: On the wall are Nixon's letter of resignation to Henry Kissinger and four flags that went to the moon, along with man-size models of *Star Wars'* Yoda and Boba Fett characters. Diapers, detergent, and tins of tuna crowd the shelves—pointing to a future foray for priceline.com, the Web site that sells air tickets, cars, hotel rooms, and loans. What else does a billionaire want? Escape from earth, of course. "Space is one of the great frontiers," says Walker, 43, echoing *Star Trek* actor and now priceline.com spokesman William Shatner. "I'd love to go on a shuttle to the moon."

For the right price, maybe he will. Since priceline.com made its debut, Walker's name-your-own-price system has turned commercial logic on its head. It proves that, for the right savings, people will buy something without knowing the brand or, in the case of airline tickets, without knowing when their flight takes off. In Walker's world, the buyer writes the price tag. There's a competing group of sellers, whose prices are matched against it by priceline.com.

At first, there weren't enough matchups—so priceline.com sometimes discounted prices below costs to make deals happen. But ultimately, Walker persuaded more than 2 million people to sign up for goods over the Web. In the process, he's forcing traditional businesses to rethink their pricing model and spawning imitators, including buyingedge.com and NexTag.com.

Now, Walker is extending the approach to fresh fields. Although he won't disclose the next items up for bid—simply smiling at the household products perched on his shelves—Walker sees no end to his potential offerings. "Even in lifesaving medicines, people will be flexible to save money," he says. How far he can stretch the concept is unclear, but priceline.com is off to a rousing start. In one year of business, revenues shot to $111.6 million in the quarter ended June 30 [1999], up from $49.4 million for the previous three months. That still meant an operating loss of $16.2 million, but the losses have shrunk from $17.6 million and $73.9 million in the prior two quarters, and analysts see profits by the middle of next year [2000]. Walker's winning ways look sustainable: He has received two patents at priceline.com and has applications in on 20 more. "This is a truly unique platform that can be transferred across product lines," says analyst Ryan B. Alexander of Wit Capital Corp. Walker wants to repeat his formula in dozens of markets. "What many people who are affluent fail to appreciate is that most of the world is on a budget," says Walker. And where does this bargain-hunting billionaire expect his business to go? Straight to the moon.[3]

Meeting-the-competition strategy
A pricing strategy whereby an organization sets prices at levels equal to those of competitors.

Undercutting-the-competition strategy
A pricing strategy whereby an organization sets prices at levels lower than those of competitors.

PRICE LEADERS AND FOLLOWERS

Price leadership strategies are generally implemented by organizations that have large shares of the market and of the production capacity in their industries. Such organizations have enough market information and enough control over their distribution systems to determine a price level that others will follow. Price leaders typically are able to make price adjustments without starting price wars and can make their announced prices stick. Price leaders are often sensitive to the price and profit needs of the rest of the industry. Some organizations, especially those in weak competitive positions, adopt a **follow-the-leader strategy** by simply pricing as the market leader does.

PENETRATION PRICING

A **penetration price** is a low introductory price. In the short run, it may even result in a loss. A penetration pricing strategy is implemented when a competitive situation is well established (or soon will be) and a low price in the introductory stage of the product life cycle will be necessary to break into the market. Penetration pricing is an alternative to skimming. Its objective is to enable a new product to become established and survive in the long run. A company achieves this objective by pricing so low that a profit is possible only if the company sells a relatively high volume and obtains a large market share. Penetration pricing is likely to be the most effective and desirable approach under one or more of the following conditions:

1. When demand for the product is very sensitive to price (elastic demand)
2. When it is possible to achieve substantial economies in the unit cost of manufacturing and/or distributing the product by operating at high volume (economies of scale)
3. When a brand faces threats of strong competitive imitation soon after introduction because there is no patent protection, no high capital requirement for production, and no other factors to keep competition out of the market (strong competitive threat)
4. When market segments do not appear to be meaningful and there is mass market acceptance of the product (mass market acceptance)
5. When acquiring a customer leads to a relationship and additional purchases (customer acquisition and retention)

Netpliance is a provider of Internet-based content, applications, and services through devices specifically designed for Internet access. When it introduced its all-in-one I-opener Internet appliance that combines an Internet terminal, keyboard, built-in mouse, and 10-inch liquid crystal display, it used a $99 penetration pricing strategy. It subsequently upgraded the product and raised its price.

The logic of penetration pricing is that the strategy will reduce or slow the threat of competitive imitation because the small profit margin will discourage low-cost imitators from entering the market. Furthermore, by increasing the size of the total market or of its market share, the marketer starts a customer relationship, establishes strong brand loyalty, and increases the brand's dominance in consumers' minds.

RealNetworks built market share with a penetration pricing strategy when it introduced its RealPlayer software as a free download at http://www.real.com. The company takes a relationship marketing view (rather than a transactional view) of the exchange process. The initial transaction—giving away the basic product offering—is merely the first of a series of exchanges. Once a relationship is developed with a customer, RealNetworks expects to trade customers up to its Plus version of the software (priced at $49.99) and hopes to sell its other software products such as RealJukebox Plus.

To restrict competitors, an organization trying to establish a monopoly might set prices low to eliminate competition and then raise prices after all competition had been eliminated. This **predatory pricing strategy** is illegal under the Sherman Antitrust Act and the Robinson-Patman Act.

Price leadership strategy
A strategy whereby organizations with large market shares and production capacities determine a price level that other, weaker organizations in the same industry will follow.

Follow-the-leader strategy
A pricing strategy whereby an organization sets prices at the level the market leader has established. It is used especially by organizations in weak competitive positions.

Penetration price
A low introductory price meant to quickly establish a product in the market.

Predatory pricing strategy
An illegal pricing strategy whereby the price of a product is set low to eliminate competition and then raised to a high level after competition has been eliminated.

TRADITIONAL PRICING

Certain prices are set largely by tradition rather than by individual marketers. These customary prices may remain unchanged for long periods. The 10-cent phone-booth call, although now a thing of the distant past, was priced at the same level for decades. Today, the typical price is a quarter. Candy bars also tend to be priced at the level of coinage (that is, so they can be paid for with coins). As chocolate and sugar prices rose or fell, the bars got smaller or larger, but the price (a nickle, dime, quarter, etc.) remained the same. It was only when candy bars had diminished to near invisibility that manufacturers broke with tradition and raised the price. Until that time, only a few bars were priced higher than the traditional price, and these were backed by appropriate supporting policies. The 10-cent bar in the 5-cent era was bigger than the others and of better quality, and it was heavily promoted. Today, candy bars that break with the going rate have similar attributes.

Exhibit 17-2 portrays the demand situation faced by firms in industries where prices have become established at particular levels. Should a company attempt to raise prices above the traditional level, the result will be considerably decreased sales. On the other hand, notice that a reduction in price will not produce sales increases that justify the price cut. Demand is thus elastic above the traditional price (P_t) but inelastic below it. The resulting curve is "kinked." This condition arises because consumers' beliefs and habits are so ingrained that price reductions are attributed to some negative change, such as a perceived lowering of quality, rather than to competitive market pressures.

The kinked demand curve also characterizes oligopolistic markets, in which a small number of marketers must price at traditional market levels to maximize profits. Oligopolists, which are highly sensitive to competitive price shifts, generally respond in kind to price reductions. Thus, there is no advantage in price reductions; they will only lead to a lower market price adhered to by all of the oligopolists.

Vending machine operators and mass transit authorities are two organizations that favor traditional pricing strategies. The Sacagawea dollar coin, which replaced the Susan B. Anthony dollar, has been well received by vending machine operators and mass transit authorities. The U.S. Mint matched the electromagnetic signature of the Susan B. Anthony coin so that machines will not have to be retrofitted to accept the new coin.

e x h i b **17-2**

Kinked Demand Curve Facing Marketers of Products Sold at a Traditional Price

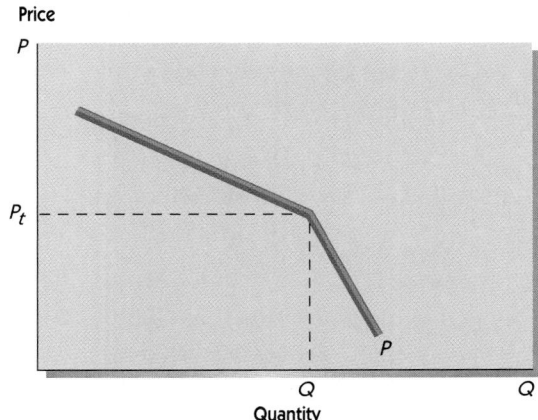

INFLATIONARY PRICING

Executives focus increased attention on pricing strategies when inflation rates are high. During periods of inflation, buying power declines for consumers as well as for many organizational buyers, and most buyers become more price conscious and sensitive to price changes. To make sure its brands offer value, Gillette sets its pricing based on a market-basket approach. Marketing managers keep daily track of a collection of lowly items, including a newspaper, a candy bar, and a can of Coke, that are all priced under a dollar. Then Gillette never raises its prices faster than the rate of increase in the price of the market basket. The company does not believe in a what-the-market-will-bear pricing strategy. Gillette believes that consumers have a relative-value consciousness. If the price of some things gets out of whack, consumers feel as if they are getting ripped off.[4]

Increased price awareness heightens price competition. Products may be altered to permit the offering of lower-priced alternatives. For example, during an inflationary period, an airline may continue to offer dependable air service while cutting some of the "free" frills and extra services rather than increasing price.

Organizations may react to inflation by changing the size or amount of the product sold. When the candy bar manufacturers raised prices and enlarged bar size, perceived value was enhanced even though price per ounce increased. Alternatively, distribution systems may be tightened in an effort to hold costs down. Advertising and personal selling messages can stress lower prices and better values when customers are known to be especially sensitive to price.

Product-Line Pricing Strategies

Many pricing strategists consider the product line, rather than individual product items, to be the appropriate unit of analysis. The objective of product-line pricing is to maximize profits for the total product line rather than to obtain the greatest profits for any individual item in the line. Marketers who do this are said to focus on *total-profit pricing* rather than on *item-profit pricing*.

CAPTIVE PRICING

Captive pricing strategy
A strategy whereby a basic product, such as a razor, is priced low but the profits from associated products needed for operating the basic product, such as razor blades, make up for the lack of profit on the basic product.

A camera manufacturer may set low prices on cameras in the hope of making significant profits on film. Firms such as Schick and Gillette sell their razors at low prices to encourage long-term purchase of blades that fit the razors. In a **captive pricing strategy**, the basic product is priced low, often below cost, but the high markup on supplies required to operate the basic product makes up for that low price.

Selling video games is much like the razor and blade business. Sony sells five pieces of PlayStation software for every one piece of hardware.[5] Only PlayStation games will fit Sony's compact disc-based PlayStation console. Marketers of products requiring consumers to repurchase operating supplies are using captive pricing strategies.

http://www.sony.com

LEADER PRICING AND BAIT PRICING

A common pricing strategy that sacrifices item profit for total profit is *leader pricing*. Most consumers are familiar with the concept of the **loss leader**, the product that the seller prices at a loss so as to attract customers, who may then buy other goods or services. Consumers are perhaps less aware of similar strategies involving *cost leaders* and *low-profit leaders*. Here again, products are priced to attract bargain-hunting customers, who may make additional purchases. The leader items, however, are sold not at a loss but at the seller's cost (the cost leader) or at a very small profit (the low-profit leader). Such pricing strategies can be quite effective. For example, when Target discount stores priced selected popular video games at two-thirds of the regular price, they tripled store traffic. Goods so priced are usually familiar, frequently purchased items that customers will be able to recognize as bargains. Reduced prices on caviar and goat meat would not accomplish the same objective.

Bait pricing involves attracting customers by advertising low-priced models of, for example, televisions. Although the bait item is available for sale in sufficient quantity, the marketer's expectation is to trade the customer up to a higher-margin model that is also available for sale. This strategy may be an effective means to sell higher-margin items.

The term *bait and switch*, however, is used when the merchant has no intention of selling the bait merchandise but only intends to convince the customer to buy more expensive goods. In fact, the item used in the bait-and-switch scheme is sometimes referred to as the "nailed-down model," so unlikely is it that it will be sold. Bait and switch has an unsavory reputation and is often the target of attention from the Federal Trade Commission.

PRICE LINING

A marketer using a **price-lining strategy** prices the products in a product line according to a number of "price points." Price points are simply specific prices. A marketer selling a full product line establishes certain price points to differentiate the items in the line.

Many retailers, especially clothing retailers, practice price lining. A dress store ordinarily does not stock dresses priced at $299.99, $299.87, $299.76, and so on, down to $55. Instead, the prices offered are $299, $249, $199, and the like. These prices are believed by the store owner to be "strong price points," or prices that are greatly attractive to buyers. The assumption is that a good number of dresses will be sold at $249 but that not many more will be sold at prices lower than $249 until the price reaches the next strong price point, $199. Similarly, if the price is raised from $249, there will be a rapid drop in sales until the next strong price point is reached.

Price lining simplifies consumers' buying decisions. Shoppers can first select a price point and then choose from the assortment in the price line based on color, style, or other product characteristics. It also simplifies the retailer's decisions about what specific prices should be selected.

PRICE BUNDLING AND MULTIPLE-UNIT PRICING

With a **price-bundling strategy**, a group of products is sold as a bundle at a price lower than the total of the individual prices. The

Loss leader
A product priced below cost to attract consumers, who may then make additional purchases.

Bait pricing
A method of attracting customers by offering low-priced items for sale with the intention of selling more expensive goods.

Price-lining strategy
A strategy whereby a seller prices products in a product line in accordance with certain "price points" believed to be attractive to buyers.

Price-bundling strategy
A strategy whereby the price of a group of products is lower than the total of the individual prices of the components. An example is selling a new car with an "options package."

Varsity Spirit trains more than 100,000 cheerleaders at more than 500 camps held on college campuses across the country. Varsity charges a small tuition fee for a 4-day session, where students learn numerous cheerleading routines and stunts. The tuition barely covers the company's costs, but Varsity gets to showcase its products. In addition to its cheerleading school, Varsity markets cheerleading uniforms, shoes, pom-poms, ribbons, jewelry, megaphones, and sundry other items. Most schools let the cheerleading squad select which supplier to use, and Varsity does quite well. This pricing strategy, which takes the total product line into account, is a strategy that wins.[6]

bargain price for the "extras" provides an incentive for the consumer. Selling a car with an "options package" is an example of a price-bundling strategy.

Microsoft Corporation combined a price-bundling strategy with a product strategy in its Microsoft Office97, a so-called suite of software. Suites are bundles of applications—for example, spreadsheets, word-processing programs, and graphics programs—sold together for a fraction of what they would cost if purchased separately. Microsoft Office97 combines Microsoft Word, Microsoft Excel, Microsoft Powerpoint, Microsoft Access, and Microsoft Explorer.

The marketer using a price-bundling strategy benefits by increasing total revenues and, in many instances, reducing manufacturing costs. Inventory costs may also be reduced when marketers bundle slow-selling items with popular items to deplete inventory.

Price bundling differs from **multiple-unit pricing** (as in a two-for-one sale) and quantity discounts because "enhanced" products or multiple products are sold rather than increased quantities of a particular product.

Multiple-unit pricing, in addition to attracting new customers through lower prices, may increase overall consumption of the product. Consumers who bring home two six-packs rather than a single six-pack may increase consumption, for example. The major disadvantage of multiple-unit pricing is that regular customers may stock up on the product and postpone future purchases until other "specials" appear.

Psychological and Image Pricing Strategies

Like any other stimulus, a price may be selectively perceived by consumers. Consumers may infer something about a brand's value or image from its price. When customers choose brands because their prices send a message, they are responding to a psychological or image pricing strategy.

REFERENCE PRICING

Retailers often use a **reference pricing strategy**, in which they choose a moderate price for a version of a product that will be displayed next to a higher-priced model of the same brand or a competitive brand. This strategy is based on the **isolation effect**, which suggests that a choice looks more attractive next to a high-priced alternative than it does in isolation. Reference pricing is also used by catalog retailers such as Service Merchandise to convey the idea that they offer bargain prices. The catalog may show "reference price," "store price," and sometimes "sale price."

> Consumers may infer something about a brand's value or image from its price.

Multiple-unit pricing
Selling more than one unit of a product at a price lower than the sum of the individual unit prices, as in a four-for-the-price-of-three sale.

Reference pricing strategy
A strategy whereby a moderate price is set for a version of a product that will be displayed next to a higher-priced model of the same brand or next to a competing brand.

Isolation effect
An effect by which a product appears more attractive next to a higher-priced alternative than it does in isolation.

High-status goods are usually priced high. Buyers of snowboarding clothing and equipment often use price as a signal of quality.

ODD VERSUS EVEN PRICING

One seldom sees consumer packaged goods priced at $2.00, $5.00, or $10.00. Instead, they are normally priced at odd amounts such as $1.87, $4.98, and $9.99. Odd prices have, in fact, become traditional.

The use of odd prices is based on the belief that, for example, a price of $1.95 is seen by consumers as only a dollar plus some small change. Advocates of odd pricing assume that more sales will be made at certain prices than at prices just one or two cents higher. However, the published research findings in this area are inconclusive about the benefits of odd pricing. There are those who suggest that a price of $1.98 is seen as $2.00 and that deeper cuts—say, to $1.75—are necessary to achieve the intended psychological effect. The practice of odd pricing does have a practical purpose. It forces clerks to use the cash register to make change, thus creating a record of the sale and discouraging employee dishonesty.

Even prices are often used to good effect by the marketers of services and high-quality merchandise. A physician charges $175 for your annual check-up. A sapphire ring costs $1,000. Even prices are said to be most effective when the objective is to create an image of high quality or to appeal to upscale consumers.

PRESTIGE PRICING

For many products, consumers use price to infer quality, especially when it is difficult to determine quality by inspection. Certain products are demanded in part because of their high prices. Perfumes, furs, and gems are among them. These products are high-status goods, and marketers often charge a **prestige price** for them to portray an image of high quality.

Prestige price
A high price meant to convey an impression of high quality.

what went wrong?

Circuit City   In 1997, Circuit City, the electronics retailer with almost 500 stores, launched a five-city experiment. In these cities, it started requiring customers returning nondefective items to pay 15 percent of the purchase price as a restocking fee if the box or packaging had been opened. Circuit City also adopted a policy nationwide of requiring the 15 percent fee for opened boxes on nondefective personal computers or peripherals.

It was another example of how retailers are getting tougher on returns. Liberal return policies were originally adopted to enhance customer service, but their misuse by a small number of customers has proven costly to retailers. Thus, in the past few years, some stores have added tags to the fronts of women's dresses, warning that the garment can't be returned if the tag has been removed. The goal is to prevent a dress from being worn for an event, then returned for a refund.

Circuit City rival Best Buy has charged 15 percent restocking fees on certain unboxed electronics products since 1995, in an effort to try to stop abuse of its liberal return policies. Best Buy says students were buying laptop computers to write term papers and then returning them. A camcorder was returned as defective; the videotape left inside showed the camera had been dunked in a swimming pool.

"There are abuses that unfortunately caused us to revise our policies," says Laurie Bauer, spokeswoman for 285-store Best Buy, based in Eden Prairie, Minnesota. The fee applies to opened boxes for nondefective notebook computers, radar detectors, camcorders, and digital cameras.

In Circuit City's case, "Some consumers were, in effect, borrowing the product," spokesman Morgan Stewart says. "Once you have an opened box, it's a markdown."[7]

Go figure.

$3 ANYWHERE

What's Your Priority?™

Now that FedEx® and UPS® have moved to zone-based pricing, Priority Mail™ makes more sense than ever.

1-800-THE-USPS ext. 2003   http://www.usps.gov   UNITED STATES POSTAL SERVICE

Distribution-Based Pricing Strategies

Many prices are based on the geographic distance separating the buyer from the point of sale or the point of production. Prices are not always higher as the buyer gets farther from the seller. However, in most cases, geographic pricing policies reflect management's attempt to recover some or all of the costs involved in shipping products long distances.

F.O.B.

F.O.B.
"Freight on board" or "Free on board"; a term used to identify the point at which title passes from seller to buyer. For example, "F.O.B. factory" means that the buyer takes title at the factory and is responsible for all shipping charges.

A common form of geographic pricing is **F.O.B.**, which stands for either "freight on board" or "free on board." The letters never stand alone but are always followed by the name of a specific place, as in "F.O.B. factory" or "F.O.B. Baltimore." This place name tells the buyer the point to which the seller will ship the goods. At that point, the buyer takes title to the goods and becomes responsible for shipping charges. A consumer in Kansas City might buy a Swedish auto "F.O.B. New York." This means that the price quoted includes shipment to New York; all other transportation costs are extra.

DELIVERED PRICING

Delivered pricing
Pricing that includes delivery within a specified area; also known as *freight-allowed pricing*.

When a department store advertises that the price of a sofa is "$1,500 delivered in our area," that store is practicing **delivered pricing**, or *freight-allowed pricing*. The delivery charges are built into the price paid by the consumer. Occasionally, ill will may develop when customers located just beyond the delivery zone lines are charged a price higher than the advertised price.

Zone pricing
A type of delivered pricing in which prices vary according to the number of geographic zones through which a product passes in moving from seller to buyer.

A variation on delivered pricing is **zone pricing**, whereby geographic zones are delineated and prices increase as the zone lines crossed in completion of the transaction accumulate. The parcel post system employs zone pricing, basing rates to mail a package on the weight of the parcel and the number of zones it will travel through before arriving at its destination. "Slightly higher in Canada" is a phrase that reflects a zone pricing policy.

A company that views the entire country as its delivery zone and charges the same prices in every location is practicing a special form of delivered pricing called **uniform delivered pricing**. When you buy through a catalog, such as Lands' End, you pay a postage-and-handling fee subject to uniform delivered pricing. Such prices are attractive to marketers because they simplify pricing and nationwide advertising.

BASING-POINT PRICING

Another distribution-based pricing system involves the selection of one or more locations to serve as basing points. Customers are charged prices and shipping fees as if their orders were shipped from these points, regardless of where the merchandise actually originates. For example, consider the situation shown in Exhibit 17-3. A buyer in Shreveport makes a purchase from a supplier in New Orleans. The goods are in fact shipped from New Orleans. However, Chicago has been specified as the basing point, so the buyer is charged as if the goods came from Chicago. The true shipping charge is $100, but the buyer must pay $200. The seller is able to pocket the extra $100 (known as *phantom freight*) because of this **basing-point pricing**.

Because this system is clearly not in the buyer's best interest and because it smacks of collusion on the part of suppliers, it has been the subject of court cases for more than 70 years. Although Supreme Court rulings made in the 1940s forbid industrywide pricing systems that include phantom freight, cases involving basing-point pricing still arise.

Uniform delivered pricing
A type of delivered pricing in which an organization charges the same price for a given product in all locations.

Basing-point pricing
Charging for shipping from a specified basing point, or location, no matter where the shipment actually originates.

e x h i b i t **17-3**

Basing-Point Pricing

Chicago basing point

Shreveport customer

New Orleans supplier

Goods from New Orleans are shipped to Shreveport at a charge of $200, as if they came from Chicago

Chicago to Shreveport $200

New Orleans to Shreveport $100

"Phantom freight" $100

Some Additional Pricing Strategies and Tactics

Pricing strategies represent logical responses to individual marketing situations. Thus, there are a great number of pricing strategies and tactics. Here are some choices available to marketers in addition to those already discussed.

The services of many professionals, such as doctors and lawyers, are often priced at a figure that suggests that the physician or attorney has been involved totally in the client's case and therefore will present a bill that is free of itemized, penny-counting entries. Thus, the professional charges $2,000 for a gall bladder operation or $700 for a quick divorce. Such prices are called *professional prices* or *gentleman's prices*.

Another sort of price is the so-called *ethical price*. Supposedly, ethical prices are lower than what could have been charged; the marketer chooses the lower price for ethical or humanitarian reasons. Drug companies claim that they set the price of insulin at a reasonable level, even though they could charge more, because it is the right thing to do.

Establishing the Exact Price

Marketers use many methods to assign specific prices to the products they sell. Here, we discuss the logic of several types of calculations: the markup on selling price or cost, the cost-plus and average-cost methods, target return pricing, and break-even analysis. See our Internet appendix E, Financial and Economic Analysis for Marketers, at http://zikmund.swcollege.com for additional details.

MARKUP ON SELLING PRICE AND MARKUP ON COST

Many marketers, especially retailers and wholesalers, rely on a comparatively un-complicated method for determining their resale prices: A simple percentage markup is added to the cost of the product to reach the selling price. When a markup is expressed as a percentage of the selling price, it is called a **markup on selling price**. For example, a cost of $1.00 and a selling price of $1.50 means a markup on selling price of 33.3 percent. The 50-cent markup is 33.3 percent, or one-third, of the selling price of $1.50. When only the term *markup* is used, it refers to markup on selling price. However, in many industries, pricing focuses on costs.

Consider an example comparing a focus on selling price with a focus on cost. Suppose an item costs a retailer $50, and the retailer sells it for $100. The markup on selling price is calculated by dividing the amount added to the cost of the product by the selling price of the product:

Markup on selling price
A markup expressed as a percentage of the selling price of an item.

$$\frac{\$50 \text{ added on}}{\$100 \text{ selling price}} = 50 \text{ percent}$$

Markup on cost
A markup expressed as a percentage of the cost of an item.

In contrast, the **markup on cost** is calculated by dividing the amount added to the cost of the product by the cost:

$$\frac{\$50 \text{ added on}}{\$50 \text{ cost}} = 100 \text{ percent}$$

As you can see, using a markup based on cost makes the retailer's markup appear higher (100 percent versus 50 percent here), even though the dollar figures are exactly the same. Distinguishing between markup on selling price and markup on cost is important. Our Internet Appendix E, Financial and Economic Analysis for Marketers, discusses formulas for calculating the relationship between these markups. Users of the markup method almost always use the selling price rather than the cost of the product in figuring the markup percentage. The reason is that many important figures in financial reports, such as gross sales, revenues, and so on, are sales figures, not cost figures.

Effective use of markup based on cost or selling price requires that the marketing manager calculate an adequate *margin*—the amount added to cost to determine price. The margin must ultimately provide adequate funds to cover selling expenses and profit. Once an appropriate margin has been determined, the markup technique has the major advantage of being easy to employ.

As Exhibit 17-4 shows, a series of markups is used as products move through channels of distribution. Certain industries have established traditional markups for the various channel members. The ultimate markup—that of the retailer—results in the price paid by the consumer.

THE COST-PLUS METHOD

Manufacturers often use a pricing method, similar to markup in which they determine what costs were involved in producing an item and then add an amount to the cost total to arrive at a price. Like markup, this cost-plus method is easy to use once an appropriate amount to add to the cost has been determined. Much government contracting is done on this basis, with the supplier of a good or service submitting the cost figures associated with a particular project and adding a reasonable profit margin to yield a total price for the project.

THE AVERAGE-COST METHOD

Identifying all the costs associated with the manufacturing and marketing of a good or the provision of a service should make it possible to determine what the average cost of a single unit of the good or service might be. Consider an example.

$$\frac{\text{All costs}}{\text{Number of units produced}} = \text{Average cost of a single unit}$$

$$\frac{\$80,000}{100} = \$800$$

(Note that to make this calculation, it is necessary to predict how much of the product will be demanded and produced.) Adding a margin for profit to the total cost figures allows calculation of a likely price for a unit of product.

$$\$80,000 \text{ all costs} + \$20,000 \text{ margin for profit} = \$100,000$$

$$\frac{\$100,000}{100 \text{ units}} = \text{Average cost of a single unit including the profit margin}$$

$$= \$1,000$$

While the average-cost method can suggest a price, there is a serious risk that the quantity demanded by the market will not match the predictions of the marketing

Markup Through a Channel of Distribution

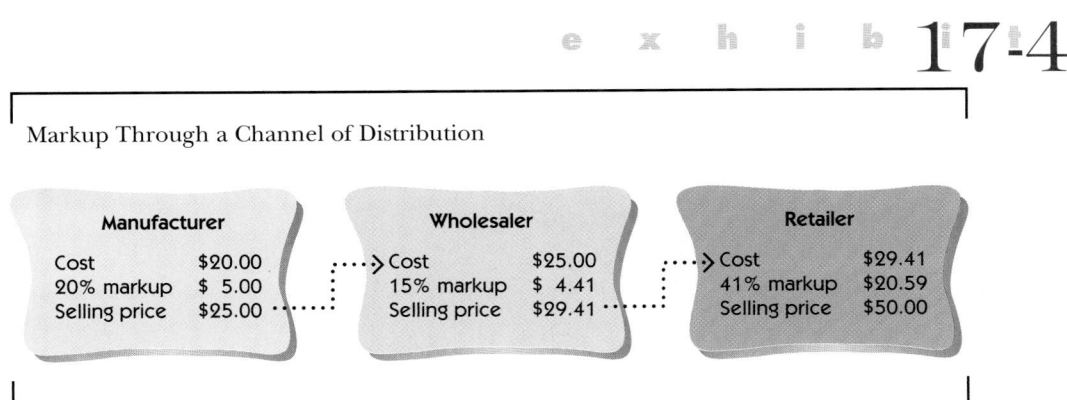

Note: At each step, markup is expressed as a percent of the selling price.

manager. If in the above example only 50 units were demanded at the price of $1,000, the firm's revenue would be only $50,000, but the costs of production and marketing would remain at $80,000. This demonstrates that it is extremely risky to base pricing decisions on costs alone. The market—the demand generated by customers—must be carefully considered in any calculation of price. Changes in demand can turn profit into loss.

TARGET RETURN PRICING

Total cost
Fixed costs plus variable costs.

Fixed cost
A cost that is incurred with the passage of time and is not a function of volume of production or sales.

Variable cost
A cost that varies directly with an organization's production or sales. Variable costs are a function of volume.

Target return pricing
Setting prices to yield a particular target level of profit for the organization.

If you've taken an accounting class, you probably remember that **total costs** are the sum of fixed and variable costs. **Fixed costs** are incurred with the passage of time, regardless of volume. **Variable costs** fluctuate with some measure of volume. These costs are used in calculating a target return price.

A marketing manager using **target return pricing** first calculates a total fixed cost figure. This figure includes such items as executive salaries, rents, and other expenses that must be paid even when no units of a product are being produced. A target return, usually represented as a percentage of investment, is added to total cost to yield a figure representing total fixed costs and target return. To illustrate, assume a fixed cost of $400,000 and a target return of $100,000, for a total of $500,000.

> It is extremely risky to base pricing decisions on costs alone.

Now the marketer must estimate demand. For an estimated demand of 1,000 units, if the total of fixed costs and target return is $500,000, each unit produced would cost $500 in fixed costs and target return.

$$\frac{\text{Fixed costs} + \text{Target return}}{\text{Units to be sold}} = \frac{\$500,000}{1,000} = \$500 \text{ per unit}$$

But the production and sale of each unit involves variable costs as well. Suppose these costs are calculated to be $75 per unit. This figure is added to the already determined cost per unit of $500 to indicate that the price per unit should be $575.

Fixed costs and target return per unit	+	Variable costs per unit	=	Suggested price per unit
$500	+	$75	=	$575

As in the case of average-cost pricing, a miscalculation of the demand for the product can be disastrous. If the firm's customers demanded only 500 units of the product, not the expected 1,000, the carefully calculated price of $575 would lead to a loss.[8]

Hotel and motel chains operate computer systems similar to the one airlines use. The systems track reservations (demand) and available rooms (supply). Travelers who book early get lower rates, and those who reserve a room late pay the highest rates. The pricing strategy, which takes fixed costs into account, uses a traditional economic model to price high when supply is low and demand is high.

BREAK-EVEN ANALYSIS

As we have seen, all marketers, whether of consumer goods, organizational goods, or services, face costs that must somehow be recovered. These include fixed costs and variable costs. Variable costs would be zero if no products were produced and marketed, but fixed costs would remain at their established level even if production and sales were zero.

Exhibit 17-5 portrays fixed costs as the horizontal line *FC*. Variable costs added to fixed costs give the total cost figures shown by the line marked *TC*. This curve rises to the right because total costs should increase as production and sales increase.

The hope is that each additional unit of goods manufactured and sold or each additional service performed and paid for will raise the firm's total revenue (total revenue equals price per unit times units sold). This relationship is shown in Exhibit 17-5 by the total revenue curve labeled *TR*. Obviously, marketers hope that total revenue will exceed total costs, resulting in a profit. If total costs exceed total revenue, the result is a loss.

At the start of operations, zero units are being produced, and total revenue is zero because no sales are being made. However, fixed costs such as rent are already being incurred. Therefore, the company is suffering a loss at this point. If all goes well, however, and sales rise, revenue will also rise. If the firm is successful, revenue will continue to rise until it meets and exceeds the costs associated with production and marketing. Now, with revenue greater than costs, the company is making a profit. The point at which costs and revenue meet is called, logically, the **break-even point**. At this point, the money coming in is equal to the money going out. (Our Internet Appendix E, Financial and Economic Analysis for Marketers, describes a formula for calculating the break-even point.)

Break-even point
The point at which an organization's revenues and costs are equal.

Price and Break-Even Analysis   Price clearly plays an important role in break-even analysis. For example, raising the price of the product may enhance revenue, allowing revenue to catch up to cost more quickly; lowering the price may have the opposite effect. It might also be demonstrated that a cost-control program would increase profit by lowering the total cost curve. In any case, every organization has a break-even point. If it achieves and surpasses that point, the

e x h i b **17-5**

Costs, Revenues, and the Break-Even Point

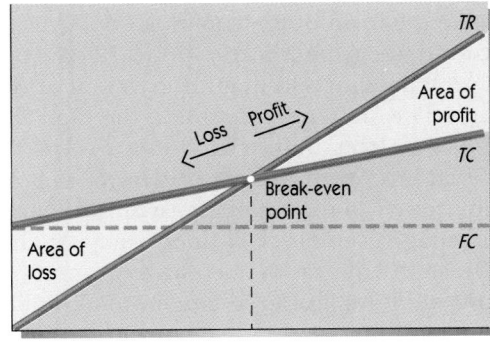

organization makes a profit. Price has an impact on when the break-even point is met. The concept, though simple, is important.

Demand and Break-Even Analysis   Break-even analysis should deal with demand as well as cost. As price changes, the quantity demanded will change. It might be expected that an increase in price will lead to fewer sales and a drop in price will generate more sales. The marketing manager's problem in employing break-even analysis is to determine just what effect a change in price will actually have on demand.

Simple manipulation of cost and revenue figures is not enough, nor are graphs (such as the one in Exhibit 17-5) that seem to portray ever-increasing profits as more and more units are sold. There is no reason to assume that a product is going to sell at either a higher price or a lower price. An effective marketer, aware of the changes and uncertainties in the marketplace, knows that raising prices will not necessarily increase revenues and lower the break-even point.

> Determining a break-even point is only the beginning. Break-even analysis may be of most use in conducting preliminary studies to eliminate certain extreme pricing situations.

In short, determining a break-even point is only the beginning. Break-even analysis may be of most use in conducting preliminary studies to eliminate certain extreme pricing situations. For example, a restaurant might be so poorly run that its costs necessitate menu prices that start at $10 for a hot dog—a price at which few are likely to be sold. Break-even points are also of use in evaluating alternative pricing strategies. But no matter how carefully costs and revenues are portrayed on a graph, the underlying problem of estimating demand remains. Thus, break-even analysis must be used with the customer in mind.

Price Adjustments

Recall that the list price is the basic, "official" price of a product. In many industries, it is common for list prices to be adjusted with rebates or discounts. Rebates reduce the list price by giving back to the consumer part of the amount paid. Rebates generally are reimbursements from the manufacturer rather than the retailer. By passing savings directly to the consumer, a rebate policy assures that the consumer, and not the retailer, will benefit from the price adjustment.

The most common price adjustments are **discounts**, reductions from the list price or reimbursements for performing a specific action, such as maintaining a sales force or carrying inventory. Common discount schemes are discussed briefly below. Notice that each discounting technique provides an incentive to potential buyers but also yields some advantage, such as speedier payment of bills, to sellers.

CASH DISCOUNTS

Cash discounts may take the form of the common "2/10 net 30" payment scheme, which indicates that payment made within 10 days of the date on the invoice will be discounted 2 percent and that full payment, with no discount, must be made within 30 days. The amount of discount, the time allowed, and when the counting of days begins vary from industry to industry. The discount offered is usually large enough that it is worthwhile for the buyer to borrow from a bank, if necessary, to pay what is owed to the supplier. An **anticipation discount**, an additional discount to encourage even faster payment, may also be offered. The purpose of each form of cash discount is to encourage prompt payment of bills. All forms of cash discounts are legal if offered equally to all similar buyers.

TRADE DISCOUNTS

Trade discounts are discounts given to members of a trade. Electricians receive discounts on wire and tape because they are in the electrical trade. Electrical dis-

---

Discount
A reduction from list price or a reimbursement for performance of a specific task.

Cash discount
A price discount offered for early payment of bills.

Anticipation discount
A discount over and above the regular cash discount, meant to encourage even faster payment.

Trade discount
A discount given to wholesalers, retail dealers, or others in a particular trade as repayment for the performance of certain functions; also called a *functional discount.*

tributors (wholesalers) get even larger discounts because they must make a profit on the products they sell to electricians. Because the recipient of the discount is performing a function, such as holding an inventory of electrical parts, these discounts are also called *functional discounts*.

The types and sizes of discounts for wholesalers, retailers, or other tradespeople vary considerably by industry. Generally, the discount rate, which reflects the intermediary's percentage margin on the goods sold, increases as the intermediary's role in marketing to the customer increases. Thus, discounts are higher in the furniture industry than in the grocery industry.

QUANTITY DISCOUNTS

There are two types of quantity discounts: noncumulative and cumulative. In the case of **noncumulative quantity discounts**, each order is treated separately. The buyer's discount is calculated on the basis of the size of a single purchase, without consideration of past purchases or planned purchases. Obviously, the purpose of this discount is to encourage large orders.[9]

Cumulative quantity discounts, on the other hand, allow the buyer an ever-increasing discount with each purchase made over some period of time—say, a year. The more the buyer orders, the larger the discount becomes. The intent of the cumulative quantity discount is to keep the customer coming back. Stated another way, the supplier's aim is to build a relationship and to tie the buyer to the seller.

SEASONAL DISCOUNTS

As you probably can guess, the **seasonal discount** is intended to help level out the marketing workload by encouraging buyers to make purchases and take delivery of out-of-season merchandise. Products such as bathing suits, winter clothing, paint, and lawn furniture are obvious candidates for seasonal discounting at various times during the year.

CHAIN DISCOUNTS

In many purchasing situations, a buyer qualifies for a series of discounts. A wholesale buyer quoted terms of 40/10/5 net 30 realizes that he or she will receive a series of discounts by using all the appropriate options. For example, for a machine with a list price of $995, the chain discount on the above terms is calculated as follows:

List price	$ 995.00
Less trade discount (40 percent of $995)	– 398.00
Balance	$597.00
Less seasonal discount (10 percent of $597)	– 59.70
Balance	$ 537.30
Less cash discount (5 percent of $537.30)	– 26.86
Price wholesaler pays	$510.44

PROMOTIONAL ALLOWANCES

A manufacturer may partially reimburse wholesalers or retailers for promotional assistance at the local level. These reimbursements may be in the form of either cash or merchandise, with the value commonly restricted to a percentage of sales or a discount off the list price.

Exhibit 17-6 summarizes the various discounts and allowances.

Pricing and the Law

Because pricing strategies can be used to harm the competition and because price so clearly affects the consumer as well as the business person, a number of

Noncumulative quantity discount
A price discount determined by the size of an individual purchase order. The larger the order, the larger the discount.

Cumulative quantity discount
A price discount determined by the amount purchased over some specified time period.

Seasonal discount
A price discount intended to encourage purchase of products during a time of year when sales are traditionally low.

17-6 Discounts and Objectives

DISCOUNT	OBJECTIVE
Cash discount	To encourage customers to pay their bills within a given period of time, such as 10 days
Anticipation discount	To encourage even faster payment of bills by offering additional discounts if the customer pays within, for example, 5 rather than 10 days
Trade or functional discount	To "reward" a customer for functions performed, such as installing a particular brand of storm windows in new houses or stocking a particular brand of clothing in a store
Noncumulative quantity discount	To encourage buyers to place a larger order each time they buy merchandise
Cumulative quantity discount	To encourage buyers to return to a particular supplier for repeat business
Seasonal discount	To encourage buyers to make purchases during the "off season"—for example, to buy house paint and bathing suits in the fall and winter and to visit winter resort areas during the summer
Promotional allowance	To encourage intermediaries to promote a product to their local customers

national and local laws have been passed that influence pricing practices. The Sherman Antitrust Act (1890) and the Clayton Act (1914) were early attempts to curb price fixing, restraint of trade, and other unfair and monopolistic practices. Additional legislation amended these acts. Here we discuss the Robinson-Patman Act, the fair trade acts and their repeal, and various state laws. Such laws, and court cases based on them, are so numerous that a service industry has grown up to supply companies with the latest information on legislation and litigation that may affect their pricing and other marketing plans.

ROBINSON-PATMAN ACT

Robinson-Patman Act

Federal law passed in 1936 and intended to halt discriminatory pricing policies by specifying certain limited conditions under which a seller may charge different prices to different buyers.

Price discrimination occurs when a manufacturer or supplier charges a lower price to one customer than to another, similar customer. The **Robinson-Patman Act** of 1936 is a federal law that makes it illegal to give, induce, or receive discriminatory prices except under certain conditions specified in the law. The act's sponsors believed it would wipe out chain stores. Under the law, a supplier of, say, meat products may not give a large discount to a supermarket chain just because that chain is an important customer. But the supplier may give the discount if a "proportional" discount is offered to the corner grocer. In the event of litigation, a judge must decide what is proportional and what is not.

The law also prohibits the granting of a wholesaler's discount, or broker's discount, to a business that does not meet criteria identifying it as a true wholesaler. The effect of this brokerage provision is that a large retailing organization cannot demand to be given a wholesaler's discount even though it may buy merchandise in larger quantities than do typical wholesalers. The law does allow for the offering of cooperative advertising and other promotional assistance if the promotional help is offered to all customers on proportionally equal terms.

The Robinson-Patman Act includes two provisions that can be used to defend prices that could appear to be discriminatory. One of these allows for the use of several prices if the competitive situation demands it. Thus, a marketer may charge one customer a lower price if this price is granted to meet the equally low price of a competitor. For example, a marketer may lower its price for a buyer in one city who is faced with a price war but charge a higher price to a buyer in another city who is not. The second provision is the so-called cost-justification provision. If the seller can prove that granting a lower price to one buyer simply represents passing on cost savings—for example, savings that result from producing and shipping in large quantities—the seller has successfully employed the cost-justification provision.

The Robinson-Patman Act, along with the Federal Trade Commission Act (discussed in Chapter 3), is one of the most important laws affecting the daily dealings of marketers. But mere observance of its major provisions is not enough to avert legal troubles. As with all legislation, its content is open to interpretation and reinterpretation by the courts and government agencies.[10]

THE REPEAL OF FAIR TRADE ACTS

Before 1975, the states were empowered under federal law to pass fair trade or resale price maintenance acts. Most states enacted laws that allowed manufacturers to fix the prices of their goods and prohibited wholesalers and retailers from offering reduced or discount prices. Although it was argued that these laws would protect small companies by forcing all businesses to charge the same prices for goods, their main purpose was to stabilize prices at comparatively high levels.

Enforcement of these laws was difficult, and growing consumer awareness that certain prices were being kept artificially high contributed to the passage of the Consumer Goods Pricing Act (1975), which repealed the right of individual states to allow price maintenance in interstate commerce.

UNFAIR SALES PRACTICES ACTS

Unfair sales practices acts are state laws that limit or prohibit the use of certain sales and marketing techniques. They commonly require that certain items be sold at prescribed markups. The markups may range from zero (thus eliminating loss leaders) to a relatively high percentage. Generally, some provision is made to allow for the sale of old or out-of-style merchandise at a reduced price. Dealers covered by such laws may charge more, but not less, than the specified markups allow. Thus, the laws are also termed *minimum markup laws*. These acts are intended to protect the small business using a relatively high markup by assuring that even a discount store must mark up its merchandise by the minimum amount. The smaller dealer then has a cushion that brings its prices closer to those charged by the chain store.

Unfair sales practices acts
State laws that limit or prohibit the use of certain sales and marketing techniques; most commonly, laws requiring that certain types of merchandise be sold at prescribed markups; also called *minimum markup laws*.

OTHER STATE AND LOCAL LAWS

Many states and cities further restrict the pricing freedom of firms within their boundaries. For example, several states set limits on the number of times per year that wholesale beer prices may be changed. Many cities require that a "fire sale" actually follow a fire and that "going out of business" sales be followed by a cessation of business operations.

Pricing and Social Responsibility

Most people in this society believe that an organization has a right to make a profit. And as our discussion of the legal aspects regulating price shows, society cares a great deal about the consumer's right to fair pricing. Laws address many ethical issues involving price. However, even some legal pricing practices can create ethical dilemmas. For example, should zoos and museums be free to the public? If public institutions such as these do charge an admission fee, should it be waived for disadvantaged segments of society?

Elsewhere in this book, we have discussed the complaint that certain marketing efforts, such as advertising, increase prices. Many ethical issues involving price are not independent of other marketing mix decisions. Changing one marketing mix element may lead to higher prices. This fact leads us to one of the most fundamental questions concerning ethical pricing: Are corporate social responsibility and the corporate profit motive compatible?

Goodwrench Service Plus dealers focus on up-front pricing because GM wants to promote the idea that its prices are fair and socially responsible. There will be no pricing surprises at a GM Goodwrench Service Plus dealer. GM's lifetime guarantee on parts and labor supports its responsible pricing strategy.

http://www.
gmgoodwrench.com

It has been argued that "welfare and society are not the corporation's business. Its business is making money, not sweet music."[11] A number of managers believe that profit maximization is the only legitimate goal of business. Furthermore, they argue that business's pursuit of economic self-interest is what's best for the country.

Pursuing goals related to social responsibility may place a company at a competitive disadvantage. Consider some examples. Ingersol-Rand developed a quiet air compressor to silence noisy jack-hammers. Unfortunately, this product, which provided a clear social benefit in the form of noise abatement, had to be sold at a 25 percent premium because of its higher manufacturing cost. In effect, the question here is "Would a buyer rather buy a jack-hammer for $5,000 or for $6,250?" And suppose a manufacturer of coal-mining equipment believes a certain safety feature will save lives. If this marketer adds the feature as standard equipment and increases the price of the equipment but other competitors are not forced to do so, will the company be at a competitive disadvantage?

It is unlikely that one manufacturer will add an expensive safety feature to a product aimed at a price-conscious market segment unless all competitors are forced to do the same. Like it or not, this kind of problem is often settled by legislation requiring that socially desirable, but costly, features be added.

Summary

Pricing is one of the most critical parts of marketing. Prices must appeal to buyers and offer them satisfaction. Costs and profit considerations are important, but prices that do not appeal to customers are of no use, no matter how they are determined. Effective marketers employ a combination of pricing strategies to arrive at prices that appeal to buyers first and then meet other organizational goals.

1) Identify the various pricing strategies.
Broadly stated, there are five categories of pricing strategies: (1) differential pricing, (2) competitive

pricing, (3) product-line pricing, (4) psychological and image pricing, and (5) distribution-based pricing.

2) Discuss the nature of differential pricing strategies.
Maintaining a single fixed price for all buyers is a one-price strategy. Organizations that sell the same product at different prices to different buyers use a differential pricing strategy. Variable pricing, second-market discounting, skimming, periodic discounting, and random discounting are differential pricing strategies.

3) Describe skimming and penetration pricing.
The skimming strategy involves charging a high price to "skim" the market. It is most appropriate when demand for a product is strong and there is little competitive pressure to lower price. A penetration strategy is employed by an organization seeking to enter a competitive market. By charging a low price, the organization hopes to establish market share quickly.

4) Show how competition affects pricing activity.
Several types of prices result directly from the competitive structure of the marketplace. Charging the going rate or pricing above or below that rate is clearly a response to competition. Similarly, charging a traditional price or following the lead of the industry's leading firms is a competition-influenced policy. Competition, though only one of many variables affecting prices, is among the most powerful influences on pricing activity.

5) Discuss the effects of inflation on pricing.
When inflation rates are high, buyers become increasingly price-conscious. Effective marketers can meet this challenge by attempting to maintain their prices or control their upward spiral. They can also alter their products, improve distribution, and use promotional methods to help allay buyer concern over rising prices. The total marketing mix, not just price, can be adjusted to respond to high inflation rates.

6) Discuss product-line pricing strategies.
Many pricing strategies consider the product line the appropriate unit of analysis. The objective of product-line pricing is to maximize profits for the total line rather than for an individual item in the line. Captive pricing, leader pricing, bait pricing, price lining, price bundling, and multiple-unit pricing are product-line pricing strategies.

7) Explain some of the psychological aspects of price.
Price influences buyers psychologically, sometimes in ways that have little to do with the product or marketing mix. For example, to most buyers, a high price implies high quality, and a low price, lower quality. Odd prices and reference pricing suggest bargains. Prestige prices are used for high-status items.

8) Show how geography influences pricing decisions.
Pricing influenced by geography includes the various forms of F.O.B. pricing, delivered pricing, and basing-point pricing. In most cases, the greater the distance a product must travel to reach its buyer, the higher the product's price.

9) Discuss such pricing tools as list price and cash, trade, quantity, and other discounts.
List price is the "official" price assigned by an organization to a product. The list price may be discounted in various ways to appeal to particular markets and to achieve certain marketing goals. The cash discount is used to encourage rapid payment by customers. The trade discount is used to reward channel intermediaries or members of specific trades by providing them with a margin of profit. Quantity discounts can be used to encourage large orders or to keep customers returning to a seller. Effective marketers use many other discounts, each with a specific purpose.

10) Describe the major legal restrictions on pricing freedom.
National, state, and local laws restrict the marketer's freedom to set prices. Pricing agreements among competitors are strictly forbidden. The Robinson-Patman Act limits the size of discounts a seller may offer a buyer. In most cases, such discounts must be proportional to the discounts offered to other, similar buyers. State unfair sales practices acts establish minimum markups that sellers must charge or in other ways restrict pricing freedom. The now-defunct fair trade acts permitted manufacturers to set and enforce prices throughout their channels of distribution. In part because price is a visible element of the marketing mix and one that strongly affects buyers, it has been a frequent target of regulation at all levels of government.

11) Identify a major ethical issue related to price.
A fundamental question concerning ethical pricing is whether corporate social responsibility is compatible with the corporate profit motive. Pursuing goals related to social responsibility may place a company at a competitive disadvantage. Ultimately, such questions are often settled by legislation requiring socially desirable, but costly, features.

Key Terms

anticipation discount (p. 504)
bait pricing (p. 495)
basing-point pricing (p. 499)
break-even point (p. 503)
captive pricing strategy (p. 494)
cash discount (p. 504)
cumulative quantity discount
(p. 505)
delivered pricing (p. 498)
differential pricing strategy (p. 488)
discount (p. 504)
fixed cost (p. 502)
F.O.B. (p. 498)
follow-the-leader strategy (p. 492)
isolation effect (p. 496)
loss leader (p. 495)

markup on cost (p. 500)
markup on selling price (p. 500)
meeting-the-competition strategy
(p. 491)
multiple-unit pricing (p. 496)
noncumulative quantity discount
(p. 505)
one-price strategy (p. 488)
penetration price (p. 492)
periodic discounting (p. 490)
predatory pricing strategy (p. 492)
prestige price (p. 497)
price leadership strategy (p. 492)
price-bundling strategy (p. 495)
price-lining strategy (p. 495)
random discounting (p. 490)

reference pricing strategy (p. 496)
Robinson-Patman Act (p. 506)
seasonal discount (p. 505)
second-market discounting (p. 489)
skimming price (p. 490)
target return pricing (p. 502)
total cost (p. 502)
trade discount (p. 504)
undercutting-the-competition
strategy (p. 491)
unfair sales practices acts (p. 507)
uniform delivered pricing (p. 499)
variable cost (p. 502)
variable pricing strategy (p. 489)
zone pricing (p. 498)

Questions for Review & Critical Thinking

1. What are the relative advantages and disadvantages of variable pricing and the one-price strategy?

2. In what competitive situations would you recommend using a penetration price? A skimming price?

3. What is the difference between periodic discounting and random discounting? How, if at all, do they differ in their purposes?

4. How might competitors influence a firm's pricing activities?

5. How does inflation affect consumers' perception of prices? How can marketers adjust their efforts to counter any negative perceptions of price?

6. Give three examples in which item profit is sacrificed for the sake of total profit.

7. Why are some prices based in part on the distances products must travel to reach the customer? Are prices always greater if the distance traveled is greater and lower if the distance traveled is less?

8. If the manufacturing cost of an item is $250, the selling expenses associated with the item are $75, and the required return is 25 percent, what will the selling price of the item be?

9. Describe the logic behind break-even analysis. Briefly explain the limitations of break-even analysis.

10. From time to time, automobile makers offer sizable rebates to customers. Why don't they simply lower the prices of their cars?

11. What is a trade discount? Why is it sometimes called a functional discount?

12. Name three products for which seasonal discounts are commonly offered. How do sellers use these discounts to sell products?

13. Using the average-cost method, determine the price you would recommend for a product if the costs associated with its production and marketing are $150,000, the margin for profit is $50,000, and you anticipate selling 5,000 units.

14. A marketer using the target return method made a mistake in predicting demand; the actual demand turned out to be half the expected demand. What would be the resulting loss per unit if the marketer used the following data to calculate price?

Expected demand: 2,000 units
Fixed cost and target return: $200,000
Variable cost per unit: $100

🅣 15. Textbooks and courses in marketing, economics, accounting, and finance discuss price. In a major corporation, who are the individuals (by job title) involved in the pricing decision? What are some potential sources of disagreement or conflict among these individuals?

e—exercises http://zikmund.swcollege.com

1. Go to the Professional Pricing Society's home page at http://www.pricing-advisor.com to access an issue of the *Pricing Advisor Newsletter,* which contains information about topics such as value-added pricing. Report on an article from a recent newsletter.
2. Go to Reverse Auction at http://www.reverseauction.com and describe this company's business model.

Address Book (Useful URLs)

World Currency Exchange Rates	http://www.rubicon.com/passport/currency/currency.html
Bloomberg's Exchange Rate Service	http://www.bloomberg.com
Consumer Price Index	http://stats.bls.gov/datahome.htm
eBay	http://www.ebay.com
Fed Law	http://fedlaw.gsa.gov
Law Mall-Antitrust	http://www.lawmall.com

Ethically Right or Wrong?

1. A retailer uses a 150-percent markup on cost for an item with a cost of $10. When the item is put on sale, the retailer advertises 50 percent off (markdown on selling price) and sells the item for $12.50. Is this deceptive?
2. A salesperson is allowed to vary the price quoted to a customer by 10 percent. The salesperson sells 100 units to one wholesaler for $3,500. The next day, another wholesaler says he will buy 100 units only if the price is $3,000. The salesperson writes up the order and says, "I hope this clears the order-processing department." Did the salesperson do the right thing?
3. A retailer's advertisement for fine china compares "our everyday price" with the "manufacturer's suggested retail price." A statement in small print at the bottom of the page says: "Manufacturer's suggested retail price is not a price at which our store offered or sold this merchandise and may not be a trade area price." Is the retailer's advertising ethical?
4. An airline arranges with a national association to offer a special discount fare to association members who are attending a convention. A travel agent uses these group fares for regular clients, who are not association members, so that they can get the lowest possible air fares. Is this good business?
5. For more than 30 years, StarKist Seafood packaged 6½ ounces of tuna in its regular-sized can. During a period of inflation, the can's weight was reduced by ⅜ ounce, but the price remained the same. Detecting this subtle change, which resulted in a 5.8 percent price increase, was a challenge for most consumers. The weight was clearly marked on the package, but the size of the can did not change. Was StarKist's action ethical?

VIDEO CASE 17-1

World Gym

World Gym–Showcase Square in San Francisco began operations in 1989. The company's objective was to meet the fitness needs of a diverse clientele, from the professional body builder to the overweight person.

World Gym's pricing plan was to have a fitness facility that targeted the common person—a fitness facility that was not on the high end or the low end, but in the middle price range. In the beginning it planned to challenge the price of the top-of-the-line facilities. It offered its services in a big cavernous space in a high-traffic area, a part of town that was becoming gentrified. There was little competition in the area. The establishment's "warehouse" space, with natural light coming in, set it apart from competitors.

The company expected its members to come from other clubs and facilities not only in the immediate neighborhood, but all around San Francisco. It saw its trade area as the neighborhoods within an 8- to 10-minute drive.

The company decided to begin by marketing its product to people who were already working out but wanted something unique. When the company opened its fitness facility, consumers readily accepted it. World Gym membership far exceeded expectations. It now has 8,000 members. As many as 2,000 people come through the door on a given day.

For years World Gym has had few serious competitors. In San Francisco, permits are required to open a gym and thus are an obstacle to potential competitors. And the cost of opening a 35,000-square-foot facility is an additional barrier to entry.

QUESTIONS

1. Was World Gym's pricing plan appropriate in a market where there was a relatively low supply of services?
2. Over time World Gym's membership exceeded expectations. Demand was strong and constant. What impact might this situation have on the company's pricing strategy? On product strategy?
3. Suppose the company learns that two new competitors plan to open fitness facilities within a mile of World Gym. How might the increased supply of services affect World Gym's pricing policy?

cross-functional insights

Many theories and principles from other business disciplines can provide insights about the role of marketing in an organization. The questions in this section are designed to help you think about integrating what you have learned in other business courses with the marketing principles explained in Chapters 16 and 17.

Monopoly and Oligopoly   Markets with only one seller are called monopolies. Markets with only a few sellers are called oligopolies.

According to economic theory, what pricing strategies are utilized by marketers operating in monopolies and oligopolies? In what industries are these situations most likely?

Competitive Pricing Strategies   Competitive pricing strategies are used by organizations that set pricing objectives based on the actions of their competitors. Dominant firms may exploit their positions. Weak firms may opt for the role of follower.

Economists use the *ceteris paribus* ("other things being equal") assumption. Do marketers setting prices agree that they should assume everything except price is held constant?

What is monetary policy? How does it influence a marketer's competitive pricing strategy?

What is the effect of a tariff on domestic equilibrium price?

Change in Supply   Supply is the quantity of a product that marketers are willing and able to sell at a given price in a given time period. A supply curve graphically represents the amount of goods or services marketers will supply at various prices.

What impact does a technological innovation in the production process have on the supply curve?

Change in Demand   Demand is the quantity of a product consumers are willing and able to buy at a given price. Usually, the quantity demanded changes as price changes, and a demand curve can be used to represent this change.

Many Americans' tastes have changed in recent years. More and more consumers enjoy Mexican and Southwestern cuisine. What impact does this have on the demand curve for salsa?

Price Elasticity   Price elasticity measures the effect of a change in price on the quantity of a product demanded. Price elasticity refers to price sensitivity.

What is the relationship between price elasticity and revenue? (Use perfectly elastic, downward-sloping, and perfectly inelastic demand to illustrate your answer.)

Consumer Price Index   The consumer price index is a measure of inflation compiled by the federal government.

How is the consumer price index calculated? How has it changed in the past five years?

Geographical Pricing   Pricing strategies are sometimes based on geographical considerations.

What roles do letters of credit and bills of lading play in a marketer's international pricing strategy?

APPENDICES

at http://zikmund.swcollege.com

Many additional resources may be found on the *Effective Marketing,* Third Edition Web site that supports this textbook. The following appendices should be particularly useful:

Appendix A, Career Opportunities in Marketing, discusses a variety of marketing careers and job opportunities. It also provides helpful tips on using the Internet to learn about career opportunities in marketing.

Appendix B, The Business Plan and Marketing Plan, explains how to develop a sound business plan with emphasis on the marketing aspects of the plan. It provides links to actual business plans.

Appendix C, Marketing Audit, presents the key components of a well-designed marketing audit and includes a sample of items to include in a marketing audit.

Appendix D, Organizing the Marketing Function, discusses ways of assigning tasks, grouping tasks into organizational units, and allocating resources to those units.

Appendix E, Financial and Economic Analysis for Marketers, explains financial concepts and many analytical ratios that marketing managers use in their decision making.

GLOSSARY

A

Account manager   A salesperson who concentrates on maintaining an ongoing relationship with existing customers.

Account service representative   A sales employee at company headquarters or at a branch office who corresponds with clients and provides customer service to established accounts; sometimes called a *sales correspondent*.

Administered strategic alliance   A vertical marketing system in which a strong channel leader coordinates marketing activities at all levels in the channel through planning and management of a mutually beneficial program.

Adoption process   The mental and behavioral stages through which a consumer passes before making a purchase or placing an order. The stages are awareness, interest, evaluation, trial, and adoption.

Advertising   An informative or persuasive message carried by a nonpersonal medium and paid for by an identified sponsor whose organization or product is identified in some way.

Advertising appeal   The central theme or idea of an advertising message.

Advertising theme   An advertising appeal used in several different advertisements to give continuity to an advertising campaign.

Agent   A wholesaler that does not take title to goods. Agents sometimes take possession of goods but function primarily to bring buyers and sellers together or otherwise help consummate a marketing transaction.

Agent intermediary   A channel intermediary that does not take title to the product. Agent intermediaries bring buyers and sellers together or otherwise help complete a transaction.

AIDA   An acronym for *attention, interest, desire,* and *action.* The AIDA formula is a hierarchy of communication effects model used as a guideline in creating advertisements.

Aided recall test   In the context of advertising, a test of consumers' memories of an advertisement, in which clues about the specific material to be remembered are provided.

Air freight   The shipment of products by air carrier.

Allowance   A reduction in price, a rebate, or the like given to a marketing intermediary in return for a large order or the performance of a specific activity.

Anticipation discount   A discount over and above the regular cash discount, meant to encourage even faster payment.

Antitrust legislation   Federal laws meant to prohibit behavior that tends to lessen competition in U.S. markets. The major antitrust laws are the Sherman Antitrust Act (1890), the Clayton Act (1914), and the Federal Trade Commission Act (1914).

Approach   The step in the creative selling process wherein the salesperson makes initial contact and establishes rapport with a prospect.

Art   Any aspect of an advertisement other than copy, including pictures, layout, and white space.

Aspirational group   A group to which an individual would like to belong.

Assembler   A marketing intermediary that performs a bulk-accumulating function.

Association creative platform   An advertising creative platform that uses an analogy or other relationship to stimulate interest and convey information.

Assorting function   An activity, performed by marketing intermediaries, consisting of combining products purchased from several manufacturers to create assortments.

Atmospherics   Physical characteristics of a store's environment, such as appearance, layout, and displays.

Attitude   An individual's general affective, cognitive, and behavioral responses to a given object, issue, or person.

Auction company   An agent intermediary that brings together buyers and sellers. Auction companies often assemble merchandise for sale in a central location and sell it by means of a bidding process.

Auxiliary dimension   An aspect of a product that provides supplementary benefits, such as special features, aesthetics, packaging, warranty, repair service contract, reputation, brand name, or instructions.

Average cost   The total costs divided by the number of units produced.

B

Backward channel   A channel of distribution for recycling, in which the customary flow from producer to ultimate user is reversed.

Bait and switch   An advertising technique, usually associated with retailers, in which a product is offered at an extremely low price to attract customers, who are then told the product is unavailable and are "switched" to a more expensive, higher-margin product.

Bait pricing   A method of attracting customers by offering low-priced items for sale with the intention of selling more expensive goods.

Barter   The exchange of products without the use of money.

Basing-point pricing   Charging for shipping from a specified basing point, or location, no matter where the shipment actually originates.

Belief   A conviction concerning the existence or the characteristics of physical and social phenomena.

Benefit segmentation   A type of market segmentation by which consumers are grouped according to the specific benefits they seek from a product.

Boycott The refusal of some group to buy certain products. A government may enforce a boycott of the products of some other country.

Brand An identifying feature that distinguishes one product from another; more specifically, any name, term, symbol, sign, or design or a unifying combination of these.

Brand equity The value associated with a brand. Where a brand has brand equity, market share or profit margins are greater because of the goodwill associated with the brand.

Brand extension A product category extension or product line extension that employs a brand name already used on one of the company's existing products.

Brand image The complex of symbols and meanings associated with a brand.

Brand mark A unique symbol that is part of a brand.

Brand name The verbal part of a brand—the part that can be spoken or written.

Break-down method A sales forecasting method that starts with large-scale estimates (for example, an estimate of GDP) and works down to industrywide, company, and product estimates. See also *build-up method.*

Break-even point The point at which an organization's revenues and costs are equal.

Broker An agent intermediary whose major role is placing buyers and sellers in touch with one another and assisting in contractual arrangements.

Build-up method A sales forecasting method that starts with small-scale estimates (for example, product estimates) and works up to larger-scale ones. See also *break-down method.*

Bulk-accumulating function An activity, performed by marketing intermediaries, consisting of buying small quantities of a particular product from many small producers and then selling the assembled larger quantities.

Bulk-breaking function An activity, performed by marketing intermediaries, consisting of buying products in relatively large quantities and selling in smaller quantities.

Business analysis stage The stage in new product development in which the new product is reviewed from all organizational perspectives to determine performance criteria and likely profitability.

Business cycle Recurrent fluctuations in general economic activity. The four phases of the business cycle are prosperity, recession, depression, and recovery.

Business model The fundamental strategy underlying the way a business unit operates.

Business-to-business marketing Marketing aimed at bringing about an exchange in which a product or service is sold for any use other than personal consumption. The buyer may be a manufacturer, a reseller, a government body, a nonprofit institution, or any organization other than an ultimate consumer. The transaction occurs so that an organization may conduct its business.

Buy phase One of the stages of the multistage process by which organizations make purchase decisions.

Buyer The buying-center role played by the organizational member with the formal authority to purchase the product.

Buying center An informal, cross-departmental decision unit, the primary objective of which is to acquire, distribute, and process relevant purchasing-related information.

Buying function Activities, performed by intermediaries, that are associated with making a purchase and thus effecting the transfer of ownership of a product.

C

Cannibalize To eat into the sales revenues of another product item in the same line.

Captive pricing strategy A strategy whereby a basic product, such as a razor, is priced low but the profits from associated products needed for operating the basic product, such as razor blades, make up for the lack of profit on the basic product.

Cash cow A high-market-share product in a low-growth market.

Cash discount A price discount offered for early payment of bills.

Cash-and-carry wholesaler A limited-service wholesaler that does not offer delivery or credit.

Catalog showroom A general mass merchandise outlet where customers select goods from a catalog and store employees retrieve the selected items from storage.

Category superstore A specialty mass merchandise outlet offering extensive assortment and depth in a specific product category; also called a *category killer.*

Census A survey of all the members of a group (an entire population).

Chain store One of a group of two or more stores of a similar type, centrally owned and operated.

Channel conflict Antagonism between distribution channel members.

Channel cooperation Coordinated efforts by distribution channel members whose marketing objectives and strategies complement each other.

Channel leader A distribution channel member that is able to exert power and influence over other channel members; also known as a *channel captain.*

Channel of distribution The complete sequence of marketing organizations involved in bringing a product from the producer to the ultimate consumer or organizational user.

Channel power The extent to which a channel member is able to influence the behavior of another channel member.

Choice criteria The critical attributes a consumer uses to evaluate product alternatives.

Closing The step in the creative selling process wherein the salesperson attempts to obtain a prospect's commitment to buy.

Closing signals Signs from the prospect revealing that he or she is ready to buy.

Closure An element of perception whereby an observer mentally completes an incomplete stimulus.

Co-branding The use of two individual brands on a single product.

Code of conduct A statement establishing a company's or a professional organization's guidelines with regard to ethical principles and acceptable behavior.

Coding Establishing meaningful categories for responses collected by means of surveys or other data collection forms so that the responses can be grouped into usable classifications.

Cognitive dissonance The tension that results from holding two conflicting ideas or beliefs at the same time; in terms of consumer behavior, the negative feelings that a consumer may experience after making a commitment to purchase.

Collaborator A person or company that works with a marketing company. Collaborators help the company run its business but are not actually part of the company.

Commercialization The stage in new product development in which the decision is made to launch full-scale production and distribution of a new product.

Commission merchant An agent intermediary similar to a broker but having certain additional decision-making powers, such as the power to make price adjustments.

Communication The process of exchanging information with and conveying meaning to others.

Communication goals In the context of marketing, what the marketer wants a promotional message to accomplish: to gain attention, to be understood, to be believed, and to be remembered.

Company A business or organization that offers products and services to consumers.

Comparative advertising A type of demonstration advertising in which the brand being advertised is directly compared with a competing brand.

Competitive advantage Superiority to or favorable difference from competitors along some dimension important to the market.

Competitor One of two or more rival companies engaged in the same business.

Concentrated marketing Development of a marketing mix and direction of marketing efforts and resources to appeal to a single market segment.

Concept testing Research procedures used to learn consumers' reactions to new product ideas. Consumers presented with an idea are asked if they like it, would use it, would buy it, and so on.

Conspicuous consumption Consumption for the sake of enhancing social prestige.

Consumer behavior The activities people engage in when selecting, purchasing, and using products so as to satisfy needs and desires.

Consumer involvement The extent to which an individual is interested in and attaches importance to a product and is willing to expend energy in making a decision about purchasing the product.

Consumer market The market consisting of buyers who use a product to satisfy personal or household needs.

Consumer orientation An organization's understanding that the organization must create goods and services with the consumer's needs in mind.

Contest In the context of a wholesaler's or retailer's sales promotion, a means of motivating a sales force by offering bonuses or prizes for sales performance.

Continuous innovation A new product that is characterized by minor alterations or improvements to existing products and that produces little change in consumption patterns.

Contract manufacturing An agreement by which a domestic company allows a foreign producer to manufacture its product according to its specifications. Typically, the domestic company then handles foreign sales of the product.

Contractual vertical marketing system A vertical marketing system in which channel coordination and leadership are specified in a contractual agreement.

Control The process by which managers ensure that planned activities are completely and properly executed.

Convenience product A relatively inexpensive, regularly purchased consumer product bought without much thought and with a minimum of shopping effort.

Convenience store A small grocery store stressing convenient location and quick service and typically charging higher prices than other retailers selling similar products.

Cookies Small computer files (downloaded onto the computer of someone who visits a provider's Web site) that track and record a user's visit.

Cooperative advertising Advertising paid for jointly by a supplier and a customer—for example, by the manufacturer of a product and a retailer.

Copy Any words contained in an advertisement.

Core competency Expertise in a critical functional area or aspect of a particular business that helps provide a company's unique competitive advantage; what a company does best.

Corporate chain A chain consisting of 11 or more stores.

Corporate vertical marketing system A vertical marketing system in which two or more channel members are connected through ownership.

Cost reduction strategy A product strategy that involves redesigning a product to lower production costs.

Creative platform The style in which the advertising message is delivered; also known as the *execution format*.

Creative process In the context of advertising, the generation of ideas and the development of the advertising message or concept.

Creative selling process The seven-step process by which creative selling is carried out: (1) locating qualified prospects, (2) preapproach planning, (3) approaching the prospect, (4) making the sales presentation, (5) handling objections, (6) closing the sale, and (7) following up.

Credit function Provision of credit to another member of a distribution channel.

Crisis management A public relations effort that involves disseminating information during an emergency.

Cross-classification matrix A grid that helps isolate variables of interest in the market. For example, a geographic variable might be cross-classified with some other variable of interest, such as income.

Cross-elasticity Elasticity in the demand for one product in relation to the prices of substitutable or complementary products.

Cross-functional activity An activity carried out by individuals from various departments within an organization and from outside the organization, all of whom have a common purpose.

Cross-functional sales team The sales representative and those who support his or her efforts in making sales and servicing accounts. Support personnel may include technical specialists and missionary salespeople.

Cross-functional team A team made up of individuals from various organizational departments who share a common purpose.

Cross-selling Marketing activities used to sell new services to customers of an existing service.

Culture The institutions, values, beliefs, and behaviors of a society; everything people learn, as opposed to the basic drives with which people are born.

Cumulative quantity discount   A price discount determined by the amount purchased over some specified time period.

Custom marketing   A marketing effort in which a marketer seeks to satisfy each customer's unique set of needs. In effect, each customer is an individual market segment.

Customer   One who buys a company's goods or services.

Customization strategy   A product line extension strategy that involves making a product in relatively small lots for specific channels of distribution or specific customers.

D

Damage in transit   Breakage, spoilage, or other injury to products that occurs while the products are being transported.

Data   Facts and recorded measures of phenomena.

Data analysis   Statistical and/or qualitative consideration of data gathered by research.

Database   A collection of data, arranged in a logical manner and organized in a form that can be stored and processed by a computer.

Data-based marketing   The practice of using databases of customers' names, addresses, phone numbers, past purchases, responses to previous offers, and demographic characteristics in making marketing decisions.

Decider   The buying-center role played by the organizational member who makes the actual purchasing decision.

Decision support system   A computer system that stores data and transforms them into accessible information. It includes databases and software.

Decline stage   The stage in the product life cycle during which the product loses market acceptance because of such factors as diminished popularity, obsolescence, or market saturation.

Decoding   In communication theory, the process by which the receiver of a message interprets the message's meaning.

Delivered pricing   Pricing that includes delivery within a specified area; also known as *freight-allowed pricing*.

Demand curve   A graphic representation of the relationship between various prices and the amount of product that will be demanded at those prices; also called a *schedule of demand*.

Demand management strategy   A strategy used by service marketers to accurately forecast the need for services so that supply is in line with demand.

Demarketing   A strategy (or strategies) intentionally designed to discourage all or some consumers from buying a product.

Demography   The study of the size, composition, and distribution of the human population in relation to social factors such as geographic boundaries.

Demonstration   An advertising creative platform in which a clear-cut example of product superiority or consumer benefits is presented.

Department store   A departmentalized retail outlet, often large, offering a wide variety of products and generally providing a full range of customer services.

Derived demand   Demand for a product that depends on demand for another product.

Development stage   The stage in new product development in which a new product concept is transformed into a prototype. The basic marketing strategy also develops at this time.

Differential pricing strategy   A strategy whereby an organization charges different prices to different buyers of the same product.

Differentiated marketing   A marketing effort in which a marketer selects more than one target market and then develops a separate marketing mix for each; also called *multiple market segmentation*.

Differentiation strategy   A strategy whereby a marketer offers a product that is unique in the industry, provides a distinct advantage, or is otherwise set apart from competitors' brands in some way other than price.

Diffusion process   The spread of a new product through society.

Direct exporting   Exporting in which a company deals directly with a foreign buyer without the assistance of a collaborator.

Direct foreign investment   Investment in production and marketing operations located in a foreign country.

Direct marketing   Marketing in which advertising, telephone sales, or other communications are used to elicit a direct response, such as an order by mail or phone; also called *direct-response retailing*.

Direct-action advertisement   An advertisement designed to stimulate immediate purchase or encourage another direct response; also called a *direct-response advertisement*.

Direct-marketing wholesaler   A limited-service wholesaler that uses catalogs or the Internet, mail or telephone ordering, and parcel delivery.

Direct-response campaign   A promotional approach intended to elicit a direct, measurable response, such as an order.

Discontinuous innovation   A product so new that no previous product performed an equivalent function. Such a product requires the development of new consumption or usage patterns.

Discount   A reduction from list price or a reimbursement for performance of a specific task.

Disintermediation   The compression, or "shortening," of marketing channels because one or more intermediaries have been eliminated.

Distributor brand, or private brand   A brand owned by a retailer, wholesaler, or other distributor rather than by the manufacturer of the product.

Diversification   A strategy of marketing new products to a new market.

Diversion in transit   Direction of a rail shipment to a destination not specified at the start of the trip.

Divisibility   The ability of a product to be sampled in small amounts by consumers.

Dog   A low-market-share product in a low-growth market.

Domestic environment   The environment in an organization's home country.

Drop shipper   A limited-service wholesaler, often dealing in bulky products, that takes customer orders and arranges for shipment of merchandise from the producer directly to the customer; also called a *desk jobber*.

Durable good   A physical, tangible item that can be used over an extended period.

Dynamically continuous innovation   A product that is different from previously available products but that does not strikingly change buying or usage patterns.

E

Early adopter A member of the group of consumers who purchase a product soon after it has been introduced, but after the innovators have purchased it.

Early majority A group of consumers, usually solid, middle-class people, who purchase more deliberately and cautiously than early adopters.

Economic system The system whereby a society allocates its scarce resources.

Economic utility The ability of a good or service marketed by an organization to satisfy a consumer's wants or needs. Economic utility includes form utility, place utility, time utility, and possession utility.

Editing Checking completed questionnaires or other data collection forms for omissions, incomplete or otherwise unusable responses, illegibility, and obvious inconsistencies.

80/20 principle In marketing, a principle describing the fact that usually a relatively small percentage of customers accounts for a disproportionately large share of the sales of a product.

Electronic interactive media Media, such as the Internet, touch-tone telephone systems, and online information services, that allow marketers to reach large audiences with personalized individual messages and that provide an opportunity for immediate interaction.

Embargo A government prohibition against trade, especially trade in a particular product.

Emotion A state involving subjectively experienced feelings of attraction or repulsion.

Encoding In communication theory, the process by which a sender translates an idea to be communicated into a symbolic message, consisting of words, pictures, numbers, gestures, or the like, so that it can be transmitted to a receiver.

Entrepreneur A risk-taking individual who sees an opportunity and is willing to undertake a venture to create a new product or service.

Environmental monitoring Tracking certain phenomena to detect the emergence of meaningful trends.

Environmental scanning Information gathering designed to detect changes that may be in their initial stages of development.

e-tailers e-commerce firms with retailing operations on the Internet.

e-tailing Computer-interactive retailing over the Internet.

Ethical dilemma A predicament in which a marketer must resolve whether an action that benefits the organization, the individual decision maker, or both may be considered unethical.

Ethnocentrism The tendency to consider one's own culture and way of life as the natural and normal ones.

Event marketing A public relations effort that involves creating an event to sponsor.

Exchange process The interchange of something of value by two or more parties.

Exclusive dealing A situation in which a distributor carries the products of one manufacturer and not those of competing manufacturers.

Exclusive distribution A distribution strategy in which only one outlet in a given area is allowed to sell a product.

Exclusive territory An area defined by geographical boundaries or population and assigned to a retailer, wholesaler, or other dealer with the understanding that no other distributors will be assigned to operate in that area.

Execution The carrying out of plans; also called *implementation*.

Experiment A research method in which the researcher changes one variable and observes the effects of that change on another variable.

Exploratory research Research to clarify the nature of a marketing problem.

Export A domestically produced product sold in a foreign market.

Export management company A company that specializes in buying from sellers in one country and marketing the products in other countries. Such companies typically take title to the products.

Exporting Selling domestically produced products in foreign markets.

Extensive problem solving In-depth search for and evaluation of alternative solutions to a problem.

Extranet The portions of an oganization's intranet that are shared by external collaborators, such as suppliers or customers.

F

Fad A passing fashion or craze that interests many people for only a short time.

Family A group of two or more persons related by birth, marriage, or adoption and residing together.

Family branding The practice of using a single brand name to identify different items in a product line.

Family life cycle A series of stages through which most families pass.

Fantasy creative platform In the context of advertising, a type of association creative platform used to link a product with the target buyer's wildest dreams and hopes.

Fashion A style that is current or in vogue.

Federal Trade Commission (FTC) Federal agency established in 1914 by the Federal Trade Commission Act to investigate and put an end to unfair methods of competition.

Feedback Communication of the receiver's reaction to a message back to the source.

Field sales manager A district or regional sales manager, so called because his or her main concern is the salespeople in the field.

Field selling Business-to-business selling that takes place outside the employer's place of business, usually in the prospective customer's place of business.

Fixed cost A cost that is incurred with the passage of time and is not a function of volume of production or sales.

Flexible manufacturing system A group of machines integrated through a central computer and able to produce a variety of similar but not identical products.

F.O.B. "Freight on board" or "Free on board"; a term used to identify the point at which title passes from seller to buyer. For example, "F.O.B. factory" means that the buyer takes title at the factory and is responsible for all shipping charges.

Focus group interview A loosely structured interview in which a group of 6 to 10 people discusses a product or focuses on some aspect of buying behavior.

Follow-the-leader strategy   A pricing strategy whereby an organization sets prices at the level the market leader has established. It is used especially by organizations in weak competitive positions.

Follow-up   The final step in the creative selling process, wherein the salesperson, after the sale has been made, contacts the buyer to make sure every aspect of the sale was handled properly.

Foreign environment   The environment outside an organization's home country.

Form utility   Economic utility created by conversion of raw materials into finished goods that meet consumer needs.

Four Cs   The microenvironmental participants that perform essential business activities: company, customers, competitors, and collaborators.

Four Ps of marketing   The basic elements of the marketing mix: product, place (distribution), price, and promotion; also called the *controllable variables of marketing,* because they can be controlled and manipulated by the marketer.

Franchise   A contractual agreement between a franchisor and a franchisee by which the franchisee distributes the franchisor's product.

Frequency   The number of times an advertisement is repeated in a given medium within a given time period, usually 4 weeks.

Full-line strategy   A product line strategy that involves offering a large number of variations of a product; also called a *deep-line strategy.*

Full-service merchant wholesaler   A merchant wholesaler that provides a complete array of services, such as delivery, credit, marketing information and advice, and managerial assistance; also called a *full-function wholesaler.*

G

Gatekeeper   The buying-center role played by the organizational member who controls the flow of information related to the purchase.

General line wholesaler   A full-service merchant wholesaler that sells a full selection of products in one product line.

General merchandise wholesaler   A full-service merchant wholesaler that sells a large number of different product lines.

Generic name   A brand name so commonly used that it is part of everyday language and is used to describe a product class rather than a particular manufacturer's product.

Generic product, or generic brand   A product that carries neither a manufacturer nor a distributor brand. The goods are plainly packaged with stark lettering that simply lists the contents.

Geodemographic segmentation   A type of market segmentation by which consumers are grouped according to demographic and lifestyle variables, such as income and age, as identified by a geographic variable, such as zip code.

Globalization strategy   A plan by which a marketer standardizes its marketing strategy around the world; also called a *standardization strategy.*

Green marketing   Marketing ecologically safe products and promoting activities beneficial to the physical environment.

Growth stage   The stage in the product life cycle during which sales increase at an accelerating rate.

H

Handling objections   The step in the creative selling process wherein the salesperson responds to questions or reservations expressed by the prospect.

Head-to-head competition   Positioning a product to occupy the same market position as a competitor.

Heterogeneity   The characteristic of services referring to the fact that the quality of delivered services can vary widely.

I

Idea generation   The stage in new product development in which a marketer engages in a continuing search for product ideas consistent with target market needs and the organization's objectives.

Image building   A promotional approach intended to communicate an image and generate consumer preference for a brand or product on the basis of symbolic value.

Import   A foreign product purchased domestically.

Import quota   A limit set by a government on how much of a certain type of product can be imported into a country.

Incentive   Something believed capable of satisfying a particular motive.

Independent retailer   A retail establishment that is not owned or controlled by any other organization.

Indirect exporting   Exporting in which a company uses the assistance of a collaborator to deal with a foreign buyer.

Indirect-action advertisement   An advertisement designed to stimulate sales over the long run.

Individual brand   A brand that is assigned to a product within a product line and is not shared by other products in that line.

Individual factor   A characteristic of a person that affects how the person perceives a stimulus.

Influencer   The buying-center role played by organizational members (or outsiders) who affect the purchase decision by supplying advice or information.

Infomediary   An intermediary, such as a vertical exchange, that serves as an electronic information broker.

Infomercial   A television commercial, usually 30 minutes long, that has the appearance of a program.

Information   Data in a format useful to decision makers.

Information search   An internal or external search for information carried out by a consumer to reduce uncertainty and provide a basis for evaluating alternatives.

Innovator   A member of the first group of consumers to buy a new product.

Inseparability   A characteristic of services referring to the fact that production often is not distinct from consumption of a service—that is, the producer and the consumer of a service must be together in order for a transaction to occur.

Inside selling   Business-to-business selling in the salesperson's place of business.

Institutional advertisement   An advertisement designed to promote an organizational image, stimulate generic demand for a product, or build goodwill for an industry.

Intangibility   The characteristic of services referring to the customer's inability to see, hear, smell, feel, or taste the service product.

Integrated marketing communications Marketing communications in which all elements of the promotional mix are coordinated and systematically planned so as to be harmonious.

Intensive distribution A distribution strategy aimed at obtaining maximum exposure for a product at the retail level or wholesale level.

Internal marketing Marketing efforts aimed at a company's own employees.

International franchising A form of licensing in which a company establishes foreign franchises. Franchising involves a contractual agreement between a franchisor (often a manufacturer or wholesaler) and a franchisee (typically an independent retailer) by which the franchisee distributes the franchisor's product.

International marketing Marketing across international boundaries; also called *multinational marketing*.

Internet A worldwide network of private, corporate, and government computers that gives users access to information and documents from distant sources.

Intranet A company's private decision support system that uses Internet standards and technology.

Intrapreneurial organization An organization that encourages individuals to take risks and gives them the autonomy to develop new products as they see fit.

Introduction stage The stage in the product life cycle during which the new product is attempting to gain a foothold in the market.

Isolation effect An effect by which a product appears more attractive next to a higher-priced alternative than it does in isolation.

J

Jingle A song or other short verse used in an advertisement as a memory aid.

Joint decision making Decision making shared by all or some members of a group. Often, one decision maker dominates the process.

Joint ownership venture A joint venture in which domestic and foreign partners invest capital and share ownership and control.

Joint venture An arrangement between a domestic company and a foreign company to set up production and marketing facilities in a foreign market.

L

Label The paper or plastic sticker attached to a container to carry product information. As packaging technology improves, labels become incorporated into the protective aspects of the package rather than simply being affixed to the package.

Laboratory experiment An experiment in a highly controlled environment.

Laggard A member of the group of final adopters in the diffusion process.

Late majority A group of consumers who purchase a product after the early majority, when the product is no longer perceived as risky.

Learning Any change in behavior or cognition that results from experience or an interpretation of experience.

Leased department retailer An independent retailer that owns the merchandise stocked but leases floor space from another retailer, usually operating under that retailer's name.

Legal environment Laws and regulations and their interpretation.

Licensing An agreement by which a company (the licensor) permits a foreign company (the licensee) to set up a business in the foreign market using the licensor's manufacturing processes, patents, trademarks, trade secrets, and so on, in exchange for payment of a fee or royalty.

Licensing agreement A legal agreement allowing an organization to use the trademark (or other proprietary rights) of another organization.

Lifestyle An individual's activities, interests, opinions, and values as they affect his or her mode of living.

Lifestyle creative platform An advertising creative platform that reflects a target market's lifestyle or hoped-for lifestyle.

Limited problem solving An intermediate level of decision making between routinized response behavior and extensive problem solving, in which the consumer has some purchasing experience but is unfamiliar with stores, brands, or price options.

Limited-line strategy A product-line strategy that involves offering a smaller number of product variations than a full-line strategy offers.

Limited-service merchant wholesaler A merchant wholesaler that offers less than full service and charges lower prices than a full-service merchant wholesaler; also called a *limited-function wholesaler*.

List price The basic price quote, before adjustment.

Location-based competition Competition based on providing place utility by delivering a product where the consumer wants it.

Logistics The activities involved in moving raw materials and parts into a firm, moving in-process inventory through the firm, and moving finished goods out of the firm.

Logo A brand name or company name written in a distinctive way; short for logotype.

Loss leader A product priced below cost to attract consumers, who may then make additional purchases.

M

Macroenvironment Broad societal forces that shape the activities of every business and nonprofit marketer. The physical environment, sociocultural forces, demographic factors, economic factors, scientific and technical knowledge, and political and legal factors are components of the macroenvironment.

Macromarketing The aggregate of marketing activities in an economy or the marketing system of a society, rather than the marketing activities in a single firm (micromarketing).

Magnuson-Moss Warranty Act Federal law requiring that guarantees provided by sellers be made available to buyers before they purchase and that the guarantees specify who the warrantor is, what products or parts of products are covered, what the warrantor must do if the product is defective, how long the warranty applies, and the obligations of the buyer.

Majority fallacy The blind pursuit of the largest, or most easily identified, or most accessible market segment. The error lies in ignoring the fact that other marketers will be pursuing these same segments.

Manufacturer   An organization that recognizes a consumer need and produces a product from raw materials, component parts, or labor to satisfy that need.

Manufacturer brand, or national brand   A brand owned by the maker of the product.

Manufacturers' agent   An independent agent intermediary that represents a limited number of noncompeting suppliers in a limited geographical area; also called a *manufacturers' representative.*

Marginal analysis   A method for determining the costs and revenues associated with the production and sale of each additional unit of a product.

Marginal cost   The net addition to a firm's total costs that results from the production of one additional unit of product.

Marginal revenue   The net addition to a firm's total revenue that results from the sale of one additional unit of product.

Market   A group of potential customers who may want a particular product and who have the resources, the willingness, and the ability to purchase it.

Market development   A strategy by which an organization attempts to draw new customers to an existing product, most commonly by introducing the product in a new geographical area.

Market factor   A variable, associated with sales, that is analyzed in forecasting sales.

Market factor index   An index derived by combining a number of variables that are associated with sales.

Market orientation   Organizational philosophy that emphasizes developing exceptional skill in understanding and satisfying customers so that the organization can offer superior customer value.

Market penetration   A strategy that seeks to increase sales of an established product by generating increased use of the product in existing markets.

Market position, or competitive position   The way consumers perceive a product relative to its competition.

Market potential   The upper limit of industry demand. That is, the expected sales volume for all brands of a particular product during a given period.

Market/product matrix   A matrix that includes the four possible combinations of old and new products and old and new markets. The purpose of the matrix is to broadly categorize alternative opportunities in terms of basic strategies for growth.

Market segment   A portion of a larger market, identified according to some shared characteristic or characteristics.

Market segmentation   Dividing a heterogeneous market into segments that share certain characteristics.

Market share   The percentage of total industry sales accounted for by a particular firm or the percentage of sales of a given product accounted for by a particular brand.

Marketing   The process that seeks to influence voluntary exchange transactions between a customer and a marketer. The marketing process involves communication and requires a mechanism or system to carry out the exchange of the marketer's product for something of value.

Marketing audit   A comprehensive review and appraisal of the total marketing operation, often performed by outside consultants or other unbiased personnel.

Marketing concept   Organizational philosophy that stresses consumer orientation, long-range profitability, and the integration of marketing and other organizational functions. The marketing concept, which focuses on satisfying consumers' wants and needs, is the foundation of a marketing orientation.

Marketing ethics   The principles that guide an organization's conduct and the values it expects to express in certain situations.

Marketing management   The process of planning, executing, and controlling marketing activities to attain marketing goals and objectives effectively and efficiently.

Marketing mix   The specific combination of interrelated and interdependent marketing activities in which an organization engages to meet its objectives.

Marketing myopia   The failure of a company to define its organizational purpose from a broad consumer orientation.

Marketing objective   A statement of the level of performance that an organization, SBU, or operating unit intends to achieve. Objectives define results in measurable terms.

Marketing plan   A written statement of the marketing objectives and strategies to be followed and the specific courses of action to be taken when (or if) certain events occur.

Marketing research   The systematic and objective process of generating information for use in marketing decision making.

Marketing strategy   A plan identifying what marketing goals and objectives will be pursued and how they will be achieved in the time available.

Markup on cost   A markup expressed as a percentage of the cost of an item.

Markup on selling price   A markup expressed as a percentage of the selling price of an item.

Mass customization   A strategy that combines mass production with computers to produce customized products for small market segments.

Mass media   Advertising media, such as television, radio, newspapers, and magazines, that reach a broad audience from many market segments and involve no personal contact or instantaneous interaction between the marketer and the target of the message.

Mass merchandise retailer   A retailer that sells products at discount prices to achieve high sales volume; also called a *mass merchandise discount store.* There are two basic types of mass merchandise retailers: general mass merchandisers and specialty mass merchandisers.

Materials management   The activities involved in bringing raw materials and supplies to the point of production and moving in-process inventory through the firm.

Maturity stage   The stage in the product life cycle during which sales increase at a decreasing rate.

Media schedule   A document identifying the exact media to be used and the dates on which advertisements are to appear; also known as the *media plan.*

Media selection strategy   Plan for determining which media are most appropriate for an advertising campaign.

Meeting-the-competition strategy   A pricing strategy whereby an organization sets prices at levels equal to those of competitors.

Membership group   A group to which an individual belongs. If the individual has chosen to belong to the group, it is a voluntary membership group.

Memory The information-processing function involving the storage and retrieval of information.

Merchant intermediary A channel intermediary, such as a wholesaler or a retailer, that takes title to the product.

Merchant wholesaler An independently owned wholesaling concern that takes title to the goods it distributes.

Microenvironment A company, its customers, and the other economic institutions that directly and regularly influence its marketing practices.

Misleading or deceptive advertising Advertising that leads consumers to inaccurate conclusions. Intentionally making false statements is an extreme case of deceptive advertising.

Missionary A salesperson who visits prospective customers, distributes information to them, and handles questions and complaints but does not routinely take orders. Missionaries really serve as customer relations representatives.

Modified rebuy An organizational buying situation in which a buyer is not completely satisfied with current suppliers or products and is shopping around rather than rebuying automatically.

Monopolistic competition A market structure characterized by a large number of sellers offering slightly differentiated products and exerting some control over their own prices.

Monopoly A market structure characterized by a single seller in a market in which there are no suitable substitute products.

Montage An advertising creative platform that blends a number of situations, demonstrations, and other visual effects into one commercial to emphasize the array of possibilities associated with product usage.

Moral behavior Individual or organizational marketing activity that embodies the ethical values to which the individual or organization subscribes.

Motivation An activated state that causes a person to initiate goal-directed behavior.

Motive An aroused need that energizes behavior and directs it toward a goal.

Motor carrier A member of the trucking industry or another carrier, such as Greyhound's package service, that transports products over roads.

Multinational economic community A collaboration among countries to increase international trade by reducing trade restrictions. Typically, a group of countries forms a unified market within which there are minimal trade and tariff barriers; the European Union is an example.

Multinational marketing group A group of countries aligned to form a unified market with minimal trade and tariff barriers among participating member countries.

Multiple-unit pricing Selling more than one unit of a product at a price lower than the sum of the individual unit prices, as in a four-for-the-price-of-three sale.

N

Need The gap between an actual and a desired state.

New product The meaning of this relative term is influenced by the perceptions of marketers and consumers. In general, it refers to a product new to a company or any recently introduced product that offers some benefit that other products do not.

New task buying An organizational buying situation in which a buyer is seeking to fill a need never before addressed. Uncertainty and lack of information about products and suppliers characterize this situation.

News release A brief written statement sent to the press or others, describing a new product, a product improvement, a price change, or some other development of interest. The release is intended to be newsworthy.

Noise In communication theory, any interference or distraction that disrupts the communication process.

Nonadopter A member of the group of consumers who never buy a particular new product or adopt a particular new style.

Noncumulative quantity discount A price discount determined by the size of an individual purchase order. The larger the order, the larger the discount.

Nondurable good A physical, tangible item that is quickly consumed, worn out, or outdated.

Nonprice competition Competition emphasizing marketing variables other than price—for example, product differentiation.

Nonprobability sample A sample chosen on the basis of convenience or personal judgment.

Norm A social principle identifying what action is right or wrong in a given situation.

North American Industry Classification System (NAICS) A numerical coding scheme developed by the governments of the partners in the North American Free Trade Agreement and used to classify a broad range of organizations in terms of the type of economic activity in which they are engaged.

O

Observability The ability of a product to display to consumers its advantages over existing products.

Observation research The systematic recording of behavior, objects, or events as they are witnessed.

Off-price retailer A specialty mass merchandise outlet offering a limited line of nationally known brand names.

Oligopoly A market structure characterized by a small number of sellers who control the market.

One-price strategy A strategy whereby an organization charges a single price for a product regardless of the circumstances surrounding the sale, the quantity bought, or any other unique aspect of the exchange.

Operant conditioning The process by which reinforcement of a behavior results in repetition of that behavior.

Operational planning Planning that focuses on day-to-day functional activities, such as supervision of the sales force.

Opinion leader A group member who, because of some quality or characteristic, is likely to lead other group members in particular matters.

Order getting An adaptive selling process that tailors sales efforts and product offerings to specific customer needs; also known as *creative selling*. An order getter is primarily responsible for developing business for the firm. Order getters seek out customers and creatively make sales.

Order taker A salesperson who is primarily responsible for writing up orders, checking invoices, and assuring prompt processing of orders.

Organizational buying behavior The decision-making activities of organizational buyers that lead to purchases of products.

Organizational market, or business market The market consisting of buyers who use a product to help operate a business or for resale.

Organizational mission statement A statement of company purpose. It explains why the organization exists and what it hopes to accomplish.

Organizational product A product or service that is used to produce other products and/or to operate an organization.

Outsourcing Buying or hiring from outside suppliers.

Ownership group An organization made up of stores or small chains, each with a separate name, identity, and image but all operating under the control of a central owner.

P

Packaging An auxiliary product dimension that includes labels, inserts, instructions, graphic design, shipping cartons, and sizes and types of containers.

Penetration price A low introductory price meant to quickly establish a product in the market.

Perceived risk Consumers' uncertainty about the consequences of their purchase decisions; the consumer's perception that a product may not do what it is expected to do.

Perception The process of interpreting sensations and giving meaning to stimuli.

Periodic discounting A pricing strategy whereby discounts are offered systematically and predictably.

Perishability The characteristic of services that makes it impossible to store them for later use.

Person marketing The use of marketing techniques, especially promotion, when the product is a person.

Personal media Personal forms of communication involving face-to-face interaction and person-to-person interaction (as by telephone).

Personal selling Person-to-person interaction between a buyer and a seller wherein the seller's purpose is to persuade the buyer to accept a point of view, to convince the buyer to take a course of action, or to develop a customer relationship.

Personality The fundamental disposition of an individual; the distinctive patterns of thought, emotion, and behavior that characterize an individual's response to life situations.

Physical distribution The activities involved in the efficient movement of finished products from the end of the production line to the consumer.

Physical environment Natural resources and other aspects of the natural world that influence marketing activities.

Physical obsolescence The breakdown of a product due to wear and tear.

Physiological need A need based on biological functioning, like the needs for food, water, and air.

Pioneer A salesperson who concentrates on selling to new prospects or on selling new products.

Pipelines Systems of pipes through which products such as oil and natural gas are transported.

Place (distribution) The element of the marketing mix that encompasses all aspects of getting products to the consumer in the right location at the right time.

Place utility Economic utility created by making goods available where consumers want them.

Planned obsolescence The practice of purposely causing existing products to go out of date by introducing new products at frequent intervals.

Planning The process of envisioning the future, establishing goals and objectives, and designing organizational and marketing strategies and tactics to be implemented in the future in order to achieve the goals.

Point-of-purchase materials Promotional items intended to attract attention to specific products in the places where those products are purchased. Signs and displays in supermarkets are examples.

Political environment The practices and policies of governments.

Population In marketing research, any complete group of people or entities sharing some common set of characteristics; the group from which a sample is taken.

Portal A Web site that offers a broad array of resources and services, such as news services, search engines, e-mail, discussion forums, and online shopping.

Positioning Planning the market position the company wishes to occupy. Positioning strategy is the basis for marketing mix decisions.

Possession utility Economic utility created by transfer of physical possession and ownership of the product to the consumer.

Posttesting In the context of advertising, testing that takes place after an advertisement has been run, to determine whether it has met the objectives set for it by management.

Predatory pricing strategy An illegal pricing strategy whereby the price of a product is set low to eliminate competition and then raised to a high level after competition has been eliminated.

Premium A product offered free or at reduced charge with the purchase of another product.

Press conference A meeting called by an organization to announce a newsworthy event to the press.

Prestige price A high price meant to convey an impression of high quality.

Pretesting Conducting limited trials of a questionnaire or some other aspect of a study to determine its suitability for the planned research project. In the context of advertising, research carried out beforehand on the effectiveness of an advertisement. It begins at the earliest stages of development and continues until the advertisement is ready for use.

Price The amount of money or other consideration—that is, something of value—given in exchange for a product.

Price competition Competition based on price. It is especially important in the marketing of products that are not distinctive, such as raw materials. Price competition is associated with possession utility.

Price elasticity A measure of the effect of a change in price on the quantity of product demanded.

Price leadership strategy A strategy whereby organizations with large market shares and production capacities determine a price level that other, weaker organizations in the same industry will follow.

Price stabilization A pricing objective aimed at avoiding widely fluctuating prices. The marketer with this objective sets prices to match competitors' prices or to maintain existing price differentials.

Price-bundling strategy A strategy whereby the price of a group of products is lower than the total of the individual prices of the components. An example is selling a new car with an "options package."

Price-lining strategy A strategy whereby a seller prices products in a product line in accordance with certain "price points" believed to be attractive to buyers.

Pricing objective The desired result associated with a particular pricing strategy. The pricing objective must be consistent with other marketing objectives.

Primary characteristic A basic feature or essential aspect of a product.

Primary data Data gathered and assembled specifically for the project at hand.

Primary demand Demand for a product class as a whole, without regard to brand; also known as *generic demand*.

Primary demand advertising Advertising aimed at stimulating primary demand; also known as *pioneering advertising*.

Probability sample A sample selected by statistical means in such a way that all members of the sampled population had a known, nonzero chance of being selected.

Problem child A low-market-share product in a high-growth market.

Problem definition The crucial first stage in the marketing research process—determining the problem to be solved and the objectives of the research.

Problem recognition The awareness that there is a discrepancy between an actual and a desired condition.

Product A good, service, or idea that offers a bundle of tangible and intangible attributes to satisfy consumers.

Product advertisement An advertisement promoting a specific product.

Product category A subset of a product class containing products of a certain type.

Product category extension A new item or new line of items in a product category that is new to the company.

Product class A broad group of products that differ somewhat but perform similar functions or provide similar benefits—for example, all automobiles made for personal use.

Product concept The end result of the marketing strategist's selection and blending of a product's primary and auxiliary dimensions into a basic idea emphasizing a particular set of consumer benefits; also called the *product positioning concept.*

Product design A product's configuration, composition, and style. This characteristic influences most consumers' perceptions of product quality.

Product development A strategy of marketing innovative or "new and improved" products to existing markets.

Product differentiation A promotional approach in which the marketer calls buyers' attention to those aspects of a product or brand that set it apart from its competitors.

Product enhancement The introduction of a new and improved version of an existing product, intended to extend the product's life cycle by keeping it in the growth stage.

Product item A specific version of a particular good or service.

Product life cycle A marketing management concept, often depicted graphically, that traces a product's sales history. The cycle has four stages: introduction, growth, maturity, and decline.

Product line A group of products that are fairly closely related. The number of different items in a product line determines the depth of the product line.

Product line extension An item added to an existing product line to create depth; also called a *line extension*.

Product line strategy The strategy of matching items within a product line to markets.

Product mix All the product offerings of an organization, no matter how unrelated. The number of product lines within a product mix determines the width of the product mix. A wide mix has a high diversity of product types; a narrow mix has little diversity.

Product modification The altering or adjusting of the product mix, typically influenced by the competitive nature of the market and by changes in the external environment.

Product obsolescence The process by which an existing product goes out of date because of the introduction of a new product.

Product placement A promotional exposure resulting from a product's being shown in a movie or on a TV show.

Product portfolio A collection of products to be balanced as a group. Product portfolio analysis focuses on the interrelationships of products within a product mix. The performance of the mix is emphasized rather than the performance of individual products.

Product sampling A sales promotion in which samples of a product are given to consumers to induce them to try the product.

Product strategy The planning and development of a mix of the primary and auxiliary dimensions of a product.

Product warranty A written guarantee of a product's integrity and the manufacturer's responsibility for repairing or replacing defective parts.

Production orientation Organizational philosophy that emphasizes physical production and technology rather than sales or marketing.

Promotion The element of the marketing mix that includes all forms of marketing communication.

Promotional campaign A series of promotional activities aimed at achieving a specific objective or set of objectives.

Promotional mix An organization's combination of personal selling, advertising, publicity and public relations, and sales promotion; its total promotional effort.

Prospecting Identifying likely customers. In prospecting, the salesperson may search lists of previous customers, trade association lists, government publications, and many other sources.

Psychographics Quantitative measures of lifestyle.

Public relations The activities involved in actively seeking to manage the nature of the publicity an organization receives.

Publicity A message about a product, organization, or event carried by a nonpersonal medium but not paid for by a sponsor. Publicity involves a third party who determines whether the message is newsworthy enough to transmit and what the nature of the transmitted message will be.

Puffery The practice of exaggerating a product's good points in advertising or selling.

Pull strategy A promotional strategy whereby a supplier promotes a product to the ultimate consumer, with the aim of stimulating demand and thus pulling the product through the channel of distribution.

Purchase satisfaction The feeling on the part of the consumer that the decision to buy was appropriate because the product met expectations.

Pure competition   A market structure characterized by free entry, a homogeneous product, and many sellers and buyers, none of whom can control price.

Push strategy   A promotional strategy whereby a supplier promotes a product to marketing intermediaries, with the aim of pushing the product through the channel of distribution.

Q

Qualifying   Evaluating a prospect's potential. Key questions are whether the prospect needs the product, can pay for it, and has the authority to make—or at least contribute to—a decision to buy.

Quality of life   The degree to which people in a society feel a sense of well-being.

Quality-based competition   Competition based on quality. Quality-based competition is associated with form utility.

Quota-bonus plan   Compensation plan whereby a salesperson is paid a base salary related to achievement of a quota and a bonus for sales exceeding the quota.

R

Rack jobber   A limited-service wholesaler that contracts with a retailer to place display racks in a store and to stock those racks with merchandise.

Rail transport   The shipment of products by train over railways.

Random discounting   A pricing strategy whereby discounts are offered occasionally and unpredictably.

Reach   The number of people exposed to an advertisement carried by a given medium.

Rebate   A sales promotion wherein some portion of the price paid for a product is returned to the purchaser.

Recall test   In the context of advertising, a research tool used to determine how much people remember about an advertisement.

Receiver   In communication theory, the one at whom a message is aimed.

Reference group   A group that influences an individual because that individual is a member of the group or aspires to be a member.

Reference pricing strategy   A strategy whereby a moderate price is set for a version of a product that will be displayed next to a higher-priced model of the same brand or next to a competing brand.

Reinforcement   Reward. Reinforcement strengthens a stimulus-response relationship.

Relationship management   The building and maintaining of long-term relationships with the parties that contribute to an organization's success; the sales function of managing the accounting relationship and ensuring that buyers receive appropriate services.

Relationship marketing   Marketing activities aimed at building long-term relationships with the parties, especially customers, that contribute to a company's success; also called *relationship management*.

Relative advantage   The ability of a product to offer clear-cut advantages over competing offerings.

Repositioning   Changing the market position of a product.

Repositioning strategy   A product strategy that involves changing the product design, formulation, brand image, or brand name so as to alter the product's competitive position.

Research design   A master plan that specifically identifies what techniques and procedures will be used to collect and analyze data about a problem.

Retail selling   Selling to ultimate consumers.

Retailer   An organization that sells products it has obtained from a manufacturer or wholesaler to the ultimate consumer. Retailers neither produce nor consume the product.

Retailer cooperative organization   A group of independent retailers that combine resources and expertise to control their wholesaling needs through use of a centralized wholesale buying center.

Retailing   All business activities concerned with the sale of products to the ultimate users of those products.

Return on investment (ROI)   The ratio of profits to assets (or net worth) for an organization, a unit of an organization, a product line, or a brand; also called the *target profit*.

Right to be informed   The consumer's right to have access to the information required to make an intelligent choice from among the available products.

Right to choose   The consumer's right to have viable alternatives from which to choose.

Right to safety   The right to expect the products one purchases to be free from unnecessary dangers. Consumers assume they are entitled to this right.

Risk-taking function   Assumption of the responsibility for losses when the future is uncertain.

Robinson-Patman Act   Federal law passed in 1936 and intended to halt discriminatory pricing policies by specifying certain limited conditions under which a seller may charge different prices to different buyers.

Role   A cluster of behavior patterns considered appropriate for a particular person in a particular social setting, situation, or position.

Routinized response behavior   The least complex type of decision making, in which the consumer bases choices on his or her own past behavior and needs no other information.

S

Salary plus commission   Compensation consisting of a regular salary plus a commission based on sales performance.

Sales branch   A wholesaling establishment that is maintained by a manufacturer for its own product and carries an inventory of the product.

Sales forecast   The actual sales volume an organization expects during a given period.

Sales forecasting   The process of estimating sales volume for a product, an organizational unit, or an entire organization over a specific future time period.

Sales management   The marketing management activity that deals with planning, organizing, directing, and controlling the personal selling effort.

Sales objectives   The specific objectives that an organization's sales effort will attempt to meet. Sales objectives should be precise and quantifiable, should include a time frame, and should be reasonable given the organization's resources.

Sales office   A wholesaling establishment that is maintained by a manufacturer for its own product and does not carry an inventory of the product.

Sales orientation   Organizational philosophy that emphasizes selling existing products, whether or not they meet consumer needs, often through aggressive sales techniques and advertising.

Sales potential   The maximum share of the market an individual organization can expect during a given period.

Sales presentation   The step in the creative selling process wherein the salesperson attempts to persuasively communicate the product's benefits and to explain appropriate courses of action.

Sales promotion   Promotional activities other than personal selling, advertising, and public relations that are intended to stimulate buyer purchases or dealer effectiveness over a specific time period.

Sales territory   The specific and prospective accounts assigned to a salesperson. They may be based on geographical divisions, customer types, or product lines.

Sample   A portion or subset of a larger population.

Sampling   Any procedure in which a small part of the whole is used as the basis for conclusions regarding the whole.

Science   The accumulation of knowledge about humans and the environment.

Screening stage   The stage in new product development in which a marketer analyzes ideas to determine their appropriateness and reasonableness in relation to the organization's goals and objectives.

Seasonal discount   A price discount intended to encourage purchase of products during a time of year when sales are traditionally low.

Second-market discounting   A differential pricing strategy whereby a product is sold at one price in the core target market and at a reduced price in a secondary market.

Secondary data   Data previously collected and assembled for some purpose other than the one at hand.

Selective attention   A perceptual screening device whereby a person does not attend to a particular stimulus.

Selective demand advertising   Advertising aimed at stimulating demand for a particular brand.

Selective distribution   A distribution strategy in which a product is sold in a limited number of outlets.

Selective exposure   A perceptual screening device whereby individuals selectively determine whether they will be exposed to certain stimuli.

Selective interpretation   A perceptual screening device whereby a person forms a distorted interpretation of a stimulus whose message is incompatible with his or her values or attitudes.

Selective perception   The screening out of certain stimuli and the interpretation of selected other stimuli according to personal experience, attitudes, or the like.

Self-concept   An individual's perception and appraisal of himself or herself.

Selling agent   An independent agent intermediary similar to a manufacturers' agent but representing a given product in every area in which it is sold, rather than in a limited geographical area.

Selling function   Activities, performed by intermediaries, that are associated with communicating ideas and making a sale and thus effecting the transfer of ownership of a product.

Service   A task or activity performed for a buyer or an intangible that cannot be handled or examined before purchase.

Service encounter   A period during which a consumer interacts with a service provider.

Service function   Activities, performed by intermediaries, that increase the efficiency and effectiveness of the exchange process. Repair services and management services provided by intermediaries are examples.

Service level   Extent of extra services provided to customers. Service level is often related to price.

Service mark   A symbol that identifies a service. It distinguishes a service in the way a trademark identifies a good.

Shopbot   A smart agent software program that performs shopping tasks for online shoppers.

Shopping product   A product for which consumers feel the need to make comparisons, seek out more information, examine merchandise, or otherwise reassure themselves about quality, style, or value before making a purchase.

Simplicity of usage   Ease of operation. This product benefit can offset any complexity in the product itself.

Single-product strategy   A product line strategy that involves offering one product item or one product version with very few options.

Single-sourcing   Purchasing a product on a regular basis from a single vendor.

Situation analysis   The interpretation of environmental attributes and changes in light of an organization's ability to capitalize on potential opportunities.

Skimming price   A relatively high price, often charged at the beginning of a product's life. The price is systematically lowered as time goes by.

Slice-of-life creative platform   An advertising creative platform that dramatizes a "typical" setting wherein people use a product.

Social and psychological need   A need stemming from a person's interactions with the social environment.

Social class   A group of people with similar levels of prestige, power, and wealth whose thinking and behavior reflect a set of related beliefs, attitudes, and values.

Social responsibility   The ethical principle that a person or an organization must become accountable for how its acts might affect the interests of others.

Social value   A value that embodies the goals a society views as important and expresses a culture's shared ideas of preferred ways of acting.

Socialization process   The process by which a society transmits its values, norms, and roles to its members.

Societal marketing concept   Organizational philosophy that stresses the importance of considering the collective needs of society as well as individual consumers' desires and organizational profits.

Software   Various types of programs that tell computers, printers, and other hardware what to do.

Sorting function   An activity, performed by marketing intermediaries, consisting of classifying accumulated products as to grade and size, and then grouping them accordingly.

Source   In communication theory, the one who sends a message.

Specialty product   A consumer product that is not bought frequently, is likely to be expensive, and is generally purchased with great care.

Specialty store   A retail establishment that sells a single product or a few related lines.

Specialty wholesaler   A full-service merchant wholesaler that sells a very narrow selection of products.

Spokesperson A person who represents an advertiser and directly addresses the audience members to urge them to buy the advertiser's product. Using a spokesperson is a variation on the testimonial.

Standard Industrial Classification (SIC) system A numerical coding system developed by the U.S. government and (until the advent of NAICS) widely employed by organizational marketers to classify organizations in terms of the economic activities in which they are engaged.

Star A high-market-share product in a high-growth market.

Still-life creative platform An advertising creative platform that makes the product or package its focal point, emphasizing a visually attractive presentation and the product's brand name.

Stimulus factor A characteristic of a stimulus—for example, the size, colors, or novelty of a print advertisement—that affects perception.

Storyline creative platform An advertising creative platform that gives a history or tells a story about a product.

Straight commission Compensation based strictly on sales performance.

Straight rebuy A type of organizational buying characterized by automatic and regular purchases of familiar products from regular suppliers.

Straight salary Compensation at a regular rate, not immediately tied to sales performance.

Strategic alliance An informal partnership or collaboration between a marketer and an organizational buyer.

Strategic business unit (SBU) A distinct unit—such as a company, division, department, or product line—of an overall parent organization, with a specific marketing focus and a manager who has the authority and responsibility for managing all unit functions.

Strategic gap The difference between where an organization wants to be and where it is.

Strategic marketing process The entire sequence of managerial and operational activities required to create and sustain effective and efficient marketing strategies.

Strategic planning Long-term planning dealing with an organization's primary goals and objectives, carried out primarily by top management; also called *corporate strategic planning*.

Streaming media Multimedia content, such as audio or video, that can be accessed on the Internet without being downloaded first.

Style A distinctive execution, construction, or design in a product class.

Subculture A group within a dominant culture that is distinct from the culture. Members of a subculture typically display some values or norms that differ from those of the overall culture.

Suggestive selling Suggesting to a customer who is making a purchase that an additional item or service be purchased.

Superior customer value The consumer's attribution of greater worth or better ability to fulfill a need to a certain product compared to its competitors.

Supermarket Any large, self-service, departmentalized retail establishment, but especially one that sells primarily food items.

Supplier An organization that provides raw materials, component parts, equipment, services, or other resources to a marketing organization; also called a *vendor*.

Supply chain All the collaborating organizations that help supply a marketing company and help distribute the marketer's products. The supply chain always includes the channel of distribution.

Supply chain management The planning, implementing, and controlling of a chain of organizational relationships to assure the efficient flow of both inbound materials and outbound finished products.

Supply curve A graphic representation of the relationship between various prices and the amount of product that will be supplied at those prices; also called a *supply schedule*.

Survey Any research effort in which data are gathered systematically from a sample of people by means of a questionnaire. Surveys are conducted through face-to-face interviews, telephone interviews, and mailed questionnaires.

SWOT Acronym for internal strengths and weaknesses and external opportunities and threats. In analyzing marketing opportunities, the decision maker evaluates all these factors.

Systematic bias A research shortcoming caused by flaws in the design or execution of a research study.

Systems concept The idea that elements of a distribution system (or another system) are strongly interrelated and interact to achieve a goal.

T

Tactics Specific actions intended to implement strategies.

Target market A specific market segment toward which an organization aims its marketing plan.

Target population The population of interest in a marketing research study; the population from which samples are to be drawn.

Target return pricing Setting prices to yield a particular target level of profit for the organization.

Tariff A tax imposed by a government on an imported product. A tariff is often intended to raise the price of imported goods and thereby give a price advantage to domestic goods.

Technology The application of science for practical purposes.

Telemarketing Using the telephone as the primary means of communicating with prospective customers. Telemarketers often use computers for order taking.

Test marketing A controlled experimental procedure in which a new product is tested under realistic market conditions in a limited geographical area.

Testimonial A type of advertising in which a person, usually a well-known or public figure, states that he or she owns, uses, or supports the product being advertised.

Tie-in A collaborative effort between two or more organizations or brands that work as partners in a promotional effort.

Time utility Economic utility created by making goods available when consumers want them.

Time-based competition Competition based on providing time utility by delivering a product when the consumer wants it.

Total cost Fixed costs plus variable costs.

Total cost concept In relation to physical distribution, a focus on the entire range of costs associated with a particular distribution method.

Total product   The wide range of tangible and intangible benefits that a buyer might gain from a product after purchasing it.

Total quality management strategy   A product strategy that emphasizes market-driven quality; also called a *quality assurance strategy.*

Trade discount   A discount given to wholesalers, retail dealers, or others in a particular trade as repayment for the performance of certain functions; also called a *functional discount.*

Trade show   A meeting or convention of members of a particular industry where business-to-business contacts are routinely made.

Trademark   A legally protected brand name or brand mark. Its owner has exclusive rights to its use. Trademarks are registered with the U.S. Patent and Trademark Office.

Transaction   A single completed exchange agreement; a one-time sale.

Trial close   A personal selling tactic intended to elicit from a prospect a signal indicating whether he or she is ready to buy.

Trial sampling   The distribution of newly marketed products to enhance trialability and familiarity; giving away free samples.

Trialability   The ability of a product to be tested by possible future users with little risk or effort.

Truck wholesaler   A limited-service wholesaler that sells a limited line of items (often perishable goods) from a truck, thus providing immediate delivery; also called a *truck jobber.*

Turnover   Sales divided by average inventory. Turnover measures the speed with which merchandise is sold.

Two-part pricing   A pricing strategy in which the marketer charges a fixed fee plus a variable usage fee, in order to adjust for losses resulting from a service's perishability.

Tying contract   An agreement tying the purchase of one product to the purchase of another. The buyer who wishes to purchase a certain product is required by the seller to purchase additional products, whether the buyer wants to purchase those products or not.

U

Ultimate consumer   An individual who buys or uses a product for personal consumption.

Unaided recall test   In the context of advertising, a test of consumers' memories of an advertisement, in which no clues are provided as to the specific material to be remembered.

Uncontrollable variable   A force or influence external to the organization and beyond its control.

Undercutting-the-competition strategy   A pricing strategy whereby an organization sets prices at levels lower than those of competitors.

Undifferentiated marketing   A marketing effort not targeted at a specific market segment but designed to appeal to a broad range of customers. The approach is appropriate in a market that lacks diversity of interest.

Unfair sales practices acts   State laws that limit or prohibit the use of certain sales and marketing techniques; most commonly, laws requiring that certain types of merchandise be sold at prescribed markups; also called *minimum markup laws.*

Uniform delivered pricing   A type of delivered pricing in which an organization charges the same price for a given product in all locations.

Unique selling proposition (USP)   A unique characteristic of a product or brand identified by the marketer as the one

on which to base a promotional campaign. It is often used in a product-differentiation approach to promotion.

Universal Product Code (UPC)   The array of black bars, readable by optical scanners, found on many products. The UPC permits computerization of tasks such as checkout and compilation of sales volume information.

User   The buying-center role played by the organizational member who will actually use the product.

V

Value   The power of one product to attract another product in an exchange.

Value chain   Chain of activities by which a company brings in materials, creates a good or service, markets it, and provides service after a sale is made. Each step creates more value for the consumer.

Variable cost   A cost that varies directly with an organization's production or sales. Variable costs are a function of volume.

Variable pricing strategy   A differential pricing strategy whereby an organization allows customers to negotiate a price that varies from buyer to buyer.

Vertical exchange   A business-to-business intermediary that specializes in using the Internet to connect and assist numerous buyers and numerous sellers in a vertical market.

Vertical marketing system   A network of vertically aligned establishments that are managed professionally as centrally administered distribution systems.

W

Warehouse club   A general mass merchandise outlet at which only "members" are allowed to shop; also called a *closed-door house.*

Water transportation   The shipment of products by ship, boat, or barge.

Wheel of retailing   The theory that new forms of retail institutions enter the marketplace as low-status, low-margin, low-price operations and then gradually trade up, opening a market position for a new low-end retailer.

Wholesaler   An organization or individual that serves as a marketing intermediary by facilitating transfer of products and title to them. Wholesalers do not produce the product, consume it, or sell it to ultimate consumers.

Wholesaler-sponsored voluntary chain   A vertical marketing system, initiated by a wholesaler, that links a group of independent retailers in a relationship with the wholesale supplier.

World brand   A product that is widely distributed around the world with a single brand name that is common to all countries and is recognized in all its markets.

World Wide Web (WWW)   A portion of the Internet; a system of Internet servers—computers that support specially formatted documents.

Worldwide information system   An organized collection of telecommunications equipment, computer hardware and software, data, and personnel designed to capture, store, update, manipulate, analyze, and immediately display information about worldwide business activity.

Z

Zone pricing   A type of delivered pricing in which prices vary according to the number of geographic zones through which a product passes in moving from seller to buyer.

ENDNOTES

Chapter 1

1. Eric Nee, "Meet Mister Buy(everything).com," *Fortune,* March 29, 1999. © 1999 Time Inc. Reprinted by permission.

2. Louise Kramer, "On the Run," *Advertising Age,* August 24, 1998, pp. 1, 35.

3. Laura Shapira, "Sara Lee Cheesecake Bites," *Advertising Age,* June 28, 1999, p. s34.

4. Julian Yudelson, "Adapting McCarthy's 4Ps for the 21st Century," *Journal of Marketing Education,* April 1999, p. 63. This article's definition has much in common with conceptualizations in Philip Kotler, "Generic Concept of Marketing," *Journal of Marketing,* April 1972, and Philip Kotler, *Marketing Management* (Englewood Cliffs, NJ: Prentice-Hall, 1997), p. 11.

5. The American Marketing Association (AMA) uses a narrower, more functional definition of marketing: Marketing is the process of planning and executing the conception, pricing, promotion, and distribution of ideas, goods, and services to create exchanges that will satisfy individual and organizational objectives.

6. The word *marketing* comes from the Latin *mercatus* ("marketplace"), which in turn comes from the word *mercari,* "to trade."

7. See the American Marketing Association's definition of marketing, as published in *Marketing News,* March 1, 1985, p. 1.

8. Neil H. Borden, "The Concept of the Marketing Mix," *Journal of Advertising Research,* June 1964, pp. 2–7.

9. E. Jerome McCarthy, *Basic Marketing: A Managerial Approach* (Homewood, IL: Richard D. Irwin, 1960).

10. Jill Lieber, "Braves Bank on Future: Converted Olympic Stadium Incorporates Latest Technology," *USA TODAY,* April 3, 1997, p. 3C.

11. Reprinted with permission from "McDonald's Tartan Choice Upsets Scottish Clan," in the May 12, 1997 issue of *Advertising Age.* Copyright, Crain Communications Inc., 1997.

12. The fact that marketing has implications that extend beyond the traditional marketer–marketing intermediary relationship is discussed in P. R. Vardarajan and Daniel Rajaratnam, "Symbiotic Marketing Revisited," *Journal of Marketing,* January 1986, pp. 7–17. See also Jagdish N. Sheth and Rajendar S. Sisodia, "Revising Marketing's Lawlike Generalizations," *Journal of the Academy of Marketing Science,* Winter 1999, pp. 71–87, and Jean L. Johnson, "Strategic Integration in Industrial Distribution Channels: Managing the Interfirm Relationship as a Strategic Asset," *Journal of the Academy of Marketing Science,* Witner 1999, pp. 14–18.

13. Matt Murray, "What Kids Eat: Snacks, Meals, Snacks, Snacks," *Wall Street Journal,* October 20, 1994.

14. For an interesting view of historical marketing philosophies, see Ronald A. Fullerton, "How Modern Is Modern Marketing? Marketing's Evolution and the Myth of the 'Production Era,'" *Journal of Marketing,* January 1988, pp. 108–125. Also see D. G. Brian Jones and David D. Monieson, "Early Development of Marketing Thought," *Journal of Marketing,* January 1990, pp. 103–113; and Terence Nevett, "Historical Investigation and the Practice of Marketing," *Journal of Marketing,* July 1991, pp. 13–23.

15. For discussions of this contemporary issue, see John C. Narver and Stanley F. Slater, "The Effect of Marketing Orientation on Business Profitability," *Journal of Marketing,* October 1990, pp. 20–35; A. K. Kohli and B. J. Jaworski, "Market Orientation: The Construct, Research Propositions, and Managerial Implications," *Journal of Marketing,* April 1990, pp. 1–18; Bernard J. Jaworski and Ajay K. Kohli, "Market Orientation: Antecedents and Consequences," *Journal of Marketing,* July 1993, pp. 53–70; Stanley F. Slater and John C. Narver, "Does Competitive Environment Moderate the Market Orientation–Performance Relationship?" *Journal of Marketing,* January 1994, pp. 46–55; Gary L. Frankwick, James C. Ward, Michael D. Hutt, and Peter H. Reingen, "Evolving Patterns of Organizational Beliefs in the Formation of Strategy," *Journal of Marketing,* April 1994, pp. 96–110; Daniel J. Goebel, William B. Locander, and Greg W. Marshall, "Communicating a Market Orientation to Other Organizational Members," in Peter J. Gordon and Bert J. Kellerman (eds.), *1999 AMA Educators' Proceedings: Enhancing Knowledge Development in Marketing* (Chicago: American Marketing Association,

1999), pp. 22–23; Brian Engelland, Michael Poletti, and Chris Hopkins, "Market Orientation, Strategic Orientation, Organizational Innovativeness and Firm Performance," in Duncan Herrington and Ronald D. Taylor (eds.), *Marketing Advances in Theory, Practice, and Education* (New Orleans: Society for Marketing Advances, 1998), pp. 228–229; Alfred Pelham, "Influence of Environment, Strategy, and Market Orientation on Performance in Small Manufacturing Firms," *Journal of Business Research,* May 1999, pp. 33–46; James M. Sinkula, William E. Baker, and Thomas Noordewier, "A Framework for Market-Based Organizational Learning: Linking Values, Knowledge, and Behavior," *Journal of the Academy of Marketing Science,* Fall 1997, pp. 305–318; and Glenn B. Voss and Zannie Giraud Voss, "Strategic Orientation and Firm Performance in an Artistic Environment," *Journal of Marketing,* January 2000, pp. 67–83.

16. Theodore Levitt, "Marketing Myopia," *Harvard Business Review,* July/August 1960, pp. 45–56. For an excellent discussion of customer value, see Robert B. Woodruff, "Customer Value: The Next Source for Competitive Advantage," *Journal of the Academy of Marketing Science,* Spring 1997, pp. 138–153; A. Parasuraman, "Reflections on Gaining Competitive Advantage through Customer Value," *Journal of the Academy of Marketing Science,* Spring 1997, pp. 154–161; and Stanley F. Slater, "Developing a Customer Value–Based Theory of the Firm," *Journal of the Academy of Marketing Science,* Spring 1997, pp. 162–167.

17. Fred. J. Burch, "The Marketing Philosophy as a Way of Business Life," in *The Marketing Concept, Its Meaning to Management,* Marketing Series no. 99. See also Theodore Levitt, "Marketing Myopia," *Harvard Business Review,* July/August 1960, pp. 45–56.

18. Theodore Levitt, "Marketing Myopia," *Harvard Business Review,* July/August 1960, pp. 45–56.

19. Lucy McCauley, "How May I Help You: Don Robinson." Reprinted from the March 2000 issue of *Fast Company* magazine. All rights reserved. To subscribe, please call 800-688-1545.

20. For research in this area, see Anusorn Singhapakdi, Kenneth L. Kraft, Scott J. Vitell, and Kumar C. Rallapalli, "The Perceived Importance of Ethics and Social Responsibility on Organizational Effectiveness," *Journal of the Academy of Marketing Science,* Winter 1995, pp. 49–56; Thomas L. Osterhus, "Pro-Social Consumer Influence Strategies: When and How Do They Work," *Journal of Marketing,* October 1997, pp. 16–29; William L. Wilkie and Elizabeth S. Moore, "Marketing's Contributions to Society," *Journal of Marketing,* Volume 63, Special Issue, 1999, pp. 198–218; Thomas W. Dunfee, N. Craig Smith, & William T. Ross, "Social Contracts and Marketing Ethics," *Journal of Marketing,* July 1999; and Ajay Menon and Anil Menon, "Enviropreneurial Marketing Strategy: The Emergence of Corporate Environmentalism as Market Strategy," *Journal of Marketing,* January 1997, pp. 51–67.

21. Roger Rosenblatt, "Reaching the Top by Doing the Right Thing," *Time,* October 18, 1999, p. 90.

22. Adapted from Burton Snowboards, www.burton.com. Retrieved December 27, 1999.

23. Excerpted with permission from *Insights and Inspiration: How Businesses Succeed,* pp. 3–4, Copyright 1995, by Connecticut Mutual Life Insurance Company, now known as Massachusetts Mutual Life Insurance Company.

Chapter 2

1. Adapted with permission from Brian O'Reilly, "The Rent-a-Car Jocks Who Made Enterprise #1," *Fortune,* October 28, 1996, pp. 125–128.

2. Pamela S. Lewis, Stephen H. Goodman, and Patricia M. Fandt, *Management* (St. Paul, MN: West Educational Publishing, 1995), pp. 5, 15.

3. "Pilot Who Left Plane for Food Gets Fired," Reuters, December 8, 1999.

4. Alfred D. Chandler, *Strategy and Structure* (Cambridge, MA: MIT Press, 1962), p. 13.

5. These materials have been reproduced by South-Western College Publishing with the permission of eBay Inc. COPYRIGHT © EBAY INC. ALL RIGHTS RESERVED.

6. Theodore Levitt, "Marketing Myopia," *Harvard Business Review,* July/August 1960, p. 45.

7. James Kim, "Dell: Built-to-Order Success," *USA TODAY,* June 30, 1997.

8. Michael E. Porter, *Competitive Strategy* (New York: Free Press, 1980). See also William L. James, John M. Planchon, and Alan Joyce, "Porter's Generic Marketing Strategies in the Computer Industry: An Empirical Investigation," *Journal of the Midwest Marketing Association,* vol. 4, no. 1 (1989), pp. 57–61; and Shannon H. Shipp, William C. Moncrief, III, and David W. Cravens, "Marketing and Sales Strategy Requirements for Competing in Turbulent Markets," *Journal of Marketing Management,* Spring/Summer 1992, pp. 55–62.

9. "Burger King Opens Customer Hot Line," *Marketing News,* May 28, 1990, p. 7.

10. Marshall Loeb, "How to Grow a New Product Every Day," *Fortune,* November 14, 1994, p. 269.

11. Sarah Schafer, "Gimme a Break," *Inc. Technology,* No. 1, 1997, p. 19.

12. Robert P. Libbon, "Data Dog: How Many Americans Eat Breakfast in the Morning," *American Demographics,* March 1999, p. 41.

13. Doug Levy, "Ads of Dubious Distinction," *USA TODAY,* December 15, 1997, p. 6b.

14. Edward O. Welles, "The Perfect Internet Business," *Inc.,* August 1999, pp. 70 +. Reprinted with permission, *Inc.* magazine, March 2000. Copyright 1999 by Goldhirsh Group, Inc., 38 Commercial Wharf, Boston, MA 02110.

15. Peter D. Bennett, *Marketing Terms* (Chicago: American Marketing Association, 1988), p. 189.

16. Lawrence Muhammad, "Lorax Pitch Leaves Loggers' Foes Fearful," *USA TODAY,* March 3, 1999. Copyright 1999 USA TODAY. Reprinted with permission.

17. Ray Billington, *Living Philosophy: An Introduction to Moral Thought* (London: Routledge, 1988), p. 17.

18. See Geoffrey P. Lantos, "An Ethical Base for Marketing Decision Making," *Journal of Business and Industrial Marketing,* Spring 1987, pp. 11–16; and R. Eric Reidenbach, Donald P. Robin, and Lyndon Dawson, "An Application and Extension of a Multidimensional Ethics Scale to Selected Marketing Practices and Marketing Groups," *Journal of the Academy of Marketing Science,* Spring 1991, pp. 90–91.

19. For a general discussion of ethical dilemmas in business, see Anusorn Singhapakdi and Scott J. Vitell, "Marketing Ethics: Factors Influencing Perceptions of Ethical Problems and Alternatives," *Journal of Macromarketing,* Spring 1990, pp. 4–18; P. J. Forrest, Daniel S. Cochran, Dennis F. Ray, and Donald P. Robin, "An Empirical Examination of Four Factors Thought to Be Influential in Ethical Business Judgments," *Proceedings of the Midwest Marketing Association,* 1991, pp. 133–138; M. Alan Miller, "A Holistic Approach to Marketing," *Proceedings of the Midwest Marketing Association,* 1983, pp. 26–31; Steven Pharr, "A Research Agenda for Marketing/Business Ethics," *Journal of the Midwest Marketing Association,* vol. 4, no. 1 (1989), pp. 133–138; and Scott J. Vitell and Anusorn Singhapakdi, "Ethical Ideology and Its Influence on the Norms and Judgments of Marketing Practitioners," *Journal of Marketing Management,* Spring/Summer 1993, pp. 1–11.

20. For an interesting study of this issue, see Michael J. Dorsch and Scott W. Kelley, "An Investigation into the Intentions of Purchasing Executives to Reciprocate Vendor Gifts," *Journal of the Academy of Marketing Science,* Fall 1994, pp. 315–327.

21. For a general discussion of ethical dilemmas in business, see John R. Schermerhorn, Jr., James G. Hunt, and Richard N. Osborn, *Managing Organizational Behavior* (New York: John Wiley & Sons, 1991), p. 27. See also Anusorn Singhapakdi and Scott J. Vitell, "Marketing Ethics: Factors Influencing Perceptions of Ethical Problems and Alternatives," *Journal of Macromarketing,* Spring 1990, pp. 4–18.

22. George Izzo, "A Theoretical Perspective of the Effects of Moral Intensity on Consumers' Ethical Judgments of Marketers' Non-Normative Behavior," in Joyce A. Young, Dale L. Varble, and Faye W. Gilbert, eds., *Proceedings of the Southwestern Marketing Association* (Terre Haute: Indiana State University and Southwestern Marketing Association, 1997), pp. 53–59.

23. For investigation of ethical awareness and values among marketing executives and marketing students, see Anusorn Singhapakdi, Kenneth L. Kraft, Scott J. Vitell, and Kumar C. Rallapalli, "The Perceived Importance of Ethics and Social Responsibility on Organizational Effectiveness," *Journal of the Academy of Marketing Science,* Winter 1995, pp. 46–56; David J. Fritzche, "An Examination of Marketing Ethics: Role of the Decision Maker, Consequences of the Decision," *Journal of Macromarketing,* Fall 1988, pp. 29–39; M. M. Pressley, D. J. Lincon, and T. Little, "Ethical Belief and Personal Values of Top Level Executives," *Journal of Business Research,* December 1982; Shelby D. Hunt, Van R. Wood, and Lawrence B. Chonko, "Corporate Ethical Values and Organizational Commitment in Marketing,"

Journal of Marketing, July 1989, pp. 79–90; R. Eric Reidenbach, Donald P. Robin, and Lyndon Dawson, "An Application and Extension of a Multidimensional Ethics Scale to Selected Marketing Practices and Marketing Groups," *Journal of the Academy of Marketing Science,* Spring 1991, pp. 83–92; Jerry R. Goolsby and Shelby D. Hunt, "Cognitive Moral Development and Marketing," *Journal of Marketing,* January 1992, pp. 55–68; David J. Burns, John M. Lansasa, and Jeffrey K. Fawcett, "Ethical Perceptions of Undergraduate Business Students: Does the Nature of the Institution Matter?" *Journal of the Midwest Marketing Association,* Spring 1990, pp. 84–156; James B. Deconinck and Paul C. Thistlethwaite, "Gender Differences in Ethical Evaluations," *Proceedings of the Midwest Marketing Association,* 1991, pp. 139–143; and Margery S. Steinberg, Robert F. Dyer, and Hiram C. Barksdale, Jr., "Marketing Ethics: An Examination of the Values and Attitudes of Today's Students/Tomorrow's Professionals," *Journal of the Midwest Marketing Association,* Fall 1989, pp. 65–67.

24. Adapted from materials found at the Second Chance Web site, http://www.secondchance.com/.

25. From the Ben & Jerry's Web site, http://www.benjerry.com. © Ben & Jerry's Homemade Holdings, Inc. Used with Permission of Ben & Jerrry's Homemade Holdings, Inc. 2000.

Chapter 3

1. Joshua Macht, "Shortcut Derails Maker of Long Golf Clubs," *Inc.,* August 1999, p. 25. Reprinted with permission, *Inc.* magazine, March 2000. Copyright 1999 by Goldhirsch Group, Inc., 38 Commercial Wharf, Boston, MA 02110.

2. See, for example, Terry Clark, "International Marketing and National Character: A Review and Proposal for an Integrative Theory," *Journal of Marketing,* October 1990, pp. 66–79; Duane Davis, Michael Morris, and Jeff Allen, "Perceived Environmental Turbulence and Its Effect on Selected Entrepreneurship, Marketing and Organizational Characteristics in Industrial Firms," *Journal of the Academy of Marketing Science,* Winter 1991, pp. 43–52; Leopoldo G. Arias Bolzmann, "Retailing in a Developing Economy: A Case Study in the Peruvian Retailing Economy," in Joseph F. Hair, Jr., Daryl O. McKee, and Daniel L. Sherrell, eds., *Advances in Marketing* (Baton Rouge, LA: Southwestern Marketing Association, 1992), pp. 250–258; Abdolreza Eshghi, Joby John, and Charlie Van Nederpelt, "Marketing Strategy in an Integrated Europe: Some Research Propositions," in Victoria L. Crittenden, ed., *Developments in Marketing Science,* Volume XV (San Diego: Academy of Marketing Science, 1992), pp. 131–135; and Ravi S. Achrol, "Evolution of the Marketing Organization: New Forms of Turbulent Environments," *Journal of Marketing,* October 1991, pp. 77–92.

3. Ian Robertson, *Sociology* (New York: Worth Publishing, 1987), pp. 64–65.

4. Unless otherwise noted, the statistics in this section are from the U.S. Bureau of the Census.

5. Population statistics are from the *Statistical Abstract* located at http://www.census.gov/statab/www/part1.html#vital.

6. For additional information see "Geographical Mobility: March 1993 to March 1994," http://www.census.gov/population/www/socdemo/mig-94.html.

7. U.S. Census Bureau, "Projections: Percentage Change of the Total Population of States: 2000 to 2025," Series A.

8. Peter Francese, "America at Mid-Decade," *American Demographics,* February 1995, p. 28.

9. "Demographics . . . It's All the Rage!" *American Demographics,* June 2000, p. 72.

10. Demographers and sociologists differ on the year that marks the beginning of Generation Y. This is in part because dates of birth define a generation, whereas important external events that occur during an age group's formative years define a cohort. Some demographers say that 1979 was the start of Generation Y.

11. Anjetta McQueen, "U.S. Enrollments Surge Again, Setting New Record," *Tulsa World,* August 20, 1999, p. A9.

12. *Statistical Abstract of the United States: 1998* (Washington, DC: U.S. Dept. of Commerce, 1999); and Peter T. Kilborn, "The Middle Class Feels Betrayed, but Maybe Not Enough to Rebel," *New York Times,* January 12, 1992, p. 1e.

13. *Money Income in the United States: 1998* (Washington, D.C.: U.S. Department of Commerce, 1999).

14. U.S. Bureau of the Census, "U.S. Population Estimates, by Age, Sex, Race, and Hispanic Origin: 1989," *Current Population Reports,* Series P-25, no. 1057 (Washington, DC: Government Printing Office, 1990), pp. 2–7.

15. U.S. Bureau of the Census, as reported in Will Lester, "U.S. Hispanic, Asian Populations Soar," *Tulsa World,* September 15, 1999, p. A10, from the Associated Press.

16. "21 Ideas for the 21st Century," *BusinessWeek Online,* http://www.businessweek.com, August 30, 1999.

17. Neil Postman, *Technopoly: The Surrender of Culture to Technology* (New York: Vintage Books, 1993), pp. 6–15.

18. James P. Ronda, "Thomas Moran and the Eastern Railroads," *The Gilcrease Journal,* Spring/Summer 1997, p. 38.

19. Neil Postman, *Technopoly: The Surrender of Culture to Technology* (New York: Vintage Books, 1993), pp. 6–15.

20. Kevin Goldman, "Video Explosions Sell Technology to Teens," *Wall Street Journal,* October 5, 1993.

21. Four excellent articles about the Internet and its impact on marketing in the 21st century are Paul Pallab, "Marketing on the Internet," *Journal of Consumer Marketing,* vol. 13, no. 4, 1996, pp. 27–39; Robert A. Peterson, Sridhar Balasubramanian, and Bart J. Bronnenberg, "Exploring the Implications of the Internet for Consumer Marketing," *Journal of the Academy of Marketing Science,* Fall 1997, pp. 329–346; John Deighton, "Commentary on 'Exploring the Implications of the Internet for Consumer Marketing'," *Journal of the Academy of Marketing Science,* Fall 1997, pp. 347–351; and Raymond R. Burk, "Do You See What I See? The Future of Virtual Shopping," *Journal of the Academy of Marketing Science,* Fall 1997, pp. 352–360.

22. "Net Results," *Advertising Age,* May 29, 2000, p. 82.

23. "MP3 Technology Rocking the Music World," CNN, http://www.cnn.com, March 1, 1999.

24. "MP3 for Beginners," http://www.MP3.com, July 13, 1999.

25. "RealNetworks' RealJukebox Reaches One Million Downloads in Ten Days," RealNetworks Company Press Release, *PRNewswire,* http://www.PRNewswire.com, May 12, 1999.

26. Mike Snider, "Nomad: High-Quality MP3 Mobility," *USA TODAY,* August 18, 1999. Copyright 1999, USA TODAY. Reprinted with permission.

27. Joshua Quittner, "Invasion of Privacy," *Time,* August 25, 1997.

28. "Broadcast.com Completes SimpleNet Acquisition," *PRNewswire,* http://www.PRNewswire.com, Tuesday, December 1, 1998.

29. Michael J. Wolf, *The Entertainment Economy* (New York: Times Books–Random House, 1999), p. 207.

30. John Huey, "Waking Up to the New Economy," *Fortune,* June 27, 1994, p. 36.

31. Excerpt reprinted with permission from Karl Schoenberger and Melanie Warner, "Motorola Bets Big on China," *Fortune,* May 27, 1996.

32. Michael D. Hutt and Thomas Speh, *Industrial Marketing Management* (Hinsdale, IL: Dryden Press, 1988), p. 39.

33. Michael D. Eisner, "Critics of Disney on the Wrong Track," *USA TODAY,* July 12, 1994, p. 10A.

34. Tim Friend, "Cosmetic Ads Must Tone Down Claims," *USA TODAY,* April 5, 1988, p. 1D.

Chapter 4

1. Clifford Krauss, "Selling to Argentina (as Translated from the French)," *New York Times,* December 5, 1999. Copyright © 1999 by the New York Times Co. Reprinted by permission.

2. The concept of the four Cs of business is copyrighted by William G. Zikmund, 1991. Use of this conceptual scheme elsewhere is not permitted without written permission from William G. Zikmund. For an alternative conceptualization, see Kenichi Ohmae, *The Mind of the Strategist* (New York: Penguin Books, 1982), p. 91.

3. For two interesting papers dealing with entrepreneurship, see Michael T. Manion, Gerald E. Hills, G. T. Lumpkin, and Rodney C Shrader, "The Recognition of New Business Opportunities: The Search for a Model," in Peter J. Gordon and Bert J. Kellerman (eds.), *1999 AMA Educators' Proceedings: Enhancing Knowledge Development in Marketing* (Chicago: American Marketing Association, 1999), pp. 317–323; and Douglas W. Vorhies, J. B. Arbaugh, and S. Michael Camp, "Managing Growth Transitions in Emerging Firms: A Conceptual Integration of Resource, Knowledge, and Life Cycle Theory," in Peter J. Gordon and Bert J. Kellerman (eds.), *1999 AMA Educators' Proceedings: Enhancing Knowledge Development in Marketing* (Chicago: American Marketing Association, 1999), pp. 324–325.

4. Patricia Sellers, "John Bryan's Sara Lee," *Fortune,* February 6, 1995, p. 24.

5. Thomas A. Stewart, "Welcome to the Revolution," *Fortune,* December 13, 1993, p. 76.

6. Reprinted by permission of Harvard Business School Press from *Real Time: Preparing for the Age of the Never Satisfied Customer* by Regis McKenna. Boston, MA 1997, pp. 3–4. Copyright © 1997 by the President and Fellows of Harvard College, all rights reserved.

7. John A. Byrne, "The Futurists Who Fathered the Ideas," *Business Week,* February 8, 1993, p. 103.

8. For an alternative view of this concept, see Michael E. Porter, *Competitive Advantage* (New York Free Press, 1985), pp. 36–43.

9. Rosabeth Moss Kanter, "Collaborative Advantage: The Art of Alliances," *Harvard Business Review,* July–August 1994, p. 97; and Joel Bleeke and David Ernst, "Is Your Strategic Alliance Really a Sale?" *Harvard Business Review,* January–February 1995, p. 104.

10. Peter F. Drucker, "The Information Executives Really Need," *Harvard Business Review,* January–February 1995, p. 59.

11. Kenichi Ohmae, "The Equidistant Manager," *Express Magazine,* Fall 1990, pp. 10–12.

12. Bureau of Economic Analysis, National Accounts Data, http://www.bea.doc/bea/dn/niptbl-d.htm

13. Philip R. Cateora, *International Marketing* (Homewood, IL: Richard D. Irwin, 1990), p. 2.

14. For some recent studies on this issue, see Lalita A. Manrai and Ajay K. Manrai, "Effects of Cultural Context, Gender, and Acculturation on Perceptions of Work versus Social/Leisure Time Usage," *Journal of Business Research,* February 1995, pp. 114–128; James W. Gentry, Sunkyu Jun, and Partiya Tansuhaj, "Consumer Acculturation Process and Cultural Conflict," *Journal of Business Research,* February 1995, pp. 129–139; and Ruby Roy Dholakia and Luis V. Domingues, "Special Section on Marketing Strategies and the Development Process," Journal of Business Research, February 1995, pp. 113–114.

15. "No Beef in India McDonald's," Associated Press, October 11, 1996.

16. Adapted with permission of the Associated Press from "Japanese Like Seafood Really Fresh," *Tulsa World,* April 27, 1991, p. C2.

17. From *DO'S AND TABOOS AROUND THE WORLD* 3rd Edition, by Roger E. Axtel. Copyright © 1993 by Parker Pen Company. A Benjamin Book distributed by John Wiley & Sons, Inc. Adapted by permission of John Wiley & Sons, Inc.

18. "Don't Drip on Me," *Time,* March 7, 1988, p. 45.

19. Laurel Wentz, "Multinationals Tread Softly While Advertising in Iran," *Advertising Age International,* November 8, 1993, p. I-21.

20. Julian Nundy, "Protesters Threaten Paris Food Fight. U.S. Sanctions on Beef Battle Put McDonald's, Coke in Cross-fire," *USA TODAY,* August 31, 1999; "Farmers Dump Manure at McDonald's," Reuters-PARIS, August 22, 1999; "Comment: Food," *Wall Street Journal,* August 26, 1999, p. A16; and "France Targets U.S. on Agriculture," United Press International, September 27, 1999.

21. Geoffrey Lee Martin, "P&G Puts Nappies to Rest in Australia," *Advertising Age,* September 19, 1994, p. I-31.

22. Adapted from "Whirlpool: U.S. Leader Pursues Global Blueprint," *Appliance Manufacturer,* February 1997, p. 21.

23. Charles Solomon, "The Gen-P Goldmine: The Pokémon Generation, from Pint-Sized to Even Older Kids, Has Helped Turn the Japanese Video Game into a Multimedia Craze," *Los Angeles Times,* October 2, 1999.

24. Joe Schlosser, "'Pokémon' Powers Kids WB!" *Broadcasting & Cable,* September 6, 1999, p. 44.

Chapter 5

1. Jennifer Lach, " Count On It: Shell Oil Recaptures the Quality of Its Once-Leading Brand." Reprinted from *American Demographics* magazine, March 1999. Copyright 1999. Courtesy of Intertec Publishing Corp., Stamford, Connecticut. All Rights Reserved.

2. See Thomas G. Exter, "The Next Step Is Called GIS," *American Demographics Desk Reference,* May 1992, p. 2.

3. "U.S. Forest Service Uses Geographic Information Systems to Plan National Forests So That Logging Is Out of Public View," *Mother Jones,* May, 1999, p. 21.

4. Ralph H. Sprague, Jr., and Hugh J. Watson, *Decision Support Systems: Putting Theory into Practice* (Englewood Cliffs, NJ: Prentice-Hall, 1986), p. 1. See also Jim Bessen, "Riding the Marketing Information Wave," *Harvard Business Review,* September-October 1994, pp. 150-160.

5. "Three Visions of an Electronic Future," *New York Times,* March 24, 1996, p. 22F.

6. Paul Schneider, "Behind Company Walls: It's the Intranet," *Arizona Business Gazette,* March 7, 1996.

7. "Technology: Sun Microsystems Planning to Unveil 'Intranet' Products," *Wall Street Journal*, March 26, 1996.

8. Andrew J. Kessler, "The Database Economy," *Forbes*, April 21, 1997, p. 168.

9. Adapted from the definition of research in the report of the American Marketing Association Committee on Definitions of Marketing Research, 1987. The official AMA definition is as follows: "Marketing research is the function that links the consumer, customer, and public to the marketer through information—information used to identify and define marketing opportunities and problems; generate, refine, and evaluate marketing actions; monitor marketing performance; and improve understanding of marketing as a process. Marketing research specifies the information required to address these issues; designs the method for collecting the information; manages and implements the data collection process; analyzes the results; and communicates the findings and their implications." See also Morris B. Holbrook, "What Is Marketing Research?" and Shelby D. Hunt, "Marketing Research: Proximate Purpose in Ultimate Value," both in Russell W. Belk and Gerald Zaltman, eds., *Proceedings, 1987 Winter Educators' Conference* (Chicago: American Marketing Association, 1987).

10. P. J. Runkel and J. E. McGrath, *Research on Human Behavior: A Systematic Guide to Method* (New York: Holt, Rinehart and Winston, 1972), p. 2.

11. A. Einstein and L. Infeld, *The Evolution of Physics* (New York: Simon and Schuster, 1942), p. 95.

12. "Rubbermaid Tries Its Hand at Bristles and Wood," *Adweek's Marketing Week*, March 5, 1990, pp. 20–21.

13. "Consumer Demand, Not New Laws, Will Protect Web Privacy," *USA TODAY*, July 7, 1998, p. 12A. Copyright 1998, USA TODAY. Reprinted with permission.

14. For further insight into problems associated with surveys, see Philip E. Down and John R. Kerr, "Recent Evidence on the Relationship between Anonymity and Response Variables for Mail Surveys," *Journal of the Academy of Marketing Science*, Spring 1986, pp. 72–82; Jon M. Hawes, Vicky L. Crittenden, and William F. Crittenden, "The Effects of Personalization, Source, and Offer on Mail Survey Response Rate and Speed," *Akron Business and Economic Review*, Summer 1987, pp. 54–63; and three articles in Joseph F. Hair, Jr., Daryl O. McKee, and Daniel L. Sherrell, eds., *Advances in Marketing* (Baton Rouge, LA: Southwest Marketing Association, 1992): Robert E. Stevens, David London, and C. William McConkey, "Does Questionnaire Color Affect Response Rates?" pp. 80–85; Ronald D. Taylor and Michael Richard, "Mail Survey Response Rates, Item Omission Rates, and Response Speed Resulting from the Use of Advanced Notification," pp. 67–72; and David Strutton and Lou Pelton, "Surveying the Elderly," pp. 264–268.

15. Gloria E. Wheeler, "Yes, No, All of the Above: Before You Conduct a Survey," *Exchange* (a publication of Brigham Young University School of Management), Spring/Summer 1979, p. 21.

16. Paco Underhill, *Why We Buy* (New York: Simon & Schuster, 1999), p. 102.

17. Adapted with permission from Gerry Khermouch, "Sticking Their Neck Out," *Brandweek*, November 9, 1998, pp. 25–34.

18. "You Say Tomato, I Say Tomahto," *Express Magazine*, Spring 1992, p. 19.

19. Adapted by permission from the Toronto Blue Jays Web site, http://www.bluejays.com.

Chapter 6

1. Adapted with permission from Beth Burkstrand, "Scrapbook Mania: Pricey Labor of Love," *The Wall Street Journal*, July 16, 1997. Reprinted by permission of *Wall Street Journal*, © 1997 Dow Jones & Company, Inc. All Rights Reserved Worldwide.

2. Adapted with permission from Barbara Carton, "Hold on to Your Tupperware—The Home Sales Party Is Back," *The Wall Street Journal*, March 26, 1997. Reprinted by permission of *Wall Street Journal*, © 1997 Dow Jones & Company, Inc. All Rights Reserved Worldwide.

3. William L. Wilkie, *Consumer Behavior*, 2nd ed. (New York: John Wiley & Sons, 1990), p. 12.

4. Kurt Lewin, *A Dynamic Theory of Personality* (New York: McGraw-Hill, 1935).

5. This model is a variation of the one discussed by John C. Mowen in *Consumer Behavior*, 4th ed. (New York: Macmillan, 1997).

6. William L. Wilkie, *Consumer Behavior*, 2nd ed. (New York: John Wiley & Sons, 1990), pp. 220–225. See also Mark E. Slama and Armen Tashchian, "Validation of the S-C-R Paradigm for Consumer Involvement with a Consumer Good," *Journal of the Academy of Marketing Science*, Spring 1987, pp. 36–45; Joseph J. Belonax, Jr. and Rajshekhar G. Javalgi, "The Influence of Involvement and Product Class Quality on Consumer Choice Sets," *Journal of the Academy of Marketing Science*, Summer 1989, pp. 209–216.

7. For an interesting article, see Jeffrey B. Schmidt and Richard A. Spreng, "A Proposed Model of External Consumer Information Search," *Journal of the Academy of Marketing Science*, Summer 1996, pp. 232-245.

8. Liveperson.com, December 1, 1999; Bruce Horovitz, "Web Site Helps with e-customer Service," *USA Today*, August 16, 1999; and Stephen C. Miller, "Anybody in There? Sites Strain to Build In Customer Service," New York Times on the Web, http://www.newyorktimes.org, September 22, 1999.

9. Marketers are interested in dissatisfaction as well as satisfaction; but since complaints are only one measure of dissatisfaction, this result is difficult to measure. See Marsha Richins, "A Multivariate Analysis of Responses to Dissatisfaction," *Journal of the Academy of Marketing Science*, Fall 1987, p. 24.

10. For an excellent literature review, see Robert D. Winsor, "Cognitive Dissonance as a Focus for Marketing Strategy: A Review and Framework," in J. Duncan Herrington and Ronald D. Taylor, eds., *Marketing Advances in Theory, Practice, and Education* (Radford, VA: Society for Marketing Advances, 1998), pp. 52–58.

11. Adapted with permission from "William Spain—Sauder (Marketing 100)," in the June 30, 1997 issue of *Advertising Age*. Copyright Crain Communications Inc., 1997.

12. A. Maslow, *Motivation and Personality* (New York: Harper & Row, 1954), p. 92.

13. Scott Bowles, "Seat-Belt Campaign Takes Graphic Turn," *USA TODAY*, February 21, 1999. Copyright 1999, USA TODAY. Reprinted with permission.

14. Matthew Grimm, "Coors Serves Taste-Test Results in Ads," *Adweek*, July 1, 1991, p. 9. For interesting studies on perception in marketing, see R. I. Allison and K. P. Uhl, "Impact of Beer Brand on Taste Perception," *Journal of Marketing Research*, August 1964, pp. 36-39; Gordon L. Patzer, *The Physical Attraction Phenomena* (New York: Plenum Publishing, 1985); William L. Rhey, Hemant Rustogi, and Mary Anne Watson, "Buyers' Perceptions of Automobile Saleswomen: A Field Study," in Joseph F. Hair, Jr., Daryl O. McKee, and Daniel Sherrell, eds., *Advances in Marketing* (Baton Rouge, LA: Southwest Marketing Association, 1992), pp. 41–46; and Donald R. Lichtenstein, Nancy M. Ridgway, and Richard Netermeyer, "Price Perceptions and Consumer Shopping Behavior," *Journal of Marketing Research*, May 1993, pp. 234–245.

15. A review of the 25-year history of subliminal cues is found in Sid C. Dudley, "Subliminal Advertising: What Is the Controversy About?" *Akron Business and Economic Review*, Summer 1987, pp. 6–18. See also Robert E. Widing II, Ronald Hoverstad, Ronald Coulter, and Gene Brown, "The VASE Scales: Measures of Viewpoints about Sexual Embeds in Advertising," *Journal of Business Research*, January 1991, pp. 3–10.

16. Debra L. Nelson and James Campbell Quick, *Organizational Behavior: Foundations, Realities, and Challenges* (St. Paul, MN: West Educational Publishing, 1994), pp. 112–113.

17. William L. Wilkie, *Consumer Behavior*, 2nd ed. (New York: John Wiley & Sons, 1990), p. 311.

18. Kenneth R. Evans, Tim Christiansen, and James D. Gill, "The Impact of Social Influence and Role Expectations on Shopping Center Patronage Intentions," *Journal of the Academy of Marketing Science*, Summer 1996, pp. 208–218.

19. See, for example, Van R. Wood and Roy Howell, "A Note on Hispanic Values and Subcultural Research," *Journal of the Academy of Marketing Science*, Winter 1991, pp. 61–67.

20. Adapted from Dennis Gilbert and Joseph Kahl, *The American Class Structure* (Homewood, IL: Dorsey Press, 1982); and from Daniel W. Rossides, *Social Stratification: The American Class System in Comparative Perspective* (Englewood Cliffs, NJ: Prentice Hall 1990), pp. 406–408.

21. See Lawrence F. Feick and Linda L. Price, "The Marketing Maven: A Diffuser of Marketplace Information," *Journal of Marketing*, January 1987, pp. 83–97.

22. Levitt material excerpted from Theodore Levitt, "The Morality(?) of Advertising," *Harvard Business Review*, July-August 1970, p. 91. Hayden material from Sterling Hayden, *The Wanderer* (New York: Knopf, 1963).

23. http://www.vtbear.com

Chapter 7

1. Reprinted from Joel Dreyfus, "The Dancing Penguin Is an Online Secretary to Help You Schedule Meetings," *Fortune*, October 25, 1999, p. 354.

2. Though these three situations are common and widely recognized, some research offers alternative viewpoints. See Erin Anderson, Wujin Chu, and Barton Weitz, "Industrial Purchasing: An Empirical Exploration of the Buyclass Framework," *Journal of Marketing*, July 1987, pp. 71–86; and Morry Ghingold, "Testing the Buygrid Buying Process Model," *Journal of Purchasing and Materials Management*, Winter 1986, pp. 30–36.

3. For an interesting article on marketing on the Internet, see Marc E. Duncan, "The Internet and Relationship Marketing: A Framework for Application," in Peter J. Gordon and Bert J. Kellerman (eds.), *1999 AMA Educators' Proceedings: Enhancing Knowledge Development in Marketing* (Chicago: American Marketing Association, 1999), pp. 72–80.

4. "A Survey of Electronic Commerce—Business-to-Business e-Commerce Is a Revolution in a Ball Valve," *The Economist,* downloaded from http://www.economist.com, June 1999.

5. "3rd Annual 50/50 1999 Internet Winners—WebBusiness," *CIO Web Business Magazine,* July 1, 1999; and Doug Bartholomew, "Trawling for $1 Billion," *Industry Week*, April 21, 1997, p. 68.

6. Ronald Henkoff, "The Hot New Seal of Quality: ISO 9000 Standard of Quality Management," *Fortune*, June 28, 1993, pp. 116–117.

7. Adapted with permission from John Larson, "The Daily Double—A Review of a Company Whose Stock Price Has Doubled Within the Last Year," *The Motley Fool*, September 27, 1999, The Motley Fool, Inc., http://www.fool.com. The information in paragraph two is based on "VeriSign to Provide Security and Trust Framework for pcsRx.com," company press release, September 29, 1999, *PRNewswire*, http://www.PRNewswire.com.

8. From a press release issued by the Executive Office of the President, Office of Management and Budget, Washington, D.C.

9. Excerpted with permission from *Insights and Inspiration: How Businesses Succeed*, pp. 135–136, Copyright 1995 by Connecticut Mutual Life Insurance Company, now known as Massachusetts Mutual Life Insurance Company.

Chapter 8

1. Adapted with permission from Wayne Friedman, "Dixie Chicks Go Mainstream in Marketing, Not Their Music," *Advertising Age*, July 26, 1999, p. 18.

2. Segmentation strategies can be very specific. See, for example, Morris B. Holbrook and Douglas V. Holloway, "Marketing Strategy and the Structure of Aggregate, Segment-Specific, and Differential Preferences," *Journal of Marketing*, Winter 1986, pp. 62–67; Jo Ann Stilley Hopper, "An Investigation of the Roles of Husbands and Wives in Family Financial Decision Making Processes: Preliminary Results," in Michael Levy and Dhuruv Grewal, eds., *Developments in Marketing Science*, vol. XVI (Miami Beach: Academy of Marketing Science, 1993), pp. 75–81; Oksana Humphreys, George M. Zinkham, and Ellen Day, "A Portrait of the Russian Consumer: 1900–1999," in Peter J. Gordon and Bert J. Kellerman (eds.), *1999 AMA Educators' Proceedings: Enhancing Knowledge Development in Marketing* (Chicago: American Marketing Association, 1999), pp. 128–132; Mary Walker and Patrice Binder, "Baby Boombers as Grandparents," in Duncan Herrington and Ronald D. Taylor, *Marketing Advances in Theory, Practice, and Education* (New Orleans: Society for Marketing Advances, 1998), pp. 36–39; Glen Riecken and Ugur Yavas, "Who Uses Prepared Food? Psychographic and Demographic Correlates," in Michael Levy and Dhuruv Grewal, eds., *Developments in Marketing Science*, vol. XVI (Miami Beach: Academy of Marketing Science, 1993), pp. 542–546; and Cynthia Webster, "Spanish- and English-Speaking Hispanic Subcultural Consumption Differences," in Kenneth D. Bahn, ed., *Developments in Marketing Science*, vol. XI (Montreal: Academy of Marketing Science, 1988), pp. 18–22.

3. David Field, "Business-Flier Plan Paying Off for United," *USA TODAY*, August 5, 1997, p. 8b.

4. Salina Khan, "More Midpriced Hotels Pamper Guests Like Rita," *USA Today*, May 23, 2000, p. 5b.

5. Reprinted with permission from "A Car or a Club?" in the November 8, 1993 issue of *Advertising Age*. Copyright, Crain Communications, Inc., 1993.

6. Ellen Neuborne, "We Are Going to Own This Generation," *Business Week*, February 15, 1999.

7. Chris Woodyard, "Generation Y: The Young and the Boundless Are Taking Over Pop Culture," *USA TODAY*, October 6, 1998. See also Stephanie M. Noble and Charles H. Nobel, "Getting to Know Y: The Consumption Behaviors of a New Cohort," in Peter J. Gordon and Bert J. Kellerman (eds.), *1999 AMA Educators' Proceedings: Enhancing Knowledge Development in Marketing* (Chicago: American Marketing Association, 1999), pp. 293–299.

8. Patrick E. Murphy and William A. Staples, "A Modernized Family Life Cycle," *Journal of Consumer Research,* January 1979, p. 17.

9. *Consumer Behavior* 3/e by Mowen, John C., © 1993. Reprinted by permission of Prentice-Hall, Inc., Upper Saddle River, NJ.

10. Judann Pollack, "Sampling, Ads May Be Key for Products Using Olestra," *Advertising Age*, April 1, 1996, p. 16.

11. Information from Patricia Sellers, "Keeping the Buyers You Already Have," *Fortune*, Autumn-Winter 1993, p. 57; and Bob Dorf, "Phone-to-Phone Marketing," *Brandweek*, September 1997, p. 27.

12. Alex Taylor III, "Porsche Slices Up Its Buyers," *Fortune*, January 16, 1995, p. 24.

13. Adapted with permission from Alex Taylor III, "Porsche Slices Up Its Buyers," *Fortune*, January 16, 1995, p. 24. Pricing information from Wilton Woods, "Not Priced for the Nineties," *Fortune*, September 22, 1993, p. 87.

14. Michael J. McCarthy, "Marketers Zero In on Their Customers," *Wall Street Journal*, March 18, 1991, p. 1B.

15. "Hot Spot: Ethan Allen," *Advertising Age*, January 13, 1997, p. 38.

16. Adapted from information at Hospitality Careers Online, http://www.hcareers.com/profile/labellemgt.

17. © 1994 SRI Consulting. All rights reserved. Unauthorized use or reproduction is prohibited.

18. Updated by SRI in April 1995 from VALS 2/Simmons Study of Media and Markets database. Used with permission from SRI Consulting, Menlo Park, CA.

19. Adapted with permission of SRI Consulting from "The VALS™ 2 Typology," © 1994, SRI Consulting.

Chapter 9

1. Adapted with permission from Stephanie Thompson, "Making Lunch Cool," *Brandweek,* October 6, 1997, pp. 18–19. © 1997 ASM.

2. Theodore Levitt, *The Marketing Imagination* (New York: Free Press, 1986), p. 79.

3. Estimates of the importance of services vary because of definitional problems. For example, U.S. government statistics omit transportation from the definition of services and thus estimate services to account for approximately 30 percent of the gross national product.

4. Rita Koselka, "Hope and Fear as Marketing Tools," *Forbes*, August 29, 1994, p. 78. Reprinted by permission of Forbes Magazine. © 1999 Forbes 1999.

5. Adapted from Dan Goodin, "Domain Ownership Isn't a Trademark," http://www.news.cnet.com, April 23, 1999.

6. For an interesting article see Kevin Lane Keller, Susan E. Heckler, and Michael J. Houston, "The Effects of Brand Name on Suggestiveness in Advertising Recall," *Journal of Marketing*, January 1998, pp. 48–57.

7. Adapted from Paul Larson, "Daily Double: VeriSign, Inc.: How Did It Double?", *The Motley Fool*, http://www.fool.com, September 27, 1999, and "VeriSign and Novell Partner to Build Trusted Internet Communities," VeriSign, Inc., company press release, October 5, 1999, http://www.verisign.com/press/.

8. Leonard L. Berry, Valerie Zeithaml, and A. Parasuraman, "Responding to Demand Fluctuations: Key Challenges for Service Business," in *A.M.A. Educators' Proceedings*, eds. R. Belk et al. (Chicago, American Marketing Association, 1985), pp. 231–234. Mary Jo Bitner, "Evaluating Service Encounters: The Effects of Physical Surroundings and Employee Responses," *Journal of Marketing,* April 1990, pp. 68–82. See also Ruth N. Dolton and James H. Drew, "A Longitudinal Analysis of the Impact of Service Changes on Customer Attitudes," *Journal of Marketing,* January 1991, pp. 1–9; Keith B. Murray, "A Test of Service Marketing Theory," *Journal of Marketing*, January 1991, pp. 10–25; Raymond P. Fisk, Stephen J. Grove, and Mary Jo Bitner, "Dramatizing the Service Experience: A Managerial Approach," in *Advances in Services Marketing and Management: Research and Practice*, eds. Teresa A. Swartz, Stephen W. Brown, and David E. Bowen (JAI Press, 1992); William H. Davidow and Bro Uttal, "Service Companies: Focus or Falter," *Harvard Business Review*, July/August 1989, p. 83.

9. Lucy McCauley, "How May I Help You: Hans Peter Brondmo." Reprinted from the March 2000 issue of *Fast Company* magazine. All rights reserved. To subscribe, please call 800-688-1545.

10. Rahul Jacob, "Why Some Customers Are More Equal Than Others," *Fortune,* September 14, 1994, p. 215.

11. Rahul Jacob, "Why Some Customers Are More Equal Than Others," *Fortune,* September 9, 1994, p. 224.

12. Excerpts reprinted with permission from Jeff Green, "Hello, There! If I Knew You Were Calling I'd Have Baked a Cake," *Brand Week,* May 15, 2000, p. 74.

13. Matthew L. Meuter, Amy L. Ostrom, Robert I. Roundtree, and Mary Jo Bitner, "Self-Service Technologies: Understanding Consumer Satisfaction with Technology-Based Service Encounters," *Journal of Marketing,* July 2000, pp. 50–64; Mary Jo Bitner, Stephen W. Brown, and Matthew L. Meuter, "Technology Infusion in Service Encounters," *Journal of the Academy of Marketing Science,* Winter 2000, pp. 138–149; Debora L. Cowles and Pamela Kieker, "Developing New Theoretical Perspectives for Predicting Consumer Acceptance of the Internet," in John P. Workman, Jr., William D. Perreault, Jr., Peter J. Gordon, and Bert J. Kellerman, *AMA Winter Educators' Conference: Marketing Theory and Applications* (Chicago: AMA, 2000), pp. 43–51; and Marc E. Duncan, "The Internet and Relationship Marketing: A Framework for Application," in John P. Workman, Jr., William D. Perreault, Jr., Peter J. Gordon, and Bert J. Kellerman, *AMA Winter Educators' Conference: Marketing Theory and Applications* (Chicago: AMA, 2000), pp. 72–80.
14. Adapted from R. A. Baron and P. B. Paulus, "Group Seekers and Avoiders: How Well-Suited Are You for Working in Groups?" in *Understanding Human Relations,* 2d ed., pp. 286–287. Copyright © 1991 by Allyn & Bacon. Reprinted by permission.
15. Mike Rosenwald, "Smith & Wesson Deal Decried in Gun Stores," *Pittsburgh Post-Gazette,* March 24, 2000. http://www.post-gazette.com/regionstate/20000324guns6.asp.
16. Information from Ben & Jerry's Web page: http://www.benjerry.com; LearNet's video *Ben & Jerry's;* and press release from Ben & Jerry's, February 20, 1997.

Chapter 10

1. Adapted with permission from etown.com and David J. Elrich, "Philips, TiVo Kick Off PVRrevolution," http://www.e-town.com, March 29, 1999.
2. Kevin J. Clancy and Robert S. Shulman, *The Marketing Revolution* (New York: Harper Business, 1991), p. 6.
3. E. M. Rogers and F. F. Shoemaker, *Communication of Innovation* (New York: Free Press, 1971). See also Vijay Mahajan, Eitan Muller, and Frank M. Bass, "New Product Diffusion Models in Marketing: A Review and Directions for Research," *Journal of Marketing,* January 1990, pp. 1–26; and Fareena Sultan, John V. Farley, and Donald R. Lehmann, "A Meta-analysis of Diffusion Models," *Journal of Marketing Research,* February 1990, pp. 70–77.
4. Adapted with permission from John Spooner, "Palm's Next Move: Taking to the Airwaves," ZDNet News, http://www.zdnet.com, October 13, 1999.
5. "Guided by Voices," *Business 2.0,* May, 2000.
6. For some products, psychographic variables may be more important than demographic variables. See Judith Waldrop, "Markets with Attitude," *American Demographics,* July 1994, pp. 22–33.
7. Chris Bucholtz, "Ironing Out the Bugs Through the Internet," *Telephony,* January 1, 1996, p. 16.
8. Kathleen Deveny, "Failure of Its Oven Lovin' Cookie Dough Shows Pillsbury Pitfalls of New Products," *Wall Street Journal,* June 17, 1993.
9. Stephanie Stoughton, "Jeans Market Now a Tight Fit for Levi's; Denim Leader Missed Marketing Opportunities, Failed to Spot Trends," *Washington Post,* February 23, 1999, p. E-01+. © 1999, The Washington Post. Reprinted with permission.
10. E. M. Rogers and F. F. Shoemaker, *Communication of Innovation* (New York: Free Press, 1971). See also Vijay Mahajan, Eitan Muller, and Frank M. Bass, "New Product Diffusion Models in Marketing: A Review and Directions for Research," *Journal of Marketing,* January 1990, pp. 1–26; and Fareena Sultan, John V. Farley, and Donald R. Lehmann, "A Meta-analysis of Diffusion Models," *Journal of Marketing Research,* February 1990, pp. 70–77.
11. Rita Koselka, "It's My Favorite Statistic," *Forbes,* September 12, 1994.
12. Based on David A. Aaker, *Managing Brand Equity* (New York: Macmillan, 1991), pp. 90–95; David Garvin, "Product Quality: An Important Strategic Weapon," *Business Horizons,* May–June 1984, pp. 40–43; and David A. Garvin, "Competing on the Eight Dimensions of Quality," *Harvard Business Review,* November–December 1987, pp. 101–108.
13. For an interesting study, see Vicki Lane and Robert Jacobson, "Stock Market Reactions to Brand Extension Announcements: The Effect of Brand Attitude and Familiarity," *Journal of Marketing,* January 1995, pp. 63–77.
14. For an interesting article, see Deborah Roedder, John Barbara Loken, and Christopher Joiner, "The Negative Impact of Extensions: Can Flagship Products be Diluted?" *Journal of Marketing,* January 1998, pp. 19–33.
15. Andrea Gerlin, "A Matter of Degree: How a Jury Decided That One Coffee Spill Is Worth $2.9 Million," *Wall Street Journal,* September 1, 1994, p. A1; and "Jury Says Coffee Too Hot," *USA TODAY,* August 19, 1994, p. B-1.

16. Adapted with permission from *Real-World Lessons for America's Small Business: Insights from the Blue Chip Enterprise Initiative 1994,* pp. 91–92. Copyright 1994 by Mass Mutual—The Blue Chip Company.

Chapter 11

1. John P. Mello, Jr., "Skateboard Champ Carves Out a Business," Inc. 500 Spotlights, *Inc.,* July 20, 1999. Originally published in *Aquent* magazine.
2. Wroe Alderson, *Marketing Behavior and Executive Action* (Homewood, IL: Richard D. Irwin, 1957).
3. For an interesting study, see Charles R. Duke and Margaret A. Persia, "Purchasing Issue Importance in Service Channels of Distribution: Tour Operators and Travel Agents," in Michael Levy and Dhuruv Grewal, eds., *Developments in Marketing Science,* Vol. XVI (1993), pp. 405–408.
4. Reprinted with permission from Mike Allen, "Jeepers, Bullwinkle . . . ," *New York Times,* April 8, 1999, p. 2.
5. For an excellent discussion of this issue, see Brad Alan Kleindl, *Strategic Electronic Marketing: Managing E-Business* (Cincinnati: South-Western College Publishing, 2001), p. 96.
6. Charles F. Hofacker, *Internet Marketing* (Dripping Springs, TX: Digital Springs Publishing, 1999), p. 94.
7. Julie Landry, "Verticalnet Gets Deep with NECX Exchange," Redherring.com, November 17, 1999.
8. Mohanbir Sawhney and Steven Kaplan, "B-to-B: Let's Get Vertical," *Business 2.0,* September 1999.
9. Adapted with permission from Eric Hellweg, "VerticalNet: Industrial-Strength Portal from Paint to Power Plants, Waste to Widgets," *Business 2.0,* September 1999.
10. Mohanbir Sawhney and Steven Kaplan, "B-to-B: Let's Get Vertical," *Business 2.0,* September 1999.
11. "Chemdex: Vertical Market Makers," *Fortune,* December 6, 1999, p. S53.
12. "Caterpillar's Backbone: A Long Dealer Network," *Business Week,* May 4, 1981, p. 77.
13. Kenneth A. Hunt, Susan P. Keaveney, and Jeffrey E. Danes, "Power and Compliance: An Investigation in a Channel Behavior Setting," in Michael Levy and Dhuruv Grewal, eds., *Developments in Marketing Science,* Vol. XVI (1993), pp. 589–593; Jeffrey C. Dilts and George E. Prough, "Perceived Environmental Uncertainty and Perceptions of the Channel Relationship," in Robert L. King, ed., *Developments in Marketing Science,* Vol. XIV (1991), pp. 96–100; David H. Strutton, Lou E. Pelton, and R. Keith Tudor, "The Relationship of Channel Structure, Climate, and Power to Exchange: Pennington Revisited," in Victoria L. Crittenden, ed., *Developments in Marketing Science,* Vol. XV (1992), pp. 11–15; William H. Redmond and Nancy Merritt, "Multifunctional Relations in Channel Partnerships," in Michael Levy and Dhuruv Grewal, eds., *Developments in Marketing Science,* Vol. XVI (1993), pp. 119–123; and Kaushik Mitra, Samantha J. Rice, and Stephen A. LeMay, "Postponement and Speculation in Exchange Relationships: A Transaction Cost Approach," in Joyce A. Young, Dale L. Varble, and Faye W. Gilbert, eds., *Proceedings of the Southwestern Marketing Association* (Terre Haute: Indiana State University and Southwestern Marketing Association, 1997), pp. 18–25.
14. For additional discussion of conflict within the channel of distribution, see Gary L. Frazier and Raymond C. Rody, "The Use of Influence Strategies in Interfirm Relationships in Industrial Product Channels," *Journal of Marketing,* January 1991, pp. 52–69; Jakki Mohr and John R. Nevin, "Communication Strategies in Marketing Channels: A Theoretical Perspective," *Journal of Marketing,* October 1990, pp. 36–51; and James C. Anderson and James A. Narus, "A Model of Distributor Firm and Manufacturer Firm Working Partnerships," *Journal of Marketing,* January 1990, pp. 42–59.
15. Adapted from Victoria Griffith, "Branding.com: How Bricks-and-Mortar Companies Can Make It on the Internet," *Strategy and Business,* Second Quarter, 1999.
16. Madeline Johnson and Charles R. Strain, "Retailers' Perceptions of Their Recycling Programs," in Joyce A. Young, Dale L. Varble, and Faye W. Gilbert, eds., *Proceedings of the Southwestern Marketing Association* (Terre Haute: Indiana State University and Southwestern Marketing Association, 1997), pp. 128–134.
17. Adapted from Burton Snowboards, http://www.burton.com. Retrieved December 20, 1999.

Chapter 12

1. Excerpt reprinted from Jennifer Owens, "Centerseat: Best Integrated Content and Commerce Experience," *AdWeek,* June 5, 2000, pp. IQ60–IQ62.

2. It is common to use sales figures to differentiate between retailers and other intermediaries. If an intermediary makes more than 50 percent of its sales to consumers, that intermediary is counted as a retailer in the U.S. government's Census of Retail Trade.

3. *Statistical Abstract of the United States: 1999*, found at http://www.census.gov/prod/www/statistical-abstract-us.html

4. See Chip E. Miller, James Reardon, and Denny E. McCorkle, "The Effects of Competition on Retail Structure," *Journal of Marketing*, October 1999, pp. 107–120.

5. Evan I. Schwartz, "Shopbot Pandemonium," *Wired*, December 1998, p. 72; and Robert A. Metzger, "Shopbots: Three Degrees of Automation," *Wired*, December 1998, p. 72.

6. Adapted from Gus Venditto, "What's a Bot?", Botspot, http://www.bots.internet.com.

7. Ronald D. Taylor and Blaise J. Bergiel, "Chain Store Executives' Ratings of Critical Site Selection Factors," *Journal of Midwest Marketing*, Fall 1988, pp. 37–49.

8. For interesting discussions of this issue, see Mary Jo Bitner, "Servicescapes: The Impact of Physical Surroundings on Customers and Employees," *Journal of Marketing*, April 1992, pp. 57–71; and Joseph A. Bellizzi, Ayn E. Crowley, and Ronald W. Hasty, "The Effects of Color on Store Design," *Journal of Retailing*, Spring 1983, pp. 21–57.

9. Paco Underhill, *Why We Buy: The Science of Shopping* (New York: Simon and Schuster, 1999), p. 33.

10. Paco Underhill, *Why We Buy: The Science of Shopping* (New York: Simon and Schuster, 1999). Reprinted by permission of Simon & Schuster Inc.

11. Bernard Stamler, "Direct Marketers Find Some Familiar Ground." *New York Times*, September 22, 1999

12. Adapted with permission from Margaret Kane, "Levi's to End Direct Sales Online," ZDNet News, www.zdnet.com, October 29, 1999.

13. U.S. Bureau of the Census, *1997 Census of Wholesale Trade*, found at http://www.census.gov/epcd/www/97ec42.htm.

14. U.S. Bureau of the Census, *1997 Census of Wholesale Trade*, found at http://www.census.gov/epcd/www/97ec42.htm.

15. Information from Hoover's Online: The Business Network, http://www.hoovers.com.

16. Internet Stock News, Friday, May 28, 1999, http://www.Internetstocknews.com.

Chapter 13

1. Jennifer Lach, "Hip Check: Lee Apparel Mined Its Own Ad History To Get Cool." Reprinted from *American Demographics* magazine, March, 1999. Copyright 1999. Courtesy of Intertec Publishing Corp., Stamford, Connecticut. All Rights Reserved.

2. Dennis Berman, "A Point-and-Click Sales Force," *Business Week*, June 28, 1999.

3. H. D. Lasswell, *Power and Personality* (New York: W. W. Norton, 1948).

4. Pierre Martineau, *Motivation in Advertising* (New York: McGraw-Hill, 1957), p. 154.

5. The hierarchy of communication effects model has been portrayed in several other forms. A common one includes awareness, interest, evaluation, trial, and adoption. Another model includes attention, interest, desire, and action (AIDA). The nature of the model depends on consumer involvement.

6. Adapted from Jane Weaver, "Girl Scout Campaign: Shedding Old Image for MTV Cool," *Adweek*, September 11, 1989, p. 68. © ADWEEK, L.P. Used with permission from Adweek.

7. Steve Lohr, "Big Blue Casts Itself as Big Brother to Business on the Web," *New York Times*, September 22, 1999. Copyright © 1999 by the New York Times Co. Reprinted by permission.

8. Bob Garfield, "Shockvertising Display Leaves Decidedly Bad Taste," *Ad Age International*, July 10, 2000, p. 4.

9. Adapted from information at http://www.boyneusa.com.

Chapter 14

1. David Batstone, "Ad It Up." Reprinted from the February 2000 issue of *Business 2.0* magazine. Copyright Imagine Media, Inc. All Rights Reserved.

2. "Campbell Launches New Soup Campaign: M'm! M'm! Good for the Body, Good for the Soul," *PR Newswire*, February 9, 1998.

3. "Ads for the Ages," *Newsweek*, October 20, 1999.

4. Excerpts reprinted from Joe Urschel, "The Song That Chevy Rocks to: Three Words That Evolved into a Corporate Hymn," *USA TODAY*, January 5, 1996. Copyright 1996, USA TODAY. Reprinted with permission.

Lyrics to "Like a Rock":
Stood there boldly sweatin' in the sun
Felt like a million, felt like number one
The height of summer, I'd never felt that strong
Like a rock
My hands were steady, my eyes were clear and bright
My walk had purpose, my steps were quick and light
And I held firmly to what I thought was right
Like a rock
Like a rock, I was strong as I could be
Like a rock, nothing ever got to me
Like a rock, I was something to see
Twenty years now, where'd they go
Twenty years I don't know
I sit and I wonder sometimes
Where they've gone
And sometimes late at night when I'm bathed in the firelight
The moon comes callin' a ghostly white
And I recall . . . I recall
Like a rock . . .

5. Adapted with permission from Jaikumar Vijayan, "Super Bowl Ads Drive IT Buildup; Dot-coms Beef Up Tech to Tackle Web Site Rush," *Computerworld*, December 6, 1999, p. 1.

6. Gene Koprowski, "Buying the Goods—The (New) Hidden Persuaders: What Marketers Have Learned about How Consumers Buy on the Web," *Wall Street Journal*, December 7, 1998, p. R10.

7. Nicholas Negroponte, *Being Digital* (New York: Knopf, 1995), p. 6.

8. Lee Fleming, "Digital Delivery: Pushing Content to the Desktop," downloaded from the Digital Information Group, 1997.

9. Brad Alan Kleindl, *Strategic Electronic Marketing: Managing E-Business* (Cincinnati: South-Western College Publishing, 2001), p. 64.

10. Eric Ransdell, "Net Effects," *Fast Company*, September 1999, p. 216.

11. CNET News.com, December 7, 1999.

12. "Strategic Relationship Enables Dramatically Enhanced Media Experiences at 1/20th the Bandwidth of Traditional Compressed Video," *PRNewswire*, http://www.PRNewswire.com, December 9, 1999.

13. Lee Fleming, "Digital Delivery: Pushing Content to the Desktop," downloaded from the Digital Information Group, 1997.

14. Jeff Sweat and Rick Whiting, "Instant Marketing," Information Week Online, August 2, 1999.

15. Jeff Sweat and Rick Whiting, "Instant Marketing," Information Week Online, August 2, 1999.

16. National ad spending by media, Advertising Age Data Place, http://adage.com/dataplace/archives/dp393.html, downloaded January 30, 2000.

17. Reprinted with permission from Margaret Kane, "Sony Glitch Reveals Subscriber e-mail Addresses," ZDNet News, November 8, 1999.

18. The initial idea for this table is based on William H. Bolen, *Advertising*, 2nd ed. (New York: John Wiley & Sons, 1984), pp. 601–602.

19. Scott M. Cutlip, Allen H. Center, and Glen M. Broom, *Effective Public Relations* (Englewood Cliffs, NJ: Prentice-Hall, 1985), p. 4.

20. Retrieved June 9, 2000 from http://www.3m.com/us/about3M/innovation/airbag/index.html.

21. "Liverpool Irate over Beatles Road Sign Ban," Reuters News Service, January 19, 2000.

22. Philip Lesley, Ed., *Lesley's Handbook of Public Relations and Communications* (4th ed.) (New York: American Management Association, 1991), p. 340.

23. Steve J. Grove and William E. Kilbourne, "A Mertonian Approach to the Analysis of Advertising's Role in Society: From Polemics to Discourse," in Robert P. Leone, V. Kumar, Peter J. Gordon, and Bert J. Kellerman, eds., *1992 AMA Educator's Proceedings: Enhancing Knowledge Development in Marketing* (Chicago: American Marketing Association, 1992), p. 441; and Joe F. Alexander, Ernest F. Cooke, and Michael A. Turk, "An Examination of That Form of Deception Called Puffery," in Kenneth D. Bahn, ed., *Developments in Marketing Science*, vol. XI (Montreal: Academy of Marketing Science, 1988), pp. 247–250.

24. See, for example, Lois J. Smith, "Children's Advertising: Difference in Advertisers' Approaches for Girls and Boys," in *Proceedings of the Midwest Marketing Association* (1994), pp. 79–84; Lois J. Smith, "Children and Television Violence: Public Policy and Advertisers' Perspectives," in *Proceedings of the Midwest Marketing Association* (1991), pp. 88–91; Michael L. Klassen, Lisa Barkema, and Fred Meisenheimer, "Nutrition Claims in Children's Food Commercials," in *Proceedings of the Midwest Marketing Association* (1993), pp. 79–82; Srivatsa Seshadri and C. P. Rao,

"Considerations in Advertising Directed toward Children," and Les Carlson, Russell N. Lacznink, and Darrel D. Muehling, "Antecedents of Mother's Perceptions of Toy-Based Programming—An Empirical Investigation," in Robert P. Leone, V. Kumar, Peter Gordon, and Bert J. Kellerman, eds., *1992 AMA Educator's Proceedings: Enhancing Knowledge Development in Marketing* (Chicago: American Marketing Association, 1992).
25. V. Kanti Prasad and Lois J. Smith, "Television Commercials in Violent Programming: An Experimental Evaluation of Their Effects on Children," *Journal of the Academy of Marketing Science,* Fall 1994, pp. 340–351.

Chapter 15

1. Adapted from Kevin McManus, "Selling," *Changing Times,* October 1990, pp. 48–56. Copyright © 1990 The Kiplinger Washington Editors, Inc.
2. Adapted from William C. Moncrief, "Selling Activity and Sales Position Taxonomies for Industrial Salesforces," *Journal of Marketing Research,* August 1986, pp. 261–270. Reprinted by permission of the American Marketing Association.
3. Kenneth R. Evans, Robert E. Kleine, III, Timothy D. Landry, and Lawrence A. Crosby, "How First Impressions of a Customer Impact Effectiveness in an Initial Sales Encounter," *Journal of the Academy of Marketing Science,* Fall 2000, pp. 512–516.
4. From *A Passion for Excellence* by Thomas J. Peters and Nancy K. Austin. Copyright © 1985 by Thomas J. Peters and Nancy K. Austin. Reprinted by permission of Random House, Inc.
5. Experienced salespeople know that they will hear the word No most of the time, or at least more than they hear Yes. Rejection is never a source of enjoyment, but there are many times when the sales representative is better off accepting a negative response gracefully and moving on to prospects who may be more likely to buy.
6. Stephen X. Doyle and George T. Roth, "Selling and Sales Management in Action: The Use of Insight Coaching to Improve Relationship Selling," *Journal of Personal Selling and Sales Management,* Winter 1992, pp. 59–64.
7. Jeff Sweat, "Software That Sells," INFORMATIONWEEK ONLINE, http://www.informationweek.com, June 14, 1999.
8. Jeff Sweat, "Software That Sells." *Information Week,* June 4, 1999.
9. Eric Sevareid, *Enterprise: The Marketing of Business in America* (New York: McGraw-Hill, 1983), p. 13.
10. Reprinted with permission from Roger D. Blackwell, *From Mind to Market* (New York: Harper Business, 1997), pp. 21–22. Copyright © 1997 by Roger D. Blackwell. Reprinted by permission of HarperCollins Publishers, Inc.
11. William H. Murphy, "Even Roses Have Thorns: Functional and Dysfunctional Effects of Sales Contests on Sales Personnel," In Robert P. Leone, V. Kumar, Peter J. Gordon, and Bert J. Kellerman, eds., 1992 *AMA Educator's Proceedings: Enhancing Knowledge Development in Marketing* (Chicago: American Marketing Association, 1992), p. 402.
12. Adapted with permission from Martha L. Stone, "CBS Hopes Web Will Bite on Bulldog," ZDNet News, October 5, 1999.
13. Reprinted with permission from Elaine Underwood, "U.S. Vintners Are Bearing Fruit with a Cultural, Culinary Approach," *BrandWeek,* September 5, 1994, p. 28–29.

Chapter 16

1. Paul Davidson, "Going Once, Going Often to Auction Sites," *USA TODAY,* November 11, 1999. Copyright 1999, USA TODAY. Used with permission.

2. During periods of inflation, price's importance in the marketing mix is rated higher by managers. See Saeed Samiee, "Pricing in Marketing Strategies of U.S.- and Foreign-Based Companies," *Journal of Business Research,* February 1987, pp. 17–30.
3. Doug Levy, "Online Shopping Easier with e-Wallets: Customers Can Just Click Instead of Re-entering Info," *USA TODAY* June 29, 1999. Copyright 1999, USA TODAY. Used with permission.
4. See Hugh M. Cannon and Fred W. Morgan, "A Strategic Pricing Framework," *Journal of Consumer Marketing,* Summer 1990, p. 62. The relationship of price and product quality over time is discussed in David J. Curry and Peter C. Riesz, "Prices and Price/Quality Relationships: A Longitudinal Analysis," *Journal of Marketing,* January 1988, pp. 36–51. See also Jerry B. Gotlieb and Dan Sarel, "The Influence of Type of Advertisement, Price, and Source Credibility on Perceived Quality," *Journal of the Academy of Marketing Science,* Summer 1992, pp. 253–260.
5. Adapted from the Toronto Blue Jays Web site, http://www.bluejays.com.

Chapter 17

1. Adapted from Dave Kindred, "Save Wrigley? Chew on This Idea," *Sporting News,* July 8, 1999.
2. For an interesting article on competitive pricing see Akshay R. Rao, Marke E. Bergen, and Scott Davis, "How to Fight a Price War," *Harvard Business Review,* March-April 2000, pp. 107–116.
3. Adapted with permission from Diane Brady, "The E.Biz 25—Jay S. Walker," BusinessWeek Online, September 27, 1999.
4. Erin M. Davies, "The Brand's the Thing," *Fortune,* March 4, 1996.
5. Robert LaForbes Franco, "Take That, Nintendo," *Forbes,* June 3, 1996.
6. R. Lee Sullivan, "School for Cheerleaders," *Forbes,* October 25, 1993, p. 118.
7. Adapted from Chris Woodyard, "Circuit City Tacks 15% Fee on Some Returns," *USA TODAY,* December 26, 1997, p. 1b. Copyright 1997, USA TODAY. Reprinted with permission.
8. The per-unit loss is $300. The fixed cost per unit is $400,000/500 = $800. The variable cost per unit remains at $75. However, because there is a loss, there is no target return per unit. The total per-unit cost (fixed cost + variable cost) is thus $875. Subtracting the selling price of $575 yields a $300 per-unit loss. Calculating the target return at 500 units would have yielded a selling price of $1,075: Fixed cost and target return per unit ($1,000) + variable cost per unit ($75) = suggested price per unit ($1,075).
9. Marketers must be careful not to structure discount schedules in ways that encourage buyers to purchase more product than they need and sell the excess on the "black market." See James B. Wilcox, Roy D. Howell, Paul Kuzdrall, and Robert Britney, "Price Quantity Discounts: Some Implications for Buyers and Sellers," *Journal of Marketing,* July 1987, pp. 60–70.
10. For an excellent discussion of the Robinson-Patman Act, see James C. Johnson and Kenneth C. Schneider, "Those Who Can, Do . . . and Those Who Can't . . . : Marketing Professors and the Robinson-Patman Act," *Journal of the Academy of Marketing Science,* Summer 1984, pp. 123–138.
11. Theodore Levitt, "The Dangers of Social Responsibility," *Harvard Business Review,* September-October 1958, p. 47.

PHOTO CREDITS

p. xxxviii: Sarto & Lund/Stone; **p. 2:** © Reinhard Eisele/Corbis; **p. 4:** © Starbucks Coffee; Courtesy of Allstate Insurance Co.; Reprinted by permission of the American Cancer Society, Inc.; BLOCKBUSTER name, design, and related marks are trademarks of Blockbuster Inc. © 2000 Blockbuster Inc. All rights reserved. **p. 5:** © VeriSign; © Cisco Systems; © Flycast; © Inktomi; **p. 6:** © Irish Tourist Council; © Lawrence Convention and Visitors Bureau; **p. 10:** © Raul Roa/AP/Wide World Photos; **p. 13:** © Lands' End, Inc.; **p. 18:** © 1997 Mirro Co.; **p. 19:** © Corbis/Bettmann; **p. 20:** Courtesy of DuPont; **p. 21:** © Jacques M. Chenet/Gamma Liaison; **p. 28:** © Chuck Nacke/Woodfin Camp & Associates; **p. 29:** Kathy Ferguson / PhotoEdit; **p. 32:** © Parmalat; **p. 34:** Courtesy of DuPont; **p. 37:** © Rayovac Corporation; **p. 39:** © Morton Salt Division, Morton International; **p. 45:** © Association of American Publishers; **p. 58:** © Chris Cole/Allsport Concepts; **p. 59:** © Golfsmith; **p. 63:** © Yahoo!; **p. 64:** © Magellan Geographix/Corbis; **p. 68:** © Andy Sacks/Tony Stone Images; **p. 72:** © Oglivy International/ Centers for Disease Control; **p. 74:** © Bruce Rowell/Masterfile; **p. 74:** © Arnie Levin; **p. 77:** © Herb Schmitz/Tony Stone Images; **p. 79:** © Federal Trade Commission; **p. 81:** © Barry Blackman/Tony Stone Images; **p. 86:** © H. Paone/New York Times Rights & Permissions; **p. 87:** © Cary Benbow/South-Western; **p. 90:** © United States Postal Service; **p. 94:** © Charles Schwab & Co.; **p. 96:** © Frank Herholdt/Stone; **p. 98:** © Telstra; **p. 102:** ILKAA UIMONEN/Corbis/Sygma; **p. 105:** © Yahoo!; **p. 106:** © Charles Krupa/AP/Wide World Photos; **p. 112:** © David Young-Wolff/Stone; **p. 113:** © Sun Oil Company; **p. 114:** © Hoover's Online; **p. 116:** © David Fields; **p. 122:** Courtesy of Focus Suites; **p. 123:** © Arnie Levin; **p. 124:** © Donna McWilliams/AP/Wide World Photos; **p. 127:** © Eric Larrayadieu/Stone; **p. 131:** Copyright 2000, USA TODAY. Reprinted with permission; **p. 134:** © SuperStock International; **p. 140:** © Dennis O'Clair/Stone; **p. 141:** © PhotoDisc, Inc.; **p. 143:** © 1997 Nissan. INFINITI and the INFINITI logo are registered trademarks of Nissan; **p. 146:** © Liveperson.com; **p. 147:** © Pioneer Electronics; **p. 150:** © Allstate Insurance Company; **p. 153:** © Travel and Leisure Golf/American Express Publications; **p. 155:** © Epson; © Daimler Chrysler; © Tropicana/PepsiCo; **p. 156:** © Lancaster Group, Inc.; **p. 157:** Reprinted with permission of PepsiCo., Inc. 1998; **p. 160:** © David Young-Wolff/PhotoEdit; **p. 161:** © Michael Newman/ PhotoEdit; **p. 163:** © Mark E. Gibson/Gibson Color Photography; **p. 170:** © VCG/FPG International; **p. 171:** © Timedance; **p. 172:** © Tyco; **p. 174:** © Dupont Lycra/DuPont; **p. 178:** © e-Stamp Corporation; **p. 179:** © Cisco Systems; **p. 180:** © Rob Lewine/Stock Market; **p. 183:** © Breezecom; **p. 190:** © Michael S. Green/AP/Wide World Photos; **p. 191:** © Paul Sakuma/ AP/Wide World Photos; **p. 192:** Photo by Joseph Higgins; **p. 194:** © Television Bureau of Advertising; **p. 195:** © K.C. Alfred/AP/Wide World Photos; **p. 199:** © Michael Newman/PhotoEdit; **p. 200:** © Foofoo.com; **p. 206:** © Snowball.com; **p. 209:** © Universal Studios; **p. 210:** © PhotoDisc; **p. 211:** © Zippo; **p. 214:** © Chrysler/AP/Wide World Photos; **p. 215:** © The Clorox Company; **p. 224:** © PhotoDisc, Inc.; **p. 225:** © Oscar Mayer; **p. 226:** © Michael Keller/Stock Market; **p. 228:** © O'Hare Hilton; **p. 231:** Printed with permission of Hershey Foods Corporation; **p. 232:** © Milan Haracek/ Bilderberg/AURORA; **p. 234:** © Felicia Martinez/ PhotoEdit; **p. 238:** © Mercedes-Benz of North America, Inc.; **p. 239:** Pizza Hut and the Pizza Hut logo are trademarks of Pizza Hut, Inc., and are used with permission. **p. 240:** © Fogdog.com; **p. 243:** © Star-Kist Foods, Inc.; **p. 244:** Courtesy of the Pillsbury Company; **p. 245:** © FAO Schwarz; © Michael Newman/ PhotoEdit; **p. 247:** © Alice M. Prescott/ Unicorn Stock Photos; **p. 248:** © Michael Townsend/Allstock; **p. 251:** © SuperStock International; **p. 252:** © Spencer Grant/PhotoEdit; **p. 260:** © Michael Caulfield/AP/Wide World Photos; **p. 261:** © TiVo; **p. 264:** © Nuvo Media, Inc.; **p. 265:** © Olympus America, Inc.; **p. 271:** © Peter Barreras/AP/Wide World Photos; **p. 270:** © Victoria Arocho/AP/Wide World Photos; **p. 272:** © Ron Heflin/AP/Wide World Photos; **p. 277:** © 3Com Corporation; **p. 279:** © Alison McKinzie/Feldman & Associates; **p. 287:** © 3M.Scotch Tape is a registered trademark of 3M. All rights reserved; **p. 288:** © Apple Computer, Inc.; **p. 294:** © Ron Frehm/AP/ Wide World Photos; **p. 300:** © Pico Van Houtryve/ AP/Wide World Photos; **p. 301:** © Pico Van Houtryve/AP/Wide World Photos; **p. 302:** © Jeff Zaruba/ The Stock Market; **p. 304:** © John T. Barr/AP/Wide World Photos; **p. 305:** © Touchstone Pictures/Kobal Collection; **p. 307:** © Stamps.com; **p. 309:** © Bonnie Kamin/PhotoEdit; **p. 314:** © Shizuo Kambayashi/AP/Wide World Photos; **p. 317:** © 1997 Gevalia Kaffe; **p. 327:** © Chanel; **p. 328:** © Mark E. Gibson/Gibson Color Photography; **p. 329:** © autobytel.com; **p. 340:** © Mark E. Gibson/Gibson Color Photography; **p. 343:** Illustration: John Porman; Ad agency: Bluefly In-house; **p. 344:** © Lands' End; **p. 348:** © Respond.com, Inc.; **p. 350:** © DiMaggio/Kalish/Stock Market; **p. 353:** © Gail Mooney/Corbis; **p. 355:** © Nordstrom, Inc.; **p. 360:** © Michael L. Weaver/Camelot Technologies; **p. 370:** © David Young-Wolff/ PhotoEdit; **p. 371:** © PhotoDisc, Inc.; **p. 372:** Courtesy of the Coca-Cola Company; **p. 374:** © Boeri USA; **p. 376:** © Christian Liewig/Corbis; **p. 379:** © 1996 GM Corporation; **p. 380:** © 1996 Bose Corporation; **p. 382:** © Chuck Nacke/Woodfin Camp & Associates; **p. 383:** © Walgreens; **p. 383:** © 1997 Fritz Hoffman; **p. 384:** © John B. Stetson Co.; **p. 387:** © Beautyscene.com; **p. 390:** © IBM; **p. 394:** © EyeWire; **p. 395:** © Michael Sexton/Michael Sexton Photography; **p. 397:** © American Dairy Association; **p. 399:** Comet Systems; **p. 401:** © Great Brands of Europe; **p. 403:** © Wm. Wrigley Jr. Company; **p. 404:** © Vlasic; **p. 405:** © GM Eventworks; **p. 406:** © The Pillsbury Company; **p. 407:** © Sideffects; **p. 408:** © 1997 HV Food Products Co.; **p. 411:** © 1997 GM Corporation; **p. 412:** © Wallpaper Council of America; **p. 413:** © Cartoon Network; **p. 415:** © Mark E. Gibson/Gibson Color Photography; © Mark E. Gibson/ Gibson Color Photography; **p. 416:** © CarPoint.com; © Tide; **p. 418:** © Harry Cabluck/AP/Wide World Photos; **p. 420:** © 1998 Jenny Craig; **p. 421:** © Robert E. Daemmrich/Stone; **p. 431:** © Spencer Grant/PhotoEdit; **p. 432:** © eToys, Inc.; **p. 434:** © Ronnen Eshel/Corbis; **p. 435:** © Fisher/Thatcher/ Stone; **p. 437:** © Michael Newman/PhotoEdit; **p. 439:** © John Feingersh/ Stock Market; **p. 443:** © Shotgun/Stock Market; **p. 446:** © David Hanover/ Tony Stone Images; **p. 446:** © PhotoDisc, Inc.; **p. 447:** © Salesforce.com; **p. 451:** © Jose L. Pelaez/Stock Market; **p. 456:** © Alese/Mort/Stock Market; **p. 457:** © Reuters/Sandy Macys/Archive Photos; **p. 466:** © eBay, Inc. **p. 467:** © PhotoDisc, Inc.; **p. 469:** © David Young-Wolff/ PhotoEdit; **p. 470:** © Jill Connelly/AP/Wide World Photos; **p. 477:** © John Bazemore/AP/Wide World Photos; **p. 480:** © Reuters/J. David Aloe/Archive Photos; **p. 486:** © NPNX/ Index Stock Imagery; **p. 487:** © Cary Benbow/ South-Western; **p. 489:** © David Young-Wolff/ PhotoEdit; **p. 490:** © Bill Aron/ PhotoEdit; **p. 493:** © U.S. Mint; **p. 494:** © Koei Co., Ltd; **p. 495:** © David Young-Wolff/PhotoEdit; **p. 496:** © Jonathan Nourok/PhotoEdit; **p. 498:** © United States Postal Service; **p. 502:** © Torleif Svensson/Stock Market; **p. 508:** © D'Arcy Masius Benton & Bowles.

NAME INDEX

SUBJECT INDEX

HyperText Markup Language (HTML), 71
HyperText Transfer Protocol (HTTP), 71

I

Iceland, 100
Idea generation, 268–269
Image building, 386–387
Import quotas, 101, 102
Imports, 95
Incentive, 149
Income, 68–69
    and pricing decisions, 473–475
Independent retailers, 339
India, 96
Indirect-action advertisements, 397
Indirect exporting, 104
Individual brand, 243–244
Individual factors, in perception, 154
Indonesia, 109
Inflation, 494
Influencer, 165, 181
Infomediary, 321–322, 359
Infomercial, 406
Information, 115. *See also* Marketing research
Information search, by consumers, 146–147
Innovators, 282
Inseparability (of services), 250–251
Inside selling, 436
Institutional advertisements, 397
Intangibility (of services), 248–249
Integrated marketing communications, 377, 392,
    425–427
    example of, 371
Intelligent agents, 72, 417
Intensive distribution, 326–327
Intermediaries
    and distribution channels, 307–308
    functions of, 306–307, 313, 315–316
    global, 104
    physical distribution and, 308–315
Intermodal service (transportation), 312
Internal marketing, 426–427
International franchising, 105
International marketing, 60, 95, 206, 246, 366. *See also*
  e-commerce
    business-to-business, 175
    cultural symbols and, 97
    ethnocentrism and, 97–98
    example of errors in, 87
    language and, 96–97
    product modifications for, 290–291
    types of involvement in, 102–104
International Organization for Standardization (ISO),
  182, 187
Internet, 3, 347, 390. *See also* e-commerce; Technology
    as advertising medium, 72, 374, 395, 414,
      415–418, 432
    and customer service, 253–254, 334
    domain names on, 239
    features of, 71–75

    intermediaries on, 321–322
    and location-based competition, 91
    privacy on, 118, 125
    as source of secondary data, 115, 116, 117, 122,
      124–125
Interstate Commerce Commission Act, 294
Intranet, 117, 177, 184
Intrapreneurial organization, 89
Introduction stage (of product life cycle), 275–276, 280
Inventory
    control of, 312–313
    management of, 303–305
Iran, 100
Ireland, 99
Isolation effect, 496
Italy, 99

J

Japan, 96, 97, 100, 106, 326
Jingles, 407–408
Joint decision making, 164–165
Joint ownership venture, 105–106
Joint ventures, 104–107

K

Kefauver-Harris Drug Amendment (1962), 78
Keiretsu, 100

L

Label, 246, 247
Laboratory experiment, 129
Laggards, 283
Language, 96–97, 109
Late majority, 283
Laws, 77–81
    federal, 78–79, 363
    Green River, 345
    international, 81
    local, 79–80
    and pricing strategies, 505–507
    state, 79
Leader pricing, 495
Learning, 156–158
Leased department retailer, 339
Legal environment, 77–81. *See also* Laws
Licensing, 104–105
Licensing agreement, 245
Lifestyle, 210
Lifestyle creative platform, 407
Likert scale, 127
Limited-line strategy, 289
Limited problem solving, 143
Limited-service merchant wholesaler, 357–358, 361
List price, 468, 504
Location-based competition, 91
Logistics, 302, 304
Logistics management, 303

Union; NAFTA
Multinational marketing groups, 81
Multiple market segmentation, 200–201, 203
Multiple-purchase offers, 459, 460
Multiple-unit pricing, 496

N

NAFTA, 80, 100, 184
National brand, 241, 242
Need, 149–152
Netherlands, The, 99
New product
    adoption process for, 281–283
    characteristics of successful, 265–267, 297
    defined, 262, 263
    development of, 267–273
    example of, 261
    and existing consumption patterns, 266, 267
    failure rates for, 265
    marketing strategies for, 40
    new-to-the-world, 263
    perspective of consumers on, 263–265
    perspective of management on, 262–263
    reasons for failure of, 273–274
New task buying, 177
News release, 423–424
Noise (in communication), 381
Nonadopters, 283
Noncumulative quantity discounts, 505, 506
Nondurable goods, 229
Nonprice competition, 470
Nonprobability sample, 130
Nonverbal communication, 443, 444
Norms, 49–50
    in consumer decision making, 160–161
North American Free Trade Agreement. *See* NAFTA
North American Industry Classification System (NAICS),
    184–185, 187
Northeast Corridor, 64
Norway, 100
Not-for-profit organizations, as marketers, 6–7
Nouveaux riches, 163
Nutritional Labeling and Education Act (1990), 80

O

Observability, 267
Observation research, 127. *See also* Marketing research
Off-price retailers, 341, 343
Oligopoly, 75, 493
One-on-one marketing. *See* Data-based marketing
One-price strategy, 488–489
Operant conditioning, 157
Operating products, 233–234
Operational planning, 33
Opinion leaders, 164
Order getting, 439, 440
Order processing, 304
Order takers, 438–439

Organizational buying behavior, 172–173
    criteria for, 181–184
    kinds of, 176–177
    roles in, 180–181
    service and, 182
Organizational market, 43. *See also* Business-to-business
    marketing
    segments of, 173, 185
Organizational mission statement, 34
Organizational products, 232–234
Outbound transportation, 304
Outsourcing, 94. *See also* Collaborators
Ownership group, 339–340

P

Pacific Islanders, 69
Packaging, 245–246, 304
Parity products, 388
Penetration price, 492
Perceived risk, of consumers, 145, 146
Perception, 152–156
Periodic discounting, 490
Perishability (of services), 249
Person marketing, 425
Personal media, 373, 374
Personal selling, 13, 176, 375, 377, 380, 384, 389, 463,
    494. *See also* Relationship management; Sales
    management
    characteristics of, 436–438
    defined, 436
    types of, 438–440
Personality, 159
Persuasion, ethics of, 389–390. *See also* Ethics
Physical distribution, 303–305
    intermediaries and, 308–315
Physical environment, 61
Physical obsolescence, 294
Physiological needs, 150
Pioneering advertising, 399
Pioneers, 439
Pipelines, 311, 312
Place, 11–12. *See also* Distribution
Place utility, 89, 302, 304, 342
Planned obsolescence, 294
Planning, 32–33. *See also* Marketing plan
    operational, 33
    relationship of, to execution and control, 47–48
    strategic, 33, 34–35
Point-of-purchase materials, 457, 459, 460
Poison Prevention Labeling Act (1970), 78
Poland, 100
Political environment, 77–81
Pop-up boxes (on Web sites), 416
Population
    in statistics, 129
    of United States, 65, 69, 83
    of world, 70, 83
Portal, 72–73, 125, 175, 321, 322
Portugal, 99
Positioning, 43, 214–216, 388, 389. *See also* Marketing

U

Ultimate consumer, 11
Umbrella branding, 243, 244
Unaided recall, 421
Uncontrollable variables, 15
Undercutting-the-competition strategy, 491
Undifferentiated marketing, 196–197, 302
Unfair sales practices acts, 507
Uniform delivered pricing, 499
Uniform resource locator (URL), 124, 240
Unique selling proposition (USP), 387–388, 404
United Kingdom, 99
United States, 63–69, 100, 101, 161, 184, 195, 246, 291, 345. *See also* Demographics
 as service economy, 75–76
 social classes in, 162
Universal Product Code (UPC), 246
Urbanization, 64
U.S. Census Bureau, 164 , 218
U.S. Consumer Product Safety Commission, 256
U.S. Department of Commerce, 359, 361
U.S. Forest Service, 115
U.S. Library of Congress, 124
U.S. Mint, 493
U.S. Patent and Trademark Office, 256
U.S. Postal Service, 498
U.S. Small Business Administration, 124
Users, 180

V

Value, 468
 cultural, and international marketing, 96
Value chain, 92–93
Variable costs, 502
Variable pricing strategy, 489
Vending machines, 341, 346, 493
Vertical exchange, 321, 323, 334, 359, 361

Vertical marketing system, 306, 323–325, 362
Vertical markets, 321
Virtual corporations, 92

W

Warehouse club, 341, 342–343
Warehousing, 304
Washington, D.C., 64
Water transportation, 311, 312
Web browser, 124
Web sites, 72–73, 330, 415–416, 417, 425. *See also* e-commerce; Internet
Wheel of retailing, 348–349
Wheeler-Lea Act (1938), 80, 294
Wholesaler, 307, 308. *See also* Intermediaries
 classifying, 356–360
 defined, 11, 355
 distribution of services by, 361–362
 marketing strategies for, 362
 sales promotions aimed at, 456–457
Wholesaler-sponsored voluntary chain, 324
Women, 68
World brand, 242
World Wide Web (WWW), 71. *See also* Internet; Web sites
Worldwide information systems, 114–115. *See also* Internet

Y

Yemen, 98

Z

Zambia, 489
Zone pricing, 498–499